DUTCH AND FLEMISH PAINTERS

Carel Van Mander

ARNO PRESS · NEW YORK · 1969

A PUBLISHING AND LIBRARY SERVICE OF THE NEW YORK TIMES

Reprinted from a copy in the library of the
Fogg Museum of Art, Harvard University

Library of Congress Catalog Card No. 71-88823

Manufactured in the United States of America by Arno Press Inc.

DUTCH AND FLEMISH PAINTERS

CAREL VAN MANDER

Dutch and Flemish Painters

Translation from the Schilderboeck

AND INTRODUCTION BY

CONSTANT VAN DE WALL

NEW YORK

MCFARLANE, WARDE, MCFARLANE

1936

PREFACE

THE first edition of Carel van Mander's *Schilderboeck* appeared in 1604. It was printed by Jacob de Meester, at Alkmaar, and published by Paschier van Westbusch, at Haarlem. A second edition of the complete *Schilderboeck* was issued in 1618 by Jacob Petersz. Wachter. The individual titles of Parts III, V and VI are dated 1616, Parts II and IV, 1617. This edition, with the biography of Van Mander probably by his brother Adam van Mander was printed by Pauwels van Ravesteyn.

The first edition of the *Schilderboeck* is scarce. There is a copy of the Prentencabinet at Amsterdam. It has marginal notes written by a Mr Houmes. These notes have been analyzed by E.W.Moes (*Oud Holland*, 1889. p.149). The second edition is not scarce; it can be found in the leading libraries in Holland. The third edition was illustrated with portraits of the artists. It has a few footnotes which have been used by later commentators. This edition is in several of the important libraries in America.

Henri Hymans should receive full credit for his translation of the *Schilderboeck* into French. Through him Van Mander's work became known to those who could not read the Dutch of the late sixteenth century. His critical analyses of statements made by Van Mander were bold and sound and were cause for further research in the history of Flemish and Dutch painting. It is to be regretted that Hymans's translation appeared in a limited edition; but it can be found in the leading art libraries in America.

The translation into German by Floerke was a result of the increased interest of German-speaking students of art of the sixteenth century in the Netherlands. The advance of the history of art as a science, and intelligent art appreciation in

PREFACE

general, called for a translation of Van Mander's *Schilder-boeck*. Floerke profited by the work of Hymans and by the work of many other scholars in various countries, during more than twenty years after the translation by Hymans had been published.

I have used each of the editions mentioned, and most of all the original edition of 1618, for my translation into English. I have verified my work with the translations by Hymans and Floerke, and, where meanings remained obscure, I have consulted art historians, philologists, and persons, that have studied the technique of the old masters. I have left the names of the artists as they were spelled by Van Mander; it will be noticed that he was frequently inconsistent. There are no paragraphs in the original text; to facilitate reading, paragraphs have been introduced. I have tried to make my translation as literal as possible for sake of truth and at the sacrifice of style. I endeavored to retain the spirit and the color of Van Mander's text.

Since French and German translations, and commentaries on the *Schilderboeck*, are not generally accessible to most English-speaking students, I have incorporated as much information as was possible in the notes, including the observations of Hymans and Floerke and those of H.E.Greve, in his *De Bronnen van Carel van Mander voor het Leven der Doorluchtighe Nederlandsche en Hoogduytsche Schilders*, The Hague, 1903, (Quellenstudien zur Hollandischen Kunstgeschichte II); this book remains a standard work for the student of Van Mander. The German translation of Part I of the *Schilderboeck*, the 'Principles' (Den Grondt der Edel vry Schilder-Const), by Dr. R. Hoecker, is generally available under the title, *Das Lehrgedicht des Karel van Mander. Text, Uebersetzung und Kommentar, nebst Anhang ueber Manders Geschichtskonstruction und Kunst-*

PREFACE

theorie. The Hague, Nijhoff, 1916, (Quellenstudien zur Hollandischen Kunstgeschichte VIII).

For students that wish to study the material offered by Van Mander, notes, indexes, and a map, have been added. I wish to express my sincere appreciation for the encouragement and advice so willingly given by Professor C.R. Morey of Princeton University, Professor John Shapley of Chicago University, Professor Walter W. S. Cook of New York University, Professor A. Philip McMahon of New York University, Professor August Vermeylen of the University of Ghent and Professor Willem Vogelsang of the University of Utrecht. I am greatly indebted to the C.R.B. Educational Foundation for the liberal, moral, and material, support given to my work. The publishers, McFarlane, Warde, McFarlane, deserve to be praised for, in the spirit of Plantin, they present this book to the New World.

CONSTANT VAN DE WALL

Department of Fine Arts,
New York University.
July, 1936

TABLE OF CONTENTS

CONTENTS

CONTENTS

CONTENTS

XII

CONTENTS

XIII

CONTENTS

CONTENTS
ARRANGED ALPHABETICALLY

CONTENTS

ARRANGED ALPHABETICALLY

INTRODUCTION
Carel van Mander and his Time
BY THE TRANSLATOR

CHARLES V was Emperor of the Holy Roman Empire (1519-1556). The period of his reign over the Netherlands was long and severe. There was great prosperity. Agriculture flourished; industry and commerce were supported by powerful capitalists. There was a safe economic stability. Antwerp had become a metropolis and Bruges was no longer a rival city. A naturally excellent harbor made Antwerp the greatest seaport of Western Europe. Transatlantic explorers had opened new territories. Antwerp was the center of world commerce, and was one of the most densely populated cities in Europe. In many respects it could be compared to modern New York.

Wealth triumphed: Ancient nobles, successful merchants, industrialists, and the clergy, had accumulated vast fortunes. At this time the University of Louvain had five thousand students; philology and theology were important departments of the university. The *Collegium Trilingue* for the study of Latin, Greek, and Hebrew, was founded at Louvain in 1517 by Jerome Busleiden. No-one did more than Erasmus to ensure the realization of its design; later, this institution served as a model for the College de France. Louvain greatly influenced the Renaissance in France. Roman Law was studied. There was more academic interest in ancient languages than in national literature. Sciences made progress. Vesalius, Mercator, and Ortelius of the Netherlands, had international reputations for their knowledge. Plantin started his famous printing house in Antwerp in 1550. He and his son-in-law, Moretus, contributed as much as any other publisher to progressive thought in Western Europe.

INTRODUCTION

Plantin taught his children to fear, honor, and love, God, the King, all magistrates and superiors—a doctrine not without potential dangers—, and to help their mother about the house. He regarded his children, from the ages four to twelve, too young for heavy work; he made them correct proofs of type matter in several languages. Plantin's five daughters worked in his printing office. Madeleine, the fourth, read proof of Hebrew, Syriac, and Greek, texts when she was thirteen years old; she worked with Arias Montanus, who supervised the printing of the famous Biblia Regia.

There was a dark side to the reign of Charles V. The wealth in the country was not distributed, and the control of it disaffected a large part of the population. The indulgence of the rich caused revolts that were more serious than the acts of paupers. The Protestant Reformation was growing.

Protestantism found fertile soil in the Netherlands. The ground had been broken by Erasmus. There was a lack of prestige and discipline within the Roman-Catholic church, which caused religious ignorance and great disrespect in the laity. In Antwerp there were many Germans and Spanish refugees that had fled from the Inquisition. Among these, there were important Jews and Moriscos whose conversion had not been accepted by the Spanish clergy. Jacques Praepositus, a friend of Luther's and an Augustin monk, became a dynamic figure in the Lutheran movement in Antwerp. Clandestine printing was disseminated to promote protestant ideas. The movement spread over Walloon territory, and, in turn, Lille and Tournai became centers for propaganda.

Calvinism entered the Southern (or Spanish) Netherlands by the way of France and was brought to Antwerp. A close relation between Flemish and English Calvinists was fostered in many ways by trade activities. Calvinism appealed to the intellectual classes and to the aristocracy. The *Institutio Christiana* (of 1536), by Calvin, converted many.

A third religious movement made a vicious attack on Roman-Catholicism in the Netherlands. Antwerp was a hotbed of anabaptists. The members of this sect were fanatics and radicals. The movement was strongest in Westphalia. It started in 1521 and it was so revolutionary Luther left the Wartburg and preached against its principles. After the defeat and death of its leader, Thomas Munzer, in 1525, there was a short lull. The movement came to its climax when Jan van Leyden established the Kingdom of Sion at Münster in Germany. He was defeated by the forces of the Bishop of Münster and pinched to death with red-hot tongs. In 1529, the first anabaptist was burned to death in Antwerp; more than seven hundred martyrs were condemned. The many victims tortured to death caused the movement to spread. The anabaptists were extremely militant; they believed in polygamy and in revolution through fire and steel. They sowed iconoclastic seeds that needed only a short time to grow and flourish.

These were the main strifes in the Netherlands during the reign of Charles V. Foreign relations were a burden to the Netherlands. Charles needed the money of wealthy merchants and weavers for his war against Francis I, of France, and against Solyman the Magnificent, Sultan of Turkey, who had ravaged Hungary and, it is said, made the Mediterranean a Turkish lake. Charles was born and baptized in Ghent (1500). Later, at Ghent, he encountered the most serious and spirited resistance against his taxation. He punished the citizens, in 1540, by executing the leaders of the opposition and by imposing excessive taxes. To achieve this he invaded the town with an army, which stayed there for a long time.

INTRODUCTION

Charles, because he was absent most the time, appointed regents for the Netherlands. His aunt, Margaret of Austria, one of the regents, held her court at Malines. She actively protected arts and letters. She was appreciated for her wisdom and tact. She had been educated at the French court. After her death, in 1530, the next regent was Mary of Hungary, the sister of Charles V. In the castles of Binche and Mariemont, built under her regency, there were brilliant festivals, and various artistic talents of the highest quality contributed to them. Triumphal arches were erected, portraits were painted of the local nobility and their guests, and engravings were made to commemorate events.

The court and the church were not alone with their demands for artists. The trade guilds ordered altar paintings for their special chapels in the cathedrals. They had their great festivals. These guilds were the same as strong, closed-shop, labor unions. The rulers were deeply interested in them, owing to their strong political influence, especially in the Chambers of Rhetoricians. To the so-called 'Land-Jewel,' a periodic jubilee of the Guild of Rhetoricians, all other guilds of rhetoric came to compete. These gatherings stimulated political interest. The rulers, because they could not afford adverse criticism, became members of these guilds and, in this way, increased national interest. The arts, if rhetoric is included, played an important part in forming political opinion in the Netherlands, particulary in Flanders.

Charles could not stop the Reformation. The attitude of his sister was significant: All heretics, whether repentant or not, should be persecuted with the greatest severity, their influence should be extinguished at once, and care should be taken to not let the provinces become entirely depopulated.

Charles was feared by the Netherlanders, owing to the incident at Ghent in 1540, but he was not hated. The feelings toward his son were different. No king of the Low Countries has been more detested than Philip II (1555-1581, in the Northern Netherlands, 1555-1598, in the Southern (or Spanish) Netherlands). But one should not forget the political situation, when Charles turned the government over to Philip (1555), was about as difficult as it could be. The religious question was not the only one. The people were troubled by the absolute despotism that Philip tried to establish, and by his tramping upon rights and privileges that generations of ancestors had worked and given their blood for. The situation was made worse because the people themselves could not agree to the fundamental issues of both state and religion.

This is not the place to discuss the war for independence of the Netherlands. Motley, in his *Rise of the Dutch Republic*, has reviewed the conflict; but his description is not always objective enough from a truly historical point of view. He has seen the conflict with the romantic, English, and somewhat protestant, eyes of the middle nineteenth century. Greater historians, Pirenne, Blok and Geyl,[1] are better authorities. Novels may often give useful background to the student: De Coster's *The Glorious Adventures of Tyl Ulenspiegl* and Felix Timmermans' *Droll Peter* are filled with the atmosphere of the Netherlands in the sixteenth century.

A disaster in the Netherlands, and one that made great consequences to the history of art, was the Iconoclasm of 1566. It was an act of fanaticism and of mob insanity. It has been explained by historians, and it is a fact, that Margaret, Duchess of Parma, the governess and half sister of Philip had refused the petition of the Nobles for moderation in the per-

[1] H.Pirenne, *L'Histoire de Belgique*. P.J.Blok, *History of the people of the Netherlands*, New York, 1898-1912. P.Geyl, *The revolt of the Netherlands*, London, 1932.

secution of the heretics. Iconoclasm flared out in Flanders and took its course toward Antwerp. Similar to a tornado, it became broad, powerful, and destructive, as it swept over Brabant and moved north. It destroyed, in only a few days, all that seemed symbolic of Roman-Catholicism. Altar paintings, sculpture, stained glass windows, and painted shrines, were smashed or burned, and with a devilish satisfaction.

Another event that led to a rabid destruction of works of art in Antwerp, was the Spanish Fury of the 4th November, 1576. The Spanish soldiers had not been paid for twenty-two months. They revolted and plundered Antwerp. Seven thousand inhabitants were killed and eight hundred houses were destroyed. The material damage was estimated at five million guilders.

The Iconoclasm and the Spanish Fury, alone, did not cause the disappearance of valuable works of art from the Netherlands. Philip II had enough Hapsburg blood in his veins to make him no ordinary art-collector. Granvelle, first Bishop of Arras, later on Archbishop of Malines, and Cardinal, was a man of refined tastes, and he and Alva must have looked for works of art that would please their king.

A patriotic Belgian, or Dutchman, that visits the Prado Museum in Madrid, is strangely and not unpleasantly surprised to find the names of his sixteenth-century artists in illustrious lettering on the entrance-wall of the museum. One should visit the former imperial collection in Vienna to realize the Hapsburgers have been extensive collectors of Flemish art.

One direct result of the Iconoclasm was the arrival of Alva. His name alone means, to the Belgian and the Dutch, the worst curse that ever came to the people in the Netherlands. The protestants, which were part of the population, left the Southern Netherlands before and during his regime.

INTRODUCTION

Many persons found it safer to leave the country altogether, because of constant spying and kidnapping by both sides. Many moved to Germany.

Migration became significant in the history of art in the Netherlands. A few words about the Flemish, Walloon, and Dutch, concerned with this migration. On the map of Europe it is plain that these people lived near to one another and that they did not integrate very much. The Flemings, in the west, the Walloons, east of Belgium, the Dutch, in what is now Holland, developed individual languages. In early history their differences and strong feelings for independence found expression in small local autonomies and in hostilities. Philip the Good (1419-1467) and Charles V experienced many difficulties when they attempted to centralize these local powers. A similar spirit existed in the rules and ordinances of the guilds; they refused to allow work to be given to strangers, or to artisans that came from a neighboring town. The racial traits of the people of the Lowlands differ little from those of the English; but, somehow, there was no amalgamation and the continental Englishman was never born in Flanders.

Local and racial differences caused tremendous difficulties for William the Silent (1533-1584) when he tried to make a strong and united front against Spain. In this, one must admire his achievements. The cause of rural misunderstandings, at the end of the war for independence (1648), was one of the terms of peace that meant the closing of the River Schelde. This choked Antwerp. Though excusable at that time for strategic reasons, the port remained sealed for about a century and a half. This encouraged the rise of Amsterdam. The Dutch Republic was contemporaneous with starving in the Southern Netherlands. Napoleon opened the harbor. The two countries were united till 1830 when their differences became too great for continued peace. Today, one can hear the organized voices of people that continue to believe a union is again possible and necessary; but bitter opposition, north and south of the border, regards such a union not only a harmless Utopia but a serious menace to their national integrity. It may be interesting for some to know there is a Flemish movement in Belgium, and its moral support comes from people in Holland. It aims at a full recognition of Flemish interests. Many Flemish poets and writers are appreciated in Holland. Artistic relations between the two countries have always been reciprocal. Political events of the sixteenth century caused a migration and a subsequent mixing of artistic personalities of the Flemish, the Dutch, and the Walloon. That was stimulating. A good artist is eager to see the work of another good artist. It does not hold that the one must follow the other. Faith and joy in work are causes for the discussion of principles and problems. This is the way an artist grows. That is why artists like to travel. Sometimes they leave their own locality, when, for some reason or other, it does not offer them a proper living. Artisans have always been international.

When Antwerp, early in the sixteenth century, was a prosperous city, altar paintings were ordered by churches and guilds for their special chapels. Private donations to the church were in the form of a work of art, to commemorate a dear relative, or to express gratitude for a blessing received. The tapestry factories in Brussels and Tournai needed designers of cartoons, and the makers of stained glass windows needed glass painters.

This was a heyday of artists. It was the time of Quentin Matsys and Joachim Patenir. Bles and other artists exported their ornate altar paintings to the Rhine provinces and to Italy. Cornelis Enghelbrechtsen and Lucas van Leyden were

INTRODUCTION

famous. Jacob Cornelisz van Oost-Sanen, in Amsterdam, and Jan Mostart, in Haarlem, were great masters of painting. Other artists won fame for the Netherlands in foreign regions. Gossart went to Italy, and Joos van Cleef visited Italy, France, Germany and England. Barend van Orley became court painter to Margaret of Austria. Jan van Schoorel, the pupil of Jacob Cornelisz., travelled through Germany. Steermarken went to Venice, Palestine and Rome, before he returned to his native country and settled in Utrecht; he became an artist with a well-known reputation. The Spanish grandees of the sixteenth century were painted by the Dutchman Antonio Moro, in an unsurpassed way. His portraits of kings and queens, and of diplomats that had the good fortune to pose for him, at the courts of Madrid, Lisbon, London and Brussels, reveal a superior character analysis similar to that of Titian, of Van Dyck and of Velasquez. In Moro's portraits one does not feel the artist's personality between oneself and the model. This cannot be said of all eminent portrait painters. No painter has brought us nearer to monarchs and given us more intimate, realistic, and artistic, aspects of their character, than Moro. When looking at the eyes of Granvelle, Philip II, Alva, Alexander Farnese of Parma, and Queen Mary of England, one wonders how far traditional historians went to reveal all the truth known of these personalities, and if they have represented the facts to us. We see them as human beings and much the same as ourselves. Moro's paintings are lasting impressions of convincing truth. Not long ago, Dutch children were taught to assume that some of these great persons were the spawn of the Devil. Moro's portraits, in their impressive silence, contradict this kind of patriotic teaching.

Let us follow the art of the Netherlands in its further development and glance at its various phases. The Iconoclasm of 1566 caused Holland the loss of most all of her early paintings and sculpture, and stained glass windows and other objects of applied art that had symbolized the glory of God for many generations. It is impossible to know much about the work of such artists as Bouts, Ouwater, Geertgen van Sint Jans, Mostart, Heemskerck, Engelbrechtsen, and many other distinguished masters. One may ask whether or not Dutch and Flemish painting would have been similar in evolution during the transition from the sixteenth to the seventeenth century, if Holland had not been deprived of the art that was destroyed. Education in art depends on what the artist sees. Were vandalism and destruction a negative influence, or were the late sixteenth and early seventeenth century artists forced to express themselves more clearly in a new idiom? Were the public and the new patrons keener and more interested in the novelties created by the artists? New wine needed new bottles. Later on, in the Southern Netherlands, where some old pictures had been preserved, faithful Roman-Catholics, such as Rubens and his followers, refilled the Belgian cathedrals.

The Protestants in Holland, it seems, wanted to keep their churches as bare as possible. The walls of old cathedrals were whitewashed. Artists were slow in taking an interest in light-effects. Stained glass windows were replaced by monotonously leaded plain glass. Dark green curtains kept the sunlight from the preacher's head, and churches were the same as austere court rooms, filled with awe and with judges to doom sinners. Often the only joyful note was the blinking brass of a lamp or a screen. These churches reflected the fear of God; the uncertainty of purgatory remained. The Last Judgement continued to be a conventional subject for art in the Calvinistic churches of Holland. The simplicity of many New England churches vividly suggests the same spirit.

INTRODUCTION

In Holland, a religious feeling that was more in the spirit of the New Testament expressed itself in the community outside the church. The religious literature of the early seventeenth century in Holland is impressive, and Carel van Mander was an important worker in this field. One cannot study the later Rembrandt without being impressed by the thoroughly religious self-expression of this Protestant, who read his Bible and interpreted the words of the Great Teacher in his own terms.

On the other hand, many artists knew how to laugh and how to express laughter; sometimes it had a very Flemish ring in it. Artists painted banqueting gods and of gay cavaliers; but one did not have to go to church to study these pictures. The paintings in guild halls, town halls, and rooms for the trustees of philanthropic institutions, prove that there was a healthy official appreciation of art.

Comparatively little of what was actual warfare has been visualized by our painters. Breughel's *Massacre of the Innocents* in Brussels is a grim story. The title was a witty excuse for the real subject. In the entire history of Flemish art, the present time included, representations of hell appear frequently; in no other country has the hell of hell been painted with such a human delight as in Flanders.

In the sixteenth and seventeenth centuries many persons collected paintings. Art dealers found and made trade profitable at Amsterdam. Paintings were exhibited and sold at the annual fairs. The wives of many artists travelled with the pictures by their husbands from place to place.

Early historians of art have underestimated the artistic movements of the sixteenth century. According to them, artists in the fifteenth century, Van Eycks, Vander Weyden, Memling, Van der Goes, and the artists in the seventeenth century, Rubens, Jordaens, Rembrandt, Hals, eclipsed the

INTRODUCTION

artists in the sixteenth century. The artistic movements that occurred in the sixteenth century received labels—Romanism and Mannerism. These labels, correct as they may be, do not focus attention directly on what was great in art during the sixteenth century. Labels are not stimulating; they simply classify according to some system or other; some historians of art seem to think labels are more beautiful than the pictures. But thanks to our modern historian: His increased interest in the eclecticism of the period, and his progress in the study of the genesis of the art of Rubens and Rembrandt, have discovered clues, in the Romanism and Mannerism of the sixteenth century, and we can detect the early stages of seventeenth-century art. Thanks to the recent interest in Van Gogh and Cézanne, and for the reproductions of their works that reach a large public. This same public will be able to observe the pictorial qualities painted by Breughel and be less concerned over his droll story of a subject. No artist has ever been more truly Flemish than Breughel. His many journeys, and his artistic experiences in France and Italy, ripened the native characteristics of his art. Breughel is as Flemish as Rembrandt is Dutch. The human element in the messages of these masters makes them great. If we have seen the light that beams from Quentin Matsys' *Genealogy of the Virgin* (in Brussels), if we have been conscious of the atmosphere of that room filled with people when Mary renders up her Spirit (on one of the wings of that same altar piece), we shall realize the greatness of art in the sixteenth century. Lucas van Leyden and Moro and their work will be remembered when the classification of the lower groups has been forgotten.

Romanism and Mannerism were the explorations of artists in new fields. There was an aristocratic, a humanistic, and a literary, background to their work. The Mannerists catered

INTRODUCTION

to a sophisticated and scholarly people. The artist made technical discoveries that were of great value to future generations—Rubens and Rembrandt. The sixteenth century had many brave pioneers in landscape, still life, and animal, painting. There was a vigorous and youthful growth in these new fields. It is interesting to study the drawings made by Flemish artists of the sixteenth century. The charming spontaneity in their Italian landscapes is aesthetically more stimulating than copies of them could be, or other copies of classical figure work.

Flemish Romanists, such as Gossart and Orley, were interested in antique sculpture, because of the plastic qualities of a single figure and, later, of group-compositions. The Dutch painter Van Schoorel was different. He was interested in the visual relation between a plastic form and the space surrounding it. A real synthesis of Italian and northern art appears in his work. Heemskerck exaggerated; he was exuberant and often too shallow. Floris was an eclectic painter and had little great pictorial character that was his own. He had numerous pupils and they worked on his paintings. His work, like Michelangelo's, was commercialized. To terminate this development, Rubens made a long and thorough study of Italian art that had, we should remember, advanced considerably during the sixteenth century.

Mannerism has been described as an epidemic. It produced exaggerated figures that had unnatural proportions, anatomically. It did not influence Breughel, though he was in the middle of it. Mannerism was abandoned at the end of the sixteenth century. It would not be right to judge the movement by its imperfections; much depends on a specific point of view. At that time, a decided search was made for new forms of expression, for new interpretations of traditional Biblical themes. There was real literary interest in art. Religious relations with Rome, political relations with Spain, and contact with the Huguenots, brought Latin up to the higher levels of society. Their art was not for the general public. Figures were made slender; action was over-emphasized and often stiffened; women were painted with long necks, turned gracefully or twisted awkwardly. Exotic costumes and head-dresses were as popular as portraits of foreigners. Facial expressions were distorted, and somewhat neurotic effects were achieved, similar to our present advertising and the pictorical designs used by industry. We should not judge the work of the Mannerists by their 'realistic' representations.

The recoil from Mannerism was stronger than the movement itself. An artistic back-to-nature movement had been stimulated by the rapidly growing interest in landscape and still life. Mannerism, while gratifying to lovely ladies and philosophical gentlemen posed in pictorially interesting settings, was not successful in painting dead fish, high game and translucent grapes. The demand for portraits brought the artists to solid ground again. The beggars of the sea made demands from life and from artists instead from the aristocracy of the Southern Netherlands.

Mannerism could be considered as an early step towards baroque painting. Some sixteenth century artists neglected local color which was the beauty of such late Gothic paintings as those by the Van Eycks. Rogier vander Weyden and Memling sacrificed the decorative quality of color to express form; and others applied decorative schemes in color that were not based primarily on observation of nature. Some artists were indifferent to the specific effects of color. Their uses of neutralized color led to new and conscious ways to render the effects of light. These ways were the special characteristics of northern artists; the highest development of these effects can be noticed in work by Rembrandt. The technique of painting changed, and mixed tones, scumbled paint, and effects obtained by spontaneous brush-strokes, were desired. A painting did not need to be as smooth as a piece of enamel. Brush-strokes were welcomed as new elements in painting. The Mannerists never realized the significance of technical liberation.

Another aspect of Mannerism, not typical of the movement, was the fashion for potboilers. It would be unfair to judge the movement by this kind of painting, though numerous examples of it may come to our attention. These pictures are nearer to resemblance than pictures of a higher quality, and this is why mistakes are made by historians that are too limited in experience to see a local school.

The Mannerists formed a link in the chain, and no chain is stronger than its weakest link. The chain was strong enough. Rubens and Rembrandt utilized the discoveries of the Mannerists for profound messages and to refine their technical achievements. Time was needed for this evolution.

Van Mander lived in this transitional, scholarly, experimenting period. Being a good teacher, he realized the need for some kind of textbook. The biographies by Van Mander are a part of such a book. After many years of thought, research, and writing, Van Mander, in 1604, faced the problem of finding an effective title for his book. He finally decided the title should be 'The Schilderboeck, in which are presented to zealous youth the Principles of the *Fine and Liberal* Art of painting. Next, in three parts, the Lives of the Famous and Illustrious Painters of Ancient and Modern Times. Finally, the Explanation of the Metamorphosis of Ovid. Also Chapters on Symbolism and Mythology. All this is for the use of Painters, Art Lovers and Poets, and for People of All Ranks, by Carel van Mander, Painter.'

INTRODUCTION

This work, for its time, was an encyclopedia of art that covered a wide field. Only the part concerning the lives of Dutch, Flemish, and some German, artists is presented in this volume.

To retain the spirit of Van Mander's great work, a few words, from the first part of his book, about the 'Principles' are needed. The 'Principles'—*Den Grondt* in Dutch, or the 'Didactic Poem'—not available in English, contain maxims typical of the author's period, which appear frequently in the biographies. Van Mander believed these maxims should be of great importance to young artists. The 'Principles' throw a beautiful light on the cultural level of Van Mander and on that of his contemporaries.[1]

In a chapter of the 'Principles,' devoted to drawing, Van Mander says drawing is the father of painting; drawing is the body, painting is the spirit. He compares drawing to the tone of a musical instrument and painting to the human voice. He wants his students to know how to draw an oval with crossed-lines as a preparation for a face. He complains that nothing was written in the Netherlands to guide young artists. He wants his students to learn the principles of drawing by making outlines and hatchings for light and shadow, first with charcoal, then with crayon and later with the pen, so that the original outline cannot be detected and strong accents can be noticed in the shadows. He recommends drawing on colored papers. Drawing he says is most useful to monarchs, captains, and soldiers, to enable them to make plans for defense works. He has no objection to the use of a frame that has intersecting threads. It is good, according to

[1]A free German translation that is an excellent and scholarly analysis of the 'Grondt' has been made by Dr. R.Hoecker: 'Das Lehrgedicht des Karel van Mander,' Haag, Martinus Nijhoff. 1916. '*Quellenstudien zur Holländischen Kunstgeschichte,*' VIII.

INTRODUCTION

Van Mander, to watch the flaying of corpses. Again and again, he emphasizes drawing from life.

He has little to say on perspective. He refers to the works of Pieter Koeck and Blum. Van Mander does not go into great detail about proportion. This was quite natural for a Flemish artist more interested in the concrete and definite message of the art of Breughel than in the theoretical pondering of Dürer. He says of Dürer, this master is unsurpassed in regard to proportion, but 'I do not care to break my head on this matter, because I need my time for painting.' Still he gives his student Vitruvius' rules for the proportions of children, and he quotes Plinius. Van Mander's theory on the action of the human body is based entirely on the theories by Alberti and Leonardo da Vinci. He warns one against impossible exaggerations and twistings of the human figure. He does not approve of artificial lacing of legs and arms. Evidently he did not like some of the work by Gossart, the Romanist, who excelled at this kind of acrobatics. Van Mander draws attention to dancing figures.

He devotes a long chapter to composition. He recommends planning a picture well beforehand, and making sketches from nature as conscientiously as possible. He likes the corners of landscape-pictures well filled with heavy foliage, accents on the open space in the center, and a small group of people against a far background. This suggests a theatrical stage-setting. He says Italians needed artists from the Netherlands for such work. He recommends a variety of poses for human figure; but he warns against cutting figures of cattle in half with the frame of the picture. He does not like much detail, and says gentlemen of importance speak few but significant words and, similarly, great masters do not need detail.

Van Mander analyses facial expressions. He advises one to

INTRODUCTION

watch nature, to look at loving couples that embrace each other and hold their heads together. One should study works of art. For expressions of emotions and passions, one should study pictures by Lucas van Leyden and Breughel's *Massacre of the Innocents*.

He devotes a chapter to light effects at dawn and sunset, to rainbows in the sky and in the mist of a waterfall; for fire, flames and volcanoes, and night effects, he selects examples by Raphael, Bassano, Goltzius, Pieter Aertsen, Dürer and Cornelis van Haarlem.

The chapter on landscape is important because Van Mander relied on his own initiative for the treatment of this subject. There were no literary examples to guide him. He advises young artists to rise early in the morning, take a sketchbook, leave the city, and study in the open, and, at the same time, listen to birds and watch the colors reflected by dew on the grass. He suggests observing how gray predominates in all colors near the horizon. Since Apelles painted thunder and lightning with only four colors, Van Mander asks why we paint landscapes in all the colors we have at our disposal. He recommends painting pictures of snow, hail and sleet; painting sky with clouds, as all the painters do in the Netherlands, and azure sky without any clouds; painting of rivulets in the meadows and the effects of muddy roads where people have slipped. Van Mander asserts that there are few Italian artists that are masters of landscape painting, and two of these masters are Tintoretto and Titian.

In a chapter about wild and tame animals, and birds, Van Mander observes that the female animals are softer and rounder than the male; he describes the beauty of a young calf. He constantly preaches that one should study from life.

Van Mander does not approve of exaggeration in painting draperies, and, as Leonardo did, he recommends the study of folds in wool. He admires the painting of satins and silks by Venetian painters, and he dislikes the abundance of the folds in work by Aldegrever.

The chapter on color harmonies and contrasts is according to Van Mander's observations of nature. He refers to flowers and to Breughel's habit of placing a spot of pure color in a mass of gray.

In the chapter that deals with painting, one is informed that underpainting should be carefully finished, after making numerous preparatory sketches. Van Mander describes Italian fresco and says it has no practical value in the Netherlands or where the climate is moist. He compares the refinement in work by the Van Eycks, by Dürer, Lucas van Leyden, with the coarse treatment of color by his own contemporaries. The technique used by Titian, in his early work, can be seen nearby and at a distance; but Titian's later work should be better seen from a distance. Van Mander warns against the use of too much white for the highlights on human flesh. This seems to be a difficult problem for young artists and amateurs. Van Mander thinks the artists of the Netherlands have not reached the perfection that the Italians have in the use of color. In paintings of the nude figure, Italian artists often used a kind of fish-color for the flesh, and at other times flesh looked like stone. Evidently, Van Mander had in mind some of Gossart's work.

Van Mander mentions the mysterious influence color can have on pregnant women and cause birthmarks on children. He admires the color of the tiger and panther, the color in the cheeks of young girls, and the colors of flowers.

The last chapter of 'Principles' is about the symbolism of color in the Bible and in mythology and heraldry; the relation of color to the planets, to the seven virtues and the seven stages of life; and, finally, the significance of red, blue, black, and white, in the four temperaments and the four seasons.

The 'Principles' may be disappointing to one searching for technical secrets, but to one interested in the philosophy of art, and in applied aesthetics, it will be delightful. The strictly technical information, concerning paints and brushes and canvases, is very meager. This book, written in verse, was the first theoretical work on painting printed in the Netherlands. It follows what might be called the Italian pattern which was popular at the time. The main source was the work of Leone Battista Alberti, but indirectly, since Van Mander knew this work in a German version by Gualtherus H. Ryff, to whom he refers. The German book was published in 1546, re-issued in 1558 at Nürnberg, and again in 1582 at Basel. When Van Mander was in Nürnberg, he may have obtained the book there.

Van Mander used Leonardo's *Treatise on Painting*, and he probably read it in a manuscript form that was not uncommon before the death of Melzi in 1570. We may assume that Van Mander did not realize the text was by da Vinci, because he quotes this master only once; though Van Mander loved to refer to an important person in his writings; he frequently mentioned authorities that were not so illustrious as da Vinci.

There were a great many didactic poems in Holland, so it will not be surprising to find Van Mander using this form for instruction, which had a long history. Van Mander was an appreciated poet who had won many prizes at the contests of the rhetoricians in Flanders; his *Gulden Harpe* reached the heart of the people.

Van Mander's book begins with a moral address to future artists. He had the spiritual welfare of his students much at heart. His admonitions and advice were—

'Do not waste time. Do not get drunk or fight. Do not draw attention by living an immoral life. Painters belong in

INTRODUCTION

the environment of princes and learned people. They must
be polite to their fellow artists. Settle disputes tactfully and
wisely. Listen to criticism, even that of the common people.
Do not become upset or angry because of adverse criticism.
Do not draw special attention to the mistakes of your master.
Food is neither praise nor blame to yourself. Thank God for
your talent and do not be conceited. Do not fall in love too
young and do not marry too soon. The bride must be at least
ten years younger than the groom. While travelling avoid
little inns and avoid lending money to your own compatriots
in a foreign country. Always examine the bedding most carefully. Keep away from prostitutes, for two reasons: It is a
sin, and they make you sick. Be very careful while travelling
in Italy, because there are so many possibilities of losing your
money and wasting it. Knaves and tricky rogues have very
smooth tongues. Show the Italians how wrong they are in
their belief that Flemish painters cannot paint human figures.
At Rome study drawing, at Venice painting. Finally, eat
breakfast early in the morning and avoid melancholia.'

It is evident that Van Mander was thoroughly justified in
writing a book concerning the completion of the education
of art students. The instruction given by the master employ-
er was seldom adequate. Van Mander's book was very helpful to numerous self-taught artists in Holland. Van Mander
gave to his readers lively, colorful, and realistic, word-
pictures in his *Schilderboeck*. He knew various languages;
he had travelled and he had kept his eyes open; he was interested in human beings. This is evident in his poetry. He
had much to give, and he always gave willingly. As an honest
and modest teacher he has mentioned the sources of his information. His introductions to some of the biographies,
specially to those of his friends, may seem exaggerated and
pompus, but they are vivid. Van Mander and Breughel loved

INTRODUCTION

to tell their stories. They tried to create an atmosphere for
their accounts of people and events. There are typical Flemish lyrical notes in Van Mander's stories. He is emotional
and depends on the emotions of others.

Van Mander, being a poet and a painter, did not always
know which of his two means of expression was the better
one for conveying his feelings. He had little or no doctrinal,
aesthetic judgement. He was driven from Flanders by the
war, not because of his religious views. He joined the Baptists
in Holland, and he found a shelter for his religious needs;
their doctrines were liberal for that time. There was no lovely madonna in their church, and Van Mander remained sensitive to that charm and must have missed it.

Van Mander was a good Flemish artist. After his visit to
Italy, he was sensitive to the beauty of the human figure. He
loved allegory and mythology for the opportunity each
offered to artists. Repeatedly he regretted that artists were
forced to paint portraits for a living. He recognized the high
artistic quality of some of their works. He knew, from his
own experience, how difficult it is to paint a portrait that will
be, to the subject's family, a satisfactory resemblance. The
people of those days in Holland knew what a war meant.
Life was concrete to them. The realities of life made the
Dutch prefer truth to beauty. Van Mander was a dreamer.
Though he had seen and enjoyed Italian art, he had not
analysed it as Quentin Matsys and Breughel had. Allegory
and mythology were subjects for painting nude figures. A
nude figure was not a sinful thing: Van Mander was born in
the country of Rubens.

Van Mander regarded a large composition of figures the
highest achievement. As both painter and poet, his experiences had made him tolerant. He had the patience to listen to
what anyone said. He was the right man to write the lives of

INTRODUCTION

Dutch and Flemish painters. His selection of artists was good. No other cross-section of the period could have been better placed.

Van Mander did not write about the work of anonymous masters; occasionally he does mention an illuminator. It was perhaps logical, as a tradition, to place the Van Eycks first in the biographies. His objections to the laws of guilds are characteristic; in this, he was in advance of his time. Van Mander hoped for the return of another time when artists should work for a wealthy aristocracy that would recognize and reward ability. But one may ask if Van Mander ever reckoned that one of his own pupils, Frans Hals, would be one of the great Dutch painters.

After reading a few chapters and becoming familiar with Van Mander's style, one does not think of the author as having lived over three hundred years ago. The problems of the artist in those days were not very different from those of today. Commercial paintings were required then; various artists became fashionable and were forgotten by subsequent generations; then, as now, many excellent artists worked almost unnoticed, and Van Mander drew attention to some of them.

Though Van Mander's knowledge of history was good, we have a different factual knowledge of his period and we can see it in perspective. He had ability and qualifications that art instructors of any period should profess. Van Mander knew how to combine his own experience, and that of others, with his knowledge of the history of art and a practical philosophy. That was appreciation for not only a limited and local style of art, but for any art that was good and healthy. That is why the warmth, and beauty, and truth, of his expressions are welcomed by a real lover of art.

BIOGRAPHY OF CAREL VAN MANDER

THE FAMILY, THE BIRTH, THE LIFE, AND THE WORKS, OF

CAREL VAN MANDER, PAINTER AND POET,

HIS DEATH AND HIS FUNERAL

BY [?] ADAM VAN MANDER[1]

I AM grateful for the opportunity to commemorate the man who, so instructively and with so much learning at his own great sacrifice, described the art of painting for students. He helped to make immortal the most important Dutch masters known. It was his privilege to do this service clearly and brilliantly in writing the *Schilderboeck*, which has been appreciated so much and so readily. Some one has been encouraged to reprint the *Schilderboeck*. I regard the undertaking as logical, just and right. Carel represents one who resurrected forgotten artists and robed them in the brilliant costume of fame. I should feel guilty before law and God, if I did not try to robe him splendidly with the gown of fame, in spite of death and mortal envy. He should live eternally and be radiant with the diamond crown of lasting fame, not to the extent, perhaps, I could wish, but as far as possible within my little power.

Worthy 'Man der Mannen', where shall I begin to trumpet the fame of thy illustrious spirit, the greatness of thy splendid, noble, examplary existence? Shall I be conceited and try to understand the great height of thy heavenly spirit with my human, terrestial mind? Of the spirit that knew how to introduce the divine matter of the holy scriptures in thy poems, which people sang and by which they were strengthened? Who in thy time has produced so much religious poetry? Have any other sweet messages been so good to the

XLI

ears of people as those thy 'Gulden Harpe' has whispered to them by its soft singing? What heart was not delighted by the Christian songs thou soundest with great joy and caused a hundred thousand inexpressible joys?[2]

Or, better, to look first with external eyes upon the work of thy high and great spirit, and to describe this noble and excellent work in painting? It cannot be praised enough.

I am in doubt as to which should come first. Thou hast excelled in poetry as well as in painting; thou hast surpassed thy contemporaries. Reason tells me I should describe both arts simultaneously. I shall begin and describe thyself, for thou art the source from which all these highly desired treasures have come. If any one wants to know from whence thou art come, from whom thou art descended, from which family and when born, let him listen:

Carel van Mander was born in the year of our Lord, 1548, on a Sunday in the month of May, in a village named Meulebeke. This village had a circumference of about nine miles, and it was situated in a pleasant valley, with meadows and houses, trees, hedges and woods. Lakes and many rivulets irrigated the land. Meulebeke was located in the center of Flanders, one mile from Putthem and one mile from Rosebeke. Before this village was destroyed by the 'Malcontents,' under command of Montigny, it had fifteen hundred mustered men. The village was situated in the region of Thielt and was part of the castellany of Courtrai. Carel's father was named Cornelis van Mander, and for a long time he was tax collector and bailiff for the lord of the village. He lived in his own house. He owned farms and land and gave land in rent. He directed loans, was a citizen of Courtrai and was sometimes a 'hoog poincter' of the castellany.

Carel's father was a freeman of the town of Bruges, since he had a manor comprised of eight properties. The house had

BIOGRAPHY

a good wall, and was surrounded by a moat; there were places for fruit and barns for cattle; there were lakes, forests, fruit trees and a pond with a mill to grind grain for the parish of Kolskamp. These possessions came to him when he married Johanna van der Beke. In political troubles he was a good fighter, and he gave a brave account of himself and his men. I could write a long story about this, but I shall pass it for sake of brevity.

Carel van Mander was baptized in the church at Meulebeke; he was held near the font by Sir Charles de Beir, who gave him the French name Charles. According to the custom of the country, and because it was easier to pronounce, he was called Carel.

Dear Reader, since in Flanders the family name of the mother is not counted, I shall inform you of Carel's ancestry on his father's side, which goes far back, and of his nobility which can be traced in a certain parchment document in the Ten Eyckhoute convent at Bruges. The Latin text of it is—

Reverendus in Christo Waltherus van Mander Episcopus Ecclesiae Tornacencis questionens interfratres et Sorores divae Trudonis Habitantis ad magnum pontem lapidium via Oostcampania, vulgo 'de groote Steenbrugghe', composit tam ad mobilia bona, una cum abbate dulcis vallis, vulgo 'Suetendaele' et Fratres in abbatia nunc quercuum vulgo 'ten Eechoute' Bruga Transposuit jussu et petitione Theodorici Elsaty Comitia Flandriae. Anno Domini MCCXLVIII Mense Augusto.

With August of the present year, 1617, three hundred and sixty nine years have passed since Walther van Mander became Bishop of Tournai. There has been another Walther van Mander: the son of Claude, the brother of the chevalier Jan van Mander. He was the great grandfather of Carel and a knight and a probationer of the Lieve Vrouwekerck at Bruges. He was sent to England by Duke Philip the Good because of his learnedness and talent in oratory. He went with the Bishop of Terwaenen. They travelled as ambassadors and to make arrangements for the marriage between Henry, Prince of Wales, and the daughter of John of Burgundy. Van Mander was richly rewarded by the Duke.[3]

Walther van Mander's epitaph appears on a metal memorial tablet under which he is buried in the Lieve Vrouwekerck in Bruges. He donated many things to this church among which was a scapula of gold embroidery, decorated with the family crest of the Van Manders. The crest is a white swan with wings spread on a black field, the swan, with a gold ring round its neck, is swimming in water. One of the dukes of Flanders, Philip the Good, honored the Van Manders with the crest after they had served the fatherland well in the war against the Scottish and English. This crest of arms, with its helmet and ornaments, was to be seen in many places and may be seen now on a blue tombstone in the church of Meulebeke, and it has been cast in the church-bells that hang in the high steeple. This should prove how illustrious the Van Manders were.

I should like to go into detail about the brave men and the pious women of the Van Mander family. I should like to mention the praise they received for their services rendered to their rulers and to the fatherland. I should like to speak of their virtues, their positions and the honors they were considered to be worthy of. To do so would make a long book which would be difficult for me to write and for you to read. I leave this as it is, and return to the task I have set for myself.

Carel was the second son. His mother nourished him with her own breasts and brought him up with his elder brother, Cornelis. Cornelis was a kind and an obedient child, willing and helpful, and he always considered seriously the matters of the household.

BIOGRAPHY

Carel, moved by a high and lively spirit, kept aloof from all common things. He surpassed his contemporaries with his wit and quick understanding. Nature, at the very beginning, had planned something special for him.

Plutarch says, children that abandon their infantile practice for the sake of something more serious that their years warrant, show signs of something good in the future; things in which a man will have his pleasure when full grown, are seen by the child at an early age. This he shows from childhood to maturity. The spirit of man is hard to really understand. It reveals itself, no matter in what vessel it is poured by God; it cannot remain hidden, as merry-making wine cannot remain hidden in living barrels, for it announces itself with songs, sweet, foolish, small talk and other little follies. That kind of spirit was in Van Mander. When he was young, when his father's girl servants had whitewashed some walls, Carel drew, with coal and red and yellow earth, the portraits of their lovers and sweethearts. One had a long crooked nose and a hump; the other had round legs, large and clumsy feet, and a hump on his shoulder where an owl was perched. He then wrote their names under the drawings. The girls were not pleased; but little Carel always knew how to get out of the trouble caused by a little joke.

One winter morning, before sunrise, when it was freezing very had, Carel promised one of his father's servants a little poem about a sweetheart who had been mean to him, providing the man would hold his tongue against the iron pump-handle while Carel read a Pater Noster and an Ave Maria. The fool was willing. He thought through the use of the art of some one else, really abuse, he could avenge the injustice done to him. They began and little Carel read. In the meantime, the man's tongue was frozen to the iron; the poor fellow could not move, and he cried and screamed with pain.

BIOGRAPHY

He wrenched himself loose and left a large piece of the skin of his tongue. Those witnessing this laughed at his stupidity and that he had been fooled by the boy.

One day Carel played another joke. It happened that the children in the neighborhood, who loved to play with Carel because of his jokes, were all together. There was a boy among them whose mother, a widow, had made for him a new, long, white tunic which he was wearing for the first time. The boy came in this outfit to see Carel. It was the season when cherries were ripe. Carel praised the tunic highly; but he made the boy believe the tailor had forgotten to put a hem on it. He told the boy, that if he would keep still, he would do it for him. The simple lad had no objections and Carel went to work. He squeezed juice from cherries and painted a double border all round, placing butterflies front and behind, and he decorated the sleeves. The boy felt proud of the way Carel had made his tunic so beautiful. His pride would have had bad consequences, if there had not been some foresight on the part of the artist. Carel had figured that the boy's mother would give him a thorough spanking, the moment she discovered the decorative borders, as the boys in those days did not wear trousers while they were small. Carel promised Joos some cherries if he would let him paint something on the lower part of his back. After much bickering the boy agreed. Carel worked with cherry juice; he placed the boy with his bare back in the sun, so that his painting would dry rapidly. He painted the face of a grinning devil on the lower part of the back. After the picture dried, he gave the promised cherries to the boy who, much excited, ran to his mother to show her how beautifully he had been decorated. When the good lady saw it all, she became very angry and she took a stick to give little Joos a beating. When she lifted his tunic and saw the devil's face,

BIOGRAPHY

she dropped the stick and fainted, crying: 'Holy Martin, Patron of Meulebeke, abide with me!' In the meantime, the news spread from one neighbor to another. The mystery was solved, and Joos got out of it without a spanking. A complaint was made to Carel's father, and, in the end, everyone had a hearty laugh.

As Carel grew older he continued to play practical jokes. He would draw all kinds of figures, and he wrote hundreds of little rhymes, on his writing paper in school, and on the walls at home and along the road. The parents and family noticed the boy had a clever and an active mind. They put him and his brother Cornelis in the Latin school at Thielt. Here Carel studied grammar and syntax and made much progress in poetry and painting. For some reason, he was taken from that school and sent to Ghent to study under a French schoolmaster. His uncle, François van Mander, living in that town, looked after him.

The boys lived there for a few years. Carel did not stop his drawing and writing of poetry. The father and uncle observed this. In time, Carel was sent to a good master painter, to learn more. They put him with Lucas de Heere who was a fine witty poet and painter. Little Carel made rapid progress in painting and poetry, considering the short time he was with de Heere. One wonders why his father took him away and sent him to a second master at Courtrai, who was the last instructor Carel had. This master was a fine painter. His name was Pieter Vlerick. Carel lived with him for more than a year, from 1568 till 1569, first at Courtrai and later at Tournai, for, at that time, Vlerick left the one city for the other. Carel has mentioned this in the biography of Vlerick, in the *Schilderboeck*.4

After our painter and poet returned to the house of his father, which stood for a long time near the church at Meulebeke, he applied himself to poetry and to writing instead of painting. He composed beautiful morality plays, one of Noah, and how he built the ark and preached to convert the people; how the deluge came and how the animals gathered and went into the ark; the sending of the dove and raven; and the sacrifice, after quitting the ark. This was arranged admirably and many persons appeared in it. Carel painted, on a large canvas, many dead bodies of men and animals floating on the water. The painting was pulled over the stage. By means of a hand pump, water was drawn up on a house and let fall with much force on the stage, as if it was rain. The spectators came in large numbers from the surrounding towns and villages to see this spectacle. They were forced back and most surprised by all the water. Many old people, weeping for the dead, were moved by fear for the living. It looked as if the ark floated on the water. Carel was busy for a long time on this spectacle. His brother Cornelis was not pleased with it all; he wanted Carel to assist him in the cloth business. When Pentecost approached, Carel knew how to prevail upon his brother; Cornelis, from his own pocket, paid for everything needed in the play. The mother said: 'You are more foolish than Carel; if you kept your money in your chest, he would not be able to do all this.'

Carel wrote farces, based upon jokes that had been played by farmers, some banquet plays, and songs and refrains, some spiritual, some serious and some foolish. He received many invitations to compete with other rhetoricians from all parts of Flanders. He won many prizes in pewter.5

Among plays, he wrote one of Nebuchadnezzar and how this illustrious prince was expelled from his realm and had to eat hay and grass with wild animals, till he had enough, was well in mind, and could return and be reinstated in his realm. Another play was about David, the royal prophet, and how

BIOGRAPHY

he secured succession for his wise son, Solomon, and gave him the plans for the building of the temple. Solomon's Judgement was another play, and he wrote a play about Hieram and the Queen of Sheba, which was performed on Pentecost, at Meulebeke. Probably fifty persons, with camels and other animals, took part in this beautiful play. The stage was arranged in an artistic manner. Adam van Mander, Carel's brother, played the rôle of Solomon, which was long. Nearly all the families of Ghent, Bruges, Courtrai, Oudenaerde, and other places, came to see the play. He wrote a play, Bride of Christ, and a farce for the wedding of his sister. He had written two plays in rhyme before he went to Rome. One was of Bael at Babel, the other one, Wisdom and Folly. These plays were given in Meulebeke, while he was in Italy. At the same time, his play of Daniel was given at Thielt. Carel became known everywhere. In the meantime, he painted things to be hung in churches and in houses.

Carel received permission from his father and mother to go to Rome. In 1574, before his departure, he wrote a parting song. He received clothing and money, and he was sent first to Ghent to his uncle François for recommendations concerning the journey, since François had once made the journey.⁶

Carel went in company with a group of young gentlemen whom he had to leave, as it was inconvenient for them to wait for him when he stopped to look at the works of art and visit masters in various cities. Carel arrived at Rome in good health. But he has written about his travels, and I refer the interested reader to his account of them.⁷

Occasionally, Carel wrote to his parents from Rome. He was there during the jubilee year, 1575, and he saw many rare things. His stay in Rome lasted more than three years. His first work was for a duke in the Italian city of Termi, for whom he made a few large pictures of scenes from the massacre of St Bartholomew's Day in Paris; one scene shows how Admiral Coligny was thrown out of a window. Carel worked with a Signor Caspare of Apulia, a pupil of Giacome de Gratisco. While Carel remained with this Italian, he painted grotesques, a work in which he was experienced, and many landscapes in fresco for various cardinals. He received permission from the Pope to wear a sword at will. He spent much time with Sprangher. The painters lived so wisely they always had money in the bank. Carel was one of the first to re-discover the catacombs in Rome, and he made many drawings of them. He made drawings of various other things, almost all the ancient monuments and what else he could find.[8]

Carel left Italy in 1577. On his return journey he went to Basel where he painted some pictures at the cemetery, called the Campo Santo. These were of the Flight of Jacob. Sprangher, who has seen these, said these paintings were exquisitely beautiful. He visited Vienna with Sprangher and assisted in making the triumphal arch erected there for the reception of Emperor Rudolph. The arch was beautifully and richly decorated. Hans Mont, the sculptor, sculptured figures.[9]

Carel longed for his home and his parents. He returned with many drawings of beautiful subjects. As he came near the village and the house of his parents, word of his arrival was given. His brother, Adam, the servants, his friends, the rhetoricians, and other members of the parish, went to meet him, with great rejoicing. His father and his mother embraced him joyfully and lovingly.[10]

After he had enjoyed himself with his friends, he began to paint. His first picture, Adam and Eve, was entirely of nudes. Standing by the tree of the fruit of good and evil, Eve is looking at Adam with love and offers him the apple; many ani-

L

mals, four-footed as well as flying, are represented; the horizon is in the distance; and many rivers flow in the background; many beautiful trees, green herbs, and beautiful flowers, are in the foreground.

Next, he painted the sinking of the world under the waters of the deluge. This picture and many others were praised by connoisseurs.

He made a memorial tablet for his brother, François van Mander, who had died and was buried in London. François had been ordered to the court of the King of Spain, to enter his bodyguard formed of nobles. On a wooden panel he painted, in oil, an elaborate and artistic border of nude putti seated on skulls and bones, holding torches upside down, and under stress of great emotion, tears roll down their rosy, fat cheeks.

At the top, he painted the crest of the Van Manders and hung the shields left and right; on the square field of the panel, he painted a Resurrection of Christ; below this, a skeleton, in a grave. François had written the epitaph. Originally, the memorial was to have been hung in the church, in memory and in honor of the father of François, above the grave of the father. In the war and the period of the iconoclasm, these pictures and other things Carel had collected were stolen or destroyed.

Carel read and wrote a great deal in his father's house, and sometimes he painted for pleasure. He visited several villages to search for a sweetheart. In the meantime, the Malcontents, the Walloons, came to take Carel's town. The farmers of the surrounding places, Thielt, Meulebeke and other villages, all together some five thousand men, took up arms.

From this time on the country side was given over to destruction. The soldiers of both sides were too heavy a burden to be carried; they strangled the population for money and goods. Carel's parents packed their jewelry, furniture, and goods, and dragged them to Bruges and to Courtrai. Refugees fled from one city to another. At the time of this ordeal, Carel composed a sonnet about the miserable situation of the fleeing girls who have been left by their sweethearts. It began:

Nog weet ik eene,	I know one,
Aerdiger geene,	There is no lovilier one.
Endie is bleven thuis.	And she stayed home.

This refers to a young and beautiful girl eighteen years old and of a humble family. Carel married her in this restless period; they had a son whom he named Cornelis after his father.[11]

Carel was forced to go to Courtrai. The soldiers had besieged Tournai and had moved along the Leie river in the castellany and were now spreading over the land round Bruges. A regiment of German soldiers, camped at Isseghem, made much trouble for the country people.

Carel went home with horses and wagons to get the wheat and bring it to Courtrai. He had loaded two or three wagons and was on his way, when at a distance of hardly an arrow's shot from the church, the Walloon regiment under Montigny attacked him. This was on Three Kings' Day, in the afternoon, in the middle of the village. The savings were lost and everything the soldiers found was taken; the men were beaten and wounded and the women and maidens were molested.

The house of Carel's father was sacked. The poor old man, who had been sick a long time, was in his bed. The blankets and sheets were snatched away from him. Adam, Carel's brother, hearing the sudden racket in his father's house, took a blade hidden somewhere and, knowing the Walloon language well, mixed among the knaves and the footmen with his sword and hacked to pieces the cabinets and chests; thus he obtained more booty and baggage than he could carry. He attacked his own mother to get her money. But they understood each other; while he held her, she was free of other bandits.

In this turmoil Carel and his wagons were caught by Walloons, and they took off all his clothing. He talked and pleaded with them, to no avail; they tied a rope around his neck and were eager to hang him unless he satisfied them with money. While this was happening, an Italian cavalier came along on horseback. Carel addressed him in Italian. The cavalier, wondering where this farmer had learned the language, inquired of him. Carel replied that he had learned it in Italy, mostly in Rome. The cavalier asked what he had been doing there. 'I painted,' replied Carel. The Italian, looking sharply into his face, recognized him. He drew his sword and, beating back the Walloons, who were on foot, he said to them: 'Be quick! Take that noose from his neck, free my friend and give him his clothing.' They did so. The cavalier wanted to help Carel regain his goods, but the marauders became too strong. Each took all he could carry and went his way.

The Italian stayed with Carel, to prevent others from causing more trouble; he would have led him into the army camp, but Carel said he had an old, sick father in the village, whose house was plundered, and he had left his wife and son at Courtrai, where he wanted to bring his father, mother, brother and sister. The cavalier remained with Carel till all the soldiers had disappeared, then he shook hands with him and said: 'A Dio Compagno sino a reviderci.'—'God bless you and I hope to meet you again.' Carel thanked him and kissed his hands. This cavalier had served under the Albanese and he had been a good friend of Carel's at Rome, at the court of the Cardinal, where Carel had been painting and had oc-

BIOGRAPHY

casionally given him a drawing. For some reason, the cavalier had left Italy and had taken part in the war in the Netherlands. Observe, how good it is to make oneself beloved by everyone. This unexpected friend apparently saved his life.

Carel went to his father and found things as miserable as they could be. He told about his experiences and how the horses and wagons and all the goods had been stolen. Adam, his brother, showed his booty and brought out their sister Janneken. She had been hiding in a dried pool between fences where Adam had put her. They took something from the booty to cover their father, mother, brothers, and sisters, and started for Courtrai. They had to carry their sick father; there was neither a wagon nor a horse to be had in the village. They went three miles this way and brought the sick man to the monastery of the grey minorites. A room was given to them with a bed and a pillow, food and drink; this was in return for the good deeds the father had done for these monks. Observe how one friendly deed is worthy of another.

While Carel was in Courtrai, in 1581, he received an order from the dean and leaders of the cloth guild and linen weavers to paint an altar panel with two wings, for twenty Flemish pounds; a portion of it was in cash that was most useful to him and his family.

The altar painting had, on the exterior, two standing figures painted in grissaille. On one side, St Catherine, with sword and a crown in her hand; the broken wheel and her tyrannical father were at her feet; Menes, her teacher of the Christian faith, was on the other side; on the interior of the wings, in six square fields, the martyrdom was shown. The sharp cutting wheel and the tyrant, about to maim and kill her, is destroyed by lightning. On each field there is a special martyr. Below each of these are two lines of verse written in gold letters. Carel composed these verses; they explain the

LIV

subject. On the central panel, on one side, the tyrant and soldiers, and on the other side, at the left of St Catherine, a number of decapitated corpses, and dogs showing their fangs and their backs humped with hair bristling. In the center, the pure and pious maiden, kneeling, with a calm face, looks towards heaven; her eyes are unbandaged, and she waits with folded hands for the deadly blow of the executioner, who stands next to her, half naked, with his sword raised to give the blow. A brilliant light from above shines on the girl; the bared part of her body glows like alabaster. The painter gave careful attention to the pose and the action and to the faces. I do not know whether Carel has made other works in Courtrai worth mentioning.[12]

Carel's second child he called Pieter, after the husband of his sister, Anna, whose name was Pieter Pype, and who had died with his wife and family, from pest. Because of this, he and his wife and child moved to Bruges in 1582. With a little baggage and a small amount of money, again on the road, they were bereft of all they had by the Malcontents. Carel and his wife were deprived of all their clothing and the smallest things were stolen. The hunger for booty was so intense, the swaddling clothes were taken off the baby, and the mother had to carry the child on her lap, wrapped in a miserable rag the soldiers had left her. Carel had nothing but a worn blanket on his body. His wife had a double pocket in her underskirt and in it a gold piece, which had not been found by the soldiers. Carel jumped into the air for joy. His wife was weeping, and Carel tried to console her, saying: 'Now, by chance, if we can reach the city, without being taken prisoners and can remain unhurt, everything will be all right again!' He sang merrily a little song. He said: 'I am going to paint very hard, and we will be able to buy clothing and food.' He took the baby on his arm and danced; he was

BIOGRAPHY

so gay his wife had to laugh. They arrived at the town and found an old acquaintance, a painter, whose name was Paulus Weyts. He gave Carel work immediately.

Carel earned money by which to live. But there was no rest in this place. The enemy was coming nearer each day, and the pest had become violent in the city. Carel left, with his wife, mother-in-law, and his children, and boarded a ship bound for Holland. He settled in the old and famous city of Haarlem, where he received drawing and painting orders.[13]

I do not intend to give the reader a list of all the things our painter-poet has produced. It would be long and too difficult for me to do, unless the beautiful lady from Crete would guide me with her thread. I shall touch on some of his works that I should recommend to your attention. You will recognize how heroic a figure he has been in art, and what a good mind he had. No-one will be so stupid as not to believe this man of all men was a good master and a good mentor for young artists.

I do not doubt Carel has experienced hateful resentment from some who were displeased by him, for the reason he allotted some too high a rank in art, and others received a lower place. This does not matter. Sensible people will take degrading remarks for what they are worth; many times these remarks have an effect different from what they were intended to have. I now ask the kind Reader to accept my appreciation, with the kindest spirit in harmony with the kindness of his own heart, and may the dear Lord reward him with the best of spiritual goods. I hope the eternal Holy Trinity will grant me this favor. Amen. Farewell!

As to the paintings and poems Carel made in Holland, I shall present some of them: He painted a Deluge in grissaille, in 1583, after he had been in Haarlem a short while. Later he painted some little scenes on roundels, which were bought

BIOGRAPHY

by Mr Rauwert at first sight. He became acquainted with Goltzius and Cornelis Cornelisz. These three artists formed a kind of academy to study models from life. Carel taught the other two the Italian method, as can be readily learned from the Ovid by Goltzius.[14]

Carel painted many grissailles because the art amateurs were pleased with them. He painted the Passion in twelve scenes, for Rauwert, a peasant wedding and other things. Jaques Razet had many of his works, among them, St John preaching, and two pictures of the Nativity. A similar subject, valued highly, is with a painter at Haarlem. Rentmaster Kolderman has a picture, by Carel, of an interrupted sermon, and another picture of the Passing under the Yoke. Jan Matthijsz., brewer at Haarlem, has a picture of David and Abigail. Carel painted a shield for the town hall at Haarlem, in memory of Jan Huygensz Linschoten. He made a very fine Story of Jephta for Master Albert. (Symonsz.) He painted a Carrying of the Cross for Melchior Wijntgis, a peasant wedding, and various other little pictures. He painted a Crucifixion, for Razet, in which he and Goltzius were done from life. There are few amateurs in Holland who have none of his works. Three of his best paintings are in the home of Kors Reyers, the goldsmith; a Carrying of the Cross, so beautifully executed connoisseurs praise it highly; the Three Magi; and Jacob Buries the Foreign Idols. He painted a landscape, with peasant houses and beautiful trees, and Christ with the Apostles healing the lepers; this was for Willem Bartjens. A little picture of Mary and Joseph is artistic. While he was at Zevenberghen he painted two pictures, for Jan de Witte, juryman at Amsterdam, the Baptism and Conversion of St Paul.[15]

Carel painted one picture for Van Assendelft and one for Barthold Claeszoon, at Delft, representing the story of the

BIOGRAPHY

Wealthy Youth. Mr Klaes Fredericksz Roch at Amsterdam, in the Warmoesstraet, has one of his last and largest paintings, The Children of Israel Passing through the Jordan with the Holy Ark of the Covenant. He had represented himself in this picture as one of the Levites, or carriers of the ark; Isaak van Gerven and his first wife are also in this picture. The figures in the foreground are active and having serious discussions. The composition is good and the background is a landscape. There are mussels and snails in the bed of the river; the greyhounds and a redhound which are growling at one another. The following verses have been written in gold round the frame. Carel composed them—

> Every Christian of this world,
> Will reach, after a long struggle,
> The Kingdom which has many joys.
> The Jordan, Death, has to be crossed.
> It is the way all flesh must walk,
> It is the last enemy to be conquered.
> If one is successful, he will reach Salvation.

He painted for Mr Jan Hendricx Zoop, master director of the Glashuis, a large piece of the children of Israel dancing round the golden calf.[16] The foreground has lustful men dancing with the women of Moabit; they are lascivious with the foreign girls and look with voluptuous eyes at the experienced and mischievous women. The women are in gorgeous costumes with beautiful folds, and wear splendid ornaments. There are beautiful green trees, painted smoothly and evenly, with little stippling. The sky is fiery. Moses, in the distance, is speaking to the Lord, in a cloud.

Jan Fonteyn has a picture which in composition is vivid and lively. It is the battle between Hannibal and Scipio, the younger. Carel painted this in 1602.

Jan van Wely ordered a bathing scene and an Amor omni-

BIOGRAPHY

bus idem. He painted for Willem a Fall of Babel, and various pictures of vases with wild flowers. These are in Hamburg.[17]

His drawings may be found in various places. He designed cartoons, for the tapestry weaver, Spierincx of Delft. He made designs, for others, for damask table cloths and napkins. He made cartoons for glass painters, mostly for the Boshuis in Amsterdam.[18]

Among prints after his works, a large one of the Prodigal Son engraved by De Gheyn, and Eight converted Sinners, Passion of Christ, Twelve Patriarchs, The Building of All the Cities, The Twelve Apostles, The Discussions of the Poets, and many little allegories. He made many drawings, for he filled books with drawings done from life.[19]

In rhyme or poetry Carel wrote, 'The Iliad of Homer,' 'Two Pictures of Haarlem,' some songs, refrains and sonnets, a translation of 'Bucolics and Georgics,' 'De Gulden Harpe,' 'Het Broodhuis,' 'De Nieuwe Wereld of Beschryvinge van West Indie,' and 'De Stichting, Vernieling en de Opkomst van de stad Amsterdam,' which is below the picture of the city, 'Schilderboeck,' 'De Uitlegging van de Metamorphoses Ovidii,' 'De Uitbeelding der Figuren,' 'Spel van Zinnen van Dina' played by Flemish rhetoricians, and much more not printed.

Carel lived at Haarlem from 1583 to 1603, and then went to the Huis te Zevenberge, between Haarlem and Alkmaar. Here he painted pictures and wrote most of his 'Schilder-boeck.' He invited there some of his most important friends, connoisseurs and amateurs, in whose honor he had written a play that was performed by his pupils in the inner court of the castle. The entrance and the gate were decorated with green, and a wreath had been worked into it; pallets, brushes, mahlsticks, and other painting equipment, were arranged in it in the festoons, and Italian antiquities, decorations with fire-weapons and shooting implements. This was strange to the one who has never been in foreign countries.[20]

Afterwards, in 1604, he went to live at Amsterdam, in a house near the Montalbaanschen toren, opposite the Waal, where the ships dock during the winter. From there he moved to a house in the Uilenburgsbrug. In 1606, in May, he went to live at the Utrechtschen Steiger, in one of the Stadsgasthuizen, number twenty-four. By this time he had finished his writings and he had begun to draw and paint.

Many of his pupils have become masters of rank. Among them, Jaques de Moschero, Jacob Martens, Cornelis Engels, Frans Hals, portrait painter from Haarlem, Ever Krynsz. from The Hague, Hendrick Geeritsz. from East India, François Venant and many others, too many to list here. His eldest son, Carel van Mander, born at Haarlem, and living at Delft, has been praised for his prolific inventions and is considered to be a bold painter and master of drawing.[18]

Carel suffered from a sickness that he thought he could overcome by his own wit; but he found that his condition became worse and was beyond hope. He called for a physician and trusted him too much. He gave the sick man so many pills he became weaker each day. Carel began to feel reconciled to death, contrary to the feeling of the doctor, who was mild and gave more consolation than cure. He encouraged his patient in vain. But providence intended differently. The potions of the physician did not help Carel. It is a great art to live when death approaches. His brothers, rightly so, were depressed by his condition. Sometimes, in an agony of pain, he would raise his hands, and his feet would become cold; his vision became weak. His brother Adam said to him: 'Brother, I think you are getting worse.' Carel replied: 'The worse, the better; it is impossible to explain to a living person, the pangs of the dying.'

BIOGRAPHY

The night passed in great fear. In the morning he sent again for the doctor, who was surprised to see the man so sick. He said: 'There need be no fear that this man will die; you are not familiar with this illness. He will recover.' These idle words were spoken by one whose wisdom had no significance when it came to surmising things above us and hidden. The physician gave Carel another potion; he took only a little bit of it and became so cold that he could not be kept warm by means of warmed cloths. They tried to console him with words, telling him to have faith in Jesus Christ, the innocent Lamb of God, who redeems the sins of the world. His good friend, Jaques Razet, said to him at his death: 'In manus tuas Domine commendo.' He was lying in his bed and did not move for a while. He breathed with great difficulty. While he was healthy he said: 'When death comes, then there is no better advice than to lie quietly and die.' Carel did so. Those with him were on their knees praying to God to be merciful. He surrendered his spirit at twelve o'clock in the afternoon of the eleventh. He did not care about anything during his sickness; he did not say a word about his wife and child; he did not recommend them to anyone. He left a widow and seven living children; three children had died.[21]

On Wednesday, Carel's body was placed in a coffin with a wreath at the head. It was carried on the shoulders of eight persons and taken to the Oude Kerck. It was a large funeral, with more than three hundred people in the procession. The coffin was placed under a grey tombstone at the left of the choir, about one step away from the wall at the south end and near a little column set in the wall, east of the little door, facing the south. The people returned to the house of death and there parted. The sad widow and children, without a breadwinner, were left to the mercy of God.

Few of his drawings and paintings have been found in the

house of death; because he tired very easily from looking at his own work he could not stand to have it round him. He had many orders, some more than ten years back and not finished.

Sir Louis Peris, living at Leyden, has Carel's last picture. The subject was taken from The Numbers xxv where is written the children of Israel who sinned with the prostitutes of the Moabites and who invited the people to offer adoration to their God. Van Mander had painted in this picture men on horseback bringing the prostitutes, a lake in which nude figures were bathing and soliciting; in a landscape at a distance people danced and worshipped idols; far away, in a hut, barely visible, Phineas thrusts a dagger through an Israelite and Moabite woman. The master intended something special in this picture, for a reason known to Pieter Putmans, the jeweler, who said that he had ordered the painting.

A few more things found were drawings and sketches; among them one of a vase with various kinds of wild flowers, showing their nature, characteristics and growth.

Many of the friends and admirers of the departed made elegies and epitaphs in honor and memory of Carel. I refer to these—[22]

It is best to have one's house prepared,
For once one must leave;
No matter how late,
Death follows rapidly,
One today, another tomorrow,
Everyone should take this well to heart,
Read, live, do well, and fare well!

BIOGRAPHY

ENCORE

Mourn! Rhymers! Mourn! Poets!
Mourn! Noble Painters!
For Cruel Death, with her iron hand,
Has pulled towards her,
Carel, who rightly may be called
'Man der Mannen.'
His body gone, his bones destroyed,
But his risen soul eats heavenly bread.
He left a name, so everlasting and so great,
It will be spoken for a thousand years.
Blessed soul, be praised forever!
As a phoenix burns to ashes,
Through its own death it creates a new one.
So your family, so the seed,
From which rises so worthy and so gloriously
The great Carel van der Mander.

G.A.BREDERO

't Kan verkeeren
(Change may come)

A DEDICATION BY THE AUTHOR

TO THE HONORABLE GENTLEMEN, MY GOOD FRIENDS

JAN MATHIJSZ. BAN AND CORNELIS GERRITSZ.
VLASMAN

AFFECTIONATE BROTHERS-IN-LAW AND ART LOVERS IN THE

CITY OF HAARLEM

VIRGIL, the illustrious poet, let Corydon, who is in love, say that one is easily attracted to a thing for which one has a great liking. This can be confirmed so immediately and readily there is no need for proving it. It is evident that man not only desires material things, but loves to cultivate what is spiritual.

Honorable gentlemen, my good friends, I regard you as being harmoniously united in mind and spirit. You have married sisters, and you are unanimously striving for the beauty and success in the fine art of painting. You have collected beautiful pictures painted by the hands of the most learned masters. You show your pictures to ambassadors and foreigners, cordially, and with kindness in your hearts.

In imitation of Bacchus, you have bestowed the products of your own art on your visitors. For a long time your honorable ancestors have practised a useful art. They have followed a profession that was discovered by the first brewer, Bacchus, or Dionysis as he is usually called. Bacchus originated the art of brewing, and various nations, in countries where it was impossible to grow vines, have been thankful to Bacchus. And as Bacchus and Egyptian kings made laws and taught trading to their people, your parents have been burgomasters and aldermen in the city of Haarlem. They were traders and they directed their own ships.

Sir Jan Mathijsz., you are a lover of art and an able gold and silversmith. You have lived in the famous city of Rome

DEDICATION

for a long time; you have visited Naples and other cities in Italy; for a little while you were a faithful companion of our Goltzius. I have reason enough for dedicating my biographies of the illustrious painters of the Netherlands to each of you. You are worthy of this honor and of many greater honors. Most sincerely, therefore, I beg you to look upon this work with friendly eyes and to accept it kindly, as a token of affection. Praying the Lord to bestow on you what is good and what will lead to your salvation, I am your obedient servant and friend,

CAREL VAN MANDER

Amsterdam
July 28, 1604

PREFACE TO THE LIVES OF THE
ILLUSTRIOUS PAINTERS OF
THE NETHERLANDS AND GERMANY

IT would be most regrettable, if in centuries to come future generations did not praise the work of great artists. The names of our illustrious artists, their lives and works, will undoubtedly remain well known; but they will become better fixed in the mind by careful descriptions. Biographies can help to prevent time from putting artists into the grave of oblivion.

Some persons, or perhaps many, will be surprised that this book has been written, and that so much effort and energy have been spent on a subject that, by some, might be regarded as of little importance. They may think only those worthy of being described with the pen are those who have gained fame by deeds of war; they may imagine that Marius, Sulla, and Catiline, and similar man-devourers, are more worthy of being kept in memory than our noble geniuses that have made the world beautiful in ancient times and at the present. It would be difficult indeed to convince me with such views.

Since there are many others capable of describing carefully, and in a learned way, the periods of bloody tragedy in the history of the Netherlands, I should be of no use for such a task; first, because of my inexperience, and, secondly, because of the worries and danger caused by differences of opinion of the people.

And if I did so, I should deserve that Cynthius pull me by the ears and say to me: 'That is not your task. You are not able to describe the cruelties of fate, when powder is exploding and there is slashing by heroes of war. But tell how artists hit their canvases with their brushes!' That is why I wish to write the book of the painters, and I do not expect anybody to find fault with me for I have done so voluntarily.

It comes to my mind that my master, Lucas de Heere from Ghent, once began to write the lives of famous painters in rhyme; but this work was lost in a corner. It cannot be expected to come to light again. This would have been a great help to me, had it happened, for I met with great difficulties in the collecting of my information.

The truth is, on the subject of the Italian painters, I have been much enlightened by Vasari's writings that deal mainly with his compatriots. He had the advantage of and could rely on the authority of the illustrious Duke of Florence, through whose influence he could get at much information. As to knowledge about the painters of the Netherlands, I have done my best to collect information myself, and to arrange it in the right order of time and place.

Though my desire to secure information was great, I obtained much less assistance than I expected. It seemed only a few persons were as interested as I, and few could share my enthusiasm because their minds were more occupied with affairs of the kitchen.

That is why I was not always able to obtain such detailed information as the dates of births or deaths, as about localities in which the artists had worked, and similar items. I believe such facts are rather important and make description truthful and beautiful. Unfortunately, it was difficult to secure information in many instances. Often when I have inquired about the birth and death of the father of some artist, the person knew almost nothing about the dates, because, at the time, pen and ink had been spared, and no note of it existed.

I could follow the method of Varro and of Pliny, and write: 'Such-and-such an artist lived in such a year; his works were produced in the time of the Emperor, Duke, or Count So-and-So.' These ancient writers mentioned a certain Olympiad to indicate the period in which an artist lived and worked. In this way I could show I had taken my task seriously.

I shall commence my story with the lives of the two illustrious brothers, Hubert and Jan from Maeseyck, who did wonders in our art. They treated colors in a beautiful way; they were so unusually skilled in drawing one is amazed at the brilliance of their work at so early a time—I could not learn about any painters, in Lower or Upper Germany, who were known or mentioned before the Van Eycks.

Next, I shall tell as much as I can about artists and men of genius that have contributed to the progress of art in the period between the Van Eycks and the present.

If I pass some artist by in silence, I hope no-one will suspect me of doing so intentionally, maliciously, and out of jealously. It will be because I lacked information and knowledge. I should not like to do injustice to any one, whether the bodies of these persons may have turned to dust, or they may be alive, and producing works, and amazing the world by the talent which the Almighty bestowed on them.

I hope that no-one finds fault with me for including contemporary masters. This can be done with greater detail, accuracy, and truth, than it can be done with those who passed away many years ago, who have been almost forgotten, and about whom one would like to have wider information. Such work has been done efficiently by an excellent writer, Vasari, who presented Michelangelo to the public, and many other artists while they were living. He glorified their names.

That is why I politely request not to be defamed, and to be thanked.

Farewell!

DUTCH AND FLEMISH PAINTERS

DUTCH AND FLEMISH PAINTERS

THE BROTHERS
JAN AND HUYBRECHT VAN EYCK
OF MAASEYCK

VARIOUS illustrious men, to be praised for the great
validity of their study and knowledge, have brought
fame, both brilliant and noble to our good and sweet
country, the Netherlands, from antiquity up to the present.
We pass over here, how our nobility made conquests by
brave warfare; won laurels of victory, in countries abroad
and far away. For did there not arise from our fragrant,
botanical gardens a paragon of science, Desiderius Erasmus
Roterdamus, regarded during the last century as the father
of that ancient and noble language spoken in the land of
Rome? Heaven generously bestowed upon us the highest
glory of scholarship, while nature, in her benevolence,
endowed us with a genius for painting. Neither the Greeks
nor the Romans, nor any other people, despite their search,
were privileged to find the method of painting discovered
by Joannes van Eyck.

Joannes, a Dutchman from the Kempen, was born at
Maeseyck on the banks of the beautiful river Meuse, whose
rivals in honor are the river Arno, the Padus, and the proud
Tiber. So art-loving Italy had to look to the Meuse, to a
bright and brilliant light shining from the banks of that river;
had to send her painters to Flanders to receive nourishment
from foreign breasts![1]

Joannes van Eyck was highly intelligent, even in his youth,

3

and his keen mind absorbed things readily. With a natural talent for drawing, he became a pupil of his brother, Hubertus, his elder by a number of years, a clever painter, although whose pupil he was, is not known. It may be assumed that few painters of ability existed in that rough, uncultured, and isolated corner of the Netherlands in so early a period; that there were no examples in art to be followed. For Hubertus was born around the year 1366; Joannes, many years later. Whether or not his father was a painter, the spirit of painting seemed to have entered into all his children. Their sister, Margriete van Eyck, became famous for her painting, too. Like Minerva, Margriete shunned Hymen and Lucina, and remained in maiden state to the end of her life.[2]

It is supposed that the art of painting with a glue and egg medium was imported into the Netherlands from Italy, because, as we have noted in the biography of Giovanni of Cimabue, this method was first used in Florence, in 1250. The brothers, Jan and Hubertus, made many paintings with a glue and egg medium, as no other method was known at that date, except one used in Italy by which painting was done on a wet ground.[3]

In the time of the two Van Eycks, the city of Bruges was enjoying an inundation of wealth from a great international trade which had centered there more extensively than anywhere else in the Netherlands. Art follows wealth for its rich rewards. Joannes went to live in Bruges because there were many wealthy merchants residing there. He painted many pictures there with glue and egg, on wood, and became famous for his noble art in the various countries to which his works were sent.[4]

According to the people of Bruges, Joannes was a learned man, clever and inventive, who studied many subjects related to painting: He examined many kinds of pigment; he studied

4

alchemy and distillation. At length, he worked out a method of varnishing his egg and glue paintings with oil, so that these shining and lustrous pictures exceedingly delighted all who saw them. In Italy, many artists had searched for this method in vain.

Now it happened in this way: Joannes had painted a panel on which he had spent much time, because he liked nicety and clarity of execution in his painting. He varnished the finished panel according to his new invention and placed it in the sunlight to dry. The parts of the panel may not have been joined or glued sufficiently, or the heat of the sun may have been too strong; the panel burst at the joints and fell apart. Joannes, much disappointed that his work was lost through the influence of the sun, took a resolve that the sun should not damage his work ever again.

Accordingly, hostile to the egg and varnish method, he set himself to discover or invent some kind of varnish which would dry within the house, away from the sunlight. He had already examined many oils and other similar materials supplied by nature, and had found that linseed oil and nut oil had the best drying ability of them all. He boiled these oils with some other substances, and produced the finest varnish on earth.

Men with active and clear minds, such as possessed by Joannes, continue to study in order to attain higher perfection. So Joannes found, after many experiments, that colors mixed with these oils could be handled easily, that they dried well, became hard, and, once dry, could resist water. The oil made the color appear more alive, owing to a lustre of its own, without varnish. And what surprised and pleased him most was that paint made with oil could be applied more easily and mixed more thoroughly than paint made with egg and glue. He no longer needed to apply color in streaks.5

Joannes was greatly pleased by this invention of treating paint with oil, and he had every reason to be, because he had created a new type of painting, to the amazement of the world. The trumpets of fame sounded forth immediately, and people from the regions of the Cyclopean archipelago, and the eternally burning Mount Etna, came to see his wonderful discovery, all of which will be described later. This noble discovery, of painting with oil, was the only thing the art of painting still needed to achieve naturalistic rendition.

If the ancient Greeks, Apelles and Zeus had come to life again in this country and had seen this new method of painting, they would not have been any less surprised than if warlike Achilles, or other hero of ancient times, had come and witnessed the thunder of cannon fire (made possible by the invention of gunpowder by a Danish alchemist and monk, Bartholdus Schwartz, in 1354). Nor would the ancient writers have been more startled had they witnessed that very useful art of book printing, of which invention the city of Haarlem may be proud.[6]

As far as I can learn, Joannes invented the process of oil painting in the year 1410. Vasari, or his printer, made a mistake in dating this invention a hundred years later, just as Vasari gives incorrectly also the date of the death of Joannes, although this artist did not die so young as a certain writer supposes. For the sake of brevity, this problem may be passed over.[7]

The Van Eyck brothers kept their invention to themselves. Many beautiful paintings were made in collaboration, by the two, and many were made by one alone. Although he was the younger, Joannes surpassed his brother in the art.[8]

The most striking work which the Van Eyck brothers did together is the altar-piece in the church of St John, in Ghent,

6

executed by order of the thirty-first Count of Flanders, Philip Charlois, son of the Duke of Dijon, who is portrayed on horseback on one of the wings. Some people believe that Hubertus began the altar-painting alone and that Joannes finished it. I believe that they began the painting together, but that Hubertus died in the year 1426, before it could be finished. Hubertus was buried in Ghent in the same church where his picture is hanging. His epitaph will be appended.

The central panel of the altar-piece represents a scene from the Revelation of St John, in which the elders worship the Lamb. The abundant detail in this scene has been executed with great care, as has the whole work. In the upper part, Mary is represented; she is being crowned by the Father and the Son. Christ holds a cross in His hand, of which the transparent crystal is ornamented with golden knobs and decorations of precious stones,—an object painted so perfectly that some painters judge the time needed for its painting alone to have been at least a month.[9]

Next to the figure of Mary are little angels singing from sheets of music. They are painted so exquisitely and so well that one can detect readily, from their facial expressions, who is singing the higher part, the high counter part, the tenor part, and the bass.

In the upper part of the right wing, Adam and Eve are represented. One may observe that Adam has a certain fear of breaking the command of the Lord, for he has a worried expression. His new bride does not offer him an apple, the fruit which artists usually use for this subject, but offers him a fresh fig,—a proof that Joannes must have been more or less learned. Augustinus, and other learned men, maintain that Eve gave a fig to her husband, for Moses does not name the fruit specifically, and states that they covered their nakedness, not with apple leaves, but with fig leaves.[10]

7

Another wing of the altar-piece represents St Cecilia.[11]

The central panel, furthermore, has two wings or double doors, which portray scenery corresponding to the subject at the center.

As has already been told, the Count of Flanders was painted on horseback on the other wing, and with him are the two painters, Hubertus and Joannes. Hubertus sits at the right of his brother because of his greater age, and looks older than his brother. He wears on his head a strange cap of precious fur with the brim turned up. Joannes wears a very decorative cap, which hangs down in the back like the slips of a turban, a black gown, and a red rosary with a medal.[12]

The painting, marvellous for its time, is excellent in regard to drawing, action of the figures, conception of subject, and precision of workmanship. The draperies are well displayed in the style of Albrecht Dürer; the blue, red and purple colors in these have not changed at all and are so fresh that they look as if they had been laid on just recently. These colors surpass in beauty those of any other painting.[13]

The learned Joannes gave the greatest concentration to this work, as though to convince Pliny of the incorrectness of his statement that painters who have to paint a hundred faces, or even a smaller number, are unable to compete with nature, who scarcely produces two similar ones in a thousand, and generally make some resembling others. In this painting are about 330 faces, of which not one is similar to another. Moreover, different expressions can be observed on these faces, such as serenity, love, and divine faith. From the mouth of Mary, who is reading a book, words seem to come.[14]

Many foreign trees are in the landscape painted on the double doors of the central panel; one can distinguish the various kinds of plants and grasses on the ground. They are rendered most beautifully. The hairs in the portraits, in the blazes and manes and tails of the horses, can almost be counted separately, so thinly and delicately are they painted. This striking work as a whole amazes every painter.[15]

A great many eminent princes, emperors, and kings have looked upon the altar-painting with the greatest delight. King Philip, thirty-sixth Count of Flanders, was eager to possess the picture, but in order not to deprive the city of Ghent of so great a treasure, had it copied by Michiel Cocxie, painter of Malines, who did it excellently.[16]

Because a beautiful blue color was needed for Cocxie's copy of the Van Eyck altar-piece, such as could not be obtained in the Netherlands, the King requested Titian to send it from Venice. It was a kind of azure, supposed to be a natural product found in some of the mountains of Hungary, and had been more easily obtained in the period before the Turks conquered the country. The small quantity needed for the mantle of Mary alone cost thirty-two ducats.[17]

Cocxie changed a few things to his own taste; for instance, the pose of St Cecilia, who was seen too much from the back, and so was not graceful, the copyist thought. This copy of the altar-piece was sent to Spain. [18]

There was once a base to the main panel of the altar-piece, which was decorated with a painting in glue and egg, representing a scene in hell in which those who are below, under the earth, have to bend their knees to the name of Jesus and the Lamb. But the paint was rubbed off and the work spoiled by senseless painters who were ordered to clean and wash the altar-piece.[19]

Count Philip, in whose company the two brothers may be seen riding, was also Duke of Burgundy. The Duke had great regard for the two, especially for Joannes. It is supposed that Joannes, on account of his peculiar talent and unusual mind, was secret counsellor to the Duke who kept him always

9

about him just as Alexander the Great appreciated Apelles for similar qualities.[20]

The altar painting of the Van Eyck brothers was shown only to a few personages of high standing or to someone who would reward the keeper very well. Sometimes it was shown on important holidays, but then there was usually such a crowd that it was difficult to come near it. Then the chapel containing the altar-piece would be filled with all kinds of people,—painters young and old, every kind of art lover, swarming like bees and flies around a basket of figs or raisins.

In the same chapel, called the chapel of Adam and Eve of the St John's church, opposite the altar-piece of the Van Eyck brothers was hung an eulogy or ode composed by Lucas d'Heere, painter from Ghent.[21]

I let it follow here, but a little changed, arranged as Alexandrine verse:

Praise to the masterpiece which can be seen in the chapel of
St John's Church.
It is a painting made by a master whose name was John.
He was born at Mæseyck; he was a Flemish Apelles.
Read this carefully, try to understand it well, and then look at the
picture.

ODE

Ye, art lovers of all generations, look at this work of Dædel! It is a treasure, a noble object, with which the wealth of Crœsus cannot be compared. It is a gift of Heaven to Flanders. I am speaking of a work of art. Observe keenly every quality in the work and ye will find a sea with its brim overflowing. This work must be praised for the great beauty which it displays.

The Father looks divine; notice the expression in the face of St John; see how lovely and sweet is the face of Mary. It looks as if one could read the words from her lips.

How well is the crown painted and the ornament!

Notice the fear of Adam; how lifelike is his figure! Whoever saw human flesh painted in such a way? It seems that he does not accept the advice of Eve who very charmingly offers a fig to him.[22]

VAN EYCK

Sweet heavenly nymphs and able angels can be noticed. They are singing rhythmically; each voice can be differentiated by the natural expression of eyes and mouth.

But it is almost in vain to praise one thing more than another. The most beautiful sparkling jewelry can be seen; it looks as if it were all real and comes forward from the picture. This is not a painting but a mirror in which ye are looking.

How venerable are the elders; and the members of the religious orders form a cortège.

Ye painters, look among other things at the fine example of drapery treatment, well done for the period of the artist.

Look at the expression of the faces of the maidens; their chastity could serve as an example to our girls.

Notice on the wings how each king, monarch, and duke is mounted in state, accompanied by a gentleman of high standing.

It is very fitting that the two painters themselves can be seen in this company. It was the younger artist who was the greater and who finished the work. He wears a red rosary on a black gown. Hubert, the elder brother, is leading.

Hubert had begun the work, as customarily. But death, which destroys everything, changed his plans. He is buried here, next to his sister, who amazed many people with her paintings, too.23

And behold how the various faces of the people differ. How many faces are there to be seen? More than three hundred and no one resembles another, and at that, so great a number!

What more praise can be given? Very few paintings have ever gained more fame. The artist had four qualities which made him so excellent a master. He was patient, he was a well-tempered man; he had a good working mind, and he was clever.

The precision of Van Eyck's work shows his humane; patient, and tempered character, and his knowledge of how to delineate everything gracefully, with proportion and according to the laws of art, so that every object painted produces the desired effect. Through his mental guidance the nature of the legend can be well understood.

His fame is still greater if we consider that he flourished at a time and in a place where no other pictures except his own could serve as examples to him.

Some Italian wrote, and this may be believed, that this Jan van Eyck had invented the process of oil-painting. He mentions three works of Jan's, one in beautiful Florence, one in Urbino and one in Naples.

Where else did anyone ever hear of so great a wonder that a new and beautiful art began in so perfect a phase? It is not known through any document who was the master teacher of these two painters from Mæseyck.

Very justly, Joannes was esteemed his whole life by Count Philip, who held him in great honor. He can be regarded as a brilliant orna-ment to the Netherlands. His work has been appreciated in various countries. This is the reason that, except for his altar painting, few of his works can be seen in this country. Another painting by him can be seen in Bruges and one in Ypres, the last not finished.

This beautiful flower faded early from the world. He was born in the humble village of Mæseyck. He died in Bruges where his remains are resting. His name and fame will live immortally.

Our Duke and King valued this painting so highly—he had a great interest in all honest art—that he ordered a copy made of the work. He paid almost four thousand guilders to Michel Cocxie, who required two years to do his copying in the chapel. He has safeguard-ed his honor. The copy was well done, from the first to the last de-tail. He was an able artist.24

The copy is now in Spain in Valladolid. It remains not only as a symbol of the appreciation of our King, of which I have spoken above, but also as a glory to the Van Eycks and Coxcy.

*Schade leer U*25

LUCAS DE HEERE.

Joannes, having finished the altar-piece in Ghent, went to live in Bruges again, and there another clever painting from his able hand remains as a splendid heritage for us. He paint-ed many pictures, transported far by merchants and looked upon by artists with the greatest amazement and envy wher-ever they went, for these painters were eager to imitate the master, but they could not find out how! Even though for-eign princes obtained some of Jan's miraculous paintings, the method remained known only in Flanders.26

The Duke of Urbino, Frederick the Second, owned a painting by Joannes which represented a bathing scene care-fully executed. Lorenzo de Medici possessed, among other beautiful works in Florence, a St Jerome by Joannes.27

Some Florentine merchants sent a splendid painting, made

12

in Flanders, by Joannes to King Alphonso I of Naples. The many figures in this painting were so ably done that the King took the greatest delight in it. A huge throng of artists came to see this marvelous painting, when it reached Italy. But although the Italians examined the picture very carefully, touching it, smelling at it, scenting the strong odor produced by the mixture of the colors with oil, and drawing all kinds of conclusions, the secret of the process remained hidden to them. The secret held until Antonello of Messina, in Sicily, went to Bruges to learn the process of oil-painting. Having mastered the technique, he introduced the art into Italy, as I have described in his biography.[28]

One of Jan's paintings, representing Mary and a praying abbott, was in the Abbey church of St Mærten in Ypres. The wings were unfinished; each had two divisions with various sections, in which were painted scenes symbolizing Mary as the burning bush, the Fleece of Gideon, and kindred objects. This work looked more celestial than human.[29]

Joannes painted many portraits from life also, and, for these he introduced backgrounds of clear and beautiful landscapes requiring great zeal and patience in their execution. His under-painting was more precise and sharper than the finished work of other artists. I remember having seen in the house of my teacher, Lucas de Heere at Ghent, a small portrait of a woman, with a landscape in the background, done only in under-painting and exquisitely smooth.[30]

Joannes had once painted in oil two portraits in a single scene, a man and a woman, who give the right hand to each other, as if they had been united in wedlock by *Fides*. This little picture came through inheritance into the hands of a barber in Bruges. Mary, aunt of King Philip of Spain and widow of King Louis of Hungary, who was killed in a battle against the Turks, happened to see this painting. The art

loving princess was so pleased with this picture that she gave
a certain office to the barber which brought him a yearly income of a hundred guilders.[31]

I have seen many drawings by Joannes which were done
with a wonderful precision.[32]

Joannes died at Bruges at a good old age and was buried in
the church of St Donæs. His epitaph may be read in Latin
Carmina on one of the columns:[33]

> Hic jacet eximia clarus virtute Joannes,
> In quo picturæ gratia mira fuit;
> Spirantes formas, et humum florentibus herbis
> Pinxit, et ad vivum quodlibet egit opus.
> Quippe illi Phidias et cedere debet Apelles:
> Arte illi inferior ac Policletus erat.
> Crudeles igitur, crudeles dicite Parcas,
> Quæ talem nobis eripuêre virum.
> Actum sit lachrymis incommutabile factum;
> Vivat ut in cœlis jam deprecare Deum.

At the tomb of the elder brother, in the St John's Church in
Ghent, a funeral tablet in the wall portrays the figure of
Death, carved in white stone, and bears a brass plate on which
an old Flemish poem has been written as an epitaph:[34]

> Those who step upon me,
> Compare yourselves with me;
> I was once as you are now;
> At present I am here below,
> Dead and buried.
> Neither advice nor medicine,
> Nor art, nor honor, nor wisdom,
> Nor great wealth, were of use
> When death came.
> Hubert van Eyck was my name.
> I am now food for the worms.
> I was once famous
> And highly appreciated for my painting.
> Rapidly I turned from something into nothing;
> In the year thousand four hundred and six,
> Let it be known,

VAN EYCK

It was on the eighteenth day of September,
That I gave my soul to God, under great pain.
Those who love art, pray to God, that
His face may shine upon me.
Refrain from sin and turn to the good,
For at the end you shall follow me.

Sometime ago, a series of the portraits of the most famous painters of the Netherlands, in the form of copper engravings, was published in Antwerp. The first of the series were portraits of the illustrious Van Eyck brothers. Some portraits were accompanied by artistic poems in Latin, called *Carmina*, composed by that great, learned poet, Dominicus Lampsonius of Bruges, secretary to the Bishop of Liége, not only a great lover of the art of painting, but himself a capable artist. I include here his words of praise of the two brothers: 35

To Hubertus van Eyck
O Hubert, the well-deserved songs of praise by our Muse, dedicated to you and your brother, are not sufficient. May I add these.36
It was through you that your brother became the greater artist, a proof of which is the altar painting in Ghent. King Philip was so impressed that he ordered Coxie to make a copy of it, who did so most ably. The King sent this to his home in the Spanish fatherland.

Joannes van Eyck, speaking about himself
I, who demonstrated the method of mixing lively colors with linseed oil, together with my brother, Hubert, very shortly amazed Bruges with this invention. Perhaps Apelles himself could not have achieved this feat. Rapidly our fame spread all over the world.

ROGIER
OF BRUGES

THE widely known city of Bruges declined when her trade moved to Sluis and Antwerp. Prosperity and fortune are unstable. Some very excellent artists lived in Bruges during the lifetime of Joannes van Eyck, and a little later. One of them, called Rogier, was a pupil of Joannes van Eyck. Joannes must have been rather old at this time, for he had kept his discovery of oil-painting secret. He did not admit anybody to the place where he was working. Finally, in his old age, he communicated the secret to his pupil, Rogier.[1]

Many works of this Rogier were to be seen in churches and old houses in the city of Bruges. He drew well, and painted as gracefully with color and glue, or in color and egg medium, as he did in oil.[2]

At this period it was fashionable to paint large canvases with tall figures in them. They were used to decorate rooms when tapestries were not used. These paintings were done with color, in egg or glue medium. Rogier was very good in this field, and I believe I have seen some of these canvases by him in Bruges. They were interesting, and commendable, considering the period in which they had been painted. Good drawing and knowledge are required to make something on a large scale. One who can work successfully on a reduced scale may readily find out that the large scale is not so easy.[3]

I do not know anything about the death of Rogier. He is still famous for the excellence of his work, through which his name will be immortal.[4]

HUGE VAN DER GOES

OF BRUGES

IT happened that parents, observing that any one who became a great master of painting, received honors and enjoyed a good fortune, encouraged their children to become artists. For this reason, Joannes van Eyck might have had many pupils if he had been very anxious to have them. Still, a certain Hugo van der Goes became a pupil of his. Intelligent and clever, he learned the art of oil-painting from his master, and became an excellent painter. His works date from around 1480.[1]

A very nice and clever little painting by Van der Goes used to hang on a pillar in the church of St James in Ghent as an epitaph to a certain Wouter Gautier. It represented an interior and a seated figure of Mary with the Infant, seen from the front. It measured no more than one and a half feet. I have seen it many times and always admired how exquisitely it was painted; the little plants and stones on the ground were admirable. The grace and chastity of the face of Mary were to be admired especially. Those old painters were best able to give venerating and devotional expressions to these spiritual beings.[2]

A painted window, the 'Descent from the Cross', was formerly to be seen in the same church; it was a very artistic work, but I do not know whether or not the drawing for it had been made by Van der Goes or by master Joannes. An altar painting representing the legend of St Catherine, a very artistic work made by Hughe, used to be in the monastery of the monk-brewers of Ghent. He had painted it while young.

Another especially good painting by Hughe still exists; it

17

has been praised most deservedly by artists and experts. This picture is in the house of Jacob Weytens in Ghent, which is surrounded by water and near the little Muyden bridge. Intended as a mantel-piece, it is done in oil, and represents the meeting of David and Abigail. The modesty of the woman cannot be admired enough. Is it not a pleasure to notice the honesty and sweetness of all the little, female figures? The painters nowadays ought to put these women forwards as an example to the models they are using at present. David is mounted in stately fashion. In short, this work is excellent for drawing, action, invention and expression.[3]

It has been said that love contributed to the success of this painting; that Cupid, in the company of his mother and the Graces, assisted in guiding the brushes. Hugo, while still an apprentice, was in love with the daughter of the house; he courted her, and painted her from life in this picture.[4]

Lucas de Heere made a poem in honor of this work of art. It is supposed to come from the mouth of one of the women in the painting and is as follows:

We are painted here, as if we were alive,
By Hughes van der Goes, illustrious artist.
He loved one of our worthy company,
Her sweet portrait shows
How love inspired the artist.
Similarly Praxiteles made the figure of Phryne
Whom he loved greatly.
The sweetheart of the painter exceeds in beauty
All of us, because he looked upon her as ideal.
Still, every man and woman has been rendered
Most artistically.
So is the horse, the donkey.
The colors are permanent, applied well
And treated beautifully.
The entire work is excellent.
Speech fails us in praise of it.
That is very unusual for us women.

HUGE VAN DER GOES

Among the many beautiful pictures which are from the hand of this master in Bruges, some of which I may not have seen, is an altar-piece in the St James Church in Bruges, regarded as the best painting Hugo ever made. It is a crucifixion, Mary, and the thieves. Hugo painted it in so lifelike a manner and with such ardor, that it pleased not only ordinary people but all people who knew about art.[5]

This painting was saved, during the senseless iconoclasm, for the sake of its artistic qualities. Afterwards, it was used by the same church as a tablet upon which to write the Ten Commandments with golden letters on a black background. This was done at the suggestion of a certain painter who did the work himself. I prefer to pass in silence the name of this man. It was a disgrace and a dishonor that such a fine work of art was spoiled and destroyed by an artist. *Pictura* must have had tears in her eyes when this happened. Luckily, the old background was very hard, the golden letters and the black over-painting formed a thick layer of greasy paint, which was washed off. The original painting reappeared undamaged.

This is all the information I could collect about this clever painter, Hughes. I do not know when and where he was buried. I recommend his name to Hebe, spouse of Hercules, for immortality.[6]

PAINTERS, ANCIENT AND MODERN

VARIOUS artists and talented men lived in Upper and Lower Germany of whom nothing but a bare name remains. Neither writers nor historians preserved any memory of them. This happened in the Netherlands especially. As usual, nearly every engraver was a painter, too; so we discover the relics and artistic works left by them either as paintings, or products of their science (prints). I mention: Sibaldus Bheem Suavius; Lucas of Cronach in Saxony, Israel of Mentz, and Hipse Martin. Their prints show how good a master each was in his own time; I cannot prove it with their paintings.[1]

I must mention Hans Memmelinck in connection with the artists in the Netherlands whose lives, works, and periods are known to me only partially. One of his works was in the Hospital of St John, in the city of Bruges. It is a reliquary decorated with rather minute figures, but executed in so masterly a style, that many times an offer for buying the shrine was received amounting to the cost of a shrine of pure silver. This master flourished before the time of Pieter Poerbus of Bruges. Poerbus used to look at this reliquary on festival days, when it was visible to the public, and he never tired of praising the workmanship. This instance shows us the excellence of this master.[2]

Geeraert van der Meire was an artist living in Ghent shortly after the time of Joan van Eyck. He had a fine technique. A certain Lieven Taeyaert, art lover, brought a painting of this artist's from Ghent to Holland, representing Lucretia, and executed most carefully. It became the property of Jacob Ravart in Amsterdam, a collector.[3]

Geeraerd Horebout was another painter in Ghent. He

20

afterwards became court painter to the King of England, Henry VIII. One of his works was in the Church of St John in Ghent. It was a set of altar-panels, placed at the left of the choir, with paintings on the outside of the wings, and sculpture in the interior. The work was ordered by Lieven Hughenos, Abbot of St Bavo. One of the wings presented a flagellation scene, expressing well the anger and cruelty of the flagellants, the patience of Christ, and the seriousness of somebody below on the panel, who is binding rods.4

A *Descent from the Cross* was depicted on the other door, with great sorrow expressed in the figures of Mary and John. The three Marys could be seen in the background, approaching the grave; they carried little lanterns into the sepulchre, and the reflection of the light on their faces was painted, too. At the very end of the sepulchre was some kind of vista.

These altar paintings by Horebout were saved during the breaking of images by a certain Marten Bierman, art lover in Brussels. He returned the pictures to the church later for the same small amount of money for which he had obtained them.

Another work by master Geeraerd is still in Ghent, in the place where the linen merchants have their department on market day. It is a round panel, painted on both sides. One side shows Christ sitting on a stone and crowned with thorns; he has been beaten on the head by somebody with a cane. On the reverse, Mary is represented with her Infant on her lap, surrounded by angels.

Still another painter lived in Ghent, but not in that very olden time. His name was Lieven de Witte. He was a good master who specialized in architectural subjects and in views in perspective, of which he produced a great many. Particularly good was his picture of an adulteress. In the Church of St John at Ghent, there are some beautiful stained glass

windows that were made from cartoons drawn by de Witte.⁵
An artist by the name of Lansloot Blondeel lived in Bruges
in the olden time. A mason in his youth, he signed his works
with a trowel. He was marvellously clever in painting architectural subjects; he pictured antique ruins and made drawings of nocturnal fires, and similar scenes. His daughter became the wife of Pieter Poerbus.⁶

Hans Vereycke was a painter who lived in Bruges, also,
and was nicknamed 'Cleen Hansken'. A good landscape artist, he worked from nature. Sometimes he put in a figure of
Mary, but not a very large one. He was a rather good por-
trait-painter, too, and painted from life. I have seen a little
cabinet of his in the Blaeuwe Huys the country home of my
uncle, Claude van Mander, in the neighborhod of Bruges.
The portraits of my uncle, his wife, and five children were
painted on its doors. Inside was a picture of Mary, in a land-
scape.⁷

Gheerhardt of Bruges was another painter of whom I do
not know anything, except that Pieter Poerbus praised him
highly, calling him an eminent artist.⁸

Jan van Hemsen was a painter who lived in Haarlem in the
olden time, and was a citizen there. He had a special way of
drawing after the antique masters, and in his style of work he
was more or less isolated from the modern artists. He painted
large figures. Some of his work was very fine and individual.
A painting in which Apostles are represented standing next
to Christ, who is on His way to Jerusalem, is now in Middelburg, at the house of Sr Cornelius Monincx, art lover.⁹

Jan Mandijn was a painter from Haarlem, good at painting
ghost scenes and diabolical subjects in the style of Jeronimus
Bos. He died in Antwerp, from which city he formerly drew
a pension.¹⁰

Another clever artist in Haarlem was Volckert Claesz.,

good at composition, drawing, and painting. Some of his pictures on canvas, in the room of the aldermen Haarlem, show a bold technique of attack on the subject, more antique in style than modern. He drew many cartoons for the glass painters at a very reasonable price.[11]

Hans de Duytscher or Singer was a painter in Antwerp who came originally from Hesse. He decorated the house of Carel Cockeel, in the Keyser street in Antwerp. One room had trees done everywhere in water-color, and linden and oak trees could be differentiated. He made many cartoons for the tapestry weavers. (However, he did not understand how to paint in the reverse very well.)[12]

Hansken van der Elburcht, called Little Hans, entered the guild at Antwerp in the year 1535; he came from the neighborhood of Kampen. The fishmongers ordered an altar painting from him and this piece is in the Onse Vrouwen Kerck. It represents Peter fishing; the figure of Christ is in the foreground; a tree is well painted, as is a storm at sea.[13]

Aert de Beer lived formerly in Antwerp, entering the guild in the year 1529. He made cartoons for the glass painters and was a very clever artist.[14]

Jan Cransse entered the guild of Antwerp in 1523. A large canvas by him used to hang in the Onse Vrouwen Kerck. It represented a washing of the feet, and is an excellent work.[15]

Lambrecht van Oort, a painter from Amersfoort, an architect, and a good artist, entered the guild of Antwerp in 1547.[16]

Michiel de Gast was admitted to the guild in 1558. He painted many Roman ruins from life, made many drawings of like subjects, and new compositions of his own on which he printed his monogram.[17]

A good water-colorist by the name of Pieter Bom lived in Antwerp and entered the guild in the year 1560.[18]

DUTCH AND FLEMISH PAINTERS

Cornelis van Dale was admitted to the guild of Antwerp in 1556. He was a specialist in painting rocks.[19]

I group together all these painters, because I do not know anything special about them and only what I have written.

ALBERT VAN OUWATER

OF HAARLEM

I TRIED to find out who have been the most excellent of our artists, in order to classify them according to their times, the older ones to be followed by the more recent. I was surprised, indeed, to hear from a reliable source that Albert van Ouwater, artist from Haarlem, became a good oil painter at an early period. I conclude, from certain well-established evidence, that he must have lived as far back as the time of the Van Eyck's, for an old, honest painter. Albert Simonsz. of Haarlem, says that beyond doubt, at the very present, in the year 1604, it is sixty years since he himself was a pupil of the painter, Jan Mostart, from Haarlem, who was seventy years old at that time. So we may figure that at least 130 years have passed since the birth of Mostart. Now Albert Simonsz., whose memory is very good, quotes Mostart as saying that he knew neither Albert van Ouwater nor Geertgen van St Jans.

Albert van Ouwater must have lived before the famous painter, Geertgen tot St Jans, because Geertgen was a pupil of Albert. I now leave it to the reader to judge at what early time oil-painting was practised in the city of Haarlem.[1]

An altar painting by Ouwater was in the Groote Kerck at Haarlem at the south side of the high altar, called the Roman altar, because it had been ordered by pilgrims who had been to Rome. The interior represented two life-size, standing figures of St Peter and St Paul. Below, at the base of the altar was an interesting landscape in which many pilgrims were painted, some walking, others resting, eating, or drinking. Albert painted the faces well; also the hands, the feet, the draperies, and the landscapes.[2]

25

DUTCH AND FLEMISH PAINTERS

The oldest painters maintain that the first and the best method of landscape painting was begun in Haarlem.3

I have seen a grisaille copy of a large, upright painting done by Albert, portraying the resurrection of Lazarus. The original had been taken to Spain in a tricky way, without any payment having been made, after the siege and surrender of Haarlem. The figure of Lazarus was beautiful for its time, a remarkable nude painting. An architectural detail in this picture was a temple, of which the columns were rather small. On one side, apostles were shown, on the other, Jews. There were pleasing female figures in this picture, too. In the background some people could be noticed looking through a colonnade of the choir.4

This artistic painting was studied by Hemskerck many times; he never tired of looking at it, and said to the owner, who was his pupil: 'Son, what did these people eat?' meaning, that these painters must have had a colossal amount of energy to have accomplished such works of art.5

This is all that time has left us of this ancient master, Albert van Ouwater, and it must serve to save him from oblivion.6

GEERTGEN TOT SINT JANS

OF HAARLEM

IN the wild, white-horned Alps and in other high mountain regions, water rushes down in little rivulets which come together and finally form a large stream hurrying to the ocean. Our art developed in the same way. Its origins were in various places, and it was perfected through contributions from men of noble genius. No harm was done to fine art when Geertgen van Haarlem became a painter. He made people see the beauty and grace of art, at an early period, and he brought to painting still greater honor and fame.

Geertgen, when young, was a pupil of the Albert van Ouwater mentioned above, whom he equalled in some respects, but whom he surpassed in composition, in the firm handling of the figures, and in expression. However, his work was not refined and was less precise than the painting of Ouwater.

Geertgen lived at Haarlem with the Knights of St John— a fact which gave him his name. However, he had not joined the order. He painted the high altar at this place. This fine piece of work was a *Crucifixion*. The wings of this triptych which were very large, were painted on both sides: one wing was destroyed by the image-breakers, or during the siege of the town; the other wing has been sawed into two pieces, and the individual parts make beautiful pictures for the room of the present superior of the order, in their new building. The one lateral part represented a miracle or an unusual event; the other, a Pieta, or the descent from the cross, in which the dead body of Christ looks most natural. Some disciples and apostles show great sorrow, especially do the holy women

27

show such grief as could not be expressed more effectively.[1] Mary is seated; her mood is sad and mournful; she seems to be subjected to the utmost sorrow and emotion. Most artists of the present day have been amazed by this work and praise it highly.

Another work of Geertgen's existed outside the city of Haarlem. It was at the Monastery of the Regular Monks, there, but was destroyed either in the war or by image-breakers. There is in the Groote Kerck at Haarlem, on the southern side, a picture of the church itself, which Geertgen made and which shows how able he was.[2]

He was a great master. When Albrecht Dürer was in Haarlem, he looked at the works of Geertgen with great admiration, and said: 'Truly, he was already a painter inside his mother's body.' He meant that Nature had predestined Geertgen to be an artist.[3]

Geertgen died young, at the age of about twenty-eight.[4]

DIRCK
OF HAARLEM

IN remote times, the city of Haarlem, in Holland, already
was known as a center for good artists—if not for the best
painters of the entire Netherlands. This reputation is an old
one, and cannot be disputed; on the contrary, it can be
proved, not only by the works of the earlier masters,
Ouwater and Geertgen te Sint Jans, but also by the works of
Dirk from Haarlem, who was an outstanding master in that
far-off day. I have not found out who Dirk's instructor was.
He lived at Haarlem in the Cruysstraet, not far from the
orphanage, in the house with the antique façade and the portraits sculptured in relief.[1]

It seems that Dirk lived also in Louvain, in Brabant, for
I saw a triptych in Leyden, of which the middle panel represented a Saviour, one of the wings, a St Paul, and the other a
St Peter, and below was an inscription in gold lettering, in
Latin: 'One thousand, four hundred and sixty-two years
after the birth of Christ, My image has been painted in
Louvain, by Dirck, who was born in Haarlem. May he have
eternal rest!' These portraits are about life-size, with beautiful hair and beards, and are very well done for the period in
which they were made.

This triptych can be seen at the house of Sr Jan Gerritsz.
Buytewegh, and it is the only example of work by Dirck to
which I can refer; it is sufficient to prove how excellent a
master Dirck had been, in what period he lived, and how
perfectly he painted. He lived a good many years before
the birth of Albrecht Dürer. His works differ greatly from
the hard, sharp-edged, unpleasing works done in the modern

manner. Lampsonius, in his *Carmina*, addresses him about as follows:

> Come and take your place, O Dirck!
> The fatherland will not exalt the glory of your work to the height of the stars by fancy praise.
> Nature, Mother of All, begins to fear
> That you will surpass her by your knowledge and your fine paintings.

ROGIER VAN DER WEYDE
OF BRUSSELS

ROGIER VAN DER WEYDE deserves a special place among those who brought fame to the art of painting. This excellent painter came from Flanders or was born of Flemish parents. His light shone in Brussels at a very early period; the past of our art was still in darkness. Nature had gifted him, and, with his keen intelligence, he enlightened the world, to the great good of the artists of his own time. He improved our art of painting greatly, through his works, by depicting the inner desires and emotions of his subjects whether sorrow, anger, or gladness were exhibited.[1]

Four famous paintings by Rogier may be seen in the city hall in Brussels, as an everlasting memorial. They represent four scenes in connection with the administration of justice. Especially to be mentioned is the picture of a sick, old father lying in bed, and cutting off the head of his own criminal son; the gravity of the father, who is grinding his teeth while performing this act of justice on his own child, is rendered realistically. Another represents a father and a son, who, in the interests of justice, have had one of their eyes pushed out.[2]

Other similar, symbolical, pictures are in Brussels. These pictures of Rogier's moved the learned Lampsonius so much, at the time when he was writing on the Treaty of Ghent, that he could scarcely keep his eyes from them. Again and again, he would cry, 'Oh, Rogier, how great a man you were!' or something similar, while he was busy with the important work of the Treaty.[3]

Another painting by Rogier was placed in the Onze Vrouwe Kerk at Louvain. It represented a *Descent from the*

Cross; two men are standing on separate ladders; they lower the body of Christ, shrouded in a white cloth; below, the body is received by Joseph of Arimathæa, and other persons; the holy women are weeping at the foot of the cross; Mary, the Virgin, is fainting, supported by St John, who stands behind her. The painting is full of expression.[4]

This work by master Rogier, his most important one, was on its way to the King of Spain and the boat sank at sea; but the painting was fished up and, as it had been packed very well and tightly, it did not seem to have suffered much; only the glue had given way. The people of Louvain were given a copy of this picture, made by Michiel Coxie, which indicates that the original must have been excellent.[5]

Rogier once painted a portrait for a queen, or other important person, and was rewarded with a pension in the form of wheat. He became wealthy and gave many alms to the poor. He died at the time of the sweating disease (called English sickness), an epidemic that spread throughout the entire country and killed thousands of people. It happened in the autumn of the year of our Lord, 1529.[6]

LAMPSONIUS ADDRESSES ROGIER AS FOLLOWS:[7]
Do not consider too great the approbation which we bestow upon you for the works of art which you have created in remote times. They are worthy of study by many artists of our own, learned epoch, provided they are intelligent enough to give it.

This can be proved by the painting in Brussels which is to teach the officials of the court not to deviate from the path of justice.

And how could we ever forget your last wishes regarding the wealth which you accumulated by your painting and which you wanted divided among the poor, to relieve them from the knell of starvation?

You left your goods on earth, where they will perish in the course of time, but the beautiful works by which we remember you, will shine in Heaven eternally.

JACOB CORNELISZ.

OF OOST SANEN IN NORTH HOLLAND

THE rapidly growing town of Amsterdam has reason to be proud of the fact that even in early times it counted among its inhabitants a painter who should be praised most highly. His name was Jacob Cornelisz., and he hailed from Oost-Sanen in North Holland. He was a great master, an illustrious artist, who rightly deserved wide fame. I could not find out at what time he was born, but he was the second teacher of Joan Schoorel, in the year 1512.[1]

Jacob Cornelisz. was already an experienced master. At that time, he had two grown children, and he also had a little daughter of about twelve years. From these data, his age and the time of his birth can be established rather well. He was born in a village in the district of North Holland called Oost-Sanen.

I could not learn how he became interested in art while living among peasants. I found out only that he was a citizen of Amsterdam and that he died in that city.

A fine altar-painting by Cornelisz. hung in the Oude Kerck in Amsterdam; it was a *Descent from the Cross*, painted artistically and with great care. There was a kneeling figure of Magdalen in it; a cloth, spread on the ground, showed many folds and wrinkles. He always painted all his draperies from life.[2]

The *Seven Works of Mercy* was another of his paintings, also in the Oude Kerck. Most of these paintings were destroyed during the iconoclasm. Some remaining fragments of the *Seven Works of Mercy* may still be seen in Haarlem at

33

the house of Cornelius Suyker, which bears the sign of the Sevensterre. They are very much worth seeing, as are some other things in his house. A *Circumcision of Christ* is very fine, an astonishing work and most carefully finished. This picture has been dated 1517, showing us when the artist flourished.3

An excellent piece by Jacob's hand is in the city of Alckmaar, with the widow Van Sonnenveldt, who is a member of the Nyeborgh family. It is a *Descent from the Cross* and portrays Mary and some others bewailing Christ, who is dead. Very interesting faces, nudes, and draperies are here; the composition is good, the workmanship, exquisite. The beautiful landscape was done by his pupil, Joan Schoorel.4

I recall seeing also some fragments of an altar painting not far from the Dam. They are from a *Crucifixion* in which Christ was stretched and raised on the cross, an excellent work.

Jacob Cornelisz. had a brother who was an artist too, and who was called Buys. He had a son by the name of Dierick Jacobsz. Many pictures painted from life by this artist may be seen in the 'Doelen' in Amsterdam. A portrait by him exists which has in it a hand painted so beautifully that it is admired by every one who looks at it. Jacob Roevaert offered a large sum of money to be allowed to cut out this hand.5

Dierick Jacobsz. died in 1567, at the age of seventy. Jacob Cornelisz. died at a great age. Occasionally, some wood engravings by him may be seen, such as nine, round Passion scenes, composed well and executed nicely. He made another set of nine Passion scenes in wood, and nine square pictures in wood, representing nine valiant knights on horseback —these are interesting and amusing.6

ALBRECHT DURER

OF NÜRNBERG

AT the time when Italy was becoming famous among the various countries for her artistic achievement, Germany was rapidly losing her darkness. A great star, rising very high, was destined to light the world for centuries. This star was an artist who had learned everything to be known in the field of drawing. Yet he had not lit his torch in Italy, nor in Greece, where the antique marbles of illustrous Greek sculptors enlightened the earth. This artist was Albrecht Dürer, and he was born in Nürnberg in the year 1470.[1]

His father was a very able goldsmith and we may assume that Albrecht learned this trade from his father, along with copper engraving, for the reason that very few paintings done by him in his youth are known. He studied painting and engraving under Hipse Marten.[2]

I do not know anything special about Hipse Marten except that he was a great artist in his time, as can be judged from the composition and from the drawing evidenced by some of his prints. A crucifixion scene must be mentioned especially in this respect, as well as an *Adoration of the Magi*, prints of Mary, a *Temptation of St Anthony*, and kindred subjects, of which only a few copies came to my attention.

Israel van Mentz has made an interesting engraving of three or four nude women (the subject may have been the three Graces), above whose heads a red globe was suspended. This work was not dated. Albrecht Dürer made a copy of this print, and this is the earliest, dated engraving by Dürer that I have seen. There is a date on the globe, 1497. Dürer

35

may have been twenty-six or more at that time. Some of his prints are not dated, and they may be his early works.3

The print of the wild man, with the skull, in the coat of arms, has been dated 1503. The beautiful print of Adam and Eve is dated 1504; the one of the small horses, 1505; the copper engraving of the *Passion*, which is an example of nice drawing and which has been engraved with remarkable precision, gives the various dates, 1507, 1508, and 1512. The print of the Duke of Saxony is dated 1524; the one of Melanchthon, 1526. This last date is the latest which can be found on Dürer's engravings. I hardly need to mention the copper engravings or wood engravings specifically; they have been done most artistically and skilfully, and are well known by artists and collectors.4

As his predecessors, in Germany, Dürer endeavored to work from life, without being too eager to select the most beautiful from the beautiful. The Greeks and Romans had applied this principle wisely and with great judgement and discrimination, as can be noticed in ancient sculpture; they opened the eyes of the Italian masters. These artists were greatly amazed by the marvellous perfection of Dürer's drawing and the clear precision of his sharp burin. The best Italian masters were benefitted by the example he set in composition, in historical costume, and in similar matters.5

It is amazing how many new, characteristic, things Dürer discovered in nature and in himself, and how he applied these to painting, in the poses, in the general composition and arrangement, and in the sweep, of the folds of draperies. Some of his later Madonna pictures show these characteristics especially well. The pose is most beautiful, the contrast between high light and dark is very striking, and the various colors observed in the draperies are rendered with fine harmony.

ALBRECHT DURER

Vasari reported that a certain Mark Antonio of Bologna had copied thirty-six small Passion scenes engraved by Dürer, and that he had these published with the signature of Alberti. Albrecht went to Venice because of this; they had been printed there. He resorted to the rulers of that city for justice; the only thing he accomplished was to have Marc Antonio remove the signature.[6]

We may assume that in his youth Albrecht devoted considerable time to literature and to the study of many subjects in science and art, such as geometry, arithmetic, architecture, perspective. The writings he left are proof of his zeal, great intelligence, and knowledge. This can be observed in that great Dædalus, a work which he wrote on proportion, and in which the measurements of the human body are described with diagrams. His book on perspective and military science is most interesting. Consequently, he was esteemed, not only by a great many of a humble class, but also by learned men and by such persons of the highest rank as Emperor Maximilian, the grandfather of our Emperor Charles V.[7]

The story is told, among other tales, that Maximilian once asked Albrecht to draw something, rather large, on a wall. The master found he was too short to reach it. The Emperor ordered one of the courtiers forward, and requested Albrecht to stand on the back of this man. The latter objected to the Emperor, in all courtesy, saying that such an act was an humiliation to nobility, and he regarded it as rather contemptible to serve as a footstool to a painter. The Emperor replied that Albrecht was already a nobleman for the excellence of his works of art; and he declared further that he could make a nobleman out of a peasant, very easily, but that it was not in his power to make an artist of a nobleman.

The Emperor allowed Albrecht to wear the coat of arms of the painters; their emblem was three white or silver blazons on a field of azure. Dürer was very much appreciated by Emperor Charles V for the perfection of his painting and for his wide knowledge.[8]

When Dürer heard of the fame of Raphael Urbino, he sent this artist his own portrait which he had painted very fluently. The high-lights had been produced by preserving the ground color of the canvas and without underpainting. I shall refer to this in the biography of Raphael.[9]

Many of Dürer's drawings can be seen in the possession of the art collectors. Sr Joris Edmheston of Brielle has a book which once belonged to Lucas d'Heere; it contains many portraits done by Dürer, one of which, representing a Cardinal, shows relief accentuated by touches of brush-work. In this book there is a figure of Mary, done very nicely with a pen, dated 1526. These are works worth seeing. Some figures relating to the subject of proportion are in the same book, and they are similar to the illustrations in Dürer's book treating this subject specifically.[10]

The same kind of pictures are in a book belonging to Sr Arnoudt van Berensteyn, of Haarlem, who is an able art collector. In this book, the figures relating to proportion are rather large and they are partly cross-hatched. Furthermore, there are some arms and hands and other subjects which are preliminary studies for the figures of Adam and Eve.[11]

Many paintings by Dürer are in various places in Italy; also drawings which are highly valued and are, accordingly, preserved with care. It is hardly possible to describe everything he has drawn, painted, and executed, from life. I shall tell as much as is within my knowledge about his painting.[12]

First of all, Dürer painted the three Magi who came from the East, in the year 1504; he represented one of the kings with a golden cup in his hand, the second one holds a globe, and the third one a small chest of gold. In 1506, he painted a

figure of Mary with two angels above her head, who crown
her with roses. In 1507, he painted a life-size picture of Adam
and Eve. In 1508, he painted a *Crucifixion* which shows the
crucifixion and many other martyr scenes, such as stoning
and beating persons to death. This picture was cleverly done,
and was exceedingly beautiful. He portrayed himself, from
life, in it, holding a little scroll on which his name can be read.
Bibaldum stands next to him.[13]

Dürer made a fine painting of a scene in heaven, in which
Christ, hanging on the cross, can be seen; the Pope, the Emperor, and the cardinals are beautifully painted below. This
painting is regarded as Dürer's best. Albrecht portrayed himself, in the lower part of this picture, in the landscape, with a
little tablet in his hand on which is written: 'Albertus Durer
Noricus faciebat anno Virginis partu, 1511.' These works, so
worth description, may be seen in Prague, in the palace of the
Emperor, in the new gallery where the painters of Germany
and the Netherlands are honored by their works.[14]

His Majesty has another excellent painting by Dürer; the
magistrates of the city of Nürnberg presented it to him for
some reason or other. This is really one of the best of Dürer's
pictures. It represents Christ carrying His cross; there is
much detail in the picture; all the magistrates of Nürnberg
have been included in it, painted from life. This work may be
seen, in Prague, in the gallery mentioned above.[15]

Another beautiful painting by Albrecht is in a monastery
in Frankfort. It is an *Assumption of Mary*; the beauty of the
figures is noteworthy; the scene representing heaven with
the angels is outstanding; all the detail has been done carefully; the hair was painted with a steady hand, and treated
artistically by a characteristic swing of the brush. Similar
skill can be noticed in the technique of Dürer's laudable
engravings. Among other interesting details in this painting,

39

there is a foot (just the heel and the middle part) of a kneel-ing apostle; it is said that much money has been offered for permission to cut out this fragment. It is almost unbelievable how much money this painting yields yearly to the monks of the monastery, through the tips given and the drinks bought by gentlemen, merchants, travelers, and others, interested in art and to whom this painting is disclosed. It was painted by Dürer in 1509.[16]

Many beautiful pictures by Dürer are in the city hall of Nürnberg, the city where he was born. I must mention some portraits of Emperors, displaying costumes with gold em-broidery similar to those worn by Charlemagne, and portraits of members of the house of Austria, and some apostolic fig-ures, full length, with beautiful draperies.[17]

The portrait of Dürer's mother can be seen, too; and there is a small self-portrait, also, in which he painted his face with long hair on it, hanging down. Some of the hair intertwines, and some is traced in gold very effectively. I can remember this well: I had this painting in my hands when I was in Nürnberg in the year 1577. As far as I know, this picture was painted by Dürer, in 1500, when he was about thirty years old. Dürer made another portrait of himself in an engraving of *The Prodigal Son*, kneeling among the pigs, and looking upward, and for whose face he used his own.[18]

A very fine painting by Dürer's hand, most carefully done, shows the Roman figure of Lucretia; it can be seen at the house of Melchior Wijntgis, a collector at Middelburg.[19]

Albrecht was an excellent man. He was respected and esteemed by people of high rank, for his fine intellect, great knowledge, and judgement.

He came to our Netherlands, and he visited artists, and looked at their works with great interest and pleasure. He was deeply interested in their personalities, especially in that

of Lucas van Leyden; the story is told of how he looked at
this artist with so much emotion that his breath and speech
failed; then he embraced him very enthusiastically, and was
surprised to find that this great man, with a great reputation,
had such a small figure. It was no less pleasant to Lucas to see
the eminent Dürer, whose fame was known to him and
whose prints he had studied with a genuinely deep interest.
These two, great, enlightened souls,—ornaments, the one to
Upper Germany, the other to the Netherlands—, made portraits of each other and enjoyed each other's friendly company exceedingly.[20]

When Dürer saw the paintings of Geertgen van St Jans,
he was utterly amazed, and said that Geertgen must already
have been a painter in his mother's body. Sometimes, when
something very ordinary or even bad was shown to him and
his opinion asked, he answered that the artist had evidently
done his best. He was very tactful and let a thing have its own
value. In this way he was not ungracious as some persons are,
who are too quick at rejecting or criticising, and thereby
make things valueless in the eyes of others. These persons
should follow the example set by this excellent master; they
should not offer their criticism to others, for is it not much
more becoming to speak about things with reserve, and con-
servatively, without sneering?

Albrecht died on the eighth of April, 1528, in the holy
week before Easter. He was buried in the cemetery of Saint
John, outside the city of Nürnberg, near some other honorable persons. This epitaph is on the gravestone:[21]

ME.AL.DV.

QUICQUID ALBERTI DURERI MORTALE FUIT,

SUB HOC CONDITUR TUMULO, EMIGRAVIT VIII

IDUS APRILIS, M.D.XXVIII.

His very intimate friend, the learned Bibaldus Pirkeymherus, of whom Dürer had engraved a portrait, composed the following epitaph in Latin:

When Albert had embellished the world,
And had rendered everything in perfection by his beautiful art, he said:
'What, did I fail to paint thus far—the high vaults of Heaven?'
He left earth suddenly, and the bright star which had been shining upon us, eclipsed.

Another epitaph:

Purity of heart, wisdom, prudence,
Artistic talent, pious devotion and faith,
Are buried here together.

Third epitaph:

If our tears could bring you, Albert, to life,
Your body in the grave would not be subjected to the action of merciless earth;
But because our tears cannot change destiny,
We can lead you to the grave only with great sorrow in our thoughts,
With tears in our eyes.

In memory of Albrecht Dürer: A very virtuous man; the greatest artist of his time, among the Germans, to master the art of painting. He brought fame to art and subjected it to strict laws, and he enlightened the future generations by his writings. For this reason and for his high moral standing and abilities, he was beloved by his fellow artists in Nürnberg, by the illustrious Emperor Maximilian, by his nephew Charles and, by Ferdinand, King of Hungary and Bohemia, who had given him a pension and many of the highest privileges.

He died at the age of fifty-seven, and was deeply mourned.

Bibaldus Pirkheymherus has written this for his faithful friend.

CORNELIS ENGELBRECHTSEN
OF LEYDEN

ONE might say that in the past the art of painting in the Netherlands has been practised with skill and not with science as it was by the Italians, who had the best of all methods—those based on the study of antique sculpture. Nevertheless, one is astonished by the fact, that at an early period, the artists of the Netherlands had a natural understanding of the human figure and, moreover, they had a beautiful and efficient technique for rendering it. This may be best seen in the clever brush strokes of Cornelis Engelbrechtsz., who was a Leyden artist. He flourished at an early period; he was born in the year 1468, in the city of Leyden.[1]

Cornelis was the first, or one of the first, painters in his native city to use oil-paints, although this process had been invented about sixty years before by Joannes van Eyck, deservedly an ornament in the crown of the school of painting in the Netherlands. I have already told this before.

I could not find out of whom Cornelis was a pupil, or whether his father practiced painting, too. The story is told that Lucas Hugensen van Leyden, whose biography will follow, had lost his father early in life, and became a pupil of Cornelis. Cornelis had two sons, both of whom were painters, and contemporaries of Lucas. There was a third, elder son, also, called Pieter Cornelisz. Kunst, who was a glass painter. Lucas, friendly with his son, became a clever glass painter himself, through this friendship. The story of the other two brothers will follow later.[2]

Cornelisz. Engelbrechtsz., of whom I want to speak here, drew well and was a clever painter in water- as well as in oil-

43

color. Some beautiful pictures of his, which were not destroyed in the cataclysm of image-breaking, have been preserved in the city hall of Leyden, by order of the magistrates, to commemorate this prominent master and citizen. However, it is to be regretted that some are hung too high for the eye, with the result that their good qualities cannot be discerned from below.

There are two altar paintings with wings, formerly in the chapel of the monastery at Marien Poel, not far out of the city of Leyden. The center panel of one portrays the crucifixion, with the two thieves, Mary, John, and persons on horseback, pedestrians—all painted very beautifully. The right door shows the sacrifice of Abraham; the left, the biting of the serpent.3

The other painting is a *Descent from the Cross*, and arranged around it are small scenes representing the seven sorrows of Mary. If I remember rightly, praying figures are represented on the wings. This was well painted.4

In the city hall of Leyden, there is a large water-color painted by Cornelisz., with large figures, an *Adoration of the Virgin*. The draperies are exceedingly fine, and one can see from this painting that Lucas van Leyden made a close study of the works of Cornelisz. This painting has somewhat deteriorated, thereby causing a great loss to art.5

But the most excellent work by Cornelisz., is a panel with two wings; it once served as a memorial tablet for the Lockhorst family, who ordered it placed above their grave in the Lockhorst Chapel. Formerly this painting could be studied in Leyden in the home of the Lockhorsts, but it has been transferred to Utrecht and, at present, it is in the home of Sr Boogaert, who married a daughter of Sr Lockhorst.6

The subject of the painting in question is the scene from the *Revelation of St John* in which the Lamb of God opens the book with the seven seals. The entire celestial hierarchy is represented, well grouped, with great variety in the beautiful faces. The whole scene is a wonderful, technical achievement. Able artists stood in awe before the picture and noted the perfection which had been attained, even though it was painted *a la prima*, a method applied very frequently and successfully in those days. Portraits of the donors, represented in prayer, are nicely executed.[7]

Cornelisz. Engelbrechtsz. was an excellent and brave master. He not only had great talent and knowledge, but put a great amount of work into his pictures and embellished them with interesting ornament. He was a keen observer of human emotions and knew how to paint them in the manner of the ancient masters.

He died at Leyden, in 1533, at the age of sixty-five.

BARENT VAN BRUSSEL
(BERNARD VAN ORLEY)

BERNARDT VAN BRUSSEL deserves to be remembered as a most efficient painter in water-color and in oil-color. He drew well, and gave good poses to his figures. He was in the service of Marguerite of Parma, Governess of the Netherlands; he was also court painter to Charles V.[1]

One of his paintings, a *Last Judgement*, is in Antwerp, in the chapel of the Alms Masters. He had the panel gilded before painting it, in order to make it more beautiful and permanent; this method gave him a fine, transparent sky.[2]

Some of his older work is at Brussels, in the Church of Saint Gudule. He made an altar painting for the Guild of the Artists in Malines, a fine work representing St Luke making a portrait of Mary. Michiel Cocxie painted the subjects on the wings which were added to it.[3]

Bernardt drew and painted very beautiful tapestry cartoons for Marguerite of Parma, for other members of the aristocracy, and for the Emperor. For the monarch, he made many hunting scenes of the woods and localities in the neighborhood of Brussels where the Emperor used to hunt. The figures of the Emperor, of the princes, and of the princesses in these cartoons, have been drawn from life; beautiful tapestries were woven after these cartoons. Bernardt was very sure in his technique and was paid well for his work.[4]

Recently, sixteen precious tapestry cartoons, designed by Bernardt, were sent to Count Maurice at The Hague in Holland. A man or woman on horseback appears in each one, life-size, and the whole set illustrates the genealogy of the House of Orange. The figures have been done from life. His

46

BARENT VAN BRUSSEL

Excellency, Duke Maurice of Nassau, ordered Hans Jordaens of Antwerp to make oil-paintings from these cartoons. Jordaens was a clever painter and lived at Delft.[5]

These cartoons, according to the date written on them, must be about one hundred years old. One can compute the period in which the master flourished. I estimate that he reached a good age. I was not able to obtain the date of his birth nor of his death, for people had not been careful enough to make record of these events.[6]

LUCAS VAN LEYDEN
PROMINENT ARTIST, ENGRAVER AND GLASS PAINTER

SOMETIMES nature seems to regard some persons as her favored children; she seems to destine them to surpass others and to rise high above them, by particularly great genius and worthy deeds, either of mind or of body. Such achievement has occurred in history; beautiful poetry relates it. Frequently, such men gave promise and caused definite expectations early in life. Some, when still youths, showed by a wise answer that a seat in the Roman Secret Council was destined for them and the hall of rulers was open to them. Others, according to the poets, showed their strength in the cradle by smothering serpents. There is a proverb which says: 'What must become a nettle, begins to sting early.'

Among the many geniuses in the fine art of painting, I do not know of one who reached excellence in the prime of life, except Lucas van Leyden. No-one, of whom I have spoken thus far, compares with him in this respect. He seemed to have been born with brushes and a burin in his hand, and with the arts of painting and drawing within him. It is almost unbelievable, although the story has been told by people who knew, that, as a child of nine, he made engravings which were finely and ably executed. Many of them may still be seen; some of these have been dated.[1]

One can calculate at what age Lucas made these engravings, for he was born in Leyden, in the year 1494, around the last day of May or the beginning of June. His father's name was Huygh Jacobsz. His father was also an excellent artist.[2]

Lucas, by endowment a master, was a pupil of his father and afterwards of Cornelis Engelbrechtsz. He had a great inspiration and strong, artistic impulses. He used his time with constant diligence, and often made day and night into one by working by candlelight. His jacks and other toys were artists' materials, charcoal, chalk, pen, brushes, burin, and kindred articles. His companions were young artists, glass painters and goldsmiths.

His mother tried to prevent him from drawing at night, not entirely for reasons of economy but for the fact that she was afraid his young, frail body and mind would be harmed by concentrating so long. He could not resist drawing from life all kinds of faces, hands, feet, houses, landscapes, and draperies, in all of which he took a great delight.3

Lucas's was a universal talent, at home in all branches of painting, as well as in oil and water-color. He painted scenery, portraits, landscapes, and human figures and he was proficient in glass painting and engraving. When he was twelve, he made a picture with water-colors on canvas, illustrating the legend of St Hubrecht, a marvelous and famous work, made for Sr van Lockhorst, who gave him as many guilders in gold as he was old in years.

At the age of fourteen, Lucas made an engraving representing Mahomet killing a drunken monk. The next year, in 1509, he engraved many subjects; he was then fifteen years old. From this year date nine round pictures, made for glass painters, of passion scenes: the olive garden, Christ taken prisoner, Christ before Annas, the Mocking of Christ, the flagellation, the crowning, the Ecce Homo, the carrying of the cross and the crucifixion. These excellent works are fine in composition. He also made a '*Temptation of St Anthony*', with a woman, beautifully dressed, standing before the Saint. This is an excellent engraving, both for its foreground and for the scenery in the background. The work is most precise.4

In the same year Lucas engraved a beautiful composition. It was a *Conversion of St Paul*; Paul was represented blind, on his way to Damascus; his blindness and the whole setting were well rendered. In this engraving there are many varieties of faces and costumes, hats, caps, draperies. All this has been done so well that, at present, great Italian artists use these prints, changing them a little sometimes, but base their works on these very engravings by Lucas.

Vasari mentions his *Conversion of St Paul* and praises him in many respects above the famous Albrecht Dürer. Vasari says: 5

'The works of Lucas are so important that he must be counted among those masters who handled the burin most beautifully. The arrangement and the composition of his subjects are most individual, and the conception and the expression are most remarkable. There is not any confusion or inefficiency; each scene seems to be the story itself; reality could not have been different. He observed the aspect of objects most accurately and rendered them more accurately according to the rules of art than did Albrecht Dürer. He treated objects in his engravings with great intelligence. According as to whether they were farther away they are rendered more lightly so that they disappear finally in the distance, similar to life where objects at a distance become less visible; Lucas observed all these phenomena so accurately and rendered the aerial perspective so beautifully that he could not have improved upon the effects by the use of colors. His observations opened the eyes of many painters.'6

This is the testimony of Vasari concerning 'Lucas from Holland', as he calls him, and this is very true, for he made wonderful compositions. A natural, aerial perspective can be noticed in his works that cannot be seen in those of Albrecht Dürer, not even in the best work of this artist, representing

St Hubertus, nor in similar works. It is also true—and again according to a statement of Vasari—that Lucas was not as skillful as Albrecht, yet he equalled him with the burin in many respects.7

If one compares the work of Lucas with that of his contemporaries, one can observe in Lucas's landscapes an entirely different and more beautiful treatment of wide, flat country, and a new and more fluent technique of engraving in the rendering of draperies and folds. I believe experts will agree with me in this respect.8

The next year, 1510, Lucas was sixteen years old, and he engraved that marvelous print, the Ecce Homo, which is a most amazing achievement for so young a boy, for its composition and for the rendering of so great a variety of national costumes, and for the representation of beautiful, modern architecture in accordance with the rules of perspective and of proportion.9

Lucas engraved another print in the same year, representing a farmer and his wife, with three cows; the farmer's wife is getting up after milking, and is showing the stiffness or fatigue from the squatting. This is an exquisite little print, and it was in great demand.10

In the same year, 1510, he made an engraving of Adam and Eve being driven from Paradise; Adam wears a skin over his body and carries a spade across his shoulder, while Eve has Cain, her first child, on her arm. This is a very fine little print. He made another, small, print—a nude woman looking for fleas on a little dog—in the same year.11

I quote these works, purposely to show and to keep in mind how perfect a fruit was produced by so young a sprout. But it would be impossible for me to tell all the works Lucas has engraved, painted, or painted on glass. I can say only that he aimed at applying his colors with great purity, and although he was an engraver, he did not neglect the practice of painting. He was most deft and careful in his printing, and never allowed proofs to leave the workshop if they showed even the slightest faults.

Consequently, Van Leyden's engravings reached fairly high prices in his own time. His best works, the larger prints, for instance, the exquisite engraving of *Magdalen*, the *Crucifixion*, the *Ecce Homo*, the *Magi*, and similar subjects, were worth one gold guilder, or twenty-eight stuyver, apiece. I have heard that his daughter said Lucas burned up many proofs which he regarded as imperfects.[12]

He never studied art in a foreign country, although Vasari writes differently and believes that all famous artists of the Netherlands once studied art in Italy. However, he makes a mistake here, as he does also regarding other things on which he was wrongly informed.[13]

Lucas married a daughter of a noble family by the name of Boshuysen; to his regret, he lost much time at banquets and having a good time, as was the custom among the rich and the members of the nobility.[14]

Some people believe that he and Albrecht Dürer tried to rival or surpass each other, that Lucas engraved the same subjects as Dürer sometimes, and that they followed each others works with the keenest interest. Finally, Albrecht Dürer came to the Netherlands and while in Leyden, made a portrait of himself, and Lucas made one of Albrecht, both on the same little panel, and they spent the time together in the most friendly way.[15]

Lucas was small and somewhat frail. He engraved a self-portrait in which he looks young, without a beard. It is a little more than half-size. He wears a large cap with feathers in it and his costume has a design of a skull in the front.[16]

Very few of his paintings can be seen nowadays, or have

even been found. But those we know are remarkable, most excellent, and most pleasing through a peculiar quality which I cannot define, a lovely grace which can be noticed.

A cabinet with two doors (diptych) must be mentioned above all his other works. It is now at the house of that great art collector and artist, Goltzius, at Haarlem, who obtained this work in Leyden in the year 1602. He bought it for a large sum and it gave him much pleasure. His great knowledge of art made him keenly interested in the works of Lucas. The subject of this painting is the story of the blind man of Jericho, Bartimaeus, son of Timaeus, who regained his sight, as is told in the tenth chapter of the Gospel of St Mark, and in the eighteenth chapter of St Luke.[17]

The work is most beautiful, the paint looks new, the treatment is most fluent, and the composition is fine. The painting on the interior of the doors completes the story. Many figures are painted in this work and they are shown in various poses, displaying great amazement at the miracle of making a blind man see. The nudes and the faces have great variety, and are warm in color and lovely. Each figure is dressed differently and the heads are covered with a variety of unusual caps, turbans and veils. Christ shows a very natural simplicity, a good-naturedness and gentleness allied with kindness, toward the blind for whom he performs the healing. Very natural and characteristic is the action of the blind man who is guided by his boy and who stretches out his right hand.

The background is beautiful and glowing in color; trees and woods are shown in the distance, so deftly and characteristically that one cannot find anywhere anything which can be compared with this work. It seems as if one were in the very fields out of doors, and had everything in nature right before his eyes. In the background of the landscape there is a little scene of Christ picking figs from a bare tree, as though the subject matter were continued by this little detail.

Some one wrote these lines of praise in honor of this wonderful work of art made by so eminent an artist: [18]

> Bartimeus received light from the light, according to the poems of St Mark and St Luke.
> This winged picture has been painted by Lucas.
> The Lamb, gentle figure, shows its kindness by performing its beautiful deed to the blind man who stretches out his hand which has been depicted very characteristically.
> The bystanders are amazed by this miracle.
> The one who beholds this picture is equally amazed, how every detail reflects artistic conception, and deep sentiments are aroused.
> This blind man attracts every one's eye and heart, but without sentiments and without eyes no-one would be moved in spite of the strongest desire of the blind.
> The blind received Light from the Light.
> Through this blind man Lucas gave light to the blind brush of the artists, so that they were able to go the right way.

This picture was painted in 1531, as is shown by the date on the exterior of the wings. On the outside, two figures have been painted, representing a man and a woman holding coats of arms, done in a broad and fluent style. Most likely this picture is the last, and also the very best work in oil, of this famous master. Apparently, he made this work his best in order to make the world more beautiful, to display wonderful things and to leave these to the world to make his name immortal, for he lived only two years longer. I place this work first, for the sake of its great merit.

Still another beautiful and splendid work of Lucas, valued highly by the magistrates, is in the City Hall of Leyden. It is a *Last Judgement* and is regarded as a most excellent piece of work. There are many nudes, of men and women in the painting, which indicate that Lucas worked from life; in the nudes of the women especially, the lovely flesh is rendered beautifully, although it was a custom of the painters to give a sharp outline to the nudes on the lighted side.[19]

On the outside of this work, two large, seated, figures of Peter and Paul can be seen; they are painted exquisitely, much better than the work on the interior; the colors are better and have been applied more fluently; this is true of the faces and the nudes as well as of the foregrounds and the backgrounds. The painting is such that foreign potentates inquired whether they might buy it; but the magistrates declined politely, stating that they did not want to part with the painting for any amount of money, for it was the work of a citizen; it was bringing still more fame to the fine art of painting.

Frans Hooghstraet, a member of the nobility, who lives outside of Leyden, possessed an excellent little painting, a diptych, showing at the interior a picture of Mary. It is a half-figure, the part below the knees being hidden behind stones. The little Infant is very lovely, He holds a bunch of grapes in His hand, with the vine hanging down. Evidently the artist intended to remind us of the allegory of Christ, "I am the vine." The drapery is painted excellently. A woman praying has been painted on the reverse, and behind her is a Magdalen, who points at Christ on Mary's lap. The background of this painting is remarkable for its landscape and flowers.

On the outside, an *Annunciation* was painted; it was very fine and it showed full figures. The draperies and the entire composition were excellent. This picture is now in the possession of Emperor Rudolph, who is the greatest collector of the present time. There was a date on this picture, 22 and the letter L, with which Lucas signed his pictures.[20]

Another fine painting by Lucas is in Amsterdam in the *Calverstraet*. It is a diptych and represents the children of

55

Israel dancing around the golden calf and having a banquet. The joy of the people and the unchaste desire in their eyes have been made very life-like. However, this painting has been smeared over with dirty varnish by some ignorant person.[21]

A beautiful water-color on canvas by Lucas is at the home of that good gentleman Sr Sonneveldt, at Leyden. Another work by Lucas is at the house of Sr Knotter, a great art lover, who paints himself. This represents the story of Rebecca and the servant of Abraham receiving a drink from the well, various beautiful girl and woman figures can be seen in this picture; they are occupied in various ways; the landscape is beautiful.

I have seen some canvases done with water-color by Lucas, in Delft, at the home of a brewer or malt producer. They illustrated the story of Joseph and displayed very original composition and a great knowledge of drawing; the draperies were very fine; especially noteworthy were the cup-bearer and the baker in the prison. However, it is to be regretted that these pictures have suffered through time and that they have been damaged by the moisture of the walls— a great evil in the Netherlands.[22]

Here and there nice portraits by Lucas can be seen, a type of work for which he had an excellent technique. There is, among other works, a portrait painted by Lucas at the home of Burgomaster Claes Ariaensz. in Leyden. It is almost life-size and shows a very natural expression. A small, lovely picture of Mary, painted by Lucas, is in Leyden at the home of Bartholomeus Ferreris, who is a painter.

I have told elsewhere how well Lucas could render emotions. He made a print representing King Saul and David; the King has a disturbed expression and shows all the signs of insanity in his features; David is playing the harp, and Saul is obviously attempting to pierce him with a lance.[23]

Similar effects can be seen in various other works of Lucas's, especially in a number of small engravings. Vasari praises Lucas, in his writings, for a print which shows a farmer who seems to be suffering from a terrible toothache. A quack pulls his tooth, and the farmer does not notice that a woman is stealing his purse at the same moment.[24]

Another small engraving by Lucas is a fine representation of an old man and an old woman who are tuning their musical instruments. This print, evidently, an illustration to a text from the philosophy of Plutarch, where a statement is made about martial law to the effect that the husband has to be obeyed in the home. There is an analogy in the fact that the largest string gives the loudest sound on most instruments; the artist placed the larger instrument in the hands of the man.[25]

The most excellent work Lucas made is an engraved portrait of Maximilian that he did when the Emperor visited Leyden and was received with great honor. It is the finest and largest portrait which Lucas ever engraved and is remarkably bold and striking in execution.[26]

After what I have written, it will appear that Lucas was a very interesting man. I do not know whether he is to be praised most for his painting and engraving, or for his glass painting. We may assume that he learned engraving from some one who did etching on armor with acids; he studied under a goldsmith, also. He made some interesting, small etchings and many woodcuts which were done most beautifully. Some of his work is on glass and is well worth preserving. Goltzio, who loves his works very much, has among other things a little piece of glass representing David approached by dancing girls; this is executed most beautifully, and it has been engraved by Jan van Sanredam.[27]

When Lucas was thirty-five years old he conceived the idea of visiting the painters in Zeeland, Flanders and Brabant. Having the means, he started out on the trip and, as far as I know, in his own boat which was well equipped.

When he came to Middelburg he delighted in the works of Jan van Mabuse, who lived there at that time, and who had made various paintings. Lucas gave a banquet, for Mabuse and the other painters, which cost sixty guilders. He did the same thing at Ghent, Malines and Antwerp, each time spending about sixty guilders at least, on the painters.[28]

He was accompanied everywhere by Jan van Mabuse who wore a costume of gold cloth, while Lucas wore a gown of yellow silk camlet which looked like gold in the sunlight. Some people believed that Lucas was regarded by the artists as a little inferior to Jan, because Mabuse's costume was more brilliant than that of Lucas.

A notion conflicting with high principles lodged in the mind of Lucas. In the latter part of his life, he regretted having made this voyage because he imagined that some envious person had administered poison to him; for, after that trip, he was never again in good health. Whether Lucas had this notion in his head rightly or wrongly, the fact is he lived six years more and, until his death, was in bed most of the time. I do not know whether he suffered from his lungs or from something else. I do know he was tortured by the delusion.

Although he was bed-ridden, he did not allow any time to be lost; he executed engravings and paintings, having tools made especially for work in this condition. His love for art became stronger than ever—as happens frequently to great masters, whose constant practice makes their love for art grow stronger every day.

Towards the end, his health decreased more and more and

no medicine could restore it. He felt he had to leave this world. Two days before he died, he had a fancy to behold the sky once more, the creation of the Lord. The maid in the house brought him out of doors for this purpose. This was his last effort; the second day thereafter he passed away. This was in the year 1533; he was only thirty-nine years old.

He was yet alive on a day which remained in the memory of people especially well, and which was called the day of the 'hot procession' in Leyden, for, during this procession, people dropped in the street, overcome by heat, and died.

The last engraving Lucas made was a small one of Pallas; it is said that this print was found in front of him on his death bed. Lucas loved and practiced his fine and noble art till the very last moment of his life.[29]

He had only one daughter. She gave birth to a son nine days before the passing away of her father. After the people of the house returned from the baptism, Lucas asked the name of his young grandson. They told him that there would be a Lucas after him. But he was not appreciative; he imagined that his family wanted him gone.[30]

The son of this daughter, Lucas Damessen, died in Utrecht in 1604 at the age of seventy-one. He was a fairly good painter, as was his brother, Joan de Hooy, who became court painter to the King of France.[31]

Lampsonius composed a poem in Latin in honor of Lucas; but I do not think it gives enough praise:

Lucas, though not equal to Dürer, but nearest to him through your artistic talent, whether you make pictures or you engrave, show your work, allow your copper prints on delicate paper to bring their message for they are worth admiration. Advance freely, if you care to; it is for your own honor; and let our poem add your name to the glory of your native town, Leyden.

JAN DE HOLLANDER

OF ANTWERP

AMONG the works of the famous artists of the Netherlands that have been published and reproduced in copper engraving, a place has been given to the paintings of Jan de Hollander, who was born in Antwerp. He was a landscape artist of distinction.[1]

He must have lived a long time ago, for he was the husband of the mother of Gilles van Conincxloy. He painted in oils and in water-colors. He used to spend much time lying on the window-sill looking at the sky, in order to improve his painting from nature. He frequently made use of a method by which he covered the ground color of his canvas or panel with a light wash, so that this ground color contributed to the final effect of the painting. Brueghel took over this method from him.[2]

Jan's wife travelled with his paintings to the markets of Brabant and Flanders, placing his works everywhere, and making good profits. Although Jan did not travel, he produced little. His landscapes are of the best. He died at Antwerp.[3]

Lampsonius addresses him as follows:[4]

> The Netherlanders have always deserved praise for their landscapes;
> The Italians painted human figures and those of gods.
> This is not so great a wonder; it can be understood easily:
> The Italian has his intelligence in his head.
> It is not an idle statement to say that the Netherlander has his wit in his hand.
> This artist from Brabant enjoyed painting landscapes well, instead of painting portraits, human figures and the Deity, badly.

60

QUINTIJN MESSIJS
OF ANTWERP

WE have made the statement that man likes to follow the individual inclination which Nature gave him at birth. But frequently there is some interference by parents, by circumstances caused by the necessities of life, and other reasons. Sometimes it happens that a person, predestined to become an artist, has had to do rough work in the beginning. We see, however, that from the moment such a person can change his activities and follow his own inclination and become an artist, even rather late in life, he makes wonderful progress and becomes successful. This was true in the life of Polydore, and in the life of Quintijn Messijs from Antwerp. He was often called the blacksmith, because he was one until he was twenty, although some persons have carelessly said he worked at the forge until he was thirty.

Before he was twenty Quintijn was seriously ill. He could hardly support himself and his poor, old mother, for whom he had been accustomed to provide. He was worried; he had to stay in bed, and he could not work; he complained to friends who visited him daily during his illness. After the worst of his illness was over, and Quintijn could sit up, his body was so weak he was unable to do the heavy work required in the smithy.

At this time Shrove-tide was approaching. In Antwerp it was an old custom for the people, who took care of the sick, the 'Lazarists', to have a procession, and to carry a torch sculptured in wood and painted. During the procession printed and colored pictures of saints were distributed to the children; these were from woodcuts, and many impressions of them were needed. Among the visitors to Quintijn there was one of the Lazarists who advised him to do some of the coloring on the little prints of the saints, and Quintijn did do so. This work stimulated his talent and caused him to devote himself with great love and diligence to the art of painting. By constant practice, and in a short time, he made remarkable progress. He became an eminent master and persisted in his work the remainder of his life.

Another story about Quintijn explains why he changed from a blacksmith to an artist. When still a smith he fell in love with a girl and began to court her. He had a rival in this courtship, and this rival was a painter. The girl loved Quintijn; but she was not pleased that he had such dirty work. She rather wished that Quintijn was the painter and her other suitor was the blacksmith. Quintijn understood this, and moved by his great love, laid down the hammers, took up the brushes and devoted himself to the art of painting. He did this to please his beloved one and to win her favor. This story has been confirmed by Lampsonius in a Latin poem or *Carmen*, which is printed under an engraved portrait of Quintijn. Lampsonius speaks as if he was Quintijn, and it will not be out of place here to quote this poem in our own language:[1]

> Quintijn Messijs, painter from Antwerp speaks:
> A rough Cyclop blacksmith was I before,
> But when my sweetheart was also courted by a painter,
> She made me understand with some reproach,
> That the thundering blows on the anvil were less pleasing to her
> Than the silent play of the brushes,
> The force of love made me a painter.
> The truth of this is indicated by a little anvil,
> Which I selected for a signature on my pictures.
> As Cypris obtained from Vulcan the arms for her son,
> O great poet, You have made a clever painter from a blacksmith.

QUINTIJN MESSIJS

Despite the romance of this tale, that courtship caused Quintijn to become an artist, the first story is regarded as the truth. According to my opinion both stories, however, may be true. Quintijn may have played with color during his illness; and, when he was well again, made the acquaintance of the girl and fell in love with her. She was also courted by a painter; but to Quintijn she may have said the few words needed to make him give up the work of a blacksmith and become an artist. By his love, by his interest in nature and by his knowledge, he achieved much and became an excellent master.

There is a work of his, a painting, most worthy of being remembered. It is in the Onze Vrouwen Kerck, in Antwerp, and it belongs to the guild of cabinet workers and furniture makers. This painting is of the *Descent from the Cross*, with the prostrate figure of Christ in the center of it. One thinks the figure may have been painted from a pose in life. It is a splendid achievement in oil-painting. The holy women and the other figures express various attitudes of sorrow. On the interior of one of the wings there is a scene of the martyrdom of St John who is being boiled alive in oil, and in the same scene there are some beautiful horses. In olden time, spectators had discussions as to how many horses' heads they could see in this picture, and some counted six, others seven, others eight. The reason for this was that the painting had deteriorated in some places, and some parts were hard to distinguish; a helmet could have been mistaken for a horse's head. The other wing illustrates the story of the daughter of Herodias, dancing before Herod to obtain the head of St John the Baptist. From a little distance the figures appear to have been painted with a decided finish; they seem to be clearly and sharply defined; but, nearby, they are somewhat coarse.[2]

The King of Spain, Philip the Second, who died recently, had a great love for art. He expended much effort to obtain this altar painting and take it to Spain. Despite the large amount of money he was willing to give for this picture, his offer was declined with due respect and politeness.[3]

This painting, by Quintijn, escaped the raving madness of the iconoclasts, and it is to be hoped that it will remain out of their destroying hands for ever.[4]

In the year 1577, during the last Stadtsberoerte, the guild of the cabinet makers sold the painting. Marten de Vos, at the sale, used his influence so effectively that the magistrates of the town declared the transaction invalid and bought the painting for themselves, for fifteen hundred guilders, in order that the town of Antwerp should not be deprived of this treasure. It is a painting that deserves to be remembered. With the money from this painting, the members of the cabinet-makers guild bought a house.[5]

Quintijn produced many more works which have been scattered and taken to various places. Occasionally, his works can be found in the rooms of art collectors who value them as preciously as they do jewelry. Bartholomeus Ferrerus, a great collector, has a painting by Quintijn. This painting is of Mary, and it shows the artist's fine technique.[6]

Quintijn's son became his pupil, and his name was Jan Messys, and he was a good painter. There is a painting by him, in Amsterdam in the Warmoestraet at the 'Lavoir', of money-changers. Various paintings by Jan Messys are in Antwerp and in other places.[7]

JERONIMUS BOS VAN AKEN

THE inclinations of artists are as many as are their technical proceedings in their works. Those who normally followed their natural talent became the best masters. Who will be able to tell of all the weird and strange ideas which were in the mind of Jeronimus Bos, and his expressions of them by his brush? He painted gruesome pictures of spooks and horrid phantoms of hell.

Van Aken was born at 'sHertogenbosch. Unable to learn how long he lived and when he died, I know that he lived at an early time. His treatment of draperies differs from that of earlier artists who painted many wrinkles and folds. His technique was sure and clever and he painted *à la prima*. This is why his paintings remain unchanged, and why they are in beautiful condition. As other old masters had done, he made his drawing of subjects on the white ground of his panel, over which he painted a transparent layer in a color, or in a shade, more or less like flesh. Frequently he used the ground for part of the final effect of the painting.[1]

Some of Van Aken's paintings are in Amsterdam. I have seen his *Flight from Egypt*. In the foreground, Joseph is asking his way, of a farmer; Mary is riding on a donkey; a strange rock can be noticed in the background; some think it is like an inn; a group of weird human figures are inducing a big bear to dance for some money. This painting is strange but amusing. Another painting, by him, on the Wael, is of a scene in hell, and in which old fathers are delivered (from their graves), while Judas, who thinks he can escape, is pulled out with a rope and hanged. It is most remarkable, all that may be seen in this picture, in the way of weirdness. How

65

cleverly and naturally he painted the flames and smoke! In Amsterdam, there is a picture that is more stately and more dignified than his usual paintings. It is the *Carrying of the Cross.* In Haarlem I have seen various paintings by Van Aken, in the house of Joan Dietringh, an art collector. There were the wings of an altar painting, with saints on it, and a holy monk disputing with a group of heretics. The monk had taken their books with his own and thrown them into a fire; the books which did not burn would be right. The book of one of the saints flies out of the fire, this book has been well painted. The burning fire and the smoking wood, covered with the ashes, are well defined. The one saint and his companions appear dignified; the others, with strange faces, are horrified. Another painting is of a miracle, before which a King and other people are terribly afflicted. The faces, the hair, and the beards are, excellent, and the figures have been done with ease.[2]

Most of his paintings are still in the church of 'sHertogenbosch, and some are in the Escorial in Spain where they are highly valued.[3]

Lampsonius addresses him in his poems as follows:[4]

Jeroon Bos, what is the meaning of your frightened face, of your pale features?

It looks as if you imagined all the spirits from hell were flying round your ears.

I could think you had listened to the roaring depth of Pluto's domain;

I could imagine the gates of hell had been opened to you.

You were so eminent an artist that you were able to paint all that has been enclosed in deepest hell.

LODEWYCK JANS VAN DEN BOSCH

THERE was once a certain Lodewyck Jans van den Bosch who was quite good at painting fruit and flowers. He represented the flowers standing in a glass of water. He had so much patience, spent so much time, and painted so precisely, that everything looked life-like. He painted on his little flowers and weeds, dew from heaven, or insects, such as beetles and little flies. His work may be seen here and there in the collections of art lovers.

How good he was at painting human figures may be noted in his pictures in the collection of Melchior Wijntgis at Middelburg. This great art lover has a beautiful painting representing St Jerome; four round pictures of fire scenes; fruit still life; vases and floral pieces; and some other small pictures—all exquisitely painted. At the home of Jaques Razet there is a beautiful painting of flowers in a glass.[1]

In my story, I place the painter next to his countryman and fellow citizen, because I do not know more to write about him except that I hope that his name and fame will remain memorable among painters.

CORNELIS CORNELISZ. KUNST

OF LEYDEN

ALTHOUGH artistic talent is not generally inherited by children from their parents, Cornelis Kunst, son and pupil of Cornelis Enghelbrechtsz., was a worthy and capable follower of his eminent father. Born in Leyden in the year 1493, he became one of the most prominent painters in Leyden in his time. However, wealth was not overflowing in the town, because the foreigners who used to bring prosperity to the city, had left, and Cornelis lived in Bruges, in Flanders, sometimes for periods of three or four years. Bruges was a prosperous and rich city, with many persons of foreign nationality attracted there by her great commerce. The result was that art was well appreciated and well paid for in Bruges. Kunst gained good money and made many beautiful pictures.[1]

Many splendid paintings were re-painted by Kunst in Leyden. Among others must be mentioned especially a painting now at the home of a certain Sr Dirck van Sonneveldt, on which can be seen a *Christ carrying the Cross*, along with the leading of the two thieves. This is a very dramatic picture; the emotion of Mary over the suffering of her son, our Lord Jesus Christ, is well expressed. The picture may well be considered as the most excellent example of Kunst's works. There is also in the same house a *Descent from the Cross*, very well done, with interesting color contrasts.[2]

A portrait of himself and his second wife can be seen at the house of Kunst's daughter, Aechtgen Cornelis, a woman at least seventy-two years old at present. She is seated in her garden outside the Koe-poort, and in the background is painted a part of the city, and the Koe-poort is represented,

68

too—all painted from life, and well executed in color.

Kunst painted many beautiful subjects for a monastery outside Leyden, at Leyderdorp, which were destroyed during the war, or were hidden.

Many of his large and small pictures are still in the possession of citizens of Leyden. They were done in oil or in water-color. I mention specially the ones in the house of Jacob Vermy, a prominent citizen.

Cornelis Cornelisz. Kunst died in the year of our Lord, 1544, at the age of fifty-one.[3]

LUCAS CORNELISZ. DE KOCK

OF LEYDEN

SINCE Cornelis Kunst inherited his artistic qualities from his father, the brother of Cornelis was not reluctant to follow in the same way.

Lucas Cornelisz. studied art under his father, Cornelis Enghelbrechtsz. He was born in 1495 in Leyden. He became both painter and cook; art hardly gave sufficient income for living. Nevertheless, he was as fine a master in oil-painting as in water-color. This still may be seen in Leyden, especially at the home of the art lover, Sr Joan Adriaensz. Knotter, who is also an artist, and who painted some canvases with water-color. His paintings were neatly done and show observation of the various effects required by the subject matter. Among others, one of the most important works is a painting of the *Woman taken in Adultery*. At the home of Sr Jacob Vermy are also many water-colors by his hand.

Lucas experienced bad times in Leyden, and he understood that, during the reign of Henry VIII in England, art was held in honor, and that there was a demand for it in that country. He travelled with his wife and his seven or eight children to England. Since then nothing has ever been heard, either of his person or of his life, except that there is in the city of Leyden a picture which has been imported from England. It is at the home of a merchant, Hans de Hartoogh, and shows a technique of painting similar to his.

At the time the Earl of Leicester was appointed governor of the Netherlands, some Englishmen came with him. They were eager to buy pictures by Lucas, because they knew about his works in England. This is all I know about Lucas.[1]

JAN VAN CALCKER

AMONG the artists gifted by nature and belonging to the Netherlands was one who seemed to be chosen for silencing the Italian painters. These artists had stated that no painter from the Netherlands could surpass or even equal their own great masters, in painting the human figure. That painter was Joan van Calcker, an eminent artist whose fame and merit cannot be trumpeted loudly enough. I regret that I have so little information about this master.[1]

Van Calcker was born in the city of Calcker, in the land of Cleves; but I do not know where he was able to follow an example which stimulated him to develop his natural talent, or under whom he started his studies. All I know is that he was living in 1536, or 1537, at Venice. He had left the Netherlands and was living at Venice with a girl from Dordrecht, whose parental home was a hostelry frequented by cut-throats and murderers. A story of this will be told later, in the life of Hemskerck.

Van Calcker was a worthy pupil of the great Titian, in Venice, whose method of painting he followed and equalled so perfectly that their technique could not be easily differentiated. Goltzius, in whose judgement I have full confidence, was in Naples at that time and some portraits by Van Calcker were shown to him; he said, spontaneously, that they had been painted by Titian. The painters who were present said: 'You are right and you judge correctly; nevertheless, the work is not by Titian but by Jan van Calcker.' His technique was so similar to Titian's that the best art experts in the world could not see the difference between them.[2]

Vasari, who knew Van Calcker at Naples, stated that his

technique in painting could not be taken as belonging to any painter from the Netherlands. He also had a remarkable technique with chalk and with the pen; his cross-hatching was very bold, and in this method he came to be almost equal to Titian.3

Van Calcker made the drawings for an important book by the famous anatomist, Vesalius; the figures were remarkably well done; they show how prominent this artist of the Netherlands was.4

Van Calcker made portrait drawings of various painters, sculptors, and architects, of Italy, which are in the books of Georgius Vasari. These are done splendidly with a very bold and steady hand and a fine technique. They really cannot be surpassed by human hands. He died at Naples, about the year 1546. His death was a most regrettable loss to art and to the glory of the Netherlands.5

PIETER KOECK

OF AELST

THE city of Aelst need not be modest and silent; she does not have to bow to other cities who boast that they have produced world renowned artists. Aelst produced Pieter Koeck. It was his native town. He lived there as a citizen.

Pieter studied painting under Bernard van Brussel, and, having a good head, he increased his knowledge rapidly. He could draw very cleverly, and became an able artist both in oil and water-color work. He was a good designer for tapestry. Pieter visited Italy and studied in Rome, as was customary. He drew most industriously and made studies of statues and architectural subjects.[1]

Pieter came back to the Netherlands, married, and soon became a widower. Some tapestry dealers in Brussels asked him to make a voyage to Constantinople in Turkey. They intended to make something outstanding in the way of a precious and beautiful tapestry for the Grand Turk. They commissioned Pieter to paint some subjects to be shown to the Turkish Emperor, but because the Turks, in obedience to the Mohammedan law, were not very eager to possess designs of human figures and animals, the enterprise led to nothing. The voyage was in vain, and great expenses were incurred uselessly.[2]

Pieter stayed in Turkey for about a year and learned to speak Turkish. Because he did not want to be idle, he made sketches of the city of Constantinople with its various surroundings, from nature, for his own pleasure.

These subjects, divided into seven sections, were publish-

73

ed as wood cuts. They show interesting aspects of Turkish life: First, how the Turkish Emperor makes his customary promenade on horseback with the Janissaries and his other attendants; secondly, a Turkish wedding, the bride being escorted by musicians and similar people, and male dancers, according to Turkish customs; third, how they bury their dead outside the city; fourth, the feast of the New Moon; fifth, how they take their meals; sixth, how they travel; and, seventh, how warfare is carried on.3

Beautiful backgrounds can be seen in these fine prints, and the treatment of the figures, in the act of carrying loads and in other activities, is most interesting. He gave very pleasing poses to little, graceful women draping them beautifully with scarfs and shawls. A great variety of costumes is shown. All this indicates how clever a master Pieter was. He represented himself, in the seventh print, holding a bow in his hand and aiming at somebody standing next to him who holds a long lance with a little flag on it.4

When he returned to Holland he was married a second time, to Maeyken Verhulst or Bessemers, by whom he had a daughter, who became the wife of Pieter Breughel, his pupil.5

At this time, 1549, Koeck wrote books on building, geometry and perspective. Since he was gifted and had learned the Italian language, he translated the books of Sebastiano Serlio into our language and thus directed in our Netherlands the art of building toward the light. Architecture had lost its bearings but now returned in the right direction. The result is that those parts in the writings of Vitruvius Pollio, which were written more or less obscurely, can now be understood easily, and it is scarcely necessary any more to read the works of Vitruvius in the original to understand the orders of architecture. The right method of building has come to us, in this way, through Pieter Koeck, and we are dropping the modern style. The ugly, modern German type of architecture is most difficult of acceptance. Since it seems to have come into use, it will be very hard to eliminate. The Italians will never adopt it.[6]

Pieter made many works, altar panels, paintings, and portraits. He was also court painter to His Imperial Majesty Charles V, in whose service he died at Antwerp, about the year 1550. His widow, Maeyken Verhulst, published his books on architecture in the year 1553.[7]

Pauwels van Aelst, who was a bastard son of Pieter Koeck, became an excellent copyist of the works of Jan Mabuse, and painted still lifes of flowers in a little glass. He lived and died at Antwerp; his widow became the wife of Gielis van Conincxloo.[8]

Lampsonius addresses Pieter van Aelst in a Latin poem as follows:[9]

Pieter, you were a clever artist
And with your works have made Aelst famous the world all over,
But you, by your great labor,
Fostered the art of those
Whose call is to build beautiful houses.
Serlius taught it to his people,
And you did so, not only to your own,
But also to the French.
You were interpreter for Serlius in two languages.

JOACHIM PATENIER
OF DINANT

THE famous and splendid town of Antwerp, prosperous in trade, attracted the most excellent artists from every land. Fine art came to Antwerp because it follows wealth. Joachim Patenier, who was born in Dinant, came to Antwerp with the others. He entered the guild of the painters in the year of our Lord 1515.[1]

Patenier had an individual style of painting landscape, both excellent and clever; the trees were somehow stippled, and he placed small figures in the landscapes most effectively. The result was that his works were in demand and sold in many countries.

Patenier used to introduce into all his landscapes a tiny figure of a man in the act of evacuating, for which reason he was nicknamed the 'Cacker.' In order to find this little figure one had to hunt for it, just as for the little owl in the works of Hendrick met de Bles.

This Patenier was a man who, although practicing a noble art, led a rough life. He indulged in drinking, and he spent whole days in the inn, spending his earnings lavishly until forced by necessity to take up his brushes which brought profit to him again. He had a pupil, Frans Mostert, and often Patenier drove him out of the house by his crankiness and drinking. Frans stood a great deal of it because he was so eager to learn.[2]

Dürer, when he came to Antwerp, took great interest in the technique of Patenier. Dürer engraved a portrait of Patenier with a copper stift, on a slate, or it may have been on some other tablet; this was an excellent piece of work.[3]

JOACHIM PATENIER

Various art collectors have fine landscapes by Patenier. At the home of Melchior Wijntgis, mint-master of Zealand, who lives in Middelburg, are three excellent works of the artist. One painting shows a variety of figures in a battle scene; it is done so well no illuminator could have wagered his work against it.

The learned Lampsonius addresses Patenier in a poem found on an engraving made by Cornelis Cort from Hoorn. (Lampsonius calls him Curtius). The engraving is made from the portrait which Albrecht Dürer had engraved so artistically. The poet wrote:

> Among all pictures,
> There is none so animated,
> As to expression and as to appearance,
> As yours, O Joachim.
> It was Curtius' hand
> That made a copper engraving of you.
> This hand did not fear to be surpassed.
> This is not the only reason
> For this achievement.
> Dürer has seen landscapes, huts and rocks,
> Which were painted by you, very cleverly,
> And he was so impressed,
> That he engraved your portrait,
> With a burin on a slate.
> Cort followed the features of this portrait,
> And by being able to accomplish this,
> He surpassed not only others,
> But himself.

HENRYCK MET DE BLES
OF BOUVINES NEAR DINANT

NATURE seems to want to show us that she blindly distributes her gifts without discrimination and, sometimes, in unknown, distant places—wherever she wants to create something new. She produced Henryck met de Bles in a lonely corner of the earth and raised him to be a star in the art of painting. He received his name 'Met de Bles' because he had a white patch of hair on the front of his head.

He was born in Bouvines, not far from Dinant, and seems to have been a follower of Joachim Patenier. He became a master without having had a teacher, according to a statement of the learned Lampsonius which is as follows: [1]

> The town of Dinant produced a painter
> Who has been praised by the painter-poet in his verse.
> The most beautiful scenery of the fatherland made him an artist.
> He scarcely received instruction from any master.
> Humble bouvines envied the glory of their neighbor.
> It produced Hendrick who was a capable landscape artist.
> But as much as humble bouvines has to cede to Dinant,
> Henryck cedes as much to you, O Joachim.[2]

I have very little information about this Joachim. I know only that his paintings can be found with various art lovers, and indicate sufficiently that he was a master who showed a great amount of patience, took a great amount of time for his paintings, and put a great deal of work into them. I mention landscapes having little trees, rocks, little cities, and a great number of people, in them. He made many small pictures in this style. The following I do know about the master:

Henryck placed in all his works a small owl which he hid

so well persons will allow each other a long time to find it, and will wager with each other that they cannot find it. This search for the little owl is quite a pastime for them.3

There are three fine landscapes by Henryck in the collection of Sr Wijntgis, as well as a small picture representing Lot. In the house of Marten Papenbroek, in the Waermoestraet, in Amsterdam, there is a grand, beautiful, and well-executed landscape in which one can see a mercer sleeping under a tree while a large number of monkeys are busy disarranging all his merchandise and hanging it in the trees.4

Some persons explain this painting as a caricature of the Pope. The monkeys could be the Martirs or Martinists, adherents of Luther, who discover the true nature of the Pope in his 'cramerye' or merchandise. But this interpretation may be wrong; perhaps Henryck did not mean this at all. Art should not be satirical.5

Another painting by Henryck is in the collection of Sr Melchior Moutheron in Amsterdam. It is a good, little picture representing Emmaus; a remarkable amount of work has been put into it. The castle of Emmaus is in the foreground and so are the pilgrims who are shown large; in another place in the picture, they are shown seated at the table. Then there are scenes in Jerusalem, such as a Passion and Ecce Homo, a Calvary with the Crucifixion, a Resurrection, and kindred subjects.

Many of Henryck's pictures can be seen in the palace of the Emperor in Italy and at other places. There is a great demand for his works in Italy, for the man with the little owl is widely famous.6

LUCAS GASSEL
OF HELMONT

WE found that, in general, the artists of the Netherlands liked very much to paint landscapes and that they had wide experience in such work. There is a difference in Italy as to appreciation; the Italians regard us as fair landscape artists, but they regard themselves as the ultimate masters in painting the human figure. We have had many artists, and we have them still, who disregard the study of the human figure, although it is the highest achievement in the field of art, and who are satisfied with painting landscapes with a few little figures and weeds as detail. One of these artists was Lucas Gassel, from Helmont, who lived and died in Brussels.[1]

Gassel painted landscapes in oil and in water-color. However, he did not paint much. He was a good, friendly man, and an interesting conversationalist. He was a friend of Lampsonius who wrote the following poem in Latin in his honor:[2]

> I greet you Lucas, worthy one,
> You, whom I honor as my father.
> You who caused me to become a lover—
>   of the art of painting already in my youth.
> When you paint
> A landscape and a hut,
> Your devotion equals your fine talent and your experience,
> And you are guided by love to your task.
> Let fame spread your virtue and your artistic name,
> Live forever old man,
> Dear to me for double reason.

LAMBERT LOMBARDUS

OF LIEGE

IN spite of most diligent and serious research, I did not succeed in getting a small Latin book written by Lampsonius, of Bruges, who in the time of Lambert Lombardus was secretary to the bishop of Liege. Lampsonius was a great lover of and an able expert in the art of painting. He was very friendly with Lambert Lombardus of Liege, and he wrote a long and detailed biography of this famous master, a work which would have been a great help to me.[1]

Lambert was born at Luvick or Luyck. He was a clever artist with a great knowledge of painting, architecture, and perspective. He is worthy of remembrance not only as a prominent artist but also, like Chaeron, as a master and preceptor of heroes. He reared such foster children or sucklings as Frans Floris, Willem Keye, Hubrecht Goltzius, and others, who have made a name for themselves and contributed honorably to his fame.[2]

Lambert visited many countries, first the Netherlands near by, then Germany, and France. He discovered some antique work done by the Franks or Germans at a time when art in Italy was almost dead because of revolutions, revolts, and other events. He made careful copies of these works before he had ever seen Roman antiquities. From these figures of the Franks he learned the first principles of art. And he obtained such knowledge of these things that he could differentiate their periods and the places where they had been made.[3]

Lambert also visited Italy and Rome where he did not idle,

and he did not return empty handed. He became the father of the art of drawing and painting in the mountainous corner of the land of Liege. For the rough and coarse barbarian style, he substituted the really beautiful antique style, an achievement for which he deserves gratitude and fame.

Lombardus lived in the neighborhood of Liege. He was an intelligent man with good judgement. He was a philosopher and a poet, and in his works he revealed a great attention to the rendering of the right poses, to the composition of the scenery, to expression, and to other elements.

Many of his works have appeared in print; among others, a large *Last Supper* which is very fine in its composition, and in expression, and other effects. So cleverly and artistically has he arranged this work, that Lombardus may well be placed among the best painters of the Netherlands, of the past and of the present. With this I recommend his name to fame.[4]

HANS HOLBEIN

EITHER some fortunate celestial influence acts upon certain artistic minds at the time of birth, or there may be benign regions where the air is so pure that it sharpens the wits and stimulates young people to grasp and understand what is superior in art and science. I will not dispute different views in regard to this matter; but more than once a great genius in our art of painting has risen in a land where no genius ever rose before. This proves that mental genius is not dependent on place or on race. It is well illustrated by the life of Hans Holbein, who left to posterity a great name and fame as an artist.

All I could find out concerning Holbein's early life is that he was born in the city of Basel, in the wild granite country of Switzerland, in the year 1498. Some people believe that he was born in Augsburg, in Suabia, but this is an error. A rather good painter with the same name did live in Augsburg, but he was not the same great Hans Holbein.[1]

I have not learned what kind of parents Holbein had, or under whom he studied. It is a mystery where or how he gained his beautiful technique which is so entirely different from the ancient and foreign technique.

I wrote to Basel, but unfortunately the man from whom I might have obtained much information died eight or ten years ago. This person was a Doctor Ammersbach, a connoisseur of art who was much interested in collecting all kinds of antiquities and who had, I believe, written an account of all that Hans Holbein had produced in his field at Basel and in England. That written document and some paintings by

83

Holbein were in Basel in the possession of one of Doctor Ammersbach's heirs. I wrote and asked him, very kindly, for the document, and explained why I should like to have it; but he replied that he could not send it to me without great effort, and that, for doing so, he felt justified in asking a good recompense.

This reply greatly surprised me, because my own labor is given voluntarily, for the love of art and not for the sake of profit; and I was also surprised that another person would not share my enthusiasm for promoting the honor of his own fellow citizen and his own town. That written refusal came to me from a Doctor Isely—one might say he ought to be named Assly, for he seemed as stubborn as the immovable rocks of Switzerland. But let the matter pass.[2]

Hans Holbein painted various beautiful pictures that are in the city hall, and in the private houses of many of the burghers, of Basel; and near the fish market in Basel there is an excellent painting of a dance. Among other artistic works by his hand at the city hall there are the famous series of paintings of the *Dance of Death*, illustrating how Death takes away people of all classes, and, as it seems, very much against their own will, for each victim is showing resistance to the very last. Some soldiers and others want to resist Death with force; but they have to go along or else be cut down. Death is taking a lovely child from its mother, without any regard for the sorrow of the parents. Death is beating a drum as a summons to war. No one, from the Pope to the humblest peasant and poorest man, escapes Death. The same series and scenes composed by Holbein have been published in a most interesting little book.[3]

Holbein never went to Italy. At Basel he became acquainted with the learned Erasmus of Rotterdam, who recognized the genius of the artist and tried to help him and to promote his interests. Erasmus esteemed the great artist; and he had his portrait painted by Holbein, who was very proficient in portraiture. Holbein's study of Erasmus was so exquisitely painted that it could not have been surpassed by anyone; and no better resemblance could ever have been achieved.

Erasmus wrote for Holbein a polite letter of recommendation to his former fellow student, Thomas More, an Englishman in London, with the hope that Holbein might go into the service of King Henry VIII and gain the friendship of that monarch, who was very fond of art. Erasmus let Holbein take his portrait with him to England, and wanted him to give it to More. Erasmus wrote that the picture resembled him very much, but that the one Albrecht Dürer had made of him lacked resemblance.[4]

Holbein was pleased indeed; and he grasped the opportunity. It seems to be true also that he was eager to leave Switzerland because he had a wife who was rather cranky, and who had so bad a disposition that he never could expect any peace or rest with her.

Holbein went to England and to Thomas More (who, owing to his great learning, was the High Chancellor to the King). He carried the letter and portrait with him as evidence of the excellence of his art.

Holbein was welcomed and well received by More, who was so delighted with the portrait of his friend, Erasmus, that he kept Holbein with him for about three years, and made him paint various things. And More, at first, neither informed the King about Holbein, nor let him see any of Holbein's paintings; he feared that had he shown some of those noble paintings to the King he would not have had enough of Holbein's services for himself. Holbein painted portraits of More and his family, relatives, and friends, and many other beautiful pictures, in the home of the Chancellor, until, finally, More was well satisfied. The King was then invited to a splendid banquet at More's house, to be shown all the pictures that Holbein had made there.5

The King, who never had seen such excellent artistic work as Holbein's, was most amazed; for he seemed to see, before his eyes, various persons whom he knew, not in the form of the actual paintings but as if they were real and alive. More saw how greatly delighted the King was, and most politely offered the paintings to the King, as a present, saying, 'They have been made for your Majesty.' The King was very thankful and wanted to know if the master who had done this work could be engaged. More replied that the master was ready to render his services, and then introduced Holbein to the King. The King was very pleased. He told More to keep the paintings; and said, 'Now that I have the master for myself, I shall obtain what I should like to have most certainly.'

King Henry VIII appreciated Holbein, esteemed him highly, and was glad to have the great artist with him. Holbein, in the service of the King, made many beautiful portraits of the King and other persons, which can still be seen in London, as I shall tell later. The King's affection for Holbein increased, and he favored him more and more, as the artist served him so well according to his wishes. There is a story about Henry's regard for Holbein, which is a beautiful pearl in the crown of the artist:

It happened that an English Earl once came to visit Holbein. He wished to see the painter's pictures, and the work upon which he was engaged at that time. This did not please Holbein, who painted every one from life, and who just then needed to have privacy in doing his work. For this reason, the artist declined to receive the Earl, and he did so with the greatest politeness possible. He asked the Earl, again and again, to pardon him for his refusal, because something prevented the possibility of the visit; and he asked the Earl to please call at another time. No matter how politely and how humbly Holbein explained the matter, the Earl refused to give up, and tried to pass the artist on the stairway, showing forcefully that a person of his Grace's importance should be more feared, and treated with more deference, by a painter. Holbein warned the Earl not to carry out his impolite intention; but the Earl persisted, whereupon Holbein grappled with him and threw him down the stairs. As he fell, the Earl exclaimed, 'O Lord, have mercy on me.'

The noblemen in attendance on the Earl had their hands full in taking care of him. In the meantime, Holbein closed his door and secured it well, climbed out through a window leading to the roof, and hurried to the King to ask that he be pardoned, without telling what had happened. The King asked Holbein repeatedly what he had done, and was willing to pardon him, if he would confess his crime. Holbein did so, openly and completely. The King responded as if it was most difficult for him to pardon Holbein, and told him not to act so boldly again. His Majesty ordered the artist not to leave, and to remain in one of the royal chambers, until more could be learned about the Earl's condition.

Very soon the Earl arrived. Carried on a royal litter, he was brought before the King, wounded and in bandages. He complained, with a very weak voice, about the painter who had treated him so badly; but the truth was only partly told, and the charge was made worse by lies, just for spite, all to the detriment of Holbein—as the King well understood.

The Earl, after finishing his complaint, asked the King to punish the culprit adequately and justly, as such injury to his personage demanded. In his temper, the Earl noticed that the King was not greatly impressed and hardly eager to fulfill his wishes, had not asked much about the case, and had re-

mained rather cool about the matter. It seemed to him that
the King was not much inclined to punish Holbein sufficiently, so the Earl gave the King to understand that he wanted to
take revenge himself.

The King became angry that the Earl should speak imper-
tinently in his Majesty's presence, as if the Earl wanted to
place himself in the position of the King. His Majesty said,
'Now you have no more dealings with Holbein, but with my
royal self.' He raised his voice and began to threaten the Earl,
and said: 'Do you imagine that I care so little for that man? I
tell you, Earl, that if it pleased me to make seven dukes of
seven peasants, I could do so, but I could not make of seven
earls one Hans Holbein, or any one as eminent as he.'

The Earl, frightened by this answer, prayed for mercy and
his life and wanted to do anything the King might order to
regain his good grace. The King commanded that at no time
should the Earl plan or commit any act of revenge on the person of Holbein, either by himself, or through others, for
anything which had taken place; otherwise the King would
punish the Earl as severely as if the offense were committed
against the person of the King himself. This ended the quarrel.

Among the pictures which Holbein painted for Henry
VIII, there is an excellent portrait of his Majesty. This portrait is full length, life-size, and so life-like that every one who
sees it is frightened; it looks as if it was alive and the head
and legs move naturally. Another of Holbein's paintings, in
Whitehall, is a great credit to the artist and shows that he was
a second Apelles. His beautiful and artistic portraits of
Henry's three children, Edward, Mary, and Elizabeth, who
were still young, are also in Whitehall.[6]

Many gentlemen and ladies of the nobility were painted
by the capable hand of Holbein. Another splendid work of

his, in the Hall of the Surgeons in London, shows the highest officials of the guild receiving their grant. In this painting, Henry VIII is shown life-size, seated in dignity on a rich throne, or chair, and with a beautiful tapestry at his feet. At both sides the guild officials are kneeling, while the King holds out, in his right hand, the grant that is being received by one of the officials with great respect and reverence. Some people believe that Holbein did not complete this painting himself, and that, after his death, the parts that were lacking were finished by someone else. If this is true, however, the finisher was able to follow the style of Holbein so cleverly that neither painters nor experts have been able to discover the difference between the hands.7

In various houses there are still so many striking and beautiful paintings by Holbein that it is amazing how he was able to produce all these marvelous works during his lifetime. Besides his pictures, he made designs for goldsmiths, for other painters, for wood engravers, and for sculptors; and what he modelled in wax was also excellent. Holbein could work in almost any medium as well as in oil and water-color, and he could do illuminating in a masterly fashion.

Before Holbein went into the service of King Henry VIII he had not done any illuminating. Among the King's workers he met an artist by the name of Lucas, who was renowned for his illuminations, and Holbein formed a friendship with him. As soon as he had seen how illuminating was done, he tried his hand at it. As he could draw better, could make better compositions, and had more knowledge and technical ability than Lucas, he surpassed Lucas, so to say, as much as the light of the sun surpasses that of the moon.8

At London, in the banquet hall of the Hanseatic League, there are two splendid water-colors on canvas, painted with great technical excellence by Holbein. One is of the *Triumph*

89

of Wealth, and the other, the *Knell of Poverty.*9

In the *Triumph of Wealth,* the god Pluto, or Dis, is shown as a bald old man seated in a graceful, golden, antique carriage; he bends forward, grasping money from a chest with one hand and strewing gold and silver coins with the other; and near him there are Fortune and Fame, or Opportunity and Glory. Bags of coins are piled on the carriage; and behind it some people are scrambling for the strewn money. On either side of the carriage there walk princes of ancient times, who are as famous for their wealth as were Croesus and Midas. The carriage is drawn by four magnificent horses which are led by female personages whose names are written either above their heads or below their feet. They help to express the meaning of the picture, for they are the producers of wealth. The nude parts—faces, hands and feet—are like flesh in color; the costumes and draperies are done in white and black; the decorative borders and ornaments are traced in shell-gold.

The point of view for this picture, and for the other one, the *Knell of Poverty,* was taken at the base line, so that all the figures come above the line of sight, which was very sensible.

The *Knell of Poverty* is as follows: Poverty is shown in the form of an aged, emaciated, hungry woman sitting in a worn-out old cart, on a bundle of straw, under a kind of thatched little roof. She looks pitiful. She is scantily covered with a torn and patched dress. Her cart is drawn by a horse and a donkey that are ugly, thin, lean, and ghastly. In front of the cart there are walking a man and a woman in a sad condition, emaciated and worn out; they are wringing their hands and loudly expressing their misery. The man carries a spade and a hammer. Hope is seated in front, on the cart, and has her eyes firmly directed towards heaven. Finally, to make the story short, this is a beautiful philosophical study, poetic in its conception, good in composition, well drawn and well painted.

Federigo Zucchero, who was in England about the year 1574, copied these pictures very carefully, with pen and wash. He said they were done so well that they might have been by the hand of Raphael of Urbino. Italians love to hold their own artists in great honor, and are inclined to regard them as superior to all artists of other nationalities.

The same Federigo expressed still greater praise to our Goltzius, who visited him in Rome. When they were speaking of Holbein and his pictures in England, Federigo said that they were superior to those of Raphael. This was a high tribute and a frank statement from a great expert. If Italy were bereft of the name of Raphael, with his fame, his reputation, and his works, she would lose an outstanding ornament from her artistic crown.

However true it may be, a similar statement confirms the fact that Holbein was an excellent pictorial genius. Federigo was deeply impressed by Holbein's portrait of a countess, life-size, full length, and dressed in black satin, which was in London, in the house of Lord Pembroke. And when, accompanied by painters and connoisseurs, Federigo saw that picture, he was so delighted by it that he said he had never seen such perfection in painting, even in Rome; he went away with the greatest admiration.[10]

An enthusiastic lover of painting by the name of Andries de Loo, who lived in London, bought all the works of Holbein on which he could lay hands. He had a great many fine portraits by Holbein. Among them was a life-size portrait of the astronomer royal, Sr Niclaes, a German or a Dutchman who lived for more than thirty years in England. Holbein's painting of him, a bust-portrait, shows him seated at a table, with curious astronomical instruments. When the King once casually asked Niclaes why it was that he could not speak better English, he answered, 'Majesty, the King, forgive me; how much English can one learn in a period of thirty years?' This answer made the King and all the bystanders laugh heartily. The portrait, fine indeed, was done in a masterly style.[11]

Another of Holbein's portraits was in the house of old Lord Cromwell; it was about a foot and a half square, painted most cleverly and as perfectly as that fine portrait of the highly learned and widely famous Erasmus of Rotterdam, which, as I said before, showed so close a resemblance. The portrait of the Bishop of Canterbury was there, too.[12]

Andries de Loo had, also, a large canvas portrait, in water-color, of the famous and beloved Thomas More, which is a beautiful and splendid composition. This picture is worthy of admiration. It was painted by Holbein as an example of his work. At the present time it is in the possession of one of the nobility, the nephew of Thomas More, also named More, who bought it from the estate of the late Andries de Loo.

The above-mentioned portrait of the Bishop of Canterbury, one of the best portraits by Holbein, is at present in the house of a member of the nobility, a certain Mr Coop, who is a lover of art, living outside of London, at Temple Bar, across from the Lord Treasurer, who has in his house many other beautiful paintings by Holbein and works by other artists.[13]

There is in Amsterdam, in the Warmoesstraet, a fine portrait, by Holbein, of a Queen of England, most admirably done. The costume, of silver cloth, looks like real silver, and some embroidery on the costume is excellently painted. This is so rare an achievement in painting that one wonders whether or not silver leaf was used under the paint. It is well worth while for one to look at this work.[14]

I have seen two self-portraits by Holbein. One, a small

round picture, like an illumination in miniature, painted with
great care, belonged to Jaques Razet, the art collector. The
other picture is a little head, about the size of the palm of the
hand, excellent in carnation. It belonged to Bartholomeus
Ferreris, a great lover of art.[15]

The eminent Holbein displayed a very definite accuracy
in all his work. He followed a system of laying in his colors
first and then painting over them—a method very different
from that of other painters. This can be seen best in his pictures at those places where the hair or a beard had to be painted. He usually painted the shadows for these parts very carefully and in the right value, and when they were dry he
painted over them the beard or hair, fluently and in a natural
manner. He applied many other similar methods to great
advantage and most effectively.

It is said that the ancient painter Tupilius, a Roman knight,
was left-handed—something never before seen and still very
unusual in artists. Holbein handled his brush and practiced
his art with his left hand. It is only very rarely that we hear of
such a thing today. However, no trace of left-handedness can
be seen in Holbein's paintings. His work is perfect.

We have spoken before about the beauty and the accuracy
of his drawings, and these details are evident not only in his
Dance of Death which came out in wood-prints, but also in a
little Bible illustrated with woodcuts. These illustrations,
printed in various other Bibles also, have been copied frequently. This little book is most interesting for its witty and
clever drawings of human figures which are remarkable for
their action. Although nearly all of the illustrations are excellent, I admire especially the little scene of Hannah, mother
of Samuel, with Elkanah, her husband; and the picture of the
announcement to David of the death of Uriah; and the picture of Abishag's visit to David; and the one of Hiram bring-

ing a letter to Solomon. How splendidly and how strikingly
that picture is done! How superior the work is to that of
other modern artists who represent Solomon on a throne,
with bare arms and with a blanket around him, as one sees too
frequently, according to old convention! But in Holbein's
picture Solomon wears a rich royal costume.[16]

In honor of the excellent Hans Holbein, the poet Nicolaes
Borbonius wrote a poem in this little book. It was a Latin
Carmen:[17]

Apelles wandered in the Elysian fields;
Zeus and Parisius were near,
And happy in that pleasant region;
They spoke lively and were noisy, though
Apelles sought solitude and was sad.
His companions found this strange and gently urged him to speak.
The great artist, downhearted and somber, sighed
And with deep emotion in his voice said:
Alas! You know not of the bad news
That came from the human world and reached the infernal regions.
O, if God could make this report untrue!
From among the mortal people, one, gifted with the power of his art,
Has made nothing of us.
We are painters only in name,
To speak without jealousy and envy,
We never were experienced and skilful in handling our brushes in our own
    time.
Holbein is the name of the man.
Holbein puts all our names in shadow and reduces them to nothing.
Many other similar complaints were made by the infernal spirits,
Who had, I believe, cause to complain.
If one could only see one of these pictures
Painted by Hans.
Hans, the most famous,
The most honored, for his splendid art.
    Then a voice said:
'No human hand has ever wrought, with brush and color, such great and
    rare achievement.'

HANS HOLBEIN

They could do nothing.
That statement was false.
God had done the work.
God alone achieved such deeds.

The poet addressed this poem to the beloved reader, with
the hope that one's heart may be strengthened by the honorable work of a great artist; and the poet urges one to turn
away from the ravisher of Ganymede and from the shameful
stealing of the Goddess of Cyprus. Two verses in Greek
have the following meaning:

Oh stranger, do you like to see pictures which appear to be alive?
Notice these, made by the hands of Holbein.

Holbein made the world more beautiful with his fine art.
Human life and all worldly things are perishable; they will
melt, will be destroyed, will come to an inexorable and un-
preventable end. Holbein died in London, choked by pest, in
the year 1554, at the age of fifty-six. His body was left rot-
ting, a corpse, soon to disappear; but he left his name and
fame to posterity and to an imperishable memory.

JAN CORNELISZ., VERMEIJEN
OF BEVERWIJK

THOSE who are endowed by the kindness of Nature with a talent for drawing well, who received benefits, and who aside from all their endowments, possess physical beauty and grace, are likely to rise higher and higher, become well esteemed, and obtain the favor of prominent people and monarchs. This happened to Jan Vermeijen, the famous artist who was honored and beloved by Emperor Charles V.

Vermeijen was born at Beverwijck, a little town not far from Haarlem, in the year 1500. His father's name was Cornelis; but I was not able to learn with whom he studied or how he began his artistic career. I know only that, through his zeal and talent, he became a painter to the illustrious Emperor Charles V, whom he accompanied like a fellow emperor to various countries and to Tunis in Barbary, in 1505. The Emperor used him frequently for making drawings of his battles, historical exploits, and victories, and from these drawings, beautiful tapestries were afterwards made. In this way, Vermeijen, portrayed many subjects from life, among which were the siege and the location of the city of Tunis. He went about this work, and about other branches of art, in an artistic and intelligent way. He was skilled in geometry and surveying, and had a good knowledge of other higher sciences.[1]

Many of Vermeijen's excellent works, which are most remarkably done and have been praised very highly, can be seen at Atrecht, in the Abbey of St Vaes. Many beautiful paintings of his are also in Brussels, including panels and portraits. The paintings which had been in the church of

St Goelen and elsewhere, were, perhaps, either destroyed or stolen by insane iconoclasts. At all events, they have been removed.[2]

He gave to the church of St Gorick a *Resurrection*, with God, the Father, in the upper part. This painting was to serve as a memorial for himself. It is at present with his son, Hans Vermeijen, an able goldsmith and modeller in Prague, who is in the service of the Emperor and highly appreciated by him. This painting was saved in time from destructive hands.

Another of Vermeijen's famous works existed as an especially important object in the same church of St Gorick, a *Nativity*, showing a fine composition and painted well. Another of his paintings represented a nude, standing figure of Christ, with one hand on his chest. This picture has been praised highly.

A self-portrait of Vermeijen is in Zeeland, at Middelburg, at the home of his daughter, Maria, widow of S. G. Pieter Cappoen. It is artistic, and executed well. The background is a landscape containing the city of Tunis, done from life, and the painter represented himself painting, protected by a group of soldiers. He added to this painting a beautiful, well-rounded woman, who is defeated, and shows a cut in the arm.

Vermeijen's daughter, Maria, also owns a portrait of the second wife of the painter, which is done very well. She was born with six fingers on each hand and, although the smallest finger had been removed from each hand, one can still notice on the hands in the picture the little protuberances where they were.

This daughter, when still a young child, was painted from life by her father; she wears a fine Turkish costume. He took pleasure in dressing her up sometimes and permitting her to join the *Omgang* in Brussels. In the possession of the same daughter also is a portrait of a young child of neighbors, who had marvelously beautiful hair. Maria has yet another picture from her father's hand, which represents a victory at sea and shows many nude figures that are done well.

Vermeijen was a great friend and close companion to Joan Schoorel. Together they bought much land in the Zype in North Holland.3

Many times the Emperor took pleasure in introducing his painter, Vermeijen, to high-ranking ladies and gentlemen of the court, for he was proud of the beautiful figure of Vermeijen, which was graceful and slender. He had a beautiful beard which was so long that when he stood up straight, he could step on it. Sometimes when he stood next to the princess, the wind would blow the beard into the face of the latter, while they were sitting on horseback. He took great care of his beard every day, and because of this splendid ornament he was called Hans with the Beard.

Hans's portrait appeared in print, and Lampsonius added a poem in Latin to it, which is as follows:4

How many subjects Vermeijen has painted,
Human people, cities and localities.
They can be noticed at a great distance,
In the background on either side of him.
O Emperor Charles V, Hans has followed you
Everywhere, on the water as well as on the land.
And he painted the pious deeds of your brave
hand with his great talent.
It was woven in tapestry which was blinking
with pure gold, afterwards.
By his art, the work received a higher value
than the material of which it was made.
He had a noble protector.
He distinguished himself not only by his art,
But also by a beard, which he allowed to wave
at request,
Which streamed down to his feet.

JAN CORNELISZ., VERMEIJEN

Vermeijen died at Brussels in the year 1559, between the ages of fifty-nine and sixty. He had a funeral with honors in the Church of St Gorick. I have mentioned this before, and where his epitaph was hung.5

JOAN DE MABUSE

THE art of painting is born first of the spirit, of the mind, and of the imagination, before its new life can be expressed by the hand. It is best practiced by those who have a quiet nature and who lead a regular life, for the reason that such people are not likely to be subjected to mental disturbances or to catastrophes of the mind, and are more able to occupy their minds in practicing the finest of all arts. This does not seem to hold true in respect to the make-up, life, and nature of Jannijn, or Jan de Mabuse, an artist born in a little town in Hainault or Artois, called Maubeuge. He was a contemporary of Lucas van Leyden and of many other gifted men.[1]

De Mabuse was an untidy man and led a most irregular life; still, in amazing contrast to this, he was as neat, as patient, and as accurate in his technique of painting as ever an artist could be. His artistic ability did not develop in him while he slept. In his youth, he was very eager to study nature carefully and to reach a high perfection. In general, the road to artistic perfection is not smooth.

Mabuse visited Italy and other countries, and was probably the first artist to introduce into Flanders the right method of composition of nude figures and poetical subjects, which were not in use in our country.[2]

The most interesting and famous of Mabuse's many works is the High Altar in Middelburgh, a very large painting with double doors which needed extra supports when they had to be opened. The famous Albrecht Dürer, when in Antwerp, came to see this work, praised it highly, and admired it greatly. The abbot who had ordered the painting was Maximilian of Burgundy, who died in the year 1524. It was a *Descent from the Cross.* Much time was spent on this excellent work of art. The painting, however, as well as the church, was destroyed by fire from heaven, or lightning, in 1568. This was a grave loss and tragedy to art.3

Many of the works of Mabuse have remained in Middelburgh, among which are some beautiful figures of Mary, and kindred subjects. But special mention must be made of an excellent work of this master at the 'Lange Delft', the house of Sr Magnus. It is more beautiful than any other picture he ever made—a rather large, upright painting, a *Descent from the Cross.* The dead body of Christ has been lowered; the figures are about a foot and a half high, nicely arranged, and carefully painted in beautiful poses; the draperies, wrinkled cloth, expressions of sorrow, and other effects, are rendered well.4

A beautiful *Lucretia* is at the home of the art collector, Melchior Wijntgis.5

Marten Papenbroeck in Amsterdam, in the Warmoestraet, has a splendid, large, upright painting, an *Adam and Eve*, almost life-size, which is done very beautifully and accurately. This picture is worth a great deal, and much money has been offered for it.6

There is also a large painting by Mabuse in Amsterdam, with Jan Nicker, representing a beheading of James, which is done in black and white, with a very little quantity of paint, like a wash-drawing, so that one may fold the canvas, wrinkle it, or squeeze it without fear of damaging it. And this picture has been painted very well.7

While he was in the service of the Marquis van der Veren, Mabuse painted also a figure of Mary. The Holy Babe in this picture was painted from life. This was painted so accurately, that any of his other works compared with this, seems coarse. A piece of the blue cloth was done so beautifully that it looked as if the picture had just been finished in the studio. Afterwards, this work could be seen in Gouda at the house of Sr Froimont.[8]

Mabuse made many fine portraits in London. There are, at least there were, in the Gallery at Whitehall, the heads of two young boys, children of the nobility, which he had painted excellently.[9]

Mabuse was for a few years in the service of the Marquis van der Veren. This nobleman, about to receive a visit from Charles V, dressed all the members of his court in white silk damask. Mabuse had frequently to think about means for obtaining money for rather low pleasures. He sold the damask which had been given him for the making of a special costume, and spent the money thus received. What should he do? The time for the festive reception was approaching. He took a piece of beautiful, white paper, had a well-cut gown made of it, and decorated it with fine damask flowers and embroidered ornaments.

The Marquis also had at his court, besides the painter, a poet, and a philosopher. He wanted these men to pass in line before a window of the palace, from which the Emperor could have a good view of them. When they passed in front of the window, the Marquis asked the Emperor which of them had the most beautiful damask costume. The eyes of the Emperor were mostly attracted by the costume of the painter, which was whitest of all, and showed the most beautiful flowers. It surpassed all the other costumes in its effect. The Marquis, for he knew everything, ordered Mabuse to serve at the table. He was asked to come near, and the Emperor, touching the material, discovered the paper.

When the Emperor was told about the trick which had been played, he was highly amused and laughed a great deal. The Marquis, however, wished for all the amount of damask, that the painter had not played such a trick to please the Emperor.

Once Mabuse, for some reason or other, took a little too much liberty, and was kept a prisoner in the town of Middelburgh. During this captivity he made many fine drawings, of which I have seen a few. They were done in black crayon. I have not been able to learn the year of his birth nor of his death.[10]

AUGUSTIJN JORISZ.
OF DELFT

GREAT renown would have come to the pleasant town of Delft, had fate not taken away its young citizen, Augustijn Joorisz., by an early death.

Augustijn was born at Delft in the year of our Lord 1525. His father was a brewer, called Jooris Jansz., who let Augustijn study with a certain Jacob Mondt from Delft, a rather mediocre artist. Augustijn stayed with him for about three years. When he left him, Augustijn went to Malines, where he studied under another master, and from there he went to Paris, in France. He lived in Paris with a Sr Pieter de la Cuffle, who was a fine engraver, and had made a print of the *Three Spinners* by Rous, and another of a ceiling decoration, which had to be seen from below. Sr Cuffle himself was not a painter. He lived in the house of his brother, and at that house there were working some goldsmiths, a painter, and a sculptor. Augustijn was given work, too.[1]

After Augustijn had worked in Paris for five years, he returned to Delft where he made a great name for himself with a small number of pictures, only five. He excelled in making large figures and fine compositions.

His brother, who is a goldsmith at Delft, has some works by Augustijn. I mention especially a fine picture of St Anne and her family, painted very well and showing beautiful modelling. It has been praised highly. No landscapes by Augustijn have been found in the Netherlands.[2]

When he had been home about five months, Augustijn was still a bachelor. He drowned in a well, and no one ever knew how this happened. There was some evidence that he

AUGUSTIJN JORISZ.

was trying to get some water, which he may have needed for a pot of white paint or for his brushes, for priming. He must have slipped, tumbled into the water, and drowned, without having been able to get assistance. This was a great loss to art, especially as he had shown such a fine beginning.3

He died Anno 1552, at the age of twenty-seven.

JOOS VAN CLEEF
CALLED FOOLISH CLEEF
OF ANTWERP

IT is likely that the most eminent artists have in their minds some hidden impulse to surpass others; for without courage and impetus, they would lose the stimulating effect from their work, and would no longer try to produce something good. Without this instinct, progress is made slowly. Still, this desire must be tempered by a proper knowledge of self, without which the result would be a decline of art, a loss, and a shame. This happened to a certain artist, one of the most remarkable who ever lived, a pearl in the crown of painting, Joos van Cleef from Antwerp. He did not belong to the family of Marten and Hendrick, as far as I know.[1]

I do not know how old he was or when he was born. I know that, in the year 1511, a Joos van Cleef entered the guild of the painters in Antwerp, and that he used to make many paintings of Mary with angels. I do not know whether this man was an ancestor of Foolish Cleef. A certain Willem van Cleeve, who entered the guild in the year 1518, was his father.[2]

This Joos van Cleef had a beautiful style of painting figures. He was exceedingly proud, and possessed a degree of self-conceit that blinded and fooled him; he thought that his works were worth more than those of other masters and could not be paid for in money to their full value. This is very likely the reason why his mind became disturbed, and he became insane. Generally, such sickness begins in this way, and is rooted in a proud and haughty disposition.

King Philip of Spain married Mary, Queen of England,

and it happened that Joos van Cleef went to England to sell his pictures to the King. He went to see Antonis Moro, who was court painter to the King, and asked his assistance, which Moro was willing to give. But on the same occasion, many beautiful paintings arrived from Italy, notably some of Titian's, which pleased the King very much, and which were bought by the monarch. Moro could not induce the King to buy from Van Cleef. Vanity drove Van Cleef so wild that he became raving mad, arguing that his paintings ought to be regarded as superior to all others, and so of greater value. He quarreled shamefully with Moro, calling him a conceited idiot, unable to appreciate masterpieces. He also said that it would be better for Moro to go back to Utrecht, to safeguard his wife from the canons of the church; and he made similar, slandering remarks. When Moro threatened him, he crawled under the table; but Moro did not regard him as worth troubling much about.3

Finally, Cleef became so mentally disturbed that he did strange things; he varnished his clothing, cape, and bonnet with turpentine varnish, and in this glittering costume went into the street. He painted the backs of his panels, too, because, he said, even if they were placed backwards, people would still see something by his hand. Whenever he got hold of paintings he had done before, he tried to destroy them, pretending he was going to improve them. This was a pity, and a great shame.

He was the best colorist of his time. He cleverly rounded his subjects, painted carnation very effectively, and did not apply heavy impasto except in the flesh color itself. Art collectors valued his paintings exceedingly, and justly so. Melchior Wijntgis, in Middelburg, owns a fine painting of Mary, for which the background is a very beautiful landscape by Joachim Patenier. There is in Amsterdam, with Sr Sion Lus,

also, a very nicely painted Bacchus, whom Van Cleef represented as a very fat old man with gray hair. He did not do this
without reason, for he wanted to prove that old age loves to
drink, and that excessive drinking results in premature old
age.4

I cannot refer to many of Van Cleef's paintings. I do not
know the time of his death. His name, for the sake of art, is
worth perpetuating in honor and fame. Lampsonius addresses him in Latin as follows: 5

> Behold! Among the great artists of the free
> Netherlands, Joos will not be forgotten by the Muses;
> He was more than a little ornament of the high art of painting.
> For the sake of your art, Joos,
> And for the art of your son,
> You would have been a very happy man,
> If you, poor man, would have remained healthy of mind.

From this poem one may conclude that Van Cleef had a
son who was not inferior to him in art. Still, there has been
another Joos van Cleef, who excelled in figure work. A certain Cornelis van Cleef also existed.6

ALDEGRAEF
OF SOEST

EARLIER in this book I should have given a place to Aldegraef, were it not for my waiting a long time in vain for detailed information from Westphalia. I believe he was born
there and lived there. He made many pictures in a large city
called Soest, eight miles from Münster, where many of his
works can be found in the churches. Special mention should
be made of an altar painting by him in the old church. It is a
Nativity, and it is well done.[1]

He painted two wings for a central panel painted by Albrecht Dürer, and this picture is in Nozenburg. There are
other paintings by him, in various other places.[2]

Engravings by Aldegraef can be seen everywhere, for he
was an able engraver, and made various, beautiful portraits
of great princes, learned men, and others. He made self-portraits, from which I judge more or less his age, and by which
the date of his birth may be guessed. He made a portrait of
Jan van Leyden, who was illegally King of Münster for a
short while; and also a portrait of Knipperdolling.[3]

A series of four small prints by Aldegraef appeared as illustrations of the story of Susanna; some small prints with little,
nude, female figures; the story of the works of Hercules; and
twelve large, dancing figures, dated 1538 and 1551, from
which we know the period of his work.[4]

These prints are excellent as to nudes, compositions, and
foreign costumes. They are engraved beautifully, with clear
lines, and are splendid material for collectors. One might wish
that he had not made the draperies so confused, with too

many folds and wrinkles. He was a good master whose name is worthy of remembrance and praise. Aldegraef died within the town of Soest and was buried very humbly.[1]

Once a painter came from Münster, who had been with Aldegraef quite a while. He had travelled with him, thought he would find him still alive, and wanted to pay him a friendly visit. He ordered a memorial stone for the artist's grave; the name and monogram on it were the same as used on his prints.

SWART JAN or JAN SWART

VRIESLAND may have been frozen and entirely withered up, but in Groningen a splendid shoot of art rose to rejuvenate the renown of the city; and the aroma of the beautiful flower which it produced was so splendid, that I could be accused readily of the worst possible neglect if I did not try to cause her perfume to spread as far as possible.[1]

All this refers to a crowning ornament in painting, the illustrious Jan Swart, frequently called Swart Jan. He was born in Oost Vriesland, at Groningen, and lived at Ter Goude for a few years at the time when Jan Schoorel came back from Italy, about the year 1522 or 1523. This Swart Jan painted landscapes, nudes, and figures, in the same style as did Schoorel.[2]

Jan Swart travelled to Italy and lived a little while in Venice, and, like Schoorel, imported into this country another method of painting which differed from the unaesthetic modern way of painting and was more in accordance with the Italian style.[3]

I cannot enumerate this painter's works. But to realize the power in them, and their virtue, one has only to look at the remarkable woodcuts which he made. They represent a group of Turks on horseback, with bows and arrows, and are done cleverly and deftly; a print of Christ is done very beautifully, too—He is preaching from the deck of a ship and some people in the foreground are listening and are seen from the back.[4]

ADRIAEN PIETERSZ. CRABETH

THIS Swart Jan had a pupil by the name of Adriaen Pietersz. Crabeth, whose father was called *Krepel Pieter*. When yet young he learned so rapidly he soon surpassed his master. He travelled to France, and, after he had been there a little while, died in the city of Autun. His death was deplored.[1]

CORNELIS
OF GOUDA

THERE was another able artist who painted portraits from life. His name was Cornelis. He was born at Gouda and was a pupil of Hemskerck. In his youth he detested drinking; but, after frequenting the court and becoming acquainted with some people of high rank, he changed his habits so completely that even great drunkards feared him. He was then on the retrograde and became a dauber. For this reason, youth should not follow him as an example.[1]

HANS BAMESBIER

THERE was yet another fine artist, who was also a portrait painter, a certain Hans Bamesbier, a High German. He was a pupil of Lambert Lombardus. This artist also became a heavy drinker, and in his old age. He lived in Amsterdam, where he died at the age of nearly one hundred years.[1]

SIMON JACOBSZ.

OF GOUDA

SIMON JACOBS from Gouda, a pupil of Carel van Iper, was a fine portrait painter. A portrait by him in Haarlem represents a glass painter by the name of Willem Tybout. This is a piece of strong and bold work. Jacobs died during the siege of Haarlem.[1]

CORNELIS DE VISSCHER
OF GOUDA

AN artist by the name of Cornelis de Visscher lived in Gouda. He was sometimes out of his mind; but he was a good portrait painter of whom much could be told. He died at sea, on a voyage from Hamburg.[1]

FRANS MINNEBROER
AND OTHER ANCIENT MASTERS
OF MALINES

BEFORE I tell you about certain other painters from Gouda, I am going to present some ancient painters from the city of Malines.

A certain Frans Minnebroer lived in Malines about 1539 or 1540. He was a clever painter in oil-color. A *Flight from Egypt* by him was in the local Vrouwe Kerck. The little family are traveling through wild scenery; the figures and trees are excellent.[1]

Outside Malines, at Hanswyck, in the Onze Vrouwe Church, a panel painted by Minnebroer represents the story of the Annunciation and of the visit of Mary to Elizabeth. The figures, landscape, and the trees of this picture are remarkably good.[2]

FRANS VERBEECK

MINNEBROER had a pupil in Malines called Frans Verbeeck, who made beautiful water-colors in the style of
Jeroon Bos. He made a painting of St Christopher, which was
to be seen in Malines, and in it many spirits appeared. In the
Katerynen Kerck a picture by Verbeeck illustrated the parable of the vineyard; people can be seen working, and weird
spooks are binding dead vines; this is painted well.

Verbeeck painted various subjects, which were sold in
many places; among others, a winter scene without snow or
ice, with leafless trees, and with houses in a fog. This looked
very natural. He is the artist who painted jolly scenes of
peasant weddings and other similar subjects.[1]

VINCENT GELDERSMAN

VINCENT GELDERSMAN was a good painter who lived in Malines, too. He painted a Leda, a half-length, with two eggs, a Susanna, a Cleopatra with the snake, and other subjects. Many copies were made of these pictures. He painted in oil-colors, beautifully and charmingly. A *Descent from the Cross* was in the Ridders Chapel of the St Rombout's Church, in which Magdalen could be seen washing the feet of our Lord amidst a crowd. This has a good deal of dramatic action in it.[1]

HANS HOGENBERGH

CERTAIN biblical subjects, such as the stories of Caleb and Joshua, and similar topics, were in the same Ridder's chapel, and were painted by a clever German painter. His name was Hans Hogenbergh and he stayed in Malines to do this work. He died there about the year 1544. He illuminated the scroll of the *Entrée* of the Emperor, which is in Bologna, and is well known by many people.[1]

FRANS CRABBE

THEN there was a Frans Crabbe, the artist who painted the high altar for the Minnebroers at Malines; also, a Passion scene in water-colors, done very well. The central panel was a *Crucifixion*. The wings were divided into various sections; there were many beautiful faces in this work, in the style of Quintijn the Smith. Crabbe was a rich man. His works were very much like those by Lucas van Leyden. He died in 1548.[1]

CLAES ROGIER

CLAES ROGIER was a good landscape artist.[1]

HANS KAYNOOT

HANS KAYNOT was a deaf artist. He came after Claes
Rogier whom he surpassed. He followed very markedly the
style of Joachim Patenier; he was a pupil of Mathijs Cock
from Antwerp, in about 1550.[1]

CORNELIS ENGHELRAMS

CORNELIS ENGHELRAMS of Malines made a painting for the St Rombout's Church called the *Feeding of the Poor*. It is one of the works of mercy and was divided into various sections; he had differentiated between the truly poor and the professional, fake beggars with their various musical instruments, such as hurdy-gurdies. These were all watercolors done on canvas. Many of his works were sent to Germany, specially to Hamburg.

A painting by Enghelrams, a *Conversion of St Paul*, can be seen in St Catherine's Church. It is a large canvas with good figures which once must have been beautiful; but at present they have deteriorated very much.

For the Prince of Orange, he painted the story of David, which is in a room of the Casteel at Antwerp. He followed a composition of Lucas de Heere for this picture. Vries painted some architectural detail, friezes, termi, and cartouches in it. The whole is done in water-color. Cornelis died in the year 1583, at about the age of fifty-six years.[1]

MARCUS WILLEMS

MARCUS WILLEMS was a pupil of Michiel Cocxie. He made many beautiful paintings, among them, a panel in the St Rombout's Church, a *Beheading of John the Baptist*. The executioner held the head forward, so it is foreshortened and looks as if it protrudes from the canvas. A little of the arm can be seen below the head.

Willems made many drawings for glass painters, for the tapestry weavers, and for other painters. He made a picture of Judith, who had beheaded Holofernes. This he made life-size, very cleverly, and with a fine treatment.

Willems designed a triumphal arch on the occasion of the *Joyeuse Entrée* of King Philip, and in it he illustrated the story of Dido cutting the hide of the ox and similar subjects. This was in the year 1549. Marcus Willems was very ready to help anybody who needed him for drawing or for other purposes. He was a good man. He died in 1561.

JAQUES DE POINDRE

JAQUES DE POINDRE was a pupil of Marcus Willems, who had married his sister. He was a good painter, specially of portraits. He painted a *Crucifixion*, an altar painting in which many portraits appeared. Once he painted a certain English Captain, by the name of Pieter Andries, who was quite a braggart and who wanted to keep the portrait without paying. Jaques, becoming impatient, painted bars in front of the face, with water-colors, so that it looked as though the captain were serving a sentence in prison; he then exhibited the picture.

The captain, when he heard about this, came and asked what kind of rogue Jaques was, to do a thing like this. Jaques answered that the Captain must be imprisoned until he should be fully paid. The Captain paid the money and demanded that the bars be removed. The other took a sponge and washed them off. Jaques made many good portraits. He went to Oostland or Denmark, where he died in 1570, or about that time.

GREGORIUS BEERINGS

GREGORIUS BEERINGS in de Schaer was a painter from Malines who worked with water-colors. He had been in Rome and was very good at painting ruins. While he was in Rome, he spent all his money, and was in a hurry to get some more. He painted on canvas a *Deluge*. Nothing but rain, air, water and the ark were in this picture; no people could be seen. When people asked him what it represented, he answered: 'It is the Deluge.' The question followed: 'Where are the people?' He said: 'They have been drowned, and when the water recedes, they will become visible; the living ones are inside the ark.'

Almost everybody wanted a similar picture, and since these pictures could be made rapidly, he soon had his purse filled again. That was a profitable business for him.

Beerings died in Malines, in the year 1570.

I have told above about the most prominent artists from Malines. The stories of Cocxie and Bol will follow in greater detail later on. I did not treat the other painters in very strict chronological order, because I did not want to omit some painters of merit without at least having made known their names, or without having at least touched on their lives, in the cases in which I had obtained but little information.

JAN MOSTART

PLACES have become famous for art: Sicyon among the Greeks; later on, Florence and Rome among the Italians. Similarly, the old and beautiful city of Haarlem was renowned in early times and produced many splendid geniuses in painting.

Jan Mostart descended from a well-known, noble family. Spurred by nature, he studied the art of painting at a very young age under a master called Jacob, from Haarlem, who was a good painter. His altar painting for the guild of the carriers was in the Groote Kerck at Haarlem.[1]

Jan Mostart, who came from Haarlem, had an ancestor that had been with Emperor Frederick and Count Floris on a crusade to the Holy Land. He had assisted in the capture of the city of Damietta in Egypt, a city previously called Pelusia. His ancestor performed a brave deed of arms, breaking three swords near the hilts on the enemy, and it was said that he was as strong as mustard. This simile was the origin of his name. He received from the Emperor three golden hilts on a red field, for his coat of arms.[2]

Jan Mostart was not only a fine painter but also a man of noble morale. He was friendly in manner, he had a beautiful figure, could speak well, was kind and polite. He was well esteemed and appreciated highly, was admired and loved by most of the nobility of the country, by people of high rank as well as by the humble. He became official painter to Marguerite, the sister of Count Philip, the first King of Spain by that name and the father of Emperor Charles V.[3]

Mostart remained in the service of Marguerite for eighteen years. He was well respected and lived wherever the court was held. A persistent painter, he produced many works and many portraits of ladies and gentlemen of rank. He was a good master of portraiture, and he made natural likenesses that seemed as if the subjects were present and alive.4

Finally, he went to live at Haarlem, where he was visited frequently by many gentlemen belonging to the Order of the Golden Fleece. It happened once that the Count of Bueren arrived at night and took his lodgings in a hostelry on the Market, called 's't-Sandt.' The next day, this gentleman, with a retinue of counts and people of rank, visited Mostart at the workshop. The artist arose from his chair respectfully, but the Count said that the painter ought to remain seated and continue his work. However, the painter laid down everything, and showed everything he had, no matter whether it had been just begun, or had been finished. He ordered the servants, his pupils, to assist him in giving the gentlemen something for breakfast. The Count went to the cupboard, and ate whatever he found, for his breakfast. The other gentlemen did the same, and a mug of beer was drunk together.

After this, something else was done. But in the afternoon, Mostart was the guest of the Count and his friends and had to sit with them at their table and enjoy himself. As has been told already, he was well loved by them.

Mostart's works have decorated many churches and private houses. The Jacobins in Haarlem had some paintings by him, an altar painting and altar frontals, among others a *Nativity*, which had great approbation and renown.

At present, nowhere can so much of his work be seen as with his grandson in Haarlem, Sr Niclaes Suycker, 'Schout' of the city of Haarlem.

First of all must be mentioned a large, upright Ecce Homo,

life-size and more than half of the figure shown. Portraits have been introduced into this picture, painted from memory and from life, among them a guard by the name of Pier Muys, who was well known in those days, for he had a comical and mean face and a head done up with plasters. He is the one who keeps Christ a prisoner.[5]

Sr Niclaes Suycker has also a *Banquet of the Gods*, in which the company looks alarmed and frightened because Discordia enters with the apple of misunderstanding. Mars is already pulling his sword. It is good in composition.

There exists also a painting by Mostart of a landscape in West India in which are many nude figures, a menacing club, and strangely constructed houses and huts. This picture is unfinished.[6]

Mostart painted the portraits of the Countess Jacoba and her husband, Van Borssele; they are well done and show fine old costumes.[7]

He made a self-portrait, too, which seems to have been almost his last work. It is taken from the front and is so large that it shows the hands which are folded. A rosary is lying before him. A naturalistic landscape is in the background. He painted a picture of Christ in the sky, who is seated as a Judge, and, on one side of Him, the Devil is kneeling with a long scroll. The latter accuses him. On the other side an angel is kneeling who prays for him.

There used to be a *Descent of St Anne* with Jacob Ravart in Amsterdam, which received high acclaim. At the home of Sr Floris Schoterbosch, Councillor at The Hague, is a picture representing Abraham, Sarah, Hagar and Ishmael, life-size, figures more than half-shown; they are dressed in old costumes, and one would say that these people could not have been dressed very differently in ancient times.[8]

Jan Claesz., painter and pupil of Cornelis Cornelisz., has

among other pictures a large painting, a St Christopher in a landscape, by the hand of Mostart. At the Princenhof is a landscape with St Hubrecht in it—a picture which shows how carefully this old painter worked and how he studied life and nature.[9]

Many pictures by Mostart were lost in the great fire in Haarlem, for his house burned down with all the pictures he had left in it.[10]

He was a man with good judgement and a fine mentality; a good artist. Marten Hemskerck testified that Mostart could paint a picture better than any of the other masters whom he had known.[11]

It has been said that Jan Mabuse asked assistance from Mostart for the work in the Abbey at Middelburg, but the offer was declined by Mostart because he was in the service of a very high-ranking lady, a Princess. His family still keeps a certain written document in which she declared Mostart to be one of her knights.[12]

Mostart died, in the year 1555, or 1556, at a ripe old age.

ADRIAEN DE WEERDT
OF BRUSSELS

I HAVE heard persons who were not entirely unqualified to speak about painting say that any one who, from early youth on, wants to improve in painting, would be benefited most by following the technique of whatever excellent master pleased him most; but one, if open to following too many examples of old masters, would become confused. I give this statement for what it may be worth. It seems to be true in the case of Adriaen de Weerdt, who had put his mind solely on painting according to the method of the Parmesan, which he desired to imitate with all his powers.

De Weerdt studied hard in his youth, first in Antwerp under Christiaen Queecborne, who was a good landscape artist living near the exchange, and who was the father of Master Daniel, painter to His Excellency in The Hague. When he returned to Brussels, he lived quietly, studied hard, and spared no effort to learn more. His parents had a little house in a lonely spot along the walls of the city, where, during the summer time, he remained by himself and practiced painting, staying away from amusements with other young people. He used to paint landscapes in the style of Frans Mostart.[1]

He went to Italy where he tried to imitate the technique of Parmeggiano. When he returned, he had changed his method entirely through this practice.

Shortly after his return to the Netherlands, about 1566, when the political troubles began, De Weerdt wanted to escape difficulties, so he went to Cologne with his mother. Many prints left his shop in that city: the *Resurrection of*

132

ADRIAEN DE WEERDT

Lazarus; the story of Ruth, with a beautiful landscape in it; a
life of Mary, with a Nativity; and kindred topics. He published also four pictures based on the *Emblemata* of Coornhert, which were known as the *Four Cravings of the Mind.*
One craves fortune, another has unchaste desires, and so on,
but the last one longs for God. The engraver was a good
master. These works were in the style of Francesco Mazzoli
of Parma.[2]

De Weerdt died at Cologne at a youthful age.[3]

I shall add here something about other ancient and more recent masters from Brussels, because I am speaking of artists
of this town.

WILLEM TONS

NOT so long ago there lived in Brussels an old and good master called Willem Tons. He was excellent at making water-colors, and at designing tapestry cartoons containing all kinds of trees, bushes, animals, birds, eagles, and similar subjects, which he did from life well and pleasingly.[1]

HANS TONS

WILLEM TONS had a son, Hans, who had been in Italy, and who painted fine water-colors.[1]

GUILLIAME TONS

GUILLIAME TONS, another son of Willem Tons, painted very well in oil—small pictures of figures in bawdy houses and kindred subjects. He went to Italy, where now he is supposed to be.[1]

HANS SPEECKAERT

HANS SPEECKAERT was an excellent young artist who was in Rome in my own time. He painted and drew very deftly. On account of his health he travelled back to the Netherlands via Florence. He returned to Rome and died there about the year 1577. He came from Brussels and was the son of an embroiderer.[1]

HENDRICK AND MARTEN VAN CLEEF

OF BRUSSELS

THE art of painting has benefited considerably from the work of a family of painters by the name of Van Cleef. There have been many good masters of this name in the city of Antwerp, among them, the two brothers, Hendrick and Marten van Cleef.[1]

Hendrick loved to paint landscapes, and travelled to Italy and to other countries, where he made many views from life, and also painted portraits which he used afterwards in his works. He did not, however, visit all the places of which he has made drawings, and some of which came out in print, namely, cities, ruins, and antiquities. He received many studies from a Hansa merchant called Melchior Lorch, who had lived a long time in Constantinople.[2]

Hendrick had a clever way of drawing subjects from life, and he was equally skilled in painting with oil-colors. He painted most of the backgrounds in the works of Frans Floris and made them so like in style that they look as if they had been done by Frans alone. Hendrick was an excellent landscape painter.[3]

He entered the guild of the painters in Antwerp in 1533. I do not know when he died.[4]

Marten van Cleef was a pupil of Frans Floris, and, in the beginning, used to paint large pictures; later, small ones, making many charming pieces on which he worked alone, and which can be seen still with collectors. He made yet others in which his brother Hendrick painted the backgrounds. Gillis van Coninghs Loo, and other painters of beautiful

138

landscapes, went to him frequently to have figures painted in the landscapes, which became much more beautiful because of them. Marten was never in a foreign country. He suffered greatly from gout and died when he was fifty years old.5

WILLEM VAN CLEEF

THERE was also a Willem van Cleef, a brother of Hendrick
and Marten. He was a good painter of large figures. He died
a long time ago.[1]

GILLES, MARTEN,
JOORIS, AND CLAES, VAN CLEEF

THE sons of Marten van Cleef were Gilles, Marten, Jooris, and Claes van Cleef. All were good painters. Marten went to Spain, and from there to India. Jooris and Gilles died. Jooris started off well in the painting of small pictures; but he died young. He was too much interested in prostitutes. Claes is now living in Antwerp.[1]

ANTONIS MORO

IT is generally for two reasons that people feel urged to follow an artistic career: One is for the sake of honor; the other for the sake of profit. Youth, endowed by nature with talent, may feel bold and courageous. An excellent artist may serve as an example by having obtained high honors, esteem, and appreciation from people of great importance. Youth may be stimulated by such an example, and so try to imitate and to equal so excellent an artist.

This happened in the case of the famous painter Antonis Moro. He followed the example of his predecessor, the canon and master painter, Jan Schoorel. Moro became a pupil of Schoorel. He was eager to study and to become a great artist. He had splendid success, specially in portraiture from life.[1]

Moro travelled in Spain. In 1552, he was at the court in Madrid where he painted a portrait of King Philip. He entered the service of the Emperor through the influence of Cardinal Granvelle. The Emperor sent him first to Portugal, to paint the Princess who was the first bride of King Philip. He painted King Joannes and also the Queen of Portugal who was a younger sister of the Emperor. For these three paintings, Moro received six hundred ducats and many precious gifts in addition to his wages, among them a golden chain worth a thousand guilders from the King of Portugal. He was received in splendor and well entertained. He made, in addition to the paintings mentioned, many portraits of the nobility, and received for each, one hundred ducats and also some gold chains, according to the wealth of the donors.[2]

ANTONIS MORO

He made several paintings at the court of Emperor Charles V. The Emperor sent him to England, to Queen Mary, second wife of King Philip. He received a golden chain and a hundred pounds sterling and, moreover, an annual pension of a hundred pounds. He had to make copies of the portrait of the Queen, on several occasions. She was a very beautiful woman. He copied her head on panels, which were given to important persons, to persons belonging to the Order of the Golden Fleece, and to Granvelle. He also gave one to the Emperor who paid him two hundred guilders for it.[3]

The story is told that he brought one of these paintings of Cardinal Granvelle, and that Granvelle sent it to the Emperor as a present. The Emperor answered: 'I do not keep a court any longer; I left everything to my son.' The painter did not receive an invitation to appear before the Emperor. He visited the Cardinal again, who said to leave the matter in his hands. The Cardinal went to the Emperor and praised not only the painting very highly, but also the beauty of the Princess. He asked the Emperor how the artist had been rewarded. The Emperor answered that the artist had not been rewarded at all. The Cardinal suggested a thousand guilders or three hundred ducats. The Emperor ordered this amount to be paid. The amount is supposed to have been paid one year and a half after the return of the artist from Spain.

After a treaty of peace was signed between the King of Spain and the King of France, Moro accompanied the King to Spain and became a very close friend of the Spanish Majesty, and of the members of the court. He made portraits of many members of the nobility. He was well esteemed and very popular. Moro became so free in his ways with the King that, on a certain occasion when the King slapped him on the shoulder, the artist playfully touched the King with his maulstick. This was a serious action, for it was a very dangerous offence indeed to touch a Lion. This familiarity would have been most harmful to Moro, if he had not been warned by a Spanish nobleman moved by friendship and real love for the artist. The fact was that members of the Inquisition were quite jealous of the artist. They were afraid that the artist was influencing the King regarding the policy to be followed in the Netherlands. Moro ran the risk of imprisonment. On a pretext, he went back to the Netherlands, receiving a formal leave of absence and promising to return.4

The King, who was just as fond of the artist himself as of his work, tried hard to get him back; but Moro constantly found excuses to elude the King, until the Duke of Alva, who had become Governor of the Netherlands, found it convenient to hold the letters which the King had written to Moro and in which he asked the artist to return. Alva engaged the artist for himself, and Moro made portraits from life of all the concubines of Alva. He received a large income from his art.5

A story went round that, when Alva ordered Moro from Utrecht to Brussels, the artist burned his easels and made presents of his paintings.

The King gave rich presents to the children of the artist and also offices, such as that of canon. Moro told the Duke of Alva that he had a daughter whose husband was a learned man. The Duke made this husband receiver for West Flanders, a position which enabled him to live in grand style. He came to Brussels many times with a great retinue, escorted by various knights.

Moro was a refined man, honorable, and eloquent.

In his youth he had visited Italy and Rome. Aside from his portraits, he painted other subjects; specially a *Resurrection of Christ*, with two angels and the Apostles, St Paul and St Peter. He knew how to deceive the eyes.6

ANTONIS MORO

Moro copied Titian's *Danae* for the King, and very excellently he did it, as well as many other subjects. At the time of his death he was working on a *Circumcision of Christ* for the Onse Vrouwe Kerck at Antwerp. This was a most promising painting.7

It was with much difficulty that I collected this information about Moro; for his children did not want to tell me anything about their father, although I addressed them in a most courteous way. It appeared to me that they did not care in the least about memories of him. I cannot say anything about the death of the artist. However, his name will be imperishable to posterity.

Antonis Moro died at Antwerp at the age of fifty-six, one year before the French Fury.8

JAQUES DE BACKER

IT is most deplorable that sometimes, suddenly and unexpectedly, death snatches away artists in their youth or while they are still prominent. This has happened often in modern as it has in ancient times. An example of this was furnished years ago by the industrious Jaques de Backer. He was born at Antwerp. His father was a very good painter, who, because of slander, went to live in France and died in that country.[1]

Jaques was sometimes called Jaques of Palermo, after a certain Antonis Palermo, an artist who was also a dealer in paintings. Jaques lived with this dealer. He was kept at a low wage and had to work hard and constantly. By his great diligence he improved with remarkable rapidity in his painting. Palermo made good profits through the work of Jaques and sent much of it to France, where he sold it for good money. Still Jaques was constantly reprimanded to do better. He was told that his paintings could not be sold. In this way, the servant artist worked like a horse, so to speak, in order to produce something valuable.[2]

De Backer never allowed any time to be lost, and on his days off, he was drawing or modelling in clay and practicing all the time. Finally, De Backer went to live with Hendrick van Steenwyck. He persisted with his usual diligence. As a result of attending to his studies too much and giving too little exercise to his body, he became ill. Some people believe that he had a fit of apoplexy and died in it; but I believe that he must have suffered from lung trouble or some internal growth. He regained consciousness while dying in the arms of the daughter of his master. He lamented his early death, saying: 'Wretched man am I; why must I die so soon?' He was not yet thirty years old. A post mortem was held; but it could not be discovered from what kind of illness the young artist had died.[3]

De Backer's paintings, everywhere, are in great demand; they decorate the cabinets or the rooms of many lovers of art. Three beautiful pictures are in the collection of Melchior Wintgis at Middelborgh—*Adam and Eve*, a *Charitas*, and a *Crucifixion*.

I have seen at the home of Sr Oppenbergh three paintings of standing figures, full length, half-size, representing Venus, Juno, and Pallas, in charming poses, with various objects in the background, and on the ground some of their things, clothing, animals, and so on.

De Backer was one of the best colorists Antwerp ever possessed; he had a good method of painting carnation; he produced high lights not merely with white, but with flesh color itself. He deserves to be praised eternally among the painters.

MATHIJS AND JEROON KOCK

ANTWERP, in our Netherlands, seems to have been the mother of artists, as was Florence, in Italy, in ancient times. Antwerp produced many artists displaying a great variety of work. This city was made still more illustrious by her citizen, Mathijs Kock, who, among others, was a prominent painter of landscapes.[1]

He was the first to paint landscapes in a better way, with more variety, according to the Italian and antique methods, and he was remarkably inventive in his compositions and arrangements. Mathijs Kock painted excellently in water-color as well as in oil.[2]

I have not much to tell about his brother, Jeronimus Kock, because he himself quit painting and became an art dealer. He had other artists working for him; he bought oil- and water-color works and let engravers work for him and make etchings. There are twelve landscapes by Jeronimus Kock which everybody still likes to see. He was very inventive in landscape painting and made etchings, but he took most of the subjects from his brother's paintings.[3]

Jeroon became rich in this way and bought one house after another. He had a Dutch wife who was called Volck or Volcktgen. He had no children.[4]

Jeroon was jolly and witty, and a rhetorician. He frequently wrote some device on his prints, such as, 'Leave to de Kock what he wants to cook and what is good for Volck' or 'Keep de Kock in honor,' and other similar phrases.[5]

He wrote on certain prints some verses in the style of the

MATHIJS AND JEROON KOCK

rhetoricians, as follows:

De Kock has to cook the greatest variety of meals,
Roasts and stews;
To the one who does not like the food,
Whether it is too hard or too tender,
It is not forbidden to spit it out.
Do not reveal the mistakes.
Blame neither the cook nor the people,
Others will do it better.

De Kock died about the same time as Frans Floris, that is, in 1570. Mathijs Kock died a long time before. Lampsonius wrote the following poem to De Kock:[6]

Mathijs, you were a fine landscape painter,
Our century has hardly seen your equal.
You will be counted among the artists
Who gave an eternal glory to the Netherlands.

WILLEM KEY
OF BREDA

SOME noble spirits are endowed by nature with splendid talents and fine mental capacity, and so gain the admiration of their fellowmen. They are still more esteemed and become worthier yet, if they show that they lead honest and virtuous lives, and are friendly and courteous to every one. This has been proved by the famous painter, Willem Key from Breda. He had a smart appearance and was always well groomed. He lived in the center of Antwerp, in the finest part of the town, near the exchange, in a large and beautiful mansion. He looked more like a senator than an artist.[1]

Willem Key was born in Breda and was a pupil of Lambert Lombardus from Liége, together with Frans Floris. He entered the guild of the painters in Antwerp in the year of our Lord, 1540. He was a man of means, indeed rich, but in his expenditures he never was a spendthrift. He was industrious at all times and always eager to profit by his work. When he came into the company of artists he would never show frivolity, as did some of the others.[2]

As to his work and his style, I may state that he was a very good portrait painter who worked from life. He followed nature closely. He had a way of giving a smooth finish to his work, which made it exceptionally pleasing, and in which he surpassed other artists. However, he was not as bold and dynamic in his work as was Floris; yet he was not without merit in his compositions, being a man with a keen mind and good judgement. Key was well rewarded for his works and always had many commissions.

A particularly fine painting of Willem Key's, which had

been ordered by Christoffel Pruyn, the Treasurer, used to be in Antwerp at the city hall. In this picture were the life-size portraits of the rulers of the town; Christ, with angels, appeared above. This painting was destroyed by fire when the rough Spanish soldiers burned the beautiful city hall in 1576.

At the Onze Vrouwe Kerck was an altar painting of Key's portraying the merchants. Its subject was Christ saying: 'All who are burdened, come unto me.' Many merchants were represented in this picture. The text was taken from Isaiah LV: 3

'Ho everyone that thirsteth, come ye to the waters, and he that hath no money, come ye, buy and eat; yea, come, buy wine and milk without money and without price.'

This painting was destroyed by the iconoclasts.

A very splendid painting by Key, in the same church, was a *Victory* or *Triumph of Christ*.

Key made a portrait of Cardinal Granvelle in a cardinal's costume, for which he received forty rycksdaelders without having asked for them.4

Finally, after he had made many paintings and portraits, he was called upon to make a portrait of the Duke of Alva. It was supposed that he did not understand any foreign language. However, while occupied with this work, he overheard some conversation between the Duke of Alva and a member of the Blood-Council, in which they said that the sentence of Count Egmont and some other noblemen would be executed; it had been decided that they should die.5

Willem Key loved these noblemen and took this affair to heart. He went home and became ill. He died on the same day on which the Counts Horn and Egmont were executed, which was on the fifth of June, 1568, on the eve of Pentecost. Some persons believe he died a few days before. Few knew the cause of his death. His faithful friends remained silent.[6]

Others say that the cruel facial expression of the Duke of Alva frightened him and made him sick, and he died consequently. But this I regard as a story. Lampsonius says about him:[7]

> Through the able hand of Key,
> People's faces have been portrayed;
> You believe you are looking at the very persons,
> So well did Key succeed.
> If we leave Moro beyond consideration,
> According to my judgment,
> Not any artist in the Netherlands
> Excelled Key.

PIETER BREUGHEL

OF BREUGHEL

NATURE was wonderfully felicitous in her choice when, in an obscure village in Brabant, she selected the gifted and witty Pieter Breughel to paint her and her peasants, and to contribute to the everlasting fame of painting in the Netherlands.

Pieter was born not far from Breda, in a village called Breughel, a name he took for himself and his descendants. He learned his craft from Pieter Koeck van Aelst, whose daughter he later married. He often carried her in his arms when she was little, and when he lived with Aelst. From Aelst he went to work with Jeroon Kock, and then he went to France and to Italy.[1]

He practiced a good deal in the manner of Jeroon van den Bosch, and made many similar, weird scenes and drolleries. For this reason, he was often called Pier den Droll. Indeed, there are very few works from his hand that the beholder can look at seriously, without laughing. However stiff, serious, and morose, one may be, one cannot help laughing, or smiling.

Pieter painted many pictures from life on his journey, so that it was said of him, that while he visited the Alps, he had swallowed all the mountains and cliffs, and, upon coming home, he had spit them forth upon his canvas and panels; so remarkably was he able to follow these and other works of nature.

He settled down, selecting Antwerp as his residence, and there he entered the guild of the painters in 1551. He did a great amount of work for a merchant by the name of Hans

Franckert, a noble and worthy man who liked to chat with Breughel. He was with him every day. With this Franckert, Breughel often went on trips among the peasants, to their weddings and fairs. The two dressed like peasants, brought presents like the other guests, and acted as if they belonged to the families or acquaintances of the bride or of the groom. Here Breughel delighted in observing the manners of the peasants in eating, drinking, dancing, jumping, making love, and engaging in various drolleries, all of which he knew how to copy in color very comically and skillfully, and equally well with water-color and oils; for he was exceptionally skilled in both processes. He knew well the characteristics of the peasant men and women of the Kampine and elsewhere. He knew how to dress them naturally and how to portray their rural, uncouth bearing while dancing, walking, standing, or moving in different ways. He was astonishingly sure of his composition and drew most ably and beautifully with the pen. He made many little sketches from nature.[2]

As long as he remained in Antwerp, he lived with a servant girl whom indeed he would have married, had it not been for the unfortunate fact that she used to lie all the time, which was repugnant to his love of truth. He made a contract or agreement with her that he would check off all her lies upon a stick. For this purpose he took a fairly long one, and he said that if the stick became full of notches in the course of time it would prevent the wedding. This happened before much time had elapsed.

At last, since Pieter Koeck's widow had finally settled in Brussels, he fell in love with her daughter, whom, as we have said, he had often carried in his arms, and he married her; but her mother requested that Breughel leave Antwerp, and make his residence in Brussels, in order that he might get his former girl out of sight and out of mind. This also happened.[3]

PIETER BREUGHEL

Breughel was a quiet and able man who did not talk much, but was jovial in company, and he loved to frighten people, often his own pupils, with all kinds of ghostly sounds and pranks that he played.

Some of Breughel's most significant works are at present in the possession of the Emperor; for example, a great *Tower of Babel* with many beautiful details. One can look into it from above. Furthermore, there is a smaller representation of the same subject. There are, besides, two *Carrying of the Cross* paintings, very natural-looking, always with a few drolleries in them somewhere. Again, there is a *Massacre of the Innocents*, in which there is much to see that is done true to life, of which I have spoken elsewhere—a whole family, for instance, begging for the life of a peasant child whom a murderous soldier has seized in order to kill it; the grief and the swooning of the mother and other events appear realistic.4

Finally, there is a *Conversion of St Paul*, also representing some very beautiful cliffs. It would be very hard to enumerate every thing Breughel did—fantasies, representations of hell, peasant scenes, and many other things.5

He painted a *Temptation of Christ*, in which one looks down from above, as from the Alps, upon cities and country borne up by clouds, through the rents in which one looks out.6

He made a *Dulle Griet*, who is stealing something to take to Hell, and who wears a vacant stare and is strangely dressed. I believe this and other pictures are also in the possession of the Emperor.7

Sr Herman Pilgrims, art lover in Amsterdam, has a *Peasant Wedding* done in oils, which is very beautiful. The faces and bare limbs of the peasants in it are yellow and brown as if they were sunburned, and they show ugly skins, different from those of city dwellers.8

He painted a picture in which *Lent* and *Carnival* are fighting; another, where all kinds of remedies are used against death; and one with all kinds of children at games; and innumerable other little, clever things.[9]

Two canvases painted in water-color can be seen in the home of Sr Willem Jacobsz., who lives near the new church in Amsterdam. They represent a *Peasant Wedding*, where many amusing episodes together with the true character of the peasant may be seen. Among the group giving presents to the bride, is an old peasant who has his little money bag hanging around his neck, and who is busy counting the gold into his hand. These are unusual paintings.[10]

Shortly before his death, the townsmen of Brussels commanded Breughel to represent in pictures the digging of the canal from Brussels to Antwerp. These pictures were not completed because of his death.[11]

Many of Breughel's strange compositions and comical subjects one may see in his copper engravings. But he has made many skilful and beautiful drawings; he supplied them with inscriptions which, at the time, were too biting and too sharp, and which he had burned by his wife during his last illness, because of remorse, or fear that most disagreeable consequences might grow out of them. In his will he left his wife a picture of *A Magpie on a Gallows*. By the magpie, he meant the gossips whom he delivered to the gallows. In addition, he had painted a picture in which Truth triumphs. According to his own statement, this was the best thing painted by him.[12]

He left behind him two sons who were able painters. One was called Pieter and studied with Gillis van Conincxloo and painted portraits from life; the other, Jan, learned water-color painting from his grandmother, the mother of Pieter van Aelst. Jan studied the process of oil-painting with a cer-

PIETER BREUGHEL

tain Pieter Goe-kindt, who had many beautiful things in his house. He went to Cologne and then to Italy, where he made a great name as a landscape painter; he also made other subjects, very small in size, a type of work in which he excelled. Lampsonius speaks of Pieter Breughel in the following lines, with the question: [13]

Who may be this other Jeroon Bos,
Who came in this world again,
Who pictures to us the fantastic conceptions of his own master again,
Who is most able with the brush,
Who is even surpassing his master?
Ye, Pieter, ye work in the artistic style of your old master.
But you rise still higher:
For reason that you select
Pleasant topics to laugh about.
Through these you deserve great merit
And with your master you must be praised for being a great artist.

JOAN SCHOOREL

OF SCHOOREL

IT is well known that in antiquity Rome was the most beautiful city and the leader of all cities. She flourished in a prosperous manner, and many nationalities were represented in her dense population. The city was adorned with excellent, artistic sculpture, and marble and bronze were transformed skilfully into the most exquisite human bodies and animal shapes.

It is also known that many times war, grinding its teeth in madness, had gripped this town with its crass hands, overthrown, and crushed it. But later, when Rome became less agitated under the peaceful rule of the popes, many beautiful pieces of sculpture in marble and bronze were discovered and delivered from their gray crypts. The statues which came to light out of darkness became a beacon to the art of painting. They opened the eyes of our art students so that they could discriminate between the ugly and the beautiful, and discover the perfection in living human figures and in the limbs of animals, in nature.

Therefore, the Italians, enlightened on this subject, had rendered the true character and poses of the human figures before the painters of the Netherlands were able to do so. The latter had a certain traditional, conventional method of working. They persistently and industriously tried to improve by studying ordinary, daily life, but they were in the dark so to speak, with little light to guide them until the moment that Joan van Schoorel brought to their attention the best artistic methods from Italy. Because he had visited Italy, and came to the Netherlands to enlighten the art of painting, he was called by Frans Floris and other artists, the Lantern Bearer and The Paver of the Way.[1]

He was born the first day of August in the year 1495, in a village called Schoorel. From this town his second name was derived. He brought wide renown to his native village.

Schoorel's parents died when he was very young. His relatives sent him to school in the city of Alkmaer, where he remained till his fourteenth year. He acquired the Latin language with zeal. He always had a natural inclination towards drawing. He copied from stained glass windows. Also, he carved with a penknife little human figures, animals, plant forms, and trees, on the white horn inkwells. For this work he was praised and loved by his fellow students in school.

His friends, noticing to what a degree he had his mind set upon the art of painting, complied with his wishes, and sent him to Willem Cornelisz., a fair artist. This master would not accept him unless a contract was signed to cover a period of three years. His friends agreed to this contract, and a certain amount of money had to be paid, in case Schoorel should not satisfy his master. The master carried this contract in his pocket, and held it many times against him. The boy was a source of great profit. During the first year, the master received more than a hundred guilders, which was a large amount in those days. The master took care that the boy should not escape, and used to say, when he was drunk: 'Joan, keep in mind that I carry you in my pocket, and in case you ever plan to run away, you must realize that something is going to happen between your friends and me!' It was most annoying to Schoorel to hear this so many times.[2]

It happened once, on a stormy, winter evening, that the master was drunk and slept. Schoorel got hold of the letter, and took it to the wooden bridge. He tore the document into many pieces which he allowed to fly away into the water. He intended still to satisfy his master conscientiously, but he took delight in the fact that the master could no longer tease him with the document. On Sundays and on holy days, in the afternoon, Schoorel usually went to a lovely woodland just outside the city of Haarlem. Here he painted a picture of the trees in color, in a clever manner quite different from that of other painters.

After his third year of apprenticeship, he took leave of the master, and went to live in Amsterdam in the home of Jacob Cornelisz., a master of great reputation, who used his colors with great purity. Cornelisz. valued Schoorel highly, regarding him as his own son. He gave him yearly a sum of money for his clever and intelligent work. He also permitted him to make paintings for himself in his free time, for which Schoorel received a neat sum, and so was able to get along well.[3]

This master had a most beautiful little daughter twelve years old. Nature had done her utmost to bestow upon this girl every beauty, poise, and friendly grace. Her charm conquered the heart of Schoorel and she gained his love. However, she was exceedingly young. In deep gratitude, Schoorel took leave of his master; but wherever he travelled, a sweet memory and an affection for this girl remained in his heart; he hoped that his love might some day be consummated in wedlock.

At this same time, Jonnijn de Mabuse was in the service of Philip of Burgundy, Bishop of Utrecht, and, although Mabuse had a very bad reputation, Schoorel went to stay with him at Utrecht, in order to learn something. It proved to be for a short time only, for this master led an irregular life, often to be found in disreputable inns, where he went to drink and to fight. Schoorel used to pay for him many times, and also risked his life for him. He saw no reason for remaining with him. Accordingly, he went to Cologne and then to Spiers. He found in the latter city a friar who was clever in representing buildings, and in foreshortening. He stayed with him for some time and made some paintings for him.4

From Spiers he went to Strasburg, and then to Basel. He visited the shops of all painters. He was very much in demand; good wages were promised because he executed clever work and accomplished more in one week than others did in a month. He did not remain long in any one place.

He visited Nürnberg and the great artist, Albrecht Dürer. He remained there for some time in order to learn more. About this time, Luther was beginning to stir the quiet world with his teachings, and Dürer took an interest in Schoorel's views on the matter.

Soon Schoorel departed for Steyer in Carinthia, where his work was in great demand by most of the nobility. He stayed with a baronet, a great lover of pictures, who rewarded him well and wanted him to marry his own daughter.5

This might have been an opportunity for Schoorel had not the god of love painted in his heart the image of the dear little daughter in Amsterdam. For the reason that his love was very great he thought only about how to become more and more skilled in his art, in order to reach his goal. He progressed rapidly and it seemed that Love taught Art.

So, leaving the city, Schoorel went to Venice, where he became acquainted with some painters from Antwerp, including a certain Daniel van Bomberge, an amateur in painting. It happened, in the meantime, that a number of persons arrived in Venice from various countries, on a pilgrimage to the Holy Land and Jerusalem. Among them was a chaplain of the Béguines from Gouda in Hollond, a very clever man and a great lover of painting. He urged Schoorel to go to Jerusalem. He was then twenty-five years old.6

Schoorel consented to go, and took his drawing materials

with him. On board the vessel he pictured various persons from life. He kept a kind of a diary in a little book and filled it with sketches of various scenes. On the way to Candia, Cyprus, and elsewhere, he drew landscapes, views, castles, little towns, and mountains.

In Jerusalem he became acquainted with the Guardian of the Zion Monastery, a man highly esteemed by Jews and Turks. With him, Schoorel travelled through the surrounding country, and on the river Jordan. He made pen-drawings of the landscapes. When he returned to the Netherlands, he made from these sketches a beautiful painting in oil, representing Joshua guiding the children of Israel with dry feet across the Jordan.

The Abbot would gladly have kept Schoorel there another year, but the Chaplain of the Béguines advised and besought him not to remain. When Schoorel left Jerusalem, he promised to send the Abbot a painting. This was sent from Venice to Jerusalem, and at the present time can be seen in the place where our Saviour was born, as many, who have been there, can testify. It is a picture of St Thomas placing his fingers in the side of Christ.7

Schoorel made a picture of the city of Jerusalem, which he utilized many times as a motif in his work; for example, in his *Christ Descending the Mount of Olives,* a work showing Christ on His way to the city, and *The Sermon on the Mount.* He also made a painting of the Holy Sepulchre; and after he had come back to the Netherlands, he painted a picture of himself with a group of knights of Jerusalem, or Keysers. This was an oblong piece done in oils, and is now preserved in the Dominican Monastery or Princenhof.8

Schoorel returned from Jerusalem in the year 1520, and went to the city of Rhodes—two years before the Turks conquered the city. He visited the Grand Master of the German

Order, the knights of which now occupy the isle of Malta. He was very well received. He made pictures of the city and its surroundings. He then went to Venice; but he left this city after a little while and visited other cities in Italy, including Rome, where he worked very hard. He made studies of antiquities, of statues and of ruins, and reproductions of the works of Raphael, and of Michelangelo—artists famous at this time—and he copied also the works of other masters.9

About the same time, Adrian VI was elected pope. He was formerly a cardinal in Spain. He had been born in Utrecht. When Schoorel came to Rome, the Pope became acquainted with him and made him director of the Belvedere. Schoorel painted many pictures for the Pope, and made also a portrait of him from life, a work which is still to be seen in Louvain, at the College founded by Pope Adrian VI. This Pope occupied the Holy See one year and thirty-five weeks and then died. Schoorel, after extensive study, returned to the Netherlands.10

When he went to Utrecht Schoorel learned, to his great sorrow, that the daughter of his former master had married a goldsmith from Amsterdam. By staying away so long he had lost his chance for his long-cherished happiness. So he went to live with a deacon from Oudemunster, named Lockhorst, who came to the court and who was a great lover of art. He made several paintings in water-color, and also in oil, for this gentleman; among others, as I have mentioned already, a Palm Sunday subject, in which Christ is represented mounted on a donkey on His way to Jerusalem. The view of the city was done from life. There are children in it, and Jews, who are spreading wreaths and cloth, and other details. This painting, which had wings, was placed as a memorial in the Dome Church in Utrecht by friends of the deacon.

About this time a riot broke out in Utrecht. One faction

was for the Bishop; the other, for the Duke of Guelders. Schoorel went to Haarlem to avoid the riot, where he was well received by the Commander of the Order of St John, whose name was Simon Saen, and who was a good friend to artists. Schoorel made some paintings for him, fragments of which may still be seen in town, among others, a *Baptism of St John*, which is a very beautiful painting and in which can be seen some exceedingly graceful women with faces that suggest the style of Raphael. They are looking upward to the descent of the Holy Ghost. A pleasing landscape is in the background with some little nude figures.[11]

Schoorel rented a house in Haarlem, for many people came to see him as he was sought as a teacher. He painted there some large panels, among others, a greatly admired one, a *Crucifixion*, for the high altar for the Old Church at Amsterdam. There is yet another painting of his on the same subject in Amsterdam.[12]

Schoorel became so famous that the members of the College of Holy Mary invited him to come to Utrecht. Schoorel was commissioned to paint the high altar of the church of this college which had been founded by Henry IV, Emperor of Rome. The interior of the altar was done in wood-carving. Schoorel painted four wings for the high altar. He received the promise of the first vacancy for canon of this College and accepted the proposal.[13]

He painted on the first of the doors the figures of the Virgin seated with the Infant, and Joseph; on the second one, he painted the kneeling figure of the Emperor and Bishop Conrad. These were all life-size. The figures had been ordered by the church at the command of the Emperor; the Bishop had to be represented as beautifully as possible, in pontifical costume. An excellent landscape was painted in the background.

Schoorel worked a number of years on the other two

doors. He had painted previously a canvas with water-color as large as the two doors, which for the time being was placed where the best doors were going to come later. This represented Abraham's Offer, and a beautiful landscape was seen in the background. King Philip, who was in this country in the year 1549, and who visited the city of Utrecht, bought this picture and transported it, with some other paintings by Schoorel, to Spain.[14]

It is to be lamented that many of Schoorel's works, such as the *Crucifixion* of Amsterdam, the beautiful wings of the altar painting of the Church of Holy Mary in Utrecht, and the beautiful panel in Gouda, which he made in the most flourishing period of his life, were destroyed by demented plebeians, and burned, with many other beautiful things, in the year 1566.

Three beautiful works by Schoorel are in existence at Marchiennes, a fine abbey in Artois: First, an altar painting representing *St Laurens tortured on a grate;* secondly, an *Eleven Thousand Virgins,* an excellent work, a panel with two wings; thirdly, a large altar painting with six wings, the interior of which is a *Stoning of St Stephen.*[15]

An altar painting with two wings can be seen in the abbey of St Vaast in Arras. It is a *Crucifixion,* located in a chapel in the ambulatory behind the choir.[16]

At Groot-Ouwer, an abbey in Frisia, is an altar painting with two wings done by Schoorel, a *Last Supper.* The figures are life-size and the faces are done from life.[17]

Schoorel made many beautiful pictures for a banker in Malines, named Willem Pieters, who had connections in Rome, and with whom he was friendly while in that city.

Schoorel also made some paintings for Count Henry of Nassau and René de Châlons, Prince of Orange; these works are at the palace in Breda.

When he came back from Italy, Schoorel received a message from the King of France, Francis I, requesting him to enter into his service and promising him a large salary. Schoorel declined the offer politely, stating that he was not interested in becoming a court painter.

He had recommended an architect to the King of Sweden, Gustavus, and on the same occasion sent a picture of Holy Mary to the King, in which the latter took a great pleasure. As a token of his gratitude, the King sent a royal present to the painter, which was accompanied by a letter signed by the King himself. The gift consisted of a beautiful ring, a case of marten skins, and an ice sledge the King used to ride in, with the entire harness for a horse. Then there was a cheese weighing two hundred pounds. The letter of the King arrived, but the seal had been cut off, and none of the presents ever reached their destination.[18]

Schoorel had great social gifts, and all the distinguished people of the Netherlands liked him. He was a musician as well as a poet and a rhetorician. He made very beautiful 'Spele van Sinne', 'Batementen', 'Refereine' and 'Liedekens.' He was a good archer, a capable linguist, speaking Latin, Italian, French, and High German. He was generous and had a jolly disposition. In the latter part of his life, however, he suffered from rheumatism and gallstones which caused him to seem old at an early age.

I ought not to pass by in silence Sr Geert Willemsz. Schoterbosch, who owns an excellent painting by Schoorel, which represents Mary presenting Jesus to Simeon in the temple (*Presentation in the Temple*). It has some splendid architecture and a beautiful vault, much gilt and gold decoration suggested by paint, and very graceful figures.

There used to be a painting by Schoorel on the wall of the Groote Houtpoort at Haarlem, but this has deteriorated.

JOAN SCHOOREL

Antonis Moro, court painter to King Philip of Spain, who in his youth was a pupil of Schoorel, and who always remained attached to his master, made a portrait of him about two years before his death, in 1560.[19]

Schoorel died in the year 1562, on the sixth of December, at the age of sixty-seven.

The following has been written under the portrait just mentioned:

> Addidit hic arti decus, huic ars ipsa decorem,
> Quo moriente mori est, hoec quoque visa sibi.
> Ant. Morus Phi. Hisp. Regis Pictor Io. Schorelio
> Pict. F. Ao. M.D.LX.

> D.O.M.
> Io. Schorelio, Pictorum sui seculi facilè principi,
> qui post aedita artis suae monumenta quam plurima,
> maturo decedens senio, magnum sui reliquit desiderium.
> Vixit annos 67. menses 4. dies 6. Obiit a nato Christo.
> Ao. 1562. 6 decembris

Lampsonius says the following in his name in verse:[20]

> Always shall I be famous,
> For having been the first,
> Who showed to the Netherlands,
> That a man who wants to become an artist
> Must visit Rome,
> Must wear out a thousand brushes,
> Must use quantity of color.
> He must also have produced many paintings
> In the style of this school,
> Worthy of praise,
> Before he may be regarded honestly an artist.

AERTGEN
OF LEYDEN

A FINE artist, who does not know how to put himself enough in the foreground, may be appreciated by people who understand art; but he may not be recognized by ordinary people, and neither he, himself, nor his works, may be duly valued. As an example, there was Aert Claessoon, a painter from Leyden, generally spoken of as Aertgen, though he was a tall fellow.

He was born at Leyden in the year of our Lord 1498. His father, a fuller, would remind Aertgen of his age by the golden year of fifteen hundred, and relate that he had started his promised pilgrimage to Rome when Aertgen was two years old. Aertgen was employed in his father's fullery till he was eighteen. That is why he was called 'Aertge the Fuller.'

Aertgen was a painter by nature. In 1516, he became a pupil of Cornelis Enghelbrechtsz. under whom he learned rapidly and soon became a master. He worked in watercolors and in oils. His subjects were seldom taken from either poetry or morale [fiction or allegory]; most of them were derived from the Scriptures. He taught the Scriptures to his pupils and used them as lessons. He was friendly and always eager to instruct them.1

On Mondays, he worked little, or hardly at all; he went with his pupils to an inn, to be merry with them. By nature he was not a drunkard. He was rather reserved and cared little about himself; he thought still more of others.

His first style of drawing was similar to the work of his master, Cornelis Enghelbrechtsoon. After he had seen work by Van Schoorel, he changed his style and made it similar to work of this artist. For the treatment of architecture he followed Heemskercken; this kind of work he did very beautifully. In his paintings he always added something that was unpleasant, and he did so with carelessness. His work had individuality, interesting composition, and a spiritual quality, for which it was valued by persons who had an understanding of art.

When Frans Floris, of Antwerp, was commissioned, in Delft, to paint the *Crucifixion* for the Cruys-Capelle in the church, he went to Leyden to see the work of Aertgen. After Floris had arrived at that city, he inquired as to where Aertgen lived; he found a humble and much dilapidated little house near the southern wall of the city. When he called, Aertgen was out. Floris asked permission to enter Aertgen's room, to see some of his paintings, because he had come far, and for this purpose alone. The request was readily granted with great pleasure. He went into a little attic, took a piece of charcoal, from the pupils who were sitting and drawing there, and drew the head of an ox, the face of St Luke, and the coat of arms of the painters, on the white wall which was low and did not offer much space; he covered the entire surface. These drawings remained on that wall until they deteriorated in the course of time. Frans finished his drawing and returned to his hostelry.

When Aertgen came home he was told that a friend from far had come to see him; that they had allowed him to go to Aertgen's room, and in his absence the friend had made drawings with charcoal in the presence of his pupils. No one knew the visitor. Aertgen went upstairs. He said, immediately: 'This must have been Frans Floris.' He then felt ashamed. He did not know what to think since a great master had come to see him. Frans, in the meantime, had asked Aertgen to come to the hostelry. Aertgen lacked courage. He did not regard himself worthy to associate with a master like Floris, although he really did want to visit with him. Frans proposed that he travel to Antwerp with him. He wanted that Aertgen's work should sell for higher prices, and he wished to make a gentleman of an artist who had lived and worked in quite poor conditions. Aertgen replied that he was as content with his sober existence as others were with their splendor. 'Let the King have his royalty; but let me live and work in peace in my poor little hut.' Aertgen remained and Floris returned to Antwerp.

As to the work by Aertgen, it was uneven and sometimes more clever than serious. One notices, specially in his large dimensions and in his tall figures, an occasional neglect of proportion, despite the interesting composition. Frans Floris, for this reason, would have had Aertgen accompany him to Antwerp so that there he could have had assistance from Floris.

Aertgen made a large number of designs for glass painters and others; these designs can be found by the hundreds in the city of Leyden. Usually he was paid seven Groote for a design the size of a full sheet of paper; as he put an unusual amount of work into his drawings, one can easily understand why he could not have become fat at that rate.

Three of Aertgen's most remarkable paintings are in the house of Sr Jan Gerrits Buyteweg, at Leyden. They are outstanding because of the beauty of the coloring. They have been painted very finely, as the nature of the subject demanded. The *Crucifixion*, with the two thieves, has Mary, the other holy women, and the disciples, at the foot of the cross in great sorrow; below them, Magdalena embraces the cross. The *Carrying of the Cross* is a composition of a large crowd of followers, among whom are Mary, other holy women and the disciples. In the painting of *Abraham and*

Isaac, the father leads his son who carries wood to the offering-place in the far distance.

The *Nativity* is in the house of the widow of the late Sr Jan van Wissenaer, former burgomaster, and collector of the city taxes of Leyden. This picture was very well planned and, although it was painted a little carelessly, it still may be regarded as one of Aertgen's best works.[2]

Among the water-colors on canvas, in the house of Joannes Adriaensz. Knotter, there is a picture of Mary with singing angels.

Sr Jan Diricks van Montfoort has a panel of the *Last Judgement* that has the portraits of the family of Dirick Jacobsz van Montfoort on the wings.

H. Goltzius, at Haarlem, has a picture of the *Red Sea* painted, by Aertgen, in oil-color; this painting is in very bad condition. The most remarkable part of this work is the painting of the various costumes, headgear, turbans, and shawls, which are very interesting and are worthy of study.

When Aertgen received an order for a picture, he went with his customer to an inn to close the bargain. After leaving the place, in the night, the artist would not return to his house; he would go to some of his friends, or loiter in a street, playing on a German flute which he always had with him. He would do this, no matter how dark it was. Two or three times he fell into the canal. In this way he lost his life.

When he could not find any company, he had a place where he would go to and sleep. He would not go home. The quarter of the fullers, where his house was located, was most unsafe at night. He had experienced the danger of going home late at night.

One night, after leaving the inn, and on his way home, near the place of the fullers, he stopped to evacuate; a drunkard attacked him from behind and stabbed his cheek with a dagger, because he had sworn to do this to the first person he met in the street. Aertgen turned and asked: 'Who did that?' The drunkard recognized Aertgen's voice and begged to be forgiven; Aertgen did so immediately. When the man was more sober, he took Aertgen to the barber, who made a dressing for the wound. After that Aertgen was afraid to go home at an unsafe hour.[3]

One afternoon, Aertgen went out with a wealthy citizen from Leyden, named Quirinck Claesz., to receive payment for a piece of work. This was for his *Judgement of Saul* which is at the present in Delft. The party separated late at night. Following his old habit, Aertgen went along the place of the fullers. He felt a certain need and took off his coat which he hung over the wall along the canal. When he was ready to get his coat, he reached for it in the wrong direction and stepped into an opening made in the wall for people to get water. He fell into the canal and drowned. This was in 1564. He had reached the age of sixty-six.

JOACHIM BUECKLAER

IT is fortunate for a beginner to have, besides his natural talent and interesting examples to follow, good and sound instruction. Joachim Buecklaer, of Antwerp, was born to be an artist, and he was very fortunate that his aunt became the wife of the famous painter, Pieter Aertsen, who was called 'Langen Pier.' By Pieter Aertsen's careful instruction, Joachim learned the way to perfection in his painting.[1]

At the beginning, it was very difficult for Joachim to paint correctly and to apply colors well. His uncle Pieter encouraged him in practicing painting; he advised Joachim to paint from life—fruit, vegetables, meats, birds, fishes, and all other subjects. By doing so Joachim became efficient and an excellent artist. He treated his subjects with great ability; and he experienced little difficulty while painting. His work was masterful.

Unfortunately, most of the things in this world, obtained without effort and without much consideration, are often neglected, or despised; things which are difficult to obtain are always in demand. The works of Joachim Buecklaer, the pictures he painted during his life time, for trifling sums of money, are at present, after his death, appreciated so much that the price paid for one picture is often twelve times the amount it brought originally. Purchasers have gladly paid good sums for this artist's work.

Joachim painted kitchen scenes. He painted a fine picture for the mint-master at Antwerp. Joachim did the work for an insignificant price. Every day the mint-master brought some

173

object to be included in the painting. Consequently, the artist could not earn his bread and cheese by painting this picture, it was so crowded with all kinds of birds, fishes, meats, vegetables and fruits.

In the Onse Vrouwe Kerck at Antwerp there was a picture, by Joachim, of *Palm Sunday;* he painted it most artistically. This painting was destroyed in the second iconoclasm.

There are two splendid kitchen pictures by Joachim in the house of Sr Zion Luz, at Amsterdam. One is of a fish-market; the other is of a fruit-market. The various details, including the figures of maids and other figures, were nicely painted. The coloring is admirable.

Sr Melchior Wijntgis, mint-master at Middelborgh, has a beautiful kitchen picture with life-size figures in it; and he has another picture of *Palm Sunday*.

In the home of Jacob Raeuwaert, in Amsterdam, I have seen an interesting little picture of a market with a background of the Ecce Homo. This painting, well done, is worthy of admiration.[2]

Hans Verlaen, a merchant in Haarlem, lives near the Kraen, and he has two large and beautiful pictures that Joachim painted of life-size figures; one, the four Evangelists, painted excellently in rich colors, and the other, St Anne.

It would be as impossible for me to mention all the places where Joachim's work has been hidden, and to praise his pictures adequately according to their real merit. It is most regrettable that an artist like Joachim had to work for very small wages, and that he was so modest about himself other people rarely esteemed him. He did his day's work here and there. He painted pictures of costumes for Antonis Moro and other artists, and earned just one guilder, or one and a half guilders a day for his work. He would paint a large and beautiful picture for five or six pounds.

JOACHIM BUECKLAER

Joachim's Ecce Homo is now supposed to be in the collection of the Emperor. Jacob Raeuwaert sold it, as far as I know, to count Van der Lip, with a picture of a fruit market by Buecklaer, and two pictures by Heemskerck, one of the *Four Extremes* (Death, Judgement, Paradise and Hell) and the other of the *Deluge*. In this painting of the *Deluge* there were beautiful nudes of men and women; and dead bodies of little children, floating on the water, whose tenacious and pitiful struggle for life could be seen in their efforts to hold their dolls and playthings in their dead little arms and hands. In the same picture Heemskerck secured other similar effects. In the same collection there was a picture, by Dierck Barentszen, of Perseus, in which people were being changed into stone. All these pictures were sold together for about a thousand Flemish pounds. They had a far greater value.[3]

Joachim died at Antwerp at the time that he was working for a military officer by the name of Vitello. This was during the latter part of the period the Duke of Alva was in the Netherlands. Joachim complained, on his deathbed, that he had to work for so little money his whole life through. He was about forty years old.[4]

FRANS FLORIS

THE Italian painters, specially some of the more unimportant among them, paint their nudes with a soft blending of the forms; they do not work out well the interior anatomical structure. They prefer to take the easiest way and do not want to bother their heads with an analysis of muscles. In this way they mar their artistic effects. The artists of our Netherlands often paint their figures too thin, and even make them emaciated, but such technique requires, nevertheless, a knowledge of muscles, of tendons, and of veins. The works of the great Buonarrotti show a thorough knowledge of the interior muscular system; he translates his forms within beautiful outlines which are the result of his great knowledge. His work shows how a really eminent master sets about rendering the highest beauty, and how much experience was necessary for this.

However, one notices in the works of the ancient masters, that difference in age were observed in the characteristics of their statues. Next to a slender, young Antinous, a masculine, sturdy Hercules, or an emaciated old Laocoön, may be seen. We may remark here that such contrasts in the treatment of a subject may be permitted whenever required.

Nevertheless, some people criticize the ancient Laocoön for being too emaciated, but this judgement indicates, in all probability, a lack of understanding on their own part; they do not comprehend the characteristics of the human body, nor the tendency for old people to lose the natural aspect of youth, to lose elasticity, become leaner and more thin.

176

FRANS FLORIS

Some people have criticized Floris, too, for the emaciated character of his figures. He is the glory of painting in the Netherlands. It has been in part Italians who expressed such an opinion, and who based their judgement only on some of the prints reproduced from his works which do not resemble the originals, and in which many fine effects have been lost.

Vasarius writes as follows about him:

'This artist is regarded as being very excellent. He treated all kinds of subjects in such a way that, according to the Netherlanders, nobody has expressed better than he the emotions of the soul, sorrow, joy, and other effects. For this reason they call him the Flemish Raphael Urbino. But the reproductions of his works in print do not justify this statement entirely. The engraver, however good he may be, never in his work reaches the same quality of the drawing and the style of the original master.'[1]

Now this is the statement of Vasari about Floris, and as has been said, he based it on prints engraved from drawings which Floris's pupils or other persons reproduced from his paintings. I believe if the writer had actually seen the fine, bold brush strokes of Floris, and the beautiful technique of his pen, he would not have been influenced in his judgement by jealousy of a foreigner, but would have sounded his praise and eulogized him.

Regarding the origin of Floris, there once lived an honest citizen in Antwerp named Jan de Vriendt who was called Floris. He was an intelligent man, in great demand for his surveying work, and he died in the year 1400. He left two sons, Cornelis and Claudius. Claudius Floris was an excellent sculptor, many of whose beautiful works may still be seen in the city of Antwerp. Cornelis was a stone cutter. He died in the year 1540, and was the father of Frans de Vriendt who was called Floris.[2]

This Cornelis, the father of Frans, had four sons who were very fine draughtsmen. Cornelis, the brother of Frans, was an excellent sculptor and an architect; Frans was a fine painter; Jaques was a good glass painter and painted pictures; Jan Floris was particularly famous for his pottery and never had a real rival in the Netherlands. King Philip took him to Spain, because of his artistic work; Jan died there while still young.[3]

Jan Floris was specially good in drawing and in painting jolly little stories and figures on pottery and on faience, of which Frans had a few objects in his home; and they were well worth seeing.[4]

Cornelis produced many fine works in Antwerp, such as the royal building of the city hall, the Ostershuys, and other buildings. He died in the year 1575.[5]

Frans, who was predestined by nature to surpass others in painting, first studied sculpture; most of the time he carved the brass work for the graves in churches.[6]

But nature wished to place him in the right environment for his vocation, and when he was twenty years old he went to live in Liége and became a pupil of the then famous Lambert Lombardus, painter at Liége. Frans imitated the style of Lombardus very closely, and kept something of this in his own paintings all through his life. A similarity in style can be noticed in the work of both the artists. I heard a story which confirms this.

Once Lambert went to Antwerp to visit his pupil, Frans, and was received very well by him. While the guests were enjoying themselves, Lambert left the company unnoticed, and came as a stranger into the workshop where a number of able assistants were busy.

He looked at the works of art there, and began to talk about their master Floris. He pointed out that the latter had been in his early youth an outstanding thief. When the pupils

178

heard such shameful talk about their master, they became angry with Lambert, and would have attacked him, had he not finally explained that Frans had been a pupil of his, and had studied so hard that he had stolen his art. The same story has been told of Apollo, in panegyric, where it is said that he was robbed of the art of painting by Zeus.

Lambert, returning to the company, asked Frans what kind of people he had in his workshop, saying that they had almost given him a beating. He told the whole story, which brought a good laugh, and he praised the pupils of Floris very much for their fine loyalty to their master.

Frans, who loved his art, travelled to Italy. In Rome he used his time very well; he made drawings, mostly in red crayon, of everything that attracted him. He made many studies of the nudes in the *Last Judgement* by Michelangelo, and drew antiques with a clever style of cross-hatching. I have seen some of these studies in prints. Some of his assistants or pupils must have got possession of this work in an irregular and secret way; they had it reproduced in prints; these things went from hand to hand and can be seen occasionally.[7]

When Frans returned to the Netherlands he was soon well known as a great master, surprising many artists and connoisseurs with his works, specially after they were exhibited splendidly in places where everybody could see them.

From the beginning, he showed what a clever painter he was and how gifted he was spiritually. He was very industrious, and his experienced hand demonstrated his excellence. He proved with his tongue that he was intelligent, too, and one could speak with him on any subject of a spiritual nature, on philosophy, on poetry, and similar topics. Later on, when wealth and abundance came to him, through the rewards he received for doing important works in large churches, and when he was pushed forward by princes and gentlemen of high rank, he was tempted by some of them, and corrupted. He began to waste his time and sacrifice himself to drinking, the great social disease of the Netherlands. He wronged fine art and his own noble spirit. He was recognized as a great painter and a great drunkard.

Floris was criticized for his drinking by various persons, especially by the poet, Dierick Volckaertsz. Coornhert, who sent him a letter and a poem which told him about a dream he had had: Albrecht Dürer appeared to Coornhert as an old dignified man; he praised the art of Frans highly, but rebuked him severely for his low living. Finally, at the end, Coornhert addresses Frans: 'If what I have dreamed may not be true, one thing *is* true: this has been said to you directly.'[8]

Against my own wishes, I shall now tell some of his adventures, and I hope that some of our fellow artists may then rather loathe him for them, than follow in his footsteps or praise him. I hope that youth, no matter how strong it may feel, will not try to gain a reputation similar to his. We, as a Germanic race, wrongly drink beyond measure and make drinking an abuse; not in every place is this habit regarded as shameful, low, and sinful; there are places where the ability to drink heavily is even praised.

By many intelligent races, this miserable, bread-stealing habit of drinking is regarded as the lowest shame in the world, more than bestial, most senseless, and a most unnatural sin; as a most destructive mother with the worst intentions, creating all kind of inabilities; a mother who has to be slandered, detested, and from whom one should take to his heels.

Frans grew so powerful through his art that he became highly esteemed by the most important people of the country, by the Knights of the Golden Fleece, by the Prince of Orange, and by the Counts of Egmont and Horn, and other similar persons. They were very friendly to the artist, and frequently came to his house to drink or to banquet. His wife, Dame Clara Floris, was sometimes raving mad, and more than bold when she wanted to be so. She could be most rude towards these gentlemen and had no consideration for any one. It was all the same to her whether she used harsh words towards the Countesses of Egmont and of Horn, or whether she addressed her servants or her maids. This hurt such a kind and courteous man as Floris again and again and irritated his spirit. It had been said that she was the cause of his rough life and his ruin, for being so exceedingly head-strong and insolent.

Although she lived in great luxury in a large and beautiful house of her own at the Meire, she often said that she did not want to finish her life in such a smoky hole—just because the kitchen was a little smoky. Consequently, Frans bought a piece of land near the hospital and built a splendid house on it. He employed his brother as architect.9

This house, or rather palace, had gates and columns in gray Arduyn, according to the ancient architectural order. The construction absorbed all the capital from the other house, including its interior furnishings, and still another five thousand guilders which Floris had deposited in the bank of Schetsen. He borrowed everywhere he could. Still worse, he not only neglected his work, but he used to have a good time every day with the people working on the house, and with the foremen. Finally, the amount of rent which was due increased, his debts increased, he had to pay always more in wages, and the work proceeded badly. It became pandemonium. He was too much of an easy mark and very neglectful. There were too many parasites and penny-scrapers round him who helped him to squander away his money.

Consequently his wife, Joffrouw Clara, and his brother Jaques quarrelled constantly, for the latter was a joker who

181

was always ready to ridicule, and he would never become angry. He used to turn Clara's arguments round and all this, because he loved to raise his glass, specially when he did not have to pay for it.

Sometimes, Dame Floris rebuked him, saying: 'Why are you back again? You are going to ruin us; you come here only to fill your stomach. I do not want to see you anymore.' And other similar remarks she made. However, Jaques, who knew how to take remarks without getting angry, just for the sake of getting his drinks, reversed her statements, and said; 'Surely, my sister, those who do not know you would believe that you do not like me, but I, who know you thoroughly, know exactly what you mean by these words. Dull heads could not understand this, but I, who know Greek, can explain the real meaning. It means: 'Beloved brother, why do you come so seldom? We openly confess that we cannot live without you nor be happy. Therefore, come every day; your company is most pleasant. I know also, dear Sister, that of my own will I should not come and help you, but you would be cross towards every one if I was not here.'

She replied at this: 'Get away, scoundrel! I do not know what more to call you to make you stay away!' He answered again: 'Now, look here, that is Greek again, it means that I must stay, that I have to come back every day, that the day is too short for my amusing you with my company, and that I have to add the night to it also. I understand that thoroughly, dear Sister; it means that by staying here night and day I show to you the greatest friendship in the world.'

In short, wherever Dame Floris found a hole, Jaques had a nail for it, with the result that the whole company had to laugh, even Dame Floris, for she liked Jaques and did not mind his teasing game so much.

As a result of all these goings-on, Floris received a great

deal of criticism, and frequently very unjustly at that. Sometimes he regretted thoroughly his lost time and his present situation. He warned his children and his pupils to be industrious and advised them to pray to the Lord that they might learn through his neglect and imprudence. He said: 'I may be careless in my old age, but in my youth I prayed to God many times for the privilege of being able to learn well and to reach salvation.'

Floris complained that, through his neglect and imprudence, he had met bad fortune, that before he started to build he had had an income of as much as a thousand guilders a year, which was a large sum in those days, and that now he had only huge debts. These he could have paid with the income from his painting very easily; but he seemed to have the habit of drinking too much, and could not tear himself away from his fellow drinkers, for these passionate servants of Bacchus loved to be with him.

He had such a reputation for his physical resistance against alcohol, that once six famous topers, swallowers of drink, Basconters, bibbers from Brussels, who envied Floris his reputation, went to Antwerp in order to test his resistance and to lay a wager with him in drinking.

Floris came out so well that, before half the dinner was over, three of the topers were already under the table. The other three remained steady a long time; then, through the long struggle, they began to lisp, and Frans gained courage. He got them under the table finally with a huge Handt-houwer or deep Frankfoorter. The one who kept up the longest, at the end had to acknowledge Frans his master. When they left the inn, this fellow conducted Frans to the court where the artist's horse was kept and where five or six pupils stood bare-headed. Floris ordered a mug of Rynschen Baey; he held it high to show how much strength he still had left. He stood on one leg, and with a single swallow emptied the mug to the health of his conquered victim. He mounted his horse and went home triumphantly in the night.

On another occasion, Floris was in the company of the directors and members of the guild of the clothiers of Antwerp, a group of thirty men, each of whom drank to his health, and he to theirs. He drank sixty times, to each of them twice. It sounds almost unbelievable, but he told it himself to his pupils at night in his bedroom that had gold leather hangings. His pupils used to be present during his undressing; they had to wish him good night. There were always two who had to assist him in taking off his shoes and stockings.

Floris always had work to do and was kept busy with large, fine altar paintings and other big pieces. The most important is certainly the St Michael altar, the altar of the Fencers, which is in the Onse Vrouwe Kerck in Antwerp and is a *Fall of Lucifer*. This wonderfully artistic composition has been painted so well that all artists and connoisseurs are astounded.[10]

The picture displays a weird mingling and falling of the nude bodies of various demons, and is an excellent study of the anatomy of muscles and tendons. The dragon with the seven heads is very venomous and terrible to behold. On one of the wings Floris painted the director of the guild of the Fencers, with a scimitar in his hand, and there was also a brown cloud in the picture which produced a nice shadow.[11]

Floris painted the high altar for the same church. It was an *Assumption of Mary*, a large canvas. The draperies of the flying angels are very fine. This was a splendid painting, graceful in its composition and painted excellently. It is to be regretted that it was smashed by evil hands during the iconoclasm. Some people believe that this painting is still saved in the Escorial in Spain, and that it is highly treasured.[12]

A *Last Judgement*, another altar panel from the hand of Floris, was in Brussels. Many beautiful nudes are in it.[13]

In the Onse Vrouwe Kerck at Antwerp there was another altar panel, a *Nativity*, on canvas, a fine piece of work.[14]

Four double wings painted by Floris were in the St Jans Kerck at Ghent, in the chapel of the Abbot of St Bavo. They were ordered by Abbot Lucas. The interior represented the story of St Luke; and the exterior had a seated figure of Mary with the Infant in her lap, and an angel, while a light came from above. At the other side, Abbot Lucas can be seen; he is painted from life and is represented kneeling. Floris has shown by this excellent painting that when he chose to be he was the best portrait painter who could be found. The picture exhibits the firm and beautiful old head of the Abbot who is in pontifical costume; he has his mitre with him and a big and beautiful water dog, or Springeul, is lying beside him. This animal has been painted so well that real dogs come to sniff at it. I have seen this happen when we had these wings at the workshop of Lucas de Heere, where they were saved from the iconoclasts, and where they served daily for our study.

There exists also a painting by Floris in which St Luke is writing his gospel, dictated by Mary, and he is arranging his writings to correspond to the gospels of the other evangelists. Another painting by Floris shows St Luke painting Mary with her Infant in her lap; the subject is rendered well; in the picture are excellent faces of old and young people and interesting heads of oxen.

Furthermore, there exists a *Sermon of St Luke*, by Floris, in which some exquisitely costumed women are listening very seriously. Next is a scene representing St Luke taken prisoner, and in the background he can be seen hung on an olive tree.

There exists also a large painting of St Macharis and another saint, which has been executed intelligently and artistically. When one looks at this beautiful work, one wonders whether this able artist really could produce in one day as much as has been said. The faces and nudes in these paintings look as if they required much time and labor, especially if one stands at a little distance from the picture; then things reveal themselves which do not seem to be there when one is looking close to; one sees things which are not there in reality.[15]

Floris's method of painting hair was clever; he gave a good depth and volume to his objects, and he painted with rather soft effects.

Frans gave a fine exhibition of his skill in painting at the time when Emperor Charles made his triumphal entry into Antwerp. He was commissioned to paint large figures; and every day he made seven of these figures, and spent also seven hours at his work. For each figure he received one Flemish pound. He worked in this way for five weeks.[16]

When he worked for his pupils, he was paid eighteen or twenty guilders a day, but he had a habit of sleeping long and did not come to the workshop much before nine o'clock. He left at seven at night, and still had done much good work.

When King Philip came to Antwerp, Floris painted a very large canvas in a single day—a *Victory*, with a group of prisoners bound and lying on the ground, and a variety of ancient arms. He made an etching of this painting that is remarkable and pleasing to look upon.[17]

Floris was exceedingly expert at painting various details—antique seats which were carved or woven, interesting vases, headgear, ornaments to be worn, footwear, boots, helmets, and similar objects.

On the exterior of his house, Floris painted *Pictura* and the other liberal arts, in yellow, as if made of brass.

The last work which Floris did, and in the process of which he died, was for the Grand Prior of Spain. The principal parts of it were a *Crucifixion* and an *Ascension*, which were painted on oak panels twenty-seven feet high. These, painted splendidly, were almost finished before he died. The other subjects, on the wings, however, were only partly begun and were still in the process of under-painting. Later on, they were finished in color by other artists, some by Frans Pourbus, some by Crispiaen, and some by others.[18]

Floris's paintings are treasured by art lovers as well as by artists. They are praised highly by many masters. At the home of St Melchior Wijntgis in Middelborgh, is a very excellent painting by Floris which represents *The Nine Sleeping Muses*. I saw also in Middelborgh a large canvas painted by him, a banquet scene of marine deities, in which many nude figures appeared.[19]

In Amsterdam, with Jan van Endt, art lover at the Dam, is a fine large picture which represents Christ calling the children and blessing them. There are splendid faces in this picture; the women wear strange costumes and wrappings; sweet, round-faced children, and other subjects, appear.

There is also a picture, an *Adam and Eve* by Floris which shows the two driven from Paradise. This is an excellent painting, well executed. Then there is still another painting a *Sorrow of Adam and Eve about Abel*.[20]

A collector in Antwerp, Claes Jongling, had very fine paintings by Floris in his new building on the Marck-Graven Leye. First of all, in one of the rooms, named the chamber of Hercules, there were about ten pieces representing the story of Hercules. In another room, the room of the seven liberal arts, were representations of these seven liberal arts. All these subjects were painted splendidly; they were excellent nude studies, and the draperies and composition were most interesting. These, and some other paintings, appeared in re-productions engraved by Cornelis Cort. They were drawn from the pictures by Simon Jansz. Kies from Amsterdam, who was a pupil of Hemskerck and Frans Floris, and who did excellent pen work and cross-hatchings with just a few strokes. But I cannot say where these paintings are now.[21]

The works of Floris have been scattered into many countries, including Spain. They are memorials to his fine art and revelations of his merits.

He was a man who always had a strong desire to paint. Even when he came home half or entirely drunk, he would pick up his brushes and then produce a great amount of work. He seemed to catch the spirit of art under these con-ditions, and to take greater delight in his work in this way. He used to say: 'When I work, I am living; when I indulge in pleasure, I am dying.' Our young men may well take this les-son to heart and follow it.

Frans entered the guild of the painters in 1539. He died in the year 1570, when he was fifty years old. He was honor-ably buried on the day of St Francis.[22]

He left a few sons who became artists. Baptiste Floris was murdered by the Spaniards in Brussels. Another son was Frans, who is at Rome and who receives approbation for little pictures that he makes.[23]

But outstanding is the fact that Frans Floris produced fine pupils. In this respect he excels all other painters in our Netherlands. His pupils became surpassing masters in all kingdoms and lands of Christianity. I have spoken with Frans Menton from Alckmaer, who was a pupil of Floris, as to the reason for this, and for the fact that, at present, the best mas-ters produce so very few good pupils. He replied that Floris had many large works to do and set his assistants to painting in the dead colors (under-painting).[24]

FRANS FLORIS

After he had sketched with chalk the subject he had in mind, Floris allowed the pupils to proceed, saying: 'Now put such and such faces in here.' He had a number of examples on panels always at hand. In this way, his pupils developed a certain bold ability, so that they could lay out large canvases themselves and could make original compositions and paint according to their inspirations.

Men with the best-equipped minds, who had studied previously with other masters for a long time, and who had great experience, came to Floris. Some of the former pupils of Frans once counted that he had had more than one hundred and twenty pupils. I shall mention some of them.[25]

BENJAMIN SAMMELING

FIRST of all, I should mention an old bachelor from Ghent, who is still living, in 1604, and who was born in 1520. He was a good colorist in his time. His pictures, in the Docksael, in the St Jans Kerck in Ghent, were inspired by the drawings of Lucas de Heere and various other works. He made good portraits.[1]

CRISPIAEN VAN DEN BROECKE

CRISPIAEN VAN DEN BROECKE, from Antwerp, was a good master. He made fine original compositions and large and beautiful nudes. He was a good architect. His works can still be seen with many collectors. He died in Holland. I do not know anything else about him; the people who did know about him did not care to give me any information.[1]

JOORIS VAN GHENT

JOORIS VAN GHENT, a pupil of Frans Floris, became a painter to the King of Spain and, later, to the Queen of France.[1]

MARTEN VAN CLEEF

MARTEN VAN CLEEF, Hendrick van Cleef, Lucas de Heere, Anthonis Blocklandt, Thomas from Zierickzee, Simon from Amsterdam, Isaack Claeszen Cloeck, from Leyden, were pupils of Floris. François Menton, of Alckmaer, who is living in Amsterdam, was an intelligent, good master in all branches of art, including drawing and engraving; he painted many portraits from life. By good teaching he has produced able pupils.[1]

GEORGE BOBA

FRANS POURBUS
OF BRUGES

JEROON FRANCKEN
OF HERENTHALS

FRANS FRANCKEN

GEORGE BOBA was a good painter and had originality. Frans Pourbus from Bruges was excellent. Jeroon Francken from Herenthals is still living in Paris in the suburb St Germain. He is a very good master who painted many fine pictures and good portraits from life. His brother, Frans Francken, was an excellent master; he entered the guild of Antwerp in 1561. He died while young.[1]

FRANS FLORIS

AMBROSIUS FRANCKEN

AMBROSIUS FRANCKEN, a third brother, at present still in Antwerp, is a good master, especially as to his compositions and figures. He is a clever painter. I knew him when, in my youth, I lived with Pieter Vlerick at Tournai, and when he was living there with the bishop.

I could have written more about these brothers, if certain persons in Antwerp had taken my questions a little more to heart.[1]

JOOS DE BEER

JOOS DE BEER, from Utrecht, lived with the Provincial of the Bishop of Doornick (Tournai) and died at Utrecht.[1]

FRANS FLORIS

HANS DE MAIER
OF HERENTHALS

APERT FRANCKEN
OF DELFT

HANS DE MAIER, from Herenthals, should be mentioned. Apert Francken, from Delft, does not practice art, but he is a great collector. He has arranged his business well and is a great admirer of Bacchus; he loves wine; he imitates the god daily and takes the greatest delight in doing so.[1]

LOYS
OF BRUSSELS

THOMAS
OF COELEN

DE STOMME
OF NIJMEGEN

HANS DAELMANS
OF ANTWERP

EVERT
OF AMERSFOORT

HERMAN
OF DEN BRIEL

LOYS, from Brussels, was a good painter, lute-player and harpist. I name also: Thomas, from Cologne, De Stomme, from Nimmegen (The Mute from Nimway), Hans Daelmans, from Antwerp, Evert, from Amersfoort, Herman van der Mast, from Den Briel, who now lives at Delft. After the death of Floris, Van der Mast went to live with Frans Francken, and there he copied a *Carrying of the Cross* by Floris, in which Christ is holding his hand on a cross more or less white. While Van der Mast was copying this work, an insect with long legs alighted upon the white of the cross of the original, and he copied this insect, too, with its shadow and all other details. When he came upstairs, the master said: 'I can see that you have not painted too industriously, for a spider is discharging on your picture;' and he sought to chase the animal away with his hat. But it did not move, and the master, seeing that it had been painted, was ashamed and insisted that Van der Mast should not wipe it off.[1]

The next day, Van der Mast showed the painting to his fellow pupil, Gheldorp, and told him the story about his master, and jokingly praised himself, because Zeus had fooled the birds only and he had fooled his own master by painting this little insect. But Gheldorp would not believe him before he was shown the painting.[2]

Van der Mast went to Paris where he lived for two years with the Archbishop of Bourges. There he painted a picture of St Bastiaen, in which the bishop's mule appeared, and various kinds of herbs, all painted from life, very realistically; some herbs appeared stepped on, and others were painted with such care that various persons, among whom was the physician of the King, recognized the species.

By this work he drew the attention of the Bishop to himself and went to live with Sr de la Queste, who was a knight, a president, and general attorney to the King of France. He was entertained here so well and was shown so much friendship that he remained for seven years. For four years he was a shield-bearer to the wife of the nobleman who was one of the ladies-in-waiting to the Queen; he rode with her in her carriage everywhere. Finally, one night, in a masquerade at a carnival, the mother of the Queen gave him a rapier and expressed the desire that he wear it to show that, now, he belonged to the nobility. This scene took place at the request of the lady-in-waiting, and in her very presence, and before other noble ladies and gentlemen. But while Van der Mast lived in this luxurious environment his art did not progress. If he had continued, as he started out, he would have attained still greater excellence in portrait painting from life, and in other branches of art.

DAMIAEN

OF GOUDA[1]

DAMIAEN VAN DER GOUDE was a pupil of Floris. He became an archer in the bodyguard of the King of Spain.

FRANS FLORIS

JEROON VAN VISSENAKEN

STEVEN CROONENBORGH
OF THE HAGUE

DIRCK VAN DE LAEN
OF HAARLEM

JEROON VAN VISSENAKEN and Steven Croonenborgh from the Hague, and Dirck van de Laen from Haarlem, were pupils of Floris. Van de Laen was very good at
painting small pictures; he had studied under Marten van
Cleef.[1]

Many other good masters were scattered in Spain and elsewhere. I recommend the glory of their art to fame.[2]

Lampsonius addresses Floris in about the following
terms:

> Floris, painter, gifted with talent,
> Who by nature was allowed to produce much
>   work,
> If you painted a great amount of work,
> To painting for a long period,
> —Painstaking filer's work and its
>   fatigue did not agree with you—
> I would like to call all painters into assembly
>   and tell them
> To do homage to you by keeping a distance,
> And they would have to do this,
> Independent of the country they were
>   natives and to the period they belonged.

Lucas de Heere, his very devoted pupil, made a panegyric
with the following meaning:[3]

DUTCH AND FLEMISH PAINTERS

Through your art, the fame of Apelles has been silenced.
When a painter has to be praised,
He has to be compared with you,
In order to receive more merit.
Your name of Floris in itself is fame,
For this is the name
Given to the greatest painter.

PIETER AERTSEN
OF AMSTERDAM

NATURE secretly, by some strange process which we cannot understand, works upon youth. This process, taking place beyond the understanding of science, and often against the wishes of the parents, rouses young people to devote themselves to some art, frequently to their benefit. This happened to Pieter Aertsen, an excellent painter from Amsterdam. Because of his great length, he was called 'Langhen Pier.' Whereas his fame travelled far, the Italians called him 'Pietro Lungo.' This means also Langhen Pier; it would not have been a bad family name.

Pieter was born in the year 1519. His parents came from 'Purmer-Landt.' His father lived in Amsterdam and wanted his son to follow the same business as he did, that of stocking maker; but his mother wanted to encourage her son in his great desire to become an artist. She said: 'Even if I have to earn the money with spinning, I shall let him study painting.'

Thus Pieter became a pupil of Alart Claessen, who at that time was one of the best painters of Amsterdam, and of whom portraits can be seen at the Doelen. From his early youth on, Pieter acquired a solid and broad way of painting. He would attempt any kind of subject and won a great reputation through his art.[1]

When he was about seventeen or eighteen, he travelled to the castle of Bossu in Hainault—famous for its beautiful pictures by various masters—with a letter of introduction from the Schout of Amsterdam, Pieter travelled from Hainault to Antwerp, and lived there with a certain Jan Mandijn who was a Walloon. I believe there have been two artists by this name; one is a painter, still in Haarlem, who painted clever drolleries in the style of Jeroôn Bos, and who had a life pension from the city of Antwerp.[2]

Pieter finally married at Antwerp and entered the guild of the painters in 1533. He began painting kitchen subjects and all kinds of food from life and he reproduced the colors so exactly that the objects looked natural. By constant practice of this sort, he undoubtedly became the very best known artist as to the handling of color; and this ability for being so sure of color helped his family to gain its reputation.

Pieter painted a kitchen subject, bought afterwards by Ravart in Amsterdam, and in this picture his second son was portrayed from life. This son, by the name of Aert Pietersz. at that time a little child, is still living. The head of an ox, being skinned by a butcher, appears in the picture among other objects. When this picture had been exhibited, Pieter was commissioned to paint the high altar of the Oude Kerck, or Onse Vrouwe Kerck, in Amsterdam.[3]

It happened that, when Pieter came to the place where the official gentlemen were going to speak with him, he sat near the fire-place and people did not know him to be the painter. He was asked where the master was. There was, among others present, the burgomaster, Joos Buyck, a splendid man, who, in the name of the city, had sworn in the King of Spain and had taken his oath to the country. The burgomaster learned by questioning that Pier was the painter and the son of Aert Pietersz., the stocking manufacturer. He said to the artist: 'If you are as good a painter as your father was a stocking maker, then you are a great artist; for since the death of your father, I have not found anybody who served me as well as he did.'

The central panel of the high altar for the Oude Kerck, was a *Death of Mary* and the interior of the wings completed the subject. The exterior contained the *Three Magi*. This was a splendid work of art; the carnation warm, and the coloristic effect excellent. Vasari writes that this painting cost two thousand crowns.4

Following upon this work, Pier was commissioned to paint the high altar of the Nieuwe Kerck in Amsterdam. Previously, Michiel Cocxie from Malines had been asked to do the work, but when he saw the artistic painting described above, and heard the small price to be paid, he was much astonished, and said: 'The artist who has made this beautiful piece of work will make the other one beautiful too.' The painting in the Nieuwe Kerck was a *Nativity* with four wings. On the interior was an *Annunciation*, a *Circumcision*, and a *Three Magi*, with a kindred subject. On the exterior was a *Beheading of St Catherine*. The cartoon of this painting, as large as the painting itself, is still in Amsterdam. It was a splendid painting, a masterpiece, bold and virile in its conception; the nudes were drawn with great care. From a distance, as it was designed to be seen, this painting produced a tremendous effect. I think no-one could see more powerful brush strokes and a more virile technique.

These beautiful memorials of the great master were destroyed by the vicious hands of raving, insane iconoclasts—a tragic loss to art. Many more of his works were ruined, including a large altar painting with wings.5

At Delft, in the Carthusian monastery, there was a *Crucifixion* by Aertsen; on the inside of the wings was a *Nativity* and a *Three Magi*, and on the outside, a *Four Evangelists* was painted. The high altar at Delft, in the Nieuwe Kerck, bore a *Three Magi* and an *Ecce Homo;* similar subjects were on the wings. There are many more altar paintings by him in such cities as Louvain and Diest; and the cartoons of the paintings he made have remained, amounting to almost twenty-five.6

Many paintings by Pieter Aertsen can be seen in Amsterdam. Jaques Walraven has a *Martha*, with large figures. At the court of Holland, with Master Claes, there is an *Emmaus*, with large figures in it, which is painted well. In the house of Jan Pietersz. Reael, there are a *Joseph* and some similar paintings. Then, there are at Haarlem, with the painter Cornelis Cornelisz., a *Martha*, and, at the Bakenisse Gracht, a picture of a fair.7

Pier was not so good at painting small pictures as at large ones. The latter is really the great thing in art and in this he excelled. He was a clever master who understood very well how to paint architectural subjects and views in perspective. He enlivened his pictures with animals and kindred details, and he would occasionally decorate them in such a way that one was reminded of a masquerade. Many times he sold his pictures for a low price, and Jacob Raeuwaert, in particular, bought many of them in this way.

A large altar painting by Pier existed at Warmen Huysen in the Northern part of Holland. It was a *Crucifixion;* someone is slashing the legs of one of the thieves with a hatchet. The interior of the wings completes the subject.

In 1566, the crowd, in its mad iconoclastic rage, smashed this painting to pieces with hatchets, although Dame Sonneveldt from Alckmaer had offered one hundred pounds for it. At the moment that the painting was about to be taken out of the church, the peasants went mad and smashed it.8

Pieter was often in an incensed state of mind, because the works which he once hoped to leave to the world were destroyed in this tragic way; and many times he had such bitter arguments with the enemies of art that he almost brought himself into danger. He died in Amsterdam in the year of our Lord, 1573, on the second of June, when he was sixty-six years old.9

PIETER AERTSEN

He had three sons who became artists. Pieter Pietersz. was a good master, and he followed closely the style of his father, his teacher; the son did many portraits from life, because, in his time, there were very few orders for large pictures. He painted a *Fiery Furnace*, for the bakers in Haarlem, which is most beautiful in composition; had he chosen to specialize in this kind of work, he would have produced remarkable things. He died in Amsterdam at the age of sixty-two. He was a highly reserved type of man, very eloquent, intelligent, and learned.10

The second son, Aert Pietersz., a man of about fifty-four years, was, in his early youth, a brilliant and industrious artist. He, too, by painting portraits from life, which he did excellently, was kept from painting 'historian' and original compositions, a kind of work for which he had a talent.11

Dirck Pietersz., the youngest, was eight years younger than Aert. He was a pupil of his father. He lived in Fontainebleau, in France, where he perished very miserably during the last war.

Pieter Pietersz., the oldest of the brothers, left a son by the same name who is following the footsteps of his father.12

MARTEN HEMSKERCK

FAMOUS FOR HIS ART

MANY times I have said that our outstanding and leading masters in various countries were born in humble villages, and that they have made these places well known and renowned. In what corner of the world is the village of Hemskerck not well known? It was the place of origin of the great artist and painter, Marten Hemskerck. He was born there in 1498. His father was named Jacop Willemsz. van Veen; he was a laborer in the fields.[1]

In his early youth, Marten felt attracted to the art of painting. He received his first instruction in art, in Haarlem, from a certain Cornelis Willemsz. who was the father of Lucas and Floris, both of whom were good painters, and who had visited Italy, Rome, and other places. Marten's father thought, perhaps, that painting did not promise anything worth while. He took his son home, and wanted him to do agricultural work, and to till the ground. It was most annoying to the young man that he was not allowed to continue in the instruction which he had received.[2]

Marten had a great aversion to peasant work, such as milking cows and similar activities. Once he came home, after milking, with a full pail on his head, and he purposely struck a branch of a tree and spilt the milk. His father became very angry because the fine milk was lost, and he chased him with a piece of wood, to give him a beating. When night came, Marten slept hidden in the hay stack. The next day, his mother supplied him with a knapsack and some travelling money. He passed, the same day, through Haarlem on his way to Delft, where he began to practise painting with a certain Jan Lucas. He was so industrious at drawing and painting in Delft, that he progressed far in a short while.

At that time, Jan Schoorel was famous for the new, extraordinary method of painting which he had imported from Italy, and which especially pleased Marten. So he went to Haarlem and worked under this master.

With his usual zeal, Marten practised so much that finally he surpassed the master, and, so well did he assimilate the style of the master, that it was very difficult to see differences between their works. The master, who was afraid that his reputation was at stake, in the opinion of some people, sent his pupil away; for he was jealous. Marten went to live and work in the house of Pieter Jan Fopsen in Haarlem, where the late Cornelis van Berensteyn used to live.

He made many things in this house: *Sol and Luna*, figures life-size, in a back room of the house, near the bedstead; an *Adam and Eve*, both figures life-size, and it has been said that both nudes were done from life.

The wife of this Pieter Jan Fopsen liked Marten, indeed, and was not satisfied that he was called just Marten; so she told everyone who came to ask for him that they had to call for Master Marten, because he deserved this rightly.

Marten lived next with a certain Joos Cornelisz. who was a goldsmith in Haarlem. Among the many works which Marten made was an altar-piece portraying St Luke, which was painted very artistically. On his departure for Rome, he honored the painters in Haarlem with this gift. One altar-piece represented St Luke seated, and painting Mary from life. She has her Infant on her lap. This painting has been done most splendidly, showing how great an artist Marten was. Nevertheless, it is in the style of Schoorel's painting, and the places where the light falls have sharp edges.3

Mary's face is very beautiful; her pose is fine, and the Infant is very sweet. A drapery in various colors hangs down from Mary's lap. It has ornaments and interesting embroidered decorations which are most pleasing; the representation could not be surpassed.

The face of St Luke was painted from life, and a baker posed for it. This is a beautiful work upon which great care has been bestowed, and which shows with how much zeal the artist followed the model. The palette at the left hand of the Saint seems to come forward from the panel. The whole subject has been painted in such a way that it has to be looked at from below.

Somebody is standing behind St Luke, probably a poet, wearing a wreath of ivy, and doubtless representing Marten himself, painted from life. I do not know what the artist wanted to express by it—whether painting and writing and poetry have to be regarded as closely related arts, for poets as well as painters must have imagination; or did he want to indicate that the very subject of this painting was a beautiful invention? I do not know the real meaning of this.

Marten also painted an angel holding a burning torch, and this picture is well done. I do not know that one can see a greater variety of faces in any other work of Marten's. The architecture in this painting shows various bare walls. Above is a parrot in its cage. Below, a little note has been nailed on the wall, and the following has been written upon it:

> This panel has been given as a memorial,
> It has been wrought by Marten,
> He painted it in honor of St Luke;
> He did so in tribute to his fellow workers.
> We ought to thank him,
> Day and night,
> For his generous gift,
> In the presence of which you are.
> Therefore, let us pray,

MARTEN HEMSKERCK

That God will give him His grace.
He passed away, Anno MVXXXII, on
The twenty-third of May.

This picture is well kept and rightly so by the government officials of Haarlem and is at present in the Princenhof, in the south hall, where many people can see it and praise it. Marten made this painting when he was thirty-four years old, as can be seen by the date of his birth. And then he went to Rome, for which place he had had a strong desire for a long time, he wanted to see the works of the ancient masters and of the Italian artists.

In Rome, Marten was the guest of a cardinal to whom he had a letter. He did not waste his time; neither did he loaf, nor go to banquets with the Netherlanders. He made drawings from antiques and from the works of Michelangelo. He made many studies of ancient ruins, architectural details, and interesting remains of ancient works that may be seen in great abundance in this city which resembles an academy of painting. Generally, when the weather was fine, he would go out to make his sketches.4

Once Hemskerck went out for his usual study. An Italian, one of his acquaintances, went into his room, without Hemskerck knowing about it. He cut two canvases off their frames, and also took away the works of art which the painter had in boxes. When Marten came home he was deeply grieved. He suspected a certain man, and went to see him. He got back nearly everything. Subsequently, he was apprehensive and did not dare to stay long in Rome, because the same Italian might do some other evil thing to him.

Marten returned to the Netherlands. He had been in Rome three years. He had made many beautiful drawings, in the time he was there, and he had earned much money.

When he arrived in Dort, he delivered there a letter which

was from a young man to his father—the lad had been a good acquaintance of his in Rome. The father was staying at an inn that was where the 'Brewery of The Little Anchor', is situated now. At that time the inn was really a murderous hole where travelling merchants and other people were killed secretly.

Marten was invited to stay a night in this place, and another art lover, Pieter Jacops, wished him to stay there; but Marten found a boat which was to sail that same night. This was great luck, for, later on, it became known that a great pit had been found, with many corpses in it, at that very place.5

A daughter of one of these murderers had been in Venice, and had lived there with that very fine artist and young man, Hans van Calcker. When she had to appear before the gentlemen of the court to be questioned, she confessed the truth. She had felt compelled to leave that gruesome house because she did not want to witness such tremendous cruelty, and because her feelings would not allow her to become a traitor to her own parents. For these reasons she was acquitted.

Hemskerck returned to his fatherland. He had changed his style of painting; it no longer resembled that of Schoorel. According to the judgement of the best painters, his style had not improved, except that he did not make such hard edges to the lighted parts. When one of the younger ones told him that, when he had worked in the style of Schoorel, he did better work than when he came from Rome, he answered: 'Son, at that time I did not know what I was painting.' The difference between his two ways of working can be seen in the Prince Hof, in the hall where there are the two wings of the altar of the Drapers. On the interior, are a *Nativity* and a *Three Magi*, two rich compositions with much detail in them. They are painted well and contain many portraits of

MARTEN HEMSKERCK

ordinary people, and also his own. The *Annunciation* is on
the exterior. The faces have been painted from life, and very
well indeed. The angel wears a strange and beautiful dress;
the slips of her under-garment are purple. This detail was
painted by Jacop Rauwaert, who at that time lived with
Hemskerck, and I heard him tell this. One can see in this
work how well Hemskerck painted architecture, and how he
liked to add decorative detail in his paintings, in contradiction to a statement which he used to make many times: 'A
painter who wants to do things well must avoid decorative
detail and architectural ornament.'⁶

One can see something very extraordinary in this painting. The angel is standing on a polished marble pavement,
and the reflection is painted as if he was standing on ice; this
happens on polished marble.

Hemskerck made large works for churches. A double-
winged painting by him existed in the Oude Kerck in Amsterdam. On the interior were subjects relating to the Passion
and on the exterior, a *Resurrection* which was done in a yellow color scheme and produced the effect of brass.⁷

A *Crucifixion* was painted by Marten for the high altar in
the Groote Kerck in Alkmaer. On the interior a *Passion* was
portrayed, and on the exterior the story of St Laurens, all
was painted most artistically.⁸

Many of the paintings of Hemskerck went to Delft. His
panels were in the Nieuwe Kerck, as well as in the Oude
Kerck. In the St Aechte Kerck was an altar panel, *Three
Magi*. He arranged this in such a way that on the interior
central panel and on each wing, one of the three Magi was
represented, and on the exterior was a *Biting of the Serpents*
in black and white. This was a most excellent work, for
which he was paid by a yearly pension of a hundred guilders.
He succeeded in obtaining many similar annuities.⁹

213

There was a double-winged high altar painted by Hemskerck in the village of Eertswout in North Holland. The panels were carved; on the interior, the life of Christ and, on the exterior, the life of Boniface, were illustrated. The whole subject was divided on the various sections; the handling was done cleverly, and the coloring was excellent.

Marten painted the high altar in Medemblick. He made two winged altar paintings, for the Lord of Assendelft—one, a *Resurrection*, the other, an *Ascension*. There was a chapel of the Assendelfts in the Groote Kerck at The Hague.

There is no end to telling of the number of panels, painted subjects, epitaphs, and portraits, Hemskerck made. He was very industrious by nature and a steady worker; he had a fluent style.[10]

Among the many paintings which he accomplished most artistically, a rather large work should be mentioned, which consisted of *Four Extreme Endings, Death, Judgement, Eternal Life,* and *Hell.* It was a superb painting that required much study. There were many nudes and human figures in various poses. A variety of human emotions is to be noticed—the pains of death, the joy of Heaven, and the sorrows and horrors of Hell. This piece was ordered from him by his pupil, Jacob Ravaert, mentioned before, who was a splendid art collector in his time; he paid Hemskerck so many golden ducats that the painter said he had enough.[11]

I have seen a little oblong picture by Hemskerck of a Bacchanalia or Bacchic festival. I saw it first with Pauwels Kempenaer, an art collector, and later on with the great collector, Melchior Wijntgens. This picture was frequently reproduced in prints; it is really the best of all the pictures he painted after he returned from Rome. The work is very 'morbido;' the nudes are in a blending of soft shades. One can see in this picture all kinds of amusements that the pagans loved. A beautiful landscape, with a splendid background in it, and a St Christopher, can be seen with Aernout van Berensteyn.[12]

Hemskerck was versatile. He had experience in painting many subjects and a very good knowledge of the nude. Sometimes he may be criticized a little for a Netherlandish dryness in the figures; also, as has been said before elsewhere, that his faces sometimes lacked a certain grace and kindness—qualities that make the work of an artist so much more beautiful.

There is no telling how many prints, after his works, were circulated. He illustrated many of the witty, allegorical poems of Dirick Volcketsz. Coornhart; he did not engrave the illustrations. He left the engraving to various artists, for whom he made a remarkable number of fine drawings, and among whom was the above-mentioned Coornhart, whose spirit, knowledge, and hands were able to understand and to execute all that is possible to be understood and to be done by man.[13]

Etchings and engravings made by Coornhart were particularly deft. They were a series on the life of the Emperor. A single exception, the one of the King of France made a prisoner, was done by a certain Cornelis Bos.

After Marten came from Rome, he remained for some time an old bachelor, and then he married a beautiful young girl named Marie, the daughter of Jacob Coninghs. The rhetoricians played a comedy in honor of the wedding. A year and a half later his wife died in childbirth. Three or four years later, Marten painted the wings to the *Massacre of the Innocents* by Cornelis Cornelisz., in the Princenhof in Haarlem; this picture has been mentioned before. Marten was married a second time to an older girl, endowed with neither much beauty nor with wisdom, but with wealth. She was so covet-

ous of the goods of others that she bought many things without paying for them, or, so to say, she found things before
they were lost. This grieved Marten very much; he advised
people not to sue her, and as an honest man, he paid for the
things she found.[14]

Marten was, for twenty-two years, a church-warden in
the city of Haarlem, until he died. When the city was besieged by the Spaniards in 1572, he had a leave of absence
from the city council and lived in Amsterdam with Jacob
Ravaert.[15]

He was by nature thrifty and niggardly. He was faint-
hearted and so easily frightened that, when the militia held
a parade, he climbed into the upper part of the tower; so
afraid was he of their shooting, he did not feel safe otherwise.
Marten always had a fear that he might come to poverty in
his old age, and for this reason he always carried gold crowns
hidden in his clothing, till his death.

When Haarlem fell into the hands of the Spaniards, many
of Hemskerck's paintings were obtained by them, under pre-
tense of wanting to buy them. The pictures were sent to
Spain. Many excellent art works by him were destroyed by
the insane image breakers. The result was that, at present, not
much of his painting is to be found in this country.[16]

Marten was a wealthy and powerful man; he did not leave
any children. He made many beautiful donations to be given
after his death. Among the gifts was a piece of land, the revenue of which was to be spent as wedding gifts for young
couples who married upon his grave. This custom has been
observed regularly.[17]

He had a blue stone pyramid, or memorial obelisk, erected
on his father's grave in the cemetery at Hemskerck. At the
highest point on the obelisk, a portrait of his father was
carved. The epitaph is in Latin and in Dutch, and a child is

standing on dead men's bones which are afire. This child is leaning on a torch and rests the right foot on a skull. This seems to be intended for an emblem of immortality. Below is written: 'Cogita mori.' At the bottom is Hemskerck's family crest: In the right field, above, there is a half double eagle; in the left, a lion; the lower half of the shield, under this, bears a nude arm which holds a pen or a brush. The upper arm is winged; the elbow is resting on a tortoise. I believe this illustrates the advice of Apelles, to be not too slow in work, and to not overload the mind with too much work. This was recommended to Protogenius, as has been told elsewhere. Marten left, also, the revenue of a piece of land for the upkeep of the pyramid, and if it should fall, the land would become the property of friends.[18]

Marten had a clever way of drawing with a pen; he could do beautiful and clear cross-hatching.

His self-portraits, in oil-color, showing various ages, are in Alckmaer in the house of Jaques van der Heck, who is a nephew of his. They are expertly and beautifully painted.

After Marten had served as a remarkable light to his time, he passed from this perishable life in 1574, on the first day of October, at the age of seventy-six, having lived two years fewer than his father. His body was buried in the Groote Kerck in Haarlem, in the chapel at the north side of the church. As his art was a beacon that will not leave his name in darkness as long as the art of painting is esteemed and kept in honor by man.[19]

RYCKAERT AERTZOON

WHO can understand and tell what kind of stimulating, pure air the sea may breathe over the corner of North Holland, so the land there will produce at times such noble and impressionable minds in painting, as it has at Schoorel, at Beverwyck, at Hemskerck, and at Wyck op de Zee? A strong vocation for art among the peasant youth was discovered, and yet they had hardly any attractive examples which they could follow.

In the seaside village of Wijk aan Zee, there lived a fisher named Aert, and his son Rijck. In an accident Rijck burned his leg badly. He was sent to Haarlem to receive medical treatment. The leg was amputated. As the boy sat often near the fire, Nature inspired him to draw. He had no examples; but his urge was so strong that he began to draw figures on the white wall of the chimney with coal from the fire. He was then asked if he wished to become a painter. He wanted this most ardently; he became a pupil of Jan Mostart. Because he had to use a crutch, he was called 'Ryck metter Stelt.' He studied hard and became a good master.[1]

Rijck painted the wings of the altar belonging to the guild of the Carriers. The altar painting itself had been done by master Jacob who was the teacher of Jan Mostart. Rijck painted on these wings a *Brothers of Joseph Coming into Egypt and Asking for Wheat*. Joseph sits, like a king, in great majesty. Rijck painted other kindred subjects on these wings. There were many pictures by Rijck in Friesland. Many paintings by him are lost, and I am not able to trace them.[2]

Rijck was a quiet, capable man, peaceful, virtuous and

218

pious. He loved the Holy Scriptures, and valued tranquillity of mind. He finally went to live in Antwerp where, for the sake of his peace of mind, he painted only the nudes in the works of other painters, and for humble wages. He did not want any of his children to study art. When he reached an advanced age, Rijck's sight began to fail; he could not see what he was making. He smeared the paint so heavily on the panels that nobody wanted to have his paintings. He had to scrape them down many times, and it sometimes made him cross that people no longer wanted his pictures.[3]

He entered the guild of the painters of Antwerp in 1520. This guild was called the 'Violiere bloem' and it had the following device: 'Uit jonsten versaemt.' This guild was formed in the year 1400.

Frans Floris painted Rijck's portrait in a picture, St Luke painting the Virgin, intended for the assembly room of the painters. Rijck's memory was beloved and cherished. Frequently Rijck said: 'Ick ben ryck en wel gestelt.' He had a pleasing and artistic face.[4]

Rijck died about a year after the Spanish Fury, in May, 1577, at the age of ninety-five.

LAMBERT LOMBARDUS had a wide reputation for high achievement in the art of the Netherlands, because he was the first to practise painting by a new, improved method. He had many pupils, and among them was Hubert Goltzius, of Venlo, who, originally, had come from Würzburg, where his family had been born.[1]

In the house of Lombardus, Hubert had seen many antique things of Roman origin, and others from Germany, and from places left by the old Franks. He became interested in these antiquities and, aided by his learning, he studied these old Roman objects. He obtained a rare knowledge, and, with the assistance of Sr Van Watervliet, published many valuable and unusual works on these topics.[2]

Hubert published in one large volume a collection of all the medals having the faces of the Roman Emperors, a work that cost much and required a great amount of labor. These medals, printed in various colors, were engraved in wood, and for the work he used a painter from Courtrai who was a man of great knowledge, and very clever. His name was Joos Gietleughen, a name, however, that did not reflect the life of the man.[3]

These portraits of the Emperors were very fine and ingenious; rather large, they began with Julius Caesar and ended with Charles V and Emperor Ferdinand. When no medal nor coin was found, an empty circle was substituted.

Hubert proved in this work that he had very accurate judgement and knowledge which he used both in producing striking resemblances, and in the descriptions of the lives of the subjects, often in the face of resentment of inaccurate writers.

The book was published by him in various languages. He lived at that time at Bruges in Flanders. He had his own printing plant where everything was at its best, and where he had the beautiful types. He did not keep an open shop.4

Goltzius published many other books which are highly valued by scholars and which are most remarkable. First of all, in the year 1563, he published a book in Latin entitled *Caius Julius Caesar—The History of the Roman Emperor from Ancient Medals*. He added to this *The Life of Julius Caesar*, a work dedicated to the Emperor Ferdinand.5

He published another Latin book in the year 1566. Its title was *Fastes*, and it dealt with the rulers and the conquests of the ancient Romans from the founding of Rome until the death of Augustus. All this material was illustrated with medals engraved by himself and with beautiful explanations. This second book was dedicated to the Senate and municipal council of Rome. Consequently, he received, in 1567, a sealed document by which the noble title of citizen of Rome was bestowed upon him because of his excellence and learning; and in this document he was declared a most worthy ornament of the city and was allowed to enjoy all the privileges of a Roman citizen. One can read this in the copy of the document printed in the book on Caesar Augustus.6

Goltzius published a second work on Caesar Augustus in the year 1574, showing the obverse and the reverse sides of medals, which was an account of Caesar in Latin, and which was divided into two volumes.7

In 1576, he published a Latin book, entitled *Cicilia et Magna Graecia*, which dealt with the history of the cities and the populations of Greece, and contained Greek medals and their descriptions. He published still other books in which he showed his great zeal and firm desire to revive the memories of the beautiful antiquity of that most illustrious empire. All of these books are excellent; they were beautifully printed in large volumes.[8]

I am not able to tell you much about his work in the art of painting with colors. I know that he was employed in Antwerp to make paintings for the Hanseatic League at the time of the festivities of the Golden Fleece. He made many works. He attacked his problems boldly with a strong technique.[9]

His first wife was the sister of the last wife of Pieter Koeck van Aelst, by whom he had some children, and being a Roman, he gave them Roman names such as Marcellus, Julius, and kindred names. While he was married to this woman, he took her to Rome, but she had no notion of it; she believed that she was in Cologne.[10]

While he lived in Bruges, Goltzius made it something of a pastime to listen to a gray monk named Brother Cornelis; and it has been said that he wrote up and published the sermons of this monk. He made a portrait of him in oil, on a portrait panel, seen almost from the front. He did this from memory and it resembled the monk very closely. He gave the portrait the same angry expression that the monk had when people provoked him with lampoons. As for its artistic value, it was done well. I have seen the picture and had it in my hand.[11]

Goltzius was married a second time, and to a woman of not very good reputation. This grieved his children and friends deeply. He lost his peace of mind, was harmed by it, and disgraced himself. This has happened to other learned and intelligent men, who, deploring the infidelities of some women, believed that they should be able to correct them through reasoning, and to ameliorate their desires, acquired by bad habits, through good education.[12]

Goltzius gave one of his books on medals, beautifully

bound, to Antonio Moro. Moro said that he could reward him only with his own art. He invited Goltzius once or twice in the morning to pose for him in order to make his portrait, but after a good breakfast he let him go home again. After three such visits, Moro painted a remarkable portrait of Goltzius within the space of one hour, or even less. It resembled the subject closely, for Moro had been making a mental picture of Goltzius all the while, and had been studying his most characteristic features.

This portrait of Goltzius is still at Bruges, in the possession of the widow of Goltzius or her friends. An engraving has been made from this painting and printed in one of Goltzius's books.[13]

The books of Goltzius were embellished with various Latin panegyrics. The following epigram was made in his honor by the English Ambassador:

> In effigiem Huberti Goltzii, ab Antonio Moro expressam, Danielis Rogerii Angli Epigramma.
>> Goltzion arte parem pingendi cernis Apelli,
>> Sculpendique parem, culte Lysippe, tibi,
>> Notitia imperii Graii, pariterque Latini,
>> Varronem similem, Pausaniaeque simul.

This means:

> Epigram by Daniel Rogier, Englishman, on the portrait of Hubert Goltzy, painted by Antonis Moro:
>> You are beholding here an artist equal to Apelles,
>> A man worthy to be compared with Lisip for his engraving.
>> A man of science equal to Varro in the Roman empire,
>> And to Pausanias the Greek.

Hubertus Goltzius died at Bruges, in the year of our Lord 1583, or at about that time.[12]

PIETER VLERICK
OF COURTRAI

AND

CAREL
OF YPRES

NOW and then it happens that young artists, from early youth, are guided and directed firmly by their natural disposition and their frame of mind. They are raised to a higher level and follow a more exalted path than do their fellow artists and contemporaries, who persist in an inferior way of working for the sake of small daily wages, hardly sufficient for a little food. The works of the latter are often not worthy of being called paintings—better, daubs, like the ones seen in some towns, and only good enough to be handled by vendors who travel from market to market.

It is to be regretted, however, that some noble minds after reaching the summit of perfection through labor, and zeal, and practice, seem to look neither forward nor round carefully enough, when the road to honor and prosperity is open to them. They could have reaped the finest fruit, enjoyed the greatest privileges, received honor, and profit, in the splendid towns where wealthy merchants live. The ancient painters are said to have visited the largest and best cities because of city-wealth. They did not follow their preference for a special region; they visited all countries and made themselves at home there.

Those who are blinded by a ridiculous, idle, and empty, love for the place where they were born, or who have an exaggerated love and affection for their parents, to such an extent that nothing can come between their parents and themselves, might be regarded as being in a most unfortunate state of mind. Their affection becomes completely useless, when they suddenly marry a poor person with whom they are hardly acquainted, and when they become a burden to their parents and friends, because they cannot carry the heavy expenses of a household. They are not able to help themselves. They remain deep in poverty, suffering under the most miserable afflictions, paying too high a price for their wilful and innate laziness and lack of energy. These people, after travel and visits to remote countries and foreign cities, dislike very much to live among foreign people as unwanted and rejected strangers. After all, man is drawn by nature to his own country and to his own people. They regret that they did not study the neighboring cities and countries, while they were still at home, among people of their own nationality, and with those who spoke their own language.

They might have selected a place which would have offered greater possibilities than their native place. They resemble birds, in this respect: It has been said that birds love to live where they were bred.

An Italian proverb may be quoted here. It expresses this idea more strongly: 'Tristo e l'augello che nasce in cattivo valle.' This means: 'Unfortunate is the bird which has been bred in a miserable valley.' Nature causes it to love its environment and to remain there, whether a region be cold or rough or bare, and only because the dear mother of the birds had built a nest there. The same tendency can be noticed when the poor birds foolishly follow bitter winter, like miserable wanderers and wretched pilgrims. They are not as careful as storks and swallows which fly in large flocks; they are not like kindred, summer-loving birds which take more pleasure in the aromatic, sweet, western wind than in the fierce, cold blasts of northern snow-vomiting blizzards.

It is said that the people who live in the wild mountains of Piedmont, in the awful Alps, where there is snow all year around, come down to the cities to buy their provisions in the markets. In these cities the conditions are more human. These people are generally in a great hurry to return to their customary poverty and frugal, miserable existence. They have large goiters, caused by drinking snow-water. I like to compare these unfortunate people to the winterbirds. And one could regard as similar to them, those artists who have excellent talents, who establish themselves in their poor, native towns, where art is hardly known, appreciated, and kept in honor.

Pieter Vlerick was one of these unfortunate persons. He was born in Courtrai in 1539. His father was a jurist, a linguist, and an attorney. When he saw that his son loved drawing, he sent him to study under a water-color painter by the name of Willem Snellaert, who lived outside the gate of Tournai; he painted on fabric and was a little better than the other painters in that city.[1]

At that same time a great deal was being said about the extraordinary, clever way of drawing and painting of Carel van Ypres, and, finally, Pieter was sent to study under this artist. He saw an entirely different style of work and assimilated it gradually. Carel often painted feet somewhat large and deformed, and Pieter accentuated them even more, because he thought the effect was better.[2]

Carel was not a tall person, but he was brave and cranky and irritable. One evening in Ypres people were baking pancakes, called 'kespen,' and each person had to turn the pan himself. When it was Pieter's turn to throw up the pancake, the buttered cake landed right in the face of the master, who certainly felt the heat of it, and it was greasy, at that. Pieter was sorry, for this incident caused a great deal of argument.

Carel, on another evening, had guests, and, rather drunk, he came into the workshop where he showed the paintings to the guests. He wanted Pieter to hold a candle; but Pieter did not light the pictures as Carel wanted, so he struck him on the head with his fist and Pieter fell down on one side and the candle on the other.

The boy could not endure this unreasonable treatment. Early the next morning he left Ypres and went to Courtrai, without taking leave of his master. The father of the boy was a severe man who did not want to believe his boy and how the event had happened; he scolded the boy badly, chided him for running away, and said that Pieter would never amount to anything. He took his horses immediately and went to Ypres. The boy, no matter how tired he was, had to go along. The distance was, as far as I know, five miles. The father wanted to find out the truth of this affair.

When they arrived in Ypres, the father noticed that Carel did not have much to say, and that he was in the wrong entirely. But the father did not want to admit that his son was in the right, in the presence of the master. Carel was paid, and the father took Pieter away with him. When they returned home, he gave Pieter little or almost no money and ordered him to leave, to seek his fortune elsewhere, and told him to be ashamed.

So it happened that the poor boy was no older than twelve or fourteen years when he finally arrived at Malines. It was on a Sunday and a Holy Day, and the people of Malines were walking outside of the town. Pieter was sitting by the road, resting.

A youth, without friends and acquaintances, and not knowing where to go, is likely to feel sad. Pieter was weeping. Some of the passersby asked him why he cried, if he had a trade, and other questions. Pieter said he was a painter. There were always many water-colorists in Malines, and one of them took Pieter home with him.

The artists there had a way of working by which the canvases had to pass through many hands. One made faces and hands, another costumes or landscapes. Pieter worked on the sections in which the lettering came. He was so good at this, and other work, that various masters tried to get Pieter away from his own master. They quarrelled over Pieter, and had arguments.

Pieter, realizing how good a master he was, left Malines for Antwerp; he thought he did not have to worry any more. He landed in Antwerp with an oil-painter who wanted him to make a copy of a *Brazen Serpent* which this artist had painted himself. He insisted that Pieter should follow his style very closely. Pieter thought the style hardly good enough for the painting of cats and dogs, but said, 'Yes.'

Pieter did not stay long in this place; he worked in one shop after another, till he finally arrived at the studio of Jaques Floris, the brother of Frans.

One evening, Pieter and his fellow pupils assisted the master in playing a joke. Jaques Floris saw his brother arriving from a distance with a light. He arranged that his pupils run at Frans with bare swords, striking the pavement with them; this clatter made Frans run as fast as he could.

When Pieter was grown up, he left the country and travelled first to France and then to Italy. He stayed a long time in Venice with Tintoretto, who took a lively interest in his work; and Pieter had an eager interest in the master. It seems that had he not craved for travel, he might have married the daughter of Tintoretto and this should not have been so bad for him. From Venice, and other cities, he went to Rome.

PIETER VLERICK AND CAREL

I believe that he had a travelling companion by the name of Hans in den Booghe.3

Pieter was in Naples, where he saw such strange scenery there as Pozzuoli and other places. In Rome, he made drawings of beautiful views of the Tiber, as seen from the city and of the castle of St Angelo, and of many ruins. He used to say that even though he had no money to count, he could count the ruins. These views were done with the pen, and most excellently. He rendered the characteristics so cleverly and surely that they could not be surpassed. He had almost the style of the pen-drawing by Hendrick van Cleef.

I have seen these works by Pieter, hung in a shop. He took them down again because they reminded him of Rome; they made his heart ache because he was not there any more. It was easier for him to earn money than to save it. He had this in common with many of his fellow Netherlanders who were too fond of good wine and who consequently and most of the time had little left.

Once at a party many of the guests left, thinking that everybody else had a bulging purse. When the bill had to be paid, no-one had any money. What could they do? They gave their stockings to the inn keeper for security; they took blacking and painted their legs; they put on their shoes and garters and left the place. It looked as if they had the finest kind of stockings. At the time, one of the artists was completing a picture. It was soon finished and sold; with the money received, their stockings were redeemed.

Pieter made many drawings in Rome, from antiquities and from Michelangelo's *Last Judgement* and his sculpture.4

Pieter also made more than one *Adoration,* in which interesting ruins were painted—a great many little figures and similar things. He became adept at working with various methods; he painted fresco, too.

At Tivoli, with Girolamo Muziano, Pieter painted the figures in the landscape which Muziano made in the palace of the court of the D'Este; and he painted other compositions which show how experienced a painter he was. He was in Rome at the time of Pope Pius IV.5

He had fantastic and serious experiences on his travels. In Germany, he and his companions lodged in places where people, after feasting and drinking in an inn, had died; they had to sleep in the beds from which the dead had been removed. By the grace of God the fellows were not harmed!

In Italy, a funny thing happened to the comrades. In a little town, they came to a painter's shop where they asked for work. The master there refused them and they went further. Then they were waved at to come back. A gentleman or citizen had asked what kind of people they were; the master had answered that they were painters looking for work; the gentleman wanted to give them work. For this reason he had called the painters back.

The comrades believed that these people wanted them to go away, for the Italians wave with a vertical, downward movement of the hand and not, as we do, with a movement upwards—this the Italians regard as an evil sign. Thus they were in doubt as to whether they should run away, or not, since they might have done something wrong. But they learned that they were really being called back.

When he returned to his native town in Flanders, Pieter was welcomed with great joy by his old acquaintances. He made water-colors on canvas; these were much admired by certain painters who knew a little more about this sort of work than the others did.

One day, on an oblong canvas, Pieter painted a *Serpent Scene* with large figures. It made a fine effect, and it was painted well. He painted a *Four Evangelists*, displaying fine heads, and a hand, on a table, represented as foreshortened. The drapery was beautiful. There was a face in it with a very serious expression. He made a canvas of *Judith* putting the head of Holofernes into a bag; the dead head is painted excellently.[6]

Vlerick painted a *Crucifixion*, an upright painting on which Mary and St John are represented; the drapery is beautiful and everything in it painted well. The dead body of Christ hangs quite differently from the way it is usually represented by other painters. Pieter painted the body in collapse as a dead body is likely to be, and the legs and knees were not in the straight position, as many painters have represented them.[7]

Pieter was excellent at rendering of architecture, at the painting of temples, and at perspective. I may say I have never seen pictures which were done so cleverly. He knew how to represent columns most effectively; he rendered colored marble beautifully, employing the relief of the flutes and the fillets; and he rendered floors and kindred details with a certain pleasing smoothness.

He enlivened temple scenes with figures; among others, Christ driving the merchants from the temple, a scene in which many figures were represented, and in all kinds of action. He painted antique water basins in which fishes were swimming while children played with them. Occasionally, Pieter painted a royal palace in which Solomon was represented seated on a very fine throne and pronouncing his first judgement, that by which the real mother of the living child was detected. He painted an *Annunciation* in which the carved, wooden chairs and benches were rendered most cleverly, and in which there was a vista into another room.

Pieter made a composition, called the *Martyrdom of the Seven Maccabees*, showing torture and cruel killing. This is a

realistic work and has been painted well. Pieter painted a
Susanna and the Elders, which looked very natural. There
was a fountain, the basin of which was a marmor shell carried
by sea gods and goddesses with split fish tails. They were
made of brass, and their various reflections were painted; also
the places where the brass had become green, covered with
moss from the water. Pieter did not hesitate to paint a picture
from one of Titian's prints which represented *Joseph and
Potiphar's Wife.* It is the scene in which Joseph is dragged to
the bed, but escapes. He painted an *Annunciation* which he
took from an engraving made by an Italian. An angel is pointing to heaven with one hand, and with the other he holds his
costume and a lily. A group of angels is descending with the
Holy Ghost in a light from above. He painted little, floating
clouds, and the rays of light on the architecture, transparent-
ly and beautifully. All was done with such knowledge that it
could not have been surpassed. Similarly, the figures, the
draperies, the faces, and the nudes, were done remarkably
well; the architecture and the floor were excellent. I have
never seen any better work in water-color. Pieter Vlerick
made a small picture of the same subject in oils, for a brewer
by the name of Jan Bonte, and this, too, was very good. He
made a few small pictures of Mary, which were fine; and a
large nude of St Jerome, kneeling, with his forearm and hand
on a skull; the body and a part of his back are seen from the
side.[8]

Pieter painted an ecclesiastical banner on the subject of
St Barbara. On one side of it, she is represented with a palm
wreath; on the other side, she is lying beheaded, and her father, with his sword in his hand, is taken away in the air and
overcome by the devil. This picture was painted in oil-color.

Pieter painted a *Passion scene* which showed Christ nude,
seated at his grave, and beside him the instruments of the Pas-

sion, similar to those placed in front of the altar during Lent. This picture, with all its details, was done in a masterly manner.

It would be impossible for me to mention all Pieter's works, especially his water-colors, which were excellent. And what is the use? Even if he had been Apelles or some other superior, ancient painter, there were no talents at Courtrai to be earned by him. It caused much comment when Pieter was able to sell his canvases for three or four pounds.[9]

He married and raised a little family. He went to live in Tournai because he had received an order for a memorial from a canon, a certain Monseur du Prez. The panel, a rather large one, was a *Resurrection*, painted at Courtrai; after the dead coloring was done, it was placed in the sun and it burst. The panel had to be re-glued and re-planed. He had a great deal of trouble with it. It was a beautiful composition.

Pieter finally went to live in Tournai about the year 1568 or 1569. This meant very much as though, according to an old saying, he had come from hell and had gone to purgatory. There was not much for him to do in this town, as it was not a town of wealthy merchants. The Walloons did not know much about the art of painting; they did not love it. He received, for a large oil-painting, no more than three Flemish pounds.

Pieter painted the wings for the picture in Tournai afterwards, and he decorated the woodwork in an exquisite way. He gilded every part of it which had to be golden. He painted the rough wood with a mixture of brown ochre and a soot color; the medium was glue. He scratched this with a little stick, and this gave an effect of some rare wood. Afterwards, the work was varnished and it looked very well.

Before he could exercise his trade freely in Tournai, Pieter had other difficulties: The painters in that place had a guild,

233

of which the dean and other officers had quite their own way of handling matters concerning art. No-one was allowed to practice painting according to his own free will, or allowed to open a workshop unless he was born in Tournai, and had worked a few years under a free, local master. They had other protective rules for barring strangers, no matter how great artists they might be. Similar rules prevailed in Paris and in other large cities, and they are very unreasonable.[10]

O Pictura, Thou art the most noble and the most enlightening art of all, the Mother of all the decorative arts, and the Foster Mother of the most noble and virtuous arts! Thou dost not have to yield place to any of thy Sisters, called the Liberal Arts. Thou wert appreciated so thoroughly by the noble Greeks and Romans, who welcomed thy artists full-heartedly, wherever they came from, and whose rulers and magistrates made citizens of them.

Oh, the present centuries are ungrateful! It became possible in nearly all cities, with the exception of Rome, for the noble art of painting to be forced into guilds by the pressure of inefficient daubers who made the most shameful laws and narrow rules. And what kind of guilds! The same as were formed for all kinds of course handwork and trades, such as weaving, the furriers' trade, carpentry, forging, and similar activities.

At Bruges, in Flanders, painting has not a guild of its own, but is associated with harness-making! At Haarlem, where noble artists have been always, the painters belong to a guild in which are also the tinkers, the tinners, and the dealers in second-hand clothing!

Although a reason exists for this affiliation in these two cities, matters have developed so far that hardly any discrimination is made between painting and the work of a cobbler, or of a weaver, or kindred activities. Ignorance and lack of common sense are the cause of this urge to form a guild. The right to be a painter must be bought with money. Masterpieces in painting have to be produced in the same fashion as the works of cabinet makers, tailors and other tradesmen— and this sounds still worse: Painting is now called a trade.

Oh noble Art, how far thou hast descended! How little appreciation is given to thy noble followers who begin to show the light they received!

Great emperors, kings and princes used to value thee highly, and to hold thee in great esteem, and give to thee from the wealth of the cities. They were in need of noble work. And at present thou art in a guild with harness makers, with tinsmiths, with tinkers, with glaziers, and with old cloth dealers. Princes, magistrates, and governments not only tolerate this, they confirm it, and take measures that scandalize and dishonor thee. Oh noble Pictura, not only are these rules maintained, but they will remain effective. No no honor to those that will be praised more for it. Oh, we are consideration is given to the disgrace to thee, Pictura. It is living in ungrateful times!

But Pieter had to produce a masterpiece. This was his *Massacre of the Innocents*—a water-color on canvas, and a fine composition. In the foreground, a building with a mêlée of soldiers and women with children; in the background, a vista of a town with a market scene and a pleasant group of houses and people.

The dean of the guild and the other daubers looked and looked at this work, and they might have looked upon a millstone. The work, however, was approved; it was accepted as a masterpiece, and Pieter was allowed to call himself a master, although he had had not a few difficulties in bringing things so far. He would not have succeeded without the assistance of the canon, who secured, moreover, the assistance of the

Bishop of Tournai. Finally, the guild granted his admission, although somewhat reluctantly.

Pieter, living at Tournai, accepted every order that came his way. He painted statues and bellows. It is to be regretted that he had to do these jobs, and that he could not devote his skill and time to something more important. He wished often that the time would come when people would say, 'Give me a measure of wheat, serve me first!'—as in the time of scarcity, when wheat is very expensive and needed, and each man wants to be served first. He often made a portrait for a small price. He once painted an altar-piece for some humble nuns, in oil-color. It was oblong, and the central rectangular panel held a *Crucifixion*; at one side, in the foreground, a thief was sitting in a cart, and consoled by a father confessor; others were digging a hole in the ground to erect a cross; some one was lying on the ground and, with his sleeve pulled up, was getting something out of the pit—probably a stone which interfered with the digging. In the center, Christ, on the cross, was somewhat dimly in the background. A ray of light came from behind a somber, dark sky, and illuminated the figure from one side, but the figure of Christ was for the most part in shadow. Pieter had the paintings and compositions of Tintoretto in mind when he painted this. The effect was not displeasing to painters and to people who understood art; but the humble little nuns were not pleased with it. Furthermore, in the background, some people were busy crucifying the other thief. Gamblers were represented, some beautiful horses with fine heads, and various details, which gave a fine effect. He received very few orders for such work; occasionally only a small one, and then there was little profit in it.[11]

Pieter had the same difficulties as other artists had, and he shared their opinions with them; they did not like strangers to become master painters; one should not paint even a

portrait. Pieter seemed to have had a liking for legal processes. He sued the guild and others. This led to his decorating a
room with grotesques for a certain lawyer. He was good at
this kind of work, worth a good deal of money in this instance, and done in order to advance his own case as much as
possible. Every day he could be seen with a bunch of papers
and letters in his hand, as if he was a barrister, or a jurist.

Pieter was very angry with a painter, Michiel Gioncquoy,
who had just come from Rome. This painter, who came from
Tournai, had painted a large number of little pictures, on
copper, in Rome, of crucifixions. He had made stencils for
these pictures, and he copied them in large numbers. He had
a special way of finishing them, neatly and accurately. The
backgrounds were black, and a little foreground was below.
He earned rather good sums from these, for the Spaniards
and other people were well pleased with this work.

I have mentioned Pieter in the biography of Sprangher.
Joncquoy criticized an arm which appeared in the *Resurrection* Pieter had made in the memorial for Monsignor du
Préz, mentioned before. He not only criticized him daily for
it, but he took paint and spoiled the thing. He meant to improve the picture; this was merely conceit and foolish self-
esteem on the part of an artist who hardly knew how to
draw, and who lacked intelligence and inventive power, all
the more discreditable to a painter who lived in the same
town where the original artist had produced the work.

Consequently, Pieter had good reason to be very angry
with Joncquoy; it was a most uncivil attitude for a man who
could scarcely be compared to him in artistic ability.

Finally, Pieter painted a picture of Venus; it has been said
that his wife posed for the nude. This painting was highly
praised. As told before, Vlerick lived where he did not reap
much benefit from his artistic achievements. The wars that

developed, the internal troubles of the country, and the disasters, did not lead to his profit.

He was made a prisoner by the soldiers between Courtrai and Tournai, and he had many consequent difficulties. He had two or three very beautiful, young daughters, and he took pleasure in dressing them in the Italian fashion; two of them died of pest and, finally, he died too, of the same disease, in 1581, on Shrove Tuesday, at the age of forty-four years and a half. He was a man with a keen, artistic, mind who thought modestly about himself.

I lived with him for about a year. Many times he said to me: 'If I did not know that you are going to be a better master than I myself, I would advise you to stop.'

Frequently he praised Frans Floris and other artists such as Veronese, Titian, Tintoretto, Raphael, Correggio. He used to speak often of a painting that was a *Crucifixion* in the church of Cremona.[13]

I should not be fair if I had omitted Pieter. He was my second and final master. Most of his works are in Tournai and Courtrai; yet, there are not so many, and they are seldom to be seen any more. He fully deserves to be mentioned, because he was an all-round artist and experienced in various kinds of art work. I recommend his name to posterity for his honesty; and may he remain famous.

When Pieter was living at Courtrai, he had a pupil by the name of Lowijs Heme, who came from this town and whose work was very similar to that of the master, specially in architectural detail and in perspective. He is the best of the painters in Courtrai.[14]

We now leave the subject of Pieter Vlerick, and return to his second master, Carel van Ypres. He came from Ypres. I do not know when he was born and under whom he studied.

PIETER VLERICK AND CAREL

Carel lived in Ypres, where he produced many works—façades of houses, panels for churches, and various other things for some of the monasteries in that neighborhood, and among these some were done on the wet lime of the wall.

I have seen a *Conversion of St Paul* in the house of the canon in Tournai, a painting done in black and white, and displaying large figures. I also saw a *Resurrection*, done in oil-colors on a panel. It was a kind of cover which could be placed over some treasure chest. This was not painted at all badly.

A Last Judgement, a large painting by Carel, was in the church of Hooghlede near Roesselaer. His pupil, Claes Snellaert, the son of the first master of Pieter Vlerick, had assisted him with the painting of some dim effect, far away in the sky, and with some other details.[15]

This Claes was fairly good at drawing, at rendering architectural detail, cartouches, and other decorative elements. He died in 1602, in the town of Dordrecht, at the age of sixty.

I have seen a *Last Judgement*, by Carel, which had been drawn on a sheet of Lombardy with a pen. The sister of Carel gave this to a painter who had taken care of her husband. I think this was a preliminary study of the previous painting. It was very fine, and there was considerable movement in the picture. It was somewhat in the style of Tintoretto. Christ was seated on clouds, and, below Him, the four Evangelists were represented.

Carel made drawings for the glass painters. A very beautiful window, for which Carel made the cartoons, is in the St Jans Kerck at Ghent. This is a realistic work of art.[16]

Carel visited Italy and other countries, and everywhere in Flanders he was well esteemed and praised for his art; he surpassed many other painters in the country; but with other painters of high achievement in Brabant and in Holland, he would hardly stand comparison. He was a somewhat cranky man that suffered from melancholy.

It happened finally that Carel came to Courtrai, where the painters wanted to show him their great friendship by feasting him. They had a good time together, chatted and joked about their wives and children; they asked about Carel's children. Then it was told that Carel had a very beautiful wife, but that he had no children. Somebody passed the remark: 'Carel, you are not worthy of such a beautiful wife, since you have no children.'

It was proved afterwards that this melancholy man took the remark to heart; he could neither put this thought out of his heart, nor forget it, in spite of all the fun going on and the amusement offered. In the afternoon, when the company went out for a walk along the river Lys that streams through Courtrai, Carel said: 'I wish I was lying at the bottom of that water.' His companions thought that he wanted to swim and cool off a little in the pleasant, clear water, because it was a very hot day in summer.

At night they returned to the inn, to the same place where they had been together previously, to have another drink after the meal. Carel was as usual very melancholy, and was sitting about very depressed. They wanted him to cheer up. Some one offered to drink his health, and after he had asked the artist whether he preferred to drink white or red wine, Carel slumped over; he had a knife in his hand, and covered by the table, he had made a wound in his body from which his blood streamed onto the table. Then he said: 'Here is the red.'

The company was very much upset. They attempted to aid the man; but he repeated that he was not worthy to live. They all felt great pity and were deeply shocked by this gruesome act. They feared this event might attract the attention of Justice, and then, if Carel died, he would be hung; that would be a great disgrace to art. They managed to get him out of town during the night. They travelled by boat along the river Lys and brought him to a convent, called Groeninghe, which had a special franchise. His wounds were dressed and he was nursed as well as was possible. The wound was not very deep, because the knife had touched a rib and had slipped.[17]

Now and then it seemed that he would recover. He reflected upon his foolishness, saying: 'What have I done?' But afterwards, he would get desperate again and begin raving in his head. He would ask for paper and draw all kinds of weird scenes, and say he was damned.

The men who nursed him, Olivier Bard, painter of Bruges, and another, had their hands full trying to control him, he developed so much strength while trying to wrestle himself free, and each time the wound would burst open again, and grow worse. This unfortunate, raving, insane creature kept this up for a few days and nights, until he died, in the year 1563 or 1564.

Some persons maintained that he had married another woman in Rome, or in Italy, and that he was always melancholy and depressed owing to his breach of faith, having lied to his first wife and having left her. He died most miserably and most unfortunately, and was buried in the convent.

I have placed the biography of the pupil before that of the master, because it seemed best to me. People will forgive me, I hope, for having done this, because the pupil surpassed the master in art, and because the pupil was my own master. In accordance with the date of his death, Carel's life should have been described long before and should have had an earlier place among my biographies.[18]

ANTHONIS VAN MONTFOORT
CALLED BLOCKLANDT

A FAMILY of fine stock, even though it may have deteriorated through misfortune, is often privileged to see some of its members climb to a remarkable degree of honor and virtuous distinction. Thus it was with Anthonis van Montfoort, who was descended from the barons and counts of the castle of Montfoort. The honorable magistrates of the city of Montfoort have informed me of his ancestry at length, and have confirmed the statement with the seal of the town.[1]

His father's name was Sr Cornelis van Montfoort; but he was called Van Blocklandt, because his ancestors had a certain fief in Blocklandt, and also from the name of the village and a manor between Gorichem and Dordrecht, called Neder Blocklandt. His father had been a steward for the Lord van Haeren and for the Baron van Moeriammez for many years, and, afterwards, he became 'Schout' of the city of Montfoort. So it happened that the Anthonis in question was named Van Blocklandt, after the place Blocklandt near Montfoort. Lord Blocklandt, nephew of Anthonis, died in 1572 without children, and bequeathed, by testament, the manor to the second brother of Anthony, who was a pensionary of the city of Amsterdam at that time.

Anthonis was born at Montfoort in 1532. He learned the rudiments of art at Delft from his uncle, Hendrick Assuerusz., who was an unimportant master, but rather good at portraits. Blocklandt was with him for a few years. But because of the reputation of Frans Floris, Anthonis had a great desire to become his pupil, which he did; he increased his knowledge during the two years he worked under Floris.[2]

242

ANTHONIS VAN MONTFOORT

Anthonis returned to Montfoort in 1552 and, at the age of nineteen years, married the daughter of an honorable citizen who was burgomaster and church-warden in that town. He did not have any children by her.

He went to live in Delft, at the Langen Dyck. He studied there very hard to get still more experience and to improve in the art of painting; he made compositions, drawings, and many portraits from life. He painted many nudes of men and women, mostly of the latter; he studied outlines, muscles, and internal, anatomical construction; the characteristics of the surface—where this was soft, where ridges were—and the action of the soft masses of the flesh. He wanted to understand and to render naturalistically all movements of the human body. Through his diligence and keen observation, he became excellent and proficient in the representation of nudes, draperies, faces, and other subjects for painting. Blocklandt became famous and well known through his extraordinarily clever work. He received many orders for large works, and he loved to make large things, deriving a real pleasure from them. In his time, he was able to find enough work to satisfy his desire for the painting of large altarpieces, wings, wood panels, canvases, and similar works.3

He seldom painted portraits from life because there was not much fame and reputation to be gained from this kind of work. He was interested especially in original composition, although he was a good master and painted most excellently from life. This can be proved by a couple of portraits, of his father and of his mother, which were done very cleverly and excellently, specially the portrait of his father with a beard which was rendered naturalistically and well. These portraits can be seen in Amsterdam in the house of Sr Assuerus, Lord of Blocklandt, nephew of our Blocklandt.

Blocklandt followed closely the style of his master Frans

Floris. He had a way of softening certain details in his paintings by means of feathers which he took from the wings of geese and other birds; he would then make cross-hatchings in the dark parts, by means of a brush, in draperies and in parts of a figure. He was very skilled in the painting of draperies, hands, feet, and faces, and he knew how to give a beautiful effect to his works. He knew how to paint hair very well, and this made his faces beautiful, as can be noticed in his bearded portraits of some old men. He was rather moderate in applying decorative detail.

Some splendid altar-pieces, panels by Blocklandt, were in the churches at Delft. A *Beheading of St James*, in the church at Ter Goude, is an excellent painting. These beautiful works were almost all destroyed during the riotous iconoclasm by mere fanaticism and insane madness. Barbaric hands stole them forever from the eyes of art lovers, and little remained.

There are some pictures and altar wings by Blocklandt in Utrecht. In the house of Jofvrouw Honthorst, very near the Dome, there is a large panel with two wings which have been painted on the interior as well as on the exterior. The interior of the panel is an *Assumption of Mary;* on the interior of the wings, a *Nativity* and something else have been painted; on the exterior of the wings, an *Annunciation* was painted.4

Some beautiful paintings by Blocklandt are in the Doelen at Dordrecht, a *Passion* and a *Crucifixion*.

As to the way Blocklandt lived: He was a quiet industrious man, not too exuberant in his style of dressing, clean, neat, and decent. He maintained a certain dignified, serious, estimable spirit in his family. He observed certain conventions and was esteemed for his great honesty. When he went out, he had himself always followed by a footman, as was necessary owing to his descent.

Blocklandt had a very clever way of laying in the under-painting. This can be proved by a work which is at Leyden with Pieter Huyghessen, art collector at the Gulden Klock. A picture representing a bathing Bathsheba, hanging upstairs, is a group of nude women. It was done by under-painting only, and he had not finished it. These unfinished things are to be valued more highly than those which he finished. This has happened more than once with painters in the olden time.

Blocklandt, during his first marriage, was without children. For a long time he had had a great desire to visit famous Roman and Italian places and to see ancient paintings and other beautiful things. Finally, he went to Italy, with a goldsmith from Delft, at the same time that Count van der Marck took Den Briel, in 1572, at the beginning of April.[5]

When Blocklandt came into Italy he saw many works, by the hands of excellent Italian masters, which pleased him very much and which he admired greatly. According to some persons, he was not much pleased with the powerful and thoroughly academic nudes in the ceiling decorations, the *Last Judgement*, by Michelangelo. This happened to many other persons when they first looked at this work, because it cannot be enjoyed except slowly and gradually, while knowledge and intelligence are increasing.

He was abroad for about half a year. He returned home, the next September, to live in the town of his father, Montfoort, and then finally, in Utrecht, where he married a second time and had three children, his first wife being dead.[6]

Blocklandt made a beautiful altar panel at Utrecht. It was intended for 's-Hertogenbosch; it represented the legend of St Catherine. This was an excellent piece of work.

Blocklandt painted still another altar panel which represented a Pentecostal scene in which the Apostles receive the Holy Spirit; an *Ascension* and kindred subjects were painted on a wing. The figures were very fine. This painting used to be in the St Geertruiden Kerck at Utrecht.

Another altar painting was at Amsterdam with the Minne brothers. It was the death and funeral of St Francis; this picture was destroyed by the iconoclasts.

Blocklandt painted a nude of Venus for a certain Keghelingen. This not very large painting is with his widow. Blocklandt always treasured this painting.7

His last work is still in Amsterdam with Wolfart van Bijler who lives at the Nes in the Tralie. It consists of some studies illustrating the life of Joseph, the patriarch; but this work was not finished.

Blocklandt lived at Utrecht, in the house of the Convent of St Catherine, where he died, in the year of our Lord 1583, at the age of forty-nine.

Blocklandt was a master who knew how to paint the nude, as may be noticed in his works, as well as in some prints. A dead *Christ* and a *Burial of Christ*, engraved by Goltzius, are worth seeing. Little portraits of women made in profile, and other pictures, show that he was fond of painting in the style of Parmegiano, whom he tried to follow.8

Blocklandt had various good pupils and assistants. One pupil, Adriaen Cluyt van Alckmaer, was good at making portraits from life; he died in 1604. The father of Adriaen, Pieter Cluyt, was a glass painter who had great experience in the painting of coats-of-arms of lords. A young nobleman studied with Blocklandt. He had already made a good start in portrait painting from life. He did not make painting his profession, and did not join the guild, because he did not want to be known as a painter, thinking this would detract from the glory of his family. In his sentiments he was different from the members of the old Roman noble family of the Fabii, who were proud of bearing the name—painter—as an attribute; they regarded this as a distinction and an honor, as can be read in folio eighty-eight. I pass over, here, the knight, Tupilius, Emperor Adrianus, and others, who tried to make their family more illustrious by means of the brush. Let us leave this topic.9

Blocklandt had another pupil, named Pieter, who came from Delft, and who was the son of a certain wealthy man by the name of Smit. Some have believed he was more clever than his master and should have become an excellent artist; however, he died young.10

Accounts of the life of Blocklandt's pupil, Michiel Meirveldt, will be given in the biographies of the living artists.

LUCAS DE HEERE

OF GHENT

I HAVE said elsewhere that many able masters came forth from the studio or art school of Fransoys Floris. As infants are eager to be nursed from the abundance in strong breasts, so did these pupils want to drink in their knowledge. Lucas de Heere was outstanding among them.[1]

He rose from an artistic environment. His father, Jan de Heere, was the most excellent sculptor to be found in the Netherlands; his mother, Dame Anna Smijters, an excellent illuminator, produced remarkably artistic work with color and brush. Her painting was astonishingly clear and sharp. She made a picture of a windmill, with every sail on the wings, and a miller in it, loaded with a bag, and climbing the mill; below, on the knoll of the hill, were a horse and wagon and people walking. This entire picture could be covered by a half of a grain of wheat.[2]

Lucas was born in the year 1534. He began to draw, in his early youth, under the direction of his father, who was an intelligent sculptor, a good architect, and who had created many beautiful works in alabaster, in marble, and in touchstone. In connection with his work his father went frequently to Namur and to Dinant, to get marble. Many times he took his little boy, who made sketches, from life, of scenes along the river Meuse, of the ruins of castles and cities. He worked with a pen, very accurately and cleverly.[3]

Lucas became quite good at drawing under his parent's instruction. Finally, he was sent to Franciscum Floris, who was a good friend of his father's. Lucas made a great artistic advance in this place. He did various things for the master and

was a real aid to Francen, especially in making cartoons for
the glass painters and tapestry weavers. All this work was
done under the name of the master, and one can understand
how experienced a designer Lucas was.

Later on, Lucas went to France where he designed many
tapestry cartoons for the mother of the King, the Queen. He
was often at Fontainebleau, where many examples of ancient
painting and other kindred things were to be seen. Returning
from France, he married a virtuous young girl, Eleonora
Carboniers, the daughter of the rent-master of the city of
Vere.4

Lucas made many portraits from life; he drew them well,
and was sure of his likenesses. He could draw any one from
memory, and the resemblance would be so good the person
could be recognized. Lucas made a portrait of Sr van Wacken with his wife and Cosijntgen; this gentleman's jester was
in it, too.5

Lucas painted an altar-piece for St Pieter's church at
Ghent, on the doors of which were painted a Pentecostal
scene with Apostles and beautiful draperies. A large epitaph
by his hand was in St Jans; an *Ascension* and a *Disciples at
Emmaus* are painted on one of the doors; on the other, Magdalena with Christ in the little garden of Gethsemane.6

Lucas's pictures and portraits are most artistic. He would
have created many if he had not wasted so much of his time
with people of high rank. He was a great favorite with them,
and he made himself well liked by his pleasant way of speaking. He was an amiable and sociable man who was appreciated for his artistic gifts. Painting and poetry, two arts having an affinity for each other, were united in him. He was
much beloved by princes, and desirable offices were given to
him.7

Lucas, at one time, happened to be in England. The Admiral in London ordered him to make pictures of all the national costumes. He finished them; but he painted the Englishman as a nude, with a heap of all kinds of silk and other materials lying beside him, and a pair of scissors and some chalk that are used by tailors. When he saw this picture, the Admiral asked Lucas what the meaning of it was. The painter answered that he had to paint the Englishman in this way because the fashions were changing so rapidly he did not know what costume to give him. If he had painted the fashion of today, it would have changed tomorrow, according to French, Italian, Spanish or Dutch fashion. For this reason, he put the cloth and the tools next to the man, and whatever might be required could be made at any moment.[8]

This story about the Admiral was circulated. When the picture was shown to the Queen, she said: 'Is our nation not foolish and inconsistent? Does it not deserve to be ridiculed by foreigners?'[9]

To state the truth frankly, however, the English and the French are to be blamed for the many changes in fashion. We people of the Netherlands, we also imitate fashions of various nationalities too often, especially those near to us, and the people with whom we are trading. The Germans and the Swiss are to be blamed least; they are satisfied with their old 'broeck oft bruick.' But we may have to go cross-legged because we have to wear wide knickerbockers in which one can hardly walk. At present we wear blouses that hang down over the belt. Later, we may squeeze into our jackets so tightly that we cannot move our arms, cannot take a breath even; and wear galley pants like slaves, some in French style, others in Spanish fashion, and others again in Portuguese fashion. In the future, trousers may be so narrow we shall not be able to put them on except by means of special devices.

Fashion is most ridiculous for our ladies, especially in regard to their 'cass' enfants' as these things have been called correctly. They look as broad-hipped and buttocked as that famous horse, Rosvayeart, and they can hardly pass through a door. At the same time they have the upper part of their body so squeezed it is harmful to them to bend, or to take a deep breath. And it is not enough that they martyr themselves as if they were placed on the torture-wheel; no, they also hurt and harm innocent, female youth with this kind of torture to such a degree that the poor girls are hardly able to gain either blood or flesh.

We have gone so far with this foolishness, and with similar errors in this country, that slenderness and an emaciated condition should be called a sickness, and not looked as features of beauty, and as something becoming. The Italians are wiser in this respect and they deserve praise. Even far back in antiq- ·uity, they liked to see splendid, full-bodied matrons well provided with flesh. They liked to see them too, at present, and they make the female costume so loose the women could be easily shaken out of them; this sort of costume really can be regarded as the best.

To return to our subject: Lucas wrote many poems, among them the *Boomgaerdt der Poesy*. Some of his verses are translations from the French, for instance, *Den tempel van Cupido*, by Marot. Many poems are his own creations, but these are not in the French meter which he used later.[10]

Lucas had begun an account of the lives of the painters in rhyme, but I have never been able to find this, despite all my efforts. It might have been of use to me, and I could have brought it to light.[11]

Lucas was a lover of antique objects, mostly medals; and he loved curiosities, for which he used to have a beautiful, appropriate cabinet. He had, among his things, tiny, brass figurines of Mercury, in pleasing poses. They were found at

251

Velseke, in Flanders, near Oudenarde, where the city of Belgis is supposed to have been. Lucas had an antique shoe, excavated in Zeeland—a sandal with many curious straps similar to those of antique statues in Rome.[12]

Although I loved my first master very much, I sent Lucas a natural, big tooth, weighing five pounds, that was found between Meulebeke and Ingelmunster, at a spot called the land of the dead; I sent him some other bones, and a piece of iron armour which was a wonderful thing to look at.

His motto was an anagram written with the same letters as his name: 'Schade leer U.'[13]

I regard this as a really clever motto. It has a didactic meaning, like a sermon; for, if one discovers harm in its beginning, not only harm to one's self, but also to others, whether one sees it, or hears about it, one can meditate on its probable cause and learn how to avoid it in the future.

Lucas died in 1584, on the twenty-ninth of August, at the age of fifty.[14]

JAQUES GRIMMAER

JAQUES GRIMMAER, from Antwerp, came into the guild of the rhetoricians and painters of Antwerp, in the year of our Lord, 1546. He had studied under Mathijs Kock, and, afterwards, under Christiaen Queburgh from Antwerp. He made various views of landscapes from nature in the neighborhood of Antwerp and elsewhere. He was a painter so excellent in making landscape that, in some respects, I do not know a better one. He painted skies in a living manner and most cleverly, observing their beauties in nature. He followed nature in everything very closely, whether he painted houses or landscapes in the backgrounds or in the foregrounds. I do not know anything special regarding his painting of figures. He was a rhetorician, too, and a very good actor. He died at Antwerp. Nis noble works are very highly valued by collectors.[1]

CORNELIS MOLENAER

CALLED SCHELEN NEEL

OF ANTWERP

IT would be unjustice to the art of painting, specially to landscape painting, if I passed in silence or did not memorialize Cornelis Molenaer, who used to be called 'Schelen Neel,' because he was so cross-eyed.[1]

Although many landscape artists have been efficient in painting trees and other details, I do not know one who had a more beautiful way of painting leaves than did Molenaer. I believe that everyone will share this view with me.

As to the composition of Molenaer's landscapes, and to the backgrounds, I can only say that everything from his hand, which can be seen, seems to please painters highly. He was not good, however, at painting the human figure. Molenaer worked in the same manner as water-color artists worked—not with a malstick. He was remarkably clever. He used to go out and work for other artists and for daily wages.[2]

He could paint, in a single day, a beautiful landscape, according to a few indications, and people used to pay him one Daelder for a whole day's work, and sometimes seven Stuyvers for a background, or a little foreground.

Molenaer was a good-natured fellow, and other painters would take advantage of him for their own benefit. He did not have much to say at home, and there was great poverty there. He loved to drink. As happens often in such cases, the wife was blamed for it. She handled the money and neglected the house work.

There was an artist who followed the style of Molenaer in his landscapes, although he never equalled him, except in his

254

figures which surpassed Molenaer's. This was Jan Naghel, from Haarlem or Alckmaer, who died, at The Hague, in 1602.3

PIETER BALTEN

OF ANTWERP

PIETER BALTEN entered the guild of the painters of
Antwerp in 1579. Pieter Balten was a fine landscape painter,
and he followed the style of Pieter Brueghel closely. He
worked with the pen, and very well. He visited many
countries and made many views from nature.[1]

Pieter Balten painted in water-color and in oil-color,
beautifully and cleverly. He was good at painting figures,
country fairs and similar subjects. His works are much in demand.

The Emperor has a painting by him which is a *Preaching
of St John;* but he had somebody paint an elephant instead of
St John, and now it looks as if all the people came to see the
elephant. I do not understand why this was done, unless the
Emperor preferred a secular topic.[2]

Pieter Balten was a good rhetorician, a poet, and an actor.
Cornelis Ketel, from Ter Goude, and Balten made poems
and little songs about each other. He died in Antwerp.[3]

JOOS VAN LIERE
OF ANTWERP

IN Antwerp there lived an artistic painter of landscapes who worked in oil and in water-color and who was good in figure work and tapestry designs. He was an excellent master. His name was Joos van Liere. He was born in Brussels. During the last political troubles, he left the Netherlands, abandoned painting, and stayed at Frankenthal where he became a member of the council. He was an intelligent man. He belonged to the followers of Calvin; he became a preacher in Swindrecht, in the Land van Waes, two miles from Antwerp. His religious friends in Antwerp came to listen to him.

Joos van Liere died in Swindrecht about a year before the siege of Antwerp, about 1583. His works are scarce.[1]

PIETER AND FRANS POURBUS
OF BRUGES

IF people could realize the energy I have spent, and the trouble I have taken, frequently almost beyond my powers, to obtain information about the lives of the famous painters of the Netherlands, they would forgive me for obtaining less than I was searching for. But who is really able to do everything he intends to do, even if he is most determined? Very few!

Still I should not like to pass in silence some of the most remarkable painters. For this reason I want to bring to your attention Pieter Pourbus, who was born in Holland, at Ter Goude. He lived from his early youth in Bruges, where he married the daughter of Lancelot Blondeel, as mentioned elsewhere. He was a good master in figure work, in compositions, and in portraits from life. Many of his paintings and other works were in Bruges.[1]

His best work, a *Legend of St Hubrecht*, was in Ter Goude, in the Groote Kerck. The interior of the panel was a *Baptism* which represented two persons being baptized by a bishop, while two other persons hold torches, in a beautiful temple; the treatment of the perspective is done very well. On the interior of one of the wings, Pieter painted a *Temptation* in which evil spirits show treasures to the Saint who is declining them; on the other wing, women are shown charming the Saint. On the exterior, on one side, Mary is mounting steps; and on the other side, she is greeting Elizabeth. These pictures were done in white and black. They are now in Delft.[2]

Pieter Pourbus was a good cosmographer or surveyor,

and he made, for Sr van den Vrye, a large painting in oil on canvas, of the property of the Vryeen; it shows all the villages and localities. He made the priming of white paint and glue too thick; the paint has cracked and peeled off in many pieces.3

The last work from his hand, that I have seen, was a portrait of the Duke d'Alençon, done from life at Antwerp.4

I have never seen a handier studio than the one Pieter had. He died about the year 1583.

Frans Pourbus was his son and pupil; afterwards, he became a pupil of Frans Floris. He far surpassed his father in art and is really the best artist from the shop of Floris. He was so good that sometimes Floris said: 'This is my master,' or 'There goes my master.' He was kind and amiable in his ways, so much so that he might have been the incarnation of politeness. He entered the guild of the painters of Antwerp in 1564.5

Frans Pourbus made many beautiful and splendid works in addition to most excellent portraits, in which he developed a beautiful and pleasing technique.

He did not travel beyond the borders of the country until in 1566, when he made arrangements to go to Italy. I saw him in his travelling costume when he arrived at Ghent, and came to take leave of Lucas de Heere. He had been taking leave of people in Antwerp, but something was holding him back; his heart was bound by the ties of love; so, finally, he married the daughter of Cornelis Floris, the brother of Frans Floris, his master.6

He excelled in painting animals from life. I have seen a picture of his representing *Paradise*, and in it one could distinguish pear trees, apple trees, and nut trees. It was a wonderful and beautiful painting, although he had done it in his youth.

I have seen various altar panels painted by Frans in the

St Jans Kerck in Ghent. President Vigilus had a panel by Frans, a *Baptism of Christ*, which had on one of the wings a *Circumcision* and some other subjects. Frans painted various portraits. In a convent at Oudenarde, a panel by Frans Pourbus had an *Adoration*, a *Nativity* and other topics, on it.7

At the home of his father, in Bruges, there was an altar panel with wings, which represented St George, painted by Frans Pourbus for the people in Dunkirk, where it is at present. The interior has a *Beheading of St George*, and in the background, the lancing of the dragon and a beautiful landscape. The legend of the Saint is illustrated on the wings—the scene in which he is forced to worship idols, and similar subject matter. This splendid and beautiful work of Frans Pourbus is sufficient proof of his excellent ability as an artist.8

Franciscus Pourbus was an ensign of the civic guard of Antwerp; one very warm day, after swinging the banner for a parade, he went to rest in the Corte gaerde and there inhaled foul air from a stinking gutter which had just been cleaned. He went home, became ill, and died. This was in the year of our Lord, 1580.9

Frans Pourbus was married twice; his second wife married Hans Jordaens, a pupil of Marten van Cleef. It was said he had not run away too soon from his master. Jordaens was an excellent master, good at figure work, landscapes and composition. He was clever in the use of accessories of peasants, soldiers, skippers, fishermen, of night effects, fire scenes, rocks, and similar interesting details. He entered the guild of the painters of Antwerp in 1579, and is now living in Delft.10

Frans Pourbus left a son by the same name, and he was very good at painting portraits from life.11

MARCUS GEERARTS

OF BRUGES

IN Bruges an artist contributed much beauty to the art of painting, and he deserves a place among the famous masters. His name was Marcus Geerarts. He was a good master, and he created various works in the city of Bruges, and elsewhere. He was a general artist, widely experienced in painting such subjects as the human figure, landscape, and architectural effect; he was skilled at composition, drawing, etching, illumination, and in all other phases of art. He was especially skilful in painting landscapes, and he introduced into his scenery a little figure of a woman, squatting on a small bridge, passing water. He made many drawings for glass painters.[1]

The preaching of new, religious ideas, in the year 1566, caused a lull in the art of painting, and Geerarts illustrated a book of animal fables by Aesop, with etchings, a beautiful and well-executed piece of work.[2]

Some time previously, Geerarts made a drawing and a large etching of the plan of the city of Bruges. It was a large map and a work upon which no improvement could have been made, I think, for he had spent a great amount of time and labor on it. One could notice a fine perfection in the rendering of every detail.[3]

Geerarts died in England. I should like to have known the date of his death, and his age; but his son did not feel inclined to supply me with this information; he believed it was not his duty to enable me to write words of praise for his father.[4]

CHRISTOFFEL SWARTS
OF MUNICH

THE man, in our own time, who has been the pearl of painting in all Germany, was Christoffel Swarts from Munich, in Bavaria. He was court painter to the illustrious monarch of Bavaria. He was an excellent painter and colorist as can be seen by his large and splendid works in the churches at Munich—especially the church of the Jesuits—and by the other paintings he did.[1]

Various beautiful compositions by Swarts appeared as prints, and were engraved by Joan Sadler; for example, a *Passion* which shows Christ falling down repeatedly, and dying, and other subjects, enable us to some extent to observe the great ability of the artist in making compositions and in rendering the poses of the human figure.[2]

Goltzio, when in Munich in 1591, made a portrait of Swarts in crayon. Swarts died in 1594.[3]

MICHIEL COCXIE

OF MALINES

SOME artists have great powers and noble minds and are impelled to surpass others in accomplishment. This has been well illustrated by the famous painter, Michiel Cocxie, who was born in Malines in the year of our Lord, 1497. Even in his youth he tried to raise himself above the plane of his fellow citizens, who were mostly at a common mental level.[1]

He was a pupil of Bernaert from Brussels and was most eager to learn. He travelled in foreign countries. He remained in Italy for a long time, and he drew most diligently from the works of Raphael and others. He painted a fresco in the old church of St Peter's at Rome, a *Resurrection*, and another fresco in the German chapel of Santa Maria della Pace; he executed various works elsewhere.[2]

In Italy he acquired a wife who, while he was in that country, often made him stay at his work and concentrate on it by her corrective remarks. By so doing she was the cause of his efficiency and prosperity as an artist. After the death of his wife he married again; there were no children by the second marriage.[3]

His first and most important work was the high altar at Halsenbergh, two or three miles outside of Brussels. This large painting, a *Crucifixion*, was an excellent work of art, and many artists of Brussels frequently came to look at it. During the troubles in the Netherlands, this splendid painting was sent to Spain by a certain Thomas Werry, a merchant in Brussels, who introduced into Spain many more beautiful things from Holland. This painting was sold through Cardinal Granvelle to King Philip.[4]

In the St Goelen Kerck in Brussels, there was an exceptional work by Cocxie, a *Death of Mary*. It was bought very cheaply, here, and sold for a very high price in Spain.

In Malines there were two wings, completing the altar of St Luke, which Cocxie had painted. The central panel was painted by Master Bernaert of Brussels. These wings were in the possession of Duke Mathias and, when he left the Netherlands, he took them with him. This was Cocxie's best work.[5]

Cocxie painted the altar, a *St Sebastian*, in the Vrouwe Kerck, in Antwerp, which belonged to the guild of the archers, and it was done very well. In the St Goelen Kerck in Brussels, a panel, a *Last Supper*, is a very creditable painting.[6]

Cocxie painted many other altar panels and paintings that can be seen in various places; he produced many pictures in the long span of his life. He became very rich and owned, among other things, three fine and beautiful houses, or palaces, in Malines. Many of his paintings cannot be bought for even a large amount of money.[7]

It has been said that Cocxie's later works were not so good as his earlier ones. He had a remarkably fluent and pleasing style of painting; he treated his decorations carefully and made graceful figures of the Virgin. He was not inventive in his composition, and for this reason made ample use of Italian examples. Consequently, he was not pleased when Jeroon Cock published a print of *The School of Philosophers* by Raphael; he had made his studies from this same painting, and had applied much detail from it to an altar painting, a *Death of Mary*, for the St Goelen Kerck at Brussels. This became known to everybody.[8]

Cocxie had a quick mind and was clever in giving an adroit answer to any one. He could be sharp with his tongue. Once he was asked to look at some beautiful, round panels and other things which a young artist had brought from Rome.

MICHIEL COCXIE

They had bruised the shoulders of the young man very much because they were so heavy to carry. Cocxie asked whether it would not have been easier to have carried these things in the heart instead of on the body, since they had made the shoulders of the young man so very sore. The other thought the package was too large to be carried in the heart. Cocxie, however, meant by the heart, the mind, and thought it would have been better for the young artist to return and be a better painter, instead of being burdened by the load of another master's work. Finally, he painted some things for the city hall in Antwerp. He fell from the scaffold and died sometime afterwards. This was in the year of our Lord 1592, and he was then ninety-five years old.9

DIRCK BARENTSEN

OF AMSTERDAM

NATURE endows some babes with a talent for art that makes them thirsty. It may be observed that these sucklings, if nourished by full, healthy breasts that give them the best food to form the most perfect education, will grow in stature and in strength and, because of their merits, will rank with the most famous artists.

Dirck Barentsen, born a painter, was nourished by the food tendered to him from the bosom of the great Titian. He became a man so remarkable that, it may be said without false statement, he achieved the distinction of having introduced into the Netherlands the Italian methods, pure and unaltered.

He was born in Amsterdam in the year of our Lord, 1534. His father, called Deaf Barent, had been a fairly good painter. He was the artist who painted, in the city hall of Amsterdam, the history of a religious sect that, in the year 1535, tried to rule the city. This was a strange picture and terrible to behold. Every detail was well rendered.[1]

When Dirck was about twenty-one years old, he went to Italy and stayed in Venice with Titian. In Titian's home he was received as kindly as if he was a son of the family. When people from his own country came to visit him, they were well treated; for his master insisted upon this.

Dirck had a fine, intelligent mind; he loved to associate with good people of importance and with learned men; he had studied literature and Latin and knew each well. In Italy he was well acquainted with the Lord van Aldegonde, a friendship and acquaintance which continued in the Netherlands. Aldegonde would not go to Amsterdam without visiting Dirck and profiting by the company of the artist. Dirck was acquainted with Lampsonius. They frequently wrote to each other in Latin. We may conclude that Dirck was a dignified and important figure. He played very well on musical instruments which he always had in his home.[2]

When Dirck had been in foreign countries for about seven years, he returned home through France. At Amsterdam he married a daughter of one of the best families. When he was twenty-eight years old he made paintings of his wife and himself, pictures still in the possession of his daughter. They are pleasing works, painted beautifully, as is also a self-portrait which he did toward the end of his life. He persisted in portrait-painting, which he did very intelligently.[3]

Dirck painted some beautiful altar-pieces. One was for the guild of the archers at Amsterdam, a *Fall of Lucifer*, showing various nudes, all well done. This picture was destroyed during the iconoclasm, except a fragment which can yet be seen at the Doelen in Amsterdam.

The most remarkable work of Dirck's is a picture of Judith, in Amsterdam. It is painted superbly. Another specimen of his best work is a picture of Venus, now in the house of Sybrandt Buyck at Leyden. At present, there is a painting by him in the 'Fraters huys' at Gouda, a *Nativity* done in the Italian style.[4]

At the house of Sr Jaques Razet in Amsterdam there is, by Dirck, a large canvas, an upright painting resembling an altar-piece. It is a *Crucifixion*, with Magdalen holding the cross.[5]

Very beautiful paintings by Dirck are in the possession of Isbranct Willemsz., a collector at Amsterdam. Numerous portraits can be found everywhere. Particularly beautiful are the portraits, by Dirck, in Amsterdam in the Doelen or guild

267

halls of the archers, which represent corporations of archers. First of all, in the Voetbooghs Doelen, there is a painting of a group of archers and a drummer. This is exceptionally good. Next, in the Cluyveniers Doelen, a guild picture shows the archers feasting at table. They are eating a certain type of fish, called 'pors' in Holland. In the St Sebastian Doelenis, there is a splendid and beautiful group in which faces of old, brown, weathered skippers appear. They are represented on a gallery, and they have a large, silver drinking horn.[6]

In this work, and in others he painted, the fine, Italian method of Titian can be observed. Dirck made a portrait of Titian; it is now in the house of Pieter Isaacks, a painter at Amsterdam.[7]

Dirck spoke Italian with the characteristic Venetian accent. He loved the country and work in the fields. He did not like the sea and sailing; otherwise he might have visited Haarlem and other cities. He was too heavy to travel by horse and wagon.[8]

There is in Amsterdam a *Last Judgement*, with the *Seven Works of Mercy*, painted by Dirck; but it remains unfinished. It is in the hospital where he died, in the year of our Lord, 1592, around Pentecost, at the age of fifty-eight.[9]

LUCAS AND MARTEN VAN VALCKENBORGH
OF MALINES

WATER-COLOR painting on canvas is especially suitable for making good landscapes. Water-colors are common in Malines. Many good masters developed in that region, as I have related.

Lucas and Marten van Valckenborgh were born in Malines. I did not learn that in their youth they ever crossed the borders of their country. They lived, most of the time, in Malines and in Antwerp, till the time of the first disturbances which began in 1566. Then they went with Hans de Vries to Aachen and to Liége, where they painted a great deal from nature. There are many beautiful views and landscapes along the river Meuse in the neighborhood of Liége. These three men, specially Lucas, were thoroughly familiar with the playing of the German flute. They often amused themselves and others with their music.[1]

The Valckenborghs returned to the Netherlands after the Prince of Orange and the provinces finally took a definite attitude against Spain.

Lucas was good at landscape and at little pictures and small portraits, in oil-colors, and illumination. Through his art, he met Duke Matthias. When the latter left the country, Lucas went with him as far as Lintz on the Danube. He remained with the Duke, and he painted many pictures; but when the Turks began their war with the Hungarians, he left.[2]

Lucas died somewhere in the region mentioned, and Marten died at Frankfort.

Marten had several sons who were able painters.[3]

HANS BOL

OF MALINES

AS I have said previously, Pieter Vlerick rose to perfection
in painting in a town where many rather ordinary artists
lived by making pictures on fabric. More than a hundred and
fifty workshops existed in Malines. Hans Bol came from
among them. He was born of a good family, in Malines, in
1534. At the age of fourteen, he studied the art of painting
there with one of the mediocre masters, and with whom he
stayed for two years. He then went to Germany, to Heidelberg, where he worked for two years. He returned to
Malines, without having had any other master or teacher. He
practised by himself, and he invented many compositions for
landscapes and other subjects. He remained in Malines and
made interesting, gay landscapes in water-colors which display his great precision and his sure methods for laying in his
painting and for finishing his work.[1]

I have seen, in the house of my cousin, Meester Jan van der
Mander, who is now a pensionary in Ghent, a large canvas in
water-color. It illustrates the story of Daedalus and Icarus
in the scene where they escape from their prison through the
open air. In it a rock was painted, surrounded by water, and a
castle was upon the rock. So cleverly and precisely had he
painted the moss and vegetation in their many colors, they
could not have been surpassed. Similarly handled was the
ancient, weird castle which seemed to have grown from the
rock. It was wonderfully beautiful. The landscape, in the
distance, was done admirably; so, too, the reflection of the
rock in the water. One could see, in the browns of the picture, the feathers that had fallen from the wings of Icarus, be-

cause of the melting wax, and they were floating on the water quite naturally.

The painting of the foreground was beautifully done, and so were some other parts of the landscape: A shepherd sitting in the foreground with his sheep and, at a little distance, a farmer plowing; both were looking in great amazement at the flying figures.[2]

At length, in the year 1572, Malines was surprised and plundered by the soldiers. Bol fled to Antwerp where he arrived bereft, and without clothes. He was received well by a lover of art, from Belle in Flanders, whose name was Anthoni Couvreur, and who gave him fine clothing. So we see that he did not lack anything to grace his art. It can be said that, as Bias did, he carried all his possessions with him.[3]

Among the various, beautiful things he made while living in Antwerp, was an illustration for a book on all kinds of animals, birds, and fishes, which he did from life, and which was well worth seeing.

At Antwerp, Bol stopped painting on fabric because he found out that people bought his canvases, copied them, and then sold them as originals. He began to paint landscapes and little sceneries in miniature style, saying: 'Let those who can imitate me now, whistle on their fingers.' In 1584 he left Antwerp because of the approaching disturbances caused by the malevolence of the art-hating Mars.

Bol went to Bergen op Zoom and, from there, to Dordrecht where he lived for about two years. He then went to Delft, and at length arrived in the rich and prosperous town of Amsterdam, where he made many beautiful and accurate, little miniature paintings. Among these there were views of Amsterdam, done from life, as seen from the water with the boats on it; other views were from the land. These were very lively pictures, and so were the views which he made of some of the villages. Bol earned much money from these pictures.4

In Amsterdam, there are still some fine miniatures from his artistic hand. In the keeping of the art lover, Jaques Razet, there is a rather large *Crucifixion* into which much detail has been introduced, and on which he worked with great zeal. There are many figures in it,—nudes, draperies, horses, sceneries, and architecture. It is a complicated subject, artistically composed, and finely rendered. A great number of prints have been made after Bol's drawings and compositions.

Bol died at Amsterdam, on the 20th of November, 1593.5

He married, only once, to a widow by whom he had no children. By her former marriage, she had a child named Frans Boels, who became a pupil of Bol's, and who made very nice, little miniature landscapes. He lived only a few years after his stepfather.6

Bol had another pupil, Jaques Saverey from Courtrai, who died, in 1603 in Amsterdam, from pest. This artist may be considered Bol's best pupil. He was industrious, painted neatly, and had great patience. His brother and pupil, Roelandt Saverey, at the present time, shows a resemblance in his work to that of his master.7

A portrait of Bol was engraved by Goltzio for an epitaph. It is a good resemblance, and it has been done excellently.8

FRANS AND GILLIS MOSTAERT
PAINTERS OF HULST IN FLANDERS

PERHAPS once a hundred times Nature allows two persons to be similar in appearance; and even then one person can be differentiated from another person by some little thing. But the twin brothers, Frans and Gillis Mostaert, resembled each other so closely their own parents did not know one brother from the other. They were born in Hulst in Flanders, not far from Antwerp. They lived with their father, who was a humble painter, in Antwerp. They were descended from old Jan Mostaert of Haarlem. Originally the family came from Holland.[1]

Once Gillis, while looking at the work of his father, sat down on a chair without noticing that his father's palette was lying on it. When his father saw that the paint on the palette was pressed down and smeared, he asked Frans to come upstairs. As Frans did not have any smears of paint on his clothing, he was not found guilty. The father then called for Gillis, who had talked things over, meanwhile, with his brother downstairs. Frans usually wore a certain cap which identified him from his brother. Gillis put on Frans' cap and, when he came upstairs, his father found him innocent too. The father then decided that both of his sons were innocent and he was very much amazed. He never found out who was guilty.

Gillis studied art under Jan Mandijn, the painter of drolleries. Frans was a pupil of that difficult master, Harry met de Bles. Both brothers became good masters. Frans made beautiful landscapes, and Gillis painted figures, particularly small ones. For a time, Frans used to paint his own figures, but eventually had them made by others. The two brothers entered

273

the guild of the painters in Antwerp in 1555. Frans died rather young, of a sweating sickness, when he was making a good reputation. His most important pupil was Hans Soens, a capable master who lived at Parma in Italy; he excelled at doing landscapes and small figures. He was so excellent that he did not have to yield place to any painter in Rome, Parma, or elsewhere.[2]

Gillis painted a picture of the Virgin Mary for a Spaniard who did not want to pay him. Whereupon, Gillis covered the painting with a size of white and glue, and arranged the drapery of the madonna in such a way that she looked as alluring and seductive as a courtesan. He then invited the Spaniard to his studio; he made things look as if he was at home. The Spaniard turned the picture round; he recognized it readily by the back, as he had marked it. When he saw this new type of Mary picture, he became very angry, and went to the Margrave. This happened in the time of the Archduke Ernest of Austria. Meanwhile, Gillis washed off the over-painting and, when it had dried well, placed the picture on the easel. The Margrave came to Gillis and said: 'What do I hear, Gillis? I am sorry that you seem to have involved yourself in trouble. What ever made you do such a thing?' Gillis invited them to look at the picture which looked all right. The Spaniard did not know what to say. Then Gillis made his complaint. He stated that the Spaniard would not recompense him for his work, and that, apparently, he had tried to cause him all kinds of trouble, so, in the end, he might get the piece for nothing. To make the story short, the Spaniard was as wrong as ever a man could be.[3]

Many similar jests can be told in connection with Gillis; for example, about a *Last Supper*, at which there was fighting, that could be transformed by washing; and a *Last Judgement*, in which he painted himself and one of his acquaintances, playing backgammon in hell. Other strange jokes of his are known; they are too long to be told here—one could write a book about them.4

When he died, Gillis left to his children the entire world, stating that there was plenty of good in it, and that they had to find for themselves a way of getting it. He died, at a good old age, in 1601. Many of his works can be seen among collectors.5

A large and beautiful painting is in Middelburg with Sr Wijntgis. It represented the Schetz. being received by the peasants as the Lords of Hoboken. This picture contains much detail and many figures. A *Carrying of the Cross* is still in existence, also a picture of Peter being delivered from prison by an angel, and various other paintings.6

MARINUS DE SEEU[1]
OF ROMERSWALEN

IT would be inconsistent with the fame of the able painter, Marijn from Romerswalen, called Marijn de Seeu, if I passed him by in silence. Many of his works were in Zeeland. He had a clever technique in accordance with the new style; from what I have seen, I should characterize it as being rather coarse and not precise. A picture, by Marijn, in the house of Sr Wyntgis, of a banker in his office, shows good composition and beautiful execution. I know neither the time of his birth nor the date of his death; he lived at the same time as Frans Floris.

HENDRICK VAN STEENWIJCK

THE works of art by Hendrick van Steenwijck have been
collected by art lovers for good reason. They have artistic
merit and they have value. That is why his name should be
found with the names of great masters. His memory deserves
to be honored always. I believe Hendrick was born in Steenwijck, and I believe he became a pupil of Hans de Vries.
He applied his talent particularly to the making of views in
perspective of modern churches. He worked with remarkable precision, and with clever and beautiful accessories. He
did his work so well, with such fine understanding and keen
observation of things, one may not expect any one else to do
similar work so beautifully.[1]

As the Valckenborghs and as de Vriese did, he left the
Netherlands to escape the cruelties that Mars, a bitter enemy
of art, inflicted on the people there. He went to and lived at
Frankfort-on-the-Main, where he died, so far as I know, in
the year 1603. He left a son who follows him in making perspective views with the various orders of antique columns.[2]

BERNAERT DE RIJCKE[1]
OF COURTRAI

WE should remember the painter Bernardt de Rycke, from Courtrai, for his great merit. He painted in a fluent and smooth style. The pleasing effect of his work can be seen in an early painting in the Church of St Marten at Courtrai—an altar-piece, painted for the Cruys Broeders, that represents a *Carrying of the Cross*. He changed his style afterwards and, in his own judgement, improved it, but I leave it to others to verify that. He entered the guild of Antwerp in 1561. He died in that city.

GIELIS COIGNET

OF ANTWERP

GIELIS COIGNET, an artist of the Netherlands, was an excellent colorist. He was of Antwerp, and he lived there with Antonis Palermo, till he went to Italy. In Italy, Coignet had a fellow worker whose name was Stello. Together, they produced various works. At Terni, between Rome and Loreto, they painted a room with grotesques, in the French style, and an altar-piece in fresco. Coignet visited Naples, Sicily, and other places in Italy, making oil-paintings and frescoes. On a bridge of a castle, during a papal festivity, Stello was killed by a fire rocket which hit him on the chest.[1]

Coignet entered the guild of the painters in Antwerp, the 'Violieren,' in 1561. He stayed there from that time on and produced many pictures—mostly paintings on canvas and wood. Sometimes he had the assistance of Cornelis Molenaer, Cross-eyed Neel, as he was called, in painting the backgrounds of his landscapes. Coignet painted many pictures for merchants. He acquired a good reputation. He was named Gillis with the Spot, because a place on his cheek had hair on it as on a mouse; this birthmark had been caused when his mother experienced a great fear during pregnancy.

Coignet left Antwerp, during the war in the time of Prince Parma, and went to live in Amsterdam; here he did well in his art. But he left that city, for the sake of his religion, or for some reason, and went to Hamburg, where he died about the year 1600.[2]

He was an entertaining and a gay man—a real wit. He was an able painter with an excellent experience in handling such varied subjects as human figures, landscapes, backgrounds,

279

and other things. He was clever at painting night effects; he often used gold to suggest candlelight, torches and lamps; the effect was realistic. But some persons criticized him for this use of gold; they did not approve of his method, on the ground that a good painter should render everything by means of color. Others, however, held that anything which improves the good effect of a painting is legitimate; they did not mind the optical illusion. Yet persons complained, for a more serious reason: That he sold copies, made by his pupils, as work of his own, after he had touched them up a little.[3]

The son of a certain Claes Pietersz., a goldsmith from Amsterdam, should be mentioned: He was one of Coignet's pupils; he was left-handed; he made a fine start; it is to be regretted that he died of languor, as did his older brother who, too, had made a good beginning.[4]

JOORIS HOEFNAGHEL
OF ANTWERP

I THINK the Netherlanders have a better custom than most other people, because parents, though wealthy, let their children learn an art or a handicraft early in youth; this kind of training may be useful in time of war, when people have to flee. We have known bad luck to affect less those who had learned an art, than those who are wealthy. The trade one has learned in one's youth can be, in time of danger, an anchor and a true salvation and prevent misery and poverty. Thus it was for Jooris Hoefnaghel, a clever man of Antwerp, born, in 1545, of rich parents. He was forced to be a merchant, and he struggled with all his strength to not be. Jooris had a great and deep love for the art of painting; but his parents would not permit him to gratify, at either home or school, the desire Nature had placed in his heart. He could hardly resist it. And when his schoolmaster took away his paper, Jooris would scrape together the sand on the floor and, with his fingers or a little stick, draw figures in it. And at home, hidden in the attic, he secretly made drawings with chalk.[1]

One day, Jooris made a picture of his own hand on a board. This was seen by an ambassador of the Duke of Savoy who was a guest in the house of the boy's father. The Ambassador said a good word for the boy, and so did his schoolmaster. Thereafter Jooris was allowed to draw as much as he wished. He received instruction in literature to which he was adaptable; he became a learned man and a good poet.

Jooris travelled and visited various countries. He wrote a large book about the things he saw and the novelties which interested him, such as agriculture, wine-presses, waterworks, ways of living, marriages and weddings, dances, festivities, and innumerable other subjects. He was busy everywhere he went; he made drawings of each city and of each castle, and various national costumes, all from life. They can be seen in a book of views of cities; to the ones that have been done quite pictorially, he signed his name, Hoefnaghel.[2]

Before he left Calis Malis, in Spain, a painter from the Netherlands sent Jooris a box of water-colors; he made a fine picture of that city, the first he had ever done in water-color. He returned to the Netherlands with many curiosities, and many pictures of strange animals, trees, and other subjects. He then received some instruction from Hans Bol.[3]

Finally, while living at Antwerp, he lost everything he had earned as a merchant. He and his father dealt together in jewelry. During the sack, called the Spanish Fury, jewelry worth many thousands of florins was concealed in a well, known to a maid of the house and to his wife. It was through the women that the Spanish soldiers, with their stealing hands, got hold of it.[4]

Jooris and Abraham Ortelius, a famous geographer, then went to Venice together. They stopped at Augsburg and visited the Fuggers who received them very well, and advised them to see an art collection in the cabinet of Duke of Bavaria, at Munich. They went there with letters of recommendation from these gentlemen. The Duke showed them everything and asked Jooris Hoefnaghel about examples of his own art. Jooris showed him a portrait of himself and of his first wife, and a miniature painting, on parchment, of animals and trees. When the visitors had returned to their hostelry, the Duke inquired through his chamberlain, or some other gentleman, how much Jooris Hoefnaghel wanted for his miniature with the little animals on it; the Duke did not want him to go away with the little paintings. Jooris had never presented himself as a painter; he was very bashful, and did not want to ask anything for his work. Ortelius encouraged him, and himself asked for a hundred golden crowns which the Duke paid immediately, and requested Jooris to remain in his service. Jooris consented and arranged to return after his visit to Italy. The Duke provided two hundred golden crowns so that Jooris's wife might come from the Netherlands; when Jooris returned to Munich, he found his wife there.5

In his art, it so happened, Jooris found more than he had looked for. As an adventure, he went to Venice, to find work as an agent or as a solicitor.

Jooris went to Rome with Ortelius. There they visited Cardinal Farnese who asked Ortelius what kind of painter Jooris was. The two miniature portraits were shown, as before, whereupon the Cardinal wanted to keep Jooris, and to pay him a yearly salary of a thousand guilders. Jooris excused himself by saying that he had given his word to the Duke of Bavaria. The Cardinal, who was a collector, found great pleasure in Jooris's works. He was regretful, because he had just lost that very excellent miniaturist, Don Julio da Caravaggio, who, after his arrival in Rome, had surrendered his able and artistic spirit to God.6

When Jooris returned, from Rome and Venice, he entered the service of the Duke of Bavaria. His work brought much profit to him; moreover, he received yearly a velvet costume and a beautiful cloak.7

Duke Ferdinand of Innsbruck gave him two hundred florins, and annually four hundred guilders, for a period of eight years. In that time, Jooris agreed to illuminate a beautifully written missal. He was witty, learned, and inventive; he made all kinds of symbolic illuminations referring to the written text, in the margins, in the initials, or wherever there was a place. He illustrated the text with various, neat, miniature scenes and delivered the finished book within the eight years. It was done so perfectly one may wonder how any one could achieve so much work, by hand, even in an entire lifetime. The Duke of Innsbruck gave Jooris two thousand gold crowns and a gold chain valued at a hundred gold crowns.[8]

Jooris Hoefnaghel made four books for the Emperor Rudolph: One for all the quadrupeds, one for the creeping, one for the flying, and one for the swimming, animals and fishes. He received a thousand golden crowns in cash. He made illustrations for a book written by the best writer of the world.[9]

Jooris entered the service of the Emperor for this work; he was rewarded well and he received a splendid yearly salary. I do not know of many of his works done in his home region. Jaques Razet, at Amsterdam, has a very nice, little piece worth treasuring.

Jooris Hoefnaghel went to Vienna to live there and avoid the noise of the court. He was very eager to study and learn. Frequently, when he could not sleep at night, he would rise at four in the morning. He was always busy painting, or composing 'carmina,' or doing something else. He was a good Latinist: With a Latin book in front of him, he could read it aloud, in Dutch, as fluently as if it was written in that language. Jooris Hoefnaghel was a very kind-hearted, generous man. He knew how to relate things clearly and eloquently. He passed away, in the year 1600, at the age of fifty-five. He left a son, Jaques Hoefnaghel, who was an experienced and excellent painter.[10]

AERT MIJTENS

OF BRUSSELS

SOME newly prepared liquors develop tremendous force, and, lacking a vent of some kind, they burst the barrel and flow away. Something similar happens, when persons are gifted with a keen intellect that, at early youth, it cannot remain hidden. It was so with the clever and able painter, Aert Mytens. He did most of his work in Italy, where he was called Rinaldo, in Latin, Arnoldus. In his youth he had been most industrious. He desired perfection in painting, in drawing, and in making casts, from life. Once he brought the body of a dead man from a place outside Brussels, where people were executed. Something funny happened there: Mytens had taken with him another artist, as helper, who followed him up the step-ladder which was always at the gallows. This assistant was supposed to hold up the dead body of a thief, while Mytens was cutting the rope; they intended to take the body down together. When the helper felt the body slipping down on him, he was so terrified, and thinking the thief was coming down to molest him, he jumped off the ladder and ran to town as fast as he could. Aert ran after his assistant, quite as fast, because he wanted to finish his work. When the farmers, at the market, saw the fleeing man and his energetic pursuer, they blamed Aert, and tried to protect the poor helper; they thought Aert was going to harm him seriously in his rage. Aert overtook the man, reprimanded him for running away, and said: 'You are not earnest enough about your study, you will never learn anything.' He used other similar expressions, and restored the man's courage; they brought the dead body home in a sack. When the artist's father heard the story, he complained to his son, and asked: 'What have you done?' He pointed out the crime and the possible trouble consequent to this deed.

Aert defended himself by expressing his desire to study and better understand the living, human body. The father went to the ruling burgomaster, a friend of his, and explained the matter satisfactorily.

Aert went to Italy while he was still very young. In Rome, he painted extensively under a certain Anthoni Santvoort, who was called Green Anthonis, and there he made many copies of the Madonna of Santa Maria Maggiore, on copper. While he was in Italy, Aert worked with Jan Speeckaert.[1]

Later, he went to Naples, worked with a Netherlander named Cornelis Pijp, and married. He made many altar paintings, compositions, and portraits in oil-color, done intelligently and effectively. He continued to do this kind of work for many years, and he had many pupils that he educated until they became masters. Many of his paintings are in churches at Naples, and others are scattered through the kingdom and through other countries.[2]

When his dear wife died, he placed his four children in the care of their grandmother, and went to visit his friends in Brussels, and his brother in The Hague. When Aert returned to Naples, he married the widow of his master, Cornelis Pijp.

Aert painted an *Assumption of Mary* in which there were the Apostles, larger than life-size, and many angels—a fine achievement. In the church outside of Naples, Aert painted the four Evangelists, each differing from the other; these pictures are in Naples.[3]

There is an altar painting by Aert, in the church of St Louis, near the palace of the Viceroy in Naples, of St Catherine. The wheel has caught fire, and a splinter hits one of the torturers. The clever painter has expressed the yells of the torturer by the characteristically open mouth, and the amazement of the crowd on horseback and on foot.4

Another altar painting by Aert, in the same church, is of St Mary beating a devil which she has subdued with a club; there are many other figures and angels in the work. The treatment of this painting is fine and the execution is clever.

Hereafter, he went to live alone with his own children and his assistants, owing to the misbehavior and the immodesty of his second wife and her children. He painted numerous, large pieces quite efficiently. I mention, especially, two paintings which were sent to Abruzzo, an *Adoration of the Magi* and a *Circumcision*, each a splendid work with graceful figures.

In time, Aert and his children went to Abruzzo and to Aquila. He took with him a painting on canvas, in a preliminary state, representing Christ crowned by night. He made in Aquila, among various other paintings, a *Crucifixion*, an exceedingly large canvas which covered an entire division of the church. Many important persons were painted in this work, in great detail, and it had a remarkably graceful composition. It was painted under such difficult conditions as standing on a ladder, and similar inconveniences sufficient to frighten and amaze most artists. Aert left Aquila and went to Rome, where he finished the above mentioned *Coronation of Christ*, and some other paintings. He received a commission for a splendid, large painting for the new part of the Church of St Peter, in which he desired to show what an artist from the Netherlands was really capable of painting.

After the marriage of his oldest daughter, he died, in Rome, in the year 1602. His *Coronation of Christ* is still at Amsterdam with Bernardt van Somer, a painter, who married his daughter. It was painted with remarkable fluency, and is quite different in treatment from the usual work of the artists in the Netherlands. Aert was an excellent master. He caused the Italians to be a little more reserved in their statements about artists from the Netherlands—that they did not know how to paint human figures well. By his works, he was able to silence their remarks and to make them speak with appreciation.[5]

JOOS VAN WINGHEN

OF BRUSSELS

BRUSSELS, the princely city, was destined to have artistic glory at the present time, for, side by side with Aert Mijtens, mentioned before, another artist is claimed by this city, the able painter Joos van Winghen.

Joos was born in Brussels in the year of our Lord, 1544. He was very industrious and wanted to learn. He went to Italy and lived with a cardinal in Rome for four years. When he returned to the Netherlands, and to his native city, Brussels, he was a painter to the Prince of Parma.[1]

Joos made various, beautiful paintings, especially an altar painting in the St Goelen Church at Brussels. He painted, according to some persons, a *Last Supper* for the church of the Celle-Broers, but the architectural details were done by Pauwels de Vries. This picture—and Joos did not make a second one of the same subject—is an excellent piece of work and the best example of his art to be seen in the Netherlands.[2]

Jan Mijtens, a doctor in Brussels, has, by Joos, an admirable painting of *Samson* whose hair is cut off. In the house of another citizen, there is a fine *Conversion of St Paul*.[3]

Joos let his heart go to another country. He gave his place with the Prince of Parma to Octavium van Veen, and he went to live with his family in Frankfort in about the year 1584. He painted some beautiful pictures in Frankfort; one was an unusually large piece that portrayed *Horrified Belgium* as a nude woman chained to a rock. Above her head, Time, flying, has come to unchain her and to set her free; Religion, represented with a Bible, is stepped on by Tyranny, who is shown as a warrior with a sword in his hand.

Joos painted two other pictures of similar subjects, but they differ in composition. These excellent works were of *Apelles*, painting the beautiful Campaspe, and falling in love with her. One picture is at Hanau, a new city about four miles from Frankfort, in the house of Daniel Forreau, a merchant, and a lover of art. The picture of *Belgium* is in the same city. The picture of *Apelles* is in the possession of the Emperor. Another painting, of *Andromeda*, is in Frankfort at the house of a doctor who is an art lover; and in the same place, there are other beautiful portraits painted from life.4

Melchior Wijntgis, at Middelborgh, has a painting by Joos. It illustrates *The Story of Pyneas*—the scene where two nude figures, embracing each other, are pierced. This is a splendid painting of figures that are life-size. Cornelis van der Voort in Amsterdam, has Joos's large picture of *Justice protecting Innocence against Tyranny*, or it may be a similar subject.5

Many drawings by Joos have been reproduced in beautiful engravings: *Night Banquet with Masquerade, Let the Children Come Unto Me, Paul Weaving a Tapestry, Four Feminine Tricks*, a *Crucifixion*, and other topics. His ability to make fine compositions, and his fluent way of painting human figures, can be noticed in these prints.6

There are very few paintings by Joos, but they are very good. He did not paint many pictures. He loved company. He loved to spend his time talking to friends and to have a glass of wine. He was not a drunkard.

Joos had a son, Jeremias, who was his pupil, and he is now about eighteen years old. He has made a good beginning with the handling of colors. Not long ago, he was studying with Francisco Badens in Amsterdam.7

Joos van Winghen died at Frankfort, in the year 1603, at the age of sixty-one.

MARTEN DE VOS
OF ANTWERP

AMONG those who made Antwerp and the Netherlands famous for the art of painting, the excellent and well-known painter, Marten de Vos, from Antwerp, is not in the background. In his early youth he devoted himself to art with the greatest zeal. He visited Rome and Venice, in Italy, and other countries. He entered the guild of Antwerp in 1559.

His father, Pieter, born in Leyden, had been a member of the guild in Antwerp since 1519. Marten had a brother named Pieter, and he was an excellent painter.[1]

Marten painted many beautiful pictures. His hand was able, and he colored his subjects cleverly. His most excellent portraits are from life. His compositions, his style, his poses for the human figure, and his artistic capacity, are shown by the numerous prints which engravers have made after his pictures. There are so many of them that he surpasses the other Marten, Marten Hemskerck, or he is his equal. Marten de Vos was a prolific artist; very able and sure in his drawing. He was a stately, tall, and heavy-set, man. He died this year, 1604, at a good old age.[2]

BIOGRAPHIES OF
FAMOUS PAINTERS OF THE NETHERLANDS
LIVING AT THE PRESENT TIME
(1604)

INTRODUCTION[1]

I HAVE described the lives of the famous and illustrious painters of the Netherlands. The threads of their lives have been spun and cut off by Atropos. As much as was in my power, I have tried to preserve their names to decorate the hall of fame with their glory for eternity. I shall now direct my efforts, as conscientiously as possible, to the lives of living artists. I have done this work about pupils and sons of famous, noble and artistic spirits now passed away; the descriptions of their lives I have been forced to leave at rest, owing to a lack of detailed information about them.

I expect the subsequent part of my work will be subjected to the criticism of persons who are inclined to judge hastily. To avoid this criticism I shall try my best to write the truth and to praise the artists, within measure, according to the merit of their capabilities and works. If, in the judgement of some one, I make a mistake and praise too abundantly, I hope to be forgiven; my good will and a too meager knowledge of facts, alone, may be blamed.

I hope, too, no-one may be elevated in spirit beyond his proper value, by the scratching of my lauding pen, and become conceited because of those things which have been lent to him for a short time—as in the story of the page, who, mounted on the horse of his master, was proud indeed, but who could be called at any moment to return all to his master. He who is modest, despite his knowledge, will be able to test the value of what is said to him or about him, through that knowledge. Correggio did so, as did Andrea del Sarto and others. They were hardly or not at all convinced that they were capable of achieving important works and that they were great masters. He who has too high an opinion of himself will always produce a great deal of the smoke of conceit, whether the bellows are working or not. It is peculiar that sometimes the best masters, with their great knowledge, no longer have good sense, when prosperity blows upon their sails very strongly. Then they sail without a compass, and lose their direction. It was the same with old Zeuxis who proudly strutted about in a mantle on which his name was embroidered in gold. Arthenaus, in his twelfth book, tells us about Parrhasius, dressed in purple and with a golden crown on his head, who, after finishing some work, wrote this poem:

> This work has been made by a man who was worldly,
> Who loved virtue and who was honorable,
> By Parrhasius, a man whose fatherland was famous Ephesus.
> I do not want to keep silent my father's name Evenor.
> I was born a Greek and became the Prince of the painters.

There is some contradiction as to loving virtue and living in worldly ways. He, moreover, was proud that he had painted supernatural beings. He painted Hercules on the Isle of Lindo, and as he had seen him in his sleep. He says, in the following lines:

> Behold here the god
> As he appeared to Parrhasius in a sleep.

In his philosophy, he followed Aristippus, who discloses the delight of the senses and of voluptuousness. He was far from sombre when he was working: Theophrastus, in his book on happiness, tells us that Parrhasius sang gaily while he painted. Parrhasius valued his own art beyond measure. He craved honor and praised his knowledge in suffocating terms:

INTRODUCTION

I now tell you, that the limit of this art has been reached.
I am restrained by what cannot be mastered,
I can go no farther.
Every mortal being experiences this
And can only complain,
When his wishes are not complied with.

The great perfection of his art has been told previously in his biography. He wanted to accentuate his own magnificence. The people of his day wore laced, leather shoes with different kinds of bows on them; but Parrhasius wore special ones made of gold. I am convinced that this man could not have been made the least bit humble by a written or spoken word, because of his character. He thought that he was so great a master he had surpassed even Zeuxis.

Parrhasius was not the only one. There are many who try to make themselves important and surround themselves with splendor. It is easier to ridicule than to improve them.

Therefore, I shall continue the work I have done so far, freely. I shall begin with the oldest of the famous painters I know and are yet alive.

HANS FREDEMAN DE VRIES
OF LEEUWARDEN

THE youth of Fredeman de Vries was not different from other young artists. At the beginning, while studying drawing, they realize neither the great task to which Nature might call them, nor the kind of work in which they might reach perfection.

Hans de Vries was born in Vriesland in 1527. His father was a constable, a 'Busschieter,' and served under Commander Ierrich Schenck. Vries went to Leeuwarden to study with a painter from Amsterdam named Reyer Geeritsen. At that time he wanted to be a glass painter. After working for five years under this artist, Vries went to Campen to study there with the town painter. This man was a mediocre artist and Vries could not advance. At the end of two years, Vries went to Malines in Brabant, where he painted many water-colors. He was frequently sick.[1]

When the Emperor Charles and his son Philip came to Malines, and to Antwerp, in 1549, Vries painted the triumphal arches. He made some money by this work, and went to Collum in Vriesland, where he made an oil-painting. Vries met there a cabinet maker, who owned a copy of a book, by Sebastiaen Serlius on Vitruvius, which had been published by Pieter Koeck. Night and day Vries worked at copying the big book and the additional little one. Vries returned to Malines and worked for an artist named Claude Dorici, who commissioned him to paint various subjects in which architectural detail appeared. He had to finish one picture, of a view in perspective, which had been started by Cornelis van Vianen, who had died. Van Vianen understood this work

298

rather well, but he had a difficult method. Vries noticed this, and diligently studied the science of perspective. He invented an easy and practical method for drawing perspectives. Going to Antwerp, he designed a perspective view, for Willem Key, of a portal with wainscoting, for a court. Thereafter, he painted a large, perspective view, based on an optical illusion, which, when placed the right way, looked out through a gate and gave the illusion of a view into a court. Some German noblemen and the Prince of Orange were deceived by this painting; they believed the building and the court were real.[2]

Vries drew many architectural compositions for Jeroon Cock. One, in fourteen parts, was of perspective views of temples, palaces, and courts; another was a series of twenty-six pieces of views into palaces, from points within and above; another, a series of ovals, of perspective views with the point of view in the center—these were used by intarsia-workers; then twenty pictures of sculpture.[3]

He illustrated a *Book of Fountains* for Geerart de Jode, and another book on architecture, with the five orders, each with five pictures. Vries made designs for courts, corridors, garden monuments, perspective drawings, and labyrinths, for Philips Galle. For the same man, he illustrated a book for cabinet makers, in which all kinds of woodwork, wainscoting for portals, beds, tables, side-tables and similar objects, were rendered in perspective. For another little book, for Pieter Balten, called *Theatrum de Vita Humana*, Vries drew the five orders. It began with the 'composita,' the Tuscan order, which represented antiquity, and continued to Melancholia; Death was represented by a ruin. These six prints were supposed to be the six periods of human existence. Vries designed trophies, cartouches, grotesques, and decorative ornaments. These works amounted to twenty-six volumes.[4]

In 1570, the daughter of the Emperor went to Spain and stopped at Antwerp. The Germans in the town ordered a triumphal arch which had to be ready in five days. Vries worked very hard and finished his part of the work. The government paid him sixty 'Rycxzdaelders.'

Vries, with his family, moved to Aix la Chapelle at the time of the Duke of Alva's Amnesty proclamation for the sake of liberty. He lived there for more than two years, and later, at Liége, for a year and a half. While peace parleys were being made through the intermediance of Count Swartzenberg, Vries returned to Antwerp. Immediately, he received an order from the treasurer of the town, Aert Molckeman, to paint a view of a summer house in perspective; he painted an open door in this picture, to increase its beauty. Pieter Breughel happened to visit while Vries was away; he took the tools and, in the doorway, painted a peasant with a soiled shirt, in intimate relation with a peasant woman. People laughed very much about this; it pleased Sr Molckeman, and he would not have the painting altered for any amount of money.5

In the mean time, through the influence of Sr de Bours, the Spaniards were moved from the Casteel which is now in charge of the citizens. Vries was appointed by the town to direct all the fortifications. He was in this service till the siege of Parma and its surrender in 1586. Vries and his family left the town and went, with letters of recommendation, to Brunswick by the way of Frankfort, where he stayed with Duke Julius till 1589, when the Duke died. Vries left the court of the Duke of Wolfenbüttel and went to the city of Brunswick; there he painted a picture for a funeral ceremony. He went to Hamburg in 1591, and painted a picture for a chapel in St Peter's Church—as ordered by Jacob Moor. It was an epitaph, a perspective, in which Christ appeared, stepping upon the devil, death and hell. Below the picture there are two doors half open. Many persons made a wager as to what really was seen—was it a real view through an open door on a stairway? Among others, a Polish Wewode, or a Duke, was there; he was the Superintendent of the royal court, and he was ready to wager a thousand Polish guilders that the door was real and had been opened. Others bet a round of beer, or a barrel of butter; those who lost wished the painter might get his hands messed with something un-mentionable.[6]

In the same chapel, and on the same canvas, Vries painted a projecting cornice, and one could believe it to be a real carving in wood, supported by two terminals. He painted a hanging lamp, as seen from below, at rather a high place; most persons imagined it was a real, burning lamp. Many persons, who had gambled on this and had lost, expressed themselves with insults to the artist, who answered them: 'After all, why did you bet?'

For the court in Danzig, Vries painted *Orpheus Charming Hostile Animals*. Danzig was a place for drinking. Peace and harmony had to be preserved, so the animals were gathered amiably. Vries entered the service of the town of Danzig. Eight of his pictures are in the new hall of the city council. They are views in perspective and allegories of government: *Justice* and *Injustice*, a *Council*, *Pietas*, in a modern temple, *Concordia*, *Liberty*, *Constantia*, *Judgement*. Another painting, for the front of the fire-place in summer, which had an arch in perspective, was a picture of *Reason* sitting on steps; a dog, painted from life, symbolized *Faithfulness*; these two figures guarded over *Discord*, *Sedition*, *Treason*, *Calumny* and *Envy*, and all kinds of other evil spirits.[7]

When he returned from Danzig to Hamburg, Vries made a painting for Sr Hans Lomer. This picture was a prospective from a little gallery of a court view into the greenery of a garden. Opposite the gallery, there was a wooden fence with a view through an open door to a pond and swans. Below, there are trees whose tops are visible above an enclosure. This picture has been admired a great deal.

For the same patron, Vries painted a ceiling decoration on canvas for a flat ceiling that had various foreshortened columns and balusters which rest on a moulding and support a square ceiling with square panels of grotesques; in the center there is an opening and, through it, one can see what seems to be higher and beyond.

Vries left Hamburg, and went from there to Prague, where his son, Pauwels, an experienced master of perspective, had decorated a ceiling for the Emperor. This was on canvas two hundred feet long and eighty feet wide. The scene was of a vault resting on columns, seen foreshortened; the vault was decorated with grotesques. A wide, round opening in the center was the point of view. In another room, with a flat ceiling, Pauwels painted a panel for each of the twelve months. In the middle, in a wide, round opening, Jupiter, with lightning, was to be seen, foreshortened from below upward, and all the other details appeared likewise—columns, trees, and houses, all according to the rules of perspective.[8]

At the wish of the Emperor, Pauwels made in the same little room still another perspective, a gallery that looked out on a court with a fountain. The Emperor was frequently deceived by the painting when he attempted to pass through to the court. He often watched the painter at work.

In the chapel there is an altar painting by Hans van Aken— a *Resurrection*. On one wing, the three Marys were painted by Sprangher, and on the other wing, the Disciples at Emmaus by Joseph Switser. Vries painted a view on the exterior; he had the wings closed and made even and smooth, and over the seam where the wings met he painted a square pillar, so one would not notice the division of the panel. The Emperor looked at it with amazement and was well pleased. Vries made many designs for fountains, and for cabinets in which the Emperor could arrange his pictures; there was, also, an arrangement which permitted the Emperor to go everywhere in his palace without being seen.9

Vries went from Prague to Hamburg where he painted two large pieces for the church of St Peter. One is of *Christ being driven out of the temple by the Pharisees*, and, opposite this, the other is of *Christ driving out the merchants*.

Following the advice of Gillis Coignet, Vries went to Amsterdam. He took with him a picture of the *Tower of Babel*; he had put so much detail in this picture his eyesight was affected. This painting is supposed to be now in Amsterdam in the possession of a certain Pieter Overlander. Vries and his family left Amsterdam and went to live at The Hague; from there he went again to Hamburg.10

He published a beautiful book on architecture illustrated by fifty plates. He had worked on this book, at various times, since the siege of Antwerp, and was assisted by his sons, Pauwels and Salomon. The book has clear and instructive explanations. Pauwels, the son, visited many countries. He is now living in Amsterdam, and doing very well in the field of art and architecture; with oils, he paints beautiful perspectives of temples, and churches, ancient and modern, and various kinds of other buildings. Salomon, the other son, was a good master. He died, in 1604, this year.11

JOANNES STRADANUS
OF BRUGES

BELGIUM is part of the Low Countries. Her daughters, the Belgian cities, rightly criticize Florence, the beautiful and the flourishing, for depriving Belgium of the flower of sculpture, Joan de Bologna, and the excellent painter, Hans van der Straet, who came from Bruges in Flanders. As Circe, importuning Calypso, or as an enchanting Alcina, Florence holds Stradanus from his fatherland; she has let his hair turn white; she may even desire to keep his dead bones to enhance her glory. At Bruges, nevertheless, Stradanus saw the first light, and this city cherishes the glory that he was born there in the year of our Lord, 1536. Stradanus is, as I understand it, a descendant of the illustrious, noble family of the Van der Straets, a family that was dispersed, routed, and reduced, in the year 1127. One of the family killed Charles the Good in the St Donaea Church at Bruges. Charles, the thirteenth Count and nineteenth Forester of Flanders, was supposed to have held the title of Count unlawfully.[1]

Hans, often called Stradanus, made a good beginning at painting in Flanders. He went to Italy, and he selected Florence as a place to live in. Here he painted many beautiful frescoes and oil-paintings. He was a good assistant to Vasari, who painted in the palace of the Duke and in various other places. Through many beautiful works, Hans Stradanus became an excellent master.[2]

Stradanus painted a beautiful, large piece in the Church of the Annunciation,—a *Crucifixion*, showing soldiers dipping the sponge in vinegar. This composition was engraved and prints of it were published. For the Duke, Stradanus drew many tapestry cartoons of scenes from *The Wars of Duke Cosimo*, and some *Hunting Scenes*, which are interesting and beautiful in composition. We are able to study these scenes in the prints by Philips Galle and others. Stradanus painted two series of Passion pictures, and many pictures of horses to show their different characteristics in different countries. Stradanus finished a painting of the *Acts of the Apostles*, begun by Hemskerck—an entire series. Various other works prove sufficiently, and bear witness to, his remarkable and clever talent, his knowledge of composition, his way of arranging and finishing pictures, and his ability in many fields of art.3

At present, in 1604, he is seventy-four years old. He is a bachelor and a worthy member of the Academy of Drawing at Florence.

If, in the future, Italy or Etruria keeps his body, Flanders will have the consolation of having a son of Bruges who embellished even beautiful Florence with the flower of his work.

GILLIS VAN CONINCXLOY
OF ANTWERP

I HAVE read some dialogues and essays, written by two or three Italian authors, on the two arts, painting and sculpture, and which one of the two is superior. These writers favor the art of painting, because the artist can paint anything the human eye can see—the sky; various kinds of weather; the sun piercing clouds and sending its rays to the earth, the mountains, and into the valleys; sometimes dark rain clouds; hail; snow; all possible variations in green, of trees and fields, when spring smiles and birds sing. The sculptor cannot possibly cut all this in stone. For various reasons, painting is a more pleasing and flexible art than sculpture. The clever work of the excellent landscape painter, Gillis van Conincxloy, from Antwerp, will confirm that statement. Because of his father and his mother, he was gifted with artistic talent.

Gillis was born in Antwerp in 1544, on the twenty-fourth of January. His parents came from Brussels. He studied with Pieter, the son of Pieter van Aelst. The wife of old Pieter was a sister of Conincxloy's mother. Later, he worked with another master, Lenaert Kroes, who painted figures and landscapes in water-colors and in oil-colors. And still later, he went to live with Gillis Mostaert, to whom he paid his board. He worked for only himself.[1]

When Gillis went to France—to Paris, Orleans, and other places—, he intended to go to Italy; but he received a marriage proposal, and married in Antwerp, where he remained permanently and suffered all the miseries of that city's political troubles till the town was besieged. Then he went to Zeeland, thinking that he could sell there the pictures he had

306

on hand, and be able to go to France. He remained in Zeeland. Later on, however, he and his family left the Netherlands and went to live in Frankenthal, in Germany, where he stayed for ten years. He then went to Amsterdam, where he now lives.[2]

Gillis painted many beautiful pictures while he was in Antwerp. He did a large painting for the King of Spain. He made a painting, for Sr Jonghelincx, who lived near Antwerp, which was sixteen feet long; Sr Jonghelincx died before it was finished. It was bought by Sr Jacob Roelandts, at the sale after the funeral, and this gentleman had it finished. This was an excellent and a beautiful landscape. The many pictures which Gillis painted for merchants, caused his works to be widely distributed. He painted for merchants in Frankfort, and for persons of rank; some of his work was for the Emperor.[3]

A beautiful and a large work by Gillis is in Amsterdam in the possession of Sr Abraham de Marez. Jan Ycket owned another splendid, large painting on canvas, on which Marten van Cleef had painted the figures. It is an excellent landscape, intelligently painted; the splendid trees, the background and the foreground, are a good composition.

Sr Burghman Claesz., at Naerden, has a canvas with a fine landscape on it, with little figures and animals. Another splendid landscape, by Marten van Cleef and Gillis, is in the possession of Cornelis Monincx, at Middelborgh in Zeeland. It was painted on a panel, over a fireplace in the best room in the house. Melchior Wijntgis has one large picture, on canvas, and two round pictures, by Gillis. Paintings by Gillis are appreciated and treasured by Herman Pilgrim, at Amsterdam, by Hendrick van Os, and by other collectors in other countries and cities.

Briefly, my opinion is: I do not know of a better landscape

painter, at present. I have noticed that Gillis now has followers in Holland. The trees, that have always been rather bare, in the pictures of other artists, now begin to grow a little, according to the style of Gillis. But nursery men and planters hardly dare acknowledge this.

BARTHOLOMEUS SPRANGHER
OF ANTWERP

WHEN Nature, by benevolence and heavenly grace, occasionally endows a mind with creative power, she gives us delightful and noble fruits, with no special effort. Ordinary minds are able to produce nothing but awkward and ugly things, with painstaking efforts. It seems almost obvious that only those who have been born to be artists may enter the realm of painting. Fortune provided the excellent painter, Sprangher, of Antwerp, with paint and brushes, when he was still in his early youth; and beautiful Pictura smiled on him constantly. She claimed him for her own, and the Graces were her dowry.

The famous city of Antwerp is always gratified by a luminous, noble mind. On the twenty-first of March, Palm Sunday, in 1546, Bartholomeus Sprangher was born of an honorable family. His father's name was Joachim Sprangher, and his mother's Roelandtsinne.

Bartholomeus's father, ✱ pious, worthy and capable man, had seen a good part of the world, as he had visited many countries, and had lived in Italy, mostly in Rome, for several years. In his youth he had been in Africa with his uncle, his father's brother, a merchant in Rome who traded in Africa, at the time Emperor Charles V besieged Tunis. While living in Rome, Bartholomeus's father became acquainted with various painters from the Netherlands—to mention one, Michiel Coxie, a painter from Malines—and he really knew something about the art of drawing.

Bartholomeus, the third son, had a liking for drawing. He never left any paper untouched, not even the ledgers in his

309

father's office, in which he drew on the margins, next to his father's writing, soldiers, drummers, and kindred subjects. Once the father lost his patience, summoned Bartholomeus—for he knew who had done this work, and the other brothers would not do such things—and, although annoyed by something else on his mind, he gave the boy a severe beating. The father's anger did not last; but it upset him. Walking along the street he met an old friend, Jan Mandijn, from Holland. Mandijn was a clever artist; he made drolleries in the style of Jeronimus Bosch, and received a yearly pension from the city of Antwerp. The father told Mandijn what had happened, and instantly an agreement was made whereby the boy should go to Mandijn every other day. As Jan Mandijn had no apprentice, this worked out well; but the painter was old, and young Sprangher stayed with him for only eighteen months before he died. Then the boy returned to his parental house.[1]

Gillis Mostart was a good friend of the boy's father; through him Bartholomeus became an apprentice to his brother, Fransoys Mostart. This man died, too—within a fortnight, of a sweating-sickness—and, again, Sprangher was without an instructor. Through the influence of Gillis Mostart, Bartholomeus was apprenticed for two years to a nobleman, Cornelis van Dalen, whose parents had encouraged him to study painting for pleasure. Van Dalen was pleased by the little things the boy had done during the fourteen days he had been with Fransoys. At the end of the two years, Bartholomeus was retained for an additional two years by the same nobleman. The boy had too easy a time with this master. Van Dalen seldom did any painting, and Sprangher passed many days at reading the many books of history and poetry which were available. It was immaterial to the master, whether or not the apprentice worked hard; the only thing the boy had to do was to keep the tools in good order for the moment when the spirit to paint came over the master. Then Van Dalen would paint a rocky scene or a landscape; other artists, such as Gillis Mostart and Joachim Beuckelaer, put in the little figures. Sprangher, when the second period of two years had passed, believed he had made little progress, and, since he disliked always going to others to have the figures painted in —one could never finish a picture with his own hands in this way—, he decided that by continued study he should be able to complete his own landscapes and figures without assistance from any one.[2]

It happened that, in Antwerp, there was a German by the name of Jacob Wickram, who had come from Spiers, and who had been a pupil of the able painter Bocxbergher. Sprangher, being friendly with Wickram, consulted him. He advised Sprangher, as soon as he had served his time, to return to his father and to draw as much as possible during the period between November, 1564, and the first of March, 1565; for, after that date, they planned to make a journey together.

Sprangher lost little time in following the advice of the young German. He copied the prints of Parmentious and Floris, with charcoal and white chalk on blue paper. He did this copying for practice; and he worked for effects in composition by the means of high lights and shadows. His friend had assured him that he would succeed. Sprangher drew various compositions within a few weeks. He thought it would be a good idea to paint some of them; but the time had come for him to go to Paris with his friend, and he could not experiment and see how he might succeed with color work.[3]

The two left Antwerp. Upon arriving in Paris, Sprangher found work with Marcus, a painter to the Queen Mother, a good miniature painter, who had been in Rome with Don Julio. For a period of six weeks, Sprangher did nothing but make portraits from crayon drawings by this master. Marcus lived in a house with white walls, very suitable for a nobleman. Before long these walls were black with Sprangher's charcoal drawings of large and small sketches of human figures. Marcus saw and understood perfectly: Sprangher would not like to paint portraits continuedly. He asked the person through whom he had met Sprangher, to visit him. He explained that it would be much better to place Sprangher with some one who could help him paint compositions with figures in them. He showed the walls with the drawings, and said that although his house was rather large it seemed to be too small for the young fellow.

Sprangher, informed of this conversation, went on the same day to another master, a fine and serious gentleman, but a mediocre artist. The next morning, the master put a primed panel, about six palms high, in front of Sprangher, and, giving him color and brushes, asked him to paint a devotional picture. Sprangher, who had neither painted nor copied any devotional subject, was much embarrassed; he left the gentleman, with the excuse that he did not understand him because he knew so little of the French language. The master unlocked a box, took three prints from it, and said to Sprangher: 'Take one of these subjects, and use your own imagination.' Then he left the shop and Sprangher to himself.

Sprangher was timid; but, when he looked around and saw some of the panels painted by the master, which were very ordinary, he was encouraged and drew a composition on blue paper with coal and chalk; it was a *Resurrection of Christ*, with the soldiers at the grave. He began to lay in the painting, and as the days were long, he did not take many of them to finish the picture. The master was deeply impressed. Some painters from the Netherlands came to see this work; they praised it beyond measure, and Sprangher regained his self-confidence. After he had painted three or four similar panels, he became a little proud. He saw himself esteemed and favorably considered by painters older than himself. The master wanted him to work all the time. Sprangher did not wish to stay any longer with this painter because he had planned to go to Lyons with his friend. Sprangher believed he would get experience no matter where he went.

He left the master and prepared for the journey to Lyons. He was not feeling well and his left arm troubled him. Without the advice of any one, he joined a ball team and used his left arm in the game. The arm became swollen, red, and sore, and he developed a high fever; it looked as if this difficulty with his arm would bring him to a bad end. Sprangher had to stay in bed for a long time. His father, at Antwerp, learned of his son's illness, and wrote to a merchant in Paris that, as soon as his son had improved, it would be best to send him back to Antwerp. When Sprangher heard of this, he refused to return to his home. He hastened and, half convalescent, departed for Lyons, and imagined that he was followed by the wagon which was to take him back to Antwerp.

Sprangher arrived in Lyons where one or two painters offered work to him, and this strengthened his idea that he knew much more than he did know. On the third day, he went on to Milan. He thought the master painters would be the same everywhere, and that they would come to him and beg for his work. The poor boy soon discovered his delusion.

At Milan, he stayed for three weeks at an inn. No painters, here, came to him. And, worse, he could not find work anywhere, and he spent all the money he had. Worse yet, he met a compatriot at the inn, who pretended very meanly that he would receive a great deal of money in a short while. Sprangher paid for the fellow's expenses at the inn. The pretender promised to return the money to Sprangher and, not only that, he promised to loan him a good amount besides. But when he found Sprangher's purse was empty, he rose one morning a little earlier than the artist, and without saying good-bye or without taking leave, he departed, taking with him Sprangher's mantle, jacket, and other things. He forgot, forever, to return them.

Poor Sprangher now realized for the first time that some of his own compatriots could be unfaithful and mischievous. He found himself in a foreign country, without money, clothing, or work. It was winter. He did not know the Italian language. He was cured of his pride. His eyes were opened by self-analysis. He realized how little he knew and why he had met this misfortune. He knew nothing about distemper, water-color painting, or fresco painting. The third day after his arrival, some one came and asked him to do a certain work; he did not dare accept, for he had never done this kind of work and had not seen any of it.

For a few weeks he went to live with a Milanese nobleman. Here he met a young artist from Malines. Sprangher stayed in his company for two or three months to learn how to handle water-colors on canvas. After about eight months in Milan, Sprangher went to Parma, where he worked for an old painter, Bernardino il Sojaro, who had been a pupil of Antonio Correggio. An agreement was made that Sprangher should work for him for two years, as an apprentice and for a small salary.[5]

Within three months Sprangher had a quarrel with the son of the master. This altercation occurred on top of a cupola or lantern, of the Church of Our Lady of Steccata, where they had gone to fight it out and not be heard by anybody. They became so raving mad, and struck each other so furiously, for an hour, they fell down exhausted. When Sprangher had regained his breath a little, he climbed higher on the scaffolding to the place where he had left his coat and his dagger. Half dead from thirst, he looked round and saw a pail which had been used for lime—the water in it looked clear and greenish from the lime. It was midsummer, and as there was nothing else to drink, he drank as much as he needed to quench his thirst.

Sprangher came down and passed by the place where the two had been fighting so furiously. He passed without interference, for the other fellow had had enough; the two did not want to fight any longer. Before Sprangher was all the way down from the cupola, he had a severe chill and a high fever; the poison of the lime was taking effect. He was in bed for more than three weeks, at the point of death, in the house of some humble painter. Sprangher never returned to the house of the master. He assisted this other painter in making triumphal arches in honor of the 'Joyeuse Entrée' of the Princes of Portugal into Parma. He then went to Rome.[6]

In Rome, he worked with an ordinary painter for a period of six weeks. Then he went to live with the Archbishop of Maxima, with whom he stayed for about fourteen days. When it became inconvenient to stay there any longer, he went to another artist, a young fellow from Tournai, called Michiel Gioncoy—who died in Tournai only recently.[7]

Sprangher remained with Gioncoy for about six months. He made some little landscapes for himself, which were very nice, and which showed witches and women flying around at night in the ruins of an old building resembling the Colosseum. He painted other, similarly weird subjects.

This work was intended for a Sr Joan Spindolo, a banker; but this gentleman was not pleased with it. The artist met the famous illuminator, Don Julio Clovio, who bought the picture and paid cash. Don Julio lived in the palace of Cardinal

Farnese. The Cardinal was interested in persons with intellect. The painting of the witches was shown to him and he was pleased with it.[8]

Don Julio did his best to persuade Sprangher to stay with him. The Cardinal, visiting Don Julio in his apartments, also expressed the wish that Sprangher would remain with Don Julio; he was willing to make Sprangher a nobleman and give him a place at his own table, so that he might enjoy Sprangher's company. Sprangher appreciated this offer and wanted to accept it, but he excused himself. He had made a promise to help a young and serious artist—his friend Michiel, who had no inventive power—who had a commission to paint a high altar and decorate the wall space and the vault above it, in the church of St Oreste. Sprangher kept his promise. He painted a *Last Supper* on the wall and four Evangelists on the vault. Sprangher had said to the Cardinal that the work was to be done somewhere outside of Rome. The Cardinal asked where, and Sprangher answered that it was at St Oreste. The Cardinal said that the entire mountain region of St Oreste, with all its people, was in his Cardinalship, and he could arrange matters. The Cardinal went to Caprarola, and Sprangher and Michiel went to St Oreste. Sr Spindolo, who supplied Sprangher with horses, regretted he had not bought the picture with the witches on it. Sprangher promised to make another at St Oreste, which would be even better. Sprangher did so. Sr Spindolo was delighted with it, and went to visit Sprangher at Oreste, accompanied by a number of noblemen—all on horseback.

Sprangher stayed at Oreste for four months. When he returned to Rome, he was received most splendidly by the old, illustrious Cardinal Farnese. He lived for three years in the palace of San Lorenzo in Damasco. Finally, the Cardinal sent Sprangher to his famous palace in Caprarola, a short day's distance from Rome, where Sprangher was to have made some landscapes in fresco; but, most unexpectedly, he was summoned back to Rome. The Cardinal had arranged to introduce him to Pope Pius the Fifth. At the palace, the Cardinal and Don Julio entered the rooms of His Holiness first, and shortly afterwards, Sprangher was allowed to enter. He kissed the feet of the Pope and received the benediction. They then discussed a picture that His Holiness had asked the artist to paint. Sprangher was made court painter to the Pope. He was given splendid living quarters in the Belvedere, just above the Laocoön.9

Sprangher painted a *Last Judgement* there; it was six feet high, and painted on a copper plate; there was much detail—five hundred faces were in it. It can be seen now in the Convent del Bosco, between Pavia and Alexandria, on the memorial monument to Pius Quintus. This picture was painted within fourteen months.10

Some time later, Vasari almost succeeded in disgracing Sprangher with the Pope, by saying Sprangher was a young fellow who was not a very able master, and he was wasting his time. Sprangher, to show how industrious he was, painted a picture, of Christ in the Garden of Olives at night, on a copper plate about the size of a sheet of paper. He presented this to the Pope, who was very much pleased with it. The Pope requested him to paint an entire *Passion* in the same dimensions, and he asked him to first make pen-drawings, so that he could judge whether they would be pleasing to him. Sprangher did not like this idea, as thus far he had drawn with only charcoal and chalk. He did them, though, to please the Pope—twelve black and white drawings on blue paper. The Pope had made Sprangher draw with the pen. While Sprangher was working at the last drawing, a *Resurrection*, the Pope died. The Pope was sick even when he saw the painting of Christ in the Garden of Olives, for Sprangher had taken the picture to his bedside. I have seen some of these drawings. They are remarkable and masterful for work with a pen. The Emperor has a few of them.

Although Sprangher had lost a powerful patron, his innate desire to make big things was renewed. His first large painting for a public place was in St Louis, the French Church, S. Luigi de Francesi; it was a wall painting, in oil-color, of St Anthony, St John the Baptist, and St Elizabeth, and, high up in heaven, Mary with angels. This was a fine work, and painted well. He painted, near Porta Latina, the legend of St John, who was boiled alive in oil; the figures are less than life-size. This picture, on the high altar, was done with oil-color on canvas, and the composition is very good.[11]

In a church near Tre Fontane, Sprangher made a painting of St Anne giving birth to the Virgin. This is an altar painting on canvas, with the figures half-size. The beautiful composition includes many little female figures, busy with Mary and the new-born babe. God and angels appear in the clouds above. I have seen Sprangher working at this picture. This picture has been reproduced in prints. These large pictures Sprangher painted at Rome. Previously, he painted many small pictures which he sold immediately after they were finished.[12]

After the death of the Pope, and in whose service he had been for twenty-two months, Sprangher began, so to speak, to waste his time. He lived with a young, successful merchant from the Netherlands, a good friend of his. This merchant led a somewhat wild life, and Sprangher did little else than follow his own inclinations. He worked only when he lacked funds.

I do not know that he ever took the trouble to make any studies of the beautiful sculpture, antique works and paintings which are so abundant in Rome. I doubt that he has ever daubed on a sheet of paper—which is astonishing—for, when he travelled from Rome to Austria, he did not have to take any examples of his work; he carried them in his heart, which was much easier.

I remember how, at the time the Duchess of Aremberg was in Rome, he painted a portrait from memory, of one of her ladies-in-waiting, for a nobleman. Everybody who knew her said the portrait was remarkably good in resemblance. He was well paid by the amorous and well satisfied nobleman. By this incident we may judge how good a memory Sprangher possessed.[13]

Sprangher desired to make large pictures. His altar paintings had brought him considerable fame; but a new opportunity came: The late, illustrious Emperor Maximilian II sent a letter to Jan de Bologne, a Netherlander, a sculptor to the Duke of Florence, and asked him to send two young artists, a painter and a sculptor, who would render their services in connection with some large works and architectural projects. Bologne had known Sprangher in Rome, and had been friendly with him, while Sprangher was working at the Belvedere. He recommended Sprangher as the painter; as for the sculptor, Bologne chose his pupil, a young man in Rome at that time, Hans Mont, who was remarkably clever. Mont had been born in Ghent, in Flanders, and had one of the finest and noblest minds in the world. He was the special reason why Sprangher agreed to go to the Emperor; for one thing is sure, Sprangher would never have left Rome at that time without Hans Mont, because he intended beginning to study seriously. Sprangher knew that he would have a fine companion and that he could consult his problems with him; this moved him to make the journey. Another reason why Sprangher was willing to go was his desire to make large pictures and make them for the Emperor. The work an artist could find and do in Rome, for public buildings, paid little more than the price of a piece of bread; almost every young artist was trying to make a name by producing altar paintings. Sprangher was eager to go for the sake of a good income. He was greedy. He anticipated the pleasure in painting large pictures.[14]

Money for the journey was sent to Sprangher, and he and his companion left Rome, in the year of the jubilee, 1575, and went to Vienna in Austria. The Emperor was at the diet at Regensburg, where his son, Rudolph the Second, was crowned Roman King. After a few months, the Emperor went to Vienna. He requested Hans Mont to make some models in wax and in clay, and Sprangher to decorate a vault in a tower of a new building, outside Vienna, called 'Fasangarten,' and to make some drawings and small paintings.

Sprangher made a little painting, on an oblong piece of copper, of Christ nailed to the Cross. The cross is being erected; there is much detail in the background and in the other parts; the whole is a fine composition. Sprangher then made an epitaph which is in the hospital of the Emperor at Vienna, and which is a *Resurrection*.

After a few months, the Emperor returned to Regensburg where Rudolph was elected Roman Emperor. A little later, in October, 1576, Emperor Maximilian passed from this life to a better one, leaving a splendid and blessed memory. Meantime, Hans Mont and Sprangher worked in the new building, and made large figures, in stucco, about eight feet high; they painted some large figures in fresco, and scenes containing figures smaller than life-size, and some figures in low relief.

Winter had come with its cold, when news came of the passing away of the good Emperor. Two days later, the pay-

master in Vienna received a letter to remind him that the
painter and the sculptor from Rome should not leave before
the new Emperor could arrive in Vienna. The artists were
well treated, and they received their payments monthly.

While waiting, Sprangher made a painting, rather moderate in size, of *Mercurius introducing Psyche into the Council of the Gods*. It had a fine vista through clouds; it was good
in composition, and it was painted well. Also, he painted a
figure of Roma, a woman seated with the god of the Tiber
river, a she-wolf, and two babes. This, on copper, was the
first picture presented to the new Emperor Rudolph.
Sprangher then painted a picture of *Mary* with some other
figures; this was most pleasing in color.[15]

Six months after the Emperor had been elected, the time
had come for him to make his 'Joyeuse Entrée' into Vienna.
For this event, the rulers of the town asked Sprangher to
make a triumphal arch on the old Bauermarket. Hans Mont
made the architectural designs, since he was skilled in architecture and he loved to do this kind of work. He made some
large figures, about eight or nine feet high, which were modelled on a skeleton of straw and covered with clay. At the
sides of the entrance, there were the figures of the Emperor
Maximilian and the Emperor Rudolph. Among the other
figures there was a nude of Neptune, an excellent figure with
an impressive and beautiful pose. Mont made a figure of Pegasus, and placed it on top of the arch, above a round opening
in which the musicians were to play, when the Emperor
passed under the arch. Pegasus was twice the natural size of a
horse. All the sculpture, of clay, was painted white to give
the brilliant effect of marble. Sprangher made paintings of
allegorical subjects; figures of the virtues were placed between *Justitia*, *Wisdom* and other subjects; they looked as
though they were made of bronze. All this work was done

cleverly and excellently. He also painted, in color, some children, larger than life-size, in beautiful poses.[16]

The arch was huge, higher than the highest house in the market-place; the rulers of Vienna wanted to produce something outstanding and something to marvel at. The work was finished in twenty-eight days, in spite of the heavy rains. I remember this very well, for Sprangher had asked me to come from Krems, where I was painting a fresco in a cemetery.

The new Emperor was not a great lover of art. The two artists, who were good friends, did not know exactly how they stood before the Emperor moved to Lintz, and gave orders that one should follow the court, and that the other should stay in Vienna and wait for the orders the Emperor would give later. Hans Mont followed the court, and Sprangher remained in Vienna.

The court finally went to Prague. Hans Mont stayed for a few months and then he learned that he was being led as buffaloes are led, by the nose. Nothing was decided for him, and he could not make a definite solution. Finally, he lost patience and, without saying anything, he left the court and never returned. The last ever heard of him was supposedly from Turkey, where he had become a Turk—surely to be regretted for the sake of art and his superb knowledge, and for the beautiful, broad style he displayed in his works. Hans Mont would not have had to yield place to any sculptor of the ancient or modern school, if the opportunity to work on large projects had been given to him. He has been my good friend from early youth. He was good-natured and keen; he could not endure rudeness; sometimes he wanted to have his own way about things. Those who enter into the service of the court must have the patience of steel.

Sprangher, hearing about Hans Mont, was sad. He left the service of the Emperor. He did some work for individual gentlemen. It was work he would not care to have accepted previously; he planned to seek his fortune elsewhere, after these orders were finished.

When the upper-chamberlain of the Emperor, Sr Ronff, was informed about the plans of Sprangher, he came to Vienna and invited Sprangher to come to see him. He asked Sprangher, in the name of the Emperor, to make no arrangements for leaving, but to prepare and be ready at any time to go from Vienna to Prague. The event really took place. When Sprangher went to Prague, he was re-engaged by the Emperor and was paid a good salary.[17]

Sprangher, having steady work to do for the Emperor, seriously contemplated marriage. He loved a virtuous, young girl of fourteen years. Her mother came from the Netherlands and her father, a rich merchant and jeweller, from a German town on the sea. Fortunately, the young girl loved Sprangher and encouraged him. The Emperor and the upper-Chamberlain invited the father to come to court, where he was requested by his Majesty to give his daughter in marriage to Sprangher; this request had so much weight that the father consented. Although he knew that his daughter really loved the artist, he proposed that Sprangher should postpone the marriage for two years, owing to the age of the girl. This was agreeable to both sides; but Sprangher influenced the father and mother to consent to ten months, and the wedding occurred while the Emperor was in Vienna.[18]

The first great work which Sprangher did in Prague, to be seen by the public, was the decoration on the front of his house. He used yellow and produced the effect of brass. At the top, he painted little children, life-size; there were painting and drawing at the right, and sculpturing and drawing at the left, of the house; in the center, there was a figure of Mercury, life-size. Below this, there were lunettes, and, in an arch, a figure of Fame; below this, in the center, a female figure of Roma, standing on a globe carried by an eagle that extended downward as far as the frieze. The frieze was decorated with prisoners and trophies of war. At each corner of the frieze there was a large statue eight feet high; one of Hercules, the other of Justice. In the center, below the frieze, a figure of a child, larger than life-size, in color, held an epitaph. The ensemble is pleasing; the figures are well modelled and the poses are beautiful.

Another work of Sprangher's, to be seen in the newer part of the city of Prague, at the church of St Gillis, is a painting with life-size figures—*Christ stepping on the Devil and Death*, and angels on each side. This is a good work.[19]

A *St Sebastian* painted by Sprangher was in the Church of St Thomas, displaying figures of archers large in the foreground; they are about four feet high. The Emperor gave this painting to the Duke of Bavaria, after the work had been in the church for about four years. Sprangher made a copy of the subject for the same church, and this may be seen in Leyden. Both pictures were impressive, owing to the action of the figures.[20]

A painting of *Justice*, with some children around her, Sprangher gave to the city hall. Later, for the Jesuit fathers, Sprangher painted a large panel of the *Assumption of the Virgin*, and the figures were about seven feet high. The twelve Apostles, and angels, appear in it. It is an excellent work.

In the convent of St James, in the older part of Prague, there is Sprangher's picture of St James and St Erasmus in bishop's costume. The figures, life-size, are standing. The martyrdom can be seen in the background and shows the intestines wound up on a reel. This is a very good work. In the Church of St Matthew, not far from St John's Church, there is a painting which Sprangher made after the death of his father-in-law; it is a *Resurrection of Christ*. The figures are life-size; the figure of Christ is perhaps the best color work Sprangher ever did. A child angel, life-size, is lifting up the mantle of Christ; praying figures, on each side, represent the father and mother of the wife of the artist. Two sculptured figures of angels, by Ariaen de Frys, are above and on the pediment, and in the pediment itself the Father is shown.[21]

These works by Sprangher may be seen by the public. Many other pictures are in the collection of the Emperor who learned to appreciate art and especially the work by Sprangher.

When the Emperor was at Vienna in 1582, he requested Sprangher to leave Prague and come to him at the diet in Augsburg; Sprangher went, with his wife and family, and returned to Vienna with the Emperor. Since the Emperor did not want Sprangher to do any more painting in the artist's home, he insisted that the artist paint in a room in His Majesty's private apartments. Sprangher worked there, in the presence of and to the great delight of His Majesty.

After he had returned to Prague, Sprangher continued to paint in the apartment of the Emperor; this was the reason why few persons could own his works. He did not have assistants, and he worked only when he desired to do so. God had supplied him with the means to live; he did not have to work for his living. He wished to please only the Emperor by working in the apartment and in the Emperor's presence. He worked there for about seventeen years. He did not have the mind of a courtier. He was not aggressive, and he never was concerned about getting things; that is why he obtained rather little. He may be proud to have remained in the grace of the Emperor for so long a time, and to have received the few things he wanted.

His patience finally brought him reward and bore fruit. In the year 1588, in Prague, it pleased His Imperial Majesty, at a banquet table filled with officers, to place a gold chain of three strands on Sprangher's neck. The royal command was that he should wear the chain at all times. This was certainly the greatest tribute which Sprangher experienced, and by it the Emperor honored not only Sprangher but the art of painting as well.

A few years earlier, the Emperor, in the presence of the deputies at Prague, had admitted Sprangher and his descendants to the nobility. Since then the artist has added to his name, 'Van den Schilde,' a name used by his ancestors for many years. It was the custom in that country, for one admitted to the nobility, to add another name to his own.[22]

So now it is Seigneur Barthelemy Sprangher van den Schilde—a title that is suited to the profession of the man, for that the word 'Schilder' has its origin in the word 'Schilde.'

It would take much space to mention all the works which Sprangher painted for His Majesty, for there were a large number, small ones and large ones. Sprangher made some illuminations for the Emperor; I can testify that he was a good master in this field. I have never seen any better illumination than his which I saw in Rome, namely, a *Dispute of the Doctors on the Sacrament.*[23]

Sprangher made only a very few paintings for his friends. The Emperor gave Sprangher his freedom, finally; considering his age, he allowed him to work in his own home on condition that he would always make paintings, small or large, for His Majesty. He is doing this daily and with a greater interest in art than ever before. Sprangher regrets the time he has lost, since now his eyes, arms and legs do not function well. According to everybody's judgement, however, the things he has made last are the best.

BARTHOLOMEUS SPRANGHER

We should like very much indeed to have in the Netherlands a number of his paintings, and some as beautiful as the one he recently sent to his good friend and art lover, Sr Pilgrim. This is a graceful picture of Venus and Mercury teaching Cupid how to read. It has a remarkable composition, and it has been praised highly and rightly so by all connoisseurs.

Sprangher has no equal in drawing, so far as I know. He handles the pen most cleverly. This is not only my personal opinion, but also that of artists who are experts. Goltzius, especially, told me that he did not know any artist equal to Sprangher.[24]

We have seen in our country his *Banquet of the Gods*, or the *Wedding of Psyche*, through an engraving made by the skilful Goltzy, in 1585. In its composition, one can notice how clever the grouping of the figures is, and how each member of the company performs his task and renders his services. Hercules is the guard; the Muses and Apollo are the musicians; Ceres is the major domo; Bacchus is in charge of the wine. Each one has a special duty, and the figures are most graceful. Sprangher has shown how unusually gifted he was in this respect, and no other artist with similar talent can be found.[25]

As to his treatment of color, I have heard him say, while he was in the Netherlands, that during the long period he stayed with the Emperor, without any other artist near him from whom he could see an example of beautiful coloring, he paid little attention to that part of his work. But he saw some pictures by Joseph Hyns Switser and by Hans van Aken, who produced excellent color effects, and since then he has changed his technique in color—these painters produced the most wonderful effects in their works![26]

From the beginning, Sprangher has always given a special Apellesque grace to his figures. Harmonia, the daughter of

Venus and Mars, has contributed her qualities and coördinated color effects and beautiful, sure, and clever drawing. Criticism of his paintings could not be justified; they cannot be surpassed.

Sprangher deserved to be accepted by the Roman Emperor and to receive high distinction. The Emperor loved art as did Alexander, and he found in Sprangher an Apelles.

Sprangher longed more and more to visit his fatherland. He finally made up his mind to come to the Netherlands, in 1602. He had been absent for thirty-seven years, since he had left the country when he was young. Sprangher visited some diets, for the Emperor, at his own expense, and not at the Emperor's, as he could have done. The Emperor gave him a thousand guilders for his journey to the Netherlands.

Sprangher received a great and a most friendly welcome from the artists in the Netherlands. At Haarlem, they feasted him nobly and he feasted them in return. The members of the old chamber of rhetoricians honored him by giving a dinner and a symbolical play in praise of painting. We were very happy to have him among us, and we regretted to have him leave us.[27]

In his native town, Antwerp, Sprangher was received with great joy. He went from this city to Cologne, and then to Prague. Daily, he is now practising art with great interest and energy. Sprangher is alone. He is growing old. He has lost his very dear, virtuous wife and children. He needs a kind and able Medea to perform magic on him, and to give him back his youth. Though he finds things different, Art will remain his faithful companion, and he will be rejuvenated daily with time-absorbing and pleasure-giving practice.[18]

Sprangher's works will be his children, even as the works by Michelangelo were his. They will enshrine his name in the temple of Fame with eternal glory. It will be written forever

that he has loyally served a Pope and two Emperors with his
brush and his colors.[28]

CORNELIS KETEL

OF GOUDA

SOME youths, when they begin to study painting, seem to be opposed by Nature; they are not able to make any progress by all their efforts. Other persons, favored by nature, should attain perfection; but they are ungrateful and depend on their parent's wealth to prevent them from being driven to work by the whip of poverty. They know there always will be food; they do not trouble themselves for the sake of their spiritual welfare. There are others who rely too much on their talent; they have too much confidence in nature, do not co-operate and are not industrious; consequently, they achieve little that is worthy of praise. The artists who willingly follow nature, when she reaches out her hand to them, and follow her constantly and stay with her and are always willing to learn and to do their best, will reap the fruit of their hard labor with great joy. This has been the good fortune of many artists. It is well known that the prudent shall be rewarded by fortune.[1]

Cornelis Ketel was remarkably industrious, even in his early youth. At the age of eleven, he felt a great love for art and wanted to study painting. He received his first instruction from one of his uncles, a fair painter, who was more of a scientist than an artist.

In zeal, Ketel surpassed the other youths of the shop. The glass painter, Dirck Pieterzsz. Crabeth, a good friend of his uncle, encouraged the boy, when he noticed how eagerly Ketel wanted to learn. He said of him: 'This will be one out of a hundred, who will succeed in reaching perfection.' This remark encouraged Ketel very much, and he continued to be

330

industrious. He made drawings from memory—some were portraits—and paintings of subjects of his own invention.[2]

Ketel was born at Gouda in 1548, on the Sunday before Palm Sunday. At the age of eighteen, he went to work under Anthonis Blocklandt in Delft, where he lived during 1565. He went to Paris in 1566, and then to Fontainebleau, because he had heard that some young Netherlanders were working together there—Jeroon Vrancks, Aper Fransen, Hans de Mayet, and Denijs van Utrecht. He was accepted readily into their circle. In the spirit of fun, they worked harmoniously to surpass one another; but, after a few months, when the King established his court there, they had to leave Fontainebleau. Ketel returned to Paris where he boarded with the glass painter to the King, Sr Joan de la Hame. There, alone in his room, he painted various compositions.[3]

The King then gave rigid orders that all foreigners who had lived for less than two years in France, and who were subjects of the King of Spain, must leave, on penalty of death —many refugees had fled from the Netherlands owing to the Iconoclasm there, or for religious and other reasons. Ketel did not believe it would be advisable to stay in France—he had escaped the massacre of St Bartholomew's Eve. He returned to Holland, with the intention of going to France and Italy some time in the future. But the times were unsafe for travelling; Ketel stayed in his native town, Gouda, for about six years. There were many, very sweetly singing, little sirens in Gouda, who were fond of him; they sang beautiful lovesongs to him.[4, 5]

Since war had not caused any work for painters, Ketel went to England in 1573. He went to London, where he visited a sculptor and architect who was a compatriot and a good friend of his uncle. This man received him kindly and did not want Ketel to go anywhere else.

While in London, he sold some of his paintings to the members of the Hansa; from them he received many orders for portraits, but none for compositions with figures. He requested his present wife to leave Holland, and to come to London. They lived here for about eight years.[6]

Ketel had always wanted to paint figures. He painted a large canvas with figures more than life-size, called *Force Controlled Through Wisdom and Prudence*. A pleasant, young, English merchant, Pieter Hachten, bought this painting from Ketel, and gave it to Mr Christoffel Hatten, High Chancellor, after he died.[7]

Ketel painted a portrait of the Queen of England, in 1578, from life, for the Duke of Hereford, at the castle of Hantworth; the Queen had been invited there by the mother of the Count, the Duchess of Somerset. Ketel also made a portrait of the Duke of Oxford, the High Chancellor, and of many other important members of the nobility, with their wives and children. Some of these portraits were life-size and full length.[8, 9]

In 1581, Ketel left England and returned to Holland to live in the city of Amsterdam, where he received many commissions for paintings from life. He painted a group of archers for the 'Cleuveniers Doelen,' of which the captain was Herman Rodenborgh Beths. Ketel portrayed his own profile in this picture. The group was arranged in a gallery composed of terminuses, instead of columns, that appeared to be carved in relief and painted, forming an unusual and very original frame for the figures. The faces were good in likeness; the poses, the textures of the silk, and clothing, are excellent. A few, small, allegorical figures, in black and white, are below in the picture, and two standing figures of Mars and Vulcan appear as if made of bronze. As an explanation, Ketel added the following lines:[10]

CORNELIS KETEL

Oh, cruel Mars, stop your bloody deeds!.
Vulcan, forge no more weapons!
Bound and under your feet are the evil spirits,
Hate, Greed, Envy, and Discord.

Ketel composed two allegorical paintings. One, the Triumph of Virtue over Vice, he named the *Triumph of Virtue*; the other, the Triumph of Vice over Virtue, he named the *Triumph of Vice*. I saw these paintings in the house of Sr Joan van Wely in Amsterdam. They are admirably painted. Ketel, by details, has given remarkable expression to the attributes of Virtue and Vice; the accessories are suited to the spirit of the figures represented. They are beautiful in composition. Ketel explained the subjects: [11]

TRIUMPH OF VIRTUE

Envy, Discord, War, and Tyranny,
Lie here subdued and bereft of power;
Wisdom rules the land with a wise policy;
And Justice guards Peace.
Behold how Love and Faith, 'fore the eyes of every one,
Embrace in friendship and kiss each other!
Love gives generously of her fruit;
The palm and the laurel crown Virtue.
Behold Truth, pure and abiding in celestial region,
And Strength and Temperance make her domain richer yet.
The clear light enhances her virtues;
Hail to the land where the law of Truth
Is respected and where obedience is constantly observed.

TRIUMPH OF VICE

Infernal Envy drives Discord before her
Through somber clouds and darkness of crime;
Furiously, Virtue is pursued with arrows;
Justice is wounded and helpless.
Naked Truth, fallen through Defiance,
Is pierced by Tyranny.
War stands with his sword,
Surrounded by the mists of Anger
Prepared to avenge.

333

Faith and Love have succumb.
Wisdom, Policy, and Peace, retreat.
Woe to the land where Evil is the sovereign!

In 1584, Hans Ophoghen commissioned Ketel to paint a picture which was of St Paul, looking up to heaven; it is life-size, a knee-piece, and Rutget Jansz. posed for it. Ketel painted the same subject again, for a brother of Hans, Thomas Ophoghen, besides five other pictures which were: St Peter, repenting; Magdalen, repentant; the Publican; Saul, falling on his sword; and Judas, hanging himself. These six pictures are at Danzig in the home of Thomas Ophoghen; they are excellent in every respect and they are beautifully painted.

In 1589, Ketel painted the *Corporaelschap* for the archers of the 'Handboogh Doelen,' whose captain was Dirck Roosencrans. The portraits are life-size, and the standing figures are in graceful poses. This picture was well painted; Ketel used a new device for the frame.[12]

Many good portraits by Ketel are in existence and are easy to find. Among them there are two, one of a merchant named Neck, life-size and full length, and one of his wife.[13]

Some of Ketel's portraits are remarkable for their preciseness: the portrait of Andries Vrericksen; the one of Jan Lammersen, holding an orange in his hand; the portrait of Secretary Haen; and the one of a goldsmith, showing just his face in half-size proportions. These persons are from Amsterdam. A portrait of a Venetian, a man who ordered a beautiful, large ship built for him in Amsterdam, is very fine. He was a 'magnifico' by the name of Francesco Morosini. Ketel made another, a reverse of this one, which he painted only with his fingers, and it also showed a close resemblance. A fine portrait of Vincent Jacobsen, the Wine Inspector from Amsterdam, has him holding a beautiful 'Francfoorder' of Rhine wine in his hand. This is an accurate painting and looks

334

well at a distance. Ketel made a portrait of a Portuguese girl, and a portrait of Simon Lock, a man from Amsterdam—this portrait, the most excellent of all, is at present in The Hague in the house of Attorney Lock.[14]

There are many other beautiful portraits by Ketel. At present, he is painting Christ and the twelve Apostles. The faces, about life-size, or, perhaps, a little larger, are excellently and finely drawn; they are portraits of painters and collectors—one is the portrait of the talented sculptor, Hendrick de Keyser, architect for the city of Amsterdam.[15]

With great interest, I saw the heads of the twelve Apostles; the hands were life-size and painted boldly. These portraits are in Paris in the home of Ketel's nephew, Jacob Ketel, engineer to the King of France. This nephew, a remarkable man in his work, was formerly in Milan in the service of the King of Spain.

Ketel was a special favorite of the Muses and, as did old Timantheus, he introduced many amusing and unexpected allegories into his works. A drawing which explains the three reasons for studying the various arts has been explained by Ketel:

> There are three motives that everyone is urged to study art for:
> Money, Honor and Love.
> He who is out for money, meets Avarice,
> To interfere with the result.
> So little is learned.
> He who aims at honor learns more.
> Vain glory may lead to the tree of the arts;
> But fruit is wanted, not the tree itself.
> He who picks unripe fruit will be somewhat satisfied;
> But he who chooses the safe route, guided by talent,
> Will be constantly forced ahead by Love,
> And zeal and patience will not fail him.
> By his work he will be led to art.
> He will be rewarded with fame,
> With money and with honor.

FORTUNE PROVOKES ENVY

Jealous Hate, and Envy, and Gossip, plot against Fame.
Renown speeds ahead and informs the world of everyones' work;
But Truth comes into the light,
Somewhat later, perhaps, but nothing can stop her.
Thus, Envy's mind is tortured.
The spider vomits its venomous thread,
While the little bees suck honey.

This little allegory, *Tree of the Fine Arts*, Ketel made and sent to Brabant; at present it is in the home of Sr Domenicus van Ossele at Hamburg, in Gruening Street. The meaning is fine and spiritual. This picture is protected from the daylight and from the sight of those who are eager to see works of art —it has been put in a box.

At the request of Raphael Sadeler, Ketel drew another allegory. In the center there are Music, Painting, and Poetry, and Love with a burning heart; Love's face is turned to Painting who is listening to Music; Affection, symbolized by a little child, is voiding; the snake represents Subtlety. This allegory proves that Love is the fountain of the Arts. Ketel emphasized the same meaning in a spiritual sense, by decorating the upper basin of the fountain with seraphic heads; the water, flowing from their mouths, suggest the sources of art in the praise of God. It is natural for artists to aspire to height, honor, and glory and this strife is symbolized by a wreath and a palm. Pictura is painting the legend of Icarus and Daedalus, to remind artists to keep their self-esteem within measure. Round this subject there is a border enclosing four other pictures: Ambition, as a spinner, and in this scene there are a stork, spurs and whips; Labor, with a shovel, a hammer, a skin of an ox, and flails; Patience has a birdcage, with a lamb and an hour-glass, and handcuffs suspended behind her; Exercise, holding an arrow which she is aiming at a ring, is resting one foot on an hour-glass and, behind her, bows are suspended. Two burning lamps hang next to each of these four representations, and they seem to protrude from the decorative border of foliage. Here is shown how practice leads to perfection, and how the four forces reveal their light to us. Similarly, all other arts are revealed to us through the unison of these virtues; they are the lights on earth.[16]

Ketel painted an allegory, in black and white, a nude man standing with one foot on the head of an ox-skin, and with the other foot on a shovel; he steps over an anchor which he is lifting up with his hand in the ring; he is holding a whip and two spurs; the struggling woman on his arm is Art, lifting a laurel wreath high with her right hand, and the man, trying to reach it with his right hand, is holding a pierced and flaming heart. The woman is resting with her toe on an hourglass which has a day bird at one side and a night bird, or bat, at the other side; with her left hand she is pointing at a little lamb which is looking up to Art; a little child, kneeling, has one arm round the neck of the lamb and, with the other, holds a palette with colors, to show that he wants to learn painting. At the other side of the stepping figure of the man, seen from the back, there is a reclining figure of a boy, who holds a horn of an ox in one hand and, in the other, a music book; he wants to be a musician—he has various musical instruments beside him. Above, in the sky, there are two little children, Genius and Desire. They stimulate the flaming heart to be diligent, as indicated by the spurs and whip which the man is holding in his hand. At the other side, Cupid, with his bow, is in the distance; he has shot his arrow into the heart of the man. Ruins in the background suggest Rome, the place where youthful artists should study.[17]

This little painting may be seen in Amsterdam, in the house of a great collector, Secretary Haen. Ketel wrote the following lines as an explanation:

DUTCH AND FLEMISH PAINTERS

O Youth, Hope will not flee;
Thus, work patiently and enduringly.
Genius and Ambition will urge you,
And put zeal to your heart.
You shall get everything you are courting.

Ketel made a large painting of naked Truth as a graceful woman sleeping on a fine couch decorated in a beautiful, antique style; She has a seraphic aureole which suggests Virtue. Deceit is a masked satyr—above, he is man, below, a goat; in the guise of Truth, he is climbing onto the couch; but his mask is cast off by the power of Virtue and Truth that are symbolized by a strong man, with eagle's wings, who resembles Time; he is pressing down the shoulders of Deceit so forcefully that Deceit's back might be broken. This painting is in Amsterdam. The following lines go with it:

Naked Truth may sleep here quietly.
Virtue will guard over her constantly,
Although beautiful Deceit might cunningly try to disturb her,
He shall find himself halted.
Virtue's strength can undo him;
He is forced down and crushed;
His back is broken.

Another allegory painted by Ketel, and fine in coloring, is in Amsterdam, in the Calverstraat, in the Hof of Hollandt, with Master Claes. It has the following explanation:

Intelligence is disarmed by Wine, Venus and Love for Money;
Abuse (an old Venom), is robing her in the costume of Folly.

Intelligence is as a conquered woman, deprived of helmet, shield and lance that are trod upon by Abuse of Woman, Wine, and Money, represented as Venus, who has tied Intel-

338

ligence to her feet with a ribbon; Cupid, or Desire, is standing behind her; he, pulling the cord of his bow, symbolizes Threefold Indulgence; he is aiming at Intelligence. Bacchus is holding a crystal pitcher in one hand and a crystal goblet of red wine in the other; he is tempting Intelligence to drink beyond her capacity; the red wine is reflected on his front. A little further along, Avarice is taking a purse from a treasure box which has on the lid a picture of Midas, who is changing everything he touches into gold. Abuse, as an old satyr, puts the fool's cap on the head of Intelligence. Secretary Haen also owns Ketel's painting of the *Seven Virtues*.

Another painting by Ketel is an allegory of the proverb: 'Desire has no rest.' This picture is of a man stepping over a bottomless pit; he is blindfolded by Sensuality; Peton, a medicinal herb, is growing behind him, and a newly born child is lying at its root—this herb symbolizes spiritual life. In front of the man, Napelles, the most poisonous herb, is growing. A skull is at its roots—symbolizing spiritual death. This allegory shows that man is so eager to get only temporal goods, that he neglects those which serve for his salvation. Smiling Fortune shields under her veil the god of Wealth and throws in the way of sensuous man all he might wish; but he has one foot on the catch of an escapement; he has no rest. The following lines by Ketel gives his explanation: [18, 19]

> Restless Man, blinded by Flesh,
> Knows not God, and thus he indulges in evil.
> He wishes all he can, no end to his desires.
> Even when Fortune smiles, he has no rest in his lust.

Further explanation is given by the poetical figures which can be seen in the distance; they illustrate the infernal tortures to which Tantalus, Sisyphus, Ixion, Tityus, and the Danaïdes were subjected. This poem is with it:

339

Climb high on Mount Zion;
Be brave and go with care.
Be wise and consult aged Experience.
Never be tempted by beautiful soap-bubbles,
For you will follow illusions.
It is only the deed that counts.
One who is manly and brave and virile,
Shall receive the grace of God,
While youth may fail,
To its own dishonor and degradation.

Besides the various allegories, painted by Ketel, I should not pass over in silence his *Mirror of Virtues* which has appeared as a print by Saenredam. There is much thought expressed in this composition. Sinful man is being punished for his ingratitude; while he is receiving Sun, he is biting Charity. Gratitude, receiving Moon, feels thankful and presses her to the heart. Various symbolical suggestions can be seen on the print. The following lines, are an explanation:

Virtue shows that the really grateful heart will never forget
Even the smallest gift;
But ungrateful Man changes rapidly what is white into black.
The one who kisses such a person as a friend,
Is bitten furiously;
If one does good to the ungrateful,
It will not be acknowledged.[20]

Although Ketel's mind was productive, he had desires that were apart from his love for painting. He obeyed these inner voices, and he found forms of self-expression which were harmless.

In 1595, Ketel felt an urge to do modelling in clay. He made a group of four, nude, male figures; one figure, bound hand and foot, was evidently suggested by a story of a groom who was thrown into the utmost darkness because he had no bridal costume; the other three figures appear to want to fling away the groom. This group is a good ensemble, full of action, and it can be looked at from any side, a great surprise to all connoisseurs and to the best sculptors. Subsequently, Ketel has modelled in wax; this kind of work has helped him in his painting and drawing. Modelling has been a custom with the Italian masters, and it has been a valuable one. The following year, Ketel made portraits that were remarkably good, as can be seen by the portraits already mentioned, and by the ones which he is now painting.[21]

In 1599, he conceived the idea of painting without brushes, by using only his hand. Many persons think this is a ridiculous notion and not in accordance with good taste—as the cravings of pregnant women for strange food. To speak, and with some reserve, about this subject, one is surprised that he succeeded so well, and that his experiment did not bear ill-formed fruit.

Ketel's first picture in this manner was a self-portrait, and he repeated it in various poses. This portrait is better in resemblance than another made by an artist with tools.[22]

After this experiment, Ketel made a picture of Democritus and Heraclitus for Sr Hendrick van Os, a collector in Amsterdam; Ketel included his own portrait in the picture of Democritus, at the request of Sr van Os. This picture, warm in color, is good at a little distance.

Once, while Ketel was working with his fingers on a portrait of Sr Morosini, and he was putting on the final touches, a brushmaker came along and expressed the wish that Ketel would get a corn at the end of each finger; for, if this method of painting became the general one the brushmaker's business would fail. A man, living in Moscow, ordered a portrait of himself to be painted in this way, so that he could show it to the great monarch, with whom he was on good terms.

Ketel made a portrait of Sr Wolfaert Hermans, the Admiral of the Molucca fleet, and it was a good resemblance. Another portrait of the excellent sculptor, De Keysez, had been used before for an apostle's portrait; this picture was painted with brushes.[23]

Ketel made three heads with his thumb and fingers: One of Mary, one of St John, and one of the Saviour wearing the crown of thorns, done so well and so carefully, the blood, and the tears in the eyes, it is difficult to believe the painting was executed without tools.

Stranger yet is the fact that, in 1600, Ketel got the idea of painting with only his feet. He wanted to find out what he could do by painting this way. This method made many persons laugh; their scorn was more than before, because feet are less able than hands for such work. But they were wrong. No-one could be harmed by this experiment, except the brushmaker. One should not find fault with strange experiments that are made by some persons to prove things possible which had seemed to be impossible, such as an artist, who, without using his hands, had come and had shown how he could help himself in another way. Do not many persons want to show their cleverness and prove that similar, unusual things exist? Some shoot a gun in a queer position, and they hit the target. I pass by the fact that some persons walk on ropes—it is easier to walk on earth. I have referred to the paintings to prove that Ketel is not guilty of fraud, although at first view his paintings look as if they were made by hand and with tools.

His first experiment was a picture of Hippocrates, the god of silence, in which he succeeded admirably. He rendered a good suggestion of silence and of the character of the philosopher whose laughing and crying are coinstantaneous.

When Ketel painted these subjects, he was always careful

to not touch any tool and to use only one leg and foot, as he had planned to do; this can be ascertained by the testimonies of many persons.

Many gentlemen of high rank fancied pictures that were painted by Ketel's foot. The Duke of Nemours bought *The Crying Philosopher* out of curiosity. A Pole, named Andreas Leczinski, the Count of Leschno, owns some heads painted by Ketel's foot.[24]

Ketel decorated his own house with such subjects as Democritus and Heraclites, with a globe between them; he painted the right of the façade by his right foot, and on the left façade, Momus and Zoilus were painted by his left foot. Above the entrance of the house, there was a picture of Time, flying at great speed, wreathed with roses, with a sickle or scythe in one hand and an hour-glass in the other. Time is accompanied by two little angels; one is Intelligence and the other is Genius. All arts are achieved through Time, Intelligence and Genius. These pictures were painted by Ketel's left hand, without a brush; they are life-size and in full color.

Between these figures there are two statues that look as if they were made of bronze. At the right of Time, Pictura is painting with a hand and with a foot. At the left, there is a statue of Smiling Patience, seated on an anvil; she is attacked by Falsehood, who is shooting three arrows at once—these arrows represent Envy, Gossip and Slander. Jealousy is trying to pull Patience backward by the braids of her hair. Furious Hate is rousing up a raving dog which threatens to devour Patience. Mortality is represented by a headless man, and a skull has four flames coming from its eye-sockets. This symbolizes the great mortality in Amsterdam in 1602, when these scenes were painted. Apparently, these horrid creatures wished to destroy Patience, who is holding a little

343

lamb in her arm and a little cross in her hand; she endures, smilingly, and her face is lifted to heaven and her Creator.

Before concluding, I should like to mention some other allegories by Ketel. A nobleman, Sr van Wulp, asked Ketel to draw something in his guest book. Knowing the interests of noblemen, Ketel drew a nobleman, on a fine horse, holding a falcon in his hand; a young lady is mounted beside him, and a greyhound is running in front of them; in the distance, a peasant is on his farm with his cows. Ketel added this poem:

> How pleasant and sweet to be accompanied
> By a most exquisite and a graceful young lady.
> The galoping horse may be praised for its vigor;
> The greyhound may be praised;
> It is beautiful and faithful.
> The peasant loves his cattle and his farm.
> Who will be surprised that the worthy nobleman
> Loves his beautiful wife, the greyhound,
> And the splendid horse?

Ketel made another allegory in which he suggested the meaning of the foregoing subject. It was a picture of a lovely, little, young, nude woman seated on the lap of a young man; she wears a fool's cap, and she is giving birth to a child. The young man has beautiful features; at the back of his head there is a skull with the tail of a scorpion which, from behind, is stinging the back of the young woman. The young man is Danger of Death, and the young woman is Foolish Youth; the wise woman, assisting at the birth, is Idle-Vanity, and the child is Voluptuousness. Elsewhere, in the picture, Wise-Experience is removing the child from Foolish Youth who is about to play with the child. Two shells lie open, like a clam, and next to them, Reason, seated like a philosopher, with a stick in his hands, drives the child into the shells. The following is an explanation:

344

CORNELIS KETEL

Foolish Youth desires to play all the time with the baby.
Idle Vanity assists at the birth of Voluptuousness;
Foolish Youth violently embraces Danger of Death,
And she is unconscious of harm;
But Wise Experience takes away Voluptuousness.
Reason makes Voluptuousness return to the shell.
He who really uses Reason, will be the master.[25]

Many persons in The Hague thought this picture was ridiculous and laughed at it, as did the Prince of Orange.

Ketel made a large painting, for Burgomaster Cornelis Florissen van Teylinghen, which was seven feet high; it illustrated an ancient allegory of Time bringing about Truth. And Ketel painted another allegory in appreciation of the connoisseur, Jaques Razet of Amsterdam. It was an illustration of the motto of this gentleman—'Hereafter, better.' It was accompanied by this explanation.[26]

The roaring Earth, like a furious sea,
Is in fear and is threatened by disaster;
Painstaking Patience, chained in steel,
Is not alarmed by Calamity,
Although Tempest is blowing at her
With a terrific fourfold strength.
Strong Faith of the Heart knows that
God will never forsake.
Constant Hope shows her:
'Hereafter, better.'

Ketel also painted some small pictures for Razet: A Madonna, with a Babe refusing the breast and reaching towards the cross which an angel is presenting; another, Christ sitting on a rock with two angels crying. Razet traded this picture to De Jode; at present it is in Antwerp.[27]

Ketel painted a large picture, life-size, without tools. It is of a nude figure of a man with an ox-skin and holding a hammer, meaning Constant Labor; two little angels are flying over his head; one is Genius and the other is Artistic Ambi-

345

tion. Genius is suggesting to the mind to paint without brush-es, only with the hands and feet; the other angel, Artistic Ambition, is agitating the brain with a little pen, and is pointing towards a mirror—this means: plans must be made by the mind and the eye. Love, holding a flame in her right hand, is urging on the work, and, in her left hand, she holds a golden arrow to her heart—this symbolizes Ambition. Intelligence is directing the foot for painting, assisted by Sight, symbolized by a mirror; Intelligence cannot achieve anything without Sight, and Sight cannot achieve anything without Intelligence.

Pictura, holding a panel on her lap, has a palette with paint in her left hand; she allows Envy to be painted by a foot; Envy is raving mad. Pictura is accompanied by Ambition and Patience; they give us to understand that, with Time, they can produce much by constant labor. Time, represented flying, has not been neglected in this picture; in one hand he is holding an hour-glass, and in the other a sickle. Ketel gives this explanation:

> Genius and Artistic Ambition are hurting the mind;
> Love is active with flame and arrow;
> Intelligence is forcing man
> To achieve the obtainable.
> Patience and Ambition,
> By constant labor,
> Reveal to Intelligence that,
> With the assistance of the Eye and of Artistic Ambition,
> Hands and feet may do the work of brushes.
> Pictura sees and tolerates
> Painting that has been done by foot.
> Envy, mad and jealous, is angry at heart and spiteful.
> Flying Time is threatening to swing his sickle unexpectedly.
> Thus the one who wants to profit
> While here on earth
> Must use time wisely.
> Virtue triumphs.28

346

CORNELIS KETEL

This is the best picture that Ketel has painted without tools. Envy was done only by one foot, and the other subjects by the thumb and fingers. It is remarkable and surprising to see how precisely the little, flying angels have been painted; their nude figures are visible in the mirror which Time is holding. This painting, an excellent and wonderful piece of work, was done for Sr Willem Jacobson, an art collector, in Amsterdam. In the frieze of this large painting there is a poem which is supposed to be the painting's own story:

> Behold the costumes.
> I have been painted by fingers, feet and thumbs
> No brush, large or small,
> Ever touched me
> When I was painted by Ketel.

Recently, Ketel painted a *Judith*, a little more than a half-figure, life-size, with tools, and it is fine in color and full of grace. It was done for Sr Christoffel Dircksen Pruys, an art collector in Amsterdam.[29]

One of Ketel's most exceptional pictures is in Danzig. It is, *Danaë* and the rain of gold, life-size and large. I believe the sketch of this work may be seen in Ketel's house, where it is hanging in the front hall. There is a joke concerning it: A peasant saw this painting while passing, and asked the wife of Ketel for permission to look at it; he thought he understood the subject, and he liked it very much indeed. He said, addressing the figure in the painting, 'My dear Lady, if you can achieve this, you do not have to worry about making your living.' And standing there, he reflected and said: 'I know what this picture means. It is the *Annunciation*; the Holy Angel is bringing the holy message!' The peasant was proud of his own judgement and intelligence. He thought cupid was an angel, and Danaë, represented nude on a beautiful couch, lying with her legs spread, was the Madonna. The simple farmer moved on as wise as he was before.

Here we leave the life of Ketel in the hands of the Almighty. His works, left to the judgement of those who can discriminate, we recommend to fame. It is much easier to criticize failures in works of art than to point out what is good, or how to improve them. Ketel was a master with much experience in all the branches of art, and in architecture, geometry and perspective. He was skilled in poetry.[30]

Among Ketel's good pupils, there was a certain Oserijn, born at Copenhagen. At first, this artist worked at home without a teacher; he had no experience in drawing. When he came to Ketel, he was asked to copy a print; he had to do it alone, as well as he could. The print was of some of the works of Hercules, as engraved by Cort after a painting by Floris. After this was finished, Ketel had him copy it once more, under his supervision; he had to draw squares on it and make a tracing. There was a great difference between the first copy and this one, in the resemblance to the original print. Soon afterwards, the pupil was put at painting.[31]

Oserijn, after studying with Ketel for three years, went to Venice, where he stayed for a year; then he went to Rome, where he remained for another year. When he returned, he was so promising an artist that the highest in painting was to be expected from him; but soon he died from a fever. His life-size portrait of the King of Denmark was only in underpainting. Some of his works are in the house of Ketel, and these are interesting.[32]

GUALDROP GORTZIUS,

NAMED GELDROP

OF LOUVAIN

PAINTING portraits from life is, as I may have related previously, the work that most young artists can find to do in these countries of the Netherlands; for this reason, and because of the profit in this kind of work, many artists seldom do any of the other kinds of pictures. This was the fate of Gualdrop Gortzius, who could paint well. Usually, he was called Geldrop.

He was born in Louvain, in Brabant, in 1553. At the age of seventeen or eighteen, Geldrop went to Antwerp, a city famous for painting. He learned the first principles from Frans Francks of Herenthals. Geldrop had worked with Franciscus Pourbus before, or after, the death of his first master.[1]

Excelling in the various branches of art, Geldrop found Pourbus to be an unsurpassed, beautiful example that he could follow in painting portraits from life. Geldrop was an industrious worker, and he succeeded so well that he became painter to the Duke of Terra Nova, with whom he attended the peace negotiations at Cologne. After that event, Geldrop remained in Cologne.[2]

This artist is one of the best painters of portraits from life. This kind of work is not the only one at which he is successfully striving. He is excellent at painting compositions that include figures, as may be seen in several of his pictures now with various collectors.

A picture of Diana is in Cologne in the house of Sr Joan Meerman; it is well painted. A life-like picture of Susanna is owned by Everhard Jabach. Two beautiful pictures, of Christ, and of Mary, are in Cologne in the possession of a clergyman who is a collector. These pictures are excellent; they have been copied and engraved by Chrispian van de Passe. A picture of an Evangelist, in the house of Jooris Haeck, a collector, is admirable. Many of Geldrop's works are owned by Frans Francken and Jaques Mollijn, in Cologne. Another painting illustrates the story of Esther and Ahassuerus; it is in Hamburg, with a collector named Gortssen.3, 4, 5, 6

Paintings by Geldrop, especially his many portraits of splendid faces, are numerous. At present, in 1604, his mind, his good spirit, and his able, artistic hand, keep him busy.

Geldrop has opened the eyes of many artists and average portrait painters by his beautiful and fluent style, and he has given these artists a vision.7

MICHIEL JANSEN MIEREVELDT
OF DELFT[1]

IN art, a master that excels deserves to be praised and freed from the spitefulness of others. For this reason, I cannot refrain from commenting on Michiel Jansen Miereveldt. He was gifted in many ways. He was certain to become a painter of portraits. He is a master in this field, and his work proves that he is not equalled or surpassed. Michiel was born in Delft in 1568. His father was an able silversmith. From what I have learned, Michiel, from boyhood on, was a quiet, a good-natured, and an intelligent, person. He went to school when he was very young; he was bright; he learned rapidly. When he was only eight, he knew the art of writing so well he could write better than any schoolmaster in the city of Delft.[2]

Michiel's father let him study painting with, I believe, Jeroon Wierincz. He made rapid progress, and at the age of eleven or twelve he could handle the burin and engrave his own compositions. He engraved a *Woman at the Well*, a subject to which he had given considerable attention. Christ, seated at the right, has a serious expression; He is instructing the woman, and His hands and face express His eagerness splendidly; the woman shows surprise. The city of Sichar is on a mountain; the entire background is hilly; and the well is in the valley, and the people draw their water from it. The Apostles are on the horizon; they are bringing food. This engraving is very clear. I saw a Judith in almost the style of Blocklandt, especially the head of Holophernes, which was done with the burin most excellently. This piece is bolder in treatment than the other engraving.

At the age of twelve, Michiel went to Blocklandt, to work

351

with colors. He was not unhappy in his painting. He copied
the figures and the style of his master. He also did other
details very cleverly. I have noticed this in a variety of his
pictures that were composed and painted in his youth, when
he began to work independently, and they pleased me very
much. It seems to me that, if he had specialized in painting
original compositions with figures, he would have made some
excellent pictures.3

That seems to be the trouble in our Netherlands, especially
at the present time. There is too little for artists to do in making compositions with figures, and young artists have little
opportunity to become proficient at painting figures and
nudes. Most of the time they have to paint portraits from life.
Most artists are attracted by a sweet profit, and, as they have
to support themselves, they take this by-path in art—the
painting of portraits from life. Artists travel along this road
without delight, in time to seek the main road,—the painting
of compositions with human figures, the road that leads towards the highest in art. Many fine, splendid talents have remained unproductive, and this is regrettable.

The term, by-path, or side-road, as I have used it, may
seem too severe. It needs, perhaps, a little softening with a
brush or a feather. I say, therefore, that something very good
can be made of a portrait; the face, the most lively part of the
human body, has a great variety of interesting expressions,
and an artist by translating one of these expressions may reveal the virtues and the expressive power of art. This kind of
portraiture has been done by many of the great masters, and
at present our contemporary, Miereveldt—or Michiel Jansen
—is doing it. He has no equal here in the Netherlands.

Splendid portraits, the best work of Michiel, are in Delft.
Elsewhere, other remarkable pictures may be seen, and they
excel other portraits by other artists. Not very long ago

Michiel painted some portraits in which he realized his great ambition. The one of an old man with a huge beard is a wonderful and beautiful work,—it is in the Sign of the Cat, at Delft. A portrait of Hendrick Egbertszoon's son with his wife, is at Leyden. The portrait of Burgomaster Gerit Jansz. van der Eyck with his wife and children, is at Delft.

Michiel has almost finished a portrait of a certain Rutger Jansz., who has a fine face, who lives in Amsterdam and who is a lover of art and of all things beautiful. Michiel has painted the portraits of Jan Govertsz., of Amsterdam, and many others. He is working at present on the portraits of the Princess of Orange, some members of the nobility and their noble children. He has painted portraits of many Delft brewers.4

A portrait of the great collector, Jaques Razet, arrived recently at Amsterdam. It is a fine likeness; the carnation is well rendered; it is alive. It has caused much criticism; but it never could be surpassed. Michiel has received many requests for his work from Duke Albertus, who promised him freedom of religion and many other promises.5

Michiel is a fine master in the painting of kitchen scenes with many kinds of objects in them. He paints from life. Besides various works in Leyden, there is a kitchen scene, painted sometime ago, now in the house of Sr Bartholomeus Ferreris. Michiel seldom finds time to do anything but his portrait-painting, and he has a good deal to do, although he has a great liking for compositions with human figures in them.

Pauwels Moreelsz., who lives in Utrecht, studied for two years under Michiel, and he is now an excellent portrait-painter.6

A certain Pieter Geeritsz. Montfort, born at Delft, and now about twenty-five years old, went to Michiel at the age of seventeen, and studied for only half a year. He has a wonderful head, and he is a keen observer in his painting. He works in an excellent manner; but he paints only for pleasure and not for profit.

Pieter Dircksen Cluyt, of Delft, was a pupil of Michiel. He is about twenty-three years old. He has a great liking for composition, and he has made a good beginning as a painter.

Another pupil, named Claes Cornelisz., of Delft, has made a good start; he is a nephew of the master.7

HENRICUS GOLTZIUS

OF MULBRACHT

NATURE is marvellous in her achievements. When she has wished a youth to become an artist, she acts with dynamic force. She lets the seed she has sown in his bosom ripen very early. It becomes visible soon, as, generously, she gives the seed vitality and fertility. Thus did Nature favor Hendrick Goltzius. He was born of splendid and honorable parents, at Mulbracht, a village in the land of Julich, not far from Venloo, in 1558, in February, a few days before the anniversary of the conversion of St Paul.[1]

Hendrick's family came from the village of Heynsbeeck, where his great-grandfather, Goltz, had lived long ago. Hendrick's grandfather lived at Venloo; he was an able artist, named Hubrecht Goltz; he had a brother, Sybrecht Goltz, who was a sculptor. Hubrecht had a son and two daughters. The daughters married painters. One daughter was the mother of Hubrecht Goltz, an excellent historian, also named Van Würzburg. Hubrecht, the historian, lived a long time at Bruges in Flanders, as stated in his biography. He took the name, Goltz, from his mother's family.[2]

Jan Goltz, the son of old Hubrecht, and a good painter, lived at Kaiserswerth, where he was burgomaster and belonged to the magistracy. He had several daughters and two sons. The younger son was named, after his father, Jan Goltz, and, after the death of his father, he became a glass painter. Through some misadventures, this Jan Goltz was not able to take glass painting very far in the world. He went to Mulbracht, and he married when quite young.

Jan's oldest son is our supposed Hendrick Goltzius—a fat,

wild, and lively, child, notwithstanding the fact that his mother, through much illness, could not nourish him sufficiently with her own milk. He was a bright and active child. Once he fell and pierced his nose with a little stick. Frequently, he had to be pulled out of the water. He was very fond of fire, and when he was a year old, perhaps a little older,—he could almost walk alone—he fell face-down into a pan of hot oil, and both of his hands were burnt on the red, glowing coals. His mother did all she could to cure his little hands. She put them between strips of wood; she put ointments on them, and all kinds of other remedies. Night and day she suffered agonies. A wise-woman, of the neighborhood, came in, took off the strips of wood, and explained that it would be better to wrap the right hand alone in a towel. Because of this treatment, the sinews of the hand grew together, with the result that, later on, Goltzius never was able to open his hand entirely. Another misfortune occurred while Hendrick was still a child. It happened when Goltzius's father, by accident, unconsciously allowed the little fellow to put a piece of orpiment (a yellow dye, of arsenic) in his mouth. The parent cleaned the child's mouth as best he could.[3]

When Hendrick Goltzius was about three years old, his father, Jan Goltz, moved away from the village of Mulbracht and went to live at Duysburgh, a little town in the land of Cleves. Here, Goltzius went to school for four years, to learn the alphabet, to spell and to read. Then Nature waited no longer to do what she had planned for him.

It is said that cats cannot abstain from catching mice. It was evident that Goltzius's mind was set upon drawing. He made little figures of men with his pen, instead of making letters. Consequently, his father conceived the idea of permitting him to study drawing and glass painting. Goltzius was taken out of school. When he was about seven or eight years old, he had filled almost all of the walls in the house with drawings. He liked to draw his own conceptions, rather than copy some one else's.

Goltzius practised ambitiously from early youth, and kept steadily at his designs for glass and at the painting of glass. I remember, when I saw some of the things he had done in his early childhood, that he displayed a remarkable boldness and an ability to express very definitely and perfectly the subject of his composition.

The frequent illness of his mother caused him to be ready to wait on the other children, and to be a servant and to help with the household duties. These deflections from his work hindered the progress of his cherished plans. He was so eager to proceed that he devoted every holiday to drawing, on walls and on what he could find. He drew camels, elephants, and other large subjects. The father saw this, but he allowed the boy to draw, to paint and to be-daub as much as he wished, as long as he did not neglect his home affairs or forget his other duties. His father did not have a fortune. Things went adversely in his business.

Goltzius, though he knew he must help in the household, often regretted he was not allowed, by his father, to go to places where he could see something beautiful in the field of art. He was patient; and, owing to his great love for art, he began to make etchings on copper. He tried to engrave in copper with his lame hand, and he succeeded so well, from the very beginning, that Cornhardt, who lived at that time four miles away, wanted to teach him how to engrave. He had drawn many panels of designs for glass painters, and Cornhardt intended to engrave these. Goltzius's father, willing to give his consent, made an agreement with Cornhardt, binding him for two years; but Goltzius, however, did not like the terms and statements of this contract; nothing was decided.

Cornhardt then said that he would give the boy a trial for a month or two, and if Goltzius did not like the work, he would be free to stop. Goltzius readily accepted this proposal, as he would be able to see the process. But Cornhardt said: 'If you leave me, eventually, you must promise me that you will not go to another master, and that you will try not to learn it yourself.' Goltzius refused and retained his freedom. He went home, to his father; not a day passed without practise at engraving. Cornhardt knew this, gave him work immediately, and advised Goltzius to follow him to Holland. Goltzius agreed, providing his parents should be allowed to go, too; if not, they would not consent to his going. Goltzius went to live at Haarlem a short while after the great fire, about the time of the feast of St John. Cornhardt took pleasure in Goltzius's first attempts, taught him the best methods (according to his own) and as much more as he was able.[4, 5]

Goltzius made engravings for Cornhardt, and for Philips Galle, for a long time. Goltzius's parents went from Germany to Holland, in the meantime, but Goltzius remained in Haarlem. He married a widow of Haarlem, who had a son, Jacob Mathan, whom Goltzius instructed from youth on, and who, by dint of his great ambition, became an efficient engraver.

Goltzius, married, and only twenty-one years old, began to ponder as to his life, and to compare his chances with those of others. He allowed melancholy spells to possess him until he seldom had a rational day. Finally, he became ill of languor or consumption. He emitted blood for more than three years. The doctors did all they could to help him, but in vain. His hypochondria had taken root too deeply, and more so as he experienced new misfortunes.[6]

Goltzius realized his life was hanging by a silken thread, so to speak. He had no medical master that could help him.

HENRICUS GOLTZIUS

All the medical men believed the disease had gone too far. But Goltzius decided to go to Italy, although he was still very weak. He hoped to improve a little, and to be able to see, before he died, the fine and beautiful art of Italy from which he had been deprived for so long a time, by his marriage.

Goltzius took his servant with him on his journey; and he left his various pupils and his printer at home. He set forth in the last part of October in 1590. He took a boat from Amsterdam to Hamburg; but a great storm and thunder caused Goltzius to continue on foot the long journey ahead. Goltzius and his servant, in frost and cold, travelled throughout entire Germany. He began to feel better, and so much the more so as he saw the changes in the varying landscapes and the different inhabitants.

Goltzius took a special delight, as they went along, in playing jokes in places where he knew painters and engravers and other artists would visit them. He let his servant play the rôle of the master and let himself be unknown. He found, in this way, what they really had in their hearts. He heard slander about himself and his work—sometimes it was jealousy, at other times it was simply a narrow mind, and often for a very good reason. Goltzius's pleasure in all this made him very healthy.

Frequently he would act as a guest, and give a feast in the hostelry where his servant, according to the wishes of his master, had invited the artists. Goltzius would be very modest and hardly find a place to sit, while the servant, at the head of the table, was thanked most graciously for the fine treat given to the artists.

When he went to Munich, passing for his servant's travelling companion, Goltzius was invited by the artistic Hans Sadeler, who took him for a cheese merchant or for somebody else who had dealings, in some way or other, with

359

cheese. He promised Sadeler's wife to send her cheese from Holland, and this was actually done, by means of a letter which he wrote home. Much was said about the prints by Goltzius—the large Hercules and other subjects. The servant was modest and received the remarks very humbly. 7, 8

It usually happens that, in one's absence, other persons speak freely and openly, and with little respect; sometimes this is abuse. The presence of a person causes reserve and, perhaps, too much potential flattery, or too much diplomatic talk. Some persons may think this attitude in Goltzius wrong and unbecoming; because an artist, in the presence of his fellow artists or others, should not keep himself unknown and a stranger; persons may reproach him with hypocrisy. I know Goltzius had sufficient reason for doing what he did, and he may be exonerated. He has explained himself openly and satisfactorily.

So, very eagerly, Goltzius went to Italy, by the way of Venice, Bologna, and Florence, and finally reached Rome, where he had so much longed to be, on the tenth of January, 1591.

For several months he remained quiet and unknown. He dressed as a German peasant, and he assumed the name of Hendrick van Bracht. He hardly thought about himself, since his mind and thoughts were no longer shackled to his body; they were occupied in seeing the works of art in Rome.

Young artists, that went to Rome in great numbers, constantly saw Goltzius in his costume and looked over his shoulder at his work; they were interested to see what this German was doing; they expected some laughable product instead of something really wonderful.

Situations occurred, as in the Roman Senate, in the time of Emperor Marcus Aurelius, when the Danubian farmer came in (this only by way of parable). The artists talked a great deal about the work of this 'Tedesco.' They came more closely together; he was friendly to them, and gave them his advice. Let it be remarked that, when Goltzius was in Rome, things were unusually expensive throughout Italy, and, at Rome, there was a deplorable fear of contagious diseases. Many thousands had died there in a short time. Everywhere, in the streets and public places, the wretched people were lying about and dying. That was true of the places where Goltzius was making his drawings from antique sculpture. This could not deter him from working, notwithstanding the stench that was intense, and he was sensitive to smell.

Goltzius had his pastimes. He would go where his prints were for sale, to listen to the judgements of the artists concerning them, for they offered useful information; he gave serious attention to their criticisms.

Towards the end of April of the same year, Goltzius went from Rome to Naples with an amiable companion, Jan Mathijsen Silversmit, and a learned young nobleman, Philips van Winghen, from Brussels. The three had donned shabby looking clothing, as there was the danger of meeting wandering outcasts in numbers that made travelling unsafe. Van Winghen, an archaeologist, described everything he saw and made notes. He was a good friend of the famous geographer, Abraham Ortelius, of Antwerp. Van Winghen showed to Goltzius many letters he had received from Ortelius saying Goltzius was in Italy. In these letters, there was mention of some scars on his figure and of the crippled right hand. It was odd that Van Winghen was so eager to see the man who was daily before his eyes, and with whom he had enjoyed friendly relations for a number of months.[9, 10]

Finally, it was clear to Jan Mathijsen, and he said: 'This must be Goltzius.' Forgetting about himself and, seeing Golt-

361

zius's shabby clothing, although the three looked equally shabby, Van Winghen said: 'No, Hendrick, you are not the one. I mean that engraver from Holland.' Goltzius laughed, as Van Winghen judged the man by his clothing. Goltzius asked: 'Would it be funny, Sr van Winghen, if Goltzius was talking with you?' 'No. You are not Goltzius,' replied the other again. At night, when they arrived at Velletri, they spoke again on the same subject. Van Winghen relied entirely on his letters. Jan Mathijsen asked: 'Why do you rave so much about your letters? This *is* Goltzius.' Van Winghen became angry and refused to believe it. When Goltzius himself confirmed it, on the road, Van Winghen said: 'By Hendrick, I can't believe it.'

When they came to Terracina, the debate started again. Goltzius knew Van Winghen could not believe the truth, and since the man had been a good, honest companion, he thought he should not leave him in the dark any longer. Goltzius extended his crippled right hand, and showed him at the same time his handkerchief marked with the same monogram he had on all his prints—an H and a G, interlaced. Van Winghen became silent and white in the face. He embraced Goltzius most kindly and heartily, and regretted he had not recognized him sooner. They finished their journey to Naples, looked at the works of art there, and saw the strange phenomenon of nature, Pozzuoli. I believe Goltzius painted, in the palace of the old Viceroy of Naples, an excellent picture of antique sculpture, a young Hercules, seated. He returned with his companions to Rome.[11]

Goltzius wished to see the naked slaves that rowed the galleys of the Pope. Through a strong wind, Goltzius and his friends arrived at Gaëta and walked to Rome. In Rome, he became acquainted with the Jesuit priests and the local artists. He made crayon portraits of many who had made names for themselves. Goltzius made portraits in Florence, Venice, and in Germany.

Goltzius returned from Rome on the third of August, 1591. I do not believe there has ever been any artist of the Netherlands who produced as many pictures, beautifully done, in as short a time, and in so bad a time.

Goltzius went to Bologna with his companion, Jan Mathijsen. They travelled on horseback and stopped, for a few days at Venice, with a good friend, Dierick de Vries.[12]

Here a good joke was played. A painter knew Goltzius was coming; he said he could recognize Goltzius by his appearance. Goltzius was informed of his boast, and arranged to let Jan Mathijsen play the part of the more prominent figure. Jan was tall and stately. He was welcomed over Goltzius and called the Jupiter of Art. The artist wanted something drawn by Jan; the latter let his companion do it, and sign it with the name of Goltzius. Thus the artist, who thought he could judge so well by appearance, found himself fooled. This created a good laugh; the artist was far from pleased.

They went from Venice to Trent, and then to Munich, where they visited the same friends among whom Goltzius had appeared before as a stranger, and who now were very much embarrassed. Goltzius visited many friends and artists, and returned home quite healthy.

Goltzius was at home only a short time before the same old sickness came over him again. I do not know the cause. He seemed to be drying up. For several years he had to drink goat's milk and milk sucked from the breasts of women. He did not believe he could recover. After many severe illnesses, and against the expectations of everyone, but with the help of God, he got well. He had to take long walks every day. He lost a great deal of time and was kept from his work.

Now, he is in fine condition, and he is working with great pleasure. In a few words, this has been an account of the life of Goltzius.

As to Goltzius' works, his prints are first. His fine ability to draw is well known everywhere. In about 1580, I remember seeing at Bruges a few fine and beautiful prints after the drawings of Adriaen de Weerdt; the engraving had been done when Goltzius was at an early age. I like especially the scenes on the subject of Lucretia; they are his own compositions. Among others, there was a print of a banquet scene, in which he had very cleverly introduced some modern costumes, a novelty and deviation from the conceptions so common to most of the artists of the Netherlands.[13]

I became acquainted with Goltzius in the year 1583, when I lived in Haarlem. I showed him some drawings by Sprangher, and he took a great interest in them. I must say this about him: From his early youth he tried to understand the beauty of the various forms in nature; and he achieved a remarkable technique by which he could imitate the work of such masters as Hemskercken, Frans Floris, Blocklandt, Federigo, Lucchero, and Sprangher. He imitated the intelligent work of Sprangher, and made an engraving of *The Banquet of the Gods* by Sprangher, a work, overflowing with sweet grace, that claims eternal fame for the artist and the engraver.[14]

Once, I saw large, upright canvases in Goltzius's house. He had drawn some excellent compositions of the seven planets on them with oiled charcoal or black crayon. The nudes looked as if they had been painted in black and white. At the same time, I saw a large, oblong canvas, painted with black and white oil-colors, representing a Roman, Musius Savola, whose hand was burnt. This was made to fit in a room somewhere in a large mansion owned at the time by burgomaster Gerrit Willemsen, of Haarlem; at present, the house belongs

364

to Goltzius, and I believe this picture is in it. I should like to mention some engravings by Goltzius, his early ones, such as the *Roman Heroes* which are fine examples of his heroic strength in drawing, and of his expert handling of the burin. I shall pass over many of his works, merely for the sake of brevity, and mention the six pieces which he did after he returned from Italy. Goltzius had studied the various styles of engraving, and he now showed these different styles in his own work, after he had mastered them with his own hand. It is remarkable that he was able to do this so quickly and perfectly. He was eager to show his work in the fair at Frankfort. His prints were ready; but hardly anyone saw them. He then played a funny trick with the print of the *Circumcision* which he had done in the style of Albrecht Dürer and in which his own portrait appeared. Goltzius had his portrait and his own monogram burned out with a hot coal or iron, and then had the print smoked and treated, so that it looked as if it was ancient, and had existed many years. His print, disguised in this way, was shown at Rome, Venice, Amsterdam, and elsewhere. The artists and the connoisseurs were amazed and pleased by it. It was sold and re-sold for high prices. The buyers were delighted to obtain a work by the great artist of Nürnberg, particularly an engraving that had been completely out of sight. It was ridiculous, that the master was so much exalted. When the question was raised, as to whether or not Goltzius could have made the engraving, some critics said he was far from able, and he could not make such an engraving in a whole lifetime; and this was the best print by Dürer that they had ever seen. Others said that Albrecht Dürer had made a special engraving which he requested be hidden for a hundred years after his death, and then, if his work should be appreciated, the engraving could be printed; this engraving, in question, was the one.[15, 16, 17, 18]

It was the same thing with the engraving of the *Three Magi*, done in the style of Lucas van Leyden. The strange thing is, that engravers, who thought they knew the various style and treatment of the different great masters, were misled by this print. This shows us what the likes and dislikes of men can do: Some, who disliked Goltzius and his work, had unconsciously exalted him above the best of the old masters. Others said that better engravers than Albrecht and Lucas never could be expected, and that Goltzius could not be compared with them.

These six engravings were sufficient to show what Goltzius was able to do. I believe this work was dedicated to the illustrious Duke of Bavaria, who honored Goltzius with a gold chain and a large and beautiful gold medal of a portrait of the Duke.[19]

After these engravings, Goltzius published a series on the Passion, in the year 1597. The work was remarkable and pleasing, and entirely in the technique of Lucas van Leyden; but not Van Leyden's poses of the figures and other details. It certainly is not inferior to the work of Lucas.[20]

I cannot remain silent concerning an engraving of *Mary*, with the dead figure of Christ on her lap. This is a small engraving, done in the style of Albrecht Dürer. It is owned by Sr Berensteyn, a collector in Haarlem. All of this work proves that Goltzius is a phenomenal Proteus or Vertumnus in art, and that he is able to play various rôles. Goltzius, when very young, engraved a wonderful plate of a woman with snakes and doves and, in the background, Christ before Pilate. This is an allegory of the saying of Christ: 'Be ye therefore wise as serpents and harmless as doves.' This little plate surpasses everything else by Goltzius, in accuracy and in keenness of sight. It is for connoisseurs to say how well Goltzius could draw with the pen. In my opinion, I never have seen better work, or even its equal, and I do not expect to see any better in the future, by any other artist.[21, 22]

Among many prints on parchment, small ones and large ones, there is one of Bacchus, Ceres, and Venus, with a Cupid tending a fire which reflects upon the figures. This picture is in Rome, I believe.[23]

A beautiful example of work by Goltzius, now in the possession of the Emperor, is of *Faunus and Fauna*. Another excellent work is with the Fuggers at Augsburg—a Pieta: Christ is lowered from the Cross and placed in front of Mary, who shows great self-control by not weeping from the suffering and great sorrow in her heart; many angels appear; the entombment is in the background. This composition and its execution cannot be surpassed. It was sent to the King of Spain, who died at the time it arrived.[24]

Goltzius conceived the idea of drawing with a pen on canvas primed with oil-color; for parchment, no matter how large the piece, was too small for his great and important conceptions. Thus, he drew a figure of a nude woman and a laughing satyr on a large canvas. He emphasized the modelling of the figures with a little paint, and then varnished the picture. Once, Franciscus Badens, a painter in Amsterdam, owned this picture. The Emperor obtained it later, and he was amazed by Goltzius's technique. He wanted to know how it had been done; he invited connoisseurs to come see it, and they were amazed. It was rare and worth seeing.[25]

Goltzius drew a figure of a nude Venus recumbent with Cupid, for Badens. The background is a scene of Venus and Cupid picking flowers; Pristera and Nymphe assist Venus, and, therefore, Cupid changes her into a dove. The composition is excellent; the action, the pose of the figures, and the treatment, with long cross-hatchings, are beyond reproach. It can be seen now in Badens's house.[26]

At present, Goltzius is busy over a large canvas on which he has worked for a long time. Several, large, nude figures appear in this picture which, from what I was able to learn by hearsay, should surpass all his previous pen-work. I did not see it at the beginning; but it must be so, or I should not have heard about it. Goltzius is very careful: He does not show his half-finished work. But when he had finished them, he shows them to any one who wishes to see them. In this respect, he is like Michelangelo.

I do not know any one else so sure of his drawing, so capable at drawing a single figure, even a whole scene, directly and free-handed, with a pen, without a previous sketch. His work is perfect, accurate, and reflects a great spiritual content.

I shall now leave the topics of the clever pen-drawing and the technique of this lord, and take up his painting. Goltzius, after he returned from Italy, had the images of the beautiful Italian paintings in his head as plainly as if he saw them in a mirror. He saw them constantly and very clearly. He found a delight in the sweet grace of Raphael, in the wonderful flesh painting by Correggio, in the fine modelling and chiaroscuro by Titian, in the beautiful textures and silks in works by Veronese and those by other Venetian masters. He was no longer pleased by the paintings made in this country.

The artists liked to hear him talk about paintings; it was food to them, and his words were fascinating. He spoke of 'glowing carnation,' of 'glowing depth,' and he used other terms which were unusual and seldom heard.

When he made a drawing, he added crayon color to the nudes; so, finally, he took to brushes and oil-color. This was only two years after he had resumed a normal diet, at the age of forty-two, 1600.[27]

Goltzius's first painting was a small one on copper, painted for Gijsbert Rijckersen at Haarlem. It was a *Crucifixion*, with Mary, St John and Magdalene; the nude figure of Christ is beautiful in color but cadaverous. It is a good study, well conceived, definite, and beautifully painted. Jerusalem is in the background; a hen with her chicken is in the foreground which is somewhat in half-tone. This is an allegory of the saying of Christ when he lamented Jerusalem.[28]

Previously and for pleasure, Goltzius had painted a life-size, seated, nude figure, in oil-color on canvas, for which Tobias Swartsenburgh of Haarlem had been the model. He had represented him as an Indian with a bow. In the background there was a small figure of St Sebastian, painted excellently. For his travelling companion, Jan Mathijsen, Goltzius painted a large panel which represented a scene in Heaven, or a *Celestial Paradise*. It may be explained as the faithful, Christian soul going towards the Church of God, dressed in white silk to symbolize pure Conscience and true Devotion. She marries Christ, her celestial husband, who is an innocent child. The celestial company rejoices and glorifies the soul with palm and crown which symbolize Persistence and Reward. Explained differently: The virgin, Saint Catherine, for constancy in faith and for suffering, is rewarded with the crown of martyrdom, and receives Christ as her husband. This painting, of nude figures, faces, draperies, silks, and other details, is excellent. Goltzius gave full justice to each detail. He avoided sharp outlines, in the nudes, in the faces, and in the shadows, to make the picture harmonious. By indicating depth on both sides of raised parts of the nude, he produced the effect of relief. He painted a large drapery in ultramarine and felicitously applied glazing, as glass painters do, by a special handling of the brush. This work is evidence of the keen eye and great knowledge of Goltzius. He did most of it from life. It is appreciated by connoisseurs, and the average person likes it for its charm and love-liness.[29, 30]

On a copper plate, Goltzius painted a seated, almost nude, figure of Christ. Two angels, kneeling beside Him, burning torches, and some instruments of the Passion, are shown. This excellent painting is now with Count van der Lip, or with the Emperor.[31]

In 1603, Goltzius painted, on a large canvas, a nude and re-cumbent figure of *Danaë*, life-size. She is sleeping, and her pose is beautiful. The carnation is painted marvellously, as is the modelling. The work reflects his great study of outline and anatomical construction of the body. There is in this picture, a shrewd old woman with a glowing face, and a figure of Mercury. I cannot describe the lovely little angels that are flying with gifts. The picture is beautifully com-posed and could not be improved in any way. This painting is at Leyden with Sr Bartholomeus Ferreris, a collector; it can be seen in his art-room.[32]

Goltzius painted many pictures for his own pleasure: One is a peasant woman from the North; but I want to mention here, especially, a portrait of Jan Govertsen, of Haarlem, who is a lover of shells—he is holding some shells in his hand; this is a perfect painting and the resemblance is excellent.

As for Goltzius's work in oil-color, this is about all that I know. Had Goltzius desired to do so, he could have sur-passed every one else in the art of glass painting. A small ex-ample of his work is in Haarlem with Cornelis Ysbrandtsen, an excellent glass painter. Goltzius did glass painting for a pastime, remembering his first trials in this field. This kind of work, as in painting and engraving, has a similar evolution; its perfection is based on drawing; I do not know any one, any master, greater than Goltzius in this kind of work.[33]

If occasional thunderstorms threaten him, he should not

be alarmed, for he is like a strong cliff. The fame of his noble work shall live; but the names of those who stupidly bark at him will perish.

Goltzius is indifferent to the events of the world; he does not care about the gossip of ordinary persons. His superb love of art makes him desire a quiet state of mind and to be alone. Art requires all for herself. He loves his own freedom but little more than he loves politeness and honesty. His motto is: 'Honesty above gold.' His actions prove that he really values honesty more than money. He is modest. He considers himself and his knowledge of nature to amount to little. He refrains from bravado. He is not inexperienced in the field of natural science.

I can remember I liked a few of his adept answers which I have now partly forgotten. As Goltzius had painted many portraits, in the year 1583, he painted two full figures, on copper, of two Polish princes who had come from France to visit the Netherlands. They were dressed in the French style which was the fashion at that time. One was the nephew of the King of Poland. Goltzius went to Haarlem to see them. In order to arrange the price, they had with them a merchant who had more wealth than wisdom, and he was to attend to the payment for the princes. When the merchant learned that more money was asked than he had expected, he said it was too much, and Goltzius, if paid in this way for his art, would earn more than a merchant. Goltzius replied that the negotiations had nothing to do with art—'I can become a merchant very easily by means of money; but you, with all your money, cannot become an artist.'34

Once Goltzius was invited out by some young German noblemen, one of whom wanted to have his portrait painted on a panel, and then, later, engraved. They urged Goltzius to drink, and soon they had many glasses in front of him.

Goltzius asked them why they had invited him to come. They answered, 'To make a drawing.' 'Why, then, Gentlemen,' he said, 'why do you ask me to drink so much? You realize I am not a beast. But suppose I did! What good would that do? How could I serve you properly?' At this, they were ashamed of themselves.

Once Goltzius pointed out something wrong in the work of one of his pupils; the pupil said he knew it and he had seen it himself. Then Goltzius said: 'Your measure is filled; you are already wealthy enough.' And he directed his efforts towards another pupil, who had space in his measure to receive something, and who gratefully and readily accepted education.

When Goltzius heard painters praising their own works and indulging in their own achievements, he said they were happy and rich, because he who is satisfied with himself is rich. 'As for myself,' he said, 'I have never been able to get that sensation from my work.'

I have heard him say, many times, that he never had done a thing entirely to his satisfaction, or which even pleased him well. He always thought of possible improvements that he could make. This is a good sentiment: The artist who feels this way should not stray from his path, as do Pygmalions who fall in love with their own products, and who are less than they realize.

Goltzius had a few pupils who became fine engravers, such as De Gheyn, whose biography will be given. Jacob Mathan, another pupil, is Goltzius's son-in-law. He visited Italy. He is living at Haarlem, and he is an excellent master in his art. Pieter de Jode, a pupil of Goltzius, was in Italy a few years. He is now living at Antwerp.[6, 35]

I shall now conclude my writing about Goltzius. This year, 1604, he is a man of forty-six years. Praise God, for he is feeling well and I am thoroughly thankful.

HENRICUS GOLTZIUS

Plato, when he felt his death approaching, thanked Genius, the God of his birthday and destiny, because he had been born a human being and a Greek, instead of a barbarian, or a beast, and because he had lived as a contemporary with Socrates. In the same way, I rejoice because I have shared, for more than twenty years, a friendly companionship with the great Goltzius, and because I have had the benefit of his knowledge.[36]

HENDRICK CORNELISSEN VROOM

OF HAARLEM

KIND-hearted parents often bestow too much love on their children, and they show over-concern in bringing them up; they want to keep them at home all the time and have them well protected in cushions. Parents may often harm their children. It is like the story of the mother monkey that hugged her young too closely. Sometimes parents are not affectionate. A child may feel deprived of affection, or he may be sent from home at an early age. He soon must realize what he should do for himself in order to be successful. The child that can shoot his own arrows and reach with his own hands, without crutches for support, will succeed in the right way.

Hendrick Vroom came from Haarlem. His mother had married twice. The harshness of his step-father forced Vroom at an early age to leave the warm nest of his mother. Fortunately, he had a very strong liking for art.

Vroom was born in Haarlem in 1566. His father was Cornelis Henricksen, and a sculptor who made pottery. He was experienced in the art of drawing, and he designed wonderful and strange drinking vessels on which one did not know where to put one's mouth; he made other similar objects that were excellently colored.[1]

A brother of Henricksen, Vroom's uncle, Frederick Henricksz., was an excellent sculptor, and was skilled in geometry, architecture and perspective; he was an architect in the city of Danzig. The grandfather of Vroom was Henrick Vroom, a fine stone cutter and sculptor. Vroom came from an artistic family.

Vroom was forced by his stepfather to paint 'Plateelen.'

374

He was experienced in this work; but he wanted to learn more, and he wanted to paint pictures. Driven from the house of his stepfather, Vroom tried here and there to find work with a master. He frequently made his living by making a 'plateel' painting—a 'pot-boiler,' in time of need. Invariably, he had to draw small boats on vases.

After visiting a few such cities as Enkhuizen and Bruges in Flanders, Vroom went to Rotterdam. He went from that city, in a Spanish vessel, to San Lucar de Barrameda in Spain and then to Seville. There he met a humble painter from the Netherlands, named Pintemony—'painter of monkeys.' Then, after painting pottery with an Italian, Vroom crossed the sea, in great danger owing to the Turks, landed at Livorno and went from there to Florence and then to Rome. He lived in Rome for some time with a Spanish canon for whom he painted; in the meantime he made a few comic studies of figures. From Rome he went to Florence to visit the illustrious Cardinal de Medici, for whom he made paintings after prints. He was in Florence for about two years, and he occupied himself by painting compositions with figures, portraits, and landscapes, on copper. Pauwels Bril visited him frequently and gave him instruction.[2, 3]

From Florence, Vroom went to Venice, where he decorated majolica and porcelain. About a year later, he moved to Milan, and here he met Valerius, an ordinary painter from the Netherlands. After a few months Vroom went to Genoa. The times were hard for one to earn one's bread. Without finding work, he went to Albissola, where he intended to decorate pottery; but there was no work for him to do in that town. He then went to Turin, in Piedmont, and worked with Jan Kraeck, the painter to the Duke of Piedmont. A few months later, Vroom crossed Mount Cenis and arrived at Lyons. On this journey, Vroom was in real danger: He stumbled and would have fallen from a high and steep place, had his pants not caught on a rock; mule-drivers freed him, though part of his pants remained frozen to the rock.4

While Vroom was at Lyons, he was invited by Sr Bottoin to go to a castle outside the city and to paint, in water-color on canvas, the Italian battle-scenes on land and water, in which this gentleman, his father and his ancestors, had taken part. Galleys and other ships, and battles between cavalry and infantry, appeared in this picture; this painting was done in six months.

Vroom went from Lyons to Paris, to visit a painter from Leyden, and then to Rouen, because of the expensiveness of living. At Rouen he was very sick and was given up to die; but he recovered, after an old woman had bandaged his head. From Rouen he went to Holland by boat and returned to Haarlem, where he was married. He painted pictures after prints, and the subjects were always ships. About a year after his marriage, Vroom went to Danzig, to the uncle previously mentioned, and there he painted an altar panel for some Polish Jesuits in that city. His uncle taught him perspective and other work in painting.5, 6

With his wife, Vroom returned to Haarlem, and, after a brief stay, he took part of his religious paintings to Spain. On the voyage, owing to a great storm one night, all on board were forced to leave the ship. In a rowboat, at great risk of losing their lives, they made for the rocky coast of the island of Los Barlingos. They tried to approach a small harbor, really an inlet, where the strong waves threw them back repeatedly, and they landed with great difficulty. The ship was wrecked in the shallow water and smashed to pieces. The cargo floated to the near-by shore of Portugal, to a monastery.

When the monks of the monastery saw the little paintings

by Vroom, they spoke to the abbot of the place and convinced him by strong argument that the sailors on the island
were Christians and not English pirates come to steal.

Vroom and his twenty-five companions had no food on
Los Barlingos, and no water to drink but the rain from the
sky. They were in great agony; in desperation they calculated that they would soon have to eat the younger ones
among them. They made a large flag of their shirts and waved
it. The monks sent a boat to them, with oil, wine and bread.
Vroom and his companions were taken to Penice and asked
if they were English. They answered negatively, for otherwise they would have been taken back and abandoned on the
island. Vroom and his company went to the church of the
monks and thanked God, most devotedly, as Vroom had
taught them. They were treated cordially by the abbot, who
served them himself at table. Vroom's little pictures that
were intact were put on exhibition; the others were lost.[7, 8]

At the end of two days, some money was given to them
and they went to Lisbon on foot. From Lisbon Vroom went
to Setubal, where he boarded a ship bound for the Netherlands. He conceived the notion that this ship would not finish
its voyage. Unwillingly, the crew put him ashore, calling him
a 'Schilder Cranckhooft.' The ship was forced to pass Texel,
and it went down in the Stroom. The skipper was Roel Jansen from Medemblik.

The sailors, who survived the earlier wreck, had seen
Vroom board the ship at Setubal and had continued their
own voyage, without knowing Vroom had put ashore. They
knew the ship went down, and at Haarlem they reported
Vroom as dead.

Vroom stayed at Setubal in a monastery, where he painted
a portrait of a priest and was given every consideration.
Another painter also lived at Setubal; Vroom painted his

own shipwreck adventures for this artist, who sold the painting for a large sum of money to a gentleman of rank at Lisbon. The artist was grateful to Vroom and wanted more marine paintings.

Vroom profited rather well from this connection and went home again. In the meantime, he had notified his wife that he was alive. His wife always had thought so, and soon she had personal proof of the holy truth of her conviction.[9]

After he returned to Haarlem, he continued to do marine paintings, at the suggestion of the guild of the painters, and he did them gradually better. As there is much navigation in Holland, the public learned to admire his paintings of ships.

At about this time, Fransoys Spiering, the excellent tapestry weaver, had agreed to make a tapestry for the Admiral of England, Lord Howard, and it was to be a scene of the naval battle between the English and the Spanish fleets in 1588. Spiering wanted me to help him do the drawing of the cartoon; but drawing of boats was not my kind of work, and I introduced him to Vroom, who would work for daily wages; he drew ten large designs of various stages of the naval battle. Vroom profited by this study and work. One day he left Zandvoort in a boat for England. He visited the Admiral, and he told him that he was the artist who had drawn the cartoons of the fleet; he was rewarded with one hundred guilders.[10]

While in London, Vroom became acquainted with Isaac Oliver, an able miniature worker, who painted a fine miniature portrait of him.[11]

Upon his return home, Vroom painted, on a large canvas, the seventh day of the battle between the English and the Spanish fleets; this painting had a remarkable amount of detail. His Excellency, Count Maurice, and Admiral Justinus, looked at it with pleased amazement.[12]

HENDRICK CORNELISSEN VROOM

Vroom made a drawing of the embarking of the fleet which left Zeeland for Flanders shortly before the battle of Nieuport. This drawing was reproduced by engraving, and Vroom presented some prints of it to the town and to the members of the States-General. He received a large sum of money for this work.[13]

Vroom is an expert at rendering ships. Every day he improves, and he has made now an almost countless number of paintings. He works rapidly and makes shore scenes composed of fish and fisher-folk and other small figures; these bring him a good profit. He is to be praised because he does not daub in his pictures. Those who want his work pay for it.

In conclusion, Vroom is a master; as to the drawings of his ships, they show good construction; he has a thorough knowledge of ropes and rigging; the direction of the wind, the sails, and other details, are well rendered. Vroom excels in painting landscapes, rocks, trees, the sky, water, waves, castles, villages, cities, figures, and other subjects, that appear in his marine paintings and make them beautiful.[14]

HANS SOENS
OF S'HERTOGENBOSCH

I SHOULD not forget to mention famous artists who are now living in hidden places. The artists of the Netherlands are more eager than the artists of any other nation in the world to travel and visit foreign countries and peoples. I shall mention here the able painter, Hans Soens, from s'Hertogenbosch. He is at present at Parma, in Italy, where he is staying with the Duke of Parma, as far as I know.[1]

I do not know with whom Soens studied the first principles of art. He came to Antwerp and lived with an excellent school teacher named Master Jacob Boon. He worked there for quite a while for himself. He then boarded with Gillis Mostaert and worked in his shop. Soens copied beautiful paintings daily, specially in the style of Frans Mostaert. He became clever at following the style of painting landscapes by this master. Nature guided his artistic hand constantly; she had given him a keen mind and the power of observation.[2]

Some of Soens's earliest works, very pleasing landscapes, are with Sr Hendrick Louwersz. Spieghel, a collector at Amsterdam. A landscape in oil, that has the dimensions which water-color artists call a double-canvas, has a road, a hedge, and many beautiful trees, in the foreground, and, among some interesting figures, one is evacuating. Soens painted some landscapes on small panels and some pictures of fires; in these pictures there are fields of corn, oats and other crops.[3]

Soens has been in Italy. He was in Rome when I was there, and we often met each other. Soens produced many works in Rome. He painted many little pictures, on copper with oil-color, for gentlemen of rank, and many frescoes in the palace of the Pope. Soens showed us some landscapes that he had painted in fresco on a frieze in one of the rooms of the Pope; the scaffold was still up, but I could see the quality of his work near by, and it was remarkable. Some painter, in the service of the Pope or someone else, said that the work was too coarse and not well finished; but these paintings appeared to be unusually good from below, from where they had to be seen.[4, 5]

One little scene in this work was of St Augustine at the sea-shore, where he finds a little child trying to lift, with a small shell, all the water of the ocean into a pond. The ocean was wonderfully well painted, to show a natural, aerial perspective, and shadows and sunshine and the flatness of the water.

Soens painted a fine landscape, in fresco, in one of the ante-chambers of the royal hall. It was an allegory with a rooster in it. This fresco is excellent in comparison with the other landscapes in that chamber, painted by Caesar de Salusto, or other artists. Caesar followed Soens very closely, as I have related previously; but I made a mistake when I wrote that he came from Antwerp.[6]

Soens is at Parma, where, from what I hear, he has done his very best work in various large landscapes. He is good at painting small-figure compositions. I have seen some of these pictures in Rome, and they were very fine, and some of them were comical.[7]

Soens is a bachelor and he is about fifty-six or fifty-seven years old. He deserves to be counted among the best of the landscape painters of the Netherlands.[8]

HANS VAN AKEN
OF COLOGNE

IT is a fact that when one is a really eminent master of painting one becomes famous. Fame is stimulating and exciting to our youthful artists, when it reaches their ears. Fame, who is informed on everything that happens in the universe, blows her trumpet and makes an artist celebrated. Deep waters and high cliffs cannot stop her; she soars high above everything on her all-knowing wings. A great artist seems to be visible at any distance, because he is so radiant. Illustrious princes and mighty rulers often invite a great painter to show his artistic and noble mind through the work of his experienced hand. An artist, while pleasing beautiful Pictura with things lovely to the eye, may rise as high in rank, and be as esteemed by princes and rulers, as is Hans van Aken.

Hans van Aken was born of honorable parents, in the famous city of Cologne on the Rhine, in 1556. His father was a splendid, serious man. He came from the city of Aachen, and he gave this city's name to his son in addition to his other name.[1]

Benevolent Nature selected the boy, and she impressed on his mind, in his early youth and afterwards, the beauty and nobility of the art of painting. She consented, however, to let him stay in school and learn to read and write till he was in his tenth or twelfth year, if he would draw as often as he could, with his pen or other tools, the various subjects she suggested to him. These were men, animals and kindred topics. And so he took his first steps on the road that she had plotted for him, and that was to lead to perfection, honor and fortune. Hans willingly obeyed. He was ambitious.

Wherever he went he observed and detected what Nature taught him. The world was a great schoolroom. He began to discriminate between the interesting things—the beautiful, the graceful, the fine—and the ugly things.

He might see a fine horse that carried its head beautifully, had a good gait and admirable proportions; or he might see a lovely woman's face; then he would do his best to paint what he had seen, as perfectly as he could. It is easy for one to identify his subjects: While a Duchess from Cologne was lying in her window looking out, Hans made a drawing of her, and by it one could recognize her.

Hans made a life-drawing of a cat, sitting on a high place; it was done with a pen. A painter, who visited the boy's father and saw this drawing, thought the boy had already received drawing instruction and was experienced; when he learned otherwise, he was much surprised and advised the boy to study art. He said, 'There is a man in this boy and a chance for him to become a great master.'

Hans then studied under a somewhat mediocre painter. He did not stay a full year with him, because he believed the artist could teach him little. Hans went to another painter at Cologne, who was named Giorgie or Jerrigh, and who was a Walloon. This artist had studied at Antwerp and had been compelled by poverty to be a good artist, specially of portraiture from life, which he did excellently.[2]

Hans made such wonderful progress under this painter that, after six years, when the painter died, he was an excellent portrait painter and had painted many fine heads. Hans was eager to draw in an ambitious manner. He followed the work of Sprangher very closely, as I judged by some of his drawings which I saw at that time.[3]

Hans was about twenty-two years old when he went to Venice. He visited a painter from the Netherlands, named

Gaspar Rems, and, instead of testing Hans at what he knew about art, he only asked him what place he had come from. When he learned that Hans had come from Cologne, he said: 'You are a 'mof,' and 'moffen' do not know much.' He sent Hans to an ordinary Italian painter and picture-dealer named Morett, who gave work to travelling painters. Morett let Hans copy some of the beautiful things which were in the local churches.4

Hans made, among other things, a portrait of himself, laughing, which he did before a mirror; this picture was intended for Gaspar. This laughing face was painted so well and so beautifully that Gaspar was astonished; he had been wrong to believe the 'moffen,' as he called the Germans, were not able to produce fine work, and he felt he had been most unfair.

Gaspar treasured this painting as long as he lived; he showed it to everyone and praised it. Hereafter, Gaspar was glad to prepare and prime the canvases for Van Aken. From this one may learn how very unjust, careless, and rude, some persons are when they regard as inferior one whom they do not know and whom they judge by the place of birth.

Subsequently, Hans went to Rome and painted many beautiful pictures. One remarkable painting was an altar panel that he painted with oil-color on zinc or lead. It was a *Nativity* with angels, and with other details in accordance with the wishes of the Jesuit priests, and it was placed in their church at the foot of the Capitol.5

I shall not mention many of Van Aken's pictures. The laughing portrait of himself has a female figure, named Donna Venusta, playing on a lute; he is standing behind her with a bowl of wine. This picture was painted so well experts said that they never had seen anything better by him or any other artist.6

Van Aken went to Florence, and there he painted many portraits from life of gentlemen and ladies of rank, for example, the illustrious Duke of Florence, Francesco, and the poetess, Donna Laura. Hans kept a copy of her portrait which can be seen in Amsterdam with his pupil, Pieter Isaacsz.7

When Hans returned to Venice, he painted some splendid pictures for a merchant from Maestricht in the Netherlands. One was a life-size painting of the *Mocking of Christ*; Christ is almost nude and leaning to one side and looking upwards; the attitude is beautiful. Another painting was a life-size *Danaë*, which picture is very fine, and it is excellent in treatment. A little Madonna with St Catherine and angels was on copper; this picture was engraved by Raphael Sadeler, and prints of it were published. It is a fine little piece. Hans's large composition, of half-figures, life-size, is of Venus with Cupid; Venus is coming out of the sea at Cyprus, and the houris give her a present of divine costume and ornaments; this illustrates one of Homer's Songs to Praise the Gods.8, 9

Hans, after his return to Cologne, made for a merchant named Boots, a beautiful painting of *The Judgement of Paris*, and it was engraved by Raphael Sadeler.10

Later on, when Hans was in Venice again, he received an invitation from Count Otto Heinrich von Schwarzenberg, court master for the Duke of Bavaria, to go to Munich and to paint a memorial picture in his mortuary chapel. This is a panel with figures more than half-size; it represents St Helena discovering the Cross, and it is a splendid work. Hans became acquainted with the Duke, through Count Otto. He painted a group of the Duke, the Duchess, and their youngest son and daughter, and this composition pleased each one. After Hans had finished various paintings, the Duke gave him a beautiful gold chain, in addition to other rewards, and

Count Otto gave him another gold chain and two hundred florins.[11, 12]

Hans went from Bavaria to Prague. The Emperor there had been inviting him to come for over four years, because he had seen the portrait that Hans had painted in Florence of Jean de Bologne, an eminent sculptor from the Netherlands. The Emperor had persisted at inviting Hans; and at last, through the representations of an ambassador, the artist went to see him. He remained and painted a Venus and Adonis for the Emperor who was much pleased, specially by the coloring which was unusual.[13]

For some reason, Hans returned to Munich and went to Augsburg. He painted a *St Sebastian*, for the Jesuit Church in Munich, that was excellent in composition. This painting was beautifully engraved by Joan Muller, an excellent copper engraver in Amsterdam. The portraits of the Fuggers of Augsburg were painted by Hans.[14]

Requested by the Emperor, Hans returned to Prague. He had married the daughter of a famous musician, Orlando de Lasso.[15]

By his art, Hans has found the most powerful and highest Maecenas of the entire world; he has been serving him ever since as a decorator of his palace. He is enjoying an Apellistic friendship with this mighty Alexander who holds him in great esteem.

Van Aken has painted many beautiful and excellent pictures for the Emperor, and they may be seen in the palace; they are in the large hall above the stables, in the galleries above the art room, and in other rooms of His Majesty's Court.[16]

A large and beautiful painting by Hans is in Amsterdam with Sr Heyndrick van Os, a collector. The figure, life-size and painted artistically, is a beautiful nude woman; she represents Peace and holds a branch of laurel; her feet rest on the paraphernalia of war. Abundance, Pictura, and other allegorical figures, are with her; they symbolize Art and how it can flourish, when there is peace.[17]

Hans is where his art is loved and appreciated most sincerely. He is as fine a man as his paintings are beautiful; he lives nobly; he is generous and kind to all artists. He is far removed from those who in conceit seek entrance into the houses of persons of high rank.[18]

I hope Hans will have a long life, and he will be happy, so that the art of painting may be glorified by him, and he by it.[19]

The first pupil of Hans van Aken is Pieter Isaacsz. He was born at Helsingfors in 1569, and went with Hans to Italy and Germany. His father came from Haarlem.[20]

Pieter studied the first principles of art with Ketel at Amsterdam, for a year and a half. He now is living in Amsterdam. He is excellent at portrait painting. He has had much experience in figure composition and in drawing.

Specially beautiful and splendid is the portrait by Isaacsz. at Leyden in the Breestraat., of a young lady named Sara Schuyrmans; it is large and knee-length; her dress is of satin; she is playing on a zither and her hands are well rendered; her face is a good likeness and is painted very carefully. This picture is sufficient proof of the greatness of Isaacsz. Two other portraits by Isaacsz. are at In de Klok; one is of Pieter Huygesze, and the other is of the first wife of this gentleman. A large painting by Isaacsz. is in Amsterdam with Sr Hendrick Franckin, a great collector, who lives at the Voorachterburgwal; it is an *Adam and Eve*. In the same place there is a painting, on copper, of St John preaching, a well-composed and very pleasing little picture. Portraits of Sr Franckin and his wife were painted by Isaacsz.[21, 22]

The best portrait by Isaacsz. is in London. It is of Pieter Semeynes, a young Englishman of Dutch origin. He had a sensitive fine face and beautiful glossy curls.

Three oval portraits are in Amsterdam with Sr Jacob Poppe. The one of Jacob must be mentioned for the face and the hair; the resemblance is excellent. In the same house there is a painting on copper of the Roman women thronged together at the Capitol. Young Papirius had been told, and had made his mother believe, the council had decided that each man should have two wives; women of all nationalities are in this picture, including the Netherlands and North Holland; some have armed themselves with pans and spits; an old, crippled woman in a little cart pulled by a dog, is there; and the capitol and the statue of Marcus Aurelius on horseback.[23, 24]

Beautiful pictures and portraits by other masters may be seen in Pieter's house. Pieter has the self-portrait by Hans van Aken, which the master sent to him about two or three years ago, and, from what I hear, it is a good likeness.[25, 26]

I must include in this group of painters another pupil of Hans van Aken. This is Joseph Switser who was born at Berne. His father was an architect and builder. When this Joseph went to Rome, he had some knowledge of drawing but did not know how to handle color. Therefore, he went to Hans van Aken, who lived in the house of Anthoni Santvoort, or Green Anthony, as he was called. Switzer studied coloring. He was more industrious than any German or Netherlander; he worked with great zeal and drew all kinds of beautiful sculpture or paintings in Rome and in Venice. He had a careful and good method of handling the pen and for making washes; his equal may not be found.[27]

Joseph was at Prague and at court there. The Emperor was so pleased with his drawings, that he sent him to Rome to make drawings of classical and antique sculpture. He is now with the Emperor at Prague. He has an excellent manner of handling colors, and his work is good.

At Prague there are many other good artists. One of them is Pieter Stevens from Malines, who is an able painter. Gielis Sadlaer, the engraver, is there; sometimes he handles brushes, for he paints well. Adriaen de Vries, the excellent sculptor from The Hague, has been seduced by sweet Pictura many times.[28, 29, 30]

I recommend to Art, these painters and many more whom I do not know, because they enrich Art all the time. Their fame will spread.

PIETER DE WITTE[1]

THE beautiful city of Florence has attracted more than one pearl of the Netherlands that she has kept for her own adornment. Pieter de Witte, the painter, has lived there with his parents for a long time, and he is there yet. They are from Bruges in Flanders.

He is a good painter of fresco and does fine work in oilcolor. He models in clay and this helps him in his painting.

He has painted many pictures for Giorgio Vasari at Rome, in the palace of the Pope—the Sala Regia. He has worked at the Dome at Florence and elsewhere, and he has made various tapestry designs and other things for the Duke of Florence.[2]

Pieter de Witte was at Munich for many years, where he worked for the Duke of Bavaria and produced many beautiful things. I saw some of his work in Florence and knew him there. He had a brother who served with the Guard of the Duke; as far as I know, his name was Cornelis. He began painting landscape in 1573, when I was there; he was good at this kind of painting, although he started late. Some of the pictures by Pieter have been engraved, and the prints reflected his artistic mind and ability; he signed them Pieter Candido. He may be about fifty-six years old, now, in 1604. I am told that he is living at Munich, so I should not accuse Florence of holding him.

MATTHEUS AND PAULUS BRIL
OF ANTWERP

ROME has always attracted painters. It is a city that seems to exist for artists, and the beauty resulting from its many works of art has compelled many painters to go there. The brothers, Matthews and Pauwels Bril, from Antwerp, went to Rome.[1]

Mattheus worked in Rome in the palace of the Pope, in the rooms as well as in the galleries. He painted some fine landscapes and procession scenes. He died in Rome, in 1584, at the age of thirty-four.[2]

Pauwels Bril began to learn under a rather mediocre painter named Damiaen Wortelmans. He painted, at first, in water-colors, on the lids of clavecins and similar objects; he did this work to keep himself alive, till he was fifteen years old. He went from Antwerp to Breda and then returned to Antwerp. When he went to France, he was then twenty years old, and he kept his friends ignorant of his going, because they would not approve of his absence so far away.[3,4]

Pauwels Bril lived for a long time at Lyons, and from there he went to Rome; his brother had gone there previously. He made rapid progress in painting landscape, although in his youth he was slow at learning.

One of his exceptional works is a large landscape in fresco. It is sixty feet long, and is in the new room of the palace of the Pope. He painted this in 1602, and it is *St Clement* tied to an anchor and in the water; angels are in the sky. This is an excellent fresco. Six beautiful landscapes by Pauwels are in the summer room of the Pope. They are from life; they represent some of the richest monasteries, outside Rome, at beautiful locations in the mountains.[5]

391

For Cardinal Matthei, Pauwels decorated a large room with landscapes and grotesques; for Asdrubale Mattei, the brother of the Cardinal, he painted six large landscapes, and in them appear the castles which belonged to this man; the castles are at a great distance. They are large and beautiful pictures.[6]

A great number of small pictures on canvas and on copper plates are distributed among various collectors. A fine little picture on copper by Pauwels is with Sr Hendrick van Os; it displays interesting and beautiful ruins with figures, like the scenery at Campo Vaccina, the old market in Rome. Some very fine landscapes by Pauwels have been engraved and are in print.[7]

Pauwels is forty-eight years old this year, 1604. He has a pupil in Rome, who is married, and whose name is Balthaser Louwers; he comes from the Netherlands and is about twenty-eight years old. His landscapes are good. Guilliaem van Nieuwlandt was a pupil of Pauwels for about a year. He came from Antwerp; he is twenty-two years old and is living in Amsterdam. He adopted the style of his master.[8,9]

CORNELIS CORNELISZ.

OF HAARLEM

THERE is an idea—and a proverb confirms it—that the misfortune experienced by one is the good fortune of another, and that good luck always follows bad luck. Heaven seems to have sympathy for men in misfortune.

The ancient city of Haarlem was a wonderful place at which the world marvelled; everyone spoke of her fabulous beauty. This city was besieged for thirty-one weeks by the terrifying and frightful Spanish forces. The fortresses were weak, but the people were brave and gallant. At that time, or a little later, a beautiful mansion on the Spaazne river was given into the care of Pieter Schilder, and he had to keep the house open. Pieter was the son of Langen Pier of Amsterdam. He was a stimulating person and the first master of Cornelis Cornelisz. Cornelis was born in Haarlem in 1562. His parents left the city, because of the siege during the years 1572 and 1573, and went elsewhere.[1]

Cornelis was very young when he developed his love for painting. He practised at home. Nature had endowed him with talent. He was certain to become an artist; he would be busy for days with a knife or a tool of some sort, carving little statues out of red brick.

Cornelis learned the rudiments of painting under Langen Pier, the Younger, who was an excellent master in all branches of art, and he was thoroughly experienced in the mixing of colors. Langen Pier II had in Cornelis a pupil that soon surpassed him as a master. In his early youth, Cornelis was named Cornelis Schilder; he inherited the second name, and he proved that he was worthy of it.

393

Cornelis went to France when he was seventeen years old. He went to Rouen, where he did not stay long because of the pest. Then he went to Antwerp, a city that was famous for its paintings, and tried to find work with some one of the best masters there. After staying a short while with Frans Pourbus, Cornelis finally went to Gillis Coignet. He stayed with this master for a year and learned a fluent style of painting. I saw a picture that he had painted, then or a little later, after his departure, and it had some female figures that were painted softly and were somewhat defused.[2]

While with Gillis Coignet, Cornelis painted from life a vase holding various kinds of flowers. In accordance with the wishes of the master, hardly any leaves appeared in this painting. These flowers were so beautifully painted, from a pictorial point of view, that Coignet kept this painting for a long time, and he would not sell it.

Cornelis, after arriving at Haarlem, practised his art courageously. He painted a *Corporaelschap*, a group of archers, from life, for the Schuttershof at the Oude Doelen at Haarlem. I was surprised to find these artists there. This picture has a fine arrangement of the figures. The various persons have been portrayed very well in their actions, manners and characteristics. The merchants are clasping hands; those that love a drink, hold mugs; each member has been characterized by some special detail. The faces are good for likeness; the costumes, the hands, and the other details, have been painted fluently. This painting should endure with others and should be appreciated.[3]

Cornelis developed a certain firmness in his painting, and he had individuality in his brush-stroke. He has continued this method faithfully ever since, without attempting to do anything differently.

He painted a large upright picture of *Charitas*. It is a seated

394

figure of a woman with some children; one child is holding a cat by its tail and crying because the cat has clawed him in the thigh. This is an excellent painting. Cornelis was badly fooled by a man who took this picture to France. Neither the man, nor the picture, nor the money for it, has been seen since. After this, Cornelis painted a large oblong picture of the extremes of *Avarice* and *Extravagance*. In the second picture, roses are thrown to pigs.4, 5

Cornelis promoted his talent very efficiently by making drawings from life. He selected the most beautiful of living models and of antique sculptures. This is the safest and the best kind of study that one can do, if one has sound judgement and is able to detect the most beautiful from the mere beautiful.

Cornelis's artistic ability did not come to him while he was asleep. He acquired it, and paid for it, with a great amount of labor. Those who think they can achieve perfection in a different way will find themselves fooled by their idleness; they will remain in the shadow of art.

Cornelis, who kept himself busy by studying in this way, painted a *Deluge*, a long canvas which eventually came into the hands of the Duke of Leicester, in England. It was a wonderful painting that reflected a great deal of study.6

At his best, Cornelis painted *The Biting of the Serpents*, an oblong painting on a large canvas. He painted another large upright picture of *The Fall of Lucifer*. These two pictures were owned by Sr Jacob Ravaert in Amsterdam.7

I cannot write enough about these two paintings, nor to say how great was the study involved in the rendering of the various poses of the nudes. It is regrettable that these pictures may not be seen by the public. Cornelis has been exceptionally careful about the drawing, choice of poses, and the proportions, in these pictures.

He has made many other pieces, both small and large, that were mostly nude figures. One picture was *The First World* or *The Golden Age*. This painting is now in Amsterdam with Sr Hendrick Louwersz. Spieghel, a connoisseur. The treatment of it is excellent. The nudes are remarkably good. The rendering of the skin, as it is on the hands and other parts of the body of a living model, was one of his special achievements.[8]

Sr Bartholomeus Ferreris, in Leyden, has another large painting by Cornelis. It is *The Deluge* or *The Fall of the Angels*, and the various nudes in it are excellent.[9]

An excellent *Adam and Eve* and twelve small pictures on panels, a series on *The Passion of Christ*, and a beautiful picture of *The Purification of the Children of Israel in the Jordan*, are owned by Sr Melchior Wijntgis, in Middelburg.[10]

Cornelis painted a large canvas of *The Massacre of the Innocents*, in the Princenhof in Haarlem. Wings, by Marten Hemskerck, have been added to this painting. It is an excellent piece of work that shows the nude butchers of children, and the agony of mothers trying to protect their children. The carnation tones vary with the various ages and with the men and women. The tender young flesh of living children, and the changes that occur in the color of the flesh of the dead, caused by loss of blood, have been clearly rendered. There is another large upright painting of *Adam and Eve*, above a door; the figures are life-size.[11, 12]

A very large painting, by Cornelis, that covers the entire wall of a room in the Princenhof, represents *The Banquet of the Gods*, or *The Wedding of Peleus and Thetis*, and Discord is throwing the apple. This is a great work and the composition is fine.[13]

Cornelis, in these and in his later pictures, has displayed an increasing regard for the color of his nudes. He has changed in his work; one can see this, when his recent pictures are shown next to the ones that he made at an earlier period.

He made a beautiful painting, in 1602, which is now with Jan Mathijssen in the See-paerd at Haarlem. It represents *The Resurrection of Lazarus*; it is pleasing to look at because it is very warm in color.[14]

A small painting by Cornelis is owned by Sr Willem Jacobsz., an art lover in Amsterdam. Most of the figures in it are about a foot in height. This painting is another version of the wedding of Thetis; the composition is pleasing, and it includes many faces in full view, nudes and other details. It is a delightful picture.[15]

There are many other pictures by Cornelis, too many to be mentioned, with various collectors. He painted excellent portraits, and better than one would expect, considering that he did not like this kind of work.[16]

He is now, in 1604, a man of forty-two years. He is in the best period of his life, and he is painting constantly. Let us leave him in hope that he will continue his quiet and pleasing work in great happiness.[17]

Cornelis had some good pupils. The best one was Geerit Pietersz., the brother of the famous organ player, Orpheus Jan Pietersz. of Amsterdam. Geerit Pietersz. learned the rudiments of painting from Jacop Lenartsz. at Amsterdam, whose father was a sailor from Zandvoort. Lenartsz. was a good painter and an excellent glass painter; he was remarkably clever and he had a splendid technique. It would have been difficult to find his equal in his time. Geerit made such progress the master finally said he could not teach him any more and he should go to a better master. With the recommendation of Jacop Rauwaert, Geerit became a pupil of Cornelis Schilder, and he was, in my opinion, his best pupil. After

Geerit had progressed in painting, for another year or two, he worked independently for three or four years in Haarlem. He practised daily, working from life, and became most proficient in the rendering of nudes. I believe, among the painters of the Netherlands, only a few are as constantly ambitious and eager, as he is, to advance in art and to gain experience. Geerit told me that he would not exchange his brushes for the sceptre of the King of Spain. He wanted to be a good painter instead of a great prince.[18, 19]

Geerit lived for some time in Antwerp, after he had been for many years in Rome. He is now in Amsterdam where he is painting, daily. His splendid pictures are making him famous. He is an excellent master. If he has the good luck to paint some large compositions, for which his mind and hands are set, one may see what he can do with his talent and knowledge. As it is, he is forced to paint portraits and other little pictures, which can be seen in Amsterdam with burghers and collectors; but they are excellent.[20]

GOVERT

Among Geerit Pieters' pupils, there was a certain Govert who was good at landscapes and small figures.[21]

PIETER LASMAN

Another pupil was Pieter Lasman of whom much is expected. He is now in Italy.[22]

JAN VAN DELFT

Cornelis Cornelissen had a pupil, from Delft, named Langen Jan. He made a good beginning, but he died early.[23]

CORNELIS JACOBS

Cornelis Jacobs, a pupil from Delft, is an able master.[24]

CORNELIS CORNELISZ.
CORNELIS ENGHELSEN

Cornelis Enghelsen, a pupil from Gouda, is a good painter and an excellent portrait painter.[25]

GERRIT NOP

Gerrit Nop, of Haarlem, was in foreign countries for a long time, at Rome and elsewhere. His return is now expected. It is to be hoped that his work will justify faith in his ability.[26]

ZACHARIAS

Zacharias, from Alckmaer, and other artists, will probably have improved in their work while they are in foreign countries.[27]

JAQUES DE GHEYN

OF ANTWERP

WILL power can be very effective and help one to great achievement. Many examples may be noticed daily, and they convince us of this fact, again and again. The life of Jaques de Gheyn is one interesting example of such achievement. From his early youth De Gheyn showed a great liking for the art of drawing and he persisted so long and worked so faithfully that he climbed higher and higher. At last he began to work with colors and to make paintings. He wished to attain perfection in art, and one most efficient means to that end is to render nature as closely as possible.

De Gheyn was born in Antwerp in 1565. His parents were from the city of Utrecht, and they came from a fine and honorable family. His father was named Jacob Jansz. van de Gheyn. I am told that he was not born on land but while his mother was embarked in a ship sailing from Harlingen to Amsterdam.[1]

De Gheyn was more than a common glass painter, as is evident from the many beautiful stained-glass windows which he made. The four large windows of the choir of the St Walbourg Church at Antwerp should be mentioned here, and those in the Minnebroer Kerck in the same city. He was appointed to make various windows for the Italian nation; these were favorably commented upon by other painters and connoisseurs.[2]

I think the large window which De Gheyn made in the west side Oude Kerck of Amsterdam is a specially lovely one because of its beautiful colors. He knew how to use pieces of stained and fired glass very artistically; he made use of the pieces that were lighter on one side and browner on the other, and the subjects of his designs appeared to be in relief.

De Gheyn made good miniature portraits. He also liked to paint in oils; but he finally made his cartoons, which he had previously painted on paper, on canvas.

Although Jaques was seventeen years old when his father died, he understood glass painting so well he was able to complete the unfinished work begun by his father. He had practised a little with the burin while his father was alive; because Jacob Jansz. van de Gheyn had urged his son most earnestly to concentrate on engraving. But Jaques continued to paint glass for a long time and to practise miniature painting.

Later, De Gheyn went to the great artist, Goltzius, in Haarlem, and received instruction in engraving for about two years. He then worked alone for a time, and, although he had a sincere desire to practise art as seriously as possible, his study suffered considerably because he was attracted by the sweet company of young folks.3

In 1595, he married and found an unusual state of rest and quiet. He began to study again and, being very ambitious, worked constantly. He kept at engraving, and he produced a number of plates after his own compositions and after the pictures of other painters. As related before, Jaques de Gheyn found painting the best medium for rendering life and nature most closely. His desire to paint became stronger and stronger. He stopped engraving and printing and deplored the time he had lost and spent uselessly at doing this kind of work. Practising very seriously, he found it was quite necessary, in order to learn all the principles of art, to work as much as possible from life and to make original compositions.4

De Gheyn wanted to work with paint, but he realized that in the beginning he would experience difficulty in distinguishing the various colors and their characteristics. He devised a method by which he could save time. This method, although unusual, was helpful to him in learning colors. He divided a panel into about a hundred squares which he numbered in a notebook. He filled each square with a color—various greys, greens, yellows, blues, reds, carnations, and other mixtures. Each color, as far as possible, had its related shadows. He made careful notes of this procedure.

As he intended to practise oil-painting; he wanted to experiment and to learn how to go about his work. His first subject was a little vase with flowers that he did from life. This picture belongs to Sr Heyndrick van Os in Amsterdam. It is carefully done and quite remarkable for a first attempt. But because De Gheyn wanted to improve on parts that did not please him in the first picture, he decided to make another study of a vase with flowers, even though he was most eager to paint figures. With great patience and care he painted a large glass with a bouquet of flowers. The Emperor bought this picture, and a little book that De Gheyn had illuminated; the subjects in the book were done from life and among them there were many small animals.5

De Gheyn realized that a fine finish in painting was not specially helpful to his artistic progress, and that he should follow another method. Therefore he worked broadly in his painting. He began to think of work on a large scale; space should offer the greatest artistic possibilities.

As an outcome of the battle in Flanders, Prince Maurice received a beautiful horse which had belonged to the Archduke. The prince sent word to De Gheyn to say he wanted the horse painted life-size. De Gheyn was delighted, and, since he wanted so much to paint a large piece, he accepted the order. He painted a picture of the horse being led by a man holding the reins. The prince was well pleased. But De

Gheyn was not satisfied: He wanted to try the subject in another way.[6]

De Gheyn painted a picture of a skull; this belongs to Reynier Antonissen in Amsterdam. In 1604, followed a *Sleeping Venus*; this is in the possession of Sr Willem Jacobsz. The picture is life-size. In it two satyrs are shown at the feet of Venus, and one of them shamefacedly lifts a thin veil covering her charms; a sleeping Cupid is in it. This work, to express my opinion freely and without flattery, is excellent in composition, pose, proportion, technical treatment, and it is fluent in style. It is remarkable as a beginning and for a large-figure composition, work that requires the best possible artistic ability. But do not imagine De Gheyn is leaving off here. His love for painting will not let his mind be idle. He is stimulated and he should do better work all the time.[7, 8, 9]

De Gheyn was the master of several pupils that became fine engravers. One is the famous Jan Sanredam, now living at Assen in Delft. There was also a certain Zacharias Dolendo; he showed a good beginning which can be noticed in some of the engravings he made, in particular a little Passion Scene which I have drawn. Dolendo had a great love for his art. He died very young. He seriously injured his lungs by strenuous dancing and intemperate drinking. He lost a great amount of blood and, finally, he could not be helped any more.[10]

Other pupils were Robert, at Amsterdam, and Cornelis, who is now in France.[11]

OCTAVIO VAN VEEN

OF LEYDEN

AND OTHER PAINTERS FROM ANTWERP AND ELSEWHERE

I SHOULD regret it if I omitted any artists of renown, though they are scattered and live far away from me. I mention first, therefore, Octavio van Veen, an excellent artist and great painter, and a man to be remembered by future generations. Van Veen, the son of a good family, was born at Leyden. Nature inspired him with a love for art. As far as I know, he has visited Rome, Italy, and other places. His ability in art is appreciated highly by the Prince of Parma.[1]

Van Veen is specially esteemed by the Archduke Albert and Duchess, in whose services he entered. He refused other good offers that were made to him by the Archbishop of Salzburg, the Emperor, the King of Spain, and the King of France, because he was proud of his fine artistic reputation. He received various invitations from royalty as the years passed, and he would have enjoyed great benefits, if he had accepted such invitations; but he preferred to stay with his acquaintances and friends.[2]

Van Veen has made many beautiful paintings and portraits. Two portraits of the Excellencies mentioned above were sent to the King of England, James II.[3]

A large painting, the *Triumph of Bacchus*, was made by Van Veen in 1604. It is of a feast, and is similar to one by Hemskerck, which belongs to Sr Wijntgis at Middelburg. The picture has been well painted and its technique is fine. The same composition has been engraved. Sr Wijntgis has another beautiful work by Van Veen's artistic hand. It is a *Zeus*, with five nude female figures.[4]

OCTAVIO VAN VEEN

Octavio's brother, Gijsberd van Veen, is a very good engraver and painter. I believe he is living in Brussels. Octavio's other brother, Pieter van Veen, is artistically inclined. He only paints for pleasure. It is a pity that he does not make painting his purpose in life.[5]

HANS SNELLINCK[1]

HANS SNELLINCK, I am told, was born in Malines, lives in Antwerp, and is a fine master and an excellent painter. He is now about fifty-five years old, in 1604. Snellinck is specially good at painting scenes with figures in them, such as battle scenes. The princes have frequently commissioned him to make such pictures. He paints realistically the smoke of cannon, and the soldiers enveloped by it and partly visible.

TOBIAS VERHAEGHT[2]

TOBIAS VERHAEGHT is an able landscape painter living in Antwerp.

ADAM VAN OORT[3]

ADAM VAN OORT is a good painter of figures.

HEYNDRICK VAN BALEN[4]
AND
SEBASTIAEN VRANCKS[5]

HEYNDRICK VAN BALEN and Sebastiaen Vrancks are each good figure painters. They studied under Adam van Oordt. Vrancks is now about thirty-one years old. He paints landscapes with horses and little figures in them.

JOOS DE MOMPER[6]

JOOS DE MOMPER paints landscapes excellently and with a clever technique. He lives in Antwerp.

DUTCH AND FLEMISH PAINTERS
FRANCISCUS SAVIUS[1]

I HEAR great praise of Franciscus Savius, at Mons in Hainault.

MARTINUS FREMINET[2]

THERE are some good masters in Paris. One is Martinus Freminet, a Frenchman. He recently entered the service of the King. He is supposed to have begun a painting, in the presence of the King, without making a drawing previously; he painted a hand here, a foot there, elsewhere a face; he finally made a very acceptable painting, to the great astonishment of the King.

DU BREUL[3]

NOT so many years ago, before the time of Freminet, Du Breul, of Paris, worked for the King. He was the son of a saddler. He was a clever and an able artist and good at drawing nudes, for he had studied anatomy with a barber. He often had his pictures painted by artists from the Netherlands. He emphasized the dark parts, using even pure black for this purpose.

Du Breul played the lute wonderfully well, and he enjoyed riding. He died young and suddenly. He came in a great hurry from St Denis, to see some guests he had invited. On his way, an old, internal wound became worse and must have opened. I have placed his biography with the living artists, since I forgot to mention this artist previously. Du Breul was a contemporary of Freminet. Each artist, when young, studied under a dauber in Paris.

BUNEL[4]
AND HIS WIFE

ANOTHER good painter in Paris is named Bunel. He works

at the court there, and lives in the suburb of St Germain. He is a stately burgher. He has a beautiful way of painting, and he mixes his colors very well.

Bunel's wife is praised, beyond her husband and other excellent masters, for her painting.

BOLLERY[1]

AN artist in Paris, by the name of Bollery, is a painter of night scenes, masquerades, Mardi-Gras, similar festivities, and all kinds of animals, in somewhat the style of Bassano. He is a proud man. He rides with a servant behind him.

FRANCOYS STELLAERT[2]

A MASTER of landscape painting, figure work, compositions, and portraits, from life, and of drawing, is Francoys Stellaert. He lives in Lyon. He is from the Netherlands; but I do not know where and when he was born.

CASPAR HUEVICK[3]

ANOTHER painter from the Netherlands is far away in Italy, at Bari in Apulia. He is working for the local bishop there, as far as I know. He is a good master and is widely experienced in all branches of painting. He is doing well with his art at that distant place. He was successful in his grain business in the last period of the high cost of living in Italy. He was an acquaintance of mine, when I was in Rome. He is Caspar Huevick. He is from Oudenaerde in Flanders. He lived a long time with Costa, the painter to the Duke of Mantua, mentioned previously. He is about fifty-four years old.

HERDER[4]

OF GRONINGEN

I SHOULD have mentioned Herder before this. He is a

clever painter from Groningen. He may be about the same age as Huevick. I knew him in Rome. While in Groningen, he was the painter to Verdugo. He deserves to be praised for his ability in all branches of art, as can be proved by his works.

HANS ROTTENHAMER[1]
OF MUNICH
AND THE LIVES OF OTHER MASTERS

IT is beneficial to young and artistic minds, if there are in their home towns artists that can stimulate them and cause them to pursue art. Many great masters of painting have gone to Munich, because the illustrious Duke there loved art. Their works have been shown in many of the public places.

Hans Rottenhamer, a good colorist, was born in Munich in 1564, and he grew up in the same place. He learned the rudiments of painting from an ordinary artist named Donauwer. When Rottenhamer went to Rome, he did paintings on metal plates, in the same manner as the artists of the Netherlands do. He did not paint as an ordinary painter; he made excellent compositions. The first thing by which he gained a reputation was a large, upright painting, on metal—the *Apotheosis of the Saints*. It was of heaven and various holy men, women and angels. The technique was fine, the draperies were well done, and the faces, the veils, and all kinds of beautiful details, were rendered in beautiful colors. He made numerous pictures on copper, large and small ones. They have been scattered to many countries and are in the possession of numerous collectors. Among these, Sr Joan Knotter, an art collector in Utrecht, has various pieces by Rottenhamer on copper. I mention specially an *Assumption of the Virgin*, and a picture of *Actaeon and Diana*; these are well composed and are lively and warm in color. Rottenhamer's pictures are treasured by collectors. His name is worthy of mention with the names of the most artistic painters.

Rottenhamer finally went to Venice and married a Venetian woman.

ADAM[1]
OF FRANKFORT

IN Rome there is an excellent painter and he is from Germany. He is named Adam. He was born in Frankfort, and he is the son of a tailor. When he went to Italy, he was an ordinary painter; but while in Rome, he made wonderful progress and, by hard work, became an able artist. He works constantly in the churches and elsewhere, and he studies the works of the masters. He is remarkable at painting compositions on copper plates.

Adam is a kind man and he likes to please everyone. At present, in 1604, he is twenty-eight or thirty years old.

DIERICK DE VRIES[2]
AND
LODEWYCK TOEPUT

TWO artists of the Netherlands, now in Venice, are Dierick de Vries from Vrieslandt, and Lodewijck Toeput, so far as I know, from Malines. I should like to tell something about these artists. I have seen various still life pictures of food and fruit-market scenes that were charming in color. So I may not omit De Vries's name here. I do not know his age.

Lodewijck lives outside Venice, at Treviso. He is a good landscape painter and he makes fine compositions. Truly, he may be called a master. I hear that he is a good rhetorician. Painting and poetry seek each other; they are good friends.

JOACHIM WTENWAEL[1]
OF UTRECHT

THE seed of a noble painter in an artistic heart must grow as most fertile plants do, and strive upwards, and climb until the highest degree of perfection in painting has been reached.

This kind of seed was in the heart of Joachim Wtenwael, a painter born in Utrecht in 1566. His father was a glass painter, and his mother's father, named Joachim van Schuyck, was a good painter for his time.

Joachim Wtenwael worked as a glazier and glass painter for his father till he was eighteen years old. He then lost interest in this work, as his mind turned towards other things. He was interested in painting, and he studied under an ordinary painter in Utrecht, Joos de Beer, for about two years. Joos was a pupil of Frans Floris. After this, Wtenwael went to Italy. When he arrived at Padua, he worked for a French bishop from St Malo. After they had travelled together through Italy for two years, they stayed in France for another two years. Wtenwael made many things for the bishop, working from memory and from original ideas.

After his return home, Wtenwael lived in Utrecht and painted many of the pictures, large and small, that now belong to various art lovers and which are very much treasured.

One may not be able to say whether Wtenwael is better at painting on a large scale or at making small pieces. This is an indication that he has good judgement and a keen knowledge, two qualities that do not often combine in an artist. Many times one sees large and small works done by the same hand, and one would be inclined to believe that they had been done by different masters.

Wtenwael is excellent and experienced in all branches of his art. His beautiful kitchen pieces were painted from life. At Gouda there is one of his very large paintings; one in Antwerp, owned by an Italian, is six feet high and ten feet long, and it represents Lot and his daughters; life-size nudes appear in this picture; the rendering of the fire, the trunks of the trees, and other details, are very interesting.

In Amsterdam there is a picture of *The Sign of Apelles* with his cousin Lucas, a painter from Utrecht; this is a beautiful, upright painting; the composition is free, the drawing is excellent, as is the coloring. In the same place there is a painting of the *Annunciation to the Shepherds*; this is a night scene and it proves how good an artist Joachim is. There are many small pictures that have been very carefully painted by Wtenwael. One picture, on copper, is a *Banquet of the Gods*. It has been done with much detail. It is owned by Sr Jan Niquet or his son, in Amsterdam.

Recently, Wtenwael delivered to Sr Jan van Weely an excellent, small, upright painting on copper—*Mars and Venus*; it is full of fine detail that has been rendered very sharply. The eye can distinguish a table, a divan, and the gods and cupids descending from the clouds. Another *Mars and Venus* is owned by Sr Melchior Wijntgis in Middelburg.

I regard Wtenwael to be worthy of a place among the best painters of the Netherlands. It is remarkable how kind Pictura is to him, since he considers her of second importance. Wtenwael is a merchant and he lets business come first; but he does not let one activity interfere with another—he finds time for each. Some say they fear that, like Arachne, who was caught in her own web because of the anger of Minerva, Pictura might change Wtenwael into the flax in which he is dealing. Wtenwael is now thirty-eight years old.

ABRAHAM BLOEMAERT
OF GORINCHEM

FATE and nature had destined that Abraham Bloemaert should be an artist. He crowned and voluntarily offered the most beautiful flowers to Pictura. Bloemaert brought fame to the town of Gorinchem, where he was born, in 1567, about Christmas time.[1]

Abraham's father, Cornelis Bloemaert, was a sculptor, architect, and engineer. He was born at Dordrecht. He fled from this town because he did not wish to take a certain oath; he hoped to escape approaching political troubles. He went to Gorinchem, after several disastrous adventures. Later, with his family, he went from Gorinchem to 'sHertogenbosch, and then to Utrecht.[2]

While he was living with his father, Abraham Bloemaert began painting, after some drawings made by Frans Floris. His father sent him to a dauber, named Gerit Splinter, to study. Splinter suggested Bloemaert paint some dummies for a fencing instructor, for Bloemaert was already a better master than Splinter was. The originals were interesting paintings by a talented artist named Heyndrick Whoeck. But Bloemaert stayed only fourteen days, because Splinter drank constantly; the figures that he had begun were left unfinished.[3]

Bloemaert went to Joos de Beer, a pupil of Floris who lived in Utrecht. De Beer was not one of the best painters. He owned many beautiful pictures which had been painted by Blocklandt and other masters. Here, Bloemaert made a picture in oil-colors, a modern banquet scene, after a painting by Dirck Barensz.; the original belongs to the painter Cornelis

413

van der Voort in Amsterdam. In the picture, one figure is playing on a harp and a woman is singing. This picture was painted intelligently, and the lavish detail was rendered with artistic feeling. Considering his youth, Bloemaert made a remarkably good copy of the original. Bloemaert's father observed this; but he was unable to make any agreement with De Beer, who did not consider this work as of much importance. The father took his son home, where he believed the boy should do well at making copies of beautiful pictures. The boy copied a kitchen subject, by Langen Pier, in which the head of an ox appeared. But Bloemaert did not accomplish much at home. His father allowed him too little time, he had to do other work instead.[4]

Subsequently, Bloemaert went to the Bailiff Van Heel, to paint. The Bailiff promised the father to help the boy with his study, and to make arrangements for sending him to Blocklandt. This did not happen. The Bailiff used the boy for a footman and for other services. Bloemaert, unable to improve his artistic ability, after a year and a half, returned home. His father sent him to Rotterdam, to the artist Uthoeck. Uthoeck, after he had seen some of Bloemaert's work, was glad to accept him as a pupil; but the artist's wife objected to the idea.

Bloemaert, now about fifteen or sixteen years old, was sent to Paris and to a certain Jehan Bassot, with whom he stayed for about six weeks. Then he went to a painter, named Maistre Herry, and he remained with him for a year and a half. Bloemaert painted from memory. He received almost no instruction. Before he returned to Utrecht, he visited Jeroon Franck from Herenthals. He went to Amsterdam, where his father was the town architect. After his father died, Bloemaert returned to Utrecht, where he has remained ever since. He married twice.[5]

ABRAHAM BLOEMAERT

Bloemaert studied ambitiously. He became a well recognized painter; he achieved this without studying with a master. He has said, to his pupils, when he wished to stimulate their interest, 'I wish that once in my life I had seen a good master paint and work with colors, so I might have been able to follow his method of painting'.

While Bloemaert was living in Amsterdam with his father, he worked in a church or other spacious place, as a workshop. He painted, among other things, a small picture, and a large one, which is now owned by Sr Zion Luz in Amsterdam. Many life-size nudes appear in this work. The anatomy of the figures is well understood and the treatment is excellent. The picture illustrates the story of Niobe, who was shot and killed by her children Apollo and Diana. A large and beautiful painting of the same subject, though different in composition, is owned by the Emperor. He and all experts are delighted by this work, which is a recent one.[6]

Somewhere in the northern part of the country there is an excellent picture of the *Banquet of the Gods*. This strikingly good work was composed and painted very well. Another *Banquet of the Gods*, painted earlier and not so large, is in the possession of Count van der Lip.[7]

Three large portraits by Bloemaert, painted at an earlier time, belong to Jaques Razet, an art collector of Amsterdam. They are round, and show Venus, Juno, and Pallas in graceful poses. Sr Razet has some other small paintings by Bloemaert; among them a skull and some additional objects which are good in execution and color. In a very small picture the foreground has some Indian trumpet-shells on which sea gods and goddesses are resting, and in the background the sea is shown. Andromeda is with Perseus and he is freeing her. The coloring has been done well and artistically.

Certain art collectors have some interesting landscapes by

Bloemaert. Most of these pictures are farm scenes, with farm implements, peasants, trees, and fields—sights to be seen often and in variety near Utrecht. Bloemaert works mostly from nature; he did these farm scenes from life. He has a clever way of drawing with a pen, and, by adding small amounts of water-color, he produces unusual effects.[8]

Bloemaert has had wide experience in various branches of painting. He gives much character and beauty to many and various subjects. Occasionally, he has introduced sunshine, or darkness, or fiery sky-effects, according to his subject. Animals, cattle, dogs, and other objects, appear in his works, and each has been done from life. He has painted many little scenes. Although they are not overloaded with detail, they are excellent. They cannot be surpassed, in my opinion.[9]

He has painted various studies of ponds, with water lilies, iris, and other flowering plants, floating on the water, and there is additional foliage in the foregrounds. These paintings are on canvas; the details are not crowded.

Because Bloemaert has not wanted anything to distract his mind from creative work, he has not been interested in painting portraits from life. Many of his subjects, compositions, and figures, which he drew with a pen and painted afterwards, in black and white oils, have been engraved in copper by the able Joan Muller. The famous Saenredam has made engravings after Bloemaert's work, because he found great interest in the drawings. Saenredam did his best to represent beautifully and artistically the work of the artist.

Bloemaert is, in 1604, thirty-seven years old; he will be thirty-eight next Christmas. He is a quiet man, and he is very able. He is thoroughly devoted to Pictura, and he tries to represent her strength and beauty. Pictura has bestowed her favors on him generously for the sake of his *bloemaert*; he adorns her with the flowers of his art. Pictura is grateful.

ABRAHAM BLOEMAERT

Fame, who sees and hears everything, has heralded Bloemaert's renown, from the town of Utrecht to all the world. Fame is the daughter of Speech. She has a thousand tongues and can tell her stories rapidly. She will add the name of Bloemaert to the list of famous painters in the hall of honor, and she will preserve his name for Immortality. She will protect it from the destructive scissors of Atropos.

PIETER CORNELISZ VAN RIJCK[1]
OF DELFT

ARTISTS who stay long in Italy and practise the art of painting usually return home with some method of work superior in beauty and quality to the style common in the Netherlands. One can notice the unusual skill and ability of these artists. This was true of the work of Pieter van Rijck, from Delft. His first study of drawing was at Delft with Jacob Willemsz.; at the end of two months he was forced to stop because he had to do other work for three years. But he had developed a love for art and he returned to it.

He worked under Hubrecht Jacopsz., a good painter and portrait artist in Delft. Pieter studied drawing for six months, and he devoted as much time to learn the colors and how to paint. Then he went with Jacopsz. to Italy, where, for fifteen years, he worked with various masters and for many princes, gentlemen of rank, prelates, monks, nuns, and other persons, throughout Italy. He made oil-paintings and frescoes.

This year, 1604, Van Rijck is thirty-six years old. He is living in Haarlem, where he has painted many beautiful works, large and small. He has made, among other things, a kitchen subject which has various kinds of birds in it, along with figures of animals and other creatures. His painting of the parable of the rich man and the poor Lazarus is in the hospital for the Lepers, outside Haarlem.

Van Rijck has a fine technique that proves he has worked much in the style of Bassano. He is an intelligent and a capable artist. His works, which can be seen here and there, show that he is a great master, good at composition and portraiture.

418

FRANCESCO BADENS
OF ANTWERP

WE have recently noticed that the art of painting in the Netherlands has changed and improved. This is in reference to color treatment, to carnation, and to the handling of shadows. Artists are working away from a stony, grey color—a somewhat cold, fishy pallidness. Warm colors, for carnations and for the tones of flesh, have come into more general use.

Francesco Badens has contributed much towards this development. He was born in Antwerp, in 1571. He was five years old when the Spanish Fury took place on the fourth of November, 1576. Badens's father, who died this year (1604) in Amsterdam, came to the Netherlands shortly after the Spanish Fury. In his early youth, Francesco lived in Amsterdam. He was taught by his father who was an unimportant painter. He had no masters.[1]

Badens travelled in Italy for about four years, in company with Jacob Mathan, the son-in-law of Goltzius, and then returned home. Badens was the first artist in Amsterdam to introduce the beautiful modern method of painting. For that reason the younger artists have called him the Italian Painter. Badens has an excellent and a fluent technique, and he uses warm, rich colors. He is as proficient at painting scenes as at painting faces and portraits.

This year (1604), at Badens's house in Amsterdam, I have seen a rather large painting of *Bathsheba*, bathing. A letter is being delivered to her, and an old emissary is whispering at her ear, while she listens. There are other nude, female figures, and details, in this picture. It is a splendid work in harmony, coloring, and composition.[2]

419

There are many excellent portraits by Badens, and he has used some of them in his compositions. He has painted many banquet-scenes and masquerades that include modern costumes. A painting by Badens, of a loving couple in Italian costume, is in the possession of Cornelis van der Voort, a painter in Amsterdam. A man is playing on a lute and two lovers are singing together.3

I should like to write more about Badens, but I am unable to do so. I have encountered a certain number of present-day artists who refused to give me any information; they consider themselves not important enough to be mentioned with really great masters. So, because artists, who have not said anything and have died, and those who are living have refused to make any statements, I travelled straight against wind and current. My voyage has been far from easy.4

JAN BADENS1

JAN, Francesco Badens's brother, was born at Antwerp, on the eighteenth of November, 1576, fourteen days after the Spanish Fury. This brother went to Italy. He made wonderful progress with his art, and a great deal was expected of him. He had much good luck in Germany and in Italy. Fortune smiled on him. He was highly respected everywhere by many of rank, and he was well rewarded. When Jan returned home, with a horse of his own, a large amount of money, and a proper outfit, he met with misfortune and was ruined; when he entered the Netherlands, the sons of Mars deprived him of everything, and he was made a prisoner. Finally, at home, after a miserable adventure, he died of languor in 1603.

DAVID VINCKEBOONS

OF MALINES

I BELIEVE people have not ever heard me in any way praise my own achievements; and even if I did, I should not praise them more than they deserve. As for my own works, they are at liberty to reveal my ability and knowledge. Work cannot praise and modestly excuse itself to connoisseurs that judge without prejudice. My own judgement may not be adequate, and I may not write impartially about the artists and do justice to their qualities. I have not tried to compare one artist with another and play the work of one against that of another. I think it best to avoid grave errors, and I make it a principle, on going into the homes of art lovers, to pay strict attention to what art works have been collected, by whose hand they were done, and for what special reason they were desirable. I may have some confidence in my own knowledge and judgement; but I gladly follow the general opinions of connoisseurs of art.

David Vinckeboons was born in Malines in 1578. When he was a young child, he was brought to Antwerp. Seven years later he went with his parents to Amsterdam; he is living there now. His father, Philips Vinckeboons, was a good painter in water-color. David started with this medium first, under his father's instruction. Later he had another master and he persisted at working entirely with oil-colors. He has painted many small pictures of charming little figures. Two of these small pictures, which should be mentioned, are those in the possession of Sr Joan de Bruyn, an art lover in Calverstraat, at Amsterdam. One picture, *Carrying of the Cross*, shows a crowd of all sorts of people; it was painted with the excellence required by the subject. The other picture, *Peasant Wedding*, is a composition of jolly peasants, horses, houses, trees, and landscape. Vinckeboons does this kind of picture very well.[1, 2, 3]

Two of Vinckeboons's small pictures were sent to Frankfort, to Messrs Caymox. One was a landscape, and in it Christ is healing the blind man on the road; the other picture was of a *Peasant Wedding*.

In the office of the Oude Mannen Gasthuis, at Amsterdam, there is a large painting by Vinckeboons. It is forty feet long and eight feet high, and it represents a lottery for the benefit of that hospital. It is a night scene; the square and the houses were done from life; the various kinds of people carry lanterns and lights. It was painted, very well, in 1603.[4]

Now, in 1604, Vinckeboons is working at two little pictures which he is doing for the painter Jan van Conincxloo. One is of Christ, preaching; the other is a *Peasant Wedding*. They are beautifully executed, and the little figures, houses, ships, and landscapes, are good in composition.

Many of Vinckeboons's landscapes contain modern figures. These pictures have been copied and engraved by Niclaes de Bruyn, who has a very good technique for engraving landscapes.

Vinckeboons enjoyed working with various mediums. At first, he painted with water-colors and made miniatures of such subjects as small animals, birds, fish, and trees, which he did from life. He was also successful at painting glass and made some interesting pieces. He handles the burin with good results, and he does some etching on copper. This is remarkable, for he has done this work without any instruction. Vinckeboons does not, however, apply himself to engraving as extensively as to painting in oil-colors. Considering his artistic talent, his ambition, his time, his labor, and the little

DAVID VINCKEBOONS

money he earns, Vinckeboons has been rewarded far too
meagerly for his beautiful and intelligent work.[5, 6]

VARIOUS PAINTERS OF
THE NETHERLANDS
NOW LIVING

RECKLESS and destructive Mars is terrifying our country with thundering batteries that raise even the grey hairs of Time. It is surprising, in spite of all this, that many artists can continue their work at the art of painting. Art requires peace and prosperity. There are so many artists in the Netherlands, that, if I should try to fully describe their lives, my book would be too long. In an attempt to finish my writing, I shall commemorate a few artists by mentioning only their names. I shall give a place to all that pass my mind.

CORNELIS FLORIS

HE is the son of Cornelis Floris, a sculptor and an architect at Antwerp. He is an excellent painter and sculptor. He lives in Antwerp. His art is not well known; he has not been adequately rewarded for his meritorius work.[1]

PAUWELS MOREELS

IN Utrecht there is an artist by the name of Pauwels Moreels. He is good at painting portraits from life. Various portraits by him may be seen; he is now working at other portraits. He does his work in a masterly fashion. Among his works the portraits that Moreels made of the Count and Countess of Cülemborgh should be mentioned. They are full length and life-size. The portrait of Sr Knotter's wife is pleasing and it is well executed. There are also many others. Though now a young man, Moreels is a pupil of Michiel Miereveldt of Delft.[2]

VARIOUS PAINTERS

FRANS PIETERSZ. GROBBER

THIS artist is an excellent portrait painter. He paints figure compositions and, if commissioned, he does excellent embroidery. He was a pupil of Jaques Savry with whom he studied landscape painting. Various large and small portraits by Grobber may be seen here and there; they are good in their resemblances and they are well executed.[3]

CORNELIS CLAESZ

THIS artist comes from Haarlem and he now lives there. He gave up navigation to draw and paint ships. He knows the rigging, the ropes, and all the characteristics of ships. He has a good technique; he is extremely careful at rendering ropes.[4]

BERNAERT AND PAUWELS VAN SOMER

THESE two painters, in Amsterdam, came originally from Antwerp. They are brothers. Bernaert married the daughter of Aert Mijtens, in Italy where he lived for several years. He is a good portrait painter. He works from life and he makes good compositions.[5]

Pauwels is a bachelor. He is excellent at all kinds of painting.[6]

CORNELIS VAN DER VOORT

THERE is in Amsterdam an especially good painter of portraits. His name is Cornelis van der Voort. He came, as far as I know, from Antwerp. He paints his subjects in a very pleasing way. They look very well. He is young.[7]

DUTCH AND FLEMISH PAINTERS

EVERT KRIJNSZ (*VAN DER MAES*)

THIS artist lives in The Hague. He recently came from Italy, where he adopted a pleasing manner of painting. His subjects are mostly compositions and portraits.[8]

RAVESTEYN

I SHOULD mention the name of a good painter and portrait-artist at The Hague, Ravesteyn. His technique is admirable.[9]

AERT JANSZ. DRUYVESTEYN

THIS artist is a young man. He lives at Haarlem. He is unusually experienced in the painting of landscapes and little figures. He only paints for his pleasure.[10]

JAQUES DE MOSSCHER

HE lives at Delft. He has had experience in all kinds of painting.[11]

THONIS ARIAENSZ.

THIS is a good artist who lives at Alckmaer.[12]

NICLAES VAN DER HECK

THIS artist lives at Alckmaer. He is a member of the Marten Hemskerck family and he is a pupil of Jan Naghel. He is good at landscapes.[13]

VARIOUS PAINTERS
PIETER GEERITSZ. MONTFOORT

HE comes from Delft. He is an excellent young man and born of good family. He is a keen observer, has a great love of art, and works with much ambition. Montfoort is about twenty-five years old. He is a pupil of Michiel Miereveldt, with whom he stayed for only a half-year. He is eagerly striving for the best in painting and in color work. He works in various ways: He makes drawings on blue paper and suggests the modelling by emphasizing the forms with touches of light and dark. He does not desire to produce a large number of pictures; he intends to paint pictures that have special quality.[14]

PIETER DIERICKSEN CLUYT

HE is from Delft. He is a pupil of Miereveldt. His father was an eminent expert on various flowers and a collector of them. Flora nourished the elder Cluyt; the botanical garden in Leyden has been entrusted to him. He wrote a learned book, in the language of the Netherlands, on flower-loving honeybees and honey. His son Pieter has ability and he is eager to attain perfection in composition, drawing, and painting.[15]

JAN ARIAENZ.

AMONG the artists of the Netherlands Ariaenz. deserves esteem. After he had visited many foreign countries he settled in Leyden. He is young and his best years should be before him. Ariaenz. has painted landscapes and various other subjects, and he has done architectural rendering.[16]

HUBERT TONS

I MUST include the name of Hubert Tons. He is one of the most able of the coming artists. He is a descendant of the Tons that I have previously mentioned. Young Tons paints good landscapes and small figures. He lives in Rotterdam.[17]

I believe many other young artists that I do not know, or that do not come to my mind, deserve a place here. Nevertheless, I wish to encourage their artistic efforts. I hope Fame will regard them as worthy and loudly call their names which should be in the book of the immortals.

If I have praised an artist too highly, let that artist be stimulated and try to win appreciation commensurately. I hope that no-one will feel I have displeased him in some way because I did not do my work perfectly.

Let no-one exalt himself by his art. Previously, I have said art was only a shadow of the Highest Essence—a flower; our life is nothing more than a fleeting shadow like a flower in a field. In time, all sceptres, drawing pens, and brushes, will be snatched away by destroying Death. We should love the best and most divine art, even as a man should love his fellow man. One should foster art and study it. Art is a road leading to sure salvation.

I should have added a few chapters on our glass painters and engravers, and on our women painters. I have mentioned the most outstanding of them in the biographies of the painters. I find my book is rather long, so I shall leave the matter, as I had intended to do at first, and write at length only about painting and painters. I think the time has almost come, after I have written about artists and how they painted, for me to turn to my brushes, to experiment and try to produce something good.

It is good to drop my tired pen for the sake of art. I have worn my pen out in my attempts to honor painting and noble artists, and to stimulate youth to study and to take a delight in painting. I have devoted much time to this book. My efforts have been my best and I have suffered not a little. Love made me begin, persist, and finish, this work.

CONCLUSION

THERE are a few facts which should be added to the lives of some of the painters, and some changes and corrections to be made.

ALBRECHT DURER

I WAS informed, later, Emperor Maximilian ordered one of his noblemen to hold the step-ladder, on which Albrecht Dürer was standing, and this nobleman ordered his page not to do it, because of the humiliation to nobility. The Emperor's reply was as has been told before. Albrecht Dürer was given the crest of arms worn by painters; the arms belonged to the nobleman. It consisted of three white shields and a red field; the crest of the painters has a blue field.[1]

QUINTIJN MACYS

THIS must be eight parts and two horses in each part; this makes sixteen portraits.

Quintijn Macys died in 1529. He was an accomplished musician. He did not learn painting from any one.

JOOS VAN CLEEF

JOOS VAN CLEEF, called Joos the Fool, was from the same family as Marten and Hendrick, a fact that I did not know. I do not know the exact date of the death of Hendrick van Cleef; it may be assumed that he died in 1589. Marten entered the guild of Antwerp in 1551.

ANTONIO MORO

MORO died in Antwerp at the age of fifty-six, one year before the French Fury.[2]

CONCLUSION

PIETER BREUGHEL, *THE YOUNGER*

I HAVE been wrongly informed: young Pieter Breughel paints from life. He copies and imitates the works of his father.

MARTEN DE VOS

HIS father, Pieter de Vos, was a Hollander, from Gouda, I believe. Marten de Vos died, on the 4th of December, 1603, at the age of seventy-two.

MIEREVELDT

MIEREVELDT was born in Delft on the 1st of May, 1567. His mother's father was a glass painter at Delft. Miereveldt did not study under Jeroon Wierincx. I have been misinformed on this matter. His first master was Willem Willemsz. He went to a pupil of Blocklandt, named Augustyn, at Delft, who was experienced at making compositions; from him Miereveldt learned the rudiments of painting; he stayed with Augustyn for about ten weeks. When Miereveldt was about fourteen years old, he went to Blocklandt, in Utrecht, and stayed with him for two years and three months. When Blocklandt died, Miereveldt returned home. Though Miereveldt's father wanted his son to paint compositions with figures, the artist painted mostly portraits for the next nine or ten years. There are many of his portraits in Delft, belonging to the burgomaster, Sr Schilperoort.3

GEERIT PIETERSZ.

OF AMSTERDAM

GEERIT PIETERSZ. made a 'Rot,' or 'Corporaelschap,' for the Sebastiaens Doele in Amsterdam, and delivered it this year—1604. I believe the captain of the group is Jan Jansz. Carel. This is an excellent and fine work as to faces, likeness-

431

es, costumes, silks, and other details. It deserves a high place in the esteem of the public. Pietersz. did not rest on this achievement. He has developed a newer and stronger ambition for painting. He intends to improve and do new work; he has never been satisfied with himself. This is a good attitude for an artist, because, if he is too easily pleased, he will not make progress. Many, who have showed great talent while they were young, failed when they grew older because of their mistaken ideas and self-esteem. They lost what they had achieved in art, and they produced nothing that pleased connoisseurs.4

OCTAVIO VAN VEEN

WHEN he was fourteen, Octavio van Veen began the study of painting with Isaac Claesz., at Leyden. In the meantime he studied literature every day. His father then sent him to Dominicus Lampsonius, secretary to the Bishop of Liége, a famous poet with a great knowledge of painting. Octavio received a good education from Lampsonius, although the Bishop did not do any painting. Van Veen, in his youth, practised art and associated with such famous masters of Christianity, as Taddeus Zuccaro and Federico at Rome. When Octavio was eighteen years old, he went to Italy and stayed there for about seven years, mostly in Rome. After he left Italy, he lived for some time with the present Emperor, later with the Duke of Bavaria, and then with the Bishop of Cologne who released him with great protestations. Octavio is now, in 1604, about forty-seven years old.5

CONCLUSION

The reader will discover that I have placed the lives of younger artists often before those of older artists who are still alive; this was done because, in some cases, I had to wait for information about the older ones. I hope the reader will not mind.

> Man fails and loses his way,
> In spite of all his efforts.
> My work is not free from errors;
> The information, the written statements,
> May be wrong;
> I desire not to hide my mistakes
> With beautiful words;
> I would let them be known to everyone.

THE END

NOTES TO THE TEXT

BIOGRAPHY OF VAN MANDER, p.xli

1 See, for the probable author of this biography, L.Koch, 'Bredero is niet de schrijver van het levensbericht van Karel van Mander,'-*Oud Holland*, XLIV, p.78.

2 'Man der Mannen,' Mander mannen; in Dutch, a play on the name Mander; a rivulet, about three miles from Meulebeke was called the Mandere, according to the map of Guicciardini's *Descrittione di tutti i Paesi Bassi*, Amsterdam, 1635. Van Mander had a cousin named Jan van der Mander. *Gulden Harpe*, a volume of poetry by Van Mander, published in 1599. See G.Kalff, *Geschiedenis der Nederlandsche Letterkunde*.

3 The daughter of John of Burgundy was the sister of Philip the Good, and the only English marriage arranged by Philip for his sister was that of Anne whom he married to John Plantagenet, Duke of Bedford and regent of France, on April 13, 1423, thereby cementing the Anglo Burgundian alliance.-Pirenne, *Hist. de Belgique*, II, p.496.

4 See Lucas de Heere and Vlerick biographies.

5 For the literary works of Carel Van Mander, see G.Kalff op.cit.

6 Carel van Mander was in Italy, from 1573 to 1577.-Floerke, I, note 344. Van Mander, in the biography of Pieter de Witte, says he was in Florence in 1573.-Floerke, II, note 700.

7 Van Mander tells about his travel in Italy in his Didactic Poem 'Den Grondt der Edel vry Schilderconst.' He was as far as Terracina, sailed the Tyrrhenian Sea, was at Florence, but did not visit Venice. See R.Hoecker, *Das Lehrgedicht des Karel van Mander*, Haag Nijhoff, 1916. p.51.

8 The catacombs of S.Sebastiano were known and visited, during Van Mander's time. The exploring of the Catacombs began May 31, 1578, at the Via Salaria.-Floerke, II, note 702.

9 Van Mander may have been in Basel; the paintings at the Campo Santo of Krems in Austria, to which he refers in the biography of Sprangher, contradict this statement. De Jongh in the third edition of Van Mander, 1764, corrected the statement accordingly.-Hymans, I, 7,1.

10 Van Mander went by way of Nürnberg. He says he held Dürers self-portrait in his hands. According to his biographer, Van Mander was more than three years in Italy; we may assume that he came to Nürnberg toward the end of the year 1573 and left early in 1577.-Floerke, II, note 704.

11 The name of Van Mander's wife was Louise Buse. *Biographie des hommes remarquables de la Flandre occidentale*, II, 1844. p.217.

12 The center panel is still in the St Martins Church at Courtrai. It is signed and dated 1582.-Hymans, I, p.13.

13 A pamphlet, published at Haarlem, deals with the arrival of the Flemings. It mentions Carel van Mander, from Meulebeke, with wife and children. 1579. 'Memoriael van de Overkomste der Vlamingen hier binnen Haerlem.'-Hymans, I, p.8.

14 This refers to Ovid illustrations published in 1589 and 1590.-Hymans, I, p.10.

435

15 The shield for Jan Huygensz Linschoten is in the museum at Haarlem. It was painted in 1596. Jacob buries the Foreign Idols,-Genesis xxxv.4. Christ healing the Lepers,-Luke xvii.12. The Children of Israel passing through the Jordan,-Joshua iii.

16 Glashuis, the glass factory. Golden Calf,-Exodus xxxii.19.

17 Willem, probably Van Mander's son.

18 Carel van Mander's son was an important designer working for Spier-incx.-*L'Art*, 1880. I, p.41-*Kronyk Historisch Genootschap Utrecht*, III, p.62, 1856; p.326, 1857.

19 Discussion with the Poets,-Acts xvii.28.

20 Van Mander evidently did not intend to stay at Zevenbergen because when he had finished the manuscript of the *Schilderboeck*, he is supposed to have said: 'It is now time for me to return to my brushes and to see whether it may be given to me to produce something worth-while myself.'-Hymans, I, p.10.

21 See Charles van Weycheusz in: *Epitaphien ojte Grafschriften ghemaeckt op het afsterven van Carel van Mander, in zijn leven cloeck schilder ende Poët, overleden zijnde op den 11-September*, 1606. Ghedruckt te Franeker, bij Rombertus Doyma (voor Paschier van Wesbusch) Boeckenvercooper, Anno 1609.-Greve, 16.

THE BROTHERS VAN EYCK, p.3

Van Mander mentions few printed sources used for his information; he quotes Vasari repeatedly; he used the second edition of the *Vite*, 1568. Unless indicated otherwise, the references to Vasari, given below, refer to the Le Monnier edition of 1846,1857.

1 Campine, Kempen, the north eastern part of Belgium, between the rivers Schelde and Meuse. Van Mander evidently used this metaphor having in mind the biography of Antonello da Messina by Vasari. Vasari, I, 163, and Vasari, IV, p.78. The visit of Antonello to Flanders is regarded fictitious at the present.-Greve, 58-59.

2 For the relation between Hubert and Jan van Eyck, see Lampsonius, Domenicus: Pictroum aliquot celebrium Germanicae inferioris effigies etc. Vna cum Doctiss. Dom. Lampsonij huius artis peritessimi Elogiis, Antwerpiae. Apud Viduam Hieronymi Cock MDLXXII.

This was a series of engraved portraits of famous artists with verses underneath; No.1 represented Joannes van Eyck; the statement given above was from this number. See Greve, 72.

Marcus van Vaernewijck describes the representation of the Van Eyck brothers on the altar in Ghent as follows: 'Joannes den ioncsten broeder, ende principael meester, is in de selve tafel ghecontrefaiet rydende te peerde, meet een rooden Pater noster, op zwarte cleederen, ende Hubertus om zyn ouderdom, sitt op een peert neffens hem, ter rechter hant,' 'Joannes the youngest brother and the most important master, has been portrayed in this picture on horseback, with a red rosary on black costume, and Hubertus is sitting, for sake of his age, on a horse next to him, at his right.

No work of Margriete van Eyck is known.-Floerke, I, note 3. See: Crowe and Cavalcaselle, *The Breviary of the Duke of Bedford*, Leipzig, 1875. Lucas de Heere stated: '...de suster...Die met haer schilderie heeft verwondert.' '...the sister... Who caused surprise by her painting.'

De Heere, Lucas: 'Den Hof en Boomgaard der poesien,' Ghend...Anno MDLXV. See Greve, 91.

3 Other methods of painting were known long before. Theophilus, Schedula diversarum artium (XII Cent.) mentions oil as a medium for painting already.

4 Van Eyck worked at The Hague. Hyman remarks, in connection with Van Mander's statement that Jan van Eyck went to live in Bruges, 'Ceci n'est point exact. Peintre et varlet de chambre de Jean de Baviere (Jean sans Pitie), du mois d'octobre 1422 au mois de septembre 1424, Jean van Eyck habita La Haye pendant ce laps de temps. Devenu peintre de Philippe le Bon le 19 mai 1425, il ne vint sans doute a Bruges qu'en cette derniere qualite.'-Hymans, I, 27,1.-Alex. Pinchart, Bulletins de L'Academie royale de Belgique, XVIII, Serie 2, 1864.-Crowe and Cavalcaselle, 40, note 1.

5 Van Mander translated almost literally Vasari's Vita di Antonello da Messina, IV, pp.75-76. Vaernewijck, Guicciardini, and Lucas de Heere, evidently used Vasari as a source. Hymans did not translate the sentence, 'en niet en hoefde so getrocken te zijn ghedaen.' The method described by Van Mander refers to tempera painting.

6 Gutenberg had priority, according to some historians.

7 Vaernewijck: 'Joannes died young.' Lucas de Heere, in 'Ode op den Agnus Dei,' 'This noble flower departed from this world early.'-Vasari, XIII, 147.-Vasari probably depended for this information on Guicciardini's Descrittione di tuttu Paesi Bassi. It is doubtful Van Mander used the same source directly, because it contains a reference to a painting by Jan van Eyck in the St Donaeskerk at Bruges, and this picture is not mentioned by Van Mander or Vasari. See Becker, Schriftquellen z. Geschichte der Altniederlandische Malerei, Leipzig, 1807.

8 Vasari, IV, 77: '...e massimamente, che egli per un tempo non volle da niuno esser veduto lavorare, ne insegnare a nessuno il segreto...'

9 The church of St Bavo was consecrated originally to St John the Baptist. It received its present name in 1540.-Hymans, I, 30,3. The altar painting was ordered by Jodocus Vydt. Philip the Good had nothing to do with this work.-Floerke, I, note 11.-Friedlander, Die Van Eyck, 1924, pl.xvii. Van Vaernewijck and Lucas de Heere believed Hubertus began the altar painting in Ghent.-Van Vaernewijck: Die Historie van Belgis, IVch.47, 'Hubertus van Eyck...who had begun the panel in the St Jans Kercke.' Lucas de Heere, speaking about Hubertus, 'He had begun the work, as he was used to do.'-Greve, 89.-See studies of E.Renders.-Hubertus was buried in the vault of the families Vydt and Borluut, September 8, 1426. An inscription on the wing states the altar was finished six years after the death of Hubert. Hubertus eeyck maior quo nemo repertus Incepit pondusque Johannes arte secundus Judoci Vydt prece fretus. VersV seXta MaI Vos GoLLoCat aCta tVerI. The chronogram indicates 1432. Opinions differ as to the share each brother had in the work. Max Dvorak: 'Das Ratsel der Kunst der Bruder van Eyck.' (Jahrb. d.kunsthist. Samml. d.allerh. Kaiserhauses, XXIV, p.161), Vienna, 1903. Mary is not crowned by the Father and the Son. Christ is blessing with His right hand and He is holding a crystal globe in His left. He is between Mary and St John.

10 Vaernewijck, IVch.47: 'Eve is holding a fig in her hand. Augustinus

believes it was a fig and not an apple, which Adam ate. The literal text mentions a fruit. After the fall, they covered themselves with fig leaves, not with apple leaves.' Lucas de Heere: 'And she is offering him a fig, which she loves.'-Greve, 91.

11 Floerke identifies the figure at the organ as a playing angel.-Floerke, I, note 15.

12 Vaernewijck, IVch.47: 'Joannes was well beloved by Philip of Charlois, the son of Duke Jan of Digion, count of Flanders. He was appointed secret councillor to his majesty, for his wisdom and keen mind. His presence and company were appreciated.'-Greve, 96.
Van Mander's description of the Van Eyck brothers is based on the portraits in the Lampsonius series.-Greve, 72. The description of the Agnus Dei painting is based almost entirely on the statements of Vaernewijck and Lucas de Heere. Van Mander has seen the painting.-Greve, 217.

13 Van Mander praises Dürer's painting of draperies in the biography of the Van Eycks and in his *Grondt der edel vry schilderconst.*-Greve, 216.

14 Vaernewijck, IVch.47: '...All those faces so well painted; some meditate, some speak, some read, some sing, and there are not two, among these three hundred and thirty faces, alike.'-Greve, 91.

15 Vaernewijck, IVch.47: '...foreign trees, which do not grow in this country...done carefully, and the time that was necessary for this work...the blades of grass to be counted with the thousand,...and the little herbs that can be recognized.'-Greve, 92.

16 Philip, II, 1556-1598.
Vaernewijck, IVch.47: 'Master Michiel de Cockxien, anno XVLIX received an order from our Noble king Philippus, the XXXVI count of Flanders, and made a lively copy.' Lampsonius, De Heere, Guicciardini, and Vasari XIII, p.149, made similar statements. Van Mander does not mention the price and the time spent on this work; De Heere mentions 4000 guilders and two years; Guicciardini speaks of 2000 ducates, plus the rest and two years.-Greve, 94.

17 Vaernewijck, IVch.47: 'It is said, Toetsianus sent the azure, at command of the king, for the color of the coat alone of 'Our lovely Lady,' thirty-two ducats were paid. It is believed this was natural (not artificial) azure...'-Greve, 94. The blue color was lapis lazuli.

18 This copy was finished in 1559, but never reached Spain. The parts have been scattered.-Hymans, I, 33,1.
Vaernewijck, IVch.47:'...and it was sent to Spain...' Similar statements of De Heere, Lampsonius, Guicciardini and Vasari.-Greve, 94-95.

19 Vaernewijck, IVch.47: refers to another cleaning, 'A representation of hell, once on the base of the principal panel, was painted by the same master, Joannes van Eyck, in water-color. Some ordinary painters, it is told, cleaned it, and the miraculous art work was washed off by their calf's hands. This base and the panel were worth more than the gold that covered the painting.'-Greve, 95.

20 About the relation between Jan van Eyck and Philip the Good, see Crowe and Cavalcaselle, pp.81-87, 99,107,124.

21 Vaernewijck, IVch.47:'...How many scenes have been painted in this. Everybody may come and see, people and emperors, and artists who know well the same art, and who value this work.'-Greve, 92.

NOTES TO THE TEXT

22 The poem was taken from Lucas de Heere's *Den Hof en Boomgaard der Poesien*, Ghent, 1565. See Ph.Bloemaert, *Levensschets van Lucas de Heere*, Gent, 1853. pp.25-28.-Greve, 78.

23 Floerke holds the fruit to be a lemon and points out the leaves, Adam and Eve cover themselves with, are not fig leaves.-Floerke, I, note 14.

24 Floerke refers to marginal notes that, in a copy of the *Schilderboeck* (evidently the one in the Royal Library at The Hague), say Hubert had begun the work alone.-Floerke, I, note 22. Greve has proved these marginal notes were not written by Van Mander.-Greve, 289.
Hubert was buried in the crypt at St Bavo. His grave was disturbed in the XVI Cent.-Hymans, I, 35,2.

25 This is not mentioned by Van Mander in the biography of Coxie.

26 Anagram and motto of the painter poet. It means, 'profit by experience.'

27 The first presentation of the altar to the public took place May 6th 1432. Jan van Eyck bought a house in Bruges in the same year.-Hymans, I, 38,5.-Weale, *Notes on Jan van Eyck*, p.8. It is believed that Jan finished the painting in Bruges and that he worked at it after Christmas 1429, after his travel to Portugal. He was called to Hesdin by Duke Philip in 1431.-Laborde,A.de, *La Renaissance des Arts a la Cour de France. Etudes sur le seizieme siecle*. Paris, 1850. p.257.-Vasari, XIII, 148.-Vaernewijck, IVch.60: Johannes van Eyck, the prince of all the painters left an example of his art at Bruges.-Guicciardini: Et medesimanete in Bruggia nella chiesa di Donatiano, e una bellissima Pittura di quel mestro con l'imagine di nostra Donna, et d'altri santi. Van Mander does not mention the subject of the painting.-Greve, 56.
Paintings by Jan van Eyck of which the dates are known:
Portrait of B.Nicholas Albergati, 1432, Vienna.
Portrait of a Man (Leal Souvenir), 1432, London.
Our Lady and Child, 1433, Ince-Blundell, Liverpool.
Portrait of a Man, 1433, London.
Arnolfini and his Wife, 1434, London.
Van der Paele Madonna, 1436, Bruges.
Portrait Jan de Leeuw, 1436, Vienna.
St Barbara, 1437, Antwerp.
Our Lady and Child, 1437, Antwerp.
Portrait of Margaret van Eyck, 1439, Bruges.
Maelbeke Madonna, 1441, Kessel Loo.
See W.H.James Weale and M.W.Brockwell, *The Van Eycks and Their Art*, London, 1912-1928.

28 Van Mander probably meant Federigo I.-Hymans, I, 39,1.

29 Vasari mentions the gift of a Flemish painting to King Alphonso I of Naples in the biography of Antonello da Messina.-Vasari, IV, p.77. The earliest work of Antonello is of 1465 or '75. It is possible that Antonello went to Flanders, but this must have been after the death of the master of the Agnus Dei.-Hymans, I, 39, note 4.

30 This description refers to the Maelbeke Madonna, of 1441. Carton and Waagen regard this painting a work of Lambert van Eyck.
Vaernewijck, IVch.61: In the church of St Maerten a panel painted by Joannes represented Mary and an abbot kneeling before her etc. Similar statements in De Heere,-Guicciardini and Vasari, (XIII p.148).
-Friedlander, *Van Eyck*, 1924. pl.XXIII-XXIV.

31 This cannot be the picture of St Barbara in Antwerp. Van Mander would have mentioned the tower and the palm in her hand.-Karl Voll, *Die Werke des Jan van Eycks*, Strassbourg, 1900. p.127.

32 Arnolfini and his Wife. London National Gallery.-Friedlander, *Van Eyck*, 1924. pl.xxi.-H.Hymans: *L'Exposition des Primitifs Flamands a Bruges*, 1902. p.18.
Vaernewijck, IVch.47: 'Vrau Marie, the aunt of our noble king Philip, married Ludovicum, king of Hungary, who died on the battle field against the Turks, had a small picture done by the same master whose name was Joannes van Eyck. It represented a wedding of a man and a woman married by Fides. The picture belonged to a barber, who was paid for it with an office which gave him an income of hundred guilders a year. See E.Panofsky, *Burlington Magazine*, March, 1934. Van Mander mentions prices of paintings only occasionally. Greve gives a list of prices.-Greve, 175. Arnolfini is holding the right hand of his wife.-Hymans, I, 40,2.

33 Van Mander does not mention which drawings and where and when he saw these.-Greve, p.219.

34 The day of his death has been calculated to be July 9, 1440. He was buried in the cemetery outside the church. His brother Lambert asked the coffin to be placed inside the church.-Crowe and Cavalcaselle, 124. -Weale, 15. The church was destroyed by the French.-Hymans, I, 41,2. Vaernewijck, IVch.47: 'Bruges where he is buried in St Donaes Kerck. His epitaph is on a column and reads: Hic jacet...Similar statements by Lucas de Heere, Guicciardini and-Vasari, XIII, p.148.-E.de Busscher: *Recherches sur les peintres et sculpteurs à Gand*, Ghent, 1866. p.11.

35 Vaernewijck, IVch.47: His sepulcher is at Ghent in the same church. The figure is holding a metal tablet, on which is engraved an old Flemish carmina, which I have spelled letter for letter: 'Spieghelt U aan my, etc.'

36 Domenicus Lampsonius was born in 1532 at Bruges. Poet, painter, savant, secretary to three bishops of Louvain. He left his notes to Vasari. He wrote a biography of Lambert Lombardus, his instructor in painting and on whom he had great influence. He died at Louvain in 1599.-Hymans, I, 42,2. The most important work of Lampsonius was: 'Pictorum aliquot celebrium Germaniae inferioris effigies' Antwerp 1572, published by the widow of Hieronymus Cock. It shows the portraits of Hubert and Jan van Eyck, taken from the Agnus Dei.-Hymans, I, 42,1.

37 Van Mander may have had the impression that the Van Eyck brothers did the painting together, from the statement of Lampsonius: 'Quas mode communes com fratre, Huberte merenti Attribuit laudes nostra Thalia tibi...etc.'-Greve, 46.

ROGIER OF BRUGES, p.15

1 Van Mander follows Vasari, by regarding Rogier from Bruges and Rogier van der Weyden as separate masters.-Vasari, I.163.-Vasari, IV.76. -Greve, 66.

2 Vaernewijck states: Master Rogier's decorations are in the churches and houses in Bruges.-Vaernewijck, IVch.60.

3 Greve calls large canvases with tall figures in them 'kamerschutten,' screens.-Greve, 281.-Vasari, XIII, 148.

NOTES TO THE TEXT

4 Rogier from Brussels and Rogier van der Weyden are identical. Van Mander's error can be explained by his use of the first edition of Vasari (Torrentino, 1550. p.84 and 379).

HUGE VAN DER GOES, p.17

Hugo van der Goes became a member of the guild of Ghent in 1463. His fee was paid by Joos van Wassenhove (Joos van Ghent), a fellow painter who became member of the guild of Antwerp in 1460 and of the Guild of Ghent in 1464.

1 It is not probable that Hugo van der Goes was a pupil of Jan van Eyck. His debut in painting was not long before 1450.-Hymans, I, 51,2. Vaernewijck mentions Hugo's father as Willem Hughe.-Vaernewijck, IVch.48.

2 Mentioned by Vaernewijck, but not described. Hymans, I, 51,3, is convinced that this work is the Madonna of the Pinacoteca in Florence. Bode does not put it on the list of identified paintings.-Bode, 'Die Anbetung der Hirtee von Hugo van der Goes in der Berliner Gallerie.' *Jahrbuch der kon.preuss. Kunstsammlungen*, XXIV, 1903. p.99.

3 The David and Abigail painting is known through copies.-Friedlander, *Hugo van der Goes*, 1926. pl.xxx.

4 Vaernewijck interprets the subject wrongly.-Crowe and Cavalcaselle, p.170. Many copies of this subject have been made.-Frimmel, *Chronique des Arts*, 1896. p.157.-Hymans, 'Une Peinture detruite de Hugo van der Goes.' *Gazette des Beaux Arts*, XX, 1898. p.346.-Friedlander, 'Hugo van der Goes, Eine Nachlese.' (*Jahrbu. der kon. preuss. Kunstsammlungen*), XXV, p.108.

5 This picture was still in the church in the year 1763.-Sanderus, *Flandria Illustrata*, II, p.81.-J.B.Descamps, *Voyage pittoresque de la Flandre et du Brabant*. Paris, 1769.-Hymans, I, 53,1.

6 Hugo van der Goes died 1482, in the Augustine Monastery Roodendale (Rooden Clooster) in the wood of Soignies near Brussels. He received the following epitaph: 'Pictor Hugo van der Goes humatus quiescit Dolet ars com simileum sibi modo nescit.'-Crowe and Cavalcaselle, p.176. -A.Wauters, *Hugues van der Goes, sa vie et ses oeuvres*, 1872.

PAINTERS ANCIENT AND MODERN, p.20

1 Hans Sebald Beham, painter and engraver was born at Nürnberg in 1500 and died at Frankfort a.M., Nov. 22, 1550.
Lucas Miller (Lucas Cranach, the Elder) was born 1472 at Cranach in Upper Franconia, died in 1553 at Weimar.
Israel von Meckenem, born at Bocholt in Westfalen and died there in 1503.
Martin Schongauer (Hupsche Marten, Bel Martino), one of the most illustrious painters of his time, born at Colmar in 1443 or 1445 (1420) and died there in 1488.

2 Hans Memling born probably at Muemling (Memelingen), near Mainz. He appears at Bruges in 1467 and died there on August 11, 1494. Buried in the Aegidius-Church. The Ursula shrine is in the St John's Hospital, Bruges.-Weale, *Catalogue de l'Exposition des Primitifs flamands a Bruges*, 1902. XXI.-Ludwig, Kammerer, *Memling*.

NOTES TO THE TEXT

Van Mander probably saw the reliquary.-Weale, W.H.J. *Hans Memling*, London, 1902. p.26.-Friedlander, VI, 1928. pl.xxi-xxii.
Van Mander may have remembered statements by Pieter Pourbus on the reliquary painted by Memling.-Greve, 165.
Van Mander does not use all the information Vaernewijck gave on .*Duytschen Hans* (Memling).-Vaernewijck, IVch.48.

3 Gerard van der Meire was not a pupil of Hubert van Eyck. In 1452 he became a member of the guild of St Luke at Ghent. He was sub-dean in 1474.-Hymans, I, 62,1. This Lucretia is probably the painting in Pesth attributed to Jacob Cornelis.-Hymans, I, 62,2.

4 Gerard Horenbout appears in the accounts of Ghent, 1510-1511 and from 1540-1541.-Hymans, I, 62,3. Lieven Hughenos became abbot in 1517.

5 Lieven de Witte, not Lieven (van Laethem) from Antwerp, according to Anonimo Morelliano was one of the painters of the Breviary Grimani. De Witte was born at Ghent in 1513 and was living in February, 1578. -Hymans, I, 64,1.

6 Lancelot Blondeel was born at Poperinghe 1496 (or 1485, or 1495) came to Bruges in 1519, became a member of the guild of St Luke; died in 1561. -Weale, *Catalogue de l'Exposition des Primitifs flamands a Bruges*, 1902. XXVII.-Friedlander, XI, 1933.
Van Mander does not use the statement by Vaernewijck; that Lancelot Blondeel and Jan van Scorel restored the Agnus Dei in 1550.-Greve, 89. Lancilloto e stato eccellente in far fuochi, notti, splendori, diavoli e cose somiglianti.-Vasari, XIII, 151... mirabile nel far apparire unfuoco vive, et naturale, come l'incendio di Troia et simile cose.-Guicciardini.

7 Hans Vereycke was probably a glass painter. Guicciardini speaks of a 'grand maistre et homme moult repute en l'art'-Hymans, I, 64,4.
Hulin de Loo identifies this master with Jan van Eeckele, (alias Van Eeck) and the monogramist J.V.E. *Catalogue Exhibition*, Bruges, 1902. The Blaeuwe Huys was destroyed in 1578. It was located outside of Bruges beyond the Porte St Croix, between the church with the same name and the Cistersian cloister. This castle belonged at the time of its demolishment to Marc Laurin. This Blaeuwhuys had to be removed for defense works.-Weale, *Beffroi*, III, p.265.-Hymans, I, 64,5.

8 This refers to Gerard David, born at Oudewater in Holland, c.1450. He died at Bruges, August 13, 1523.-Hymans, I, 54,6.

9 Jan Sanders van Hemishem (Hemixem or Hemessen) near Antwerp, born c.1504, pupil of Hendrik van Cleve at Antwerp, became a free master in 1524, in 1548 he became dean of the guild of St Luke at Antwerp. He died at Haarlem, between 1555 and 1556.-F.J.Van den Branden, *Geschiedenis der Antwerpsche Schilderschool*, Antwerpen, 1883. Van Mander may have received information about Jan van Hemsen from Albert Simonsz.-Greve, p.136.
Christ on His Way to Jerusalem.-Matthew, 9. 9-13.-Mark, 2. 13-17.-Luke, 5. 27-32.

10 Jan Mandyn was born in 1500 at Haarlem, settled at Antwerp before 1530. He became the instructor of Gillis Mostart (c.1550) and of Sprangher (1557); died early in 1560.-Hymans, I, 76.-Van den Branden. p.159. See note: He signed in full a *Temptation of St Anthony*, in the Corsini Gallery, Rome.-Hermann Dollmayr, 'Hieronymus Bosch und

die Darstellung der vier letzten Dinge in der niederlandischn Malerei der XV und XVI Jahrhunderts.' *Jahrb. der kunsth. Samml. des allerh, Kaiserhauses*, XIX.

11 The only date known about Volckert Claesz is 1524, for the burial of his daughter in the St Bavo at Haarlem. No picture of him is known. -Hymans, I, 65,3.

12 Hans de Duytscher entered the guild of St Luke at Antwerp in 1544; was registered as 'maître Jean l'Allemand' peintre de grandes figures sur toile.-Hymans, I, 66,1.

13 He was registered at the guild 1535-1536. Immerzeel places his birth in 1500. The Miraculous Catch is no more at the Onze Vrouwe Kerck at Antwerp. Kramm regarded Van Elburcht as the oldest marine painter. -Hymans, I, 66,2.

14 Born at Antwerp 1490, died 1542, (Immerzeel). Son of the painter Jan de Beer, who appears in the Antwerp guild in 1504 (Wurzbach). He was the first instructor of Lambert Lombardus.-Hymans, I, 66,3.

15 Jan Cransse, dean of the guild 1533-1536, was living in 1548. The Washing of the Feet is no more in 'Onse Vrouwen Kerck'.-Hymans, I, 66,4.

16 Lambrecht van Oort, (van Noort) was born at Amersfoort c.1520 and died at Antwerp in 1571. Lambert van Noort was the father of Adam van Noort, the master of Rubens. He painted a number of windows in the Groote Kerk at Gouda.-Hymans, I, 66,5.-Van den Branden, p.389.

17 Michiel de Gast (Michael Gast) made an agreement with the painter Laurens from Rotterdam to make drawings for him. Nov. 25, 1538. -Bertoletti, *Artisti belgi ed olandesi a Roma nei secoli XVI e XVII*, 1880. p.44.
The Gast entered the guild as son of a master in 1558.-Hymans, I, 67,1.

18 Pieter Bom, born at Antwerp 1530 (Wurzbach), entered the guild in 1564 and became dean in 1598-99. He died at Antwerp, Nov. 29, 1607. -Hymans, I, 67,2.

19 Cornelis van Dalem, a member of the guild in 1556, must not be confused with the famous glass-painter Cornelis van Dalem, who was praised by Guicciardini and who became a member of the guild in 1534.-Hymans, I, 67,3.

ALBERT VAN OUWATER, p.25

1 It was difficult for Van Mander to place ancient Dutch painters in chronological order, owing to lack of definite dates.-Greve, 34.

2 For early painting in the Netherlands see-Van der Kellen, *Les peintures murales dans l'eglise de St Bavon a Haarlem*, 1861.-A.Pit, *Les origines de l'art Hollandais*, Paris, 1894.

3 A.J.Wauters refers to a similar statement by Johannis Molanus: (Dirck Bouts) clerus inventor in describendo rure.-Joannis Molani, '*Doctoris Lovaniensis Theologi*,' *Annales urbis Lovaniensis*, Louanii, 1572.-A.J. Wauters, *Thierri Bouts de Haarlem et ses fils*, Bruxelles, 1863.

4 W.Bode, 'Die Auferweckung des Lazarus von Ouwater in der Koniglichen Gemalde Galerie zu Berlin,' *Jahrb. d.K.Pr. Kunstsammlungen*. XIX, pp.27 to 116. The altar painting disappeared, but the picture of the Resurrection of Lazarus reappeared. It is now in the Kaizer Friederich Museum, Berlin; found in Genoa in 1889. It had come there because Philip II of Spain had given it to the Balbi family.

NOTES TO THE TEXT

Staatl. Museen zu Berlin, *Beschreibendes Verzeichnis der Gemalde im Kaiser Friedrich Museum und Deutschen Museum*, Berlin, 1931. -W.Bode, *Jahrb. der pr. Kunstsammlungen*, XI, 1890. p.35.-M.J.Friedlander, *Die Altniederlandische Malerei*, III, 1925. p.57 and 112. Ph.Ackermann attributes the painting to a member of the Meiren family. *Art in America*, XVI, 1928.

5 Van Mander received this information about Heemskerck probably from Jacob Rauwert.-Greve, 155.

6 There is little known about Van Ouwater.
Ouwater is the name of a town in Zuid-Holland; see Franz Duelberg, *Die Leidener Malerschule*. p.13.
The records of the church of St Bavo at Haarlem show that in 1467 a grave was opened for the daughter of Ouwater and that the Salvator chimes were rung.-Van der Willigen, *Les artistes de Haarlem*, Haag, 1870. p.49.

GEERTGEN TOT SINT JANS, p.27
Crucifixion-Friedlander, V, 1927. pl.ix-x.

1 The interior and exterior pictures of the remaining wing have been separated and are in the Imperial Gallery at Vienna. (Cat.645) The pane had been in the collection of archduke Leopold Wilhelm at Brussels, who had inherited the picture from King Charles I of England.
One side shows the Burning of the bones of John the Baptist, the other side Christ lamented.
Notizen zum Klassischen Bilderschatz, IX, No.1243 and 1256.-Floerke, I, note 74.

2 There is a picture (in the Ryksmuseum at Amsterdam) by Geertgen, of a Holy Family, which shows the interior of a church; this is not identical with the picture mentioned by Van Mander, it shows the ability of the master at architectural construction.-Duelberg, *Die Leydener Malerschule*. p.31.
Friedlander gives a criticism on this in *Repertorium für Kunstwissenschaft* XXII, 1899. p.331.-Floerke, I, note 74a.

3 Dürer was not in Haarlem on his visit to the Netherlands.-Crowe and Cavalcaselle, p.207.

DIRCK OF HAARLEM, p.29
1 Dirk Bouts, Dieric de Louvain, was born in Haarlem after 1400, and died at Louvain May 6, 1475. He was appointed painter to the town in 1468. He was probably a pupil of Ouwater, founder of the School of Louvain. -Kat. *Alte Pinakothek*, Munich. p.25.-Friedlander, III, 1925.

ROGIER VAN DER WEYDE, p.31
1 Born at Tournai in 1399 or 1400. He became a master of the guild August 1, 1432, and died at Brussels June 16, 1464. He was a pupil of Robert Campin from Tournai after March 5, 1427. Not a pupil of Jan van Eyck. He worked at Tournai and Brussels. Painter to the town in 1436. He worked for a short while at Louvain and at Bruges. He was in Italy, 1449-1450, probably at the court of Lionelle d'Este at Farrara. -*Beschr. Verz. der Gemalde Galerie*, Berlin, 1931. p.526.-Crowe and Cavalcaselle, p.221.-Friedlander, II, 1924.

444

NOTES TO THE TEXT

2 The pictures in Brussels were destroyed in 1695 during the siege of Brussels by the French. The inscriptions had been copied before, and give a general idea of the subject matter. The Burgundian tapestries at Bern, which have the same inscriptions, probably represent the same subjects. See E.Muentz, *la Tapisserie*, Paris, Quantin, 1882. p.151. The four subjects of the paintings were: Justice for Trajan, Pope Gregory receiving the head of Trajan, Archambaud de Bourbon beheading his nephew, Archambaud shows the Host he received after the bishop refused it to him.-*Bulletin de l'Academie royale de Belgique*, 2 serie, XVII, 1864. p.54.
-G.Kinckel, *Die Brusseler Rathausbilder*, Bern, 1867.-Wurzbach, article on C.Ed.Taurel, 'De Christelijke Kunst in Holland en Vlaanderer,' Amsterdam, Buffa. *Kunst Chronik*, 1883. p.528.
Probably an error on the part of Van Mander, to attribute this subject to Van der Weyden. One picture by Holbein, in the Town hall of Basle, is of the legend of Zaleukos from Lokris, who has his own right eye and the left eye of his son torn out as a punishment for the latter's adultery. As a judge he had passed this sentence on himself and in this way saved one eye of his son.-A.Woltmann, *Holbein und seine Zeit*, 1866-68. p.298. -Hymans, I, 100,1.
3 Lampsonius did not take part in the Pacification of Ghent. As secretary to the Bishop of Liége, Gerard de Groesbeke, he may have taken part in negotiations for the Perpetual Edict of 1577.-Hymans, I, 100,1.
4 The 'Descent from the Cross' belonged to the archers of Louvain; they gave it to Mary of Hungary. It is now at the Escorial. There are copies of this painting in the Kaiser Friederich Museum at Berlin, in the Prado (probably the one by Cocxie), in St Peter's Church at Louvain, in the Bridgewater Collection at London. The picture shows one stepladder. -Hymans, I, 101,1.-Beschr. *Verz. d.Gemalde*, Berlin, 1931. p.530.-Friedlander, II, 1924. pl.ii,vii.
5 Van Mander may have taken the information from-Joannis Molani, 'Doctoris Lovaniensis Theologi:' *Annalis urbis Lovanensis*, Louanii, 1572. 'Magister Rogerius...decinxcit Lovanii...summum altare, quod opus Maria regina a Sagittarius impetravit, et in Hispanias vehi curavit, quamquam in mari periisse dicatur, et ejus et novum altare, ad examplar Rogerii expressum opera Michaelis Coxenii, sui pictoris.'-Greve, 122.
6 Van Mander exaggerated the benevolent act of Rogier, see-A.Pinchart, *Bulletin des commissions royales d'art et d'archeologie*, VI, p.478,
7 Lampsonius, No.3: 'tua, de partis pingendo extrema voluntas Perpetua est inpum quod medivina fami.'

JACOB CORNELISZ., p.33
Jacob Cornelis van Oostzanen is master of the monogram IMA. Oost Zaandam is a village on the river Zaan, near Amsterdam.
1 According to the catalogue of the Ryksmuseum of 1898 he was born in 1480 (?) and died at Amsterdam after 1533. He worked in that city from 1510 to 1532.-P.Scheltema, *Historische Beschrijving van de Schilderijen van het Raadhuis te Amsterdam*, No.30, Amsterdam, 1879.
2 Hymans believes the Descent from the Cross in the Louvre, attributed to Quentin Massys and to Lucas van Leyden, is identical with the painting mentioned here.-Hymans, I, 109,1.

NOTES TO THE TEXT

3 L.Schleiber found 1506 to 1530 the extreme dates for the work of Jacob Cornelis.-L.Schleiber, 'Die Gemaelde des. Jacob Cornelis van Amsterdam des Monogrammisten.' *Jahrb. d.K.Preuss. Kunstsammlungen,* III, 1882. p.13.-J.Six, 'Dirk Jacobsz, Twee Amsterdamsche Schutterstukken te St Petersburg, *Oud Holland,* XIII, 1895. p.94-96.-A.Riegel, 'Das Hollandische Gruppen Portrait,' *Jahrb. d. Kunsts. des X all. Kaiserhauses,* XXIII, 1902.

4 The Widow Van Sonneveldt probably informed Van Mander about Jan van Scorel.-J.Six, 'Dirk Jacobsz, Twee Amsterdamsche Schutterstukken te St Petersburg, *Oud Holland,* XIII, 1895.

5 Van Mander refers to group-pictures of the civic guard, of which there are two, in the city hall and in the Ryksmuseum.-H.Riegel, *Beitrage zur niederlandischen Kunstgeschichte,* Berlin, 1882.-P.Scheltema, *Historische Beschrijving der Schilderijen van het Raadhuis te Amsterdam.*

6 Bartsch, *Le Peintre Graveur,* VII, p.444, mentions 21 engravings by Jacob Cornelis.-Passavant, III, places the number at 127 engravings. The series of the knights is not identified definitely.-Floerke, I, note 90. -E.Fetis, *Doc. iconographiques et typographiques de la Biblioteque Royale de Belgique,* 1877.

ALBRECHT DURER, p.35

1 Albrecht Dürer was born May 21, 1471.
Van Mander means Rome and Florence.
He knew about Dürer's trip to Venice (1505-1507) through Vasari.
-Floerke, I, note 91.-Hymans, I, 113,2.
Van Mander probably derived the date of Dürer's birth from the grave of Dürer in Nürnberg, which he must have seen.-Greve, 171.

2 Vasari says about Hupse Marten: 'Dopo questo Martino, comincio Alberto Duro'-Vasari, IX, 260.

3 The group of four women. Bartsch, 185. The engraving of Dürer is reproduced in *Klassiker der Kunst,* IV.
The originator of the engraving is master W, whom Thausing identified as Wolgemut, Thausing compared the technique of Dürer with that of Wolgemut and showed that Wolgemut produced the original.-Hymans, I, 114,5.
The original and the copy show the date 1497, which is possible for Wolgemut, but not for Dürer. (Thausing, I.) Lehrs has proved the prints with the monogram W are not by Wolgemut, but the W belonged to Wenzel von Olmutz, who copied Dürer.
Thode, 'Die Jugendgemälde Albrecht Duerers;' *Jahrb. d. preuss. Kunstsammal,* XII, 1891.
The oldest copper engravings by Dürer are, The Holy Family and the Love Declaration.(*Klassiker der Kunst* I, K, IV.); both prints show his usual monogram and for this reason were not made before 1496. -Thausing, I.

4 Vasari, IX, p.61, mentions the horses of 1505: '...a duo cavalli per carta...'
Reproductions of these prints are in *Klassiker der Kunst,* IV.

5 Vasari states about Jacopo di Ponturmio: '...ma sopra tuto vi era un bellissino paese, tolto per la maggior parte da una stampa d'Alberto Duro'-Vasari, XI, 47.

446

NOTES TO THE TEXT

6 Marc Anton copied this series without introducing Dürers monogram.
-Hymans, L.115,1.-Thausing, I, 341.-Vasari, Sansoni, V, 406.

7 Books on proportion: *Hierin sind begriffen vier Buecher von mensch-licher Proportion, durch Albrechten Duerer von Nurnberg erfunden zu Nutz allem denen, so zu dieser Kunst Lieb tragen,* 1528.
Dürer finished the first volume, the other three were edited by friends and the entire set appeared October 31, 1528, published by his widow and printed by Jeronymus Andrea.-Thausing, II, 317.
Book on perspective and Military Science:
Unterricht zur Befestigung der Stadte, Schlosser und Flecken, 1527.
Unterweisung der Messung mit dem Zirkel und Richtscheit in Linien, Ebenen und ganzen Korpern, 1525.

8 This story and the correction of it by Van Mander are to be considered as fiction.-Thausing, II.
See emblems of painters:-F.Warnecke. *Das Kuenstlerwappen.*-S.Mulder, 'Utrechtsche Schildersvereenigingen,' *Oud Holland,* 1904. XXII, p.1.

9 Vasari writes about the portrait: 'Per queste e molto altre opere essendo passata la fama, di questo nobilissimo artefice insino in Francia ed in Fiandra, Alberto Durero tedesco, pittore mirabilissimo ed entagliatore di rame di bellissime stampe, divenne tributario delle sue opere a Raffaello, e gli mando la testa d'un suo ritratto condotta da lui a guazzo su una tela di bisso, che da ogni banda mostrava parimente, e senza biacca; lumi trasparenti, se non che con acquerelli di colori era tuita e macchiata, e de'lumi del panno aveva campato: chiari: la quale cosa para maravi-gliosa a Raffaello.'-Vasari, VIII.
Van Mander writes about Raphael: 'His fame spread round the world rapidly. Albrecht Dürer sent him his portrait, done in wash on canvas, without the use of white for highlights, saving the light of the canvas. Raphael regarded this as something remarkable and expressed his grati-tude by sending him many drawings. This portrait was in Mantua among things which belonged to Giulo Romano.' This portrait has disappeared.
-Thausing, I.

10 Hymans believes the picture in the Louvre, Tete de Vieillard (Cat. 1900) represents the Cardinal.-Hymans, I, 117,1.
Drawings by Dürer are in the British Museum.-A.Springer, *Albrecht Dürer,* 1892.

11 There are many studies by Dürer in the Albertina Collection, Vienna.
-Thausing, I.

12 About Dürer, Vasari states 'Ma troppo sarei lungo se io volessi tutte l'opere raccontare, che uscirono di mano ad Alberto.'-Vasari, IX.

13 The Three Magi (1504), Florence, Uffizi, 434 (Cat.1891)-Bode, *Cicerone,* II, 742.-*Klassiker der Kunst,* IV, 24.
Madonna with the Finch, 1506. Berlin Kaiser Friedrich Museum.
-*Klassiker der Kunst,* IV.-M.J.P.Richter, *Kunst Chronik,* 1883.
Adam and Eve, (1507). Madrid, Prado Museum. Old copies are in the Pitti Collection, Florence.-*Klassiker der Kunst,* IV.
Crucifixion of 1508: Van Mander means the Martyrdom of the ten thousand Christians under King Sapor of Persia.-*Klassiker der Kunst,* IV.
Van Mander did not see the picture; it came into possession of Rudolph II in 1600; Sprangher may have informed Van Mander.

447

NOTES TO THE TEXT

14 The description of the painting of 1511 refers to The Adoration of the Holy Trinity.-*Klassiker der Kunst*, IV.-*Thausing*, II.

15 The Carrying of the Cross by Dürer is not known.-Floerke, I, note 108. Various drawings of the subject by Dürer exist.-Hymans, I, 118,5.

16 The Assumption of Mary refers to the 'Hellersche Altar.' The central panel was lost in a fire in 1674. It had been acquired by the elector Maximilian of Bavaria in 1615. The wings and a copy of the center panel are in Frankfort.-*Klassiker der Kunst*, IV.-Thausing, II. -Floerke, I, note 109.-Ephrussi. *Albert Dürer*, 1882. A similar anecdote about a detail in a picture is told in the biography of Dirck Jacobsz. Van Mander saw the picture in Frankfort, on his return trip through Germany.-Greve, 214.

17 Charlemagne and Emperor Sigismund, painted in 1512. Germanisches Museum, Nürenberg.-*Klassiker der Kunst*, IV. Portrait of Maximilian I (1519), at Vienna. Dürer gave the paintings of St John, St Peter, St Paul, and St Mark, to the magistry of his city. October 7, 1526.-Munich. Alte Pinakothek.

18 The picture of his mother is lost.-Floerke, I, note 112. Dürer's self-portrait of 1500 (according to Van Mander), is in the Alte Pinakothek. Thausing dates this portrait between 1503 to 1509.-*Klassiker der Kunst*, IV. The other self-portrait, Dürer as Prodigal Son, see *Klassiker der Kunst*, IV. Engraving, (Bartsch 28). Vasari states: '...ed in un'altra il Figluol prodigo, il quale stando a uso di villano ginocchioni con le mani incrocicchiato, guando il cielo, mentre certi porci mangiando in un trogolo...'

19 Lucretia, Munich Alte Pinakothek.-Thausing, II.-*Klassiker der Kunst*, IV. This picture was in the collection of the dukes at the end of the XVI Century. Melchior Wyntgis or Wyntgens, mint-master of Zeeland, lived at Middelburg from 1601 till 1612. In 1615, he was 'conseiller et maître extra ordinaire de la Chambre des Comptes pour les Affaires du pays et duche de Luxembourg.'-Hymans, I, 120,1.-A.Pinchart, *Archives des Arts*, III, 1881.

20 Dürer was in the Netherlands during 1520 and 1521.-See Thausing, 'Dürer's Briefe, Tagebucher und Reise,' *Wiener Quellenschrifte*, III, 1872. Dürer's portrait of Lucas van Leyden at Lille.-Hymans, I, 120,3.-Reproduced in *Oud Holland*, XVII, 1899.

21 Van Mander gives the wrong date for the death of Dürer; should be April 6, 1528. For a history of the graves see Thausing, II. Van Mander quotes the epitaphs, probably from Dürer's book on proportion.-Greve, 116. Van Mander may have received material about Dürer from Goltzius.-Greve, 148.

CORNELIS ENGELBRECHTSEN, p.43

1 Van Mander's information about Engelbrechtsen came from Aechtgen Cornelis, probably.-Greve, 134.-Franz Duelberg, *Die Leydener Malerschule*, II, C.Engelbrechtsz. Berlin, 1899.

2 The father of Engelbrechtsen has been recorded as a town guard in

NOTES TO THE TEXT

Leyden, February 6, 1457. He was a carpenter. According to some he was a wood-engraver.-Hymans, I, 123,1.
It is a supposition of Duelberg that Engelbrecht the carpenter was the father of Cornelis Engelbrechtsen.-Duelberg, *Die Leydener Malerschule*, p.41.
Pieter Cornelisz Kunst appears in the records of the town guards, 1499 and 1519.
The town guard records show he was paid in 1527 for painting a crest of arms on the glass of a lantern. He did some other work on glass in 1523 for the convent of Marienpoel.-Hymans, I, 123,3.

3 The Crucifixion:-Duelberg, op.cit.-Max.J.Friedlander, Franz Duelberg, 'Die Leydener Malerschule,' in *Rep. für Kunstwissenschaft*, XXII, 1899. Marienpoel is between Leyden and Oegstgeest.-Friedlander, X, 1932.

4 The Descent from the Cross.-Leiden, Stadsmuseum (Cat.1886).-Greve, 208.-Friedlander, X, 1932.

5 The Adoration of the Virgin.-Leiden, Stadsmuseum (Cat.1886).-Greve, 208.

6 Apparently the Lockhorst memorial is lost.-Friedlander, X, 1932.

7 Hymans did not translate the phrase: '...en is nochtans weel al ten eersten opghedaen, ghelijck sij doe veel voor een veerdighe fraey wijse hadden.'-Floerke, I, note 126.

BARENT VAN BRUSSEL (Bernard van Orley), p.46.

1 Lampsonius states about Bernard van Orley: 'Quam tibi quod carus Belgarum Margari rectrix.' He was painter to Marguerite of Austria; after her death he was in the service of Mary of Hungary. It is not known that he had an official title of painter to the emperor.-Hymans, I. 127,1.-Friedlander, VIII, 1930.

2 The Last Judgement by Van Orley went to the St Elizabeth Hospital, Antwerp.-Reproduced in Taurel, *L'Art Chretien*, II, p.43.

3 St Luke painting the Madonna is not by Van Orley but by Gossart. This picture was painted in 1515. Archduke Matthias took it with him in 1580; it is now at Prague, with the wings painted by Coxcie.-Hymans, I, 127,4. -Friedlander, VIII, 1930.

4 These tapestries, *Belles chasses de Guyse*, or *Belles chasses de Maximilian*, are in the Louvre.
Alph.Wauters, *Bernard van Orley*, Brussels, 1881.-Hymans, I, 128,1.

5 Greve refers to a painting by J.Mijtens, (Museum of Rennes) in which these tapestries appear.-Greve, 256. These tapestries were woven with gold and silver threads and decorated the castle at Breda. They have not been retraced. There are four drawings in the Kupferstichkabinet at Munich, which represent princes and princesses of Orange.-Hymans, I, 128,2. The archives of the Guild of St Luke at Antwerp mention various masters with this name. Four masters with this name can be found in the catalogue of the Museum at Antwerp. Jordaens, mentioned here, refers to the artist that registered at Delft and died there in 1613. He married the widow of Frans Pourbus, the elder.-Hymans, I, 128,3.

6 According to Alph.Wauters, Bernard van Orley was born between 1490 and 1501. He died at Brussels January 6, 1542.-A.Wauters, *Bernard d'Orley*, Bruxelles, 1881.

NOTES TO THE TEXT

LUCAS VAN LEYDEN, p.48

1 Sometimes called Lukas Huighensz, or Lukas Jacobsz.-Friedlander, X, 1932.
2 Van Vaernewijck states: '. . . There is a painted panel in the same cloister. (St Peter's cloister at Ghent); it is behind the high choir. It was made a long time ago by Master Hugo van Leyden, in Holland. . .'-Hymans, I, 137,1.
3 See about Lucas van Leyden's early life:-Franz Duelberg, *Die Personlichkeit des Lucas van Leyden. Oud Holland,* 1899, p.65.-Elsevier, 'Ouders van den Schilder Lucas van Leyden,' in *De Navorscher,* 1858. p.245.-Greve, 133.
4 Mahomet killing a Monk,-Bartsch, p.126. Nine round passion scenes. Bartsch, pp. 57 to 65.-Vasari, IX.
   Temptation of St Anthony,-Bartsch, p.117.
5 The Conversion of St Paul,-Bartsch, p.107.-Vasari, IX.
6 Vasari stated: '. . . il quale, se bene non aveva tanto disegno quanto Alberto, in molte cose nondimeno lo paragonava rol bulino.'-Vasari X.
7 St Hubert,-Bartsch, p.57.
8 Marc Antonio used the landscape of the engraving of Mohammed for engraving the 'Bathing Soldiers' by Michelangelo.
   Francesco Verdi, pupil of Perugino, borrowed an entire group from Lukas van Leyden in his 'Baptizing of Christ' Uffizi Gallery, Florence. -Floerke, I, note 143.-Vasari, X.
9 Ecce Homo,-Bartsch, p.71.
10 Farmer and his wife with cows,-Bartsch, p.158.
11 Adam and Eve driven from Paradise,-Bartsch, p.11.
   Nude woman with dog,-Bartsch, p.154.
12 Magdalen,-Bartsch, p.122.
   Crucifixion,-Bartsch, p.74.
   The Magi,-Bartsch, p.37.
13 Van Mander criticises the information of Vasari, who was informed by Lampsonius.-Vasari, XIII.-Greve, 47.
14 Elizabeth, daughter of Jakob van Boschuysen and Adele Heerman. -Hymans, I, 141,5.
15 Dürer did not visit Leyden. The meeting took place at Antwerp in 1521.-Hymans, I, 141,6.-Floerke, I, note 117.
16 Hymans doubts this engraving represents Lucas van Leyden and compares it with the drawing by Albrecht Dürer and the engraving in the series of Lampsonius.-Hymans, I, 142,1.
17 The Blind Man of Jericho.
   Leningrad, Ermitage, (Cat.1895).-Friedlander, X, 1932.
18 The poem is probably by Cornelis Ketel, *Obreen's Archief,* VI, p.100-106.-Greve, 151.
19 The Last Judgement, Leyden Museum (Cat.1886).-J.C.Overvoorde and W.Martin Stedelijk Museum te Leiden.-Greve, 243.
   Probably painted in 1526 in memory of Claes Dircz and exhibited in the St Pieterskerck, hidden in the St Jacobshospital during the Iconoclasm of August 26th and transported to the room of the magistrates in the town hall in 1577. Later, moved to the Stedelijk Museum. See Van Dulberg, *Repertorium für Kunstwissenschaft,* XXII, 1899, p.30.-Friedlander, X, 1932.

NOTES TO THE TEXT

20 Madonna and Annunciation, Munich, Alte Pinakothek.-Friedlan ᵗᵉr, X, 1932.
21 The Children of Israel dancing around the Golden Calf. This picture was sold at auction in Amsterdam, May 7-8, 1709. Sale Jacob Cromchout and Jasper Loskart. See Geerard Hoet, *Catalogus van Schilderjen met derselver Pryzen*, 1752.
22 The Story of Joseph appears in a series of five engravings by Lucas van Leyden,-Bartsch, pp.19-23.
23 Saul and David, Bartsch, p.27. '...Fece poi in un carta in rame un Saul a sedere en Davit giovinetto che gli mona intormo.'-Vasari, IX.
24 Farmer with Toothache,-Bartsch, p.157.
25 Old Man and Old Woman tuning Instruments,-Bartsch, p.155.
26 Portrait of Maximilian,-Bartsch, p.172. Lucas van Leyden engraved this portrait in 1520, after the death of the emperor. Maximilian visited Leyden in 1508.-Hymans, I, 147,3.
27 The print by Saenredam, (Bartsch, III, p.254) No.109, A.Bredius mentions, in *Obreen's Archief*, V, p.293, a box containing eight square glass paintings by Lucas van Leyden which appeared at an auction in 1662. The subjects are not mentioned. There is a glass Painting in the Ambrosiana Library at Milan which Bredius wants to identify as an o-riginal work of Lucas van Leyden.-*Repertorium für Kunstwissenschaft*, XI, p.390. The self-portrait by Lucas of 1525, Bartsch, p.173, is an etching. Bartsch has described twenty wood-engravings; but it has not been proved that these engravings are by the hand of Lucas.-Hymans, I, 147,3.
28 Jan van Mabuse, also called Jan Gossaert. Lucas van Leyden was enrolled as free master in the guild of St Luke, Antwerp, in 1522.-Hymans, I, 148,2.
29 Pallas,-Bartsch, p.139.
30 This daughter was not born from his marriage with Elizabeth Boschuysen. Her name was Marie; she married the painter, Dammasz, or Damissen Claesz, in 1532. There exists a testament of a certain Lucas Jansz van Wassenaer, which was discussed in the Court of Holland in 1645, and in which is mentioned that Lucas van Leyden left a daughter named Marguerite, who married a certain de Hoey by whom she had four sons: Cornelis, Lucas, Huigh and Jan. About the last one, see -Hymans, I, 149,3.-P.A.Leupe, 'Adversaria betreffende onderscheidene kunstenaars en hunne werken, Lucas van Leyden,' in *Obreen's Archief*, II, 1879-80, p.144.
31 Jan de Hoey, named, in France, Doe, Dhoe, Valet de chambre et peintre ordinaire du roi, was born in Leyden in 1545, according to De Jongh, and was a pupil of Lucas Dammasz. After working in Leyden, he went to Italy and to France. He was conservator of the picture collection of Henri IV. He died in France in 1615 at the age of seventy. -Hymans, I, 149,4.

JAN DE HOLLANDER, p.60

1 Called himself Janne van Amstel, was born in Amsterdam; he became free master of the guild in Amsterdam in 1528. On February 1, 1536, he was registered in the civil records of the town of Antwerp as: Jan Amstel, Aertssone, van Amsterdamme, painter.

451

NOTES TO THE TEXT

-Gillis van Conincxloo,-Van den Branden, *Geschiedenis der Antwerpsche schilderschool.*

2 Gillis van Conincxloo may have informed Van Mander about Jan de Hollander.-*Oud Holland,* 1885.-*Journal des Beaux Arts,* 1870.-Greve, 144. Gillis van Conincxloo the Younger, see his biography. His mother, widow of Jan van Amstel, was named Adriana van Doornicke. She was a daughter of Jan van Doornicke. Her sister, Anna, was the wife of the painter, Pieter Coecke van Aelst.-Van den Branden, op.cit. p.287.

3 Glück identifies him by the 'Braunschweiger Monogrammist.' If this is not true, there is no known painting by him.-Gustav Glück, *Zu einem Dilde des Hieronymus Bosch in der Figdorschen Sammlung in Wien.* -*Jahrb. Kon. Preuss. Kunsts.,* XXV, 1904. p.183.

4 Lampsonius, No.11: 'Propria Belgarum laus est bene pingere rura.' -Greve, 73.

QUINTIJN MESSIJS, p.61

1 Messijs, also Massys and Matsys and Metsys.
The portrait of Quintijn was engraved by Jan Wiericx after the self-portrait (the artist) gave to the Guild of St Luke at Antwerp. The painting has been lost.-Hymans, I, 160,3.-Friedlander, VII, 1929.

2 The Descent from the Cross is at the present in the Antwerp Museum. A copy is in Amsterdam.
There are only four heads of horses in this painting. Salome does not dance; she is carrying the head of John the Baptist.-Hymans, I, 160,3,4,5. -Friedlander, VII, 1929.

3 King Philip died September 13, 1598. Van Mander's statement, the king died recently, indicates that the biography of Messijs was written shortly after 1598.-Greve, 31.

4 Van Mander mentions names of various persons who saved works of artists. See, biographies of Gerard Horebout, Frans Floris.-Greve, 130.

5 The triptych now in the Museum of Antwerp, Descent from the Cross, was ordered by the Guild of the cabinet makers in 1508. It was finished in 1511.-Van den Branden, pp.62,234,237.
The painting became the property of the town, May 15, 1582, not in 1577.-Hymans, I, 161,3.

6 Hymans believed the picture of Mary was the one in the Rijksmuseum at Amsterdam (Cat.1891).
A similar picture is listed in the inventory of the Amsterdam art dealer, Duarte, in 1682, and was valued at 300 florins.-Hymans, I, 161,4.
The Amsterdam painting is an old copy.-Greve, 248.-Friedlander, VII, 1929.

7 According to the catalogue of the Berlin Museum, Quentin Messys was born at Louvain c.1466 and died between July 13 and September 6, 1530, at Antwerp. Jan Matsys was born in 1509 and died in 1575.-Van den Branden, p.136.

JERONIMUS BOS VAN AKEN, p.65

1 His family came from Aachen, Aken in Dutch. He was born at 's-Hertogenbosch (den Bosch, abbreviation in Dutch) c.1460, died in 1516.

452

NOTES TO THE TEXT

Alex. Pinchart, Notes sur Jerome van Aeken, dit Bosch, et sur Alard du Hameel, *Bulletin de l'Academie royale de Belgique*, 1858, IV, p.407; and in *Archives des sciences lettres et beaux arts*, I, pp.267-275.-Friedlander, V, 1927.

2 Van Mander probably saw the Flight from Egypt in Amsterdam. -Greve, 190. This painting has disappeared.-Floerke, I, note 189. The picture seen by Van Mander on the 'Wael,' may have been the one now in Hampton Court (Cat.1897), or the one in Prague, (Cat.1889).-Greve, 191.

No painting of this subject can be considered as an original by Bosch. Anonymus Morcelliano says three pictures by Bosch, in the possession of Cardinal Grimani in Venice (1521) are, a representation of Hell— 'la tela del inferno cun la gran diuersita de monstri fo de mano de Hieronimo Bosch.'-*Wiener Quellenschriften*, Neue Folge, I.-Floerke, I, note 190.

The Carrying of the Cross is probably the picture retouched by Lambert Lombard and of which a large engraving was published by Cock. The engraver is not known. This work seems to have been in Bonn in 1584, according to a document in the archives of the University found by Gottfried Kinkel; it is assumed that the picture disappeared after the fire in the cathedral, where it was kept.-Hymans, I, 170,3.

In 1584, Gerhard von Haen, a canon in Bonn, bought a picture from a Netherlander who had been expelled because he was a Catholic. This picture was placed on the high altar. It was a triptych and represented the Entry of Christ into Jerusalem on the center panel. On the wings were the Birth of Christ and His Resurrection.

See Dollmayr, 'Hieronymus Bosch und die Darstellung der vier letzten Dinge.' *Jahrbuch der kunsthistorischen Sammlungen des Allerh Kaiserhauses*, XIX.

There is a Carrying of the Cross in the Escorial to which Van Mander refers. See C.Justi, 'Die Werke des Hieronymus Bosch in Spanien,' *Jahrbuch der Kon.preuss. Kunstsamml.X.* This is considered a painting by Breughel. See,-L.Maeterlinck, *Le genre satirique dans la peinture flamande*, Bruxelles, 1903.

3 The paintings once in 'sHertogenbosch do not exist. According to J.B.Gramaye, *Antiquitates Belgicae*, these pictures were in the St John's Church at 'sHertogenbosch in 1611.

When Frederik Hendrik of Orange had conquered the city in 1629, he allowed the Catholic clergy to take these pictures with them.-T.van Westrheene, in *Kunster-Lexikon de Meur*, I.

The drawings for the windows of the chapel of the Liebfrauenbruederschaft of the same church can be traced to Bosch.-C.Justi, 'Die Werke des Hieronymus Bosch in Spaniem,' *Jahrbuch der Kon.preuss. Kunsts*, X, 1889, p.121.

There are eight pictures in the Prado Museum attributed to Hieronymus Bosch, but they are not all authentic.-Hymans, I, 170,6.-C.Justi, *Jahrb. Kon.preuss.Kunsts*, 1889, X, p.124.-Gustav Glück: 'Zu einen Bilde von Hieronymus Bosch in der Figdorschen Sammlung in Wien,' *Jahrb. Kon. preuss. Kunsts*, XXV, 1904, p.179.

Van Mander does not mention Jan Mandijn as a follower of Bosch. -Greve, 40.

NOTES TO THE TEXT

Van Mander does not mention engravings made after the work of Bosch, though Vasari does.-Vasari, IX.-Greve, 50, p.191.
4 Lampsonius, No.4.

LODEWYCH JANS VAN DEN BOSCH, p.67

1 According to Siret, *Dictionnaire des Peintres*, van den Bosch died in 1507. A work by this artist appeared at the inventory sale of Jean Chrysotome de Backer van Eindhoven, which took place at The Hague in 1662. See A.Bredius, 'Een Kunstverzamelaar der XVII Eeuw,' *Obreen's Archief*, V, 1882-83, p.296.

CORNELIS CORNELISZ. KUNST, p.68

1 The second son of Cornelis, Engelbrechts., see the biography of this artist.-Hymans, I, 176,1.
2 The works of Cornelis Cornelisz Kunst do not appear in the Bruges inventories.-Hymans, I, 176,2.
No painting can be attributed definitely to Cornelis Cornelisz Kunst. -Floerke, I, note 200.
3 M.C.E.Taurel doubts Van Mander is correct in the date of the death of the artist. He believes it was in 1533.-Hymans, I, 177,1.

LUCAS CORNELISZ. DE KOCK, p.70

1 According to the Catalogue of Hampton Court (E.Law.1881) De Kock died in 1552. A number of portraits of members of the court of Henry VIII have been attributed to him, and copies of heads from pictures by Lucas Cornelisz. De Kock went to England in the reign of Henry VIII. He painted a series of reduced copies of the portrait of the high constable of the castle of Queenborough, which are at Penshurst.-Hymans, I, 181,1.

JAN VAN CALCKAR, p.71

1 Jan van Calckar is not to be confused with Jan Joest or Joosten in Calcar. -Hymans, I, 181,1.
According to the catalogue of the Berlin Museum, he was born in 1499.
2 No picture by the artist can be traced in Italy.
There is a portrait by him in Paris (Vesalius) and one in Berlin.-Floerke, I, note 203.
3 'Conobbi ancora in Neapoli, e fu mio amicissimo, l'anno 1545, Giovanni di Calker, pittore fiammingo molto raro, e tanto pratico nella maniera d'italia, che le sue opere non crano conosciute per mano di fiammingo; ma costui mori giovane in Napoli, mentre si sperava gran cose di lui.' -Vasari, XIII.
4 Andreae Vesalii Bruxellensis. *De humani corporis fabrica libri septem*, Basel, 1543.-Choulant, *Geschichte und Bibliographie der anatomischen Abbildungen*, Leipzig, 1852.-Hymans, I, 182,3.
According to Vasari, these pictures were drawn by himself and by his pupils, and engravings were made after the drawings by Cristofano Coriolano.
Passavant believes Coriolano to be the German engraver Lederer, born in Nürnberg in 1540.-Hymans, I, 183,1.
5 Van Mander probably guessed at the date of Calcar's death, figuring

454

NOTES TO THE TEXT

Vasari knew the painter in Naples in 1545; the first edition of Vasari's work came out in 1550.-Greve, 61.

PIETER KOECK, p.73

1 Pieter Koeck, also Coecke and Coucke, called Pieter van Aelst. He was born August 14, 1502.
In 1527, having been a pupil of Bernard van Orley, he became a free master of the guild. He married and had two children, Pieter (1559) and Michiel.
Van den Branden, p.151.-Hymans, I, 184,1,2,3.-Friedlander, XII, 1935.

2 Van der Meeyen, Dermoeyen, also d'Armoyen.-See Wauters, 'les Tapisseries bruxelloises,' p.141, in *Essai historique sur les tapisseries et les tapissiers de houte et de basse lice*, Bruxelles, 1878.
There was a gobelin weaver in Brussels by the name of Pieter van Aelst. He was not Pieter Coeck.-Hymans, I, 184,5. He became a widower after 1529.-Hymans, I, 184,4.
Wauters believes the real purpose of this trip was to learn the secrets of the dyeing process used in the orient. There is no proof the Sultan did not receive the artist with the greatest courtesy. Braun in his, *Civitates orbis terrarum*, 1574, affirms that Sulieman was pleased with the works of Pieter Coeck, and had his portrait made by the artist. He gave numerous presents to Coeck.
Gentile Bellini painted the portrait of Mahomet II.-Hymans, I, 186,1.

3 These engravings appeared with the following titles: *Les moeurs et fachons de faire de Turcz avecqu les Regions y appaertenantes ont este au vif contrefaictez par Pierre Coeck d'Alost luy estant en Turquie l'an de Jesu Christ MD33, lequel aussy de sa main propre a pourtraict ces figures duysantes a l'impression d'ycelles*. They were reproduced in 1873, -W.Stirling Maxwell, *The Turcs in 1533*.-Max Rooses, in *Onze Kunst*, 1902. p.172. On the versos of the engravings described by Van Mander there is printed: 'Maria Verhulst veufve dudict Pierre d'Alost trespasse en l'an MDL etc.' They appeared as follows:
1.Voicy les montaignes du pays de Slavonie...2.Quant on parvient aux champaignes et platz pays...3.Vecy la maniere et de quelle sorte des Turcqz mangent...4.La qualite et assiete du pays de Macedonie...5.La maniere turquoise comment en en quelle mode de pompes ils font les funerailles...6.La Vraye assiette ou qualite de la ville de Constantinople avec tous leurs moschees ou temples...7.La ville de Constantinople, etc.
There were ten engravings divided into seven parts; the ensemble formed a frieze.-Hymans, I, 186,3.-Friedlander, XII, 1935. pl.xxix.
Van Mander did not use the information about Pieter Coecke van Aalst in the fourth volume of George Braun, *Civitates orbis terrarum*, which appeared between 1572 and 1575.

4 He represented himself on the first print, not on the seventh.-Hymans, I, 187,1.

5 Maria Verhulst, from Malines, was a miniature painter. She was the mother of his three children: Pauwels, Katelijne and Maria. The latter became the wife of his pupil, Pieter Breughel.-Van den Branden, p.153.

6 Pieter Coeck published, in February 1539, a résumé of the works of Vitruvius, titled: *Die inventie der Colommen met haren Coronementen ende maten wt Vitruvio ende andere diversche auctoren opt cortste ver-*

455

NOTES TO THE TEXT

gadert voer schilders, beeldsniders, steenhouders, etc., ter begheerten van goeden vrienden uitgegheven door Peeter Coecke van Aelst. This octavo edition is extremely scarce. The Flemish editions of Serlio appeared: III, in 1546; IV, in 1549; I, II, and V, in 1553, after his death. The Flemish editions alternated with French editions and various volumes appeared in 1545,1547 and 1550, published in Antwerp. The author in the French editions assumes the title: 'Libraire jure de Charles-Quint.'-Hymans, I, 187,3.
An English edition of Serlio was issued in London in 1611.
It follows the Antwerp editions.-Hymans, I, 187,4, and Hymans in, *Bulletin du Bibliophile belge*, 1874. Hymans believes Serlio died in 1552.
7 Last Supper, Brussels. Hymans suggested the 'Avontmael Christi,' after which Georgi Chisi made an engraving, was not by Lambert Lombardus but by Pieter Coecke.
No signed work by Pieter Koeck is known.-Hymans, I, 188,1.
Pieter Koeck died December 16, 1550 in Brussels, and was buried in the church of St Gery, which does not exist. The epitaph of the master has been copied and published. He was forty eight years old. He received the title of 'Painter to the Emperor and to Mary of Hungary.'-Hymans, I, 188,2.
8 Pauwels van Aelst was the natural son of Pieter Koeck and Antonia van der Sant.-Van den Branden.
9 Lampsonius, No.16.

JOACHIM PATENIER, p.76
1 Born in c.1490.-Hymans, I, 192,2. He died in 1524 in Antwerp.-Van den Branden, p.113.-Friedlander, IX, 1931.
2 Frans Mostart was born in 1534. He was not a pupil of Patenier.
3 Van Mander bases this information on Lampsonius, who states: 'exaravit in palimpsesto ahena cuspide tuos vultus.'
For further information see-N.de Roever, 'Amsterdamsche Potten en Plateelbakkerijen,' *Oud Holland*, 1883, I, p.50.-M.Thausing, 'Duerers Briefe,' *Tagebuecher*, p.117.-Lippmann, *Bemerkungen zu Zeichnungen von A.Duerer in Nachbildungen*, II, p.17.

HENRYCH MET DE BLES, p.78
1 Lampsonius, No.14: Text in prose. Van Mander.
2 Lampsonius does not refer to Herri met de Bles, but to Patenier.
3 The Italians called him 'Civetta,' the French, 'Le maître Chouette' or 'Henri à la Houppe.'
4 The picture of the Mercer is now in Dresden (Cat.1902); Van Mander saw it.-Greve, 186.
5 Pieter Breughel treated the same subject.-Floerke, I, note 229.
This story is older than Luther's.-Hymans, I, 198,2.
6 There are pictures by Herri met de Bles in Venice, Naples, Padua, and Genoa.-Hymans, I, 200,1.
Bles was born c.1480 and died c.1550, most likely at Liége.-Wurzbach.

LUCAS GASSEL, p.80
1 According to an engraved portrait, Lucas Gassels by Jacob Bink, in 1529 (Bartsch 93); Gassels must have been born c.1500.

456

NOTES TO THE TEXT

There are a number of works by this artist in the style of Herri met de Bles. The dates of these pictures range from 1538 to 1561. A picture in the Belvedere Collection, Vienna, is dated 1548. Hieronymus Cock published a series of engravings after the works of Lucas Gassel.-Hymans, I, 204.

2 Lampsonius, No.21: Van Mander's information based almost entirely on poem of Lampsonius.-Greve, 73.

LAMBERT LOMBARDUS, p.81

1 The book Van Mander tried to get was, *Lamberti Lombardi, apud Eburones pictoris celeberrimi vita, pictoribus, sculptoribus, architectis, aliisque id genus artificibus utilis et necessaria*; Brugis, Fland, ex officina Huberti Goltzii, 1565. It contained seven pages with a portrait of the master, engraved by Suavius, his brother-in-law. This work was dedicated to the famous geographer, Abraham Ortelius, not by Lampsonius, but by Hubert Goltzius.-Hymans, I, 207,1.

If Lampsonius had been alive at the time this biography was written, Van Mander could have written to him for the necessary information. This indicates the biography was written after 1599, the year Lampsonius died.-Greve, 31.

'Costui, dico, mi mando gia scritta latinamente la vita di detto Lamberto...'-Vasari, XIII, 156.

Most likely Van Mander knew about the little book through Vasari. The copy owned by Vasari is preserved at Florence.-Greve, 70.

2 See the biographies of these artists; Dominicus Lampsonius (born at Bruges 1532, died at Liége in 1599) was a pupil.

3 Van Mander borrows much for this paragraph from the preface of Hubrecht Goltzius, *Le vive imagine di tutti quasi gl'imperatori*, 1557.
-Greve, 104.

4 The engraving of the Last Supper is the one by Giorgio Ghisi (Bartsch 6). It shows an inscription by Hieronymus Cock, dated 1551, and a dedication to Cardinal Granvelle. The original picture is in the Francis Amory collection at Louvain.-Hymans, I, 208,1.

HANS HOLBEIN, p.83

1 Hans Holbein the Younger, born at Augsburg, c.1497. Pupil of his father. In the Upper Rhine region, 1514-15; at Basel, 1515 till October 1517; in Luzern, till September 1519, and probably in Italy; in Basel, 1519-26; in London, 1526-28; for the third time in Basel, 1528-1531; in London again from 1532-43, with a few interruptions; in Basel in 1538. Worked mainly for Henry VIII and for the wool merchants. Died, late in 1543, in London from Pest.

His father was born, probably at Augsburg, c.1460, and died there in 1524.-Paul Ganz, *Klassiker der Kunst*, XX, 1912.

2 Van Mander refers to Basilius Amerbach, son and heir of Bonifazius Amerbach, friend and heir of Erasmus. The collection of Bonifazius (the inventory was made by the son), was bought by the city of Basel in 1661 for 9000 Reichstaler. Holbein painted the portrait of Amerbach in 1519; it is at the present in Basel.-Hymans, I, 273,1.-A.Woltmann, *Holbein und seine Zeit*, Leipzig, 1866. p.263.

Van Mander probably did not agree to the fee.-Greve, 151.

457

NOTES TO THE TEXT

3 The pictures in the town hall were begun in 1521; they were done in fresco. They reflect great love for justice and a strong republican virtue; they were a warning against despotism.-Woltmann, *Holbein und seine Zeit*, Leipzig, 1866. p.298.
Façade of the Hauses zum Tanz in the Eisengasse near the Rheinbrücke; it has disappeared.-Woltmann, p.289.-*Klassiker der Kunst*, XX, pp.159, 162. Holbein did not paint any Dance of Death. This type of composition, which decorated the Dominikanekloster at Basel, dated from the fifteenth century.-Hymans, I, 214,1.
'Les simulachres et historiees faces de la Mort,' published first at Lyon in 1538. Wood-engravings by Hans Luetzelburger, 41 prints. Octavo. -Hymans, I, 214,2.

4 Greve was not able to trace this in a letter to Thomas More; he found it in a letter to Henricus Botteus, dated 1528: 'Pinxit me Durerus, sed nihil simile.' *Opera Omnia*, Basel, 1540. III, p.632.-Greve, 216.
Erasmus mentioned twice the portraits of him by Dürer. He wrote to Pirkheimer, on July 30, 1526, about an engraving made in 1526 (*Klassiker der Kunst*, Holbein, p.154): 'Alberto Durero, quam gratiam referre queam, cogito. Dignus est aeterna memoria. Si minus respondet effigies mirum non est. Non enim sum is, qui fui ante annos quinque.'
Erasmus refers to a portrait, in the letter to Henricus Botteus, dated March 29, 1528: 'Unde statuaris ille nactus sit effigiem mei demiror, nisi fortasse habet eam, quam Quintinus Antverpiae fudit aere. Pinxit me Durerus, sed nihil simile.'-Floerke, I, note 243.-*Klassiker der Kunst*, XX, p.207.

5 Holbein took a letter from Erasmus to More. It is not true that he entered the service of the King and that More made use of Holbein for himself alone. Holbein was appointed Peintre du Roi in 1536. After Holbein's return to Basel More was appointed High Chancellor.
Van Mander's remarks about the wife of Holbein are not confirmed. -Hymans, I, 218,1.-*Klassiker der Kunst*, XX, pp.69,227.

6 The mural painting in Whitehall was finished in 1537. Represented in it were: Henry VIII and Elizabeth of York; the background showed renaissance architecture. The painting was destroyed by fire in 1698. Remegius van Leemput made a reduced copy of it, under the reign of Charles II, which is now at Hampton Court.-Woltmann, II, p.165.
The cartoon for the left side of the painting, with the two royal figures, is in possession of the Duke of Devonshire, in Hardwick Hall. The portraits of the royal children were part of the large mural painting. -Hymans, I, 218,1.-*Klassiker der Kunst*, XX, pp.120,125,181,222,227.

7 The privilege of the guild of the barbers and surgeons was granted 1540-41. The picture by Holbein must have been made afterwards; it is partly by Holbein, partly by an inferior artist. It has been restored very much and is at Monkwell Street, 33-36, London.-Hymans, I, 218,2.-*Klassiker der Kunst*, XX, p.130.

8 The illuminator referred to, was Lucas Horebout, mentioned by Guicciardini as a great miniaturist. He was the son of Gerard and the brother of Susanna Horebout, both in the service of the king. Albert Dürer, in the Netherlands, admired their works very much. Lucas died in 1544 in London.-Hymans, I, 219,1.

9 Van Mander may have received information about Holbein's painting in

NOTES TO THE TEXT

London from Ketel, who was in this city from 1573 to 1581. These pictures have disappeared since the seventeenth century. The Hanseatic League, in 1616, offered them to Henry, Prince of Wales. Sandrart saw the pictures in 1627 in the Arundel collection, and Felibien has seen them in Paris.-Hymans, I, 219,2. The original sketch for the Triumph of Wealth is in the Louvre; engravings and copies are in existence.-H.Janitschek, *Geschichte der deutschen Malerei*, 1890. p.465.-*Klassiker der Kunst*, pp.175,176,177.

10 The portrait of princess Christine of Denmark, widow of the duke of Milan, now in possession of the Duke of Norfolk; Holbein painted this in Brussels for Henry VIII.-Hymans, I, 221,1.-*Klassiker der Kunst*, XX, p.121.

11 Nicolaus Kratzer from Munich. The picture of 1528 is now in the Louvre. The same Nicolaes of which Dürer writes in his diary: 'Ick hab conterfeitet Herren Nicolaum ein Astronomus, Der wohnt bei den Konig von England.' Antwerp, 1520.-*Klassiker der Kunst*, XX, p.73.

12 Lord Thomas Cromwell, later Earl of Essex, was beheaded in 1540. Woltmann stated it was in the Ridgway collection, in London, in 1877. -Hymans, I, 221,3.-*Klassiker der Kunst*, XX, p.106.

13 William Warham, Archbishop of Canterbury. There are two portraits, one in the Louvre, one in the palace of the archbishop at Southwark; each is dated 1527.-Woltmann, II, pp.139-144.-*Klassiker der Kunst*, XX, p.71.
This picture, was painted in 1528, has disappeared. A sketch for it is in the National Museum at Basel, some studies for it are in Windsor Castle.-Woltmann, II, p.164.

14 This is the picture of Jane Seymour in the Imperial Collection, Vienna. -Floerke, I, note 255.-*Klassiker der Kunst*, XX, p.119.

15 The originals cannot be traced.-Woltmann, II, p.167.-Hymans, I, 222-4. -*Klassiker der Kunst*, XX, pp.134,150,227.

16 Van Mander refers to the second edition: *Historiarum veteris testamenti icones ad vivum expressae*, Lugduni, sub scuto Coloniensi, 1539. (Melchior et Gaspar Trechsel fratree excudebant). It contains a latin poem by Nicolaus Bourbon and Holbein is hailed as master.-Woltmann, II, p.172.

17 Nicolas Bourbon de Vandoeuvre, born 1503; poet to Marguerite de Navarre; later a protégée of Anne Boleyn; returned to France in 1536 and became the mentor of Jeanne d'Albret.-Hymans, I, 223,2.
Holbein painted his portrait; the drawing is in Windsor Castle; later Holbein made the woodcut for the *Nugae*, a collection of verses by Bourbon, Lyon, 1538.

JAN CORNELISZ. VERMEIJEN, p.96

1 Court painter to Marguerite of Austria; received a pension of 100 pounds Flemish; his allowance is dated 11-May, 1529. He drew a view of the siege of Bougie, in 1551.-Hymans, I, 225,2.-Friedlander, XII, 1935. Vermeyen received £50 on 27-November, 1530 from the executors of the testament of Marguerite for painting portraits, probably those of Charles V, Ferdinand and his wife Anna, and Mary of Austria.-Engerth, *Oesterr. Jahrb*. IX, Vienna, 1889. p.419. The tapestries are in Madrid. There are twelve, woven by Willem van Pannemacker, from 1548-1554.

NOTES TO THE TEXT

The cartoons remained in Brussels and were discovered in the eighteenth Century; they were believed to have been made by Titian, according to Mariette. They are now in the Belvedere Collection in Vienna.-Hymans, I, 225,3.
The 'Capture of Tunis' cartoon is missing. There are six preparatory studies for these cartoons by Vermeyen; they are in the castle of the Duke of Koburg. These are oil paintings.1-The Siege of Goleta; 2-The Counter-attack of the Turks; 3-The Capture of Goleta; 4-The Battle of Tunis; 5-The Capture of Tunis; 6-The Going aboard of the Army. Three pictures by Vermeyen are in the Mansi Gallery at Lucca: 1-The Capture of Tunis, with inscription: THUNETUM EXPUGNATUM Ao 1535. 2-The Battle of Pavia, with inscription: CAPTIO REGIS FRA. Ao 1525. 3-The Capture of Rome, with inscription: ROMA CAPTA, Ao 1527.
See: Eduard Ritter von Engerth, 'Nachtrag zu der Abhandlung uber die im kaiserlichen Besitze befindlichen Cartone, darstellend Kaiser Karls V Kriegsz ug nach Tunis, von Jan Vermayen,' in *Oesterreichisches Jahrb.* IX, Vienna, 1890. p.419, and XI, p.113.-*Oud Holland*, 1896. p.95.-Emil Jacobsen, *Niederlandische Kunst in den Gallerien Mansi zu Lucca.* -Hofstede de Groot, in *Bull Oudheidk*, III.-Greve, 274.
The Council of Brabant allowed him in May of 1536 to make an engraving of the battle of Tunis and to publish the same. This permission was renewed in March of 1538.-Hymans, I, 226,1.
2 There is only one picture by Vermeyen in the Museum of Arras–an entombment of Christ. It came from a Franciscan convent in Arras. -Hymans, I, 226,2.
Portraits of the Thurn and Taxis family, painted by Vermeyen, were in the church of Notre Dame du Sablon at Brussels. In 1794 the French took them away; they have not been traced.-Hymans, I, 226,3.
Hans is mentioned by Quad, *Teutscher Nation Herrlichkeit*, Cologne, 1609, as an excellent goldsmith and sculptor.
3 This refers to land claimed from the sea. Schoorel had worked out a plan for claiming the Zype, and he had begun the work with permission of the emperor; work was stopped and resumed under Philip II.-Hymans, I, 228,3.
4 Lampsonius, No.15.
5 Van Mander was probably informed by the daughter of Vermeyen, who was alive in 1604, at Middelburg.-Greve, 75,160.

JOAN DE MABUSE, p.100
1 Mabuse was born c.1470 at Maubeuge in Hainault. He entered the guild of St Luke of Antwerp in 1503; died there in 1541.
2 Mabuse made this journey with Philip, Bastard of Burgundy, bishop of Utrecht, 1517-1524.
Vasari was the first to note the Italian influence on the work of Mabuse. -Vasari, XIII, p.151.-Hymans, I, 232,3.
3 The High Altar at Middelburg was in the convent of the Premonstratensians.-Hymans, I, 233,1.
The fire was on 24-January, 1568. The Polish ambassador valued the work at 80,000 guilders.-Hymans, I, 233,3.
Alex. Pinchart, *Bulletin des Comissions d'art et d'archeologie*, Bruxelles, 1865. IV, p.322.

NOTES TO THE TEXT

4 Lange Delft is a street at Middelburg.
5 The Lucretia is probably the little picture in the Galleria Colonna in Rome. There was a Lucretia by Mabuse at an auction sale at The Hague in 1662; it was sold for 60 guilders.-Hymans, I, 233,4.-A.Bredius, 'Een kunstverzamelaar der XVII Eeuw, Johan Chrisothomus de Backer,' in Obreen's Archief, V, p.296.
6 It is in the gallery of Hampton Court. This picture seems to have been in the possession of Henry VIII. There is a duplicate of it in the Berlin Museum (Berlin, Cat.1898. p.408).-Hymans, I, 234,1.
7 In 1619 Duke Charles de Croy had an Adoration of the Magi by Mabuse, 'crayonnée de blanc et de noir.'-Pinchart, Archives, I, p.164.
8 Adolph of Burgundy, Heer van Beveren, whom he accompanied to Middelburg in 1528.-Hymans, I, 234,3. Floerke does not agree with Hymans, that this refers to the picture in Munich; he believes the picture in Palermo is the one in question.-Floerke, I, note 277.-Hymans, I, 234,4.
9 At Hampton Court; it is of the children of King Christian II of Denmark. -Hymans, I, 234,5.
10 The statement about Mabuse's captivity has not been confirmed. -Hymans, I, 236,1.

AUGUSTIJN JORISZ., p.104

1 Hymans titled the picture, 'Les trois Graces' d'apres le Rosso.-Hymans, I, 241,3.
2 This brother probably supplied the information about Augustijn.-Greve, 151.
None of the mentioned pictures has been found.
3 Hymans remarks: 'This shows us that he applied a tempera technique, which was in vogue at Malines.'-Hymans, I, 242,2.

JOOS VAN CLEEF, p.106

1 Van Mander in his Conclusion says Joos van Cleef, Foolish Cleef, belonged to the family of Marten and Hendrick van Cleef. This statement may be true, but it has not been proved.-Hymans, I, 243,2.
2 This is evidently Joos van Cleef, alias Van der Beke, called van Cleve, see Van den Branden, p.128. He was dean of the guild of St Luke in 1519, 1520 and 1525; in 1523, 1535; in 1536 he took four pupils. Firmenich Richartz, Zeitschrift für Bildende Kunst, 1894, and Carl Justi Jahrbuch der Preuss. Kunsts. 1895. p.23, identify him as the master of the Death of Mary. According to Justi a picture by him, of a Madonna surrounded by four angels, is in the collection of Weid Blundell at Ince Hall near Liverpool.-Floerke, 285.
3 The wedding of Philip II and Mary Tudor was on July 25, 1554, London. Hymans remarks: 'A cette epoque, van Cleef n'existait plus depuis longtemps.'-Hymans, I, 244,1.
Floerke states: 'Bald darauf muss der 'Sotte Cleef' gestorben sein.' -Floerke, I, note 287.-Fr.Winkler fixes his death in 1540.-Winkler, Alt Niederlandische Malerei, Berlin, 1924. p.245.
4 This picture, with the landscape painted by Patenier, who died 1525, cannot be by the hand of Sotte Cleef, but must have been painted by Joos van Cleef the elder.-Floerke, I, note 288.

461

NOTES TO THE TEXT

5 Lampsonius, No.12: 'Quam propria, nati tam feoix arte fuisses.-Greve, 71.

6 Cornelis was born in Antwerp, 1520. He was the son of Joos van Cleef the elder. The self-portrait of Joos van Cleef the younger and the portrait of his wife are at Windsor Castle. The engraving in the series of Lampsonius corresponds to this picture.-Van den Branden, p.128. -Floerke, I, note 289.

ALDEGRAEF, p.109

1 Heinrich Aldegrever, whose real name was Heinrich Trippenmaker, was born at Paderborn in 1502. He lived at Soest, where he died in 1560. -Janitschek, *Geschichte der Deutsche Malerei*, 1890. p.529. There is at Soest only one religious picture in the Peterskirche which represents a Passion.-Hymans, I, 249,3.
Janitschek mentions only a two winged altar painting in the Wiesenkirche.-Janitschek, *Geschichte der Deutsche Malerei*, p.529.

2 -A.Woltmann, *Alg. Kunstler Lex*, I, p.242. Karl Voll, 'Albrecht Dürer's Paumgartner Altar,' *Monatsberichte uber Kunst und Kunstwissenschaft*, *Jahrg.* III, pp.39-42. In Nürnberg, there was only one painting by Dürer, the Paumgartner Altar, now in the Pinakothek at Munich.-Hymans, I, 249,4. The painting found not long ago, on the back of the painting, was an Annunciation by Dürer.-Floerke, I, note 292.

3 Bartsch describes the engravings by Aldegrever in his *Peintre Graveur*, VIII.
Passavant, Nagler, and Woltmann, mention a few unpublished prints. The total of his engravings was more than three hundred. Some portraits engraved by Aldegrever appeared in the 1764 edition of the *Schilderboeck*, Pt. IV.-Greve, 27. Aldegrever born in 1502.-Hymans, I, 249,6.

4 Susanna.-Bartsch, 30-33, of 1555.-Vasari, IX, p.296.
Little nude Figures:-Bartsch, 143.-Floerke, I, note 297.
Hercules:-Bartsch, 83-95, of 1550.
Dancing Figures:-Bartsch 152-159 of 1551, and 144-151, 160-171, of 1538.

SWART JAN OR JAN SWART, p.111

1 Metaphor based on the meaning of the Dutch words, vriesland, (English: freezing country), and groningen (English: green).

2 Born in c.1469, died at Autun, c.1535. His education based principally on the works of Lucas van Leyden.-Floerke, I, note 301.

3 Confirmed by Lomazzo, *Trattato dell'arte pittura*, Milano, 1584, Lomazzo named him Giovanni de Frisia da Groningie.-Hymans, I, 253,3.

4 A painting in the Alte Pinakothek at Munich, of John the Baptist preaching, has been attributed to him.-Bartsch, VII, p.402.-Hymans, I, 254,1. Christ preaching from a ship:-Passavant, *Peintre Graveur*, III, p.14, No.1. Not mentioned by Bartsch.

ADRIAEN PIETERSZ. CRABETH, p.112

1 Adriaen Pietersz. Crabeth was the elder brother of the glass painters Dirck and Wouter Crabeth, who have painted the windows in the Johanneskerk at Gouda. He died at Autun May 17, 1553.-Hymans, I, 254,2.

NOTES TO THE TEXT

CORNELIS, p.113

1 Information probably obtained from Ketel.-Greve, 152.

HANS BAMESBIER, p.114

1 Hymans says there is nothing German in this name Bamesbier, which means in Flemish, Beer of the Fall, Beer of St Bavo, October 1st. This master is unknown in Germany and in Holland. He was born c.1500 and died c.1598, according to Wurzbach.-Hymans, I, 255,1.

SIMON JACOBSZ., p.115

1 He painted the windows of the Groote Kerck at Gouda, 1570 to 1597, and other windows in Haarlem; he died and was buried in the St Bavo July 25, 1599.-Hymans, I, 255,2.-Chr. Kramm, *De Goudsche Glazen*, Gouda, 1853.
Van der Willigen, *Les Artistes de Haarlem*, p.203.

CORNELIS DE VISSCHER, p.116

1 His portrait is in Hondius. There is a portrait of William of Orange in the Rijksmuseum at Amsterdam, painted by Michel Jansz Miereveldt, (Cat.1898). It has the inscription: 'FACIEM HUIUS AD PRINCIPALE CORNELII DE VISSCHER FECIT M A MIEREVELD. Cornelis de Visscher undoubtedly was the father of the famous engraver. A portrait of a man in the Belvedere at Vienna was done by Cornelis in 1572.-Hymans, I, 255,4.

FRANS MINNEBROER, p.117

1 Frans Minnebroer means Frans the Minorite monk. A note found by E.Neefs suggests this painter belonged to the order and his name was Crabbe. Frequently this artist was called N.Frans. E.Neefs, *Histoire de la peinture et de la sculpture a Malines*, 1876. I, p.214.
2 No work of Minnebroer is known.-Floerke, I, note 313.

FRANS VERBEECK, p.118

1 Frans Verbeke, son of Carel, was admitted to the guild at Malines, August 25, 1531. He became dean in 1563. He died July 24, 1570. No work by him is known.-Hymans, I, 256,3.

VINCENT GELDERSMAN, p.119

1 Born c.1539. No work by him is known.-Hymans, I, 257,1.

HANS HOGENBERGH, p.120

1 According to E.Neefs, Hans Hogenberg, born c.1500 at Malines, descended from a family of Louvain; he died c.1544. All his works are lost. -Hymans, I, 257,2. The name of the master who made the scroll is Nicholas Hogenberg. See *The Procession of Pope Clement VII and the Emperor Charles V after the coronation at Bologna on the 24th of February 1530*, designed and engraved by Nic.Hogenberg, reproduced in facsimile, with an introduction by Sir W.Stirling Maxwell, Edinburgh, 1875. Nicholas Hogenberg is probably the brother of Hans Hogenberg. He died September 23, 1539.-Hymans, I, 257,3.

NOTES TO THE TEXT

FRANS CRABBE, p.121

1 Frans Crabbe, alias van Espleghen, was admitted to the guild of Malines in 1501; dean 1533 and 1549. He died February 20, 1553. (Neefs. op. cit.). No work by him is known. Passavant believes Frans Crabbe can be identified as the Master with the Crab.-Bartsch, VII, p.257.-Passavant, III, p.15.-Hymans, I, 257,4. This is the only place where Van Mander mentions Quinten the Blacksmith.-Greve, 210.

CLAES ROGIER, p.122

1 Claes Rogier died at Malines in 1534.-Hymans, I, 258,1.

HANS KAYNOOT, p.123

1 Jan Keynooghe, son of Jacob, was admitted to the guild at Malines, August 10, 1527. He was living in 1570. No work by him is known.-Hymans, I, 258,1.

CORNELIS ENGHELRAMS, p.124

1 Cornelis Enghelrams, born at Malines in 1527, admitted to the guild September 17, 1546, died June 8, 1580. His son, Andries, was a painter. None of his work is known. Neefs mentions a painting which appeared at an auction at Malines in 1830. Anthonis Wierinx made a series of engravings of the church fathers from paintings by Enghelrams.-Hymans, I, 258,3-4.

MARCUS WILLEMS, p.125

1 Marcus Willems was born c.1527 at Malines. None of his work is known. -Hymans, I, 260,1.

JAQUES DE POINDRE, p.126

1 Born at Malines, 1527. In 1559 he had a pupil, Willem de Vos, whose portrait was etched by Van Dyck. The portrait of a bishop, dated 1563, is the only known work by De Poindre.-Hymans, I, 260,1.

GREGORIUS BEERINGS, p.127

1 Gregorius Beerings in de Schaer, means Beerings was born in a house called de schaer—the scissors. Beerings was born in 1526 at Malines, entered the guild of St Luke on September 17, 1555, died in 1573. His sons Pauwels and Gregorius were painters. No work by him is known. -Hymans, I, 261,1-2.-E.Neefs, op.cit. p.198.

JAN MOSTART, p.128

1 Jacob van Haarlem, is an unknown master.-Floerke, I, note 326.

2 Schrivelius names him, Joh. Sinaius Mostardt (Harlemum, 1647. p.275), and states: 'Hic Joh. Sinapius a Sinapi acrimonia nomen accepit.' It may be assumed that Van Mander Latinized the name Mostart.-Floerke, I, note 327.

3 Philip the Fair, King of Castile.-Hymans, I, 262,3.

4 Hymans says the inventories of the pictures owned by Marguerite of Austria do not mention works by Mostart. Van Mander's statement that Mostart worked eighteen years for Marguerite can be doubted; the list of expenses of this princess, from 1521 to 1530, once mentions the painter in January 1521: 'A ung pictre qui a presente a Madame une paincture de

464

NOTES TO THE TEXT

feu Nostre Seigneur de Savoye faict au vif, nomme Jehan Masturd (sic):
XX philippus.' This spelling proves the painter was not known at the
court; Barent van Orley was court painter at that time.-Hymans, I, 263,1.
For portraits painted by Mostart see Friedlander, X, 1932.-R.Stiassny,
Rep. für Kunstwissenschaft. XI, p.359.
5 Ecce Homo:-Friedlander, X, 1932. pl.ix-x.
6 West-Indian Landscape:-Friedlander, X, 1932. pl.xii.
7 Hymans says these portraits were not made from life, because Jacoba
died in 1436, and her husband in 1470, before the probable birth of Mostart, c.1470. The pictures in question are in the Museum at Antwerp.
-Hymans, I, 264,2.-Scheibler, in *Rep. für Kunstwissenschaft*, XI, p.379,
12.
8 Abraham, Sarah, Hagar and Ishmael:-Friedlander, X, 1932. pl.vi.
The Descent of St Anne: was probably sold at the auction of the collection of J.C.de Backer, The Hague, 1662, for thirty-five guilders.-Hymans,
I, 264,3.
9 The accounts of Delft mention Jan Claesz as living there in 1615.
-Hymans, I, 265,1. The Princenhof at Haarlem was a Dominican convent.
-Hymans, I, 265,3.
10 October 23, 1576.-Hymans, I, 265,3.
11 Van Mander may have received this information from Jacob Rauwert.
-Greve, 155.
12 The owner of this document was probably Nicolaes Suycker of Haarlem, who evidently gave Van Mander information about Mostart.
-Greve, 159.

ADRIAEN DE WEERDT, p.132

1 Christiaen van den Queeckborne (van Queboorn), the second one having this name, was born at Antwerp in 1515. He was free master of the
guild in 1545, dean in 1551 and 1557, town painter of Antwerp 1560, and
died there in 1578. Daniel van den Queeckborne was the father of the engraver Crispyn, born at The Hague in 1604. He entered the guild of Antwerp in 1577 and married Barbara van den Broeck soon afterwards. She
distinguished herself as an engraver. Daniel went to Holland, after the
surrender of Antwerp to Parma in 1584, and he became painter to Prince
Maurice.-Hymans, I, 268,1.
Adriaen de Weerdt is not mentioned in the records of the guild of
St Luke of Antwerp.-Hymans, I, 268,1. The engraving of the story of
Ruth has been dated 1573.-Hymans, I, 269,2.
2 Four Cravings of the Mind engraved by Goltzius (probably). G.Rath-
geber, 'Beredeneerde geschiedenis der Nederlandsche Schilder,' *Houts-
nij en Graveerkunst*, Amsterdam, 1844. German edition, 1843. p.271.
3 Probably 1590. No work by him is known. The Italians named him
Adiano dal Hoste.-Hymans, I, 269,3.

WILLEM TONS, p.134

1 Van Mander probably knew Hubert and Willem Tons in Rome.-Greve,
11.
He lived at the end of the sixteenth Century.-A.Wauters, *Les Tapisseries
bruxelloises*. p.128. A portrait in water-color by Willem Tons appeared

NOTES TO THE TEXT

in the catalogue of the paintings of the Rubens collection sold in 1640.
-Hymans, I, 270,1.

HANS TONS, p.135

1 According to Felibien (*Entretien sur les vies des plus excellens peintres*, Paris, 1685. I, p.553), Hans Tons was a pupil of Barent van Orley and a great landscape painter who worked at the 'Belles Chasses' of Maximilian.
-Hymans, I, 270,2.

GUILLIAME TONS, p.136

1 Guilliame Tons entered the guild of St Luke at Antwerp as a pupil of Henri Ghysmans. No painting by the Tons is known. Rubens owned a little painting by Willem Tons, in water-color.-Hymans, I, 270,3.
Van Mander says, in the Errata of the edition of 1604, 'Among the painters of the younger generation, Hubert Tons was an inventive artist and a descendent of Willem Tons. He must not be forgotten. He was good at painting landscapes containing small figures. He is now living at Rotterdam.'
Hymans says, 'It is unfortunate Van Mander does not specify which Willem Tons he had in mind. Van Mander's remark has been omitted in the second edition. Hubert entered the guild of St Luke at Antwerp in 1596.'-Hymans, II, 350,2.
There are two pictures by him mentioned in the inventory of H.Saftleven, 1627 at Rotterdam, 'A dog' and 'Three small dogs.' *Obreen's Archief*, V. p.119.

HANS SPEECKAERT, p.137

1 According to the biography by Van Mander, Speeckaert was in Rome, 1575-1577.
The title of the last chapter of the *Lives of the Italian Painters* is, 'About various Italian painters who were at Rome in my time, between 1573 and 1577.'-Floerke, I, note 344. According to Nagler, Jan Speeckaert was a pupil of Hans van Aken and was living at Rome in 1582. A signed painting by him is in the Belvedere Collection at Vienna. A number of his works have been engraved by G.Sadeler, Chrispijn van de Passe, Cornelis Cort, P.Perret.-Hymans, I, 271.

HENDRICK AND MARTEN VAN CLEEF, p.138

1 Hendrick van Cleve was born c.1525, Marten in 1527. They entered the guild of Antwerp in 1551 as pupils of Frans Floris.-Hymans, I, 272,1.
2 Van Mander refers to *Ruinarum varii prospectus, ruriumq aliquot delineationes*, by Philipp Galle, dedicated to Van der Haept. A series of thirty-seven prints.-Hymans, I, 272,2.
Melchior Lorch, born in 1527 at Flensburg, died at Rome in 1586.
-Hymans, I, 272,3.
3 Hendrick van Cleve painted backgrounds in paintings by Marten van Cleve.-Greve, 202.
4 Van Mander, in his Conclusion, says Hendrick van Cleve died in 1589.
5 In the year 1581.-Van den Branden, p.297.

WILLEM VAN CLEEF, p.140

1 Willem van Cleef died in 1564.-Van den Branden, p.294.

466

NOTES TO THE TEXT

GILLES, MARTEN, JOORIS, CLAES VAN CLEEF, p.141
1 Claes died at Antwerp, August 20, 1619.
Gillis was in Paris in 1588, and he was alive in 1604.

ANTONIS MORO, p.142
1 Moro was called Moro van Dashorst, after a property called Dashorst. He was born at Utrecht in 1512 and entered the guild of Antwerp in 1547 as free master.-Van den Branden, 276.
2 The portraits of John III and Catherine are in the baptismal chapel at Belem.
Raczynski, *Les Arts en Portugal*, p.291.
Pinchart says the bride of Philip, later king of Spain, was Maria the sister of the king; the daughter of John III died in 1545. The portrait of Maria of Portugal is in the Prado, Madrid.-Hymans, I, 276,3.
3 Moro's trip to England was in 1553. He returned to Utrecht in 1555. -Hymans, I, 276,3.
The portrait of Queen Mary is in the Prado, Madrid. There are many portraits of Mary Tudor in English castles; there is an oval picture of her in the Belvedere Collection in Vienna.-Hymans, I, 277,2.
See Th.Frimmel, *Kleine Gallerie Studien*, 1894-97. II, p.34.
4 The king started his journey to Spain August 20, 1559. There are a number of portraits of Philip II attributed to Moro.-Hymans, I, 278,1.
5 A fine portrait of Alba by Moro is in the Museum at Brussels.-Hymans, I, 278,2.
6 It is known that Moro was in Rome in April, 1550.-Hymans, I, 280,1.
7 Moro's copy of a work by Titian is probably the copy mentioned by Castan in *Monographie du Palais Granvelle à Besancon*.-J.A.Crowe and G.B.Cavalcaselle, *Titian, His Life and Times*, II, p.229.
8 Van Mander says in his Conclusion, 'Antonio Moro died at Antwerp, at the age of 56, one year before the French Fury.' Max Rooses remarks that Van Mander probably wanted to write Spanish Fury (Nov.4, 1576). Chevalier de Burbure found, in the Archives of the Church of Notre Dame at Antwerp, a note referring to the death of Moro, which indicates he was dead in 1578.
See Rombouts en van Lerius, *Les Liggeren et autres archives de la gilde de St Luc*, I, p.159.
The French Fury was in January and February 1583.-Van den Branden, p.243.
In Hubrecht *Goltzius's Sicilia et Magna Graecia*, there is an engraving by Hubrecht Goltzius after a painting by Moro. This was supposed to be in the house of the widow of Moro.-Brussels Cat.1900.-Greve, 107.

JAQUES DE BACKER, p.146
1 Jaques de Backer is not listed in the *Liggeren* of the Guild of St Luke at Antwerp.-Hymans, I, 286,1.
2 Antonio Palermo came from a Malines family and was a burgher of Antwerp in 1547. He helped in the decoration of the town at the entry of the Infante Philip in 1549. He was dean of the guild in 1555, 1561, 1570 and 1571. He died at Antwerp c.1588.-Hymans, I, 286,2.
3 Hendrick van Steenwijck was a free master in 1577.-Hymans, I, 286,3.
Catherine of Palermo was the widow of Pieter Goekindt, a pupil of her

467

brother.-Hymans, I, 287,1. Nagler and Siret fix the date of de Backer's death in 1560. Pinchart believes de Backer was born c.1560, because he painted a Last Judgement for the sepulchre of Christopher Plantin, who died in 1589.-Hymans, I, 287,2.

MATHIJS AND JEROON KOCK, p.148

1 Mathys and Jeroon Kock were sons of Jan Wellens, alias Cock, a painter. Mathys was born c.1509, Jeroon soon afterwards.-Van den Branden, 289. -Hymans, I, 289,2.
2 A picture of the Tower of Babel in the Belvedere Collection at Vienna has been attributed to him.-Hymans, I, 289,3.
3 Jeroon gave a strong impulse to the art of engraving in Flanders. The number of his own engravings is very small. The landscapes after the works of Mathys Cock are etchings, dated 1551 and 1558.-Hymans, I, 289,4-5. Van Mander does not mention the engravings specifically. -Vasari, IX, pp.256-299.-Greve, 50.
4 Volquaera Dircx continued the business after the death of her husband. She published the series of artist portraits collected by Lampsonius. -Hymans, I, 290,1.
5 This motto appears on plate No.1 of the 1563 reprint of Johan Fredeman de Vries' *Scenogrpahia sive Perspectivae*.-Greve, 118.
6 Jeroon de Kock died October 3, 1570.-Hymans, I, 290,2.
Frans Floris died October 1, 1570.
Mathys de Kock died before 1548; his wife is mentioned in the register of the guild of St Luke at Antwerp as a widow on this date.-Hymans, I, 290,3.

WILLEM KEY, p.150

1 Willem Key lived in Antwerp at Korte Clarastraet, No.1.-Van den Branden, 268.
2 Vasari says, about Key, 'E stato condiscepolo di costui (Frans Floris) sotto la disciplina d'un medesimo maestro (Lamb. Lombardus) ha imparato, Guglielmo Cay di Breda.'-Vasari, XIII, p.152.
Key was born c.1520, and entered the studio of Lambert Lombardus in 1540. In 1542 he became free master of the guild of St Luke at Antwerp, in 1553 he became a dean.-Van den Branden, 267.
3 Isaiah lv.1.
4 Perhaps the portrait in the Besancon museum.-Hymans, I, 296,2.
5 The Museum at Brussels has a portrait of the Duke of Alva attributed to Moro. Hymans believes this anonymus picture is by Key. The portrait of the painter in Hondius's *Theatrum honoris*, shows a portrait of Alva in the background. It is a copy from one of the portraits in the Lampsonius series with the portrait of Alva added to it.-Hymans, I, 296,3.
6 In the biography of Johan Fredeman de Vries, this artist worked for Key; this makes it possible to assume that Van Mander was informed about Key by de Vries.-Greve, 161.
7 Lampsonius, No.20.

PIETER BREUGHEL, p.153

1 Pieter Breughel was born c.1525.

NOTES TO THE TEXT

Two engravings and various drawings have the word Rome; Breughel was in Italy in 1553.-Hymans, I, 299,3.

2 Van Mander may have known Breughel at Antwerp.-Greve, 9. Hans Franckert is mentioned in 1546 in the registers of St Luke at Antwerp as coming from Nürnberg. There are two paintings by Breughel, in tempera, in the Museo Nacional, Naples. The Blind leading the Blind, done in 1568, and the picture of the Monk robbed by a man enveloped by a globe. This last picture has the title,

'Omdat de werelt is soe ongetru
Daer om gha ic in den ru.'
(The world is so unfaithful
Therefor I wear mourning)

Reproduced in, Rene van Bastelaer and G.H.de Loo, *Pieter Bruegel l'Ancien, son oeuvre et son temps*, Brussels, 1905. The Kampine refers to the Campine Anversoise.-Hymans, I, 300,2.

3 Breughel married Maria Coecke in 1563.-Van den Branden, 265.

4 The Tower of Babel is in the Vienna Museum, dated 1563. A smaller picture of the same subject is in the Prado.-Hymans, I, 302,3.
The Carrying of the Cross, in the Vienna Museum, dated 1563, was copied by Pieter Breughel the Younger.-Hymans, I, 302,4.
The Massacre of the Innocents is in the Vienna Museum, and the same subject can be found in the museum of Wurzburg, Hampton Court, Brussels, Antwerp. The picture in Vienna is dated 1563. Van Mander was in Vienna with Sprangher and may have seen the imperial collection. -Greve, 13.

5 The Conversion of St Paul is dated 1567.-Hymans, I, 302,7.

6 The Temptation of Christ was engraved by Hieronymus Cock. The painting was owned by Rubens.-Hymans, I, 303,1.

7 The Dulle Griet, dated 1564, and may have been in the collection of the emperor; it came from Sweden. The Swedes sacked the Gallery of Rudolph II at Prague in 1648 and took more than 700 pictures to Stockholm.-Hymans, *Gazette des Beaux Arts*, XVIII, 1897.

8 There is a Peasant Wedding in Vienna. A similar painting was mentioned in the inventory of the Amsterdam art dealer Diego Duarte and was listed for the enormous sum of 225 guilders.-Hymans, I, 303,3.

9 The Lent and Carnival of the Vienna Collection is dated 1559. The Remedies against Death was in the possession of Count Brandis at Vienna in 1870. A copy of this painting is in the Lichtenstein Gallery, dated 1597.-Hymans, I, 303,5. The Childrens Play painting is in the Vienna Collection, dated 1560.

10 Pieter Breughel often repeated the Peasant Wedding picture.

11 The opening of the canal was in 1565; Breughel died in 1569. Hymans remarks that it may be possible Breughel made preparatory paintings for this work. A painting by Breughel (no Christian name mentioned) was at an auction at Amsterdam, May 6, 1716; its description was: 'A Heu with many people on board, sailing on the Schelde River to Brussels.'-G.Hoet, *Catalogus*, I, p.197.
Hymans questions this was really a work by old Pieter Breughel. -Hymans, I, 303,8.

12 The best engravings after Breughel were made by P.A.Mirycenis (Van der Heyden). Most all of these were published by Hieronymus Cock,

NOTES TO THE TEXT

publisher of the engravings from the works of Hieronymus Bosch. See M.J.Schretlen, *Dutch and Flemish Woodcuts of the XV Century*, London, 1925. The Magpie on a Gallows, dated 1568, is now in the Museum, Darmstadt. See Bredius, *Nederlandsche Kunstbode*, 1880. p.285.

13 Van Mander may have received information about Breughel and his sons from Gillis van Coninxloo, who was living in Amsterdam in 1604. -Greve, 144. Pieter Breughel the Younger, named Helschen Breughel, was born the end of 1564 at Brussels. He was a free master of the guild of Antwerp, and died at the beginning of 1536.-Van den Branden, 440. Jan Breughel, Fluweelen Breughel (Velvet Breughel), born 1568 at Brussels, was at Rome in 1593. On May 30, 1596, he was at Milan, in 1601, he became burgher of Antwerp and dean of the guild of St Luke. He died January 13, 1625.-Van den Branden, 444.
Pieter Goekindt married Catherine of Palermo, see biography of Jaques de Backer. Lampsonius, No.19.

JOAN SCHOOREL, p.158

1 Vasari remarks about Joan van Schoorel: 'Giovanni Schoorl...il quale porto in Fiandra molti nuovi modi di pitture cavati d'Italia...'-Vasari, XIII, p.151.
2 Willem Cornelisz must be Cornelis Willemsz of Haarlem.-A.van der Willigen, *Les Artistes de Haarlem*, 1870. pp.40-56.
3 Jacob Cornelisz refers to Jacob Cornelisz van Oostsanen.
4 Philip of Burgundy, bastard of Philip the Good and Bishop of Utrecht, 1517-1524. See biography of Mabuse.
5 It is possible Schoorel was in Carinthia for a long period. The altar painting in the church of Obervellach in Carinthia has the crests of the families Lang von Wellenburg from Augsburg and Frangipani, and the date 1520. The altar painting of the genealogy of the Virgin, painted on pine wood, was not done in Venice, but in the Alpine region. Since Apollonia Lang had properties in the region of Obervellach, through her first marriage with Julian, Count of Lodron, it may be assumed that the painting was originally intended for this place.-Floerke, I, note 411.
6 Daniel van Bomberghe from Antwerp was a printer of books in Hebrew. He died at Venice in 1549.-Hymans, I, 310,3. The date of the pilgrimage must have been c.1519.-Hymans, I, 310,4.
7 The painting St Thomas placing his fingers in the side of Christ was painted for the monastery of Zion. This monastery was removed to the interior of Jerusalem in 1559; most likely the painting has been preserved there.-Hymans, I, 311,2.
8 The painting of the Holy Sepulchre has been lost.-Floerke, I, note 415. -Friedlander, XII, 1935. pl.LXVII. The painting of the Knights of Jerusalem is in Haarlem. The painting came from the Chapter House of the Knights of St John. It was evidently a mistake by Van Mander—the Jacobin Monastery.-Hymans, I, 311,4.-Friedlander, XII, 1935. pl.LXX.
9 Van Mander, speaking of the Grand Master of the German Order, means the Order of the Knights of St John.-Hymans, I, 312,1.
10 Adriaen VI, Adriaen Florisz. Boeyens from Utrecht, Teacher of Charles V, and elected Pope January 9, 1522.-Hymans, I, 312,2. The

470

NOTES TO THE TEXT

portrait of the pope is still at the College. Many copies exist. A letter from Schoorel to Adriaen de Marselaer in Antwerp, dated May 26, 1524, shows the picture of Adriaen VI was made two months before the death of the Pope.-Hymans, I, 312,3. See C.Hofstede de Groot, 'De wetenschappelijke resultaten van de tentoonstelling van oude kunst te Utrecht gehouden in 1894,' in *Oud Holland*, XIII, 1895. pp.34-56.

11 The Archives of the Chapterhouse of the Knight Hospitalers at Haarlem show Schoorel painted for the order the Baptism of Christ (dated 1520, now in the Museum), Adam and Eve, a Crucifixion, Maria Magdalen (Rijksmuseum). During the troubles in 1573, a number of paintings were transported to Utrecht, to Frederick Uttenham, knight of the Order; these were, Christ carrying the Cross, assisted by two angels; Christ between the Thieves, (this is probably in the Museum at Haarlem) and a small picture of St Cecilia. (Stedelijk Museum Haarlem).-Hymans, I, 313,3.
Baptism of St John.-Friedlander, XII, 1935. pl.LXV.
Hymans says the various figures in the Baptism of St John, dated 1520, are faithful copies of Raphael's work. If the dating is correct, these copies must have been made from drawings or from engravings, for Schoorel's stay at Rome was between 1522 and 1524.-Floerke, I, note 423.

12 There is a Crucifixion in the Museum at Bonn, signed and dated 1530, another in the Aartsbischoppelijk Museum at Haarlem, a third in the Museum at Antwerp; these three paintings are small.-Hymans, I, 313,5.

13 Schoorel became Canon of the Cathedral at Utrecht, October 16, 1528. -Taurel, *l'Art chretien en Hollande*, II, p.69.

14 Abraham's Offer has not been located.

15 The Abbey of Marchiennes was in a little town of the same name, west of Douai. The pictures do not exist.

16 The Crucifixion at Arras has been lost.-Hymans, I, 314,3.

17 Groot Ouwer, see *Groningsch Jaarboekje*, 1893. p.24.

18 The museum at Stockholm has a picture of a woman looking through a book, attributed to Van Schoorel.-Hymans, I, 315,1.

19 Schoorel's birth and death may have been derived from the portrait Moro made of Schoorel, since the inscription on this portrait was independent of the portrait. It is in the Museum of Braunschweig and is one of the most important works by Moro.-Hymans, I, 316,2.

20 Lampsonius, No.17.

AERTGEN, p.168

1 The information about Aertgen may have been given by Aechtgen Cornelis, daughter of Cornelis Cornelisz Kunst.-Greve, 134.

2 Probably the Nativity by Aertgen was owned by Rubens, later on listed in the catalogue of his collection as Nativity by Artus van Leyden (No. 1890). Two other pictures by the same master are mentioned, No.194, a bawdy house, and No.219, Une epitaphe a dix clotures.-Hymans, I, 325,1.

3 The engraving Suyderhoef made after the self-portrait of Aertgen shows the scar on the right cheek of the painter.

JOACHIM BUECKLAER, p.173

1 The Aunt married Pieter Aertsen in 1542.-Van den Branden, 165.

NOTES TO THE TEXT

Beuckelaer was accepted as free master of the guild in 1560. He was married, probably, in November of the same year.-Van den Branden, 318.

2 For various pictures of the Ecce Homo exist: See E.Jacobsen; 'Neue Erwerbungen des Rijksmuseums,' *Repertorium*, XXIV, 1901. p.168. There is a picture by Joachim Beuckelaer in the Museum at Dresden, signed and dated 1567. It is of the four Evangelists.

3 A fruit-market picture by Beuckelaer is in the Belvedere Collection at Vienna, dated 1567; a similar subject, a little different, is in the castle at Prague, dated 1561. There is a picture of a female cook in the Museum at Prague.-Hymans, I, 331,1. See O.Granberg, *La Galerie de Tableaux de la Reine Christine de Suede*, Stockholm, 1897. pp.20-53.

4 Joachim Beuckelaer died at the end of 1573. He accepted a pupil the same year, Jaques Comperis. According to the portrait engraved by Hondius, Beuckelaer was more than forty years old; according to Van den Branden he was near sixty.-Van den Branden, 321.-Hymans, I, 331,3.

FRANS FLORIS, p.176

1 The Vasari statements are in, Vasari, XIII, p.151.

2 Jan de Vriendt was free master of the guild of St Luke in 1533. He became dean in 1538.-Hymans, I, 334,1.
Cornelis de Vriendt died September 17, 1538.-Van den Branden, 175.

3 According to Rooses, Frans Floris was born c.1516. He was twenty when he became a pupil of Lambert Lombardus. Lambert went to Italy in 1538; Floris entered the guild in 1540 as free master; we may assume that Floris was a pupil before 1538.-Rooses, *Geschiedenis der Antwerpsche Schilderschool*, Ghent, 1879.
Cornelis, the brother of Frans the sculptor, was born in 1514.-Van den Branden, 174,3.
Jaques the glass painter was born in 1524.-Van den Branden, 174,5.
He died in 1581; his daughter married Frans Pourbus the elder.-Hymans, I, 335,2.
Pieter Vlerick, the second teacher of Van Mander, was a pupil of Jaques Floris; through him anecdotes about Frans Floris may have come to Van Mander.-Greve, 160.

4 Jan de Vriendt is the first pottery maker whose name appears in the records of the Antwerp guild of St Luke, entered in 1550. July, 1581, he became a superintendent of the Pardo.-Hymans, I, 335,3.

5 Van Mander must have known Cornelis Floris and the latter gave the information about his father and his uncle.-Greve, 146.

6 Floerke believes Van Mander refers to the 'niello' process, by which a design, incised on a metal plate, is filled in with a black alloy.
Reproductions of this kind of work are in: E.de Busscher, *Recherches sur les Peintres et Sculpteurs a Gand, XVI siècle*, 1865.
Hymans believes it refers to the beautiful ornamental sculpture in high relief in brass found in churches and cemeteries in Germany.-Hymans, I, 335,4.-Floerke, I, note 454.

7 The Last Judgement was finished in 1541, under Paul III.

8 Dierick Volckaertsz Coornhert, poet, theologian, and engraver. He was the last teacher of Goltzius, who engraved a splendid portrait of him (Bartsch, 164). He was born at Amsterdam in 1522 and died at Gouda,

472

NOTES TO THE TEXT

1590. There is a portrait of him by Cornelis van Haarlem in the Rijks-museum, Amsterdam.-Hymans, I, 338,2.

9 The hospital is the St Elisabeths Gasthuis. The name of the street is at present, rue aux fleurs.

10 The Fall of Lucifer is in the Museum at Antwerp, dated 1554.

11 The wings of the Fall of Lucifer do not exist.-Hymans, I, 342,2.

12 Hymans did not find any reference to this painting. The picture by Floris was replaced by an Assumption of Mary by Rubens, in the XVII Century.-Hymans, I, 342,2.

13 The Last Judgement is in the Museum at Brussels, formerly in the Notre Dame du Sablon, dated 1566. Another Last Judgement, signed and dated 1565, similar to the one in Brussels, is in the castle at Prague. -Hymans, I, 342,4.

14 This Nativity is in the Museum at Antwerp.-Hymans, I, 343,1.

15 The painting of St Macharis has disappeared.

16 The Entrance of Charles V and his son Philip into Antwerp was in 1549.

17 The print published by Hieronymus Cock is dated 1552; the second entrance of Philip II was in 1556.-Hymans, I, 344,2.

18 Van Mander says the Crucifixion in the Museum at Seville, was attrib-uted to François Frutet by Spanish writers. Eduard Fetis identified this master as Frans Floris.-Hymans, I, 344,3.

19 The Nine Sleeping Muses is in the Museum at Turin; the painting is mentioned in the inventory of Duke Charles de Croy in 1612, as 'Les Sept Arts liberaux dormans par la vertu de Mars.'-Hymans, I, 345,3.

20 There is another Adam and Eve picture in the Belvedere, Vienna. -Hymans, I, 344,4.

21 The Works of Hercules was offered for sale at The Hague in 1697; they were sold in 1751 with the collection of de Hogendorf.-Hymans, I, 345,5.
The Markgraveleye was outside Brussels. The word suburbano can be found on an engraving of Cornelis Cort, after the series of the liberal arts.-Hymans, I, 346,1.

22 Anecdotes about Frans Floris may have been told by Lucas de Heere, a pupil of Frans Floris.-Walpole, *Anecdotes*, 1862. II, p.153.-L.Cust, 'A notice of the life and works of Lucas de Heere,' Westminster, 1894, article in, *National Biography*.

23 Baptist Floris made a portrait of Frans Francken the elder.-Van den Branden, p.349.
The son, Frans, was born 1545; he is not mentioned in the records of the guild at Antwerp.-Hymans, I, 346,5.

24 According to de Jongh (third edition of the *Schilderboeck*), Frans Menton died January 24, 1615 at Alkmaar.

25 Floris was free from the obligation of seeing all his pupils registered in the guild; for this reason a small number is known.-Hymans, I, 347,1.

BENJAMIN SAMMELING, p.190

1 Sammeling was born in 1520. He was Sub-Dean of the guild at Ghent in 1583 and in 1598. The painting of the Docksael (jube) was in 1559. This referred to decorative work for the festival of the Order of the Golden Fleece, in this church.-E.de Busscher, *Recherches XVI Siècle*.
No authentic work of Sammeling is known.-Hymans, I, 347,2.

473

NOTES TO THE TEXT

CRISPIAEN VAN DEN BROECKE, p.191

1 Crépin van den Broecke was born at Malines, was free master at Antwerp in 1555, burgher in 1559 and died at Antwerp in 1591. Works by this master are in the museums at Brussels, Antwerp, Arras, Madrid. -Hymans, I, 347,3.
This artist finished two paintings by Frans Floris, after Floris died, a Crucifixion and a Resurrection.-Greve, 221.

JOORIS VAN GHENT, p.192

1 Jooris van Ghent is unknown.-Hymans, I, 348,1.

MARTEN VAN CLEEF }p.193
FRANÇOIS MENTON }

1 See the biography of Anthonis Blocklandt.
Nothing is known about Thomas van Zierickzee.
Simon van Amsterdam is mentioned, in a manuscript in possession of Kram, as a remarkable painter, 'obiit mensis julii 1620.' Isaac Claessen Cloeck was perhaps the father of the engraver Nicolaes Clock.-Hymans, I, 348,7.
According to de Jongh, (third edition of the *Schilderboeck*), Frans Menton died January 24, 1615 at Alkmaar.

GEORGE BOBA }p.194
FRANS FRANCKEN }

1 Boba was one of the artists of the School of Fontainebleau. He made a series of six etchings, landscapes after the paintings of Primaticcio, (Bartsch, XVI, p.363).-Hymans, I, 349,1. Frans Pourbus has a separate biography. Jeroon Francken was born in 1540 and died at Paris in 1610. A triptych by this artist, in the Museum at Brussels, is dated 1571 and represents an Adoration of the Magi. It has the monogram of Frans Floris connected with that of Hieronymus Francken, who probably finished the work after the death of the master.-Hymans, I, 345,1 and 349,3.
Frans Francken was born in 1542, was free master in Antwerp in 1569, dean in 1587, and died in 1616.-Hymans, I, 349,4.

AMBROSIUS FRANCKEN, p.195

1 Ambrosius Francken born in 1544 at Herenthals. According to Van Mander (in biography of Ketel) he painted in 1566 at Fontainebleau. Cited by De Laborde among the artists who in 1570 worked at the decoration of the castle. He entered the guild of St Luke at Antwerp in 1573, became dean in 1581, died in Antwerp in 1618.-Hymans, I, 349,5. -Van den Branden, 339-356.-See biography of Vlerick.

JOOS DE BEER, p.196

1 Joos de Beer registered in the guild of Utrecht in 1550, became dean in 1582, 1583 and 1585. His most important pupils were Joachim Utewael and Abraham Bloemaert. See the biographies of these artists. No picture by Joos de Beer is known. He died c.1596, (Wurzbach).-Hymans, I, 350,1.

NOTES TO THE TEXT

HANS DE MAIER, p.197

1 Hans de Maier entered the Antwerp guild as a pupil of Frans Floris in 1559. He worked at Fontainebleau. He was there November 8, 1569. He was a free master of the guild at Antwerp in 1575, and took pupils until 1610. No work by him is known.-Hymans, I, 350,2.

Van Mander calls Apert Francken, Franssen, and says he, and Frans Francken, and de Maier, worked in Fontainebleau in 1566. The real name of the artist was Van der Houven; he was a brewer.-Hymans, I, 350,3.

LOYS; HERMAN, p.198

1 Nothing is known about De Stomme of Nijmegen.-Hymans, I, 350,4.

Hans Daelmans was registered in the Antwerp guild in 1561 as son of a master, with Melsen Salebos.-Hymans, I, 350,5.

Evert of Amersfoort is unknown.-Hymans, I, 350,6.

Herman van der Mast is probably the artist registered in the guild of The Hague in 1580. A Dirk van der Mast registered in the guild of Delft, as son of a master, in 1627; he was probably the son of Herman.-Hymans, I, 350,7.

A picture of a young man and his wife, by Herman van der Mast, is in the Rijksmuseum; the portrait of the man is signed Mast, that of the woman, 1547.

E.Jacobsen, 'Neuerwerbungen des Rijksmuseums,' *Repertorium für Kunstwissenschaft*, XXIV, pp.180. 1901.

2 Gheldorp was Geldorp Gortzius. See his biography.

DAMIAEN, p.200

1 Nothing is known about Damiaen. Stirling, Passavant, Meisel, Viardot did not find any trace of this artist in Spain.-Hymans, I, 352,1.

JEROON VAN VISSENAKEN } p.201
DIRCK VAN DE LAEN

1 Jeroon van Vissenaken entered the Antwerp guild, as son of a master, in 1579; he accepted pupils in 1616 and 1617.-Hymans, I, 352,2.

Nothing is known about Dirck van der Laan. He may have been the father of Christopher van der Lamen, an excellent painter. Van Dyck made a portrait of the latter.-Hymans, I, 352,4.

Steven Croonenborgh is not known by his works. There are four portraits in the Prado attributed to Anna van Croonenburg.-Hymans, I, 352,3.

2 Marten de Vos was a pupil of Frans Floris, see His biography.-Hymans, I, 352,5.

3 Lucas de Heere, *Hof en Boomgaerd der Poesien*, Ghent, 1565. p.45, poem to M.Franchois Florus, excellent Schilder.-Greve, 81.

PIETER AERTSEN, p.203

1 Pieter Aertsen was born at Amsterdam c.1508; buried at Amsterdam June 3, 1575; lived at Antwerp between 1535 and 1566. *Catalogue Amsterdam Rijksmuseum*, 1898.

Alart Claessen not to be confused with Alaert Claeszoon van Leyden who was never in Amsterdam.-Hymans, I, 352,3. *Oud Holland*, VII, 3.

NOTES TO THE TEXT

The architect of the famous castle of Bossu was Jacques du Broeucq. The cornerstone was laid, March, 1539; Charles V occupied the castle in 1544, Philip II in 1549. The castle was destroyed in 1555 during the war with France; there is no record of the paintings there.-Hymans, I, 354,1.

2 There was only one Jan Mandijn.
Pieter Aertsen became a free master in 1535. He married Katelijne van den Beuckelaere, the aunt of Joachim Beuckelaere.-Van den Branden, 165.

3 The similarity of the picture, with his second son in it, to a painting by Joachim Beuckelaer in Naples makes it doubtful whether Beuckelaer was the originator. *Jahrb. d.K. Pr. Kunsts*, XI, p.35.

4 Vasari writes, 'Pietro Aertsen, detto Pietro Lungo fece una tavola, con le sue ale, nella sua patria Amsterdam, dentrovi la Nostra Donna ed altri Santi; la quale tutta opera costo duemila scudi.'-Vasari, XIII, p.153.

5 See J.Six, *Nederlandsche Spectator*, 1886.
There is a fragment of the altar painting of the Nieuwe Kerck in the Rijksmuseum at Amsterdam, probably part of the Nativity. It has been indicated in the catalogue as a fragment of a painting destroyed by fire in the city hall, July 7, 1652; it was in the Weeskamer (room of the orphans) of the city hall.-Floerke, I, note 511.

6 One wing of one of the altar paintings at Delft is in the Rijksmuseum, Amsterdam. Its subject is the Representation in the Temple; on the back King Balthasar is shown.-Hymans, I, 356,1.

7 None of the pictures mentioned in this paragraph has been found. A picture of a fair by Pieter Aertsen was sold at auction in Amsterdam in 1757. -Hoet, III, p.183.

8 Dame Sonneveldt probably told of this event to Van Mander.-Greve, 157.

9 The expenses for the funeral and chimes were paid by his son Pieter and by Jacob Rauwert; the latter was a good friend of Van Mander. -Greve, 156.

10 The Fiery Furnace by Pieter Pietersz is in the Museum at Haarlem, dated 1575. Pieter Pietersz was born at Antwerp c.1540.-Hymans, I, 358,1.

11 Aert Pietersz was born at Antwerp c.1550.
Various group portraits by him are in Amsterdam.-*Oud Holland*, VII, 24.-Hymans, I, 358,3.

12 Pieter Pietersz II, alias Jonge Lange Pier, was born in 1578, probably at Haarlem.-*Oud Holland*, VII, 14.

MARTEN HEMSKERCK, p.208
1 The portrait of his father is in the Metropolitan Museum, New York, dated 1532. He died in 1535.-Van der Willigen, *Les Artistes de Haarlem*, p.157.-Taurel, *l'Art chretien*, II, p.98.-Hymans, I, 362,1.

2 Master Cornelis Willemsz was cited as having done work for the St Bavo at Haarlem in 1481 and 1482. He painted, in 1523, with his pupils, a series of heraldic shields for the Wassenaer family. He sold his house in 1540.-Hymans, I, 362,2.

3 The St Luke painting is in the Museum at Haarlem. (Catalogue 1897).

476

NOTES TO THE TEXT

A second picture of St Luke, painted by Heemskerck after his Italian trip, is in the Museum at Rennes.-Hymans, I, 363,1.

4 Two of Marten van Heemskerck's sketch-books, in the Kupferstich Kabinet at Berlin, show a number of studies of antique Roman architecture, sculpture and various christian churches; these sketches were done between 1536 and 1538; they have historical value.-*Jahrb.Preuss. Kunsts*, V, p.327; XII, p.117; articles by Jaro Springer.-Floerke, I, note 522a.

5 Compare this to the biography of Jan van Calcar.

6 Heemskerck received the contract for the paintings in the Princenhof from the St Bavo Kerck at Haarlem; he was paid 150 guilders. The centerpiece of the altar was a piece of sculpture which was replaced in 1604 by a painting by Cornelis van Haarlem, representing the Massacre of the Innocents. The work is now in the Mauritshuis at The Hague. -Hymans, I, 366,2.-Floerke, I, note 525.

7 Van Mander, speaking of the Oude Kerck in Amsterdam, meant the Old Sint Nicolaas Kerck.-Hymans, I, 367,1.

8 This series of paintings, begun in 1538, was bought in 1542 for 750 guilders and a life rent of twenty guilders a year. There is a Crucifixion by Marten van Heemskerck in the Hermitage at Leningrad.-Hymans, I, 367,3.

9 The Biting of the Serpents, at the Museum at Haarlem, is dated 1551.

10 Hadrianus Junius says about Heemskerck: '...tum...nullum tam occupatum habeat diem, quo non aliquid agens, lineam ducendo artem exerceat...tum etiam operum multidune, quae infinita prope sunt in omni genere.'
Hadrianus Junius, *Batavia*, Lugd. Bat, 1588.

11 As to The Four Endings, see Waagen, II, p.358. The painting, in Hampton Court, is signed.-Hymans, I, 368,1.

12 The Bacchanalia is in the Belvedere, Vienna. Jan Dirk de Bry made an engraving after it. The composition was originally from Giulio Romano. The engraving by De Bry does not show the name Heemskerck.-Hymans, I, 368,2.

13 De Jongh, (third edition of Van Mander) states burgomaster S.van Huls of The Hague collected 648 engravings.

14 The series of The Life of the Emperor was published by Hieronymus Cock. The first edition, 1556, and the second, 1558, were dedicated to Philip II. Three editions were engraved by Philip Galle, Ch.de Mallery and Jan Boel; the print by Cornelis Bos is No.2 of the series.-Hymans, I, 369,3.
The Massacre of the Innocents, in the Rijksmuseum, by Cornelis Cornelisz is dated 1590.
The painting mentioned by Van Mander is the one in the Mauritshuis.

15 Heemskerck was warden of the St Bavo church at Haarlem.
Philip Galle, the engraver, dedicated to Ravaert (Rauwaert) the series, *Acta Apostolorum*, 1575, done after works by Heemskerck in memory of the kind hospitality he had received from his pupil.-Hymans, I, 370,4.

16 There is no work under the name of Heemskerck, in Spanish Museums. -Hymans, I, 370,5.

17 The last of these ceremonies was on November 12, 1781.-Van der Willigen, p.169.

477

NOTES TO THE TEXT

Jacob Dircks van der Heck, Heemskerck's principal heir, was the son of his sister.-Hymans, I, 370,6.
18 For articles on this monument see *Navorscher*, VII, pp.170,310, VIII, p.19.-Van der Willigen, p.126. *Noord Hollandsche Oudheden*, II, p.91. Reproductions in *Eigen Haard*, 1901.-Hymans, I, 365,-Greve, p.172.
19 Van Mander did not use all the information given by Vasari in the descriptions of engravings by Hieronymus Cock after paintings by Heemskerck.-Vasari, IX, pp.256-299.-Greve, 50.

RYCKAERT AERTZOON, p.218
1 Jan Mostart was at Haarlem.
2 No work by Rijckaert is known. A picture of a Madonna by him appeared in an inventory made in Rotterdam in 1627. *Obreen's Archief*, 1882-83.
3 In 1555 Lambert Aertszen, son of Rijckaert, was accepted in the guild of Antwerp as son of a master. He married Katharina, the daughter of Rogier van der Weyden, the great-granddaughter of the Rogier. -Hymans, I, 374,2.
4 The painting by Frans Floris is in the Museum at Antwerp. Floris represented himself grinding paint.-Winkler, *Altniederlandische Malerei*, Berlin, 1924. p.314.

HUBERT GOLTZ, p.220
1 For a detailed biography of Goltzius see W.J.H.Weale's *Beffroi*, III. Hubert Goltzius was born at Wurzburg, October 30, 1526. *Beffroi*, III, 248.
2 Marc Lauwerin, or Laurin, Lord of Watervliet. It was through the mediation of Abraham Ortelius a mutual friend, Goltzius settled in Bruges. They associated themselves for the publication of the books on medals. *Beffroi*, III, 253.
The fact is mentioned in the works by Goltzius and in Guicciardini's *Descrittione di tutti Paesi Bassi*, 'Il medisimo Laurino ha non solamente fauorito, ma preso totalmente in braccio et in protettione Huberto Goltzio Herbipolta Venliniano eccellente Scultore...etc.'-Greve, 121.
3 Hubrecht Goltzius, *Le vive imagine di tutti quasi gl'imperatori*, 1577. Information about Hubrecht Goltzius was obtained by Van Mander from the works of Hubrecht.-Greve, 104.
Gietleughen. This name, literally translated, means Stream of Lies. Hymans says according to Weale this artist was named Josse van Gulleghem, after a place near Courtrai.-Hymans, I, 376,4.
4 The book of the portraits of the emperors was issued in German, Latin, French and Italian. *Beffroi*, III, 250.
Goltzius lived more in Antwerp and stayed there after 1546.-*Beffroi*, III, 248.
5 Hubrecht Goltzius, *Caius Julis Caesar sive Historiae Imperatorum Caesarumque Romanorum*, 1563.
At the back of this book is a list of persons, among which appears Rutgerus Goltzius, Herbipolitanus, Pictor venloniensis Auctoris Pater. Van Mander evidently did not notice this, as in the genealogical list of the Goltzius family, he does not give the name of the father of Hubrecht Goltzius.-Greve.
6 The Roman Senate took this decision May 9, 1567.-*Beffroi*, III, 260.

NOTES TO THE TEXT

7 The title of the second work on Caesar Augustus is, *Caesar Augustus sive historiae imeratorium caesarumque Romanorum ex antiquis numismatibus restitutae...Liber secundus: accessit Caesaris Augusti vitae et res gestae*, Brugis Flandrorum, 1574.

8 *Graecia sive historiae urbium et populorum Graeciae ex antiquis numis matibus restituae*, libri quator..., Brugis Flandrorum, 1576.
For its contents see *Beffroi*, III, 263, note 38.
The other books Van Mander refers to may be *Siciliae historiae posterior*, of 1576. The works by Goltzius were hard to get even in Van Mander's time and this is evidently why Van Mander does not mention titles. The second part of *Siciliae historiae posterior sive corum, quae post pacem sub Augusto terra marique partam usque ad hoc saeculum gesta sunt...-Beffroi*, III, 263.

9 The convention of the Hanseatic League was in 1555, at the time of Philip II, in the cathedral.

10 The first wife was Elisabeth Verhulst, alias Bessemers, from Malines. -Hymans, I, 378,6. The names of these children were Marcellus, Scipio, Julius, Aurelius, Maria, Sabina, Katharina. They helped him with his work.-*Beffroi*, III, 262.

11 The portrait of brother Cornelis is in the Town hall at Bruges. A Latin inscription gives the name of the person and the words: AD VIVUM DELIN. MDLXXIII. He was named Cornelis Adriaensen, born at Dordrecht 1521, died at Bruges 1581 and was one of the most fiery defenders of Spanish ideas in-Hymans, I, 380,2.

12 The name of the second wife was Marie Vynck. She was the widow of Martin de Smet van Westwinkel; she re-married after the death of Hubert, March 24, 1583.-*Beffroi*, III, 268.

13 The portrait of Goltzius in the Museum at Bruges is dated 1576.

PIETER VLERICK, p.224

1 No trace of Willem Snellaert can be found. His son Nicolaes (Claes) Snellaert was born at Courtrai.
He lived at Dordrecht where he is entered in the records of the guild of St Luke in 1586. He died January 15, 1602. *Obreen's Archief*, I, p.184. -*Oud Holland*, XII, 107 and XXII, 59.

2 Pieter Vlerick went to Carel van Ypres c.1550.

3 Hans in den Booghe's death is mentioned in the *Liggeren*, 1585-1586.

4 Floerke believes the word 'rondt' used by Van Mander does not refer to sculpture but to the vaults of the Sistine Chapel.-Floerke, I, note 579.

5 Girolamo Muziano, born 1528 at Aquafredda near Brescia, died at Rome 1590; Pope Pius, 1559 till 1565.

6 Hymans believes the Serpent Scene is the picture attributed to Van Oost, hanging in the St Martin's Church at Courtrai.-Hymans, I, 389,1.

7 A picture somewhat similar to this description is in the Martin's Church at Courtrai; it is not certain Vlerick painted it.-Hymans, I, 389,2.

8 The Martyrdom of the Maccabees, Susanna and the Elders, has disappeared. These pictures were painted with tempera and were subject to deterioration.-Hymans, I, 390,1.
There is a print of Joseph and Potiphar's wife after Titian, signed M.G.F. (Mathieu Greuter?).-Hymans, I, 390,2.

9 Talents, in the sense of money.

479

10 The statutes for painters at Tournai were severe and prescribed in detail the colors to be used by painters and with a prohibition against their use by others.

11 Pieter Vlerick was registered as sub-dean of the guild of goldsmiths, painters and glaziers at Tournai, June 15, 1575.
There is a triptych in the St Nicolas church at Veurne (Furnes) with a Crucifixion similar to the painting described by Van Mander.-Hymans, I, 394,2.-*Bulletin des Commissions royales d'art et d'archeologie*, XXII, p.251.

12 Michiel Gioncquoy, in 1573, was in Rome.
He was accepted in the guild of Tournai, October 19, 1581.
He was listed as burgher of Antwerp, July 6, 1584.
In 1586 he was in Antwerp.
Ph.Rombouts et Theodore Van Lerius, *Les Liggeren et autres archives de la gilde anversoise de Saint-Luc*, I, pp.283,294,305.

13 The picture in the church of Cremona is probably the one by Pordenone, still in the cathedral.-Hymans, I, 396,2.

14 The name Lowijs Heme is not listed. He is perhaps the artist who painted the picture of St Martin in the St Marten Church at Courtrai. -Hymans, I, 396,3.

15 Claes Snellaert was admitted to the guild of St Luke at Dordrecht in May, 1586. *Obreen's Archief*, I, p.184.

16 The window in the St Jans Kerck (St Bavo) has disappeared. Hymans believes a triptych in the St Walpurgis Church at Veurne (Furnes), a Nativity, to be done by Carel van Ypres. It is signed with a monogram. -Hymans, I, 397,3.

17 The real name of Carel van Ypres was Carel Foort. He died June 22, 1562.-Hymans, *Bulletin de l'Academie*, 1897.

18 The biographies of Vlerick, Carel van Ypres, and Jaques Floris, are evidently based on information by Van Mander at Courtrai and at Tournai, 1568-1569.

ANTHONIS VAN MONTFOORT, p.242

1 Hadrianus Junius stated: '(Ant.Bl.Montfoort) extulit partu.' Hadrianus Junius, Batavia, 1588.-Greve, 68.

2 Blocklandt's name does not appear in the records of the guild at Antwerp; Floris undoubtedly was freed from the obligation of having his pupils registered.-Hymans, I, 401,2.

3 Junius stated: 'Qui in repraesentandis venuste vultibus minime durus, in reddendis historijs nulli facile secundus audit, idque loqui mihi videntur nonnulla quae spectavi opera prope spirantia solaque anima defecta.' Hadrianus Junius, Batavia, 1588.

4 The Beheading of St James is in the Museum at Gouda.-Hymans, I, 403,1.

5 The taking of Den Briel was the great victory for the Watergeuzen (Gueux) under de La Marck.-Hymans, I, 405,1.

6 Blocklandt is listed as free master in the records of the guild of the Saddle Makers at Utrecht in 1577; the saddle makers and the painters were united in one guild.-S.Muller Fz. *De Utrechtsche Archieven*, Utrecht, 1880. p.14.-Hymans, I, 405,1.

7 Van Mander probably received information from this lady.-Greve, 139.

NOTES TO THE TEXT

8 The Burial of Christ is in the Bisschoppelijk Museum at Haarlem. The engraving is dated 1583,-(Bartsch–265). Goltzius made engravings after other pictures of Blocklandt.-Hymans, I, 406,1.

9 Adriaen Cluyt, glazier, entered the guild at Dordrecht, January 25, 1647. *Obreen's Archief*, I, 219.
Van Mander seemed to know Cluyt rather well; we may assume that he asked him about Antoni Blocklandt.-Greve, 142.

10 Ketel was a pupil of Blocklandt.-Hymans, I, 406,4.

LUCAS DE HEERE, p.248

1 Lucas de Heere, or Mijnheere, of Mijnsheeren.-*Oud Holland*, XXI, 1903. Lucas signed his painting The Queen of Sheba before Solomon, in the St Bavo at Ghent, LUCAS DERUS INVENIT ET FECIT, ANNO 1559.-E.de Busscher, *Recherches XVI siècle*, p.28.

2 Jan d'Heere was a sculptor and architect. He made a new choir in the St Bavo at Ghent for the festival of the order of the Golden Fleece in 1559. In 1529, he executed the mausoleum for Isabella of Austria, Queen of Denmark, in the St Peter's Abbey at Ghent. He died in 1578. -E.de Busscher, *Recherches XVI siècle*, p.28.-Hymans, II, 2,1.

3 One of the miniatures of the reduced copies of the Brevarium Grimani, in the Bibliotheque Royale at Brussels, shows a mill on a hill, corresponding with the description given by Van Mander.-Hymans, II, 1,4.

4 Van Mander refers to Catherine de Medici; Lucas must have been very young when he went to France; in 1554, at the age of twenty, he was in England, by his dated portrait of Mary Tudor. His other English portraits are dated 1555, 1557 and 1558. In 1559, he was in Ghent.-M.Rudelsheim, *Oud Holland*, 1903. XXI, p.86.
Lucas married c.1560.-M.Rudelsheim, *Oud Holland*, 1903. XXI, p.87.

5 Adolph of Burgundy, Seigneur de Wackene, Gotthem and Cappelle, later vice-admiral of the North-Sea fleet, died July 7, 1568.-E.de Busscher, *Recherches XVI siècle*, p.35.

6 The altar painting for St Pieter's church was lost, during the religious troubles in 1566.-Hymans, II, 3,2.

7 Lucas had the title, Greffier de la chambre des comptes et pensionnaire du prince d'Orange et de Sainte-Aldegonde.-De Busscher, *Recherches XVI siècle*, p.41.

8 The admiral in London was Edward Lord Clinton, Earl of Lincoln; he died in 1584.-*Oud Holland*, XXI, 86.-De Busscher, op.cit., 38.-Hymans, II, 3,4.

9 A collection of water-colors in the archives at Ghent have the same subject as mentioned by Van Mander. The title is, *Theate de tous les peuples et nations de la terre avec leurs habits et ornements divers tant anciens que modernes, diligemment depeinte, au naturel, par Luc Dheere, peintre et sculpteur Gantois.*
The collection was dedicated to Adolph of Burgundy and completed in c.1576.
According to Walpole, the inspiration to depict the Englishman nude with cloth and scissors next to him is based on an epigram by Andrew Borde (Andreas Perforatus) who lived under the reign of Henry VIII: 'I am an Englishman and naked I stand, Musing in my mind what rayment I shall wear.'-E.de Busscher, op.cit., p.185.-Hymans, II, 4,1.

481

NOTES TO THE TEXT

10 The Ode to the Agnus Dei at Ghent was in this collection.-Greve, 48.
-M.Blommaert, *Annales de la Societe royale des beaux-arts et de litter-ature de Gand*, 1852.

11 Nothing has been found of the manuscript by de Heere.-V.van de Haeghen, *Memoire sur des Documents faux, relatifs aux anciens peintres, sculpteurs et graveurs flamands*, Bruxelles, 1899. pp.75-100. -Greve, 126.

12 See for the discovery at Velseke,-Vaernewijck, *Historie van Belgis*, 1574. p.117b.

13 Schade leer U—Profit by Experience.

14 Van Mander lost his master in 1568, returned to his parents and became a pupil of Pieter Vlerick. The reason for this change was Lucas de Heere had been banished for his adherence to the Reformation. -Hymans, II, 6,1.
There is a portrait by Lucas de Heere painted of Henry VIII in 1564 or 1567, according to Lionel Cust. On one side Mary and Philip and the god of war were represented, on the other side, Queen Elisabeth, and behind her the goddesses of peace and welfare. The motive is clear; if we knew the exact date of the picture we would know when Lucas changed from Catholicism to Protestantism.-*Oud Holland*, 1903. XXI, p.87.
A portrait of Lady Jane Grey by Lucas de Heere was sold in London February, 1905 for 13.330 Marks.-Floerke, II, note 28.

JAQUES GRIMMAER, p.253

1 Grimmaert, or Grimmer, was born c.1526.-Van den Branden, p.297. The first master of Grimmaert was Gabriel Bouwens, in 1539. He became a free master in 1547. Adriaen Collaert engraved a series of twelve landscapes after Grimmaert's work. The first of these prints is marked, Jacopo Grimmer, By Antwerpen.-Hymans, II, 11,4. Grimmaert died shortly before May, 1590. There is a large landscape by him in the City Hall of Antwerp.-Van den Branden, p.298.

CORNELIS MOLENAER, p.254

1 Cornelis Molenaer entered the guild of St Luke at Antwerp in 1564. -Hymans, II, 15,1.

2 Van Mander may have received information from Nicolaes van der Heck, a pupil of Jan Nagel.-Greve, 150.

3 Two large paintings by Molenaer are mentioned in an inventory, dated The Hague, 1623. *Obreen's Archief*, II, p.146, article by P.A.Leupe.

PIETER BALTEN, p.256

1 Pieter Balten was known by the name of Pieter Balthasar, Custos, Custodis, and de Coster.-Hymans, II, 17,1.
Balten entered the guild in 1540; he was dean in 1569.-Hymans, II, 17,2.

2 The painting with the elephant has disappeared.

3 De Busscher believes Balten died in 1598.
Lucas Kilian engraved his portrait in 1609.-De Busscher, *Biographie nationale de Belgique*, I, p.680.
There is a signed picture in the Rijksmuseum at Amsterdam, which represents a St Martins Markt.-Floerke, II, note 43.

NOTES TO THE TEXT

JOOS VAN LIERE, p.257

1 Joos van Liere was dean of the guild of St Luke at Antwerp in 1546. -Hymans, II, 19,1.
None of the works by Joos van Liere has been traced.-Hymans, II, 19,2.

PIETER AND FRANS POURBUS, p.258

1 Pourbus, Poer-bus, Poederbusse. The literal meaning of the word is gunpowder container. The family name Poer-bus appears frequently in documents of the time.-Van den Branden, 278,1. Pieter Pourbus was born at Gouda c.1510. He died at Bruges January 30, 1584. He was master of the guild at Bruges in 1543.
The name of the daughter of Blondeel was Anna.-Van den Branden, 278.

2 The paintings in Delft have disappeared.

3 The view of the Vryeen was taken from the belfry; it was finished in 1566 and was paid for with 3,352 livres, 14 escalins parisis. In 1597 it was replaced by a copy by Pieter Claeissens which is in the city hall in Bruges.-Hymans, II, 22,1.-Weale, *Bruges et ses Environs*, 1875. p.26.

4 The portrait of the Duke d'Alençon has not been recovered. There is no reference to Pieter Pourbus being in Antwerp, though many authors assume that he was. The portrait must have been made in 1582, if it was done in Antwerp.-Hymans, II, 22,2.

5 Frans Pourbus was born in 1545 at Bruges. He became master of the Antwerp guild in 1569 and died in that city September 19, 1581.-Van den Branden, 278.

6 Frans Pourbus married Susanna Floris, daughter of Cornelis de Vriendt. -Hymans, II, 22,6.

7 The painting Paradise has disappeared.-Hymans, II, 23,1.
The altar panel mentioned by Van Mander is the triptych of Christ and the Doctors, which is in the first chapel south of the choir in the St Bavo. Among the doctors are various portraits: Alva, Charles V, Philip II, and one of the artist himself. On the interior of the wings: Baptism of Christ and Presentation in the Temple; the exterior of the wings: The Saviour and the donor, Viglius; its date is 1571. There is also a picture of the Deeds of St Martin, in twelve scenes, dated 1572.
The paintings in Oudenarde have disappeared.-Hymans, II, 23,2,3,4.

8 The Beheading of St George is, since 1852, in the Museum of Dunkirk; it was in the St Eloi Church. It was signed FRANCISCUS POURBUS IV, ET PICTOR, 1577. The painter put his own portrait in this picture.-Hymans, II, 23,5.

9 Frans Pourbus died September 19, 1581.-Van den Branden, 282.

10 Frans Pourbus's second wife was Anne Mahieu; he married her in 1578. Hans Jodaen died at Delft c.1604.-Van den Branden, 283.-Hymans, II, 24,3.

11 The son of Frans Pourbus was born at Antwerp in 1569, and he died in Paris in 1622.

MARCUS GEERARTS, p.261

1 Marcus Geerarts was born c.1530. In 1558 he was second Vinder of the guild of St Luke at Bruges, according to a contract dated July 16, 1561. He accepted the task of finishing the large triptych of the Passion, order-

483

NOTES TO THE TEXT

ed from Van Orley by Marguerite of Austria, at his death it was unfinished.-Hymans, II, 29.

2 The Aesop had the title *De Waerachtige Fabulen der Dieren*, Bruges, Pieter de Clerck, 1567. The Privilege is dated June 7, the dedication to Hubert Goltzius July 18. The work opens with an ode, by Lucas de Heere, but written by the poet Eduard de Dene from Bruges. The book is illustrated with 107 etchings by Marcus Geeraerts. The second edition, in Latin, was published at Antwerp in 1579.-Hymans, II, 28,1.

3 The plan of the city of Bruges comprises ten prints, made in 1562. -Hymans, II, 28,2.

4 Geeraerts died in 1590.-D.Guilmard, *Les Maîtres Ornemanistes*, Paris, 1880-81. p.483.
Marcus Geeraerts the younger, born 1561, died in 1635 at London. There are important works by him in England. Wenzel Hollar engraved his portrait, after a self-portrait of 1627.-Hymans, II, 29,1.

CHRISTOFFEL SWARTS, p.262

1 Christopher Swarts, Schwartz, born near Ingolstadt, 1550, was a pupil of Melchior Bocksberger of Munich, with whom he made a contract in 1560.-Hymans, II, 31,1.
The king of Bavaria was William V, 1579-1597.
The Fall of the Angels and the Martyrdom of St Andrew are in the Michaelis Hofkirche.

2 The series of the Passion is in eight engravings in folio; its title is, *Praecipua Passionis D.N.Jesu Christi Mysteria ex Seren. Principis Bavariae Renatae Sacello desumta. Pinxit Chr.Schwarz Monach.Joan Sadeler Belga sculpsit Monachii*, 1589. These engravings were executed after the paintings in the Frauenkirche at Ingolstadt. The original drawings are at Nymphenburg.-Hymans, II, 31,4.

3 Schwartz died in 1597; a drawing by him of this year is in the Kupferstichkabinet at Dresden.-Floerke, II, note 72.

MICHIEL COCXIE, p.263

1 Cocxie, or Van Coxie, or Coxcyen.
The first instructor of the artist was his father, Michel van Cocxie. Bernaert was Bernaert van Orley.-Hymans, II, 33,2.

2 Van Mander mentions the German chapel of Santa Maria della Pace, but probably meant the Santa Maria dell'Anima. In the Santa Maria della Pace are the sibyls of Raphael. These two churches are opposite each other; this explains the confusion. Santa Maria dell'Anima was the place of worship for German catholics and those from the Netherlands. In the third chapel are the frescoes by Coxcie.-Hymans, II, 33,4.

3 Van Coxie returned to the Netherlands in 1539, for in November of the same year he enrolled with the guild of the painters in Malines.
The wife of Van Coxie was Ida van Hesselt; the artist married her at Hasselt.
Alph.Wauters, *Bulletin de l'Academie royale de Belgique*, 1884. I, p.63. Ida van Hesselt died in the spring of 1569; she left two sons, Raphael, born 1540, Willem, and a daughter, Anna.-Hymans, II, 33,7.

4 The Crucifixion, Christ between the Thieves, is in the Escorial. The

painting was copied, in 1623, by H.de Clerck for the high altar in the church of St Josse ten Noode, a suburb of Brussels.-Hymans, II, 34,2.

5 The central panel of the altar of St Luke was not painted by Bernaert van Orley, but by Mabuse.
The wings represented the Evangelist St John at Pathmos and John the Baptist, boiled in oil.

6 The St Sebastian painting, in the Museum at Antwerp, is signed and dated 1575.-Hymans, II, p.34,5.
The Last Supper is a triptych in the Museum at Brussels; the left wing represents the Footwashing of the Apostles, the right wing, Christ in the Olive Garden.

7 See about Coxcie's presumable wealth:-E.Neefs, *Histoire de la peinture a Malines*, Gand, 1876. I, p.154.

8 The engraving of the School of Philosophers was by Giorgio Ghisi of Mantua (Bartsch—24), dated 1550, and made in Antwerp.

9 Coxcie died March 10, 1592. He was restoring the painting of Solomon's Judgement, which he made for the city hall of Antwerp in 1583.-Van den Branden, 330.
The painting is undoubtedly the one in the Museum at Antwerp, attributed to F.Floris.-Hymans, II, 36,4.

DIRCK BARENTSEN, p.266

1 The father of Dirck Barentsen was Barent Dircksz.
See C.E.Taurel, *L'Art Chretien*. In the city hall, Taurel believes there were six paintings by Deaf Barent, which represented the punishments with which the Anabaptists were threatened; they were reproduced in Domselaer, *Beschryving van Amsterdam*.-Hymans, II, 41,2.

2 Philips Marnix, Lord of Aldegonde, born at Brussels, 1538, Burgomaster of Antwerp in 1584, which city he defended against Alexander Farnese.

3 The portraits mentioned have disappeared.-Hymans, II, 42,6.
There is a portrait of the Duke of Alva by Barentsen in the Rijksmuseum (Cat.1898).

4 The Judith and the Venus paintings have disappeared.
The Venus picture was in the house of Gerbrant Buyck, in 1671.-*Oud Holland*, VII, p.152.
There is a large triptych of the Nativity in the Museum at Gouda; the interior wings have the Death and the Assumption of the Virgin, the exterior the Annunciation.-Hymans, II, 43,2.

5 The Crucifixion has been lost.

6 The group portrait of the archers, with the drummer in it, is lost.
The painting of the Archers of the Cluyveniers Doelen, in the Rijksmuseum, is dated 1566; it represents a group of people and a woman carrying perch on a dish.-Hymans, II, 44,3.

7 The portrait of Titian is lost. For Pieter Isaacks see the biography of Hans van Aken.

8 The portrait of Barentsen himself does not show his heaviness.-Hymans, II, 45,1.

9 The Last Judgement picture has not been found.-Hymans, II, 45,2.
The funeral of Barentsen was on May 26, 1592.-Hymans, II, 45,3.

NOTES TO THE TEXT

LUCAS AND MARTEN VAN VALCKENBORGH, p.269

1 Lucas was born in 1530, Martin in 1542.-E.Neefs, *Histoire de la peinture et de la sculpture à Malines.*
   Lucas was admitted to the guild of St Luke of Malines August 26, 1560 and became a free master in 1564. Martin joined the guild of Malines in 1559 and in 1564 the guild of Antwerp. The flight from Antwerp was in 1567.-Hymans, II, 47,2.
   Hans Vredeman de Vries was a noted architect and painter. See his biography. He left Malines 1563. He left Antwerp in 1570, after the proclamation of Pardon by Philip II, and went to Aachen and Liége.
   Matthias left the Netherlands in 1580.
2 The work done for the Duke, for the most part, is in the Belvedere Collection at Vienna, dated 1580 to 1598.
3 Various facts indicate that Lucas was in Nürnberg in 1622, the year when Sandrart must have known him there.-Hymans, II, 48,3.-Fetis, *Artistes belges a l'Etranger*, II, p.144.
   The date of the death of Marten is not known. His son, Marten, died in 1636 at Frankfort a.M.-Hymans, II, 48, 4 and 5.

HANS BOL, p.270

1 The name of the father of Hans Bol was Simon Bol.-E.Neefs, *Histoire de la peinture et de la sculpture à Malines.* p.202. E.Neefs says Hans Bol received his first instruction from his uncles Jacob and Jan. Hans Bol returned to Malines and joined the guild February 10, 1560.-Hymans, II, 52,5.
2 Bol painted Daedalus and Icarus many times. There are two pictures in tempera on oak in the Museum at Stockholm; these pictures were in Prague. An engraving by Adriaen Collaert is of one of the Stockholm pictures in reverse.-*Repertorium für Kunstw.* XXVI, p.135.
   Aegidius Sadeler also made an engraving of the subject. Hymans discovered a miniature painting by Bol at an antique dealer in Malines; this was dated 1580, and it corresponded perfectly with the description given by Van Mander.-Hymans, II, 54, 1 and 2.
3 Hans Bol entered the guild of St Luke at Antwerp in 1574; he obtained his citizenship September 1575.-Hymans, II, 54,3.
4 Many engravings of his drawings were made by Galle, Sadeler, Collaert, Hendrick Goltzius, Chrispijn van der Passe, Pieter van der Heyden, Nicolas de Bruyn, Hieronymus Cock. Hans Bol himself made etchings. -Hymans, II, 56,1.
5 Hymans doubts Bol died in 1593, because he saw an oil painting on parchment of the Adoration of the Shepherds signed with golden letters. H.Bol.F.1595.-Hymans, II, 56,2.
6 Another pupil of Hans Bol was Jooris Hoefnagel.-Greve, 141.
7 Roelandt Savery was born at Courtrai in 1576. He died on February 25, 1639 at Utrecht, where he had lived since 1619.-*Cat. Rijksmuseum*, 1898.
8 Goltzius engraved a portrait of Bol, dated 1593 (Bartsch—162), and a smaller one later (Bartsch—162).-Hymans, II, 56,6.

FRANS AND GILLIS MOSTAERT, p.273

1 Frans and Gillis Mostart were born c.1534.-Van den Branden, 301.
   Gillis painted landscapes. Hendrick Goltzius engraved a series of the

NOTES TO THE TEXT

twelve months after originals by Gillis. In 1595 he received 98 guilders and 8 stuivers for a moonlight picture and a fire scene, which were made for Archduke Ernst of Austria, now in the Belvedere, Vienna.-Hymans, II, 60,1.-Floerke, II, note 125.
According to the records of the guild, Frans had a pupil in 1553; Gillis became a member in 1554.-Van den Branden, 301.
2 Frans Mostart died in 1560.-Hymans, II, 60,3.
3 Ernst of Austria was governor in 1594.
4 Sprangher's father was well acquainted with the Mostarts; he may have given information to Van Mander about them.-Greve, 159.
Gillis Mostart married Margaretha Baes in 1564; they had five sons and five daughters; the youngest, Gillis, born in 1588, became a painter and was accepted as son of a master in the guild of St Luke at Antwerp in 1612.-Van den Branden, 306.
5 Gillis van Conincxloo may have given this information about Gillis Mostart; he studied under him.
Hans Soens and Sprangher may have given information.
6 Gaspar, Balthazar, and Melchior Schetz of Antwerp. Melchior Schetz was the treasurer general for Philip II.-Hymans, II, 61,2.

MARINUS DE SEEU, p.276
1 There is a painting of a Tax Collector in his office, in the Alte Pinakothek at Munich, dated 1542.

HENDRICK VAN STEENWIJCK, p.277
1 Hendrick entered the guild of St Luke at Antwerp in the year 1577. The presence of Hendrick van Steenwijck in Frankfort indicates that he had left the country for religious reasons.-Hymans, II, 663,4.
2 The son was born probably at Frankfort in 1580, died at London in 1649, where he had been active since his twenties. *Cat. Dresden Museum*, 1899. Van Mander does not mention Jacques de Backer as his pupil. -Greve, 161.

BERNAERT DE RIJCKE, p.278
1 The Carrying of the Cross, by Bernaert de Rijcke, at the same place, is signed and dated 1560.-Hymans, II, 68,2. Bernaert de Rijcke was born c.1535. He died January 1, 1590.-Van den Branden, 332.

GIELIS COIGNET, p.279
1 Coignet or Congnet was born c.1538.-Van den Branden, 272.
2 Coignet left Antwerp for sake of his religious views.-Hymans, II, 70,5.
The only evidence of Coignet's stay in Amsterdam is the engraving representing the Last Supper, which Jan Muller made after one of his paintings. It has a dedication to Jacques Razet and is dated 1594—(Bartsch-28).
-Hymans, II, 71,1.
Coignet died December 27, 1599, and was buried in the Jacobi Kirche at Hamburg, a protestant church.-Hymans, II, 71,2.
3 Gillis Coignet must have been able to inform Van Mander about Cornelis Molenaer; the latter painted backgrounds in the work of Coignet.-Greve, 143.
4 Pupils registered with Coignet in Antwerp were: Simon Ijkens 1570,

NOTES TO THE TEXT

Jacob Hermans 1571, Gaspar Dooms 1574, Robert Huls 1584. Another pupil was Cornelis Cornelisz van Haarlem.-Hymans, II, 71,3 and 72,1.

JOORIS HOEFNAGHEL, p.281

1 The father of the artist was Jacob Hoefnaghel, a jeweller; his mother Elisabeth Vezeler, or Veselaers, was the daughter of a goldsmith who sold work to Frances I, of France.-Hymans, II, 74,3.
Jan Sadeler engraved a portrait of Hoefnaghel which had the inscription: AETAT 48.1591. According to this Hoefnaghel was born c.1543. -Hymans, II, 74,2.

2 The drawings were in the Imperial Library at Vienna.-Greve, 236.

3 Calis Malis, Caliz, is near Almeria.-Hymans, II, 76,2.

4 Hoefnaghel married Susanna van Onchem or van Onssen at Antwerp, November 12, 1571.-Hymans, II, 76,4. The Spanish Fury was on November 4, 1576.

5 The Fuggers, Anton and Raymond founded the church of St Maurice at Munich and owned a famous art collection.-Hymans, II, 77,1. The Duke of Bavaria was Albrecht V, 1550 to 1579.
The portrait of Hoefnaghel engraved by Sadeler, had the inscription: GEORGIUS HOVENAGLIUS ANTWERP QUI PICTURAM DELICATIOREM QUI PICTURAM EO PROMOVIT SUMMUS UT PRINCIP; PLACEAT ALBERTO AUSTRIACO IPSI IMP. RUDOLPHO AUGUST. JOAN SADELERUS, AMICUS AMICO PORTERITATI.-Greve, 172.

6 Hoefnaghel and Ortelius were in Rome in 1578, according to an inscription under a view of Tivoli in the *Civitates* by Bruin.-Hymans, II, 77,4. -Fetis, *Les artistes belges a l'étranger*, I, 108.
Giulio Clovio from Croatia, died at Rome in 1578 at the age of 80. He was a pupil of Giulio Romano. Vasari gives attention to him.-Hymans, II, 78,1.

7 In 1579 Hoefnaghel gave Plantin six copies of the first two volumes of Bruins *Civitates*.-Rooses, *Geschiedenis der Antwerpener Schilderschool*, 106-108.

8 The manuscript by Hoefnaghel, made for the Duke of Innsbruck, was in the Imperial Library in Vienna.
Waagen (in his *Die vornehmsten Kunstdenkmaeler in Wien*, p.66) says it is remarkable that Hoefnaghel finished the work in this time. The Breviarum Grimani is the only manuscript Hoefnaghel's work may be compared to.
Two dates in the manuscript prove the work was begun in 1581 and finished in 1590.-Hymans, II, 78,3.

9 Nagler says the series never reached the Emperor and it was in the hands of an antiquary in Munich in 1830. Jacobus Hoefnaghel published in 1592 a series of four books, each containing twelve prints of insects, flowers, etc., taken from the works of his father; the title: *Archetypa studiaque patris Georgii Hoefnaghelii Jacobus F. genio duce ab ipso sculpta, etc.*-Hymans, II, 78,4.

10 Jacques Hoefnaghel was a pupil of Abraham Lisart at Antwerp in 1582. He was a good engraver and miniature painter.-Hymans, II, 79,4. An interesting work by him, in the Museum at Valencia, Spain, has the words, 'Albertus Durer Norimbergensis faciebat post Virginis partum 1510. Coloribus sic illustrabat Jacobus Hoveneglius. Antwerp 1600.'

488

NOTES TO THE TEXT

AERT MIJTENS, p.285

1 Anthoni Santvoort is not A.van Santvoort, the engraver in Brussels in the middle of the XVII Century.-Hymans, II, 84,1.
2 See the biography of Speeckaert.
3 In the biography by Van Mander his sister Anna married Pieter Pype; it would indicate that the two Pype's were closely related.-Greve, 153. The Assumption of the Virgin has not been found.-Hymans, II, 84. There is no work by Mijtens in the Museum at Naples.
4 The church of St Francesco di Paola, built in 1817, is at the place of the little church of the Anjou's.-Floerke, II, note 170.
5 No painting by Mijtens has been found in Naples.-Hymans, II, 83,2.

JOOS VAN WINGHEN, p.289

1 According to Van Mander, at the end of this biography, Joos van Winghen was born in 1542.-Hymans, II, 81,2. Alexander Farnese. Baldinucci believes, wrongly, this was in Parma. -Hymans, II, 81,3.
2 The Church of the Celle-Broers was dedicated to St Gaugericus. -J.B.Descamps, *Voyage pittoresque de la Flandre et du Brabant*, 1779. p.51. For Pauwels de Vries, see the biography of Fredeman de Vries.
3 The Samson was engraved by Raphael Sadeler in 1589. The original painting is in the Museum in Düsseldorf.-Hymans, II, 87,6.
4 Joos van Winghen was among the burghers sent by the city of Brussels to Alexander Farnese to negotiate the capitulation of the city. Van Winghen probably left the city afterwards.-Hymans, II, 88,2. The drawing for Horrified Belgium is in the Kupferstich Kabinet, Berlin.-Rathgeber, *Annales*, No.3241. There are two compositions almost identical of Apelles painting Campaspe in the Belvedere at Vienna, Nos.950 and 951. No.950 belonged to Emperor Rudolph II, and No.951 to the Duke of Buckingham. -Hymans, II, 88,4.
5 The Story of Pyneas was engraved by Jacques Granthomme. The Justice was engraved by Egbert Jansz.-Hymans, II, 88,7-89,1.
6 The Night Banquet was engraved by J.Sadeler. The painting is in the Rijksmuseum, Amsterdam. Jean Sadeler made an engraving of Let the Children Come Unto Me, dated 1588. Four Feminine Tricks was engraved by R. and J.Sadeler in a series representing Solomon's Idolatry, Sardanapolis and the Prodigal Son. The Crucifixion was engraved by Chrispijn van der Passe, 1599.-Hymans, II, 89,2-90,1,3,4.
7 Jeremias was born at Frankfort in 1587.-Gwinner, *Kunst und Künstler in Frankfort*.-Hymans, II, 90,5.

MARTEN DE VOS, p.291

1 Marten de Vos was born c.1531.-Hymans, II, 92,1. Van den Branden does not agree with Van Mander about the brother; the latter was the father of Willem de Vos of whom Van Dyck made a portrait etching. -Hymans, II, 92,4.-Van den Branden, 217.
2 The Museum at Antwerp has various religious pictures by Marten de Vos. A double portrait by him of Aegidius Hoffman and Margaretha van Nispen, signed and dated 1570, is in the Rijksmuseum at Amsterdam.

NOTES TO THE TEXT

See *Repertorium für Kunstw.*, XXIV, p.192.-Floerke, II, note 196. -Hymans, II, 92,5.
Hymans says few artists have given so many drawings to engravers. The engravings made after his drawings amounted to hundreds and gave work to nearly all the engraving shops in Antwerp. Goltzius made engravings after work of Vos. All these works show great virtuosity but lack of taste.-Hymans, II, 93,1. Marten de Vos died December 4, 1603, at the age of 72.

BIOGRAPHIES OF LIVING ARTISTS ETC., p.295
(INTRODUCTION)
1 Van Mander did not make a special chapter of this introduction; it was included in the biography of Hans Fredeman de Vries.

HANS FREDEMAN DE VRIES, p.298
1 Jerrich Schenck was governor of Friesland.-Hymans, II, 100,2.
Reyer Geeritsen, Reyer Gerbrants is recorded as a citizen of Leeuwarden, 1544.-Eeckhoff: *de Stedelijke Kunstverzameling te Leeuwarden*, 1875. p.281.
2 Van Mander means by the large book of Pieter Koeck his translation of the works on architecture by Serlio.
The little book is *De inventie der Colommen met haren ornementen ende maten ut Vitruvic ende andere diversche auctoren, etc.*, *Antwerpen ter begheerten van Goede Vrienden*, 1539.-Hymans, II, 100,6. De Vries can be traced to Malines in 1561.-Neefs, *Histoire de la peinture et de la sculpture à Malines*, I, p.167. Dorici, Dorizi, was admitted to the guild of St Luke at Malines in 1536 as a citizen of the town. He was born in 1517 and died in 1565.-Hymans, II, 101,2.
Nothing is known about Cornelis van Vianen.
De Vries left Malines between 1563 and 1564 and settled at Antwerp. In 1555 a series of ornamental designs by De Vries were published by Gerard de Jode.-Hymans, II, 101,4. The prince of Orange was William the Silent; he left Antwerp in April, 1567. Willem Key died in June, 1568.-Hymans, II, 101,6.
3 This book was re-edited in 1601 by Theodore Galle under the title: *Variae architecturae formae*.
The first edition is dedicated by Cock to Cardinal Granvelle. The ornamental frame of the dedication has been retained in the second edition. -Hymans, II, 101,8.
A modern edition in lithography has been issued at Brussels and at Paris. Van Mander mentions twenty six pieces, should be twenty.-Greve, 118.
4 The Book of Fountains, for Geerart de Jode, was titled: *Artis perspectivae plurium generum...multigenis fontibus, etc. Excudebat Antwerpiae Gerardus De Jode, Anno* 1560. 30 plates.-Hymans, II, 102,3.
The book on architecture and the five orders was translated into French in 1597 by Theodore Kemp.-Hymans, II, 102,4.
5 Anna of Austria, daughter of Maximilian II, bride of Philip II came to Antwerp August 26, 1570. The General Amnesty of Philip II excluded all suspected of heresy. Vredeman de Vries and the Valckenborghs moved away.-Hymans, II, 103,1. Various fortification plans by De Vries

NOTES TO THE TEXT

can be found in the series *Architecturae*, published by Gerard de Jode in 1577.-Hymans, II, 103,5.

6 The St Peter Church at Hamburg was destroyed by fire in 1842; part of the tower remained and was saved in the reconstruction.-Hymans, II, 104,1.

7 The picture Orpheus Charming Hostile Animals exists; it was painted in 1592.-A.Lindner, Danzig, 1903. p.60.
The ceiling decorations by De Vries, in the red room of the town hall at Danzig, have been replaced by later paintings; part of the cycle mentioned by Van Mander exists.-A.Lindner, Danzig, 1903. pp.51-53.

8 Pauwels de Vries was born at Antwerp in 1567. He married in Amsterdam in 1601 and became a burgher of this city February 14, 1604. -Kramm, *Levens en Werken.-Obreen's Archief*, II, 275.

9 Hans van Aken was born in 1562 in Cologne, and died in 1613. Joseph Switser was Joseph Heintz, court painter to Rudolph II, born June 11, 1564, at Basel, son of the town architect Daniel Heintz. Joseph was in Rome from 1585 till 1587. He was appointed court painter. He died at Prague in October, 1609.-Berthold Haendecke, *Joseph Heintz, Hofmaler Kaiser Rudolph II.-Oesterreich. Jahrb.* 1894. XV, p.45.

10 The Tower of Babel painting has not been found.

11 De Vries was in Holland in 1604: he tried on February 8 to be admitted as professor of architecture at the University of Leyden; he failed despite support by Prince Maurice.-Hymans, II, 106,6.

JOANNES STRADANUS, p.304

1 Joan de Bologna, Giovanni da Bologna, Jean de Boullogne, was born at Douai 1524, died at Florence 1608. According to his epitaph in the church 'Santissima Annunziata' at Florence, Stradanus was born in 1523 and died November 2, 1605 at the age of eighty-two. Borghini states that Stradanus was for three years a pupil of Lugo Piero Ollandese. This was Pieter Aertsen from Antwerp. The guild records at Antwerp show that Stradanus became free master in 1545.-Hymans, II, 110,1,3,5.

2 Before settling at Florence Stradanus stayed some time at Lyon and at Venice. According to Borghini, Stradanus specialized originally in designing cartoons for tapestries.-Hymans, II, 111,1,2.-Wauters, *Les Tapisseries bruxelloises*, Brussels, 1878. p.164.-E.Muntz., *la Tapisserie.* p.230.

3 The Crucifixion is in the Church of the Nunziata. The engraving was of the Crucifixion made by Philip Galle.-Hymans, II, 111,3,5.
Philip Galle's series of engravings, after the tapestry cartoons of the wars of Duke Cosimo, was titled, *Medicae familae, gestarum, victoriae et triumphi*, 1583. The hunting scenes were engraved by Philip Galle and Goltzius. The title was, Venationes, ferarum, avium, pixcium, pugnae. -Hymans, II, 111,6,7.

4 See J.A.F.Orbaan, *Stradanus te Florence*, Rotterdam, 1903.

GILLIS VAN CONINCXLOY, p.306

1 Pieter, son of Pieter van Aelst, was born in 1559.-Hymans, I, 184,3.-Van den Branden, 151. Lenaert Kroes is not in the records of the guild of St Luke of Antwerp. There was a Leonard Kroes in Bruges at the end of the fifteenth Century.-*Le Beffroi*, I, p.117.

2 Gillis married Maria Robroeck, the widow of Pauwels van Aelst in 1570.

NOTES TO THE TEXT

He entered the guild of Antwerp in the same year and remained till January 1585.-Sponsel, 'Gillis van Coninxloo und seine Schule,' *Jahrb. der. preuss. Kunst-samml.* X, p.57.

Gillis was living in 1604 and probably gave Van Mander information about old Pieter Breughel and his sons, about Jan de Hollander, Pieter Breughel II, and Pauwels van Aelst, about Joos van Lier and about Gillis Mostart.-Greve, 143-144.
3 The picture does not exist.-Hymans, II, 118,9.
Two landscapes are in the Lichtenstein Collection, dated 1598 and 1604. A large landscape, a Judgement of Midas, is in Dresden.-Sponsel op.cit. p.70.
The engraver Nicolaes de Bruyn (born at Antwerp 1571 and died at Amsterdam 1635) made thirteen landscapes after Coninxloo.-Hymans, II, 121.-Sponsel, op.cit., 61,1.

BARTHOLOMEUS SPRANGHER, p.309
1 Jan Mandijn was born in 1500 at Haarlem, settled at Antwerp before 1530. He became the instructor of Gillis Mostart c.1550 and of Sprangher in 1557. He died early in 1560.-Hymans, I, 76.-Van den Branden, 159.
2 Jacob Wickram may be Georg Wickram from Spiers. There is nothing in the records of the guild about him.-Hymans, II, 125,2.
3 Hans Bocksberger from Salzburg was a fresco painter. He made the mural decorations at Landshut between 1542 and 1555. He made drawings for the wood engravers.-Janitschek, *Geschichte der deutschen Malerei*, p.537.
4 Marc Duval, named 'le Sourd,' also Bertin, after his stepfather, was an excellent engraver of portraits. He died at Paris September 13, 1581. His daughter Elisabeth worked in the same genre.-Hymans, II, 126,1 and 2.
5 Bernardino Gatti, named 'il Sojaro' or 'Sogliato' from Cremona, died in 1575 at the age of eighty. He finished an Adoration of the Magi in the church of the Madonna della Steccata at Parma, which was begun by Michelangelo Anselmi.-Müller, *Kunstlerlexikon*, II, p.159.
6 The wedding of Maria of Portugal and Alexander Farnese of Parma was in November, 1565, at Antwerp.-Hymans, II, 129,1.
7 Van Mander became acquainted with Sprangher in Rome.-Greve, 13.
8 Giulio Clovio from Croatia, died at Rome in 1578 at the age of 80. He was a pupil of Giulio Romano. Vasari gives attention to him.-Hymans, II, 78,1.
9 The famous castle of Caprarola was built by Vignola, 1547 to 1559, for Alexander Farnese.-Floerke, II, note 273.
The Palace of St Laurence of Damascus is the Cancelleria, but Van Mander refers to the Palazzo Farnese in the immediate vicinity.-Floerke, II, note 274.
10 The Last Judgement by Sprangher is in the Museum at Turin.-Hymans, II, 131,1.
11 The painting for the church of S.Luigi de Francesi does not exist. The present church of S.Luigi was dedicated in 1589. Hymans knew an engraving after the painting by Crispijn van der Passe.-Hymans, II, 132,1. The church near the Porta Latina is not the S.Giovanni a Porta Latina but the S.Giovanni in Oleo. According to Greve (p.269) the picture is in the S.Giovanni a Porta Latina.-Floerke, II, note 278.

NOTES TO THE TEXT

12 The engraving after the St Anne painting was made by Matthaeus Greuter, 1566-1638.-Hymans, II, 132,2.

13 The Duchess of Aremberg, Marguerite de la Marck, the last of her name, was the wife of Jan de Ligne, Prince of Aremberg since 1565; she died in 1597.-Hymans, II, 132,2.

14 Jan de Bologne, Giovanni da Balogna, was born at Douai in 1524 and died at Florence in 1608. Nothing more known about Hans Mont. His successor, with Emperor Rudolph, was Adriaen de Vries from The Hague.-Hymans, II, 133,1.

15 The Mercurius introducing Psyche into the council of the Gods is in the gallery at Hampton Court. Oval picture on copper.-Hymans, II, 135,1.
The Roma was engraved by J.Matham and Rafaello Guidi.-Hymans, II, 135,2.

16 Van Mander visited the Imperial collections in Vienna and became acquainted with the works of Breughel and of Dürer.-Greve, 13.

17 The upper-chamberlain was Wolgang Rumpff, baron von Wielros und Weittrach. Sprangher dedicated his picture the Wedding of Psyche to him. This was engraved by Hendrick Goltzius (Bartsch—277). -Hymans, II, 136,2.

18 The girl's name was Christine Muller. Sprangher painted her portrait, which is in the Belvedere in Vienna. In 1500 Gillis Sadeler made an engraving of this portrait, with that of Sprangher, surrounded by allegorical figures.-Hymans, II, 137,1.

19 The painting Christ stepping on the devil and Death has disappeared. -Floerke, II, note 290.

20 There is one picture in the Pinakothek at Munich, and there are three in the Schleisheim Gallery, representing Apollo, Mydas, and Marsias, Lot and his daughters flee from Sodoma, Susan and the Elders.-Cat. 1898.-Floerke, II, note 292.

21 The convent of St James was destroyed in 1689.-Hymans, II, 138,3.

22 See, for emblems of painters,-E.F.A.Warnecke, *Das Künstlerwappen*. -S.Muller Fz, *Schilders-Vereenigingen te Utrecht.-Oud Holland*, 1904. XXII, p.1.

23 According to Von Perger (*Mitteilungen der Zentralkommission*, X, p.230) the inventory of the collection at Prague mentions no less than twenty-seven paintings by Sprangher.-Hymans, II, 140,2.

24 The statement about Goltzius shows that Van Mander valued the judgement of this artist.-Greve, 148.

25 The Wedding of Psyche was engraved by Goltzius in 1587. The engraving consists of three pages (Bartsch—277). According to Nagler, the drawing was in the collection Gruenling in 1823.-Hymans, II, 140,3.

26 Joseph Heintz, court painter to Rudolph II, 1564 to 1609.

27 This meeting with Sprangher must have been important to Van Mander: because Sprangher could give information about Van Aken, Heinz, Adriaen de Vries, Hoefnaghel, Cornelis van Dalem, Wickram, Pilgrim; Sprangher's father knew Michiel Coxcie, Jan Mandijn and Gillis Mostart.-Greve, 14.

28 Sprangher died c.1627; at that time his son Matthias was alive.-Hymans, II, 143.

NOTES TO THE TEXT

CORNELIS KETEL, p.330

1 See the biographies of Vlerick and of Bloemaert.

2 Dirck Crabeth and this brother Wouter are the originators of the twelve most beautiful windows in the S Jans Kerck at Gouda. They were executed in the years 1555-1577. Dirck died in 1577.-Floerke, II, note 303.

3 Nothing is known about Denijs van Utrecht.

4 For Joan de la Hame, see De Laborde, *La Renaissance des Arts a la cour de la France*, p.396.-Hymans, II, 148.

5 St Bartholomew's Day, August 23-24, 1572.

6 The name of the wife of Ketel was Adelheid Gerrits.-Hymans, II, 148,6.

7 The full length portrait of Hatten is at Ditchley in the collection of Viscount Dillom; it was shown in the exhibition at Manchester, 1857. -Hymans, II, 149,1.

8 The queen was Elisabeth.
The mother of the count was Lady Frances Howard, sister of Lord Admiral Nottingham.-Hymans, II, 149,3.

9 The Earl of Oxford was Sir Edward Vere.-Hymans, II, 149,5.
Vertue mentions the portraits of William Herbert, Earl of Pembroke, Lord Admiral Lincoln, Henry Fitzalan, Count Arundel.
G.Scharf mentioned to Hymans the portraits of Sir Thomas or Sir William Gresham at Titsey Park, with G.Leveson Gower. (This portrait is signed and dated 1579) and the portrait of Sir Martin Frobisher, at the University of Oxford, for which the artist was paid five pounds sterling. -Hymans, II, 149,6.

10 Ketel had a son baptised in Amsterdam on November 16, 1581 with the name Raphael.-Hymans, II, 149,7.
The picture at the city hall at Amsterdam, dated 1588, shows little that corresponds with the description by Van Mander.-Hymans, II, 149,8.

11 These pictures according to Vertue were in the Duke of Buckingham's collection.-Hymans, II, 150,1.

12 Rutger Jansz published a mystical book in 1602; his portrait was painted by Miereveldt.-Hymans, II, 151,1.
Van Mander's error; Ketel painted the picture of St Paul in 1588; it was done for the Voetboogh Doelen.-Catalogue, 1898, No.754.-Greve, 197.

13 Jacob Houbraken made an engraving after the portrait of Jacob Cornelis van Neck, who became burgomaster of Amsterdam in 1622. -Hymans, II, 151,3.

14 Van Mander presumably meant Andrea Morosini, born in 1557, died in 1618. Francesco Morosini was born in 1618. Jacob Matham made an engraving after the portrait of Vincent Jacobson (Bartsch—169). -Hymans, II, 152,1,2.

15 Hendrick de Keyser, born at Utrecht in 1565, died at Amsterdam in 1621.-Hymans, II, 152,3.

16 This composition is undoubtedly the one engraved by J.Sadeler and cited by Kramm.-Hymans, II, 154,1.

17 Apparently Ketel was never in Italy. Sandrart however, stated that he was, but did not prove it.-Hymans, II, 166,1.

18 Peton. Tobacco was called Petum. Napelles refers probably to Aconitum Napellus, a poisonous herb.

19 Escapement: Part of the movement in a timepiece.

494

NOTES TO THE TEXT

20 Jan Saenredam made an engraving of this picture (Bartsch—106). *-Peintre Graveur*, III, p.253.
21 The story of the groom is in Matthew xxii.13.
22 One of these portraits probably served for the engraving by H.Bary. The original is in the gallery of Hampton Court.-Hymans, II, 158,2.
23 Wolfart Hermanszoon defeated the Spaniards in 1601, near Bantam. -Hymans, II, 158,4.
24 The Duke of Nemours was Henri de Savois, 1572-1633. His portrait was engraved by Thomas de Leu. (Robert Dumesnil-No.466).-Hymans, II, 159,1.
25 Anagram in Dutch.
26 Cornelis Florisz van Teylinghen was burgomaster of Alkmaar during the siege by Spaniards in 1573.-Hymans, II, 161,2.
27 The Madonna with Babe was engraved by Quirin Boel. Christ seated on a rock was engraved by Pieter de Jode the Elder, pupil of Goltzius. -Hymans, II, 162,3.
28 Virtue Triumphs was Ketel's motto.
29 Fiorillo has seen this picture together with an affidavit at a merchant in Frankfort a-M, named Kaller.-Hymans, II, 163,2.
30 Ketel was buried August 8, 1616, in the Oude Kerck at Amsterdam. See A.D.de Vries Azn. 'Biographische aanteekeningen Testament of Ketel.' *-Oud Holland*, 1885. II, p.74.
31 According to Hymans, Van Mander confused Isaac Isaacsz. with Pieter Isaacsz. about whom he writes in the biography of Hans van Aken. There is in the Museum at Copenhagen a painting by Isaac Isaacszen in the style of Veronese, and it is dated 1632. This painter is mentioned in an official deed in 1631 as being alive on June 18, and is indicated as the heir of Pieter Isaacsz, painter to the king of Denmark.-*Obreen's Archief*, II, p.147.
   The portrait of Christian IV, engraved by Jan Muller (Bartsch—56), is signed Pieter Isaacsz. The original painting is in the Kaiser Friederich Museum at Berlin. The Berlin Catalogue by Bode (1898) indicates Pieter Isaacsz as a pupil of Cornelis Ketel at Amsterdam; the date of his death is given September, 1625.-Hymans, II, 164,1.-Floerke, II, note 358.
32 Ketel had seen work by Holbein at London, by Blocklandt at Gouda and Delft, and by Jan Gossaert.-Greve, 152.
   Van Mander used about twenty poems by Ketel in his *Schilderboeck*. -Greve, 151.

GUALDROP GORTZIUS, p.349

1 Frans Francken died October 3, 1616 at Antwerp. Geldrop was entered in the *Liggeren* as his pupil.-Hymans, II, 168,2.
2 The Duke of Terra Nova was Carlo d'Aragona.-Hymans, II, 168,3.
3 Everhard Jabach was a banker; he gave Rubens the order for painting the Crucifixion of St Peter for the church in Cologne.-Hymans, II, 169,1.
4 The ecclesiastic was probably Wilhelm Quadt, who used to write remarks on engravings by Chrispijn van de Passe made after the works of Geldorp.-Hymans, II, 169,2.
5 Van den Branden (p.351) says that, in the death inventory of Frans Francken February 17, 1617, there is a picture of St Andreas by Geldorp the Elder, and a Susan by Joris Geldorp the Younger, probably identical

495

with Geldrop Gortzius and Jorge Geldorp II, his son, who was accepted as master in the guild of Antwerp in 1610.
6 This painting has not been found.
7 According to the catalogue of the Mauritshuis at The Hague, Gortzius died in 1616, or in 1618 at Cologne.-*Kat. Mauritshuis*, 1895. p.122.-Floerke, II, note 369.

MICHIEL JANSSEN MIEREVELDT, p.351
1 See under Miereveldt in Conclusion.
2 According to de Jongh (II, p.85) the father of Miereveldt died November 8, 1592. According to the same source the father was an engraver, though this statement is not accepted.-Hymans, II, 171,2.
3 According to the records of the guild at Delft, founded in 1613, Miereveldt is entered as master. In 1625 he became a member of the guild of painters at The Hague.-Hymans, II, 170,3, and 172,2.-*Obreen's Archief* 1877-1878. I, p.4.
4 The Princess of Orange was Louise de Coligny; she died at Fontainebleau November 13, 1620. She was the fourth wife of William the Silent, whom she married in 1583. There is a little portrait of her by Miereveldt in the Mauritshuis at The Hague on which she is represented as a widow —probably a preliminary study.
5 There is no reference to Miereveldt in the southern Netherlands. The inventory of his pictures, published by Henri Havard, mentions small portraits of Albert and Isabella.-Hymans, II, 174,4.-Henri Havard, *L'Art et les artistes hollandais*, I, p.52.
6 Pieter Dircksen Cluyt, Paulus Moreelsz and Pieter Montfoort may have informed Van Mander.
7 Miereveldt died June 27, 1641.

HENRICUS GOLTZIUS, p.355
1 The Conversion of St Paul is celebrated on January 25. If Goltzius was born in February the statement should be 'after' the Conversion.
2 See the biography of Hubert Goltz from Venloo.
3 Hymans makes Hendrick's father Jan Goltzius, his brother and eliminates one generation, though Van Mander calls the older Hubert Goltz the great-grandfather of Hendrick. Jan I died at Kaiserswerth, his younger son Jan II went to Mulbrecht, where Hendrick was born. Hubert Goltzius II was an uncle of Hendrick.-Floerke, III, note 383.
4 See the biography of Frans Floris.
5 The great fire at Haarlem was on October 23, 1576. The festival of St John is celebrated June 24th. The arrival of Goltzius must have been in 1577.-Hymans, II, 181,1.
6 Philip Galle was born in 1537 at Haarlem and died March 29, 1612 at Antwerp. Goltzius engraved his portrait in 1582.-Hymans, II, 183,2.
The name of the widow Goltzius married was Margareta Bartsen. -Hymans, II, 183,3.
Jacob Matham was born at Haarlem October 15, 1571.
He entered the guild in 1600 and died in the same town January 20, 1631. -Bartsch, *Peintre Graveur*, III, p.131.-Hymans, II, 183,4 and II, 198,2.
7 The engraver Hans Sadeler, born in 1550 at Brussels, died at Venice in August 1600.-Hymans, II, 184,1.

8 The large Hercules, (Bartsch—142) was engraved in 1589.

9 The name of the silversmith was Jan Matthijsz Ban and he came from Haarlem. See the dedication of the *Schilderboeck*.
Philip van Winghe came from Louvain. He went through Italy with the famous Bosio and Giacconius. At Rome he excavated the Catacombs of St Calixtus and died in 1592 at Florence in his thirtieth year.-Hymans, II, 186,2.-Ed. van Even, *Messager des Sciences historiques de Belgique*, 1877. p.162.

10 There is a diary by Van Winghe, in the Royal Library at Brussels, and an engraved portrait by Jacob Matham, after a drawing by Goltzius. The oval portrait is surrounded by the inscription, B.M.PHILIPPO WING-HIO HENRICUS GOLTZIUS AMICITIAE ERGO DELINEABAT ROMAE. In the left corner, Jac. Matham, in the right, Sculpsit.
Below ten latin poems, an elegy ends with the words, Florentiae jacuit, anno M.D.XCII.
Another portrait by Van Winghe was engraved by Gisbert van Veen, after a drawing by his brother Octavio.-Hymans, II, 186,3.
Goltzius engraved the portrait of Ortelius, 1527-1598 (Bartsch—180). -Hymans, II, 186,4.

11 The Farnese Hercules is a standing figure. Goltzius made an engraving after this sculpture (Bartsch—143). The figures at the base may be Van Winghe and Mathijsz Ban.-Hymans, II, 187,1.

12 For Dierick de Vries see the biography of Hans Rottenhamer. Goltzius drew his portrait in 1590.-Hymans, II, 181,1.

13 The banquet scene was The Banquet of Young Tarquinius (Bartsch —104).

14 Goltzius drew a portrait of Zucchero in 1606.-Hymans, II, 189,2.
Sprangher's Banquet of the Gods was engraved by Goltzius in 1587 (Bartsch—277).

15 Roman Heroes (Bartsch 94-103) engraved in 1586, among them a Mucius Scevola.-Hymans, II, 190,3.

16 This series is known as the Masterwork of Goltzius (Bartsch 15-20) and is dated 1593.-Hymans, II, 190,4.

17 The Circumcision (Bartsch—4) Goltzius repeated in a painting which is in the Hermitage at Leningrad. Another painting of the same subject is in the Museum at Stockholm.-Hymans, II, 190,5.

18 There are two paintings of this subject, one in the Hermitage and the other in the Lichtenstein Collection.-Hymans, II, 191,1.

19 The Duke of Bavaria was William V.

20 The Passion (Bartsch 27-38).

21 Mary with the dead figure of Christ (Bartsch—41).
Arnout van Beerensteyn's portrait was engraved by Goltzius.-Hymans, II, 192,5.

22 Woman with Snakes and Pigeons (Bartsch—93).

23 Goltzius made an engraving of this subject (Bartsch—155) and it is considered one of his most beautiful works.

24 Philip II died in 1598.

25 See the biography of Francesco Badens.

26 The Venus and Cupid has disappeared.-Floerke, II, note 423.

27 The Golden Age, in the Museum at Arras, is dated 1598. The Museum of Oldenburg has a Deluge dated 1592.-Hymans, II, 194,1.

NOTES TO THE TEXT

28 Christ lamenting Jerusalem. The painting has not been found.
29 This painting has been lost.
30 Celestial Paradise has been lost.
31 A painting of this description, reported by Hofstede de Groot, was with an art dealer in Dresden in 1890.-Greve, 227.
32 The Danaë picture appeared twice for auction at Amsterdam, first in 1754, the auction Tonneman, later the auction Braamkamp, in 1771. It brought 410 guilders. It has been lost.-Hymans, II, 196,1.
33 Cornelis Ysbrandsz Kusseus, or Kuffeus, from Haarlem, painted, in 1597, a window for the St Janskerk at Gouda. Gillis van Breen made engravings after his drawings. He died in 1618 at Haarlem.-de Jongh, II, 112, note.
34 The two portraits, mentioned by Weigel, one is indicated as a young man of twenty-two, the other as one of twenty-seven. Both the prints are dated 1583.
    The King of Poland was Stephan Bathori.-Hymans, II, 197,2.
35 Pieter de Jode the Elder was born in 1570 at Antwerp. He entered the guild of St Luke in 1599, became Dean August 9, 1634.-Hymans, II, 198, 3.
36 Hendrick Goltzius died on January 1, 1617, from the inscription on the portrait engraved by Jacob Matham.-Hymans, II, 199,1.

HENDRICK CORNELISSEN VROOM, p.374

1 As to the weird ceramics designed by Cornelis Henricksen see the article by N de Roever, in-*Oud Holland*, 1883. I, p.48.
2 The real name of Pintemony is not known.-Hymans, II, 210,2.
3 Ferdinand de Medici, later on Ferdinand I, 1587-1608, Archduke of Tuscany.-Hymans, II, 210,3.
4 Albissola, about five miles from Savona, the birth place of Sixtus IV and Julius II.
    Jan Kraeck, also Carrach, Carracka, Caraqua, was court painter to Emanuele Filibertos of Savoy and his successor Carlo Emmanuele. He died at Turin in 1607. In the document of his appointment he is indicated as 'fiammingo.' Works of his are in the museum of Chambery. His ashes and those of his wife rest in the cathedral at Turin.-Hymans, II, 211,2.
5 Probably Jan de Hoey. Vroom went to Rouen to find work in ceramics. -Hymans, II, 211,3,4.
6 Vroom married Joosje Cornelisse.-A.van der Willigen, *Les artistes de Haarlem*, 1870. p.320.
7 Penice, a city Estremadura.
8 The word Vroom is also an adjective in Dutch and means pious. Keep with the pious.
9 Vroom was at Haarlem at the end of 1596. On January 28, 1597, the Magistracy allowed him to resign his office as commissary of the guild of St Luke.-Van der Willigen, op.cit.
10 Spierings was a weaver at Delft.-J.van de Graft, *De tapijtfabrieken der XVI en XVII eeuw*, Middelburg, 1868. p.68.
    Engravings after the tapestries can be found in, John Pine, *The Tapestry Hangings of the House of Lords*, representing the several engagements between the English and the Spanish fleets. London 1783. -Hymans, II, 214,4.

498

NOTES TO THE TEXT

11 Oliver 1566-1617 was a miniature painter.
12 Justinus of Nassau, natural son of William the Silent, was born in 1559; Admiral of Zeeland 1586; died in 1631.
13 The engraving was dedicated to the Magistracy of Haarlem.-Hymans, II, 215,2,3.
14 Vroom died in 1640 at Haarlem and was buried February 4.-*Cat. Rijksmuseum*, 1898.

HANS SOENS, p.380

1 According to Immerzeel, Hans Soens was born in 1553.
  The local Duke was Ranuccio I, son of Alexander Farnese 1569-1622. -Hymans, II, 219,2.
2 Jacob Boon is mentioned as a master among the members of the guild of St Luke at Antwerp in 1559.-*Liggeren*, I, p.215.
3 This landscape has disappeared.-Floerke, II, note 461.
4 For the description of the palace of the Pope, see Pistolesi, *Il Vaticano descritto ed illustrato*, Rome, 1838. VIII, p.86.-Hymans, II, 220,3.
5 Under Gregorius VIII Soens painted various landscapes in the Vatican, the ones in the Sala Ducale. His chief assistants were Mattheus Bril and Cesar de Salusto (Cesare Piemontese).-Hymans, II, 220,2.
6 As to the allegory, see Pistolesi, op.cit.
7 Soens decorated the Chapel of Santa Maria to Bianca, which no longer exists.-Hymans, II, 231,1.
8 The date of Soens' death has not been determined.
  Immerzeel states that he died in 1611 at Parma.-Van der Aa, *Biographisch woordenboek*.-Hymans, II, 221,3.

HANS VAN AKEN, p.382

1 Aken, Aachen, Aaken. See W.Schmidt, in *Meyers Alg. Kuenstler Lexikon*, I, p.39. Merlo fixes the date of the birth of Van Aken at 1552. -Merlo, *Nachrichten von dem Leben und Werken Kolnischer Kuenstler*, p.1.
2 E.Jerrigh; his name is not in the *Liggeren* of the guild of St Luke at Antwerp. Hans van Aken, according to Merlo, became a pupil of Jerrigh in 1568.-Hymans, II, 224,1.
3 Jerrigh did not die in 1574, because there is, in the Wallraf Richardtz Museum at Cologne, a picture of an Annunciation signed and dated 1601. -*Catalogue*, 1875. No.445.-Hymans, II, 224,2.
4 Gaspar Rem, born in 1542, entered in the records of the guild of St Luke at Antwerp as a pupil of Willem van Cleef in the year 1554. There is a self-portrait, dated 1614, in the Belvedere, Vienna.-Hymans, II, 224,3.
5 The Nativity was perhaps the composition engraved by Gillis Sadeler in 1588.
  The picture does not exist.-Hymans, II, 226,2.
6 The portrait has been lost, and there is no engraving of it.-Hymans, II, 226,3.
7 Francesco de Medici, 1574-1587, Laura Terracina, famous for her poetical works and her beauty.-Hymans, II, 226,4,5.
8 Merlo op.cit. calls this merchant Van Vlaaten.
  The Mocking of Christ was engaged by G.Andre (Merlo-34).-Hymans, II, 227,2.

NOTES TO THE TEXT

9 The Virgin with St Catherine in 1589 (Merlo-95).
Van Mander apparently meant St Elisabeth, not St Catherine.-Hymans, II, 227,3.

10 The first visit of Van Aken to Cologne must have been in 1588, his second in 1600.-Cat. *Wallraf Richartz Museum*, 1875. p.76.
For the Judgement of Paris see Jhr.B.W.F.van Riemsdijk, *Oud Holland*, 1899. XVII, p.123.
The Judgement of Paris was painted, according to Merlo, in 1589. Greve mentions the picture in the collection Van Leeuwen at Amsterdam and a copy in the Museum at Stockholm.-Greve, 179.

11 Van Aken was in Munich in 1590. According to Sandrart, the epitaph was in the Franziskaner Kirche.-Hymans, II, 227,6,7.

12 Van Aken painted the portrait of the count, this was engraved by Lukas Kilian.-Hymans, II, 227,10.

13 The emperor was Rudolph II, 1576-1612.
Hymans believes Van Mander refers to a portrait of the great sculptor, after which Gijsbert van Veen made an engraving in 1589.-Hymans, II, 228,2.
Van Aken is mentioned in the accounts of the imperial court of 1592 as court painter, receiving a pension of two hundred florins.-Schmidt, in *Meyers Keunstler Lexikon*.

14 The St Sebastian is in the S.Michaelishofkirche in Munich.-Hymans, II, 228,4.

15 Van Aken returned to Prague in 1601. He seems to have been in Cologne in 1600. The wedding was in 1596. The name of the bride was Regina. The mother of Van Aken went to Prague where she died. -Hymans, II, 228,7,8.

16 The inventory of the imperial collection enumerates 27 pictures by Hans van Aken. There are a dozen in the Belvedere Collection, the rest were probably having been taken by the Swedes. The portrait of Rudolph II was engraved in 1603 by Gillis Sadeler.-Hymans, II, 229,1.

17 The painting is probably the engraving by C. Du Bois: Allegory of Peace mentioned by Merlo, No.122.-Hymans, II, 229,2.

18 The emperor made Van Aken a noble in 1594.-Hymans, II, 229,3.

19 Van Aken painted Rudolph II's portrait, and this was engraved by Gillis E.Sadeler in 1603.
Hans van Aken died January 6, 1615 at Prague.-Hymans, II, 229,1,4.

20 Pieter Isaacsz may have given Van Mander information about Hans van Aken.
Pieter Isaacsz was not born in 1569, if a picture of his is dated 1576. See E.Jacobson, *Repertorium*, XXIV, p.178.
In 1587 he was at Munich with Hans van Aken; in 1590 in Holland again. He had a house in Amsterdam in which he was living in 1607. In 1606 he received three hundred guilders from the city of Amsterdam for the decoration of the town piano; Carel van Mander shared the work with him. He was in Denmark from 1607 till 1610. See de Roever, *Oud Holland*, 1885. III, p.174.

21 Clara Schuyrmans, see *Iconographia Batava*, No.1074.

22 Pieter Huygesz, see *Verslag omtrent Rijks Verzamelingen van Geschiedenis en Kunst*, XXI, 1898.

23 Jacob Poppe, *Iconographia Batava*, No.6029.

NOTES TO THE TEXT

24 The Revolt of the Roman Women is in the Rijksmuseum. See E.Jacobson, *Repertorium*, XXIV, p.178.

25 The Museum at Basel has a small painting by Pieter Isaacsz representing Vanity, signed and dated 1600.-Floerke, II, note 500.

26 Jan Saenredam made an engraving after the self-portrait of Van Aken (Bartsch—105).
Van Mander apparently did not know Van Aken, or he would not have said 'from what I hear.'

27 Joseph Heintz was born at Basel in 1565 and died at Prague in 1607.

28 Pieter Stevens. Latinized Petrus Stephani, was born at Malines in 1540, died at Prague in 1604. The Sadelers made engravings after his work. Pictures by him are in the Belvedere Collection, and in the castle at Prague.-Hymans, II, 232,2.

29 Gielis Sadeler was born in 1570 at Antwerp and died at Prague in 1629. He was the son of the art dealer Gillis Sadeler, nephew and pupil of Jan Sadeler. His name is entered in the *Liggeren* of the guild of St Luke at Antwerp in 1585. He made a series of paintings reproduced by engravings. He followed his uncles Jan and Raphael to Germany and to Italy.-Hymans, II, 232,3.

30 Adriaen de Vries was born at The Hague in 1506. He was in Italy and entered the service of Carlo Emmanuele of Savoy (Bertolotti p.203). He became the successor of Hans Mont in Prague. He created the Mercury and Hercules fountain in Augsburg in 1599; the sculpture was cast in 1602.-Hymans, II, 232,4.

PIETER DE WITTE, p.390

1 Pieter de Witte was an architect.-Hymans, II, 236,1.

2 The Sala Regia, the hall that enters the Sistine Chapel, begun by Antonio da Sangallo the Younger under the rule of Paul III, was finished in 1573. There are large frescoes in it by Vasari, Salviati, and Zuccari.-Floerke, II, note 507. Van Mander met Pieter de Witte and Vasari at Florence.
Vasari worked in Florence in 1564. If de Witte was born in or about 1548, as is evident from his age which is 56, he must have worked with Vasari when he was sixteen years old. This is doubtful: Vasari's dates are 1512-1574.-Hymans, II, 236,2.
Munz found de Witte's name in the accounts, 1559-1560, of the Ducal family.-E.Muntz, *Histoiree de la Tapisserie, Ecole Italienne*, Paris, 1878-1884. p.66.-Hymans, II, 236,3.
This would make the age given by Van Mander quite doubtful.

3 De Witte went to Munich in 1576 and worked there under Duke Albrecht V, William V and Elector Maximilian I. There are many pictures by de Witte in the Munich and Schleisheim galleries.-Floerke, II, note 510.

4 There is a landscape, signed C. de Witte, in the Lichtenstein collection at Vienna attributed to Caspard de Witte from Antwerp.-Hymans, II, 236,5.

5 The engravings, after work by Pieter de Witte, are numerous and by the best masters of the period, for example the Sadelers.-Hymans, II, 237,1.

6 Pieter de Witte, or Peter Candid, died in 1628 at Munich *Cat. Alte Pinakothek*, Munich, 1898.

MATTHEUS AND PAULUS BRIL, p.391

1 Van Mander may have met the Bril brothers in Rome.-Greve, 11,166.
2 The pope was Gregory XIII, 1566-1572.
   Mattheus worked in the Sala Ducale and was assisted by Jan Soens and in the Sala di Consistorio; the ceiling is the work of Perino del Vaga. -Hymans, II, 241,2.
   The epitaph published by Bertolotti shows Mattheus died at the age of thirty-six.-Hymans, II, 241,3.
3 Damiaen Ortelmans became free master of the guild of Antwerp in 1545. He is enrolled as painter on canvas, which refers to tempera work. Paul Bril was not registered.-Hymans, II, 241,4.
4 The Bril family came possibly from Breda.-Van Gooi, *Beschrijving van Breda*, p.306.-Bertolotti, *Artisti Belgi ed Olandesi a Roma*, Florence, 1880. p.379.
5 The fresco of St Clement is in the Sala Clementina named after Pope Clement VIII, 1592-1605.-Hymans, II, 242,1.
6 Girolamo Mattei died in 1603.-Hymans, II, 242,2.
7 A picture in the Museum at Bordeaux is the same as the one described in the possession of Van Os.-Greve, 195.
8 Paul Bril died at Rome on October 7, 1626, at the age of seventy-two. -Hymans, II, 242,3.
9 Willem van Nieuwelandt, born in 1584 at Antwerp, son of the painter Adriaen van Nieuwelandt, was a pupil of Jacob Savery at Amsterdam in 1599. In 1602 he went to Rome to Paul Bril, and returned to Amsterdam in 1629 where he died at the end of 1635.-Van den Branden, 636.

CORNELIS CORNELISZ, p.393

1 The siege of Haarlem lasted from December 11, 1572 till July 13, 1573.
   The father of Cornelis Cornelisz. was named Cornelis Thomasz. Pieter Schilder, the son of Pieter Aertsen, also Pieter Pietersz., was born in Amsterdam in 1541 and died there in 1603.-Hymans, II, 251,2,3.
2 Frans Pourbus referred to by Van Mander, was Frans Pourbus the Elder.
3 The merchants had a special way of grasping each other's hand during the bidding of a sale.
   This Corporaelschap is in the Museum at Haarlem and it is dated 1583. *Cat. Haarlem Museum*, 1897, No.38.
   There is a second painting in the same collection, dated 1599, No.41.
4 The Carita painting was bought by the Museum at Valencia in 1855. -Hymans, II, 252,2.
5 The Avarice and Extravagance painting cannot be found.-Hymans, II, 252,3.
6 A Deluge, by Cornelis Cornelisz, is in the museum at Braunschweig, dated 1592. This is probably a small replica of the painting mentioned by Van Mander.-Hymans, II, 253,1.
7 The Biting of the Serpents is in the Museum at Darmstadt; it is signed C.Haerlemesis, 1597.-Hymans, II, 253,2.
   The Fall of Lucifer cannot be found.-Hymans, II, 253,3.
8 A Golden Age in the Museum at Braunschweig, No.166, is dated 1615, cannot be the picture mentioned by Van Mander, who died in 1606. -Hymans, II, 253,4.

NOTES TO THE TEXT

9 The Deluge and Fall of the Angels mentioned here may be the pictures in the Museum in Darmstadt.

10 A picture of Adam and Eve, in the Hamburger Kunsthalle, has the signature of Cornelis Cornelisz and is dated 1622.-Hymans, II, 253,6. The same subject is in the Museum at Karlsruhe. This master made many replicas.
The Purification of the Children of Israel in the Jordan is probably the painting mentioned in the catalogue of Hoet and Terwesten, sold at Amsterdam in 1767. Sale Capello.-Hymans, II, 353.

11 The Massacre of the Innocents is at The Hague, Mauritshuis, dated 1591; another painting of the same subject in the Rijksmuseum at Amsterdam, signed C.CORNELI II. FECIT. AO 1590.

12 The large painting of Adam and Eve is in the Rijksmuseum at Amsterdam, dated 1593.

13 The Banquet of the Gods is in the Mauritshuis at The Hague. It was painted in 1593 for the Princenhof at Haarlem.

14 Jan Matthijsen Ban was a friend of Goltzius and of Van Mander. The painting of the Resurrection of Lazarus has been lost.-Hymans, II, 254,5.

15 There is a Wedding of Thetis at Hermannstadt. Catalogue, 1901, No. 192.-Greve, 207.

16 There is, in the Rijksmuseum at Amsterdam, a portrait of Dirk Volckertsz Coornhert, poet, engraver, and scientist, who died on October 29, 1590. There is a replica of this picture in the Museum at Augsburg, and a copy of it in the Museum at Dresden.

17 Cornelis Cornelisz died November II, 1638, at Haarlem.

18 Jan Pietersz Sweling, a famous composer, and organist of the St Nicolaeskerk at Amsterdam. He was born at Deventer in 1561 and died at Amsterdam on October 16, 1621. His portrait, painted most probably by his brother, is in the Museum at Darmstadt.-Hymans, II, 256,2.
Gerrit Pietersz is not mentioned in the Liggeren of the guild of St Luke at Antwerp. De Busscher, in his Recherches sur les Peintres a Gand, speaks in detail about a Gerard Pietersz who became a member of the guild of Ghent in 1590, and who is not mentioned after 1600. This painter had come from Bruges and his presence in Ghent has been established.-Hymans, II, 256,6.

19 Nothing is known about Jacob Lenartz.-Floerke, I, note 551.

20 See Conclusion by Van Mander.

GOVERT, p.398
21 Govert, Govert Jansz. Two landscapes by this master appeared in the inventory of Rembrandt and were indicated as landscapes with figures. -Hymans, II, 257,3.
Abraham Govaerts from Antwerp was a different artist.

LASMAN, p.398
22 Pieter Pietersz Lasman, was born at Amsterdam in 1583, where he was buried on April 4, 1633. In 1602 he was a pupil of Gerrit Pietersz; he studied in Rome under Elsheimer and Caravaggio and worked later in Amsterdam, where he became the teacher of Rembrandt. Cat. Rijksmuseum, 1898. p.33.

NOTES TO THE TEXT

JAN VAN DELFT, p.398

23 Nothing further is known about Jan van Delft. In the Catalogues mentioned by Hoet, there are various pictures by a certain Lange Jan, who painted scenes of the Old and New Testaments, pictures of saints, mythological subjects, etc. They were by Jan van Bockhorst, born at Muenster 1605; died there on April 21, 1668.-Hymans, II, 258,1.

CORNELIS JACOBSZ., p.398

24 Cornelis Jacobsz Delff, a still-life painter, brother of the engraver Willem Jacobsz Delff, born at Delft in 1571 and buried there.-Hymans, II, 258,2.

CORNELIS ENGHELSZEN, p.399

25 Cornelis Enghelszen Verspronck, pupil of Van Mander. He became a member of the guild of Haarlem in 1593; died after 1637.-Hymans, II, 258,3.

GERRIT NOP, p.399

26 Gerrit Nop left no important works. Van der Willigen found his name among the control registers of the Haarlem Civic Guard of 1609. -Hymans, II, 258,4.

ZACHARIAS, p.399

27 Zacharia Paulusz painted, according to Houbraken (*Schouburgh, Ed. Wurzbach*, p.186), in 1620, The Directors of the old Schutters; in 1627 and in 1628, he made a group of six officers of the Schutters at Alkmaar; in 1643 and in 1644 he accepted various pupils, Adriaen Jansz Dekker, Dirck Barentsz, JJ Regtop and Pieter Jansz. *Obreen's Archief*, II, 36. His picture can be seen in the Museum at Alkmaar.-Hymans, II, 258,5.

JAQUES DE GHEYN, p.400

1 Jacob Jansz van de Gheyn was enrolled as free master of the guild of St Luke at Antwerp in 1558. He was registered as a glass-painter; in 1570 accepted a pupil.-Hymans, II, 262,1. Van Mander knew de Gheyn in Haarlem and the latter informed him about his father.-Greve, 147.

2 The two churches mentioned were destroyed during the French occupation.-Hymans, II, 262,2.

3 De Gheyn worked under Goltzius from 1585 till 1587, the time Goltzius adopted his new style. The engravings by de Gheyn follow after 1586. There is none in the year 1585.-Hymans, II, 264,2.
Jaques de Gheyn was in Antwerp in 1591, called there by the Jesuits. -Hymans, II, 264,3.-Pinchart, *Archives*, III, 320.

4 De Gheyn married Eva Stalpart van de Wiele.-Hymans, II, 264,4. -Kramm, p.1559.

5 The painting bought by Rudolph II was in the Collection Hoogendijk, The Hague, No.227.-Greve, 227.
The paintings, mentioned under his name in the Catalogues of Hoet Terwesten, are flower pictures only. In 1577, at the Nieuhoff Auction at Amsterdam, a similar work was sold for twenty guilders.-Hymans, II, 265,1.

504

NOTES TO THE TEXT

There is no painting by De Gheyn in the Belvedere at Vienna.-Hymans, II, 265,2.

6 The Archduke was Albert I. The horse was a white Spanish colt, caught by Prince Ludwig Guenther van Nassau in the Battle of Nieuwpoort. See *Nederlandsche Kunstbode*, 1880. p.239. The painting is in the Rijksmuseum and is signed DE GHEYN FE. 1603. There is another picture of a horse painted by de Gheyn in the museum. -Hymans, II, 266,1.

7 The skull painting, probably a traditional Momento Mori subject, has not been identified.-Hymans, II, 266,2.

8 The Sleeping Venus painting has not been found.-Hymans, II, 266,3.

9 Jaques de Gheyn was buried on April 2, 1629, in the Groote Kerck at The Hague. *Nederlandsche Kunstbode*, 1881. p.421.

10 Jan Saenredam, born at Zaandam in 1565, died at Assendelft in 1607. He was a pupil of Hendrick Goltzius. Zacharias Dolendo was born at Haarlem in 1561. His engravings show the influence of Goltzius. -Hymans, II, 266,5,6.

11 Robert, Robert de Baudouz, born in 1575 at Brussels, Burgher of Amsterdam in 1598, was alive in 1648.-Hymans, II, 267,1. *Obreen's Archief*, II, p.5; III, p.221; V, p.40.
Cornelis was probably Cornelis Drebbel, born at Alkmaar in 1572, who died at London in 1634. He made engravings after Van Mander and Goltzius.-Hymans, II, 267,2.

OCTAVIO VAN VEEN, p.404

1 Octavio van Veen was born in 1558. (*Cat. Rijksmuseum*, Amsterdam, 1898). His father, Cornelis van Veen, was Raadspensionaris and Burgomaster of Leyden, 1561 to 1565, 1581 to 1591.-Hymans, II, 271,2.

2 Van Veen painted Alexander Farnese of Parma more than once. His brother Gijsbert van Veen made an engraving after one of these portraits.-Hymans, II, 271,4.
Van Veen was painter to Archduke Ernst, Governor of the Netherlands, for whom he made many portraits (1595).-Hymans, II, 271,5.
The monarchs Van Mander refers to were Philip III, of Spain, and Henry IV, of France.

3 There is a picture of the Infanta Isabella at Hampton Court. Pinchart published a bill of 700 pounds payable to Gijsbert van Veen for painting a portrait of the Archduke and Archduchess, sent to the king of England.-Pinchart, *Archives des Arts*, I, p.284.-Hymans, II, 273,9.

4 The Triumph of Bacchus by Van Veen has not been found. The picture of Zeus has not been found.-Hymans, II, 274,3.
Octavio van Veen died on May 6, 1629, at Brussels.-*Cat. Rijksmuseum*.

5 Pieter van Veen was born at Leyden in 1562 and he died at The Hague in 1629.-Hymans, II, 274,4.

6 Gijsbert was born in Leyden c.1558, and died at Antwerp in 1628. He was a painter and an engraver.

HANS SNELLINCK, p.405

1 Hans Snellinck was born at Malines in 1549 and died at Antwerp on October 1, 1638. He painted many pictures in tempera.-Van den Branden, 431.

TOBIAS VERHAEGHT, p.405

2 Tobias van Haecht was born in 1561 at Antwerp and was registered in the guild in 1590 as son of a master. He died at Amsterdam in 1631. He was the first teacher of Rubens.-Van den Branden, Op.cit., 383.

ADAM VAN OORT, p.405

3 Adam van Noort, the second teacher of Rubens, was born in 1562, second son of the painter Lambrecht van Noort at Antwerp. He entered the guild in 1587 and died soon after, September, 1641.-Van den Branden, 389.

HEYNDRICK VAN BALEN, p.405

4 Heyndrick van Balen was born at Antwerp in 1575 and died there on July 17, 1632. He became a member of the guild of St Luke in 1593.-Van den Branden, 463.

SEBASTIAEN VRANCKS, p.405

5 Sebastiaen Vrancks was born at Antwerp in 1573 and became free master of the guild of St Luke in 1600. He died at Antwerp on May 19, 1647. -Van den Branden, 470.

JOOS DE MOMPER, p.405

6 Joos de Momper was born in 1564 at Antwerp. His father was Bartholomeus de Momper. He died in the same city in 1635.-Van den Branden, 309.

FRANCISCUS SAVIUS, p.406

1 This can refer to only François Sayve, le Sayve, Saive, le Save, who became a free master in the guild of St Luke at Antwerp in 1599.-Hymans, II, 290,4.

MARTINUS FREMINET, p.406

2 Martin Freminet, born at Paris on September 23, 1567; died on June 18, 1618 in the same city.-Hymans, II, 300,1. The King was Henri IV.

DU BREUL, p.406

3 Toussaint du Breuil, born c.1560, died on November 22, 1602.-Hymans, II, 300,3 and 4.

BUNEL AND HIS WIFE, p.406

4 Jacques Bunel, born c.1558 at Tours, died in October 1614 at Paris. He worked in the Louvre and at other places.-Hymans, 303,2.
The wife of Bunel was Marguerite Bahuche. She was born at Tours. She painted portraits. She died some time before October 9, 1632.-Hymans, II, 303,3.

BOLLERY, p.407

1 Nicolas Bollery, born c.1565 at Paris, died there in October 1630, was a son of the painter Jerome Bollery; according to Felibien he worked in the Louvre.-Hymans, II, 300,6.

NOTES TO THE TEXT

FRANCOYS STELLAERT, p.407
2 Francoys Stellaert is evidently Frans Stella. Felibien says he came from Malines and he died at the age of twenty-four at Lyon in 1605.-Hymans, II, 301,1.

CASPAR HUEVICK, p.407
3 The dates of birth and death of Caspar Huevick are not known. There is, in the town hall of Oudenarde, a large painting of the Last Judgement, which probably came from the Walburg church, and an allegory, dated on the frame, 1582.-Hymans, II, 304,5.

HERDER FROM GRONINGEN, p.407
4 Francesco Verdugo was governor, for Philip II, of Friesland, Gelderland, and Groningen.-Hymans, II, 305,1.
According to Immerzeel Herder died in his native town in 1609. Nothing more is known about him.-Immerzeel, II, 34.

HANS ROTTENHAMER, p.409
1 The father of Hans was Thomas Rottenhamer a court painter and evidently his first teacher.-Hymans, II, 306,1.
Hans Donauer, court painter under Wilhelm V, is the artist who made the decoration for the aquarium at Munich.-Hymans, II, 306,2. Hautle, *Die kgl. Residenz in Muenchen*, p.22. Rottenhamer came to him in 1582 and remained his pupil for six years, then he went to Italy.-Hymans, II, 307. Rottenhamer was a pupil of Tintoretto at Venice. Many pictures by Rottenhamer are in Venice.-Hymans, II, 306,4. The Assumption of the Virgin cannot be found.-Floerke, II, note 611. The Acteon and Diana Rottenhamer painted frequently. There are copies in Munich and Schleissheim.-Floerke, II, note 612. Rottenhamer died in 1623 at Augsburg.

ADAM FROM FRANKFORT, p.410
1 Adam from Frankfort, Adam Elsheimer, was baptized on March 28, 1578 at Frankfort. He was a pupil of Philip Uffenbach in the same city. *Catalogue Dresden*, 1899. Adam from Frankfort died at Rome c.1620. -Hymans, II, 308,2.

DIERICK DE VRIES AND LODEWYCK TOEPUT, p.410
2 Van Mander probably was informed about de Vries and Toeput by Goltzius.-Greve, 148.
Toeput's name in Italian was Pozzoserrato.

JOACHIM WTENWAEL, p.411
1 Joachim Wtenwael, Uitenwael, Utenwael, Wttewael. See, C.M.A.A. Lindeman, *Joachim Wtewael*, Utrecht, 1929. Van Mander was informed about Wtenwael and his father Van Schuyck by Wtenwael himself. Van Mander knew Lucas Wtenwael, a brother of the painter at Amsterdam. Justi found in the Chapel of the Conception at Osuna in Andalusia, an Annunciation of the XVI Century with the signature: GERALD WITVEL DEUTRECHT.-C.M.Justi, *Pr.Jb.*, 1884. V, p.160.
According to Muller, Wtenwael's father was named Antonis.-J.Muller,

NOTES TO THE TEXT

Utrechtsche Archieven, 1880. p.14. Joachim van Schuyck has been registered in the records of the guild of the saddle makers, with which the painters were affiliated, in 1569.-J.Muller, op.cit., p.60.-Hymans, II, 314,3.
Van Mander refers to Charles de Bourgneuf, Bishop of St Malo, 1587 to 1596.-Hymans, II, 314,5.
Joachim was accepted as master in the guild of the saddle makers in 1592 and in 1611 became a member of the newly founded guild of the painters. -Muller, op.cit., p.14,126,19.
In the Museum Kunstliefde at Utrecht there is a self-portrait of Wtenwael dated 1601, and a portrait of his wife, as a woman selling fruit.-*Cat.*, 1885. No.88.-Hymans, II, 315,1.
In the Museum at Berlin there is a picture of Lot and his daughters. The large picture, mentioned by Van Mander, has not been found.-Hymans, II, 315,2.
Wtenwael's cousin was probably Lucas Dammertsz (Wtenwael) whose name appears among those of the painters in the guild of the saddlers in 1569.-Muller, op.cit., p.69. There is an Annunciation to the Shepherds, dated 1607, in the Belvedere at Vienna.-Hymans, II, 315,4.
A Banquet of the Gods, dated 1602, (on copper 31 x 42 cm.) is in the Museum at Braunschweig.-*Cat.* 1898. No.174. There is in the Alte Pinakothek at Munich a Wedding of Peleus and Thetis (on copper 16 x 21 cm.). *Cat.* 1898. No.304.
There is a Mars and Venus by Wtenwael at The Hague, at the Mauritshuis; it is on copper (21 x 16 cm.) which may be the one described by Van Mander.-Hymans, II, 316,3.
Jan van Weely was a jeweler and amateur painter at Amsterdam. Jan van Weely is mentioned in the biography of Ketel also.-Hymans, II, 316, 2. Wtenwael died at Utrecht on August 13, 1638.

ABRAHAM BLOEMAERT, p.413

1 The introduction to this biography, in the original Dutch, is an intricate anagram on the name Bloemaert. Bloemaert was born December 1564 at Utrecht and died there on January 27, 1651.-Kramm, 101.
2 See about Cornelis Bloemaert, P.Scheltema, in *Obreen's Archief*, 1879. II, p.274.
Cornelis Bloemaert became a master of the guild of the Saddle Makers in 1576 and he was a dean in 1594.-Muller, *De Schilders Vereenigingen te Utrecht*, 1880. p.14,58.
3 Gerrit Splinter is mentioned in the list of the members of the guild of the saddle makers as a painter, not as a 'cleerschriver ofte bastertschilder' (letterer) a category mentioned in addition to the regular painters. -Muller, op.cit., p.60.
4 The Modern Banquet was most likely the picture that appeared at an auction sale at Amsterdam in 1708. It was engraved by Jan Sadeler; a man is playing on a guitar, not on a harp.-De Vries, in Taurel, *l'Art chretien*, II, p.175.-Hymans, II, 320,4.
Van Heel was not registered in the guild.-Hymans, II, 320,7.
Bloemaert was at Amsterdam approximately from 1588 till 1594. See *Obreen's Archief*, II, p.274.-Greve, 140.
5 Nothing is known about Bassot and Maistre Herry.

NOTES TO THE TEXT

6 Jeronimus Francken lived in Paris from 1566 until his death in 1610.-Van den Branden, 340.

7 The Banquet of the Gods owned by Van der Lip went to the National Museum at Stockholm.-Greve, 108.

8 The Venus Juno and Pallas painting was engraved by Boetius.-Hymans, II, 323,6.

9 'That may have been so at the time that Van Mander wrote. Bloemaert produced a number of portraits; some of them are in the Louvre and in the Museum at Stockholm.'-Hymans, II, 324,2.

PIETER CORNELISZ VAN RIJCK, p.418

1 Jacob Willemsz from Delft, died on May 5, 1601.-Hymans, II, 329,1.
Hubert Jacobsz from Delft was in Venice for a long time. He received the additional name, Grimani, according to Van Bleyswijck. He died in 1628, or 1629, at Briele.-Van Bleyswijck, *Beschrijvinge van Delft*, p.846. -Hymans, II, 329,2.

FRANCESCO BADENS, p.419

1 Francesco's father was Josse Badens, accepted in the guild of St Luke at Antwerp as son of a master in 1569.
He had a brother and an uncle, Josse and François who were pupils of Jan de Hollander.-Hymans, II, 331,2.

2 There is a painting in Stockholm entitled Merry Company, the only known work by Badens.
Egbert van Panderen made an engraving after a painting by Badens, S Jerome.
Bacchus, Venus and Ceres were reproduced by B.Lens.
Goltzius made a number of engravings after Badens.-Hymans, II, 332,1.

3 See about the Lovers in Bode, *Studien*, p.165.

4 This last paragraph is significant as to the method followed by Van Mander.-Greve, 137.

JAN BADENS, p.420

1 The information about Jan Badens came undoubtedly from Francesco. -Greve, 137.

DAVID VINCKEBOONS, p.421

1 The name of Philip Vinckeboons appears in the records of the guild of St Luke at Antwerp in 1580. He is listed there on September 30, 1586; on March 8, 1591, he became a burgher at Amsterdam.-Hymans, II, 334,2.

2 The Carrying of the Cross is probably the one in the Museum at Augsburg. A similar painting is in the Pinakothek at Munich. Since this picture is dated 1611, it cannot be the painting in question.-Hymans, II, 335, 1.

3 Christ healing the Blind was engraved by J.v.Londerseel. The painting is not known.-Hymans, II, 335,6.
A Peasant Wedding is in the Museum at Braunschweig, No.652. -Hymans, II, 335,4.
There is a John the Baptist Preaching in the Museum at Schleissheim, dated 1621. No.964.-Floerke, II, note 675.

NOTES TO THE TEXT

4 The Lottery is in the same place. See N.de Roever, *Oud Holland*, III, 193, note 1.
5 There are two authentic etchings by Vinckeboons: a woman begging, with two children, dated 1604, and The Emptied Nest, with the inscription, DIE DEN NEST WEET DIE WETHEN, MAER DIE HEM ROOFT DIE HEEFTEN. -Hymans, II, 336,2.
6 David Vinckeboons died in 1629 at Amsterdam.

CORNELIS FLORIS, p.424

1 Cornelis Floris, son of Cornelis and nephew of Frans Floris was born at Antwerp in 1551. He was a pupil of Jeroon Francken in Paris. He was a free master of the guild at Antwerp in 1577 and died on May 12, 1615 in the same city.-P.Genard, *Journal des Beaux Arts*, 1869. p.36.-*Liggeren*, I, p.264.

PAUWELS MOREELS, p.424

2 Pauwels Moreels was a painter and architect, born at Utrecht in 1571, where he died a few days before March 19, 1638. He was in Italy before 1604. He enrolled in the guild of the saddle makers at Utrecht, and during the years 1611, 1612, 1615, and 1619, was dean of the newly founded guild of St Luke. He painted genre pictures and some historical subjects. There is a self-portrait by him in the Mauritshuis at The Hague. *Cat. Mauritshuis*, 1895. p.253.

FRANS PIETERSZ GROBBER, p.425

3 Frans Pietersz Grobber was born at Haarlem in 1570; died there in March 1649. He was dean of the guild of St Luke. Four banquet scenes of officers of the Town Guard done in 1600, 1610, 1619, are in the Museum at Haarlem.-Hymans, II, 342,2.

CORNELIS CLAESZ., p.425

4 Cornelis Claesz van Wieringen was born at Haarlem. He died in the same city October, 1643.-Hymans, II, 343,1.-Van der Willigen, *Les Artistes de Haarlem*, p.11.

BERNAERT AND PAUL VAN SOMER, p.425

5 Barent van Somer was registered in the *Liggeren* of the guild of St Luke at Antwerp in 1588 as a pupil of Philip Lisart.-Hymans, II, 343,3.
6 Pauwels van Somer was born in 1576 and according to Vertue (Walpole, *Anecdotes of Painting in England*, Ed.Dalaway, London, 1828, II, p.6.) he died at London on January 5, 1621. There are some pictures by him at Hampton Court.-Hymans, II, 343,4.

CORNELIS VAN DER VOORT, p.425

7 Cornelis van der Voort was born in 1576 at Antwerp and was buried at Amsterdam on November 2, 1624. In the Rijksmuseum at Amsterdam there are a number of Burgherweer, and Regenten pieces, and some portraits, by him.-*Cat. Rijksmuseum*, 1898.

EVERT KRIJNSZ., p.426

8 Evert Krijnsz van der Maes was a pupil of Van Mander. He is listed in

NOTES TO THE TEXT

the guild of St Luke at The Hague in 1604.-Hymans, II, 344,2.-*Obreen's Archief*, III, p.260.

RAVESTEYN, p.426
9 Jan Anthonisz van Ravesteyn was born c.1572. He is entered in the guild of St Luke at The Hague on February 17, 1598 and in the year 1656 assisted in the founding of a new painters' society at The Hague. Twenty-five portraits by him are in the Mauritshuys at The Hague.-*Cat. Mauritshuis*, 1895.

AERT JANSZ DRUYVESTEYN, p.426
10 Arnold Jansz Druyvesteyn was born at Haarlem in 1567 and died there on August 5, 1617.-Hymans, II, 346,2.

JAQUES DE MOSSCHER, p.426
11 Jacob Fransz de Mosser was a pupil of Van Mander. He entered the guild at Haarlem in 1593 and in 1613-1624 was a dean of the guild of St Luke at Delft. He worked at Haarlem between 1640-1650, assisted by Adriaen van Ostade.

THONIS ARIAENSZ, p.426
12 There is nothing definite known about Thonis Ariaensz.

NICOLAES VAN DER HECK, p.426
13 A certain Claes Dirksz van der Heck became a member of the guild of St Luke at Alkmaar. Houbraken mentions various paintings by him. -Houbraken, ed, *Wurzbach*, p.163.

PIETER GEERITSZ MONTFOORT, p.427
14 Pieter Geeritsz Montfoort has been mentioned in the biography of Van Miereveldt.

PIETER DIRCKSEN CLUYT, p.427
15 Pieter Dircksen Cluyt was the son of the famous naturalist Theodorus Augerius Clutius. No picture by him is known.-Hymans, II, 349,2.

JAN ARIAENSZ FROM LEYDEN, p.427
16 Vosmaer presents Ariaensz as a landscape painter.-Vosmaer, *Rembrandt, sa vie et ses oeuvres*, La Haye, 1877. p.28.

HUBERT TONS, p.428
17 Hubert Tons is registered in the guild of St Luke at Antwerp in 1596.

ALBRECHT DURER, p.430
1 This story and its original version are fiction.-Thausing, II, 169.

MORO, p.430
2 Van Mander means the Spanish Fury.

NOTES TO THE TEXT

MIEREVELDT, p.431

3 The portrait of Schilperoort was in the inventory of Miereveldt.-Havard, *L'Art et les Artistes hollandais*, I, p.52.

GEERIT PIETERSZ, p.432

4 See about the painting of the Corporaelschap which Geerit Pietersz made for the S.Sebastiaens Doelen, *Oud Holland*, XV, p.135.

OCTAVIO VAN VEEN, p.433

5 Isaack Claesz from Leyden was Isaac Claesz. Swanenburgh; died in 1614; was the father of Willem Swanenburgh the teacher of Rembrandt.

A series of sixteen paintings representing the Life and Passion of Christ, and a series of six compositions of the Triumph of the Church, by Octavio van Veen, are in the Museum at Schleissheim.-Hymans, II, 272,4.

APPENDIX A

ARTISTS AND THEIR WORK
*Indicates work seen by Van Mander

Aachen, *See* Aken.

Adam van Frankfort,*See* Elsheimer.

Aelst, Pauwels van, flower pictures; copies of work by Gossart (Mabuse).

Aelst, Pieter van, *See* Koeck.

Aert Claessen, *See* Aertgen van Leyden.

Aertgen van Leyden, *Crucifixion, Christ on the Cross between the Thieves; Mary, Mary Magdalen, Disciples; *Christ carrying the Cross,Mary,Disciples; *Abraham and Isaac, J.Gerritsz Buijtenwegh, Leyden; *Nativity, Widow Joan van Wassenaer, Leyden; *Mary and Choir of Angels, Johan Knotter; *portrait, Family of Dirck Jacobsz van Montfoort; Last Judgement, Jan Diericksz Montfoort; *The Passage of the Red Sea, Goltzius, Haarlem; *Solomon's Judgement, Delft.

Aertsen, Pieter, kitchen scenes; *kitchen scene, Rauwert; Death of the Virgin, Adoration of the Magi, altar, Oude Kerk, Amsterdam; Nativity, Annunciation, Circumcision, Beheading of St Catherine, altar, Nieuwe Kerk, Amsterdam; *cartoon of the same, Amsterdam; Crucifixion, Nativity, Four Evangelists, Carthusian Monastery, Delft; Adoration, Ecce Homo, altar, Nieuwe Kerk, Delft; Altar paintings, Louvain, Diest and elsewhere; *Martha, Walraven, Amsterdam; *Emmaus, Meester Claes, Hof van Holland; *Joseph, Jan Pieterz. Reael; *Fair, Bakenisse Gracht; Crucifixion, Warmenhuizen.

Aertsz, Rijckaert,(Met der Stelt), *Joseph's Brothers in Egypt asking for Wheat, Jacob van Haarlem, Haarlem.

Aken, Hans van, copies after Venetian paintings;self-portrait;Nativity; self-portrait; self-portrait, with Donna Venusta; portrait of Franciscus Maria de Medici, Duke of Florence; portrait of Madonna Laura (Terracina); *copy of Madonna Laura, Pieter Isaacsz., Amsterdam; Mocking of Christ; Danaë; Madonna and St Catherine; Venus and Cupid; Judgement of Paris; Discovery of the Cross by St Helena; portrait, William V, Duke of Bavaria, with wife and children; portrait, Jean de Bologne; Venus and Adonis, Rudolph II; St Sebastian, Munich, St Michaelis Hofkirche; portrait, The Fuggers, Augsburg; *Peace, Van Os, Amsterdam; self-portrait, Pieter Isaacs, Amsterdam; Resurrection, Prague; drawings; portrait of a Duchess; a cat; *drawings after Sprangher.

Aken, Jeronimus Bos, *See* Bosch.

Alart Claessen (teacher of Pieter Aertsen), portraits, Doelen, Amsterdam.

Aldegraef (Aldegrever), Nativity, Soest Westphalia; wings to altar painting (probably Paumgartner altar), Nürenberg; *portraits of Princes and learned men. engr. (Bartsch 182-190); *self-portrait. engr. (Bartsch 188 or 189) 1537; *portrait Jan van Leyden. engr. (Bartsch 182); *portrait Knipperdolling. engr. (Bartsch 183); *Susan and the Elders. engr. (Bartsch 30-33) 1555; *Nude Women. engr. (Bartsch 103-106, 117-136, 131-137); *Works of Hercules. engr. (Bartsch 83-95,

513

96, 97) 1550; *Twelve large Dancers. engr. (Bartsch 160-171) 1538; *eight small Dancers. engr. (Bartsch 144-151, and Bartsch 152-159) 1538 and 1551.

Alkmaer, Zacharias (Paulus) van.

Amersfoort, Evert van.

Amstel, Jan van, *See* Hollander.

Amsterdam, Simon van, *See* Simon.

Antonello of Messina.

Ariaensz, Jan, landscape; architectural subjects.

Ariaensz, Thonis.

Ariaensz, Pieter, *See* Aertsen.

Augustijn Jorisz, *See* Jorisz.

Augustijn, Jan, figure compositions.

B

Backer, Jaques de, *Adam and Eve, *Charitas, *Crucifixion, Wyntgis Middelburg; *Venus, Juno and Pallas, Sr Oppenbergh.

Badens, Francesco, *lovers, Cornelis van der Voort, Amsterdam; *Bathsheba, Badens; *portraits, Masquerades, Banquets.

Badens, Jan.

Bahuche, Marguerete, wife of Bunel.

Balen, Heyndrick van, figure compositions.

Balten, Pieter Balthasar, John the Baptist, Emperor, Vienna; fairs.

Bamesbier, Hans, portraits.

Bard, Oliver.

Barent de Doove, *See* Bernard de Doove.

Barentsen, Dirck, *Fall of Lucifer, *Judith, *Portrait, Dirck.

Barentsen and his Wife, *Venus, Sybrandt Buyck, Amsterdam; *Nativity, Gouda; *Crucifixion, Razet, Amsterdam; *portrait, Guild of the Archers, Voetboogs-Doelen, Amsterdam; *portraits, Isbrandt Willemsz, Amsterdam; *portrait, Banquet of the Archers, Kloveniers Doelen, Amsterdam; *portrait, Group of Skippers, St Sebastiaens Doelen, Amsterdam; *portrait of Titian,

Pieter Isaacs, Amsterdam; *Last Judgement and Seven Works of Mercy, Hospital, Amsterdam; *Perseus, Rauwert, Amsterdam; *modern banquet, Cornelis van der Voort, Amsterdam.

Bassano, Jacopo.

Bassot, Jean.

Baudoux, Robert.

Beer, Aert de, cartoons for glass painters.

Beer, Joos de.

Beerings, Gregorius, Deluge.

Beham, Hans Sebald, *See* Bheem.

Bellini, Gentili.

Bernard de Doove, Riot at Amsterdam, 1535, City Hall, Amsterdam.

Beuckelaer, Joachim, *See* Buecklaer.

Bheem, Sibaldus (Suavius).

Bles, Herri met de, Owl (signature), *three landscapes, *Lot, Wyntgis Middelburg; *Mercer and Monkeys, Marten Papenbroeck, Amsterdam; *Emmaus, Passion of Christ, Ecce Homo, Calvary, Crucifixion and Resurrection, Moucheron, Amsterdam.

Blocklandt, Anthonis, *portraits of his Father and Mother, Assuerus, Lord of Blocklandt, Amsterdam; nudes; altar paintings, Delft; Beheading of St James, Gouda; Assumption of Mary, Nativity and Annunciation, Honthorst, Utrecht; Passion of Christ, Crucifixion, Doelen, Dordrecht; *Bathsheba, Pieter Huyghensen, Leyden; St Catherine, 'sHertogenbosch; Pentecost, Ascension of Christ, Apostles, Utrecht; St Francis, Amsterdam; Venus, widow of artist; Life of Joseph, Wolfert Byler, Amsterdam; Dead Christ; various paintings, Joos de Beer.

Blocklandt, Hendrick Assuerus, portraits.

Bloemaert, Abraham, copies after Uthoeck, Barentsen, Pieter Aertsen; *Niobe, Simon Luz, Amsterdam; *Niobe, Banquet of the Gods, Vienna; *Venus, Juno, Pallas, Razet, Amsterdam; Banquet of the Gods, Count van der Lip; *Skull; *Sea Gods, Andromeda, Razet, Amsterdam; *landscapes; drawings, paintings in black and white.

Bloemaert, Cornelis.

Blondeel, Lansloot, nocturnal fires; antique Ruins.

Boba, George.

Bocksberger, Jan.

Boels, Frans, landscapes (miniature).

Bol, Hans, *Dedalus and Icarus, Jan van Mander, Ghent; Crucifixion, Razet, Amsterdam; *landscapes; illuminations; *views at Amsterdam; Razet, Amsterdam; *views of villages; drawings for various engravers.

Bollery, Nicolaes, nocturnal scenes; masquerades; mardigras; animals.

Bologne, Jean de.

Bom, Pieter, water colors.

Bomberghe, Daniel.

Bos, Cornelis, *Francis I taken prisoner by Charles V.

Bosch, Jeronimus (van Aken), *Flight from Egypt, *Hell, *Carrying of the Cross, Amsterdam; *Saints, Joan Dethring, Haarlem; *Monk disputing with Heretics, Miracle, paintings, 'sHertogenbosch and Spain.

Bosch, Lodewijck Jans van den, *still life, flowers in a glass of water, Razet, Amsterdam; still life, flowers, insects, beetles, *St Jerome, fire scenes, Wyntgis Middelburg.

Bouts, Dirck, *head of Christ, heads of Peter and Paul, J.G.Buytenwegh, Leyden.

Breughel, Jan, landscape.

Breughel, Pieter I, Tower of Babel, Tower of Babel, Carrying of the Cross, Carrying of the Cross, *Massacre of the Innocents, Conversion of St Paul, Temptation of Christ, Dulle Griet, Emperor,

Vienna; *Peasant Wedding, Pilgrims, Amsterdam; Fight between Lent and Carnival; Remedies against Death; children plays; *Peasant Wedding, Willem Jacobsz, Amsterdam; Digging of the Canal, Brussels-Antwerp; Magpie on a gallows; Triumph of Truth; *Sinnekens (published by J.Cock).

Breughel, Pieter II (Helsche-Breughel), portraits.

Breul, Matheus du, nudes.

Bril, Matheus, landscapes.

Bril, Paulus, St Clement tied to Anchor, landscape, Six Monasteries, Landscapes, Vatican; Landscapes for Cardinal Matthei; Castles of Asdrubale Mathei; *Campo Vaccina, Van Os, Amsterdam; *landscapes (prints).

Broecke, Chrispiaen van den, nudes.

Brueghel, See Breughel.

Brugge, Rogier van, See Weyden, Rogier van der, decorative hangings on canvas.

Brussel, Barent van (Bernardt van Orley) See Orley.

Brussels, Loys van, See Loys.

Bruyn, Nicolas de, *engravings after Vinckeboons.

Bueckelaer, Joachim, kitchen scenes, Mintmaster, Antwerp; Palm Sunday, Onse Vrouwenkerck, Antwerp; *fish market, *fruit market, Simon Luz, Amsterdam; *kitchen scene, *Palm Sunday, Wyntgis, Middelburg; *Market with Ecce Homo, Rauwert, Amsterdam; *Evangelists, Verlaen, Haarlem; *fruit market, Rauwert, Amsterdam; *St Anne, Verlaen, Haarlem.

Bunel, Jaques.

Buys.

C

Caesar de Salusto, See Salusto.

Calcker, Jan van, portrait drawings, Naples; anatomical drawings for Vesalius; portraits of Italian artists for Vasari.

APPENDIX A

Candido, *See* Witte, Pieter de.
Carracka, *See* Kraeck.
Claessen, Alaert.
Claeszoon, Alaert, *See* Aertgen.
Claeszoon, Cornelis (Van Wieringhen), ships.
Claeszoon, Isaac (Swanenburgh) van Leyden, *See* Swanenburgh.
Claeszoon, Jan.
Claeszoon, Marinus (van Romerswalen),*See* Romerswalen.
Claeszoon, Volckert, paintings, Schepen Camer, Haarlem; *cartoons for glass painters, Haarlem.
Cleef, Claes van.
Cleef, Cornelis van.
Cleef, Gillis van.
Cleef, Hendrick van, landscapes; portraits; antiquities; cities, ruins; *backgrounds in the works of Frans Floris; *backgrounds in the works of Marten van Cleef; drawings (some of them in prints).
Cleef, Jooris van, small pictures.
Cleef, Joos van (foolish), *Virgin in a Landscape by Patenier, Wyntgis, Middelburg; *Bacchus, Simon Luz, Amsterdam.
Cleef, van, son of Foolish Cleef.
Cleef, Joos van, (neither Foolish Cleef, nor his son, according to Van Mander), figure compositions.
Cleef, Joos van (Ancestor of Foolish Cleef, who entered the guild of Antwerp in 1511), Mary with Angels; Bacchus.
Cleef, Marten van I, figures in the landscapes of his brother Hendrick; figures in the landscapes of Gillis van Coninxloo.
Cleef, Marten van, II.
Cleef, Willem van, large figures.
Cloeck, Isaac Claeszoon.
Cluyt, Adriaen, portraits.
Cluyt, Pieter (Father of Adriaen Cluyt from Alkmaer), heraldic designs.
Cluyt, Pieter Diericksen, from Delft.

Cluyt, Pieter (son of Pieter Diericksen from Delft), figure compositions.
Cock, Jeroen, *See* Kock, Jeroen.
Cock, Mathys, *See* Kock, Mathys.
Cock, Lucas Cornelisz de, *See* Kock, Lucas Cornelisz.
Cocxie, Michiel, drawings after-Raphael; Resurrection of Christ, Rome; St Barbara; *Crucifixion, Halsenberg, near Brussels;*Death of the Virgin, St Gudule, Brussels; St Luke altar, wings to central panel by Orley, Malines; *St Sebastian, Ons Vrouwkerck, Antwerp; *Last Supper, St Gudule, Brussels; copy of the Agnus Dei, and Descent from the Cross by Van der Weyden.
Coeck, Pieter, *See* Koeck, Pieter.
Coelen, Thomas van.
Coignet, Gielis, landscape backgrounds in the works of Cornelis Molenaer; figure compositions; landscapes; light effects, candles, torches, lamps; lottery; Judith and Holofernes; frescoes, Terni; room with grotesques in French style; altar painting.
Conincxloy I.
Conincxloy, Gillis van II, painting for the King of Spain (begun by Jongheling), Roelandts; *large painting, Abraham de Marez, Amsterdam; *landscape, Jan Ycket; *landscape, Burgman Claesz, Naarden; *landscape, Cornelis Monincx, Middelburg; *large painting and two round ones, Wyntgis, Middelburg; *paintings, Pilgrim and Van Os, Amsterdam.
Conincxloy, Jan van.
Coornhert, Dirck Volckertsz, *engravings and wood engravings after Heemskerck; *Life of Charles V.
Cornelis van Gouda, portraits.
Cornelis van Vianen, *See* Vianen.
Cornelisz Claes.
Cornelisz, Cornelis, female figures;

APPENDIX A

vase with flowers; *portraits, Corporaelschap, Oude Doelen, Haarlem; *Caritas; *Avarice and Extravagance; *Deluge; *Biting of the Serpents, *Fall of Lucifer, Rauwert, Amsterdam; *Golden Age, H.L.Spieghel, Amsterdam; *Deluge and Biting of the Serpents, Ferreris, Leyden; *Adam and Eve, *Passion of Christ (12 small paintings), *Purification of the Children of Israel, Wyntgis, Middelburg; *Massacre of the Innocents, Princenhof, Haarlem; *Adam and Eve; *Peleus and Thetis, Princenhof, Haarlem; *Resurrection of Lazarus, Jan Matthysen Ban, Haarlem; *Wedding of Thetis, Willem Jacobsz, Amsterdam; *portraits; *Platonic Cave, (mentioned in Van Mander's Grondt) Amsterdam.

Cornelisz, Floris.

Cornelisz, Jacob (van Oost-Sanen), *Descent from the Cross, Mary Magdalen, Cornelis Suycker, Haarlem; *Seven Works of Mercy (1517), Oude Kerck, Amsterdam; *Circumcision of Christ, Cornelis Suycker, Haarlem; *Crucifixion, Near the 'Dam', Amsterdam; *Descent from the Cross, Sonneveld, Alkmaar; *Passion of Christ, wood engravings (Bartsch 1-12); *Passion of Christ, wood engravings, second series, squares; *Valiant Knights, wood engravings, nine. 'Nine Worthies.'

Cornelisz, Lucas (son of Cornelis Willemsz), glass painting.

Cornelisz, Pieter, glass painting.

Cornelisz (Kunst), Cornelis, *Carrying of the Cross, Dirck van Sonnevelt, Leyden; *Descent from the Cross; *portraits, self-portrait with his second wife, Aertgen Cornelis, Leyden; Murals for Monastery, Leyderdorp; *small painting, Jacob Vermy, Leyden.

Cort, (Cornelis), *portrait, Joachim Patenier, engraving; engravings, drawings by Kies after Heemskerck.

Coster, Pieter, See Balten.

Crabbe, Frans, Crucifixion, (water color).

Crabeth, Adriaen Pietersz.

Crabeth, Dirck Pietersz (Cripple Pieter).

Cranach, Lucas, engravings.

Cransse, Jan, Washing of the Feet of Christ.

Croonenborg, Steven.

Cuffle, Pierre de la, Three Spinners (Graces); ceiling decorations.

Custos, Pieter, See Balten.

D

Daelmans, Hans.

Dale, Cornelis van, rocks.

Damessen, Lucas.

Damiaen van Gouda.

Dammerts, Lucas.

David, Geerard.

Delft, Cornelis Jacobsz, See Jacobsz. Cornelus.

Delft, Jacob Willemsz.

Delft, Jan van (Lange Jan).

Denys van Utrecht.

Dolendo, Zacharias, *Passion of Christ engravings, after drawings by Carel van Mander.

Donauwer.

Dorici, Claudius.

Drebbel, Cornelis.

Druyvesteyn, Aert Jansz, landscape with little figures.

Du Breul, (Toussaint), See Breul.

Dürer, Albrecht, *Three Graces with Globe, 1497, engr. Bartsch 75; *Carrying of the Cross, engr. Bartsch 21; *Three Magi, engr. Bartsch 5; *Virgin, engr. Bartsch 27-32; *St Anthony, engr. Bartsch 47; *Wild Man, 1503, engr. Bartsch 101; *Adam and Eve, 1504, engr. Bartsch 1; *two small horses, 1505, engr. Bartsch 96-97; *Passion, 1507,1508,1512, engr. Bartsch 3-18; *portrait Duke of Saxony, 1524, engr.

517

APPENDIX A

Bartsch 104; *portrait Melanchton, 1526, engr. Bartsch 105; *portrait, self-portrait, Prodigal Son, engr. Bartsch 28; *portrait, Cardinal, drawing, Virgin, 1526, drawing, human proportions, drawing, in book of Lucas de Heere; *human proportions, arms, hands, drawing, and Adam and Eve, studies, drawings, Collection Arnoudt Berensteyn; Three Magi, 1504; Virgin with two Angels, 1506; Adam and Eve, 1507; *Crucifixion, 1508; Christ in Heaven, Pope and Emperor, 1511; Carrying of the Cross, Nürnberg; *Assumption of Mary, 1509, Frankfort; *Portrait Charlemagne, city hall, Nürnberg; *portrait Member House of Austria, *standing Apostles, *portrait Dürer's Mother, *self-portrait (long hair), City Hall, Nürnberg; *portrait Bilibald Pirckheimer, engr.; *Small Passion, 36 wood engravings; *Lucretia; *Altar painting in Nürnberg, wings by Aldegrever, Nürnberg; *portrait Erasmus, engr.; *portrait Lucas van Leyden, drawing; *portrait Patenier.

Duval, Marc, portraits.

E

Elburcht, Hansken van den, St Peter fishing, Onse Vrouwe Kerck, Antwerp.

Elsheimer, Adam van Frankfoort, figure compositions; etchings.

Engelbrechtsen, Cornelis, *Christ on the Cross between the Thieves, Abraham's Sacrifice, Biting of the Serpents, *Descent from the Cross, Seven Sorrows of Mary, *Adoration of the Virgin, City Hall, Leyden; *Lamb of God, epitaph Lockhorst, St Peter's Church, Leyden.

Enghelrams, Cornelis, See Inghelrams.

Enghelsen, Cornelis (Verspronck),

portraits.

Evert van Amersfoort, See Amersfoort.

Eyck, Hubrecht van, *Adoration of the Lamb.

Eyck, Jan van, *Adoration of the Lamb, Coronation of the Virgin; St Cecilia, Adam and Eve, Ghent; bathing scene, Frederic II, Urbino; St Jerome, Lorenzo de Medici, Florence; Mary and Praying Abbot, Burning Bush, Gideon's Fleece, St Martin's Church, Ypres; a painting, Alphonso I, Naples; a painting (Van der Paele-Madonna), Bruges; man and woman (Arnolfini); *woman with landscape, Lucas de Heere, Ghent; *drawings.

Eyck, Margriete van.

F

Floris, Baptiste.

Floris, Claudius, sculpture.

Floris, Cornelis I.

Floris, Cornelis II, architecture; City Hall, Ostershuys, Antwerp.

Floris, Cornelis III.

Floris, Frans I, *drawings in Rome; nudes; Fall of Lucifer, Assumption of Mary, Onse Lieve Vrouwe Kerck, Antwerp; Last Judgement; Nativity; St Luke, Abbot Lucas, St Luke writing the Gospel; St Luke Painting the Virgin, Sermon of St Luke, St Macharius; St Luke Taken Prisoner, St Bavo Chapel, Ghent; trophies, Triumphal Gate 1549, Antwerp; *Victory (painting and etching) 1552; Pictura; Crucifixion; Resurrection; *Nine Sleeping Muses, Wyntgis Middelburg; *Banquet of Sea Goddesses; *Christ Blessing the Children, *Adam and Eve Driven from Paradise, *Adam and Eve Mourning Abel, Van Endt, Amsterdam; Hercules Series of Ten Paintings, The Liberal Arts, Claes Jonghlingh, Antwerp; St Luke; Carrying of

engr. Bartsch 4; *Three Magi, engr. Bartsch 5; *Passion 1597 engr. Bartsch 27-38; *Mary and Christ, engr. Bartsch 41, Berensteijn, Haarlem; *Woman with Snakes and Pigeons, engr. Bartsch 93; Bacchus, Ceres, Venus and Cupid, drawing, Rome; *Faun and Fauna, Rudolph II, Vienna; *Pieta, Fuggers, Augsburg; Laughing Woman and Satyr, drawing, Badens, Amsterdam; Crucifixion 1600, Gijsbert Rijckersen, Haarlem; *Indian with Bow, Tobias Swartsenburgh, Haarlem; *Celestial Paradise, Jan Matthysen Ban, Haarlem; *Christ, Man of Sorrows, Van der Lip, Vienna; *Danaë, 1603, Ferreris, Leyden; *peasant woman from the north; *portrait, Jan Govertsen, Haarlem; *portrait, Polish Princes engr.; *glass painting; *portrait, Christoffel Schwartz, 1591, Munich; *portrait, Hans Bol, engr. Bartsch 162; *Descent from the Cross, engr. after Blocklandt.

Goltzius, Hubert, the Elder, See Goltz.

Gortzius, Gualdrop, portraits; Diana, Johan Meerman, Cologne; Susan, Everhard Jabach, Cologne; Mary and Christ, engr. Francken 129; Mary and Christ, engr. Francken 84; Evangelist, engr. Francken 225-228, Joris Haeck; Esther and Ahasuerus, Gortssen, Hamburg; various subjects, Frans Francken, J. Mollijn, Cologne.

Gossaert, Jan (Mabuse), Descent from the Cross, *Virgin, Middelburg; *Descent from the Cross, Magnus, Langen Delft; *Lucretia, Wyntgis, Middelburg; *Adam and Eve, Papenbroeck, Amsterdam; *Beheading of St James, Joan Nicker, Amsterdam; Mary with Holy Infant, Froimont, Gouda; Portrait, Two young Boys, Withal; altar painting, to which Coxie painted the wings, wrongly attributed by Van Mander to Orley.

Gouda, Cornelis van, See Cornelis van Gouda.

Gouda, Damiaen, See Damiaen.

Govert, Jansz, landscape with small figures.

Grimani, See Jacobsz, Hubert (from Delft).

Grimmaer, Jaques, landscapes near Antwerp.

Grobber, Frans Pietersz, portraits, figure compositions, embroidery work, landscapes.

Groningen, Herder van, See Herder.

H

Hals, Frans.

Hame, Joan de la, *glass painting.

Haarlem, Cornelis van, See Cornelis Cornelisz.

Haarlem, Dirck Bouts van, See Bouts.

Haarlem, Jacob van, *altar painting for Stevedors, Groote Kerck, Haarlem.

Heck, Niclaes van der, landscapes.

Heel, van.

Heemskerck, See Hemskerck.

Heere, Jan de, *sculpture, Ghent.

Heere, Lucas de, *landscape sketches River Meuse, drawings; cartoons for glass painters; tapestry cartoons; tapestry cartoons for Catherine de Medici; *portrait, Sr van Wacken, his wife and Cosijntgen; Pentecost, Ghent; Epitaph, St John's Church, Ascension, Emmaus, Disciples, Christ and Magdalen, St John's Church, Ghent; national costumes, London, poetry, 'Boomgaerdt der Poesy'; lives of the painters; drawings, followed by Inghelrams; drawings followed by Sammelingh.

Heintz, Joseph (Switser), drawings of classical sculpture; Emmaus, wing to a central altar painting by Hans van Aken, the

APPENDIX A

other wing, the Three Marys by Sprangher, Prague.

Heme, Louis, architectural subjects; perspective views.

Hemessen, *See* Hemsen.

Hemsen, Jan van, *Christ and Apostles, Cornelis Monincx, Middelburg.

Hemsen, Katherine van.

Hemskerck, Marten van (van Veen), Sol and Luna, Adam and Eve, Pieter Jan Fobsenm, Haarlem; *St Luke, Princenhof, Haarlem; drawings after Michelangelo; *Nativity, Three Magi Annunciation, Princenhof, Haarlem; *Resurrection, Oude Kerck, Amsterdam; *Crucifixion, Passion of Christ, St Laurens, high altar, Alkmaar; *Three Magi, Biting of the Serpents, Aechte Kerck, Delft; *Life of Christ, St Boniface, Eertswout, North-Holland; *altar painting, high altar, Medemblick; *Ascension, Assendelft Chapel, The Hague; *Resurrection, Assendelft Chapel, The Hague; *The Four Extremes: Death, Last Judgement, Eternal Life and Hell, Jacob Ravaert, Haarlem; *Bacchanalia, Kempenaer and Wyntgis, Middelburg; *St Christopher and landscape, Arnout Berensteyn; *illustrations to poems by Coornhert; *Life of the Emperor (Coornhert after Hemskerck), Van Mander, Haarlem; wings to the Massacre of the Innocents by Cornelis Cornelisz; Epitaph to his Father; *self-portraits, Van der Heck, Alkmaar; Christ, Van Mander, Haarlem.

Henricksen, Cornelis, *faience, vases, pottery.

Henricksen, Frederic, sculpture, architecture.

Herder van Groningen.

Herman van der Mast, van den Briel, *See* Mast, Herman.

Herri, Master.

Heuvick, Caspar, *See* Huevick,

Gaspar.

Hoefnaghel, Jaques.

Hoefnaghel, Jooris, sketchbook with variety of subjects; national costumes; city views; Calis Malis; strange animals; portrait, the first Mrs Hoefnaghel; self-portrait; miniatures on parchment, animals, Duke of Bavaria; book of quadrupeds, creeping animals, etc.; missal for Ferdinand of Innsbruck; *small painting for Razet, Razet, Amsterdam.

Hoeven, Apert Franssen van der, *See* Francken, Apert.

Hoey, Jan van, *See* Joan de Hooy.

Hoghenberg, Hans, Caleb and Joshua, St Rombout, Malines; *Emperor Charles V in Bologna.

Holbein, Hans, Dance of Death, (Haus zum Tanz), Basle; Dance of Death, City Hall, Basle; portrait of Erasmus, Zndries de Loo, London; Dance of Death, wood engravings; portrait of Thomas More; portraits of friends of More; portrait of Henry VIII; portrait of Edward, son of Henry VIII; portrait of Mary, daughter of Henry VIII; portrait of Elizabeth, daughter of Henry VIII; portraits, Grant to the Surgeons, Hall of the Surgeons, London; Triumph of Wealth, Knell of Poverty, London; portrait of Countess in black satin (Christine of Milan), Penbroeck, London; portrait of Sr Niclaes, Astronomer to Henry VIII; portrait of Thomas, Lord Cromwell, Andries de Loo, London; portrait of William Warham, Bishop of Canterbury, Mr Coop; *portrait of Jane Seymour, Rauwert, Amsterdam; Bible illustrations, 1539, wood engrs.; *self-portraits, Razet, Ferreris, Leyden; portraits of Thomas More and Family.

Hollander, Jan van Amstel, de, landscape.

521

APPENDIX A

Hooy, Joan de.
Horebout, Geerard, *Flagellation of Christ, Descent from the Cross, St John's Church, Ghent; *Coronation of Christ, Mary with Holy Infant, Lijnwaet-Arm, Ghent.
Horebout, Lucas, illumination.
Houven, Apert Franssen van der, See Francken, Apert.
Huevick, Gaspar.

I

Inghelrams, Cornelis, Feeding of the Poor, Conversion of St Paul, St Rombout, Malines; Story of David, Prince of Orange.
Isaacsz, Isaac.
Isaacsz, Pieter, *portrait of Sara Schuyrmans, Breestraet, Leyden; *portrait of Pieter Huygheszen, *portrait of the wife of Pieter Huygheszen, In de Clock, Leyden; *Adam and Eve; *John the Baptist, on copper; *portrait of Pieter Semeynes; *portrait of Hendrick Franckin and wife, Franckin, Amsterdam; *portrait of Jacob Poppe, *Revolt of the Roman Women, Jacob Poppe, Amsterdam.
Israel van Meckenem (Mentz), Nude Women, (Graces) copied by Dürer, Bartsch 185.

J

Jacob (van Haarlem), altar painting, Groote Kerck, Haarlem.
Jacobsz, Cornelis from Delft, still life.
Jacobsz, Dierick; *portraits, Doelen, Amsterdam.
Jacobsz, Hubert (from Delft), portraits.
Jacobsz, Huygh.
Jacobsz, Simon from Gouda; *portrait of Willem Tybout, glass painter.
Jan, Langen from Delft.
Janssen, Michiel, See Miereveldt.
Jansz, Govert, See Govert.
Jan van Amstel, See Hollander.
Jan van Delft, See Jan, Langen from Delft.

Jan Swart, See Swart.
Jerrigh, portraits.
Jode, Pieter de.
Joncquoit, Michiel, See Gioncoy.
Jordaen, Hans, figure compositions, landscape, peasants, soldiers, skippers, fishermen, fire scenes, rocks, tapestry designs, genealogy house of Orange, after Orley.
Jorisz, Augustijn, five paintings, St Anne and her Family, Delft; Three Spinners; ceiling decorations.

K

Kaynoot, Hans.
Ketel, Cornelis, portraits of Members of the Hanseatic League; Force Controlled through Wisdom; portrait of the Queen of England, (Elizabeth) 1572; portrait of the Duke of Oxford; *portraits, archers under Captain Herman Rodenborgh Beths, 1581, Cloveniers Doelen, Amsterdam; *Triumph of Virtue, *Triumph of Vice, Joan van Wely, Amsterdam; *St Paul (portrait Rutger Jansz), Hans Ophogen; *St Paul, St Peter, Magdalen, Publican, Saul's Death and Judas, Thomas Ophogen, Danzig; Portraits, Archers under Dirck Roosencrans, Handboog-Doelen, Amsterdam, *Portraits, Mr Neck, Mrs Neck, Andries Vrericksen, Jan Lammersen, Secretary Haen, A Goldsmith, Francesco Morosini, Vincent Jacobson, A Portuguese Girl; *Christ and the Twelve Apostles (artists' portraits); *portrait of Simon Lock, Procureur Lock, The Hague; *Apostles, Jacob Ketel, Paris; *Tree of the Fine Arts, Domenicus van Uffele, Hamburg; *Music, Pictura and Poetry; *Hope, Genius and Ambition; *Truth and Virtue; *Desire has no Rest; *Three Reasons for studying Art; *Music, Pictura and Poetry in a spiritual sense;

522

*Intelligence Disarmed; *The Seven Virtues, Secretary Haen, Amsterdam; *Mirror of Virtues; *sculpture, Story of the Groom; *self-portrait 1599; *Democritus, *Heraclitus, Hendrick van Os, Amsterdam; *Portrait, A Moscovite; *Portrait, Sr Wolfaert Hermans; *Portrait, Hendrick de Keyser (Apostle); *Christ, Mary and John (heads); *Harpocrates; *Heraclitus; *heads, Andreas Lescinski; *mural decorations for the house of Ketel: Democritus, Heraclitus, Momus, Soylus, Time, 1602; *Allegory Van Wulp; *Allegory Van Wulp; *Time and Truth, Cornelis Florissen van Teylingen; *Allegory Morality, Razet, Amsterdam; *Mary and Holy Infant; *Christ with Angels, Razet, de Jode, Antwerp; *Constant Labor, W. Jacobson, Amsterdam; *Judith, Christoffel Dircksen Pruys, Amsterdam; Danaë, Danzig.

Key, William, *Portraits, The Rulers of Antwerp, City Hall, Antwerp; *Christ, All who are burdened, come unto me, Onse; Triumph of Christ, Onse Vrouwen Kerck, Antwerp; Portrait, Duke of Alva; Portrait, Granvelle.

Keynooge, See Kaynoot.

Kies, Simon, drawings after Frans Floris; Hercules, after Frans Floris, engraved by Cort.

Kock, Jeroen de, landscapes; etchings, twelve landscapes after Mathys de Kock; *The School of Athens, after Raphael.

Kock, Mathys de, landscapes.

Kock, Lucas Cornelis de, *Adulteress; *water-colors on canvas, Knotter, Leyden; *water-colors, Jacob Vermy; *painting, Hartoogh, Leyden.

Koeck, Pieter (Van Aelst), tapestry designs; studies of statues and monuments; *The Customs of the Turks, 7 woodcuts?; *books on architecture; *translation of the works of Serlio; altar paintings; portraits.

Koeck, Pieter II.

Kraeck, Jan.

Krijnsz, Evert (van der Maes), portraits, figure compositions.

Kroes, Leonard, figure compositions, landscapes.

Kunst, Cornelis Cornelisz, See Cornelisz Kunst.

Kunst, Pieter Cornelis, glass painting.

L

Laen, Dirck van der, small figures.

Lampsonius, Dominicus.

Langen Jan from Delft, See Jan, Langen.

Lasman, Pieter.

Lenartsz, Jacob, glass painting.

Le Sayve, Frans, See Savius.

Leyden, Lucas van, See Lucas.

Liere, Joos van, landscape, figure compositions, tapestry designs.

Lombardus, Lambert, architecture, studies of mediaeval Frankish works of art; *Last Supper.

Louwers, Balthasar, landscape.

Loys van Brussels.

Lucas van Leyden, glass painting; Legend of St Hubert, Van Lockorst; *Mahomet Killing a Monk, engr. 1508, Bartsch 126; *Passion of Christ, nine engr. 1509, Bartsch 57-65; *Temptation of St Anthony, engr. 1509, Bartsch 117; *Conversion of St Paul, engr. 1509, Bartsch 107; *Ecce Homo, engr. 1510, Bartsch 71; *Farmer and Wife and Cows, engr. 1510, Bartsch 158; *Adam and Eve Driven from Paradise, engr. 1510, Bartsch 11; *Nude Woman and Dog, engr. 1510, Bartsch 154; *Magdalen, engr. Bartsch 122; *St Hubert engr. Bartsch 57; *Crucifixion, engr. Bartsch 74; *Ecce Homo, engr. Bartsch 71; *Adoration of the Magi, engr. Bartsch 37; Portrait of Albert

Dürer, drawing; *self-portrait, etching Bartsch 173; *Bartimius, the blind man of Jericho, 1531, Goltzius, Haarlem; *Last Judgement, Peter and Paul, City Hall, Leyden; *Mary and Infant holding grapes; Annunciation and Magdalen, Frans Hooghstraet, near Leyden; *Children of Israel Dancing round the Golden Calf, Kalverstraet, Amsterdam; *Rebecca, water-color, Knotter or Sonneveldt, Leyden; *Joseph, water-color, Brewer, Delft; *portrait, Claes Ariaensz, Leyden; *Virgin, Ferreris, Leyden; *Temptation of Christ, engr. Bartsch 41; *Saul and David, engr. Bartsch 27; *Tooth Pulling, engr. 1523, Bartsch 157; *Musical Duet, engr. 1524, Bartsch 155; *David Approached by Dancing Women, glass painting, Goltzius, Haarlem; *Portrait, Emperor Maximilian, engr. Bartsch 172; wood engravings; *Pallas, engr. Bartsch 139.

M

Mabuse, Joan Gossaert, See Gossart.

Maes, Evert Krijnsz van der, See Krijnsz.

Maier, Hans de.

Mander, Carel van, *Passion of Christ.

Mandijn, Jan, ghost scenes and diabolical subjects; drolleries.

Marcus Geerards, See Geerarts, Marcus.

Marcus Willems, See Willems, Marcus.

Marinus de Seeu, *Banker in His Office, Wyntgis, Middelburg.

Martin. Hipse (Schöngauer), engravings; Carrying of the Cross, engr. Bartsch 21; Adoration of the Magi, engr. Bartsch 5; Madonnas, engr. Bartsch 27-32; Temptation of St Anthony, engr. Bartsch 47.

Mast, Herman van der, Carrying of the Cross, after Frans Floris; St Sebastian.

Matham, Jacob, engravings after Italian masters.

Matsijs, See Messijs.

Meckenem, Israel van, See Israel.

Meire, Geeraert van der, Lucretia, Rauwert, Amsterdam.

Memmelinck, Hans, St Ursula, St John's Hospital, Bruges.

Menton, Francoys, engravings; *portraits.

Messijs, Cornelis.

Messijs, Jan, *Money Changers, Lavoir, Rauwert, Amsterdam.

Messijs, Quintyn, Coloring of early woodcuts; *Descent from the Cross, St John Boiled in Oil, Salome, Presenting the Head of St John to Herodias, Onse Lieve Vrouwe Kerck, Antwerp; *Virgin, Ferreris, Leyden.

Miereveld, Michiel Janssen, *Samaritan Woman, engr.; *Judith, engr.; *portraits, Hendrick Egbert and wife, Leyden; *portrait, Old Man with Beard, *portrait, Burgomaster Gerit Jansz van der Eyck with wife and children, Delft; *portrait, Rutger Jansz, *portrait, Jan Govertsz, Amsterdam; portrait, Louise de Coligny, Princess of Orange; portraits, Brewers, Delft; *portrait, Jaques Razet, Amsterdam; *kitchen scene, Ferreris, Leyden; portrait, Paulus van Berensteyn, portrait, Mr Schilperoort, Delft.

Mijtens, Aert, Madonna in the Church of St Maria Maggiore, Rome; altar paintings; figure compositions; portraits; Assumption of Mary, near Naples; Evangelist, St Catherine, St Maria del Secors, Naples; Adoration of the Magi, Circumcision, Abruzzo; Christ Crowned at Night, Van Somer, Amsterdam; Crucifixion, Aquila.

Minnebroer, Frans, Flight into Egypt, Onse Lieve Vrouwe Kerck, Malines; Annunciation

APPENDIX A

and Visitation, Van Hanswijck, Malines.

Molenaer, Cornelis (Schelen Neel), landscapes, figure compositions.

Momper, Joos de, landscapes.

Mondt, Jacob.

Mont, Hans, *triumphal gate at Vienna for Rudolph II; *wax models for Maximilian II; *sculpture, Vienna.

Montfort, Anthonis Blocklandt, See Blocklandt.

Montfort, Pieter Geeritsz, drawings.

Moreelsz, Pauwels, portraits, Count and Countess of Culemborgh; portrait, Mme Knotter, Knotter, Leyden.

Moretto.

Moro, Antonis, portraits, King Philip II of Spain, Mary, Princess of Portugal, John III of Portugal, Catherine, Queen of Portugal, Queen Mary Tudor, Spanish Nobility, Concubines of Alva; Resurrection of Christ; Danaë (copy after Titian); *Circumcision, Onse Lieve Vrouwe Kerck, Antwerp; *portrait, Joan Schoorel; Peter and Paul; *portrait, Hubrecht Goltzius, Widow Goltzius, Bruges.

Mosscher, Jaques de.

Mostart, Frans, landscapes.

Mostart, Gilles, small figures; Virgin; Last Supper; Last Judgement; *Carrying of the Cross; *portraits, Messrs Schets, Lords of Hoboken; *St Peter delivered from Prison, Wyntgis, Middelburg.

Mostart, Jan, Portrait, Margaretha, sister of Philip II; *Nativity; altar painting, Jacobins, Haarlem; *Ecce Homo, portrait Pier Muys, *Banquet of the Gods, Peleus, Thetis, Discordia, Mars, *West Indian landscape, *self-portrait, *portraits, Jaqueline of Bavaria and Van Borselen, Niclaes Suycker, Haarlem; *Descendence of St Ann, Rauwert, Amsterdam; *Abraham, Sara, Agar and Ismael, Schoterbosch, The Hague; *St Christopher, Jan Claesz, Haarlem; *St Hubert, Princenhof, Haarlem.

Muller, Joan, engravings of paintings by Bloemaert and Hans van Aken.

Mytens, Aert, See Mijtens.

N

Nagel, Jan, landscapes, figures.

Nieuwlandt, Willem van, landscapes.

Noort, Adam van, See Oort, Adam van.

Noort, Lambert van, See Oort, Lambert van.

Nop, Gerrit.

Nymegen, de Stomme van.

O

Oliviers, Isaac, miniature portraits; portrait, Hendrick Cornelisz Vroom.

Oort, Adam van, figure compositions.

Oort, Lambert van, architecture.

Oost Sanen, Jacob Cornelisz, See Cornelis Jacob van Oost Sanen.

Orley, Bernard van (Barent van Brussel), Last Judgement, Aelmosseniers Capelle, Antwerp; St Luke Painting the Virgin, Malines; tapestry cartoons for Marguerite and Maximilian, Charles V, Count Maurice, series of sixteen.

Ortelmans, Damiaen, See Wortelmans.

Oserijn, Isaac, portrait, Isaac, grandfather of Oserijn; *drawings after engravings by Cort; *portrait, Christian IV, King of Denmark (sketch).

Otto Venius, See Vaenius.

Ouwater, Albert van, St Peter and St Paul, St Bavo, Haarlem; Resurrection of Lazarus, Apostles-Jews, pupil of Heemskerck, Rauwert (?); *Copy of the Resurrection.

Cross, engr. Bartsch 21; Three Magi, engr. Bartsch 5; Virgin, engr. Bartsch 27-32; Temptation of St Anthony, engr. Bartsch 47.

Salusto, Caesar de, fresco painting, landscape.

Sammeling, Benjamin, *Decorations in the St John's Church Ghent after drawings by Lucas van Leyden, St John's Church, Ghent; portraits.

Sanders, Jan (van Hemsen), *See* Hemsen.

Sanredam, *See* Saenredam.

Santvoort.

Savery, Jaques.

Savery, Roeland.

Savius, Franciscus.

Sayve, Frans Le, *See* Savius.

Schilder, Pieter Pietersz, *See* Pietersz, Pieter.

Schilder, Cornelis Cornelisz, *See* Cornelisz, Cornelis.

Schongauer, Martin, *See* Martin, Hipse.

Schoorel, Joan, sculpture, small figures of animals, plants, portraits, landscapes (Candia, Cypris, Jordan River), drawings; Passage of the Jordan, Jerusalem; Thomas and Christ, Monastery Sion; Jerusalem, Christ Descending the Mount of Olives, Palm Sunday, Lockhorst, Utrecht; Sermon on the Mount; Holy Sepulchre; *Knights of Jerusalem, Princenhof, Haarlem; copies of Raphael, Michelangelo and antique sculpture, Rome; portrait, Pope Adrian VI, Louvain; *Baptism of St John, Simon Saen, Haarlem; *Crucifixion, Oude Kerck, Amsterdam; Rhodus; Crucifixion, Amsterdam; Mary, Christ and Joseph, kneeling figure of Emperor and Bishop Conrad, Abraham's Offer, College of St Mary, Utrecht; St Laurens, Marchiennes; altar painting, Gouda; Eleven Thousand Virgins, St Stephen, Marchiennes;

Crucifixion, Arras; Last Supper, Grootouwer, Frisia; Virgin, sent to Gustav Wasa; *Presentation in the Temple, Schoterbosch, Haarlem; mural decorations, Groote Houtpoort, Haarlem; works, Willem Pietersz, Malines; works, 't Huys, Breda; landscape in Descent from the Cross by Jacob Cornelis van Oost Sanen, Amsterdam; Crucifixion, Oude Kerck, Amsterdam.

Schuyck, Joachim.

Schwartz, Christoffel, Fall of the Angels and Martyrdom of St Andrew, St Michaelis Church, Munich; Passion of Christ.

Simon Jacobsz, *See* Jacobsz, Simon.

Simon van Amsterdam.

Singher, Hans (de Duytcher), decorations in the house of Carel Cockeel, Antwerp; tapestry cartoons.

Sint Jans, Geertgen tot, *See* Geertgen.

Smit, Cornelis de.

Smit, Pieter.

Smijters, Anne, miniature (windmill).

Snellaert, Claes, decorative painting.

Snellaert, Willem, painting on fabric.

Snellinck, Hans, battle scenes.

Soens, Hans, copies of Frans Mostart; landscapes, H.L.Spieghel, Amsterdam; landscape, St Augustine, landscape with rooster, Vatican, Rome; small figure compositions, fire scenes, H.L.Spieghel, Amsterdam.

Sojaro, Bernardino Gatti.

Somer, Bernaert van, portraits, figure compositions.

Somer, Pauwels van, portraits, figure compositions.

Speeckaert, Hans.

Spierinck, Frans.

Spierinck, Karel Philip.

Splinter, Gerrit.

APPENDIX A

Sprangher, Bartholomeus, land-
scapes (figures by Mostart and
Beuckelaer); copies of prints by
Parmentius and Floris, drawings;
portraits after drawings by
Marcus (Duval); Resurrection
of Christ, drawing, Paris; Trium-
phal Arch, Parma 1565; landscape
with witches, Spindolo, Rome;
Last Supper; *Last Judgement,
Christ in the Garden, Pius V,
Rome; *Passion of Christ, series
of twelve drawings, Rome;
*Resurrection of Christ (No. 12
of the previous series); *Mary in
Heaven, St Anthony, John the
Baptist, St Elizabeth, St Luigi de
Francesi, Rome; *St John Boiled
in Oil, St Giovanni Porta Latina;
*St Ann Giving Birth to Mary,
SS Vincenso, Rome; *portrait, a
Lady in Waiting to the Duchess
of Arembers, Rome; *mural deco-
ration, Fasangarten, Vienna; *Cru-
cifixion; *Resurrection, Imperial
Hospital, Vienna; *stucco deco-
ration and frescoes, Fasangarten,
Vienna; *Mercurius Introducing
Psyche into the Council of the
Gods, Vienna; *Roma, *Virgin
and figures, Rudolph II, Vienna;
*Triumphal Arch for Rudolph
II, *Justitia and Wisdom, trium-
phal arch, Vienna; mural decora-
tions, house of Sprangher, Fly-
ing Mercury, mural decoration,
Roma on Globe, Hercules and
Justice, house of Sprangher,
Prague; Christ Stepping on the
Devil and Death, St Gillis,
Prague; St Sebastian, St Thomas
Church, Prague; Justice and
Children, City Hall, Prague; As-
sumption of the Virgin, Jesuits,
Prague; St James and St Erasmus,
St James Monastery, Prague;
Resurrection of Christ, Epitaph
St Matthew, Prague; *Dispute of
the Doctors on the Sacrament,
Rome; *Venus and Mercury;
*Wedding of Psyche, Haarlem;

*The Three Marys; fresco; land-
scapes for Cardinal Farnese,
Rome; figure compositions.
Steenwyck, Hendrick I, Church
views.
Steenwyck, Hendrick II, church
views.
Stella, Frans See Stellaert.
Stellaert, Fransoys, landscapes, fig-
ure compositions, portrait.
Stelt, Met der, See Aertsz,
Rijckaert.
Stephani, Pieter, See Stevens.
Stevens, Pieter.
Stomme van Nymegen, See
Nymegen.
Stradanus, Joannes, frescoes, Ducal
Palace, Florence; Crucifixion,
Annunziata, Florence; tapestry
cartoons, engraved by Philip
Galle; crusades, hunting scenes;
Acts of the Apostles; horses of
various countries, engraved by
Galle, Wierix, Goltzius; Passion,
two series, engraved by Galle,
Wierix, Collaert, C van de Passe.
Straeten, Hans van der, See
Stradanus.
Suwari, Bernardo, (Sojaro), See
Gatti.
Swanenburgh, Isaac Claeszoon.
Swart, Jan, figure composition,
landscapes, nudes, Turks on
horseback, wood engr. Bartsch
VIII; Christ Preaching, wood
engr.
Swarts, Christoffel, See Schwartz.
Sweling, Geerit Pietersz, See
Pietersz, Geerit.
Switser, Joseph, See Henitz.

T

Thomas van Zierickzee.
Thonauer, Jan, See Donauer.
Titian, Danaë.
Toeput, Lodewyck (Pozzoserrato),
landscapes, figure compositions.
Tons, Guilliame, bawdy houses,
genre.
Tons, Hubert, landscapes, small fig-
ures.
Tons, Jan, water-colors.

Tons, Willem, tapestry cartoons, water-colors, birds, trees.

U

Utewael, Antonie, glass painting.

Utewael, Joachim, glass painting; kitchen scene, Gouda; Lot and his Daughters, Antwerp; *Annunciation to the Shepherds, Lucas Utewael, Amsterdam; *Banquet of the Gods, Jan Ycket, Amsterdam; *Mars and Venus, Joan van Weely; *Mars and Venus, Wyntgis, Middelburg.

Utewael, Lucas, *See* Dammerts.

Uthoeck, Hendrick, mannequins.

Utrecht, Denys van.

V

Vaenius, Otto, portraits, Archduke Albert and Isabella; *Triumph of Bacchus, 1604; *Zeus and five nude figures, Wyntgis, Middelburg.

Valckenborgh, Lucas, landscapes, Meuse Region, illumination, small portraits.

Valckenborgh, Marten, landscapes, Meuse Region.

Valerius.

Veen, Gysbert van, painting, engraving.

Veen, Marten van Hemskerck, *See* Hemskerck.

Veen, Octavius van, *See* Vaenius.

Veen, Pieter van.

Verbeeck, Frans, St Christopher, Malines; water-colors; Parable of the Vineyard, St Catherine Church, Malines; peasant weddings, winter scenes.

Vereycke, Hans (Cleen Hansken), *Virgin in landscape and portraits of Claude Van Mander and family, Blauw Casteel, Bruges; landscapes.

Verhaecht, Tobias, landscapes.

Vermeijen, Jan Cornelis, various works, Arras, Brussels; naval victory, battles scenes; tapestry cartoons for Charles V; Siege of Tunis; Resurrection, Nativity, Christ, Hans Vermeijen, Prague; self-portrait, portraits, second wife of Vermeijen, daughter of Vermeijen, young girl, Daughter, Middelburg.

Verspronck, *See* Cornelis Enghelsen.

Vianen, Cornelis van, perspectives.

Vinckeboons, David, *landscape with figures, *Carrying of the Cross, *peasant fair, Joan de Bruijn, Amsterdam; *Christ healing the Blind, France; *Nocturnal Lottery, Oude Mannen Gasthuis, Amsterdam; *Christ Preaching, *peasant wedding, Jan van Coninxloo; miniatures of animals, birds, fishes and trees, glass painting, etchings, engravings, water-colors.

Vinckeboons, Philip, water-colors.

Visscher, Cornelis de, portraits.

Vissenaken, Jeroen.

Vlerick, Pieter, cartouches for lettering; Brazen Serpent (a copy), views of Tiber, drawing, Castle St Angelo, drawing, pen drawings; Last Judgement, copy of Michelangelo; studies of Sculpture by Michelangelo, *Adoration of the Magi, Rome; frescoes, figures in landscapes, Muziano, D'Este Court; water-colors on canvas; *Biting of the Serpents, *Four Evangelists, Courtrai; *Judith with the head of Holofernes; *Crucifixion; architectural subjects; *Christ driving Merchants from the Temple; Children playing in water; *Solomon's Judgement; *Annunciation; *The Seven Maccabees; *Susan and the Elders, marine deities; *Joseph and Potiphar's wife, after Titian; *Annunciation (Caraglio, B.3), *Annunciation, Jan Bonte; *Virgin; *St Jerome; *St Jerome; *St Barbara; *Passion of Christ; *water-colors; *Resurrection, Epitaph du Prez, Tournai; *altar painting, *Massacre of the Innocents, water-

color, Tournai; *decorations on bellows, *coloring of statues, *portraits; *Crucifixion; *Venus;
Volckert Claeszoon, See Claeszoon, Volckert.
Voort, Cornelis van der.
Vos, Marten de.
Vos, Pieter de.
Vrancx, Sebastiaen, landscape with horses.
Vredeman de Vries, See Vries.
Vriendt, Claudius de, See Floris, Claudius.
Vriendt, Cornelis de I, See Floris, Cornelis I.
Vriendt, Cornelis de II, See Floris, Cornelis II.
Vriendt, Frans de I, See Floris, Frans I.
Vriendt, Jaques de, See Floris, Jaques.
Vriendt, Jan de I, See Floris, Jan I.
Vriendt, Jan de II, See Floris, Jan II.
Vries, Adriaen de, Two Children, Epitaph Michael Peterle, Annaberg.
Vries, Dierick de, still life of food.
Vries, Jan Fredeman de, water-colors, Malines; Triumphal Arch, Antwerp 1549, Antwerp; glass painting, Leeuwarden; perspective views, begun by Vianen, Malines; perspective methods; perspective view of portal, Willem Key, Antwerp; perspective view into a court, Gillis Hofman, Antwerp; perspectives of temples, courts, palaces, series of twenty-six views in palaces, intarsia workers, reproductions of memorial sculpture, Jeroon de Kock, Antwerp; book of fountains, five orders of architecture, Gerard de Jode; courts, corridors, garden ornaments, designs for cabinet makers, Philip Galle; Theatrum de Vita Humana, (architectural orders); decorative designs, trophies, cartouches, grotesques; Triumphal Arch, 1570, entree daughter of the Em-

peror; perspective of a summer house, Aert Molckeman, Brussels; military architecture, Antwerp; painting, epitaph, Brunswick; Christ Triumphant over Devil, Death and Hell, Jacob Moor, St Peter's Church, Hamburg; Orpheus charming the hostile animals, Allegories of Government, Danzig; perspective of a pond with swans; perspective of a garden, ceiling decoration, perspective of balcony, Hans Lomel, Hamburg; decoration on altar wings (Sprangher, Heintz and van Aken), Prague; designs for fountains, Rudolph II, Prague; Christ and the Pharisees, St Peter's Church, Hamburg; Christ driving the Merchants from the Temple, St Peter, Antwerp; *Tower of Babel, Pieter Overlander, Amsterdam; *Perspectiva*, book on architecture.
Vries, Paulus de, ceiling decorations, twelve months, Rudolph II, Prague; *Perspectiva*, book on architecture; perspective views of temples, churches, etc.; Last Supper (architectural detail in the painting by Van Winghen).
Vries, Salomon de, book on architecture, perspective.
Vroom, Cornelis Hendricksz, *sculpture, *faience.
Vroom, Hendrick Cornelisz, faience decoration; ships, Haarlem; figure studies; portraits, landscapes (under direction of Paulus Bril); battle scenes, Bottoin, Lyons; altar painting, Polish Jesuits, Danzig; portrait, Priest, Setubal; shipwreck, St Huves; tapestry cartoons, Armada 1588, (ten); *seventh Day of the Battle of the Armada and Salamis; Dutch Fleet, Battle of Nieuwpoort; fishermen; castles, villages, cities; water-colors.

W

Weerdt, Adriaen de, landscapes; *Resurrection of Lazarus; *Ruth, 1573; *Four cravings of the Mind, for Coornhert; *Life of the Virgin, Nativity; drawings, engraved by Goltzius.

Weyden, Rogier van der, *decorative hangings; Justice four paintings, City Hall, Bruges; Descent from the Cross; Joseph Arimathea, Two Marys, John, Onse Lieve Vrouwe Kerck, Louvain; portrait, A Court Lady.

Wickram, Jaques.

Wierincx, Jeroon.

Wieringen; Cornelis Claesz, See Claesz, Cornelis.

Willems, Marcus, St John the Baptist, executed, St Rombouts, Malines; cartoons for glass painters, tapestry cartoons; Judith and Holofernes; Triumphal Arch, Philip II, 1549; Dido cutting the hide of the Ox, Malines.

Willemsz, Cornelis.

Willemsz, Jacob van Delft, See Delft, Jacob Willemsz.

Willemsz, Willem.

Winghen, Jeremia van.

Winghen, Joos van, Last Supper, St Gudule, Brussels; Samson, Jan Mijtens, Brussels; Conversion of St Paul, Brussels; Belgium Horrified, Apelles Painting Campaspe, Daniel Forreau, Hanau; Andromeda; portraits, Frankfort; Apelles painting Campaspe, Imperial Collection, Vienna; *Pyneas Wyntgis, Middelburg; *Justitia Protecting Innocence against Tyranny, Cornelis van

der Voort, Amsterdam; *Nocturnal Banquet, engr. by Sadeler; *Christ, Let the Children Come Unto Me, engr. by J.Sadeler; *St Paul Weaving a Tapestry, engr. by J.Sadeler; *Four Feminine Tricks, engr. J. and R.Sadeler; *Crucifixion, engr. Chr. van de Passe, 1599.

Withoeck, Hendrick, See Uthoeck.

Witte, Cornelis de, landscapes.

Witte, Lieven de, Adulteress; cartoons for the windows of St John's Church, Ghent.

Witte, Pieter de, frescoes, sculpture in clay; fresco, Sala Regia, Vatican, Rome; fresco, Dome, Duomo, Florence; tapestry cartoons, Duke Cosimo, Florence.

Wortelmans, Damiaen.

Wttewael, See Utewael.

Y

Ypres, Carel van, decorative paintings, altar paintings, house decorations, frescoes, Ypres; *Conversion of St Paul, Tournai; *Resurrection of Christ; *Last Judgement, Church, Hooghlede; *Last Judgement, pen drawing; *Nativity, glass painting, St John's, Ghent.

Ysaacsz, Pieter Isaacsz, See Isaacsz.

Z

Zacharias, Paulusz from Alkmaer.

Zeeuw, Marinus de, See Marinus de Seeu.

Zierickzee, Thomas van, See Thomas.

Zucchero, Federigo, copies of Holbein's Triumph of Wealth and Knell of Poverty.

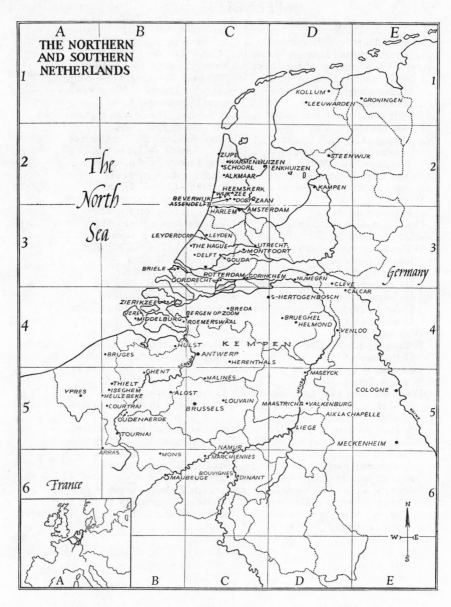

THE NORTHERN
AND SOUTHERN
NETHERLANDS

The
North
Sea

Germany

KOLLUM •
• LEEUWARDEN • GRONINGEN

• STEENWIJK

ZIJPE
• WARMENHUIZEN
• SCHOORL ENKHUIZEN
• ALKMAAR
• KAMPEN
HEEMSKERK
BEVERWIJK WIJK ZEE
ASSENDELFT • OOST ZAAN
HARLEM • AMSTERDAM

LEYDERDORP • LEYDEN
• THE HAGUE UTRECHT
• DELFT MONTFOORT
GOUDA
BRIELE
ROTTERDAM GORINCHEM NIJMEGEN
DORDRECHT • CLEVE
• CALCAR
ZIERIKZEE • S-HERTOGENBOSCH
VERE • BREDA
• MIDDELBURG BERGEN OP ZOOM BRUEGHEL
ROEMERSWAAL • HELMOND
HULST KEMPEN • VENLOO
• BRUGES • ANTWERP
• HERENTHALS
• GHENT
• MALINES • MASEYCK
YPRES • THIELT COLOGNE
• ISEGHEM • ALOST
• MEULEBEKE • LOUVAIN MAASTRICHT • VALKENBURG
• COURTRAI BRUSSELS AIX LA CHAPELLE
OUDENAERDE LIEGE
• TOURNAI MECKENHEIM
ARRAS NAMUR
• MONS • MARCHIENNES
France BOUVIGNES
MAUBEUGE • DINANT

N
W E
S

A B C D E

Reference Map

APPENDIX B

LOCALITIES, ARTISTS AND REFERENCE MAP

Abruzzo Italy, Aert Mijtens.
Aix la Chapelle (D-5),
  Lucas & Marten van
    Valckenborgh,
  Jan Fredeman de Vries.
Arbissola Italy,
  H.C.Vroom.
Alkmaar (C-2),
  Marten van Hemskerck.
Alost (B-5),
  Pieter Coeck.
Amsterdam (C-3),
  Pieter Aertsen,
  Francesco & Jan Badens,
  Dirck Barentsen,
  Abraham Bloemaert,
  Hans Bol,
  Gielis Coignet,
  Gillis van Conincxloo,
  Jacob Cornelisz van Oost Sanen,
  Jaques Jansz de Gheyn,
  Marten Hemskerck,
  Cornelis Ketel,
  Carel van Mander,
  Willem van Nieuwlandt,
  Geerit Pietersz,
  Joan Schoorel,
  Paulus de Vries,
  David Vinckeboons.
Antwerp (C-4),
  Paulus Bril,
  Cornelis Cornelisz,
  Hansken van den Elburcht,
  Cornelis Enghelrams,
  Geldorp (Gortzius),
  Jaques Jansz de Gheyn,
  Willem Key,
  Jan Mandijn,
  Willem van Nieuwlandt,
  Bernard van Orley,
  Gerrit Pietersz,
  Hans Soens,
  Marten de Vos,
  Jan Fredeman de Vries.
Aquila Italy,
  Aert Mitjens.

Arras (B-6),
  Joan Schoorel,
  Jan Cornelisz Vermeijen.
Assendelft (C-2),
  Marten Memskerck,
  Jan Sanredam.
Augsburg Germany,
  Hans van Aken,
  Hans Holbein.
Autun France,
  Dirck Pietersz Crabeth.
Bari Italy,
  Gaspar Huevick.
Basel Switzerland,
  Hans Holbein,
  Carel van Mander,
  Joan Schoorel.
Bergen op Zoom (C-4),
  Hans Bol.
Beverwijk (C-2),
  Jan Cornelisz Vermeijen.
Bois le Duc ('sHertogenbosch),
  Jeronimus Bos (van Aken),
  Cornelis Bloemaert,
  Anthonis Blocklandt,
  Hans Soens.
Bologna Italy,
  Hendrick Goltzius,
  Hans Hogenbergh.
Bouvignes (C-6),
  Joachim Patenier,
  Bles.
Breda (C-4),
  Matheus Bril,
  Willem Key,
  Joan Schoorel.
Briele (B-3),
  Herman van der Mast.
Brueghel (D-4),
  Pieter Breughel.
Bruges (B-4),
  Cornelis Cornelisz Kunst,
  Joannes van Eyck,
  Marcus Geerarts,
  Huge van der Goes,
  Hendrick Goltzius,

APPENDIX B

Hubert Goltzius,
Carel van Mander,
Claude van Mander,
Hans Memmelinck,
Pieter Pourbus,
Hans van der Straeten,
Hendrick Cornelisz Vroom,
Pieter de Witte (Candido).
Brunswick Germany,
Jan Fredeman de Vries.
Brussels (C-5),
Pieter Breughel,
Michiel Cocxie,
Frans Floris,
Lucas Gassel,
Anthonis More,
Bernard van Orley,
Gijsbert van Veen,
Jan Cornelis Vermeijen,
Rogier van der Weyde,
Joos van Winghen.
Calcar (D-3),
Jan van Calcker.
Caprarola Italy,
Bartholomeus Sprangher.
Cleve (D-3),
Jan van Calcker.
Cologne Germany (E-5),
Hans van Aken,
Geldorp (Gortzius),
Jan Schoorel,
Adriaen de Weerdt.
Constantinople Turkey,
Pieter Coeck.
Courtrai (B-5),
Louis Heme,
Carel van Mander,
Bernaert de Rijcke,
Jaques & Roeland Savery,
Pieter Vlerick.
Cremona Italy,
Pieter Vlerick.
Danzig Denmark,
Cornelis Ketel,
Jan Fredeman de Vries,
Frederick Henricksz Vroom,
Hendrick Cornelisz Vroom.
Delft (C-3),
Pieter Aertsen,
Hans Bol,
Pieter Diericksen Cluyt,

Marten Hemskerck,
Augustijn Joorisz,
Michiel Janssen Miereveld,
Pieter Cornelisz Rijck.
Denmark,
Jaques de Poindre.
Dinant (C-6),
Joachim Patenier.
Dordrecht (C-3),
Cornelis Bloemaert,
Marten Hemskerck,
Claes Snellaert.
Duisburg Belgium,
Hendrick Goltzius.
Eertswout,
Marten Hemskerck.
Elsinore Denmark,
Pieter Isaacsz.
Enkhuizen (C-2),
Hendrick Cornelisz Vroom.
England,
Joos van Cleef,
Marcus Geerarts,
Hans Holbein,
Lucas Cornelisz de Kock,
Anthonis Moro.
Fasangarten,
Bartholomeus Sprangher.
Florence Italy,
Hans van Aken,
Hendrick Goltzius,
Hans van der Straeten,
· Hendrick Cornelisz Vroom,
Pieter de Witte (Candido).
Fontainebleau France,
Lucas de Heere,
Cornelis Ketel,
Dirck Pietersz.
France,
Lucas de Heere.
Frankfort Germany,
Gillis van Conincxloy,
Adam Elsheimer,
Joos van Liere,
Hendrick van Steenwijck,
Marten van Valckenborgh,
Jan Fredeman de Vries,
Joos van Winghen.
Genoa Italy,
Hendrick Cornelisz Vroom.
Ghent (B-5),

534

APPENDIX B

Hubrecht van Eyck,
Joannes van Eyck,
Frans Floris,
Huge van der Goes,
Lucas de Heere,
Geerard Horebout,
Carel van Mander,
Benjamin Sammeling,
Lieven de Witte,
Carel van Ypres.
Gorichem (C-3),
Abraham Bloemaert.
Gouda (C-3),
Dirck Barentsen,
Anthonis Blocklandt
(Montfoort),
Cornelis Ketel,
Pieter Pourbus.
Groningen (E-1),
Herder van Groningen,
Carel van Ypres.
Groot-Ouwer,
Joan Schoorel.
The Hague (C-3),
Evert Krijnsz (van der Maes),
Aert Mijtens,
Jan van Ravesteyn,
Jan Fredeman de Vries.
Hamburg Germany,
Gielis Coignet,
Cornelis Enghelrams,
Hendrick Goltzius,
Cornelis de Visscher,
Jan Fredeman de Vries.
Haarlem (C-3),
Dirck Bouts,
Cornelis Claesz (van Wieringen),
Cornelis Cornelisz,
Geertgen tot Sint Jans,
Jaques de Gheyn,
Hendrick Goltzius,
Marten van Hemskerck,
Simon Jacobsz (van Gouda),
Carel van Mander,
Jan Mostart,
Albert van Ouwater,
Pieter Pietersz II,
Joan Schoorel,
Bartholomeus Sprangher,
Hendrick Cornelisz Vroom.
Heemskerk (C-2),

Marten van Hemskerck.
Heidelberg Germany,
Hans Bol.
Helmond (D-4),
Lucas Gassel.
Herenthals (C-4),
Jeroon Francken.
's-Hertogenbosch,
See Bois le Duc.
Heynsbeeck,
Hendrick Goltzius.
Hulst (B-4),
Frans Mostart,
Gillis Mostart.
Iseghem (B-5),
Carel van Mander.
Kampen (D-2),
Jan Fredeman de Vries.
Kollum (D-1),
Jan Fredeman de Vries.
Krems Austria,
Carel van Mander.
Leeuwarden (D-1),
Jan Fredeman de Vries.
Leyden (C-3),
Jan Ariaensz,
Cornelis Enghelbrechtsen,
Otto Vaenius,
Pieter de Vos.
Leyderdorp (C-3),
Cornelis Cornelisz Kunst.
Liege (D-5),
Lambert Lombardus,
Otto Vaenius,
Jan Fredeman de Vries.
Lisbon Portugal,
Hendrick Cornelisz Vroom.
Liverno (Leghorn) Italy,
Hendrick Cornelisz Vroom.
London England,
Joan Gossaert,
Lucas de Heere,
Hans Holbein,
Cornelis Ketel,
Carel van Mander,
Hendrick Cornelisz Vroom.
Los Barlingos Spain,
Hendrick Cornelisz Vroom.
Louvain (C-5),
Dirck Bouts,
Geldorp (Goltzius),

535

APPENDIX B

Joan Schoorel,
Rogier van der Weyde.
Lyons France,
Matheus & Paulus Bril,
Bartholomeus Sprangher,
Hendrick Cornelisz Vroom.
Maeseyck (D-5),
Hubrecht & Joannes van Eyck.
Malines (C-5),
See Mechlin.
Marchiennes (C-6),
Joan Schoorel.
Maubeuge (B-6),
Joan Gossaert.
Mechlin,
Gregorius Beerings,
Hans Bol,
Michiel Cocxie,
Frans Crabbe,
Cornelis Enghelrams,
Vincent Geldersman,
Hans Hoghenberg,
Augustijn Jorisz,
Hans Kaynoot,
Frans Minnebroer,
Jaques de Poindre,
Claes Rogier,
Hans Snellinck,
Pieter Stevens,
Lodewijck Toeput
(Pozzoserrato),
Frans Verbeeck,
David Vinckeboons,
Pieter Vlerick,
Jan Fredeman de Vries.
Medemblik,
Marten van Hemskerck.
Meulebeke (B-5),
Carel van Mander.
Middelburg (B-4),
Joan Gossaert,
Jan Cornelis Vermeijen.
Milan Italy,
Bartholomeus Sprangher,
Hendrick Cornelisz Vroom.
Mons (Bergen) (B-6),
Franciscus Savius.
Montfoort (C-3),
Anthonis van Montfoort,
Blocklandt.
Mulbracht,

Hendrick Goltzius.
Munich Germany,
Hans van Aken,
Hendrick Goltzius,
Jooris Hoefnaghel,
Hans Rottenhamer,
Christoffel Schwartz,
Pieter de Witte (Candido).
Namur (C-6),
Frans le Sayve.
Naples Italy,
Joannes van Eyck,
Hendrick Goltzius,
Aert Mijtens.
Nijmegen, Nimwegen (D-3),
De Stomme van Nijmegen.
Nürnberg Germany,
Hendrick Aldegraef,
Albrecht Dürer,
Carel van Mander,
Joan Schoorel.
Oostzaan (C-2),
Jacob Cornelis van Oost Sanen.
Oreste,
Gioncoy,
Bartholomeus Sprangher.
Orleans France,
Gillis van Conincxloy.
Oudenarde (B-5),
Caspar Heuvick,
Carel van Mander,
Frans Pourbus.
Padua Italy,
Joachim Utewael.
Paris France,
Abraham Bloemaert,
Nicolaes Bollery,
Toossain du Brevil,
Jaques Bunel,
Jeroon Francken,
Martinus Freminet,
Augustijn Jorisz,
Cornelis Ketel,
Herman van der Mast,
Bartholomeus Sprangher,
Hendrick Cornelisz Vroom.
Parma Italy,
Hans Soens,
Bartholomeus Sprangher.
Peniche,
Hendrick Cornelisz Vroom.

APPENDIX B

Pozzuoli Italy,
Hendrick Goltzius.
Prague Bohemia,
Hans van Aken,
Hans Mont,
Bartholomeus Sprangher,
Pieter Stevens,
Jan Cornelis Vermeijen,
Jan Fredeman de Vries.
Rhodes,
Joan Schoorel.
Roemerswaal, Romerswael (B-4),
Marinus de Seeu.
Rome Italy,
Hans van Aken,
Matheus & Paulus Bril,
Michiel Cocxie,
Adam Elsheimer,
Hendrick Goltzius,
Herder van Groningen,
Joseph Heintz,
Gaspar Heuvick,
Jooris Hoefnaghel,
Dominicus Lampsonius,
Carel van Mander,
Aert Mytens,
Willem van Nieuwlandt,
Gerrit Nop,
Geerit Pietersz,
Hans Rottenhamer,
Joan Schoorel,
Joan Soens,
Bartholomeus Sprangher,
Otto Vaenius,
Hendrick Cornelisz Vroom,
Pieter de Witte.
Rotterdam (C-3),
Abraham Bloemaert.
Rouen France,
Cornelis Cornelisz,
Hendrick Cornelisz Vroom.
Saint-Malo France,
Joachim Utewael.
San Lucar Spain,
Hendrick Cornelisz Vroom.
Schoorel (C-2),
Joan Schoorel.
Setubal,
Hendrick Cornelisz Vroom.
Seville Spain,
Hendrick Cornelisz Vroom.

Sichar,
Miereveldt, M.J.
Soest Germany,
Hendrick Aldegraef.
Spain,
Michiel Cocxie,
Damiaen van Gouda,
Antonis Moro.
Speyer, Spires Germany,
Joan Schoorel.
Steenwijk (D-2),
Hendrick van Steenwijck.
Strasburg Germany,
Joan Schoorel.
Thielt (B-5),
Carel van Mander.
Tivoli Italy,
Pieter Vlerick.
Tournai (B-5),
Joos de Beer,
Ambrosius Francken,
Carel van Mander,
Pieter Vlerick.
Trent Italy,
Hendrick Goltzius.
Treviso Italy,
Lodewyck Toeput.
Tunis,
Jan Cornelis Vermeijen.
Turin Italy,
Hendrick Cornelisz Vroom.
Utrecht (C-3),
Anthonis Montfort,
Abraham Bloemaert,
Cornelis Bloemaert,
Jaques de Gheyn,
Pauwels Moreelsz,
Joan Schoorel,
Joachim Utewael.
Valkenburg (D-5),
Lucas & Marten van
Valckenborgh.
Venice Italy,
Hans van Aken,
Jan van Calcker,
Albrecht Dürer,
Hendrick Goltzius,
Isaac Isaacsz,
Hans Rottenhamer,
Joan Schoorel,
Jan Swart,

APPENDIX B

Lodewyck Toeput,
Pieter Vlerick,
Hendrick Cornelisz Vroom.
Venloo (D-4),
Hendrick Goltzius,
Hubert Goltzius.
Vere (B-4),
Mabuse.
Vienna Austria,
Pieter Breughel,
Jooris Hoefnaghel,
Carel van Mander,
Bartholomeus Sprangher.
Warmenhuizen (C-2),
Pieter Aertsen,
Joan Schoorel.

Wolfenbüttel,
Jan Fredeman Vries.
Würzburg Germany,
Hubert Goltzius.
Wijk-aan-Zee (C-2),
Rijckaert Aertsz.
Ypres (A-5),
Joannes van Eyck.
Zierickzee (B-4),
Thomas van Zierickzee,
Marinus de Seeu (Romerswael).
Zwijndrecht,
Joos van Liere.
Zype (C-1),
Jan Cornelis Vermeijen.

APPENDIX C

INDEX TO SUBJECTS

APPENDIX C

Pieter Koeck.
Lambert Lombardus.
Lambrecht van Oort.
Johan Fredeman de Vries.
Pauwels de Vries.
Salomon de Vries.
Lieven de Witte.
ARCHITECTURAL DETAIL
BY ARTISTS:
Pieter Aertsen.
Jan Ariaensz.
Herri met de Bles.
Lansloot Blondeel.
Dirck Bouts.
Jan Breughel.
Pieter Breughel.
Hans Bol.
Jan van Calcker.
Hendrick van Cleef.
Joos van Cleef.
Geerard David.
Albrecht Dürer.
Adam Elsheimer.
Jan van Eyck.
Hubert van Eyck.
Cornelis Engelbrechtsen.
Michiel de Gast.
Marcus Geerarts.
Geertgen tot St Jans.
Huge van der Goes.
Jan Gossaert (Mabuse).
Louis Heme.
Jan van Hemsen.
Jooris Hoefnaghel.
Pieter Koeck (Van Aelst).
Lucas van Leyden.
Marinus de Seeu (van
Roemerswael).
Memling.
Quintyn Messijs.
Jan Mostart.
Cornelis Jacob van Oost Sanen.
Albert Ouwater.
Joachim Patenier.
Pieter Pourbus.
Roeland Savery.
Joan van Schoorel.
Hendrick van Steenwijck I.
Hendrick van Steenwijck II.
Jan Fredeman de Vries.
Paulus de Vries.

Salomon de Vries.
Rogier van der Weyden.
BATTLE SCENES:
Bernard de Doove,
Riot at Amsterdam, 1535.
Pieter Isaacsz.,
Roman Women in Revolt.
Joachim Patenier,
Hans Snellinck,
Joannes Stradanus,
Crusades.
Jan Cornelisz. Vermeyen,
Siege of Tunis,
Naval Victory.
Hendrick Cornelisz. Vroom,
Battle scenes on water and land
for Bottoin,
Battle of Nieuport,
Seventh day of the battle between
the Armada and the British
Salamis.
COPIES:
(Mentioned by Van Mander).
Hans van Aken, after Venetian
artists, Bartholomeus Sprangher.
Abraham Bloemaert, after Dirck
Barentsen, Pieter Aertsen,
Hendrick Uthoeck.
Michiel Cocxie, after Van Eyck,
Rogier van der Weyden.
Marcantonio, after Dürer.
Herman van der Mast, after Frans
Floris.
Antonis Moro, after Titian.
Aert Mijtens, after Italian artists.
Joan Schoorel, after Raphael,
Michelangelo, antique sculpture.
Hans Soens, after Frans Mostart.
Sprangher, after Marcus Duval,
Frans Floris, Parmentius.
Pieter Vlerick, after Michelangelo.
Federigo Zucchero, after Holbein.
DECORATIVE ARTS:
Ceramics—
Jan Floris.
Cornelis Henricksen (Vroom).
Hendrick Cornelisz Vroom.
Embroidery—
Frans Pieter Grobber.
Memorials—
Cornelis Enghelbrechtsen,

APPENDIX C

Lockhorst, Leyden.
Lucas de Heere, St John's
    Church, Ghent.
Hemskerck, Monument to
    Father.
Sprangher, St Matthew Church,
    Prague.
Pieter Vlerick, Du Prez, Tournai.
Jan Fredeman de Vries, Designs.
    St Peter's Church, Hamburg.
Fabrics—Painted
Rogier van der Weyden.
Willem Snellaert.
Glass Painting, (and cartoons):
Aert de Beer.
Volckert Claeszoon.
Pieter Cluyt.
Lucas Cornelisz.
Pieter Cornelisz Kunst.
Jaques Floris.
Marcus Geerarts.
Reyer Geeritsen.
Jaques de Gheyn, St Walburg
    Church, Antwerp; Minnebroer
    Church, Antwerp; Oude
    Kerck, Amsterdam.
Jaques de Gheyn II.
Hendrick Goltzius.
Joan de la Hame.
Lucas de Heere.
Jacob Lenartsz.
Lucas van Leyden.
Antonie Utewael.
Joachim Utewael.
David Vinckeboons.
Jan Fredeman de Vries.
Marcus Willems.
Lieven de Witte, St John's
    Church, Ghent.
Carel van Ypres.
Cornelis Ysbrandtsen.
Heraldic Designs:
Pieter Cluyt.
Albrecht Dürer.
Illumination and Miniatures:
Hans Bol.
Jaques de Gheyn II.
Jooris Hoefnaghel.
Hans Holbein.
Isaac Oliviers.
Anne Smijters.

Bartholomeus Sprangher.
Lucas van Valckenborgh.
David Vinckeboons.
Mural Decoration, (see techniques,
    fresco):
Pierre de la Cuffle.
Augustijn Jorisz.
Cornelis Ketel.
Cornelis Cornelisz Kunst.
Joan van Schoorel.
Hans Singher.
Claes Snellaert.
Bartholomeus Sprangher.
Pauwels de Vries.
Jan Fredeman de Vries.
Tapestry Cartoons:
Jeronimus Bosch.
Lucas de Heere.
Pieter Koeck van Aelst.
Joos van Liere.
Bernard van Orley.
Hans Singher.
Joannes Stradanus.
Willem Tons.
Jan Cornelisz Vermeijen.
Hendrick Cornelisz Vroom.
Marc Willemsz.
Pieter de Witte.
Triumphal Arches, Trophies:
Frans Floris.
Hans Mont.
Bartholomeus Sprangher.
Jan Fredeman de Vries.
Marcus Willems.
Carel van Mander.
Miscellaneous:
Michiel Cocxie, decoration, City
    Hall, Antwerp.
Pieter Vlerick, cartouches for
    lettering; Bellows; Coloring of
    statues.
Jan Fredeman de Vries, designs
    for cabinet makers, intarsia
    workers.
Carel van Ypres.
FIGURES (nudes etc.):
Hendrick Aldegraef.
Heyndrick van Balen.
Anthonis Blocklandt.
Matheus du Breul.
Chrispiaen van den Broecke.

541

APPENDIX C

Jan van Calcker.
Joos van Cleef.
Marten van Cleef.
Willem van Cleef.
Gielis Coignet.
Cornelis Cornelisz.
Albrecht Dürer.
Marcus Geerarts.
Simon Kies.
Dirck van der Laen.
Lucas van Leyden.
Joos van Liere.
Cornelis Molenaer.
Gillis Mostart.
Jan Nagel.
Adam van Oort.
Geerit Pietersz. (Sweling).
Pieter Pourbus.
Jan Swart.
Hubert Tons.
Hendrick Cornelisz. Vroom.
FIGURES, (compositions no
    specific subject):
Jan Augustijnsz.
Volckert Claeszoon.
Pieter Diericksen Cluyt.
Elsheimer.
Ambrosius Francken.
Martinus Freminet.
Frans Pieter Grobber.
Hans Jordaen.
Evert Krijnsz. van der Maes.
Leonard Kroes.
Aert Mijtens.
Pieter Cornelisz Rijck.
Hans Soens.
Bernaert van Somer.
Pauwels Somer.
Frans Stellaert.
Lodewijck Toeput.
FIRES, (artificial effects etc.):
Lansloot Blondeel.
Nicolaes Bollery.
Lodewijck Jans van den Bosch.
Gielis Coignet.
Hans Jordaens.
Hans Soens.
GENRE:
Banker in his office, Marinus de
    Seeu.
Banquet, Francesco Badens.

—, Dirck Barentsen.
—, Abraham Bloemaert.
—, Hendrick Goltzius.
—, nocturnal, Joos van Winghen.
Bathing scene, Joannes van Eyck.
Bawdy Houses, Guilliame Tons.
Canal-Digging, Pieter Breughel, I.
Children's plays, Pieter Breughel, I.
Children playing in water, Pieter
    Vlerick.
Fairs, Pieter Aertsen.
—, Pieter Balthasar Balten.
Farmer and wife, etc., Lucas van
    Leyden.
Fisher-folks, etc., Hendrick
    Cornelisz. Vroom.
Fish-Market, Joachim Buecklaer.
Fruit Markets, Joachim Buecklaer.
—, Dierick de Vries.
Genre, Guilliame Tons.
Hunting Scenes, Joannes Stradanus.
Indian with bow, Hendrick
    Goltzius.
Kitchen-scenes, Pieter Aertsen.
—, Joachim Buecklaer.
—, Michiel Janssen Miereveld.
—, Pieter Cornelis Rijck.
—, Joachim Utewael.
Lent and Carnival, Pieter
    Breughel, I.
Lottery, Gielis Coignet.
—, David Vinckeboons.
Lovers, Francesco Badens.
Mardi-Gras, Nicolaes Bollery.
Masquerades, Francesco Badens.
—, Nicolaes Bollery.
Mercer, and monkeys, Herri met de
    Bles.
Money-Changers, Jan Messijs.
Musical Duet, Lucas van Leyden.
Peasant Weddings, Pieter
    Breughel, I.
—, Frans Verbeeck.
—, David Vinckeboons.
Peasant Woman, Hendrick
    Goltzius.
Peasants, soldiers, etc., Hans
    Jordaens.
Tooth-pulling, Lucas van Leyden.
LANDSCAPES:
Jan Ariaensz.

APPENDIX C

Herri met de Bles.
Abraham Bloemaert.
Frans Boels.
Hans Bol.
Jan Breughel.
Pieter Breughel.
Mattheus Bril.
Paulus Bril.
Niclaes Bruyn.
Hendrick van Cleef.
Gielis Coignet.
Gillis Conincxloy.
Cornelis van Dale.
Aert Jansz Druyvesteyn.
Lucas Gassel.
Marcus Geerarts.
Jansz Govert.
Jaques Grimmaer.
Frans Pieter Grobber.
Niclaes van der Heck.
Lucas de Heere.
Marten Hemskerck.
Jooris Hoefnaghel.
Jan van Amstel, de Hollander.
Hans Jordaen.
Jeroon de Kock.
Mathijs de Kock.
Pieter Koeck van Aelst.
Leonard Kroes.
Joos van Liere.
Balthasar Louwers.
Cornelis Molenaer.
Joos de Momper.
Frans Mostart.
Jan Mostart.
Jan Nagel.
Willem van Nieuwlandt.
Joachim Patenier.
Pieter Pourbus.
Claes Rogier.
Caesar de Salusto.
Joan van Schoorel.
Hans Soens.
Bartholomeus Sprangher.
Fransoys Stellaert.
Jan Swart.
Lodewijck Toeput (Pozzoserrato).
Hans Tons.
Willem Tons.
Lucas van Valckenborgh.
Marten van Valckenborgh.

Frans Verbeeck.
Hans Vereycke.
Tobias Verhaecht.
David Vinckeboons.
Pieter Vlerick.
Sebastiaen Vrancx.
Hendrick Cornelisz Vroom.
Adriaen de Weerdt.
Cornelis de Witte.
MISCELLANEOUS,
Religious Subjects:
Adoration of the Lamb, Van Eyck.
Angel Choir, Van Eyck.
Dispute of the Doctors, Sprangher.
Fall of Lucifer, Dirck Barentsen.
—, Cornelis Cornelisz.
—, Frans Floris.
Hell, Jeronimus Bosch.
Miracle, Geertgen tot St Jans.
—, Jeronimus Bosch.
Monk disputing Heretics,
    Jeronimus Bosch.
Susanna and the Elders, Aldegraef.
—, Vincent Geldersman.
—, Gualdrop Gortzius.
—, Pieter Vlerick.
MISCELLANEOUS SUBJECTS:
Drolleries, Jan Mandijn.
Dulle Griet, Pieter Breughel I.
Ghost Scenes, Jan Mandijn.
—, Frans Verbeeck.
Mannequins, Hendrick Uthoeck.
National Costumes, Lucas de Heere.
—, Jooris Hoefnaghel.
Nine Valiant Knights, Jacob
    Cornelisz.
Owl (as signature), Herri de Bles.
Remedies against Death, Pieter
    Breughel I.
Sketch book, Jooris Hoefnaghel.
Turks on Horseback, Jan Swart.
MYTHOLOGY:
Andromeda, Joos van Winghen.
Apelles painting Campaspe, Joos
    van Winghen.
Bacchus, Joos van Cleef.
Bacchus, Ceres, Venus, Cupid,
    Hendrick Goltzius.
Triumph of Bacchus, Otto Vaenius.
Danaë, Hans van Aken.
—, Hendrick Goltzius.

543

APPENDIX C

—, Cornelis Ketel.
—, (copy after Titian), Moro.
Dedalus and Icarus, Hans Bol.
Democritus and Heraclitus,
Cornelis Ketel.
Diana, Gualdrop Gortzius.
Diana and Acteon, Hans
Rottenhammer.
Dido, Marcus Willems.
Fastes, Hubert Goltz.
Faun and Fauna, Hendrick
Goltzius.
Three Graces, Pierre de la Cuffle.
—, Augustijn Jorisz.
—, Israel van Mentz.
—, Albrecht Dürer.
Harpocrates, Cornelis Ketel.
Works of Hercules, Aldegraef.
Hercules, Frans Floris.
—, Hendrick Goltzius.
—, seated, Hendrick Goltzius.
—, after Floris, Simon Kies.
Hercules and Justice, Sprangher.
Leda, Vincent Geldersman.
Lucretia, Albrecht Dürer.
—, Hendrick Goltzius.
—, Jan Gossaert.
—, Geeraert van der Meire.
Mars and Venus, Joachim
Utenwael.
Flying Mercury, Sprangher.
Mercury and Psyche, Sprangher.
Muses, Frans Floris.
Niobe, Abraham Bloemaert.
Orpheus, Jan Fredeman de Vries.
Pallas, Lucas van Leyden.
Judgement of Paris, Hans van
Aken.
Perseus, Dirck Barentsen.
Peleus and Thetis, Cornelis
Cornelisz.
Vedding of Psyche, Sprangher.
Thetis, Cornelis Cornelisz.
Venus, Dirck Barentsen.
—, Anthonis Blocklandt.
—, Jaques de Gheyn.
—, Pieter Vlerick.
Venus and Adonis, Hans van Aken.
Venus and Cupid, Hans van Aken.
—, Hendrick Goltzius.
Venus, Juno and Pallas, Abraham

Bloemaert.
—, Jaques de Backer.
Venus and Mercury, Sprangher.
Zeus and Five Nude Figures, Otto
Vaenius.
Banquet of the Gods, Abraham
Bloemaert.
—, Hendrick Goltzius.
—, Marten van Hemskerck.
—, Jan Mostart.
—, Joachim Utenwael.
Banquet of Sea Goddesses,
Abraham Bloemaert.
—, Frans Floris.
Golden Age, Cornelis Cornelisz.
Laughing Woman and Satyr,
Hendrick Goltzius.
NEW TESTAMENT:
Christ,
Dirck Bouts.
Albrecht Dürer.
Cornelis Ketel.
Jan Cornelisz. Vermeijen.
Adoration of the Magi,
Pieter Aertsen.
Albrecht Dürer.
Hendrick Goltzius.
Marten van Hemskerck.
Lucas van Leyden.
Aert Mijtens.
Frans Pourbus I.
Pieter Vlerick.
Adultery, the woman taken in,
Lucas Cornelisz. de Kock.
Lieven de Witte.
Apostles, and Christ,
Cornelis Ketel.
Jan van Hemsen.
Ascension,
Anthonis Blocklandt.
Lucas de Heere.
Marten van Hemskerck.
Baptism of Christ,
Frans Pourbus I.
Pieter Pourbus.
Joan Schoorel.
Bartimeus, the Blind man of Jericho.
Lucas van Leyden.
Blind, Christ healing the,
David Vinckeboons.
Burdened, All who are,

544

Willem Key.
Burial of Christ,
Anthonis Blocklandt.
Children, blessing of the,
Frans Floris.
Joos van Winghen.
Circumcision,
Pieter Aertsen.
Jacob Cornelisz. (van Oost
Sanen).
Hendrick Goltzius.
Aert Mijtens.
Antonis Moro.
Frans Pourbus I.
Coronation of Christ,
Geerard Horebout.
Aert Mijtens.
Cross, carrying of the,
Aertgen van Leyden.
Jeronimus Bos.
Pieter Breughel I.
Cornelis Cornelisz. (Kunst).
Albrecht Dürer.
Frans Floris.
Herman van der Mast (copy of
Floris).
Gillis Mostart.
Bernaert de Rijcke.
David Vinckeboons.
Cross, descent from the,
Cornelis Cornelisz. (Kunst).
Jacob Cornelisz. (van Oost
Sanen).
Cornelis Enghelbrechtsen.
Geertgen tot St Jans.
Vincent Geldersman.
Huge van der Goes.
Jan Gossaert.
Geerard Horebout.
Quintijn Messijs.
Rogier van der Weyde.
Crucifixion,
Aertgen van Leyden.
Pieter Aertsen.
Jaques de Backer.
Dirck Barentsen.
Herri met de Bles.
Anthonis Blocklandt.
Hans Bol.
Michiel Cocxie.
Jacob Cornelisz. (van Oost

Sanen).
Frans Crabbe.
Albrecht Dürer.
Cornelis Enghelbrechtsen.
Frans Floris I.
Geertgen tot St Jans.
Michiel Gioncoy.
Huge van der Goes.
Hendrick Goltzius.
Marten van Hemskerck.
Lucas van Leyden.
Aert Mijtens.
Jaques de Poindre.
Joan Schoorel.
Bartholomeus Sprangher.
Joannes Stradanus.
Pieter Vlerick.
Joos van Winghen.
Dead Christ,
Anthonis Blocklandt.
Ecce Homo,
Pieter Aertsen.
Herri met de Bles.
Joachim Buecklaer.
Lucas van Leyden.
Jan Mostart.
Emmaus, Christ at,
Pieter Aertsen.
Herri met de Bles.
Lucas de Heere.
Joseph Heintz.
Feeding of the Poor,
Cornelis Inghelrams.
Flagellation of Christ,
Geerard Horebout.
Garden, Christ in the,
Bartholomeus Sprangher.
Groom, the,
Cornelis Ketel (sculpture).
Last Supper,
Michiel Cocxie.
Lambert Lombardus.
Gillis Mostart.
Joan van Schoorel.
Bartholomeus Sprangher.
Paulus de Vries.
Joos van Winghen.
Lazarus,
Cornelis Cornelisz.
Albert van Ouwater.
Pieter Cornelisz. van Rijck.

545

APPENDIX C

Adriaen de Weerdt.
Martha,
 Pieter Aertsen.
Mary, and Christ,
 Gualdrop Gortzius.
 Chrispiaen van de Passe.
Mary, Christ and John,
 Cornelis Ketel.
Mary Magdalene,
 Jan Cransse.
 Lucas de Heere.
Merchants, driving away of,
 Pieter Vlerick.
 Jan Fredeman de Vries.
Mocking of Christ,
 Hans van Aken.
Mount, Sermon on the,
 Joan Schoorel.
Nativity,
 Aertgen Van Leyden.
 Pieter Aertsen.
 Hans van Aken.
 Hendrick Aldegraef.
 Dirck Barentsen.
 Anthonis Blocklandt.
 Frans Floris I.
 Marten van Hemskerck.
 Jan Mostart.
 Frans Pourbus I.
 Jan Cornelisz. Vermeijen.
 Adriaen de Weerdt.
 Carel van Ypres.
Palm Sunday,
 Joachim Buecklaer.
 Jan van Hemsen.
 Joan Schoorel.
Passion of Christ,
 Herri met de Bles.
 Anthonis Blocklandt.
 Cornelis Cornelisz.
 Jacob Cornelis (van Oost Sanen).
 Zacharias Dolendo.
 Albrecht Dürer.
 Hendrick Goltzius.
 Marten van Hemskerck.
 Lucas van Leyden.
 Carel van Mander.
 Christoffel Schwartz.
 Bartholomeus Sprangher.
 Joannes Stradanus.
 Pieter Vlerick.

Pentecost,
 Anthonis Blocklandt.
 Lucas de Heere.
Pharisees, and Christ,
 Jan Fredeman de Vries.
Pieta,
 Hendrick Goltzius.
Preaching of Christ,
 Jan Swart.
 David Vinckeboons.
Presentation of Christ,
 Joan Schoorel.
Prodigal Son,
 Albrecht Dürer.
Publican,
 Cornelis Ketel.
Resurrection,
 Hans van Aken.
 Herri met de Bles.
 Michiel Cocxie.
 Frans Floris.
 Marten van Hemskerck.
 Antonis Moro.
 Bartholomeus Sprangher.
 Jan Cornelisz. Vermeijen.
 Pieter Vlerick.
 Carel van Ypres.
Samaria, the woman of,
 Michiel Janssen Miereveld.
Sepulchre, the holy,
 Joan Schoorel.
Shepherds, annunciation to the,
 Joachim Utewael.
Sorrows, the Man of,
 Hendrick Goltzius.
Temptation of Christ,
 Pieter Breughel I.
Thomas, and Christ,
 Joan Schoorel.
Triumph of Christ,
 Willem Key.
 Bartholomeus Sprangher.
 Jan Fredeman de Vries.
Vineyard, the parable of,
 Frans Verbeeck.
Virgin,
 Aertgen van Leyden.
 Joos van Cleef (Foolish Cleef).
 Michiel Cocxie.
 Albrecht Dürer.
 Van Eyck.

Frans Floris.
Jan Gossaert (Mabuse).
Lucas van Leyden.
Quintijn Messijs.
Aert Mijtens.
Gillis Mostart.
Joan van Schoorel.
Bartholomeus Sprangher.
Hans Vereycke.
Pieter Vlerick.
Adoration of the Virgin,
Pieter Aertsen.
Cornelis Enghelbrechtsen.
Huge van der Goes.
Hendrick Goltzius.
Jan Gossaert (Mabuse).
Geerard Horebout.
Cornelis Ketel.
Lucas van Leyden.
Annunciation,
Anthonis Blocklandt.
Marten van Hemskerck.
Lucas van Leyden.
Frans Minnebroer.
Pieter Vlerick.
Assumption,
Anthonis Blocklandt.
Albrecht Dürer.
Frans Floris.
Aert Mijtens.
Hans Rottenhammer.
Bartholomeus Sprangher.
Coronation,
Van Eyck.
Death of the Virgin,
Pieter Aertsen.
Michiel Cocxie.
Flight into Egypt,
Jeronimus Bosch.
Frans Minnebroer.
Life of the Virgin,
Adriaen de Weerdt.
Seven Sorrows of Mary,
Cornelis Enghelbrechtsen.
Visitation,
Frans Minnebroer.
Pieter Pourbus.
Mary with Angels,
Aertgen van Leyden.
Joos van Cleef (Foolish Cleef).
Albrecht Dürer.

See also Christ,
Nativity,
Adoration of the Magi,
Mary and Christ,
Mary, Christ, and John,
Descent from the Cross.
Apostles, Evangelists etc.,
Pieter Aertsen.
Anthonis Blocklandt.
Joachim Bueckelaer.
Gualdrop Gortzius.
Jan van Hemsen.
Cornelis Ketel.
Aert Mijtens.
Albert van Ouwater.
Joannes Stradanus.
Pieter Vlerick.
Last Judgement,
Aertgen van Leyden.
Dirck Barentsen.
Frans Floris I.
Lucas van Leyden.
Gillis Mostart.
Bernard van Orley.
Bartholomeus Sprangher.
Pieter Vlerick.
Carel van Ypres.
OLD TESTAMENT:
Abraham and Isaac,
Aertgen van Leyden.
Cornelis Enghelbrechtsen.
Joan Schoorel.
Abraham, Sarah, etc.,
Jan Mostart.
Adam and Eve,
Jaques de Backer.
Cornelis Cornelisz.
Albrecht Dürer.
Joannes and Huybrecht van
Eyck.
Frans Floris I.
Jan Gossaert.
Marten van Hemskerck.
Pieter Isaacsz.
Lucas van Leyden.
Angels, the fall of,
Christoffel Schwartz.
Babel, the tower of,
Pieter Breughel I.
Jan Fredeman de Vries.
Bathsheba,

547

Francesco Badens.
Anthonis Blocklandt.
Bible illustrations,
  Hans Holbein.
Burning Bush,
  Joannes van Eyck.
Caleb,
  Hans Hoghenberg.
David,
  Huge van der Goes.
  Cornelis Inghelrams.
  Lucas van Leyden.
Deluge,
  Gregorius Beerings.
  Joachim Bueckelaer.
  Cornelis Cornelisz.
Esther and Assuerus,
  Gualdrop Gortzius.
Fiery Furnace,
  Pieter Pietersz. I.
Gideon,
  Joannes van Eyck.
Golden Calf,
  Lucas van Leyden.
Joseph,
  Pieter Aertsen.
  Rijckaert Aertsz.
  Anthonis Blocklandt.
  Lucas van Leyden.
  Pieter Vlerick.
Joshua,
  Hans Hoghenberg.
Judith,
  Dirck Barentsen.
  Gielis Coignet.
  Cornelis Ketel.
  Michiel Janssen Miereveld.
  Pieter Vlerick.
  Marcus Willems.
Lot,
  Herri met de Bles.
  Joachim Utewael.
Maccabees,
  Pieter Vlerick.
Paradise,
  Hendrick Goltzius.
Paradise, terrestrial,
  Frans Pourbus I.
Passage of the Jordan,
  Joan Schoorel.
Purification, Children of Israel,

Cornelis Cornelisz.
Phyneas,
  Joos van Winghen.
Rebecca,
  Lucas van Leyden.
Red Sea, passing the,
  Aertgen van Leyden.
Ruth,
  Adriaen de Weerdt.
Samson,
  Joos van Winghen.
Saul,
  Cornelis Ketel.
  Lucas van Leyden.
Serpent, the brazen,
  Pieter Vlerick.
Serpents, the biting of,
  Cornelis Cornelisz.
  Cornelis Enghelbrechtsen.
  Marten van Hemskerck.
  Pieter Vlerick.
Solomon's Judgment,
  Aertgen van Leyden.
  Pieter Vlerick.
PERSPECTIVE:
Albrecht Dürer.
Louis Heme.
Cornelis van Vianen.
Jan Fredeman de Vries.
Pauwels de Vries.
Lieven de Witte.
PORTRAITS:
Hans van Aken:
  Duchess.
  William V, Duke of Bavaria,
    Duchess & children.
  Fugger.
  Jean de Bologne.
  Self-portrait.
  Self-portrait with Donna
    Venusta.
Aertgen van Leyden:
  Family of Dirick Jacobs.
Hendrick Aldegraef:
  Jan van Leyden.
  Knipperdolling.
  Princes.
  Self-portrait.
Francesco Badens.
Hans Bamesbier.
Dirck Barentsen:

APPENDIX C

Banquet of Archers.
Dirck Barentsen and his wife.
Group of Skippers.
Guild of the Archers.
Titian.
Anthonis Blocklandt:
  Cornelis van Montfoort and his
    wife, (the artist's father and
    mother).
Cornelis Bos:
  Francis I taken prisoner by
    Charles V.
Pieter Breughel II.
Jan van Calcker:
  Portrait of Italian painters,
    sculptors and architects in the
    books of Vasari.
Alart Claessen.
Hendrick van Cleef.
Adriaen Cluyt.
Cornelis Cornelisz.:
  Corporaelschap (group of
    archers).
Cornelis van Gouda.
Cornelis Cornelisz. Kunst:
  Self-portrait with his second
    wife.
Cornelis Cort:
  Joachim Patenier.
Albrecht Dürer:
  Cardinal.
  Duke of Saxony.
  Emperors (Charlemagne, etc.).
  Erasmus.
  Lucas van Leyden.
  Melanchton.
  The artist's mother.
  Patenier.
  Self-portrait.
  Self-portrait with long hair.
  Self-portrait as the prodigal son.
  Small self-portrait.
Marc Duval.
Cornelis Enghelsen.
Joannes van Eyck:
  Arnolfini.
  Count Philip the Good of
    Flanders.
  Joannes and Huybrecht van Eyck
    on horseback.

Frans Floris I.:
  Abbot Lucas.
Jeroon Francken I.
Vincent Geldersman:
  Cleopatra.
Jaques de Gheyn:
  Miniature portraits.
Joos Gietleughen:
  Roman Emperors engraved for
    the books of Hubert Goltz.
Huge van der Goes:
  Girl.
Hubert Goltz:
  Medals of the Roman Emperors.
  Monk.
Hendrick Goltzius:
  Hans Bol.
  Jan Govertsen.
  Jesuit Priests.
  Musius Savola.
  Polish Princes.
  Roman Heroes.
  Christoffel Schwartz.
Gualdrop Gortzius.
Jan Gossaert:
  Two young boys at Whitehall.
Frans Pietersz. Grobber.
Lucas de Heere:
  Sr Van Wacken, his wife and
    Cosijntgen.
Jooris Hoefnaghel:
  The first Mrs Hoefnaghel.
  Self-portrait.
Hans Holbein:
  Archbishop of Canterbury
    (Willem Warham).
  Countess Christine of Milan.
  Edward, son of Henry VIII.
  Elizabeth, daughter of Henry
    VIII.
  Erasmus.
  Friends of More.
  Grant to the Surgeons.
  Henry VIII.
  Lord Thomas Cromwell.
  Mary, daughter of Henry VIII.
  Thomas More.
  Sr Niclaes, Astronomer to Henry
    VIII.
  Queen of England (Jane
    Seymour).

549

APPENDIX C

Pieter Isaacsz.:
Pieter Huyghesz.
Pieter Huyghesz.'s first wife.
Jacob Poppe.
Sara Schuyrmans.
Pieter Semeynes.
Dierick Jacobsz.
Hubert Jacobsz.
Simon Jacobsz:
Willem Tybout, glass-painter.
Jerrigh.
Cornelis Ketel:
Archers under Dirck
Roosencrans.
Archers under Captain Herman
Rodenborgh Beths.
Elizabeth, Queen of England.
Goldsmith.
Secretary Haen.
Hanseatic League members, in
London.
Heads in the Leczinski
collection.
Heraclitus, the crying
philosopher.
Sr Wolfaert Hermans.
Vincent Jacobsen.
Hendrick de Keyser.
Jan Lammersen.
Simon Lock.
Francesco Morosini.
Francesco Morosini (second one,
reversed).
A Muscovite.
Mr Nock.
The Duke of Oxford.
A Portuguese girl.
Self-portrait.
Andries Vrericksen.
Willem Key:
Duke of Alva.
Rules of Antwerp.
Pieter Koeck (van Aelst).
Evert Krijnsz (van der Maes).
Lucas van Leyden:
Albrecht Dürer.
Emperor Maximilian.
Self-portrait.
Francoys Menton.
Michiel Janssen Miereveld:
Brewers at Delft.

Burgomaster Gerit Jansz van der
Eyck, with his wife and
children.
Jan Govertsz.
Old Man with a huge beard.
Princess of Orange (Louise de
Coligny).
Jaques Razet.
Rutger Jansz.
Aert Mijtens.
Pauwels Moreelsz.:
Count and Countess of
Culemborgh.
Mme Knotter.
Antonis Moro:
Concubines of Alva.
King John III of Portugal.
King Philip II of Spain.
Princess of Portugal (Marie,
sister of the King).
Queen Catherine of Portugal.
Queen Mary Tudor.
Joan Schoorel.
Spanish nobility.
Gillis Mostart:
Messrs Schets, Lords of Hoboken.
Jan Mostart:
Jacob of Bavaria, and van
Borssele.
Pier Muys.
Self-portrait.
Isaac Oliviers:
Miniature portraits.
Cornelis Hendricksz. Vroom.
Isaac Oserijn:
A Grandfather.
Aert Pietersz.
Geerit Pietersz.
Pieter Pietersz. I.
Jaques de Poindre:
Pieter Andries.
Frans Pourbus I.
Frans Pourbus II.
Pieter Pourbus:
Duc d'Alencon.
Jan van Ravesteyn.
Pieter Cornelisz. Rijck.
Benjamin Sammeling.
Joan Schoorel:
Kneeling figure of the Emperor,
and Bishop Conrad.

APPENDIX C

Knights of Jerusalem.
Pope Adrian VI.
Bernaert van Somer.
Pauwels van Somer.
Bartholomeus Sprangher:
  Lady in waiting of the Duchess
  of Aremberg.
  Portraits after the crayon
  drawings of Marcus.
Fransoys Stellaert.
Otto Vaenius:
  Archduke Albert and Isabella.
Lucas Valckenborgh:
  Small portraits.
Hans Vereycke:
  Claude van Mander and family.
Jan Cornelisz. Vermeijen:
  A Daughter.
  The Artist's second wife.
  Self-portrait.
  A Young Child with beautiful
  hair.
Cornelis de Visscher.
Pieter Vlerick.
Cornelis van der Voort.
Marten de Vos.
Hendrick Cornelisz. Vroom:
  Portrait of a priest at Setubal.
Joos van Winghen.
Rogier van der Weyden:
  Portrait painted for a Queen.
SAINTS:
St Andrew, martyrdom,
  Christoffel Schwartz.
St Anne,
  Joachim Buecklaer.
  Augustijn Jorisz.
  Jan Mostart.
  Bartholomeus Sprangher.
St Anthony, Temptation,
  Lucas van Leyden.
St Anthony, with other saints,
  Bartholomeus Sprangher.
Apotheosis of saints,
  Hans Rottenhammer.
St Augustine,
  Hans Soens.
St Barbara,
  Michiel Cocxie.
  Joannes van Eyck.
  Pieter Vlerick.

St Boniface,
  Marten van Hemskerck.
St Catherine, Beheading of, and
Madonna,
  Pieter Aertsen.
  Hans van Aken.
  Anthonis Blocklandt.
  Huge van der Goes.
  Aert Mijtens.
St Cecilia,
  Joannes and Huybrecht van
  Eyck.
St Christopher,
  Marten van Hemskerck.
  Jan Mostart.
  Frans Verbeeck.
St Clement,
  Paulus Bril.
St Elizabeth, with other saints,
  Bartholomeus Sprangher.
St Erasmus, and St James,
  Bartholomeus Sprangher.
St Francis,
  Anthonis Blocklandt.
St George,
  Frans Pourbus I.
St Helena,
  Hans van Aken.
St Hubert,
  Lucas van Leyden.
  Jan Mostart.
  Pieter Pourbus.
St James, beheading of,
  Anthonis Blocklandt.
  Jan Gossaert.
St James, and St Erasmus,
  Bartholomeus Sprangher.
St Jerome,
  Lodewijck Jan van den Bosch.
  Joannes van Eyck.
  Pieter Vlerick.
St John, the Baptist,
  Pieter Balthasar Balten.
  Pieter Isaacsz.
  Joan Schoorel.
  Bartholomeus Sprangher.
  Marcus Willems.
St John, boiled in oil,
  Bartholomeus Sprangher.
  Quintijn Messijs.
St Lawrence,

551

APPENDIX C

Marten van Hemskerck.
Joan Schoorel.
St Luke,
  Michiel Cocxie.
Frans Floris, I.
Marten van Hemskerck.
Bernard van Orley.
St Macarius,
  Frans Floris I.
St Mary Magdalene,
  Jan Cransse.
Vincent Geldersman.
Lucas de Heere.
Cornelis Ketel.
Lucas van Leyden.
St Thomas More,
  Hans Holbein.
St Paul,
  Pieter Breughel I.
Cornelis Inghelrams.
Cornelis Ketel.
Lucas van Leyden.
Joos van Winghen.
Carel van Ypres.
St Paul and St Peter,
  Dirck Bouts.
Lucas van Leyden.
Albert van Ouwater.
St Peter,
  Hansken van den Elburcht.
Cornelis Ketel.
Gillis Mostart.
St Sebastian,
  Hans van Aken.
Michiel Cocxie.
Herman van der Mast.
Bartholomeus Sprangher.
St Stephen,
  Joan Schoorel.
St Thomas, and Christ,
  Joan Schoorel.
St Ursula,
  Hans Memmelinck.
Virgins, eleven thousand,
  Joan Schoorel.
SCULPTORS:
Claudius Floris.
Cornelis Floris II.
Sybrecht Goltz.
Jan de Heere.
Frederick Henricksen.

Cornelis Ketel.
Hans Mont.
Joan Schoorel.
Cornelis Henricksen Vroom.
Pieter de Witte.
STUCCO DECORATION:
Bartholomeus Sprangher.
SHIPS:
Cornelis Claeszoon (van
  Wieringhen).
Hendrick Cornelisz. Vroom.
STILL LIFE:
Pauwels van Aelst.
Abraham Bloemaert.
Lodewijck Jans van den Bosch.
Cornelis Cornelisz.
Jaques de Gheyn, II.
Dierick de Vries.
TECHNIQUES:
Drawings,
  Pieter Aertsen, cartoon for altar
    painting.
  Hans van Aken, drawings after
    Sprangher.
  Jan van Calcker.
  Hendrick van Cleve, drawings
    for 'Ruinarum varii prospectus,
    rurumque aliquot delinationes.'
  Marcus Duval, portraits.
  Michiel Cocxie, after Raphael.
  Frans Floris I, after Michelangelo.
  Jan Gossaert (Mabuse), black
    crayon drawings.
  Lucas de Heere, river Meuse.
  Marten van Hemskerck, after
    Michelangelo.
  Joseph Heintz, classical sculpture.
  Jooris Hoefnaghel, sketchbook.
  Pieter Koeck van Aelst, sculpture.
  Lambert Lombardus mediaeval
    sculpture.
  Pieter Geeritz Montfoort,
    drawings on blue paper.
  Bartholomeus Sprangher,
    Resurrection of Christ.
Pen Drawings,
  Abraham Bloemaert.
  Hendrick Goltzius.
  Bartholomeus Sprangher.
  Pieter Vlerick.
Embroidery,

APPENDIX C

Frans Pietersz Grobber.
Engraving,
  Aldegraef (Aldegrever).
  Nicolas de Bruyn.
  Dirck Volckertsz Coornhert.
  Jacob Cornelisz van Oost-Sanen.
  Cornelis Cort.
  Lucas Cranach.
  Zacharias Dolendo.
  Albrecht Dürer.
  Philip Galle.
  Jaques de Gheyn.
  Joos Gietleughen.
  Hendrick Goltzius.
  Gualdrop Gortzius.
  Hans Holbein.
  Lucas van Leyden.
  Hipse Marten (Schöngauer).
  Jacob Matham.
  Françoys Menton.
  Joan Muller.
  Gielis Sadlaer.
  Joan Sadlaer.
  Raphael Sadlaer.
  Jan Saenredam.
  Gysbert van Veen.
  David Vinckeboons.
Etching,
  Adam Elsheimer (van
  Frankfort).

Marcus Geerarts.
Jeroon de Kock.
Lucas van Leyden.
David Vinckeboons.
Fresco,
  Gielis Coignet.
  Caesar de Salusto.
  Hans Soens.
  Bartholomeus Sprangher
  Joannes Stradanus.
  Pieter Vlerick.
  Pieter de Witte.
  Carel van Ypres.
Watercolor,
  Pieter Bom.
  Jooris Hoefnaghel.
  Lucas Cornelisz de Kock
  Lucas van Leyden.
  Joan van Schoorel.
  Hans Singher.
  Hans Tons.
  Willem Tons.
  Frans Verbeeck.
  David Vinckeboons.
  Philip Vinckeboons.
  Pieter Vlerick.
  Jan Fredeman de Vries.
  Hendrick Cornelisz Vroo:.
Coloring of Woodcuts,
  Quentijn Messijs.

APPENDIX D

COLLECTIONS MENTIONED BY VAN MANDER

(from Greve, *Bijlage*, I)

P   oil painting,
W   water-color,
S   sculpture,
F   fresco,
G   stained glass,
D   drawings, cartoons,
I   illumination,
*   seen by Van Mander,
B   known from printed sources.

The figures indicate the number of works of each kind.

ALKMAAR,
Kerk: Heemskerck-*P
v.d.Heck,J.:Heemskerck-*P2
v.Sonneveldt (widow): Jacob
    Cornelisz-*P
AMSTERDAM,
Oude Kerk: Jan de Gheyn-*G
    : Heemskerck-*P2
    : Jac. Cornz.v.
    Oostzanen-P2
Oude Kerk: Pieter Aertsen-P2
    : v.Scorel-*P
Nieuwe Kerk: Pieter Aertsen-P2
Kerk: Blocklandt-P
Handboogdoelen: Ketel-*P
Kloveniersdoelen: Ketel-*P
    :Dirk Barentsen-*P
Schuttersdoelen:
    Dirk Barentsen-*P
Voetboogdoelen:
    Dirk Barentsen-*P
Sebastiaansdoelen:
    Dirk Barentsen-*P
Sebastiaansdoelen:
    Geerit Pietersz-*P
Op de Doelen: Dirk Barentsen-*P
Op de Doelen: Allart Claessen-P
Op de Doelen: Dirk Jacobsz-*P
Gasthuis: Dirk Barentsen-*P
Mannengasthuis: Vinck-Boons-*P
Stadhuis: Doove Barent-P
Assuerus (Heer v.Blockl.):
    Blocklandt-*P2
Badens, F.:Badens-*P
    : Hen. Goltzius-*D2

Bruyn, J.:Vinck-Boons-*P2
v.Bijler, W.:Blocklandt-*P
Claes (Meester) in t'Hof van
    Holland: Ketel-*P2
Claes (Meester): Pieter Aertsen-*P
Dirk Barentsen (daughter of): Dirk
    Barentsen-*P3
v.Endt,J.:Floris-*P3
Francken H.:Pieter Isaacs-*P3
Haen: Ketel-*P3
Jan Govertsz: Miereveldt-*P
Isbrandt Willemsz: Dirk
    Barentsen-*P
Ketel, C.:Ketel-*P5 *D *S
    :Isaac Oserijn-*D
de Marez, A.:v.Coninxloo-*P
Moucheron, M.:Bles-*P
Nicker, J.:Gossaert-*P
v.Os,H.:H.v.Aken-*P
    :P.Bril-*P
    :Ketel-*P2
    :v.Coninxloo-*P
    :Jac. de Gheyn-*P
Overlander, P.:J.Vredeman de
    Vries-*P
Papenbroeck M.:Bles-*P
    :Gossaert-*P
Pieter Isaacs:H.v.Aken-*P2
    : Dirk Barentsen-*P
Pilgrims, H.:P.Breugel I-*P
    :v.Coninxloo-*P
    :Sprangher-*P
Poppe, J.:Pieter Isaacs-P2
Pruys, C.Dz.:Ketel-*P
Rauwert, J.:Beuckelaer-*P2

APPENDIX D

:Corn.Cz.v.Haarlem
-*P2
:Dirk Barentsen-*P
:Heemskerck-*P
:Holbein-*P
:J.Matsys-*P
:v.d.Meire-*P
:J.Mostart-*P
:Ouwater-*P
:Pieter Aertsen-*P2
Razet, J.:A.Bloemaert-*P5
:Bol-*I2
:L.Jz.v.d.Bosch-*P
:Ketel-*P3
:Dirk Barentsen-*P
:Hoefnagel-*I
:Holbein-*P
:Miereveldt-*P
Reaal,J.Pz.:Pieter Aertsen-*P
Reynier Antonisz.:
Jac. de Gheyn-*P
Rutger Jansz.:Miereveldt-*P
Sion Luz: Beuckelaer-*P2
: Bloemaert-*P
: J.v.Cleve-*P
v.Somer.:Mijtens-*P
Spieghel, H. Lz.:Corn. Cornelisz
van Haarlem-*P
Spieghel, H. Lz.:Soens-*P3
v.d.Voort, C.:Badens-*P
:Dirk Barentsen-*P
:v.Winghen-*P
Walraven, J.:Pieter Aertsen-*P
v.Wely,J.:Ketel-*P2
:Wtenwael-*P
Willem Jacobsz: P.Breughel I-*W
: Ketel-*P
: Corn.Cz.-I
Haarlem-*P
: Jac. de Gheyn-*P
Wttewael, L.:Wtenwael-*P
Ycket, J.:v.Coninxloo-*P
:Wtenwael-*P
? :H.Bosch v.Aken-*P2
:Dirk Barentsen-*P
:Blocklandt-P
:H.Bosch (v.Aken)-*P2
:Corn. Cornelisz van
Haarlem-*P
(op de Wael): H.Bosch
(v.Aken)-*P

(niet wijt van den Dam):
Jb. Cornz. v.Oostzanen-*P
: (in de Kalverstraat)
Luc. van Leiden-*P
:v.Scorel-*P
ANTWERP,
Aelmoeseniers kapel. v.Orley-P
O.L.V.Kerk: Beuckelaer-P
: Key-*P2
: Coxie-*P
: Cransse-P
: Floris-*P3
: Hansken v.d.Elburgt
-P
: Q.Matsys-*P3
: Moro-*P
: v.Orley-*P
Burgkerk: Jan de Gheyn-*G4
Minnebroederskerk: de Gheyn-*G
Stadhuis (City Hall): Key-*P
Cockeel, C.:Singher-W
Hofman, G.:J.Vredeman de Vries
-P
de Jode, P.:Ketel-*P
Jonglingh, C.:v.Coninxloo-P
: Floris-P17
Key: Vredeman-P
Roelandt, J.:v.Coninxloo-P
? :Enghelrams-P
:Cl. Floris-S
:P.Pourbus-*P
:J.Vredeman de Vries-S
(with an Italian)
Wttewael-P
: (mintmaster
Antwerp) Beuckelaer-P
AQUILA,
Kerk: Mijtens-P
ARRAS,
Abdij van St Vaes: v.Scorel-P
Abdij van St Vaes: Vermeyen-P
AUGSBURG,
Fugger: H. van Aken-P
: Hendr. Goltzius-*D
BASLE,
Haus zum Tanz: Holbein-*P
(City Hall): Holbein-*F
BOSCO,
Klooster: Sprangher-*P
BREDA,
Slot: v.Scorel-P

APPENDIX D

BRIEL,
Edmheston, G.:Dürer-*D
BRUGES,
St Donaeskerk: J.v.Eyck-BP
St Jacobskerk: v.d.Goes-*P
St Janshospitaal: Memling-*P
Goltzius (Wed.v.Hub.): Moro-*P
v.Mander, G.:Vereycke-*P
? :Hub. Goltzius-*P
:P.Pourbus-P
:v.d.Weyden-*W
BRUNSWICK,
? : J.Vredeman de Vries-P3
BRUSSELS,
St Gorickkerk: Vermeyen-P3
St Gudule: Coxie-*P2
: Floris-*P
St Gudule: Vermeyen-P
: v.Winghen-P
Stadhuis: v.d.Weyden-P4
Molckeman, A.:J.Vredeman de
Vries-P
Mijtens, J.:v.Winghen-P
? :(in een ander's
Burgherhuis) v.Winghen-P
CAPRAROLO,
Paleis Farneze: Sprangher-*P
DANZIG,
Stadhuis: J.Vredeman de Vries-P9
Ophogen, Th.:Ketel-*P6
? :Ketel-*P
:Vroom-P
DELFT,
St Agathakerk: Heemskerck-P
Karthuizer klooster:
Pieter Aertsen-P
Nieuwe Kerk: Pieter Aertsen-P
Kerk: Blocklandt-P?
:P.Pourbus-*P
v.Berensteyn, P.:Miereveldt-P
v.d.Eyck, G.Jz.:Miereveldt-P
Joorisz (brother of Augustijn J.):
Augustijn Joorisz.-P
Schilperoort: Miereveldt-P
? :Aert Claesz-P(by een brouwer)
:Lucas v.Leiden-*W(in de Cat)
:Miereveldt-*P
DIEST,
Kerk: Pieter Aertsen-P
TOURNAI,
Kerk: Vlerick-*P

du Pres: Vlerick-*P
Vlerick, P.:Vlerick-*P20,*D3
? (in eenig Canonicks huys)
:Carel van Ypres-*P
DORDRECHT,
Doelen: Blocklandt-P
DUINKERKEN,
Kerk: P.Pourbus-*P
EERSTWOUD (N.H.),
Kerk: Heemskerck-*P2
FLORENCE,
Annunziata: v.d.Straeten-P.F.
Laurens de Medici: J.v.Eyck-BP
Hg. Cosimo: Lde Witte-D
FONTANA DI TREVI,
S.S.Vincenzo ed Anastasio:
Sprangher-*P
FRANKFORT,
Klooster: Dürer-*P
Forreau, D.:v.Winghen-P2
? :Gortzius-P
:Vinck-Boons-*P2
:(tot eenē Doctoor)
v.Winghen-P
GHENT,
St Bavo (St John's): J.en H.v.Eyck
-*P
: Floris-*P
: J. de Heere-*S
: L. de Heere
-*P2
: Horebout-*P
: Carel van
Ypres-*G
: F.Pourbus-*P
: Sammeling-*P
: L.de Witte
-*G
St Jacobskerk: v.d.Goes-*P
Vrouwenbroerskl.:v.d.Goes-BP
St Pieterskerk: L. de Heere-*P
De Heere, L.:Dürer-*D
: J.v.Eyck-*P
: Floris-*P
v.Mander, J.:Bol-*P
Vigilius: F.Pourbus-*P
Weytens, J.:v.d.Goes-B
? (op de Vrydaghmarckt)
:Horebout-*P2
GOUDA,
Groote Kerk: P.Pourbus-*P

APPENDIX D

: v.Scorel-P
Fraterhuis: Dirk Barentsen-*P
Kerk: Blocklandt-P
Froimont: Gossaert-P
? : Wtenwael-P
THE HAGUE,
v.Assendelft: Heemskerck-*P2
Lock: Ketel-P
Prins Maurits: de Gheyn-*P
: Jordaen-P8
: van Orley-D8
Schoterbosch, F.: J.Mostart-*P
v.d.Wulp: Ketel-*D2
GROOTOUWER (Fr.),
Kerk: v.Scorel-P
HAARLEM,
Jacobijnenkl.: J.Mostart-P
Jacobijnenkl.: v.Scorel-*P
St Janskl.: Geertgen v.St Jans-*P2
: v.Scorel-*P
Regulierskl.: Geertgen v.St Jans-*P
Groote Kerk: Geertgen v.St Jans-*P
: Jacob v.Haarlem-*P
: Ouwater-P
: Pieter Pietersz-*P
: Rijckaert Aertsz-*P
Leprozenhuis: Rottenhamer-*P
Prinzenhof: Corn.Cz.v.Haarlem
-*P3
: Heemskerck-*P3
: J.Mostart-*P
: v.Scorel-*P
Schuttershof: Corn.Cz.v.Haarlem
-*P
Schepenk.: Volckert Claesz-*P
Ban, J.Mz.: Corn.Cz.v.Haarlem-*P
: Hendr. Goltzius-*P
v.Berensteyn,A.: Dürer-*D
: Hendr.Goltzius
-*P
: Heemskerck-*P
v.Berensteyn, C.: Heemskerck-*P2
Cornelis Ysbrantsen: Hendr.
Goltzius-*G
Cornelis Cz.v.Haarlem: Pieter
Aertsen-*P
Dehtring, J.: H.(Bosch) v.Aken-*P3
Fopsen, P.J.: Heemskerck-*P2
Gerrit Willemsen: Hendr.
Goltzius-*P
Goltzius (Hendr.): Aert Claez.-*P

: Hendr.
Goltzius-*P*D2
: Lucas v.Leiden
-*P*G
Gijsbert Rijckersen: Hendr.
Goltzius-*P
Jan Claesz.: J.Mostart-*P
Jan Govertsen: Goltzius-*P
Schoterbosch, G.Mz.v.Scorel-*P
Suycker, C.: Jacob Cornelisz.-*P2
Suycker, N.: J.Mostart-*P6
Tybout, W.: Simon Jacobsz-*P
Verlaen, H.: Beuckelaer-*P2
? (op de Houtpoort): v.Scorel-P
? (Bakenissegracht): Pieter
Aertsen-*P
HALSENBERG, near Brussells,
Kerk: Coxie-*P
HAMBURG,
St Pieterskerk: J.Vredeman de
Vries-P3
Gortssen: Gortzius-P
Lomel, H.: Vredeman-P2
v.Uffelen, D.: Ketel-*P
HANAU,
Forreau, D.: v.Wingen-2
'sHERTOGENBOSCH,
Kerk: Carel van Ypres-*P
? : H.(Bosch) v.Aken-P
YPRES,
Kerken, kloosters: Carel van Ypres
-*F*P
St Maarten: J.v.Eyck-BP
JERUSALEM,
Kerk: v.Scorel-P
COLOGNE,
Boots: H.v.Aken-P
Francken, F.: Gortzius-P
Haeck, J.: Gortzius-P
Jabach, E.: Gortzius-P
Meerman, J.: Gortzius-P
Mollijn, J.: Gortzius-P
? : Gortzius-P2
KOLLUM (Friesland),
Kerk: J.Vredeman de Vries-P
COURTRAI,
St Maarten: de Rijcke-*P
Bonte, J.: Vlerick-*P
? : Vlerick-P
LEYDEN,
St Pieterskerk: Corn.

557

APPENDIX D

Engelbrechtsen-*P
Stadhuis:-*P3
   : Lucas v.Leiden-*P
Aechtegen Cornelis: C.Cornelisz
  Kunst-*P2
Buyck, S.:Dirk Barentsen-*P
Buytenwegh,J.Gz.:Aert Claesz.-*P3
    :Dirk Bouts-*P
Claes Ariaensz.:Luc.v.Leiden-*P
Ferreris, B.:Corn.Cz.v.Haarlem-*P
   :Hendr. Goltzius-*P
   :Holbein-*P
   :Luc.v.Leiden-*P
   :Q.Matsys-*P
   :Miereveldt-*P
de Hartogh, H.:L.Cz.de Kok-*P
Hendrik Egbertsz.:Miereveldt-P
Hooghstraet, F.:Luc.v.Leiden-*P
Knotter, J.Az.:Aert Claesz-*P
   :Luc.Cz.de.Kok-*W
   :Luc. van Leiden-*W
   :Moreelse-*P
   :Rottenhamer-*P2
Lockhorst: Luc. van Leiden-W?
   : v.Scorel-P
Pieter Huyghessen: Blocklandt-*P
   : Pieter Isaacs
      -*P3
v.Sonneveldt, D.:C.Cornelisz Kunst
  -*P
   :Luc.v.Leiden-*W
Vermy, J.C.:Luc.C.de Kok-*W
   :C.Cornelisz Kunst-*P
v.Wassenaer(weduwe): Aert
  Claesz-*P
? (in de Breestraet): Pieter Isaacs
      -*P
LOUVAIN,
O.L.V.kerk:Coxie-P
   : v.d.Weyden-P
Universiteit: v.Scorel-P
Kerk: Pieter Aertsen-P
LONDON,
Whitehall: Gossaert-P2
   : Holbein-P2
   : v.Veen-P
Chirurgijnshal: Holbein-P
Coop: Holbein-P
Jacob I.:v.Veen-P2
Howard: Vroom-*D
de Loo, A.:Holbein-P4

Pembroke: Holbein-P
  ? : Ketel-P
   : (een Admiraal)L.de
Heere
   : (in verscheyden
Heerenhuysen)
   Holbein-P
LYONS,
Bottoin: Vroom-W
MAASTRICHT,
  ? (Koopman te M.):H.v.Aken-P4
MADRID,
Koninkl.coll.:H.Bosch (v.Aken)-P?
   :v.Coninxloo-P
   :Coxie-*P3BP
   :Floris-P
   :Moro-P
   :v.Scorel-P2
   :v.d.Weyden-P
MARCHIENEN (Artois),
Abdij: v.Scorel-P3
MALINES,
St Catherinakerk: Enghelrams-P
   : Verbeeck-P
St Romboutskerk: Enghelrams-P
   : Geldersman-P4
   : Hoghenberg-P
   : Marcus Willems
   -P
   : v.Orley-P
O.L.V.Kerk: Minnerbroer-P
Minnebroederskl.:Crabbe-W
Kerk: Coxie-P
Dorici, G.:Vredeman de Vries-P
Willem Pietersz.:v.Scorel-P
? (buyten Mechelen)
  : Minnebroer-P
   :V ⸱beeck-P
   :Vredeman-S
MEDEMBLIK,
Kerk: Heemskerck-P
MIDDELBURG,
Kerk: Gossaert-P
Cappoen (widow): Vermeyen-P5
Magnus: Gossaert-*P
Monincx,C.:v.Coninxloo-*P
   :v.Hemsen-*P
Wyntgis,M.:de Backer-*P3
   :Beuckelaer-*P2
   :Bles-*P2
   :L.Jz.v.d.Bosch-*P4

558

APPENDIX D

:J.v.Cleve-*P
:v.Coninxloo-*P3
:C.Cz.v.Haarlem-*P3
:Dürer-*P
:Floris-*P2
:Gossaert-*P
:Heemskerck-*P
:Marinus de Zeeuw
-*P
:Moro-*P3
:Patenier-*P4
:v.Veen-*P2
:v.Winghen-*P
:Wtenwael-*P
? :Gossaert-P.*D

MUNICH,
St Michaëlsk.:H.v.Aken-P
:Schwartz-P
Hertog.Coll.:H.v.Aken-P
:Hoefnagel-D
:Sprangher-P
Gr.v.Schwartzenberg: H.v.Aken-P

NAARDEN,
Burghman Claesz.:v.Coninxloo-*P

NAPLES,
Alphons I: J.v.Eyck-BP
St Louis: Mijtens-P2
: Sprangher-P2
? : Kerk (buiten Napels)
Mijtens-P
: (binnen N.) Mijtens-P

NURNBERG,
Stadhuis: Dürer-*P4
Kerk: Aldegrever-P
: Dürer-*P

ST OREST,
Kerk: Gioncquoy-P
: Sprangher-P

OUDENARDEN,
Klooster: F.Pourbus-*P

PARMA,
? :Stradanus-S

PARIS,
Aartsbiss.v.Bourges: H.v.d.Mast-P
Katherina de Medici: L.de Heere
-D
Ketel,J.:Ketel-*P

PRAGUE,
Kerk: H.v.Aken-P
: Heinz-P
: Sprangher-P2

: Vredeman-P
Matthiask: Sprangher-P
: J.Vredeman de Vries-P
St Gillisk.:Sprangher-P
St Jacobskl.:Sprangher-P2
Stadhuis: Sprangher-P
Kerk: Sprangher-P
Huis v.Sprangher: Sprangher-P
Keizerl.coll.:Dürer-P2
:J.Vredeman de Vries
-P3
Vermeyen,H.:Vermeyen-P3

ROME,
Kerk: H.v.Aken-P
St Pietersk.:Coxie-BP
St Maria de la Pace: Coxie-BP
S.Luigi de' Francesi: Sprangher-*P
S.Giovanni a Porta Latina:
Sprangher-*P
Pausel.Coll.:M.Bril-F
:P.Bril-F
:Soens-*F2
:Sprangher-*P*D
Spindola,J.:Sprangher-P2
:P.Bril-F7
:Cognet-F
:Soens-*P
:Sprangher-P*F13
:Vlerick-P2

SION,
Klooster: v.Scorel-P

SOEST,
Oude Kerk: Aldegrever-P

STOCKHOLM,
Royal Coll.:v.Scorel-P

URBINO,
Frederik II: J.v.Eyck-BP

UTRECHT,
S.Geetruidenk.:Blocklandt-P
Domkerk: v.Scorel-P
St Mariencoll.:Scorel-P
Blocklandt (wid.): Blocklandt-P
v.d.Boogaert: Cornelis
Engelbrechtsen-*P
v.Honthorst: Blocklandt-P
Kegheling (wid.): Blocklandt-P

VENICE,
Rems,G.:H.v.Aken-P

WARMENHUIZEN (N.-H),
Kerk: Pieter Aertsen-P

559

VIENNA,
Imperial Coll.:H.v.Aken-P
:Balten-P
:Beuckelaer-*P
:Bloemaert-*P2
:P.Breughel I-P6
:Dürer-P4
:Jac.de Gheyn-*P*Ill
:Hendr.Goltzius-*D2
:Heinz-P
:Hoefnagel-Ill
:Luc.v.Leiden-*P
:Mont-*S
:Sprangher
 -*P6.*F.*S2
:J.Vredeman de
 Vries-P
:P.de Vries-P

:v.Winghen-P
Bard: Carel van Ypres-*D
de Beer: Blocklandt.
v.Coninxloo,J.Vinck-Boons-*P2
Hg.v.Innsbrück: Hoefnagel-I
Kempenaer,P.:Heemskerck-*P
Lescinski,A.:Ketel-*P
Leycester: C.Cz.v.Haarlem-*P
Gr.v.d.Lip.:Beuckelaer-*P2
:Bloemaert-*P
:Dirk Barentsen-*P
:Hendr.Goltzius-*P
v.Montfoort,J.Dz.:Aert Claesz-*P
Hg.v.Nemours: Ketel-*P
Ophogen,H.:Ketel-*P
Oppenbergh: de Backer-*P
v.Teylingen,C.F.:Ketel-*P
v.Vianen,C.:Vredeman de Vries-P

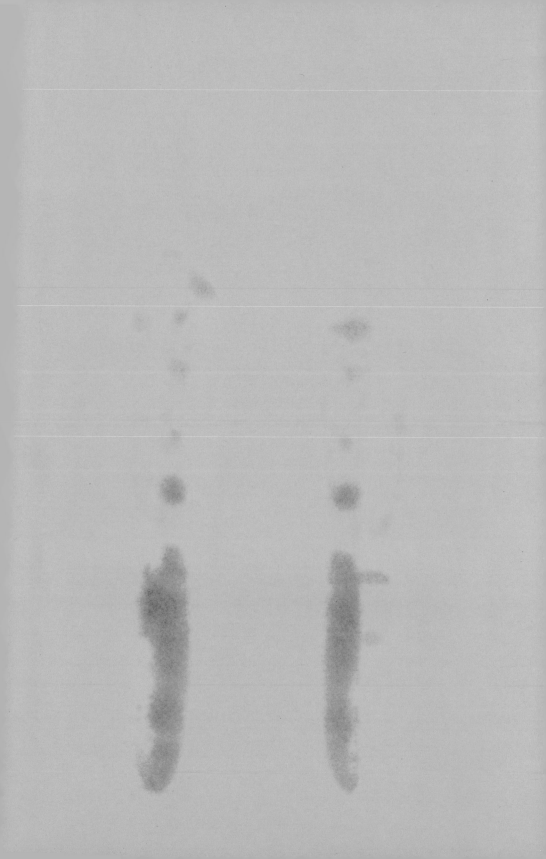

DATE DUE

GAYLORD   PRINTED IN U.S.A.